BENCHMARK SERIES

Microsoft® FRONTPAGE 2002

Independence Community College
Independence, Kansas

STONEY GADDY

EMCParadigm

Developmental Editor Michael Sander
Cover and Text Designer Jennifer Wreisner
Desktop Production Desktop Solutions
Copyeditor Sharon R. O'Donnell
Proofreader Joy McComb
Indexer Nancy Fulton

Publishing Team: George Provol, Publisher; Janice Johnson, Director of Product Development; Tony Galvin, Acquisitions Editor; Lori Landwer, Marketing Manager; Shelley Clubb, Electronic Design and Production Manager.

Acknowledgment: The author and publisher wish to thank Mary A. Walthall, Ph.D., St. Petersburg College, Clearwater Campus, Clearwater, Florida, for her academic and technical contributions.

Library of Congress Cataloging-in-Publication Data

Gaddy, Stoney
Microsoft FrontPage 2002 / Stoney Gaddy.
p. cm. – (Benchmark series)
Includes index.
ISBN 0-7638-1611-6
1. Microsoft FrontPage. 2. Web design and publishing. I. Title. II. Series.

Text: ISBN 0-7638-1611-6
Order number: 01577

Published by **EMC**Paradigm
875 Montreal Way
St. Paul, MN 55102

(800) 535-6865
E-mail: educate@emcp.com
Web Site: www.emcp.com

Printed in the United States of America
10 9 8 7 6 5 4 3 2 1

CONTENTS

FRONTPAGE

UNIT 1: CREATING, MODIFYING, AND ENHANCING FRONTPAGE WEBS AND PAGES

Investigating FrontPage 2002

Planning and Creating an Initial FrontPage Web

Working with Graphics and Photo Galleries

Creating and Customizing Hyperlinks

Modifying and Enhancing FrontPage Webs and Pages

CHAPTER 1

INVESTIGATING FRONTPAGE 2002

PERFORMANCE OBJECTIVES

Upon successful completion of chapter 1, you will be able to:

- **Locate Web presence providers around the world based on location, cost, and services**
- **Locate domain registration companies**
- **Open Microsoft FrontPage 2002**
- **Explore Microsoft Office Tools on the Web**
- **Use the many features of Microsoft FrontPage 2002 Help**
- **Find FrontPage 2002 Help on the World Wide Web**
- **Add buttons to the toolbar**
- **Personalize menus**

Chapter 1 IRC

Designing and developing Web sites can be a challenging, yet rewarding experience. Many different types of Web sites have been developed for the World Wide Web, including news and information, special interest, electronic commerce, product and technical support, and education and reference. Individuals from all points of the globe are putting themselves into position to become Web developers. No matter what type of Web presence you intend to design, Microsoft FrontPage 2002 makes it easier to focus on designing and developing Web content rather than on programming.

In this chapter you will explore World Wide Web fundamentals and locate Web presence providers as well as domain registration companies. You will become familiar with many components of the FrontPage 2002 window. As Microsoft strives to make each of its Office suite applications integrate seamlessly, you will explore the commonalities and new features among the Office XP programs. The Help feature can be utilized to locate answers to common questions about FrontPage 2002. FrontPage 2002 toolbars can be customized to add tool buttons, and menus can be personalized for individual preferences.

Exploring World Wide Web Fundamentals

The World Wide Web

The World Wide Web is an interlinked system of computers that supports graphics, multimedia, and text. The navigability of the Web gives it an advantage over paper forms of communication. For example, a number of items are instantly available on the Web page shown in figure 1.1. Tim Berners-Lee, at the European Organization for Nuclear Research (Centre Européen pour la Recherche Nucléaire, or CERN), developed the World Wide Web between 1989 and 1990. The Web was introduced in December 1990 at CERN in Switzerland and made available on the Internet in 1991.

FIGURE 1.1 **A Web Home Page**

Web Pages

Located on the World Wide Web are pages created by companies, individuals, educational institutions, government agencies, and other groups to convey information, sell products and services, communicate, and present multimedia in the form of video and audio. Web pages are primarily created using a coding language called Hypertext Markup Language (HTML). A new standard in Web page coding is Extensible Markup Language (XML). XML allows developers to create their own customizable tags to define, transmit, validate, and interpret data between applications and technologies; it will be covered in greater detail in chapter 9. Both are cross-platform languages recognized by PC, Mac, Linux, UNIX, and other platforms. Basic components of a typical Web page are described in figure 1.2.

FIGURE 1.2 *Typical Web Page Components*

Element	*Description*
Background	Can consist of solid colors, tiled patterns and images, a sidebar, or a watermark.
Page Banner or Title	Identifies contents of page; may also include addresses, contact information, slogans, and graphics.
Page Content	Includes the information that brought the visitor to the page and may contain a combination of text, graphics, tables, animation, and/or multimedia.
Graphical Images	Make up a large part of a Web page, including banners, figures, photos, animation, buttons, and hyperlinks.
Hyperlinks	Interconnect users to Web pages through content associations; can consist of both textual and graphical elements.

Web Browsers

Millions of people access the World Wide Web each day using a software program called a Web browser. Browsers enable users to navigate the Web using textual and graphic hyperlinks. Web browser software programs interpret HTML and other codes for display on the screen. Some content, such as Macromedia Flash animation, requires an additional browser plug-in player to be installed before the browser can interpret it. The two most popular Web browsers today are Microsoft Internet Explorer (see figure 1.3) and Netscape Navigator.

URLS

Accessing a Web page is as easy as entering its address, the Uniform Resource Locator (URL). The URL has four parts (see figure 1.4). The protocol is the standard method of transmission between computers. The domain name refers to an individual's or organization's Web site and links users to its home page. The path identifies a folder, or subweb, that has been created on the Web site. A particular Web page may be located several subwebs or folders into the site. The fourth part of the URL refers to the Web page file or document stored on the host computer. Most Web pages will end in either .htm or .html.

FIGURE 1.3 ***Microsoft Internet Explorer 6 Browser***

FIGURE 1.4 ***Components of a URL***

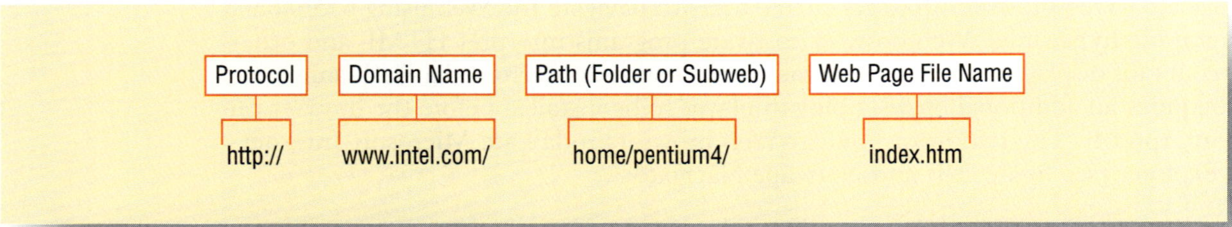

Web Servers

Web content is stored on Web servers located at businesses, Web Presence Providers (WPPs), sometimes called Internet Service Providers (ISPs), educational institutions, and domain hosting sites throughout the world. Web servers are fast and large-storage-capacity computers that store and dispense Web pages as requested by users. While most home users connect and disconnect as needed, most Web servers are kept running 24 hours per day.

(Note: In several exercises in each chapter, you will be opening documents that you have downloaded from the Internet Resource Center. The IRC *icon on the first page of each chapter will inform you that you must download files for that chapter.*

You will be performing two kinds of activities in this text. The first, involving chapter-specific files you create and files you download in separate chapter folders from the Internet Resource Center, can be performed using a small-capacity storage device such as a floppy disk, and then deleted at the end of each chapter. The others, involving the ongoing creation and expansion of the EMCPWebs FrontPage Web, must be performed on a large-capacity storage device such as a CD-RW, Zip disk, hard drive, or network storage folder. Consult with your instructor regarding which storage device can best be utilized and supported by your institution. When that decision is made, download to your chosen storage device the EMCPWebs Files *and the* EMCPWebs Images *folders. The contents of these folders will be drawn on throughout the text.*

Before beginning each chapter, create a chapter folder on your floppy disk, download the student files for that chapter from the Internet Resource Center, and then make that folder the active folder. Steps for creating a folder, downloading files from the Internet Resource Center, and deleting a folder are presented on the inside of the front cover. Before you begin exercise 1, download the Chapter 1 data files from the Internet Resource Center to the Chapter 1 *folder you have created on your disk, and then make* Chapter 1 *the active folder.)*

exercise 1

LOCATING WEB PRESENCE PROVIDERS

1. Open your Web browser.
2. Key the URL **http://www.microsoft.com/frontpage** in the browser address bar and then press Enter.

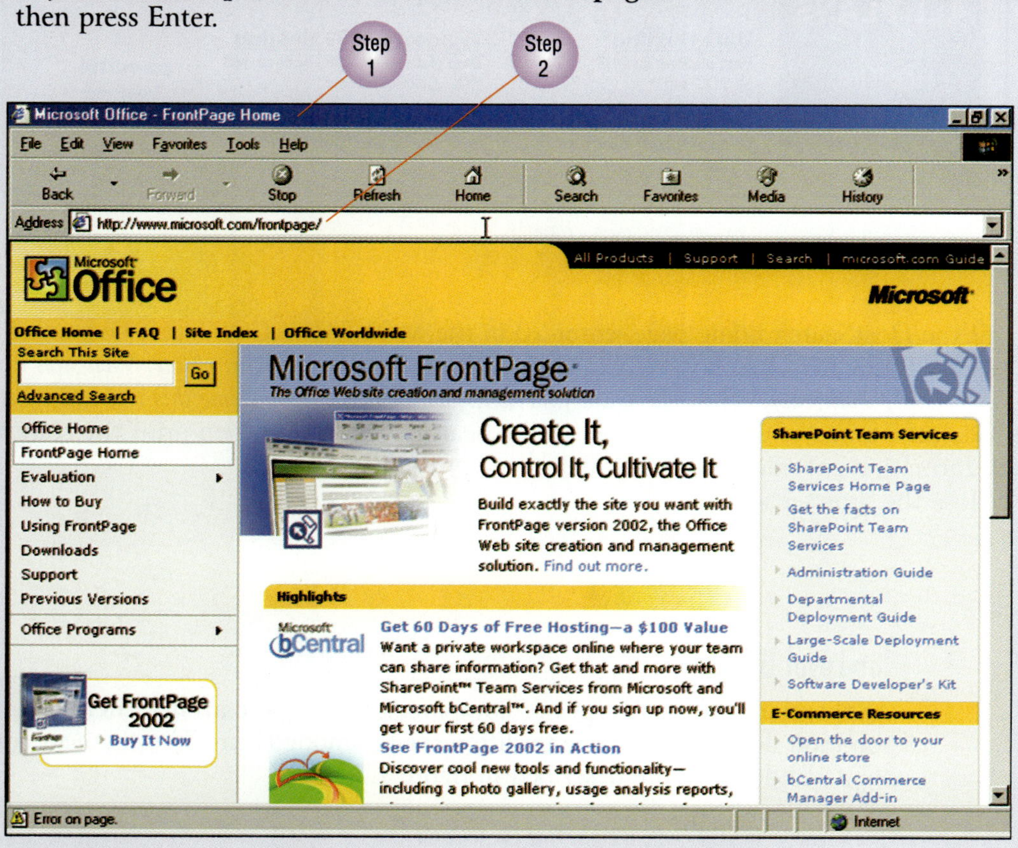

3. At the official Microsoft FrontPage Web site, locate the *Web Hosting* section and then click the *Find a Web Presence Provider* link.
4. Use the Locate a Web Presence Provider form to locate the WPP closest to your community.
5. Access the site of the closest WPP and then print the home page.
6. Key the URL **www.hostsearch.com** in your browser address bar and then press Enter.

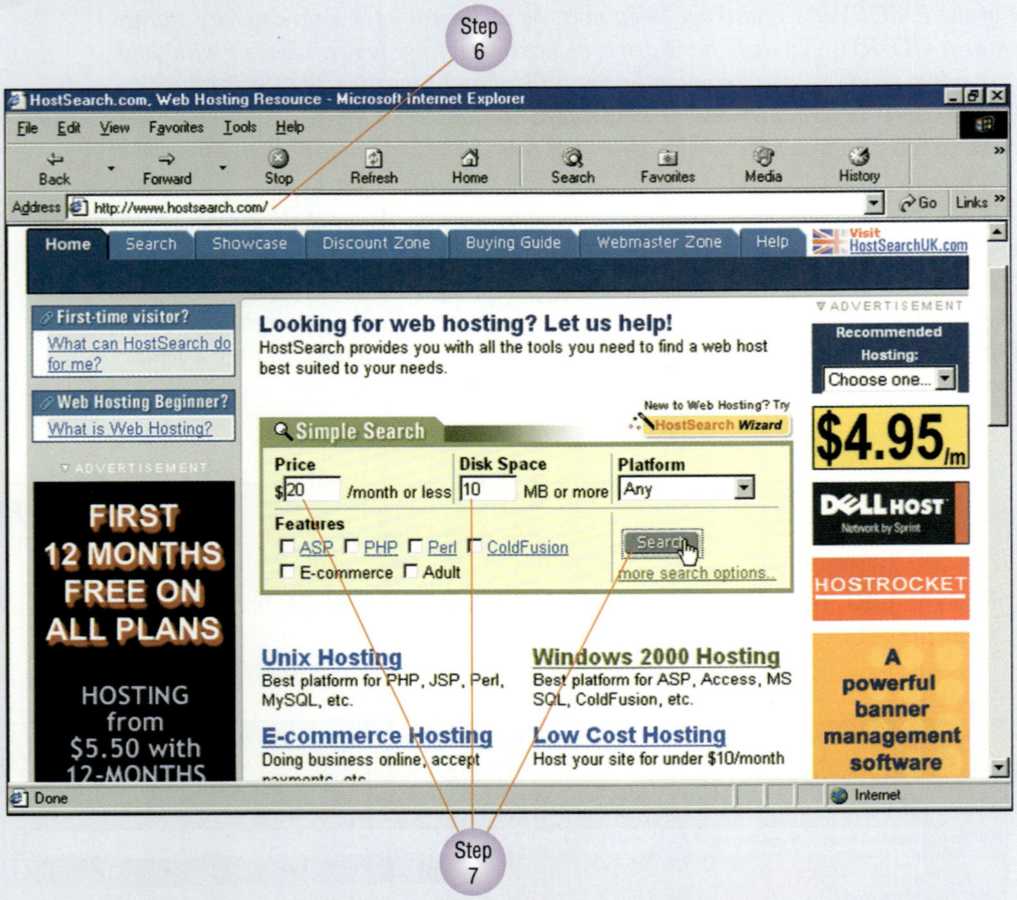

7. At the HostSearch home page, enter 20 in the MONTHLY COST text box, enter 10 in the DISK SPACE text box, and then click the Search button. *(Note: Web sites are notoriously changeable. This reflects the function of HostSearch at the time this text was written.)*
8. Click the name of one WPP listed in the Search Results and then print the company information provided by HostSearch.
9. Close the browser window.

Top-Level Domains

As there are different types of companies and organizations, there are different top-level domains available to differentiate among them. The six most common top-level domains are described in figure 1.5.

FIGURE

1.5 ***Most Common Top-Level Web Domains***

Top-Level Domain	***Description***
.com	Intended for commercial entities that buy and sell products and services.
.edu	Intended for four-year educational institutions. Schools and two-year colleges are typically registered in their country domains (.us) and sometimes as .net.
.net	Typically reserved for ISPs or networking sites.
.gov	Typically reserved for federal government institutions or agencies. Many state and local government agencies use country domains.
.us	A country domain intended for K–12 schools (K12), community colleges (CC), technical schools (TEC), state government agencies (STATE), councils of government (COG), libraries (LIB), museums (MUS), and several other unit types.
.mil	Reserved for the U.S. military.

The Internet Domain Name System (DNS)

The Web sites you access on the World Wide Web have each been registered through a domain registration company, sometimes called a registrar. The registrar, in turn, registers the domain name in the Internet domain name system (DNS), a hierarchical directory of all of the domain names that have been registered. To find out if the domain name you want is already taken, InterNIC has a Whois search for potential domain owners. Only registrars accredited by the Internet Corporation for Assigned Names and Numbers (ICANN) are authorized to register .com, .net, and .org names. ICANN is a nonprofit corporation that has assumed responsibility for many technical aspects of the Internet as well as management of the DNS. More information about ICANN can be accessed at www.icann.org.

exercise 2 LOCATING DOMAIN REGISTRATION COMPANIES

1. Open your Web browser.
2. Key the URL **www.internic.net** in the browser address bar and then press Enter.

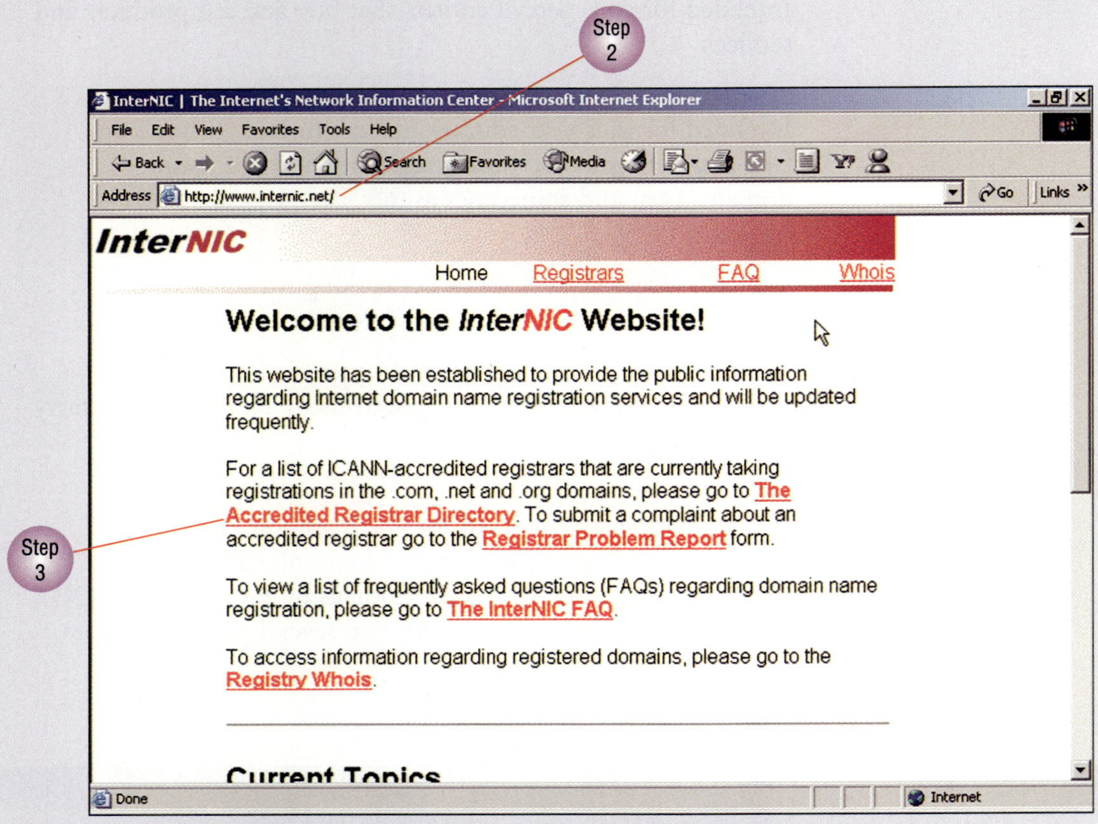

3. At the official InterNIC Web site, locate the *Accredited Registrar Directory* link and then click it.
4. Click the *Listing by Location of Registrar* link.
5. Locate a domain registrar in your country and then click the company logo image link.
6. Print the domain registration company's home page.
7. Close your browser window.

exercise 3 PERFORMING A WHOIS SEARCH

1. Open your Web browser.
2. Key the URL **www.internic.net** in the browser address bar and then press Enter.
3. At the official InterNIC Web site, locate the *Registry Whois* link and then click it.
4. Key your first and last names, all lowercase, no spaces between names, in the Registry Whois text box. Key **.com** after your last name and then click the Submit button.

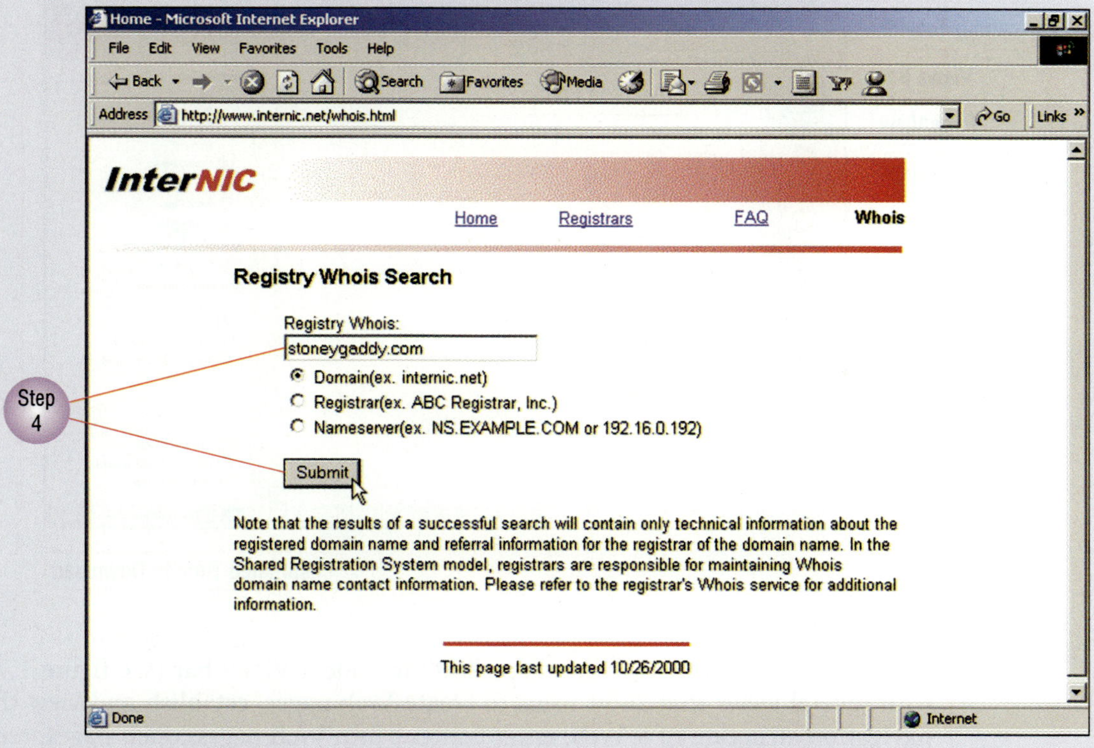

5. Key the address **amazon.com** in the Search again text box and then click the Submit button.
6. Print the Whois Results Web page.
7. Close the browser window.

Exploring the FrontPage 2002 Window

FrontPage 2002: The HTML Editor

Microsoft FrontPage 2002 is an HTML editor that provides Web designers, from beginner to highly skilled, with the canvas and tools to create, save, and edit complex Web sites as well as simple Web pages. An HTML editor is a software program that allows users to create Web sites and pages in a manner that is often easier than keying HTML code directly into a text editor. Typical HTML editor features include a What You See Is What You Get (WYSIWYG) user interface, buttons and commands that make coding requirements almost nonexistent, wizards and templates for common page elements (e.g., frames, forms, tables), and seamless publishing capabilities. Figure 1.6 identifies the parts of the FrontPage 2002 window.

FIGURE 1.6 ***Microsoft FrontPage 2002 Window***

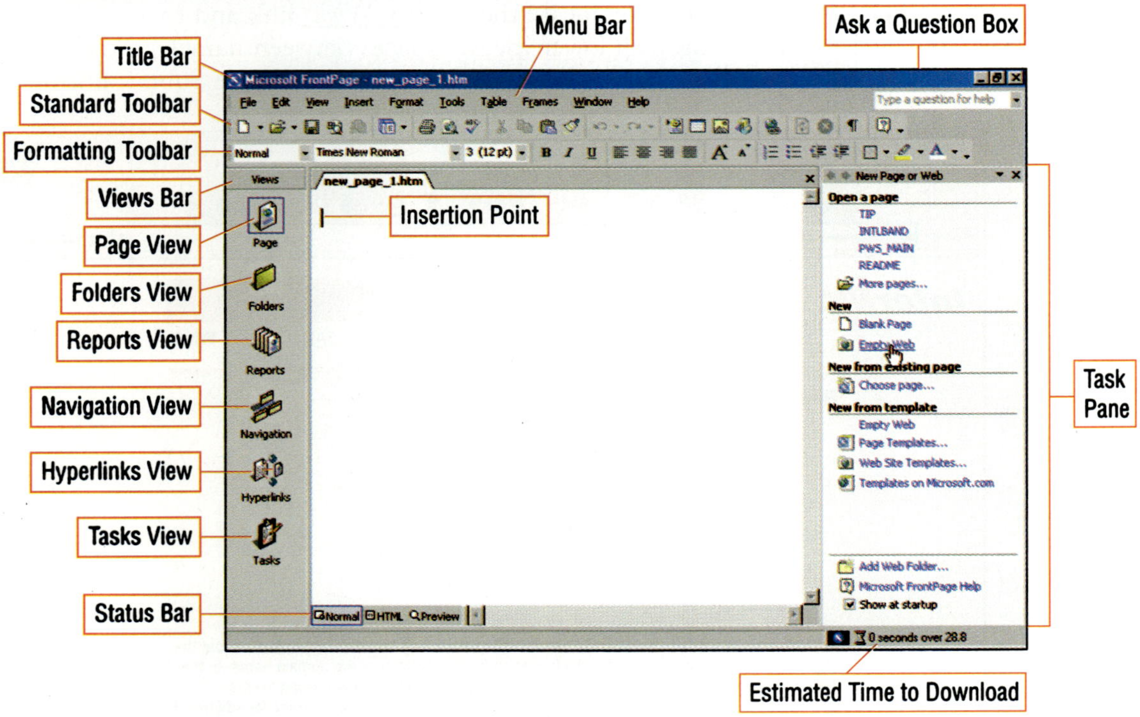

The Views Bar

The integrated features of FrontPage 2002 include a Views bar (see figure 1.7) with several views that allow users to create Web pages, establish and view the navigation structure of a Web, enter content into Web pages, open pages, rename pages, analyze pages, and assign tasks to Web designers. When you first begin to create Web content, knowing the organization of FrontPage 2002 views and the features they include is crucial to developing the site effectively and efficiently.

FIGURE 1.7 ***Views Bar***

exercise 4 — OPENING AN EXISTING FRONTPAGE WEB

1. Click the Start button Start on the Windows taskbar.
2. Point to *Programs* and then click *Microsoft FrontPage*. (This procedure may vary depending on your operating system.)

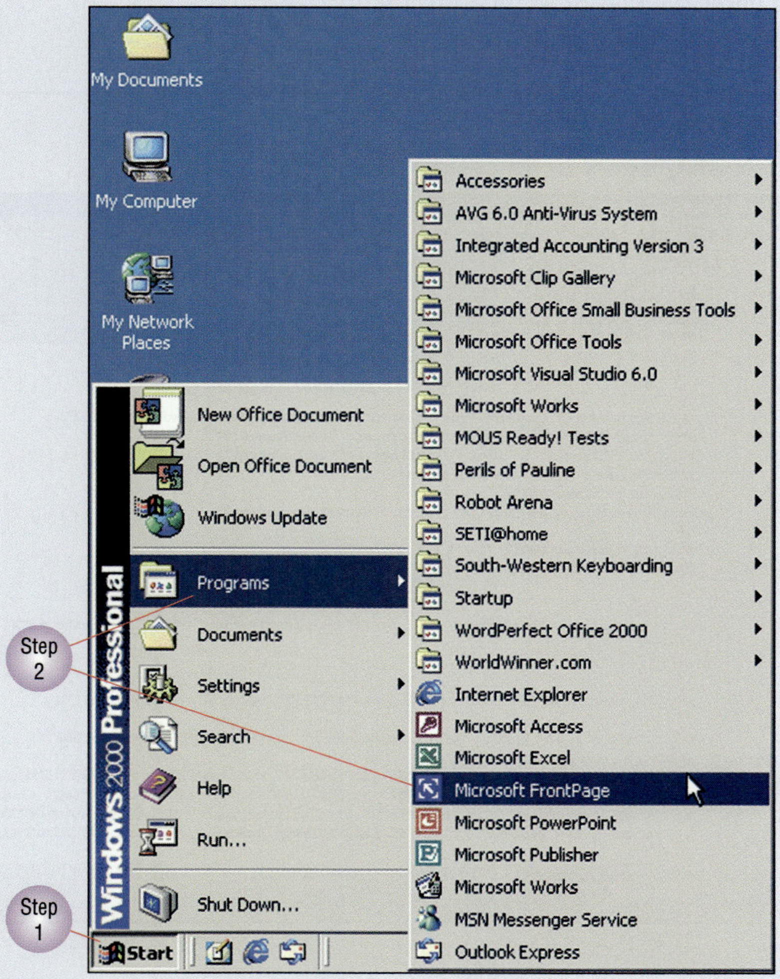

3. Close the New Page or Web Task Pane.
4. Click File and then click Open Web.
5. Open the chapter01web FrontPage Web, located in your *Chapter 1* folder.

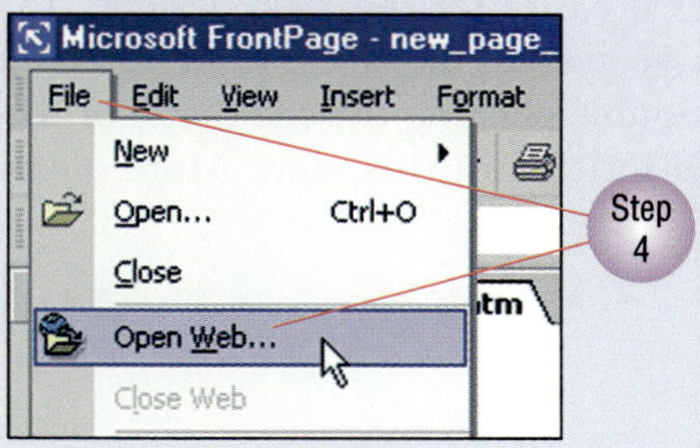

Page View

The Page view in FrontPage 2002 is the canvas upon which Web pages are created. Creating Web pages in FrontPage is very similar to creating word processing and desktop publishing documents. Text and graphical elements are inserted in the page as they are intended to be seen in a Web browser. Users needing to insert HTML tags that FrontPage does not include, or to code elements from other languages such as JavaScript, can click the HTML tab at the bottom of the page (see figure 1.8) and enter the tags or scripts directly.

FIGURE 1.8 **Page View, HTML Mode**

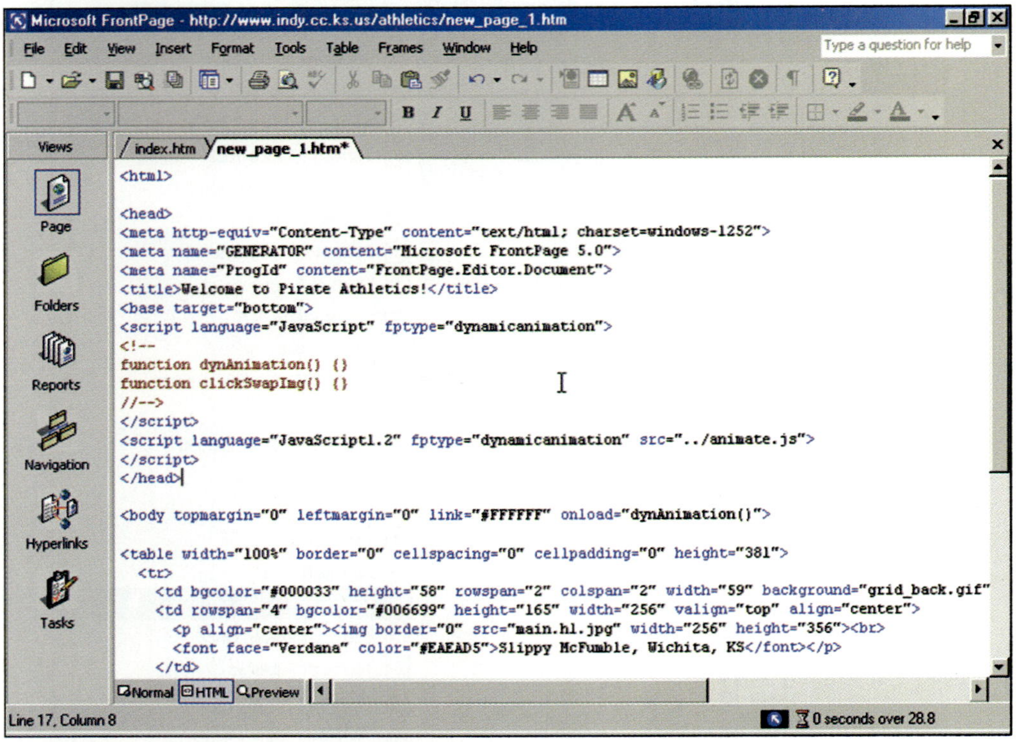

Folders View

The Folders view is an organized page, graphic, and file structure of your FrontPage Web (see figure 1.9). The contents of the Folders view are in alphabetical order, which makes it easier for the Web designer to locate and open the necessary Web page in a large system of pages, folders, and subwebs. Web pages can easily be opened by double-clicking the file name or icon. Web pages can also be renamed, deleted, and retitled in this view. More on the Folders view will be covered in chapter 2.

FIGURE 1.9 Folders View

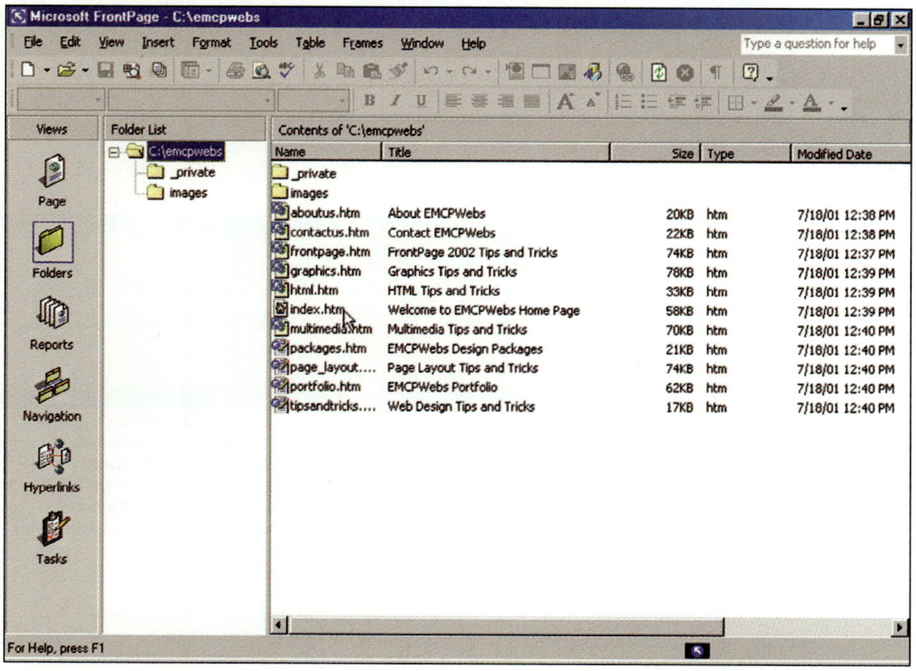

exercise 5

OPENING MULTIPLE WEB PAGES INTO PAGE VIEW

1. With the chapter01web FrontPage Web open, click the Folders view button.

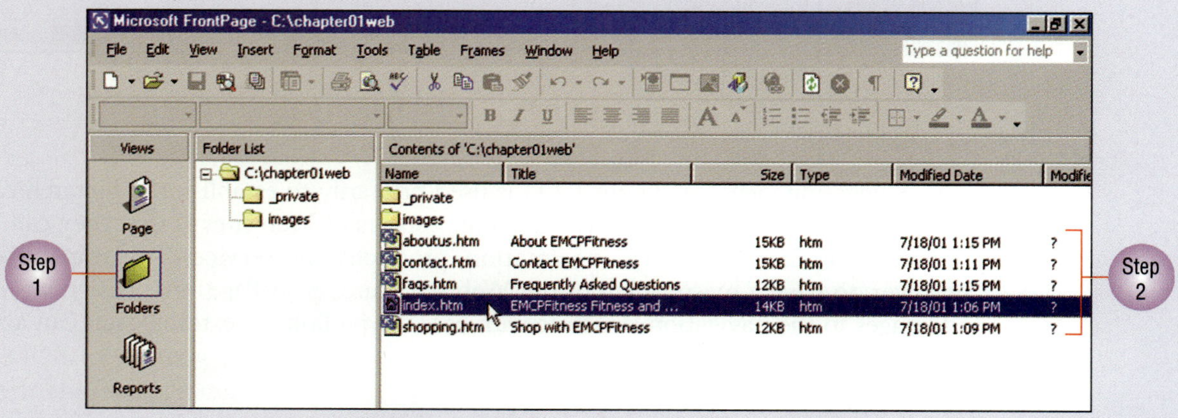

2. Double-click in turn the following Web page files: index.htm; aboutus.htm; faqs.htm; and contact.htm.
3. Explore the remaining views for the chapter01web FrontPage Web.

Reports View

Pages, graphics, and files in your Web can be analyzed by running reports to list slow pages, unlinked pages, recently added or changed files, broken hyperlinks, component errors, uncompleted tasks, categories of files, and the published status of Web pages, graphics, and files (see figure 1.10).

FIGURE 1.10 **Reports View**

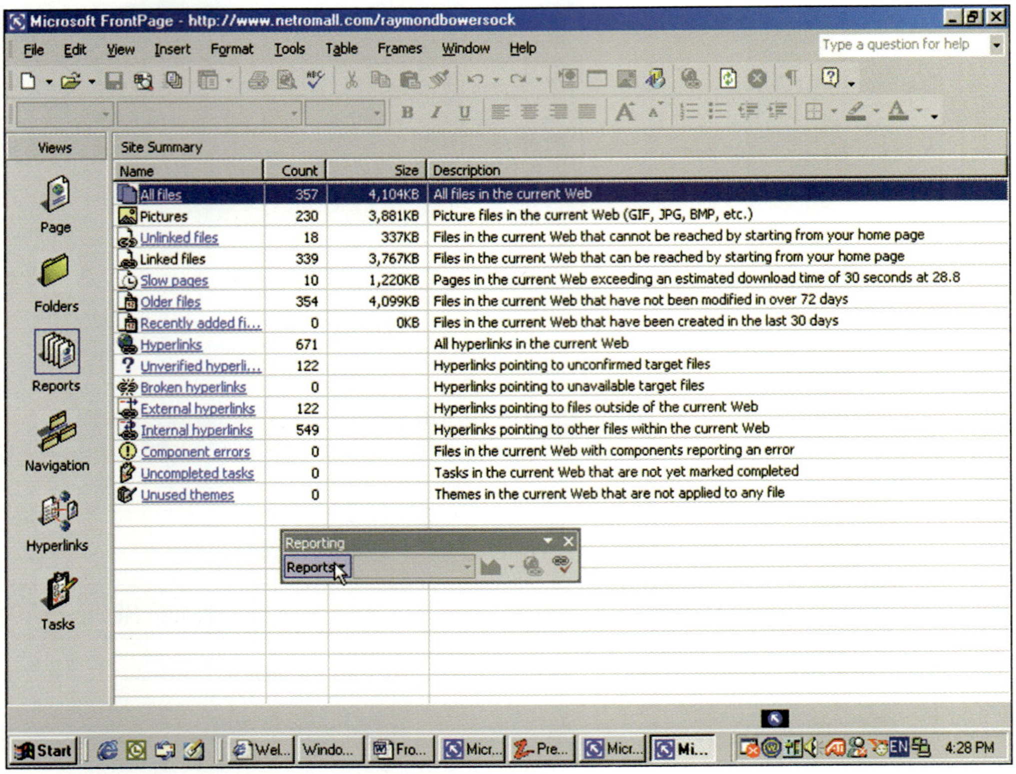

Navigation View

The Navigation view (see figure 1.11) is used primarily to establish the hierarchical structure of a Web site. One of the dynamic aspects of Web sites is that they can be constantly updated with new information, products, and services. It is imperative, however, to have a master plan of the Web structure. FrontPage Web designers can add pages to the navigation structure with ease. Hyperlinks to external sites can also be added in the Navigation view.

FIGURE

1.11 **Navigation View**

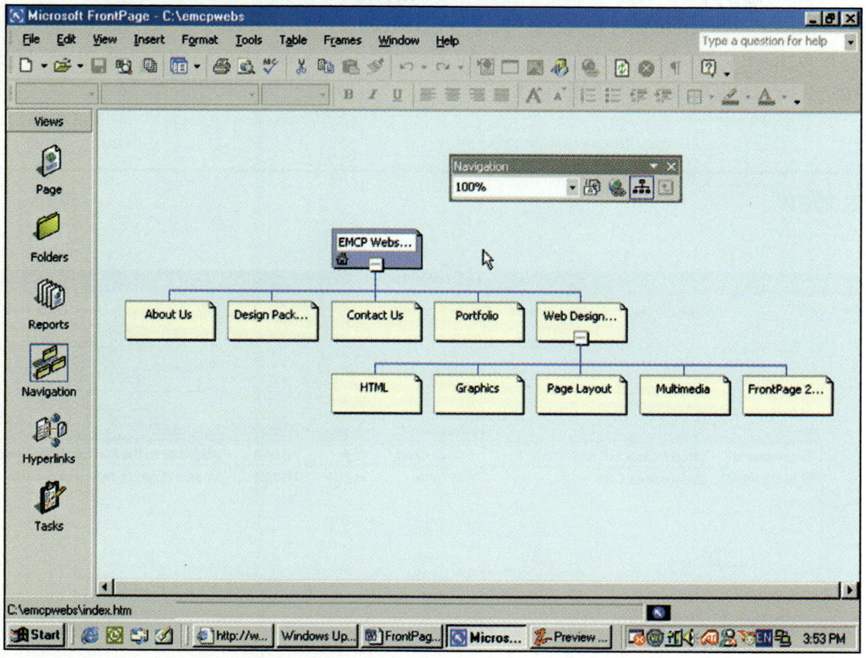

Hyperlinks View

The Hyperlinks view (see figure 1.12) allows Web designers to view exactly how internal and external pages, graphical images, and application documents are hyperlinked within the current Web. Any broken hyperlinks that need to be fixed or deleted can be easily seen as well.

FIGURE

1.12 **Hyperlinks View**

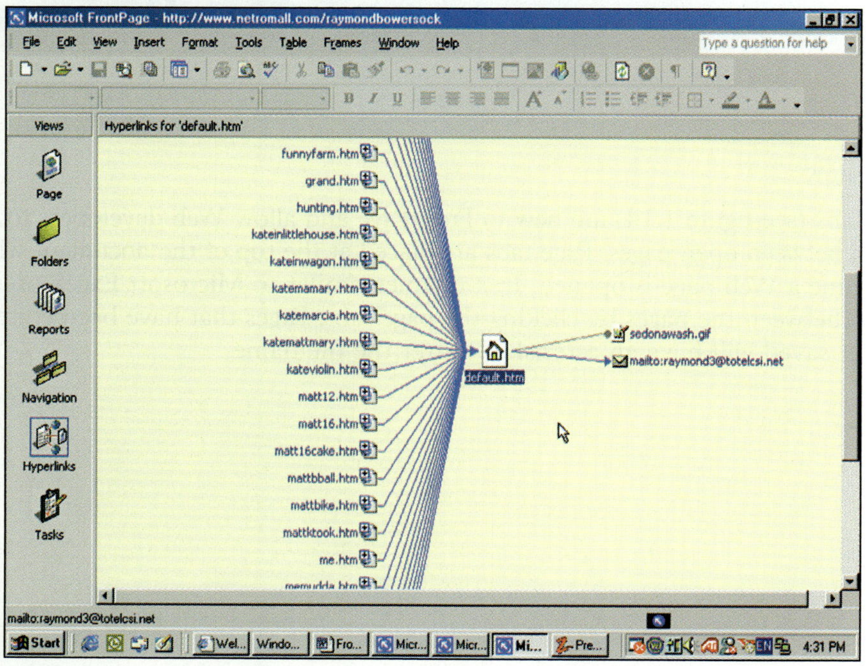

Tasks View

FrontPage Webs may be modified by multiple persons in various capacities within an organization. The Tasks view (see figure 1.13) allows users to determine and assign tasks to specific designers. The Webmaster and users alike can assign tasks, establish priority levels, view and apply descriptions of the task, and view the date and time the task was established.

FIGURE 1.13 **Tasks View**

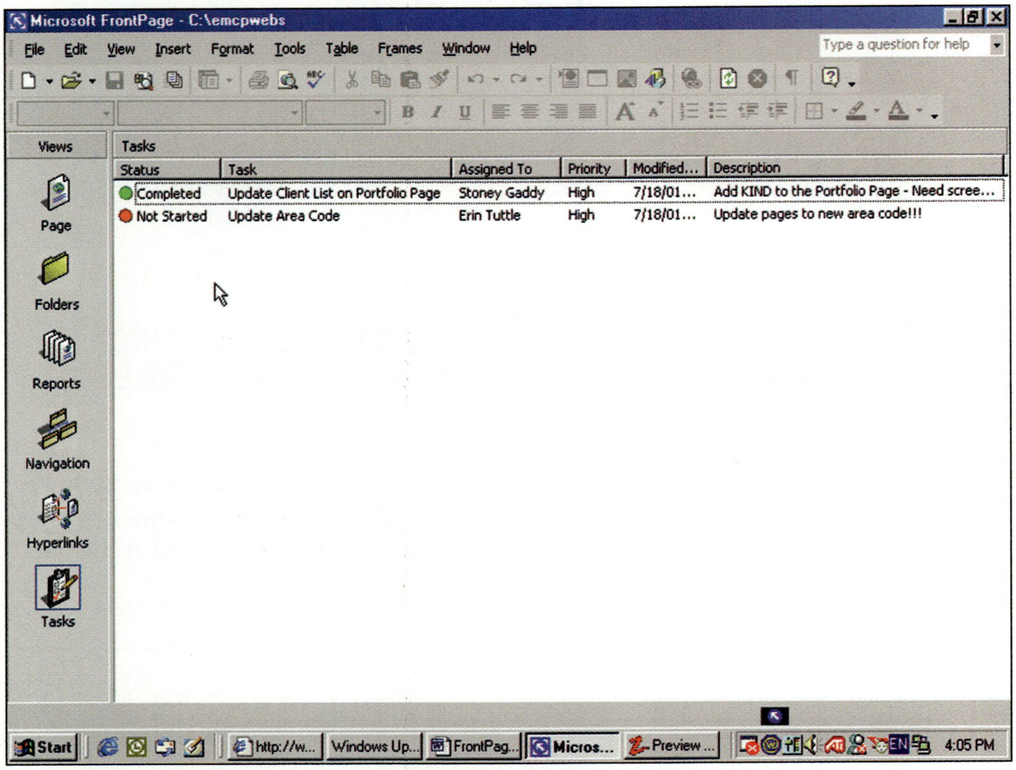

Page Tabs

Page tabs (see figure 1.14) are new to FrontPage and allow Web developers to easily switch between open pages. Page tabs are placed at the top of the document window each time a Web page is opened. In a manner similar to Microsoft Excel, users can switch between the pages by clicking the page tabs. Pages that have been edited but not yet saved will have an asterisk (*) after the file name.

FIGURE 1.14 **Page Tabs**

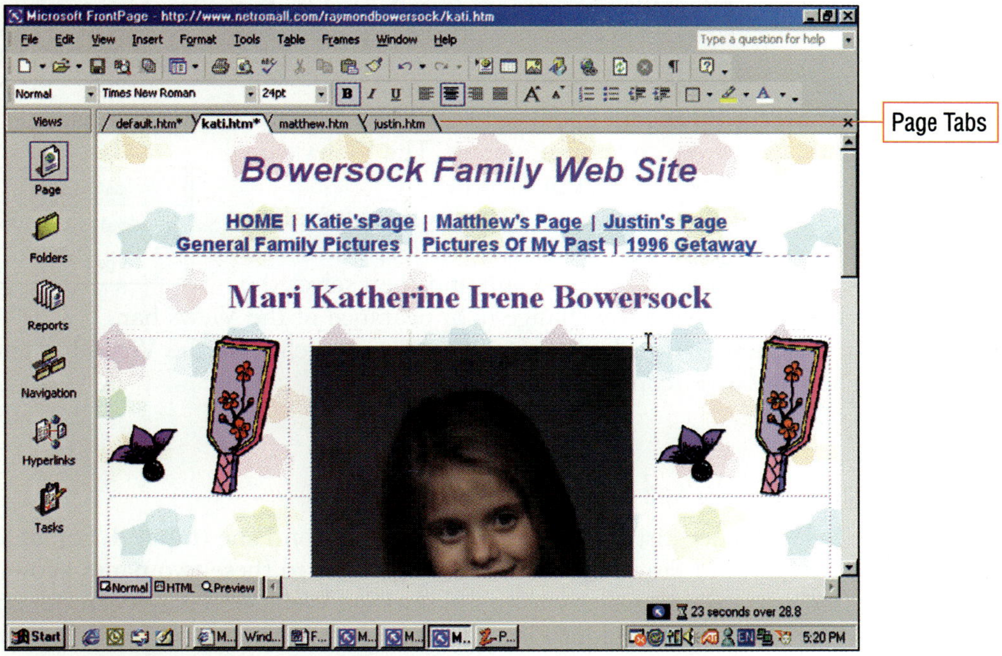

exercise 6

SWITCHING BETWEEN OPEN WEB PAGES USING PAGE TABS

1. Ensure that the index.htm, aboutus.htm, faqs.htm, and contact.htm pages of the chapter01web Web are open in Page view.

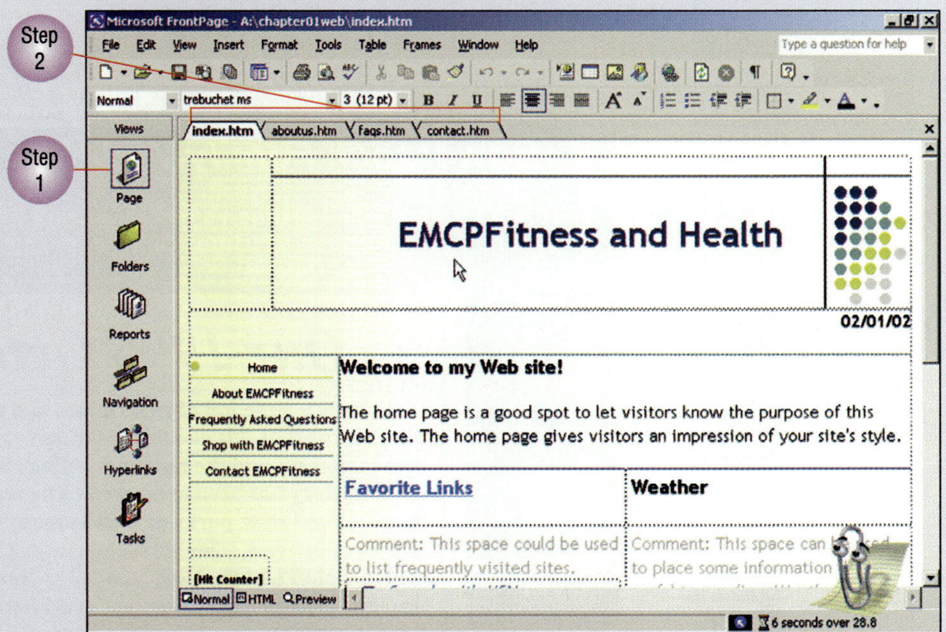

2. Click each of the page tabs to navigate between the pages.
3. Close each Web page without saving any changes that you may have made.

Once you begin developing your site content, it is common practice to turn off the Views bar for a realistic view of how the page will look in a Web browser.

exercise 7

HIDING AND DISPLAYING THE VIEWS BAR

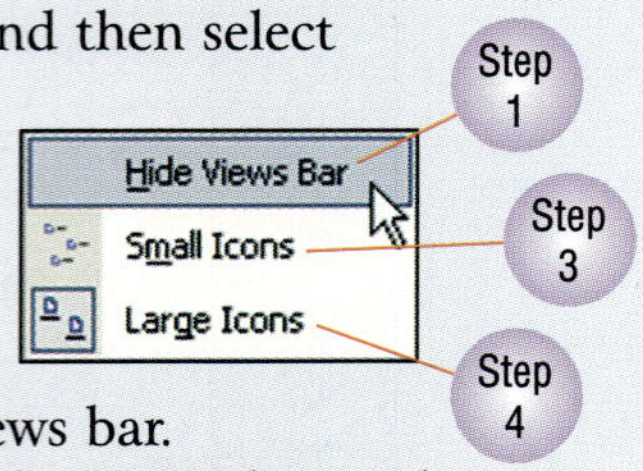

1. With FrontPage 2002 still open, right-click the Views bar and then select Hide Views Bar from the pop-up menu. The Views bar will disappear from your screen.
2. To reinstate the Views bar, click View on the Menu bar and then click Views Bar. The Views bar reappears.
3. Right-click the Views bar once again and then select the Small Icons view. Note the change in appearance of the Views bar.
4. Return the Views bar to Large Icons view by right-clicking the Views bar and then clicking Large Icons.

Folder List and Navigation Pane

The Folder List (figure 1.15) and Navigation Pane (figure 1.16) are additional new features in FrontPage 2002. Having access to these two panes allows users to easily open and edit pages within a FrontPage Web. Web pages can be renamed and/or retitled in the Folder List. The navigation structure as well as page titles can be modified in the Navigation Pane. Users can navigate between the two panes, which alternately occupy the same position on screen, by using either the View menu or the buttons at the bottom of the pane.

FIGURE 1.15 *Folder List*

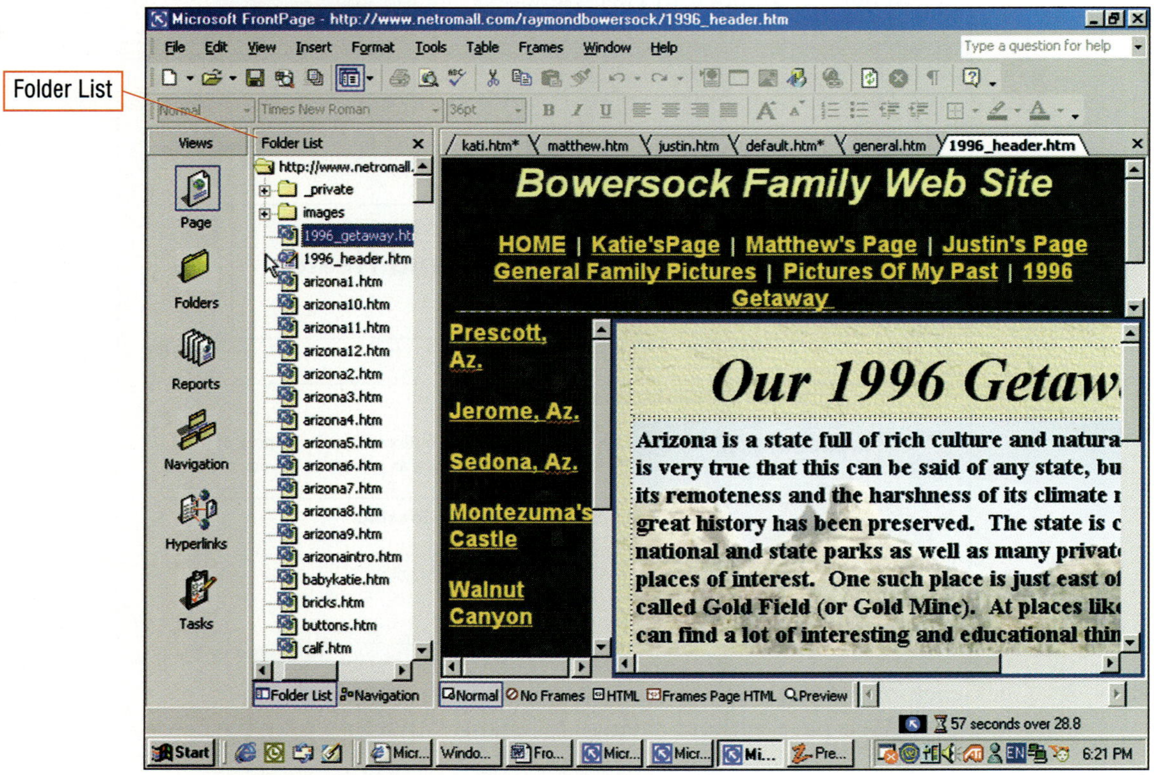

FIGURE

1.16 Navigation Pane

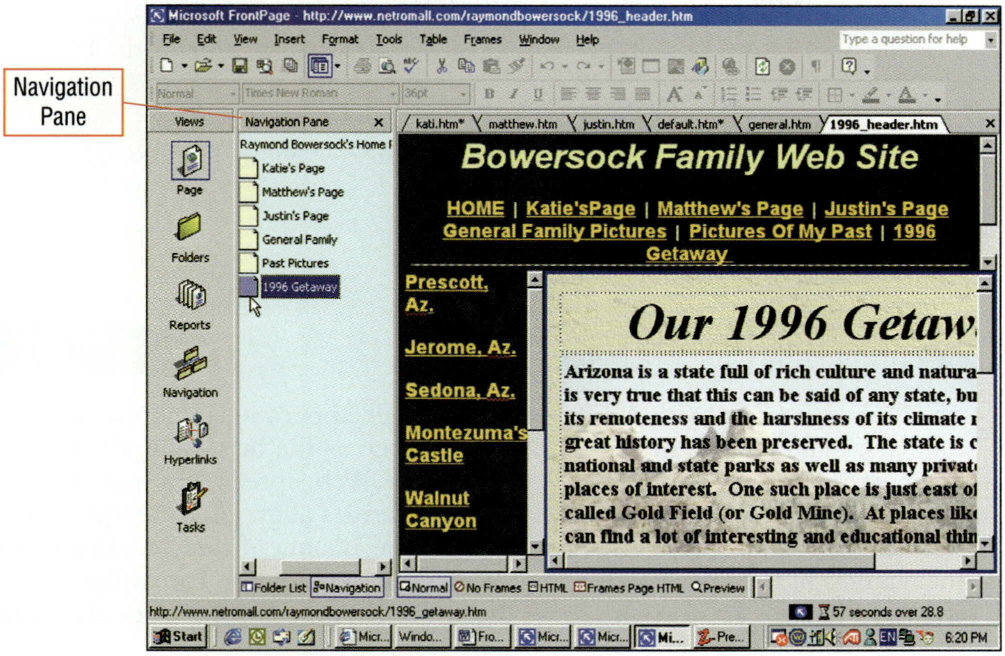

exercise 8

EXPLORING THE FOLDER LIST AND THE NAVIGATION PANE

1. With the chapter01web open, click the Toggle Pane down-pointing triangle on the Standard toolbar.
2. Select Folder List.

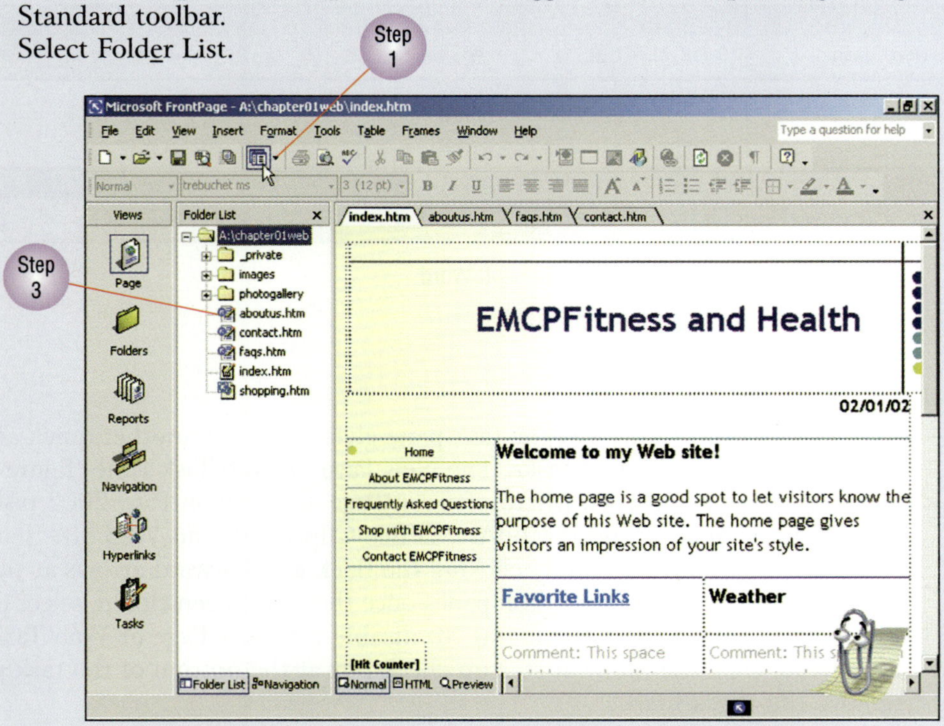

3. Double-click the *aboutus.htm* Web page file icon.
4. Click the Toggle Pane down-pointing triangle once again.
5. Select Navigation Pane.
6. Double-click the *Frequently Asked Questions* Web page title.
7. Return to the Folder List by clicking the Folder List button at the bottom of the Folder List pane.
8. Click the Close button in the upper right corner of the Folder List.
9. Close each of the open Web page files in Page view without saving anything.
10. Close Microsoft FrontPage 2002.

Exploring FrontPage 2002and Office XP

The Microsoft Office XP suite has several bundled applications that include similar toolbars, dialog boxes, menus, and features such as the task pane, the Office Clipboard, improved search tools, tools on the Web, speech and handwriting recognition, and help on the Web. These similarities allow easy transfer of data from one application to another and decrease the amount of time required to learn the features of each new application. As you can see from the Formatting toolbars shown in figure 1.17, the features of the Office XP programs are not only similar but frequently identical.

FIGURE 1.17 ***Formatting Toolbars in FrontPage and Word 2002***

(a) Microsoft FrontPage

(b) Microsoft Word

The Task Pane

New in Microsoft Office XP, the task pane gives users yet another quick access method to frequently used tasks. The New Page or Web Task Pane (figure 1.18) is shown each time you open Microsoft FrontPage. Other FrontPage 2002 task panes include Basic Search, Insert ClipArt, Office Clipboard, and Web Site Templates. Task panes can be switched by clicking the Back and Forward arrows at the top of the pane. To access the Office task panes once they have been closed, select the Task Pane command on the View menu. To disable the New Page or Web Task Pane at Startup, click the Show at startup check box at the bottom of the task pane to remove the check mark.

FIGURE 1.18 ***New Page or Web Task Pane***

exercise 9 DISABLING AND ENABLING THE NEW PAGE OR WEB TASK PANE AT STARTUP

1. Click the Start button, point to *Programs,* and then click *Microsoft FrontPage*.
2. In the New Page or Web Task Pane, click the Show at startup check box to remove the check mark.
3. Exit FrontPage.
4. Open FrontPage once again.
5. Click View on the Menu bar and then click Task Pane.
6. Click the Search button on the Standard toolbar.
7. Click the Back arrow on the task pane.
8. Click the Show at startup check box to insert a check mark.
9. Close the task pane.

The Office Clipboard

The Office Clipboard (figure 1.19), new to FrontPage 2002, allows users to paste content that has been cut or copied from FrontPage as well as other Office applications. With the Office Clipboard Task Pane open, users can cut or copy multiple selections of information and images. Items can be pasted into FrontPage by clicking visual representations on the Office Clipboard Task Pane. The FrontPage 2002 Clipboard will be discussed further in chapter 5.

FIGURE 1.19 ***Office Clipboard***

Data Integration

One of the purposes of software suites is to simplify integrating components among the applications and their files. Integration objects from Office XP applications for FrontPage 2002 Webs can include text, tables, images, Excel spreadsheet components (see figure 1.20), charts, Access database components, PowerPoint presentation slides, and Outlook calendars. In this book you will develop skills in copying, pasting, and inserting data and files into FrontPage Webs.

FIGURE 1.20 ***Excel Spreadsheet Inserted into a Web Page***

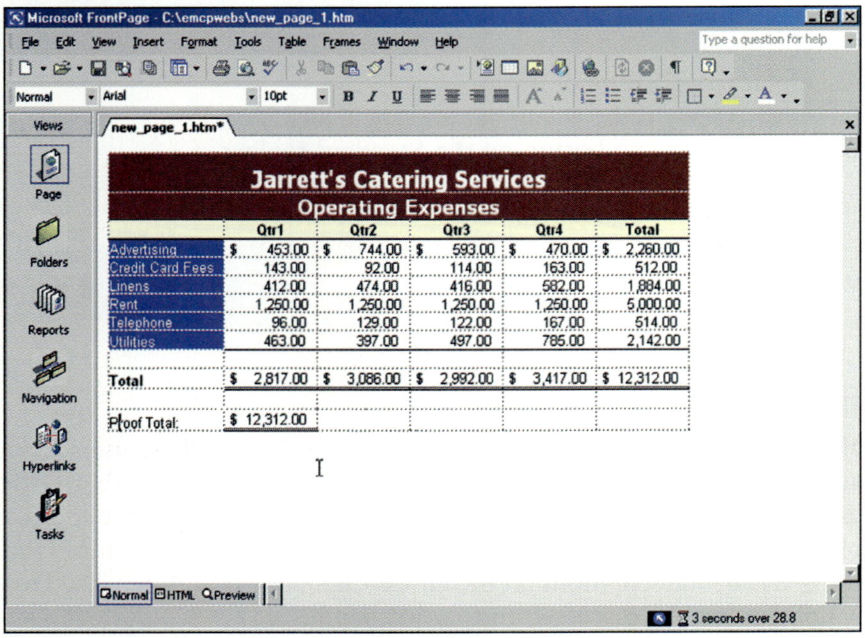

Improved Search Capabilities

The Find feature for locating text within a document has been a staple of Microsoft Office applications for many years. Microsoft Office XP has a new search feature to find documents for editing without leaving the application. With files stored on diskettes, hard drives, CD-ROMs, ZIP disks, file servers, Web servers, and even e-mail servers, having all-inclusive search capabilities is very important. To open the Basic Search Task Pane (see figure 1.21), click the Search button on the Standard toolbar. Enter the keyword(s) into the Search text: text box and then click the Search button. Other search options include searching specified locations and searching by document type. For quicker searches, Fast searching should be enabled. With Fast searching capabilities enabled, the files stored on your hard drive are indexed and stored. The Fast searching feature of file indexing is very similar in nature to search engines that index Web sites throughout the World Wide Web for quick results.

FIGURE 1.21 **Basic Search Task Pane**

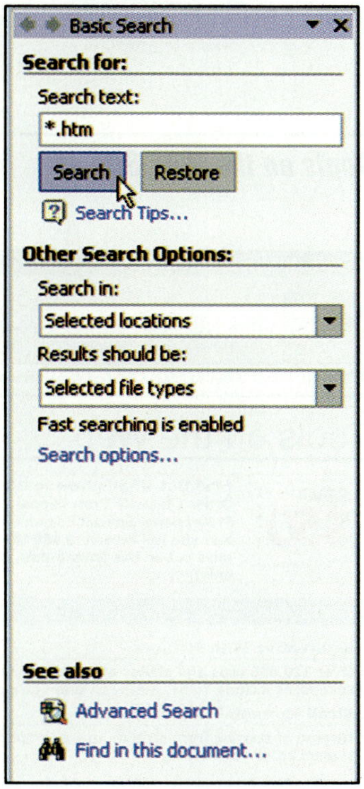

exercise 10 SEARCHING FOR A WEB PAGE FILE TO EDIT

1. With FrontPage open, click the Search button on the Standard toolbar.
2. At the Basic Search Task Pane, key **fpread10** in the Search text: text box.
3. On the Results should be drop-down menu, click *Office Files* and *Outlook Items* to remove the check marks.
4. Click the Search button in the task pane.

5. Point to the *FPREAD10* icon in the Search Results area and then click the down-pointing triangle.
6. Click *Edit with Microsoft FrontPage*.
7. Close FrontPage.

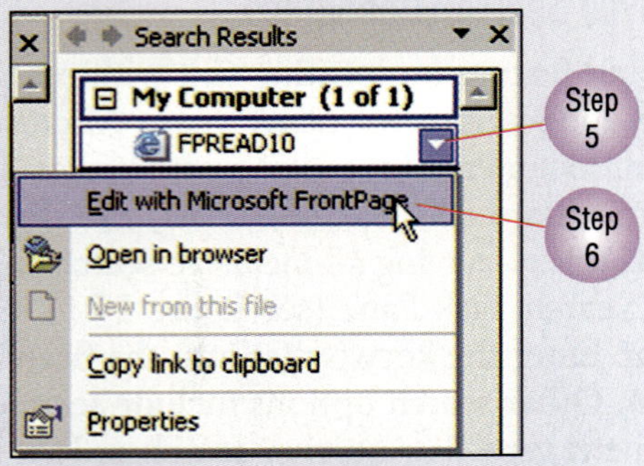

Office Tools on the Web

New in Office XP applications is access to the Microsoft Office Tools on the Web site (see figure 1.22). Among the features available on the Tools on the Web site are timesaving tips, Microsoft Office product update downloads, a variety of Web services, and links to additional resources and tools.

FIGURE 1.22 ***Microsoft Office Tools on the Web Site***

exercise 11

ACCESSING TIMESAVING TIPS FROM MICROSOFT OFFICE TOOLS ON THE WEB

1. Open FrontPage.
2. On the Menu bar, click Tools and then click Tools on the Web.
3. At the opening Office Update Worldwide map, click the country of your preference.
4. Click the *Assistance Center* link on the left-side navigation bar.
5. Click one of the Spotlight articles that interests you.

6. Print the Assistance Center Web page that appears.
7. Close the Web browser and exit FrontPage.

The Office Language Bar

The Office Language bar (see figure 1.23) is another new tool for Office XP users. Speech and handwriting recognition tools can be accessed from the Language bar. The Language bar tool is installed automatically with the typical Office XP or individual application installation process. To access the Language bar, click the language indicator EN on the Windows Status bar and then click the Show the Language bar command. English users will see an "EN" on the button. Click the Language bar minimize button to remove the bar from the screen.

FIGURE 1.23 **Microsoft Office Language Bar**

Speech Recognition

Speech recognition capabilities have been in development and widely available for the last 10 years. To utilize the speech recognition tools on the Language bar, click the Microphone button. The first use of this feature will require an accuracy and reliability configuration test of your voice and microphone (see figure 1.24). The Microphone tool has two modes: Dictation and Voice Command. The *Dictation* mode is used to process your voice into text output that appears on the screen. The *Voice Command* mode is used for such tasks as formatting text and objects, inserting images and objects, and other tasks that are typically accessed through menus and toolbar buttons. To change the font color of text, for example, say "Color, Blue." The more you use the speech recognition tool, the better the recognition capabilities will become as it grows more familiar with your speech patterns. It is recommended that you use a high-quality close-talk headset microphone when employing any speech recognition software.

FIGURE 1.24 **Training Your Speech Recognition Tool**

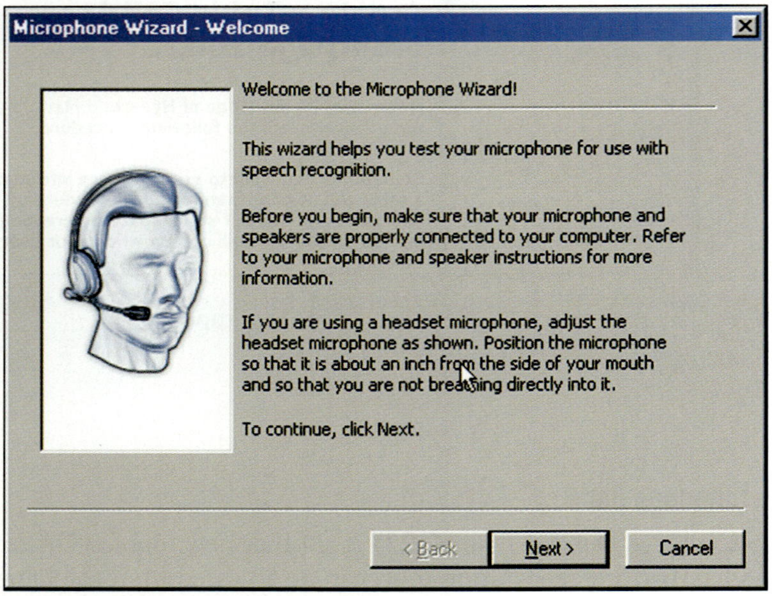

Handwriting Recognition

Handwriting recognition tools allow users to convert natural handwriting into text in any Office program. There are several handwriting tools that allow text entry without having to use the keyboard. The tools include the Writing Pad (see figure 1.25), Write Anywhere, Drawing Pad, On-Screen Standard Keyboard, and On-Screen Symbol Keyboard. Common uses of the handwriting recognition tools include meetings and seminars where keyboarding may be distracting. The Drawing Pad makes meetings and seminars even more effective by allowing the user to draw diagrams, flowcharts, images, and other types of sketches. While a mouse can be used for text entry, it is recommended that you have a high-quality graphics tablet with stylus pen.

FIGURE

1.25 Microsoft Office Writing Pad

As you can see, Microsoft Office XP and FrontPage 2002 have many new features to assist users in making work easier in the various applications. While this textbook aims to teach how to use FrontPage 2002, there are new trends, technologies, and tools dealing with Web design of which designers need to keep abreast.

Additional Microsoft Office highlights, tips, tools, resources, and upgrades can be found at www.microsoft.com/office. The official Microsoft FrontPage Web site can be accessed at www.microsoft.com/frontpage.

exercise 12

TOURING MICROSOFT OFFICE XP AND FRONTPAGE 2002

1. Open your Web browser.
2. Key **www.microsoft.com/office** in the browser address bar and then press Enter.

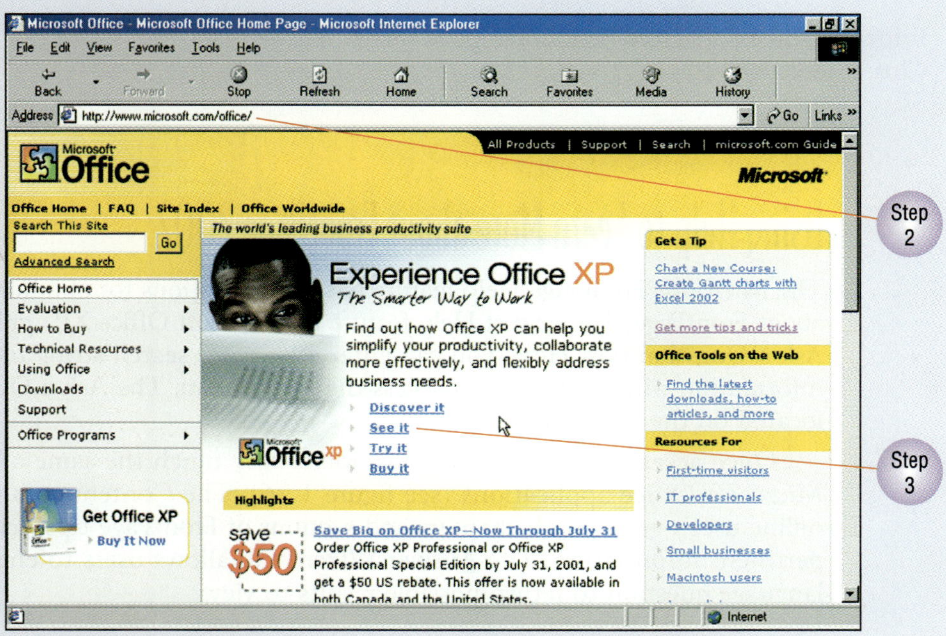

3. Click the *See it* link on the official Microsoft Office Web site.
4. At the Office XP Demo page, click the start demo button. If you do not have the Macromedia Flash Player installed on your system, click the Macromedia Flash Player link. (Check with your instructor first.)
5. Maximize the pop-up window to view the tour in full screen.
6. Close the window once the tour is finished.
7. Return to the Office XP Demo page and then click the *Office Programs* link.
8. At the Office Programs submenu, select the *FrontPage* link.

9. Print the Microsoft FrontPage home page.
10. Close the Web browser.

Using Help to Learn More about FrontPage 2002

The Microsoft FrontPage Help feature has several options for obtaining information about FrontPage. The newest Help feature in Microsoft Office XP applications is the Ask a Question box. Here, you can enter a keyword search string to locate needed information without having to access the Help menu. The Ask a Question box is located on the Menu bar.

Once accessed, the Help window looks very much the same as in previous Microsoft Office applications (see figure 1.26). The Contents tab includes an online user's guide, with chapters and sections of FrontPage tips, tricks, and other pertinent information. The Answer Wizard tab allows users to enter a natural-language question to return possible results to view.

FIGURE 1.26 ***Microsoft FrontPage Help Window***

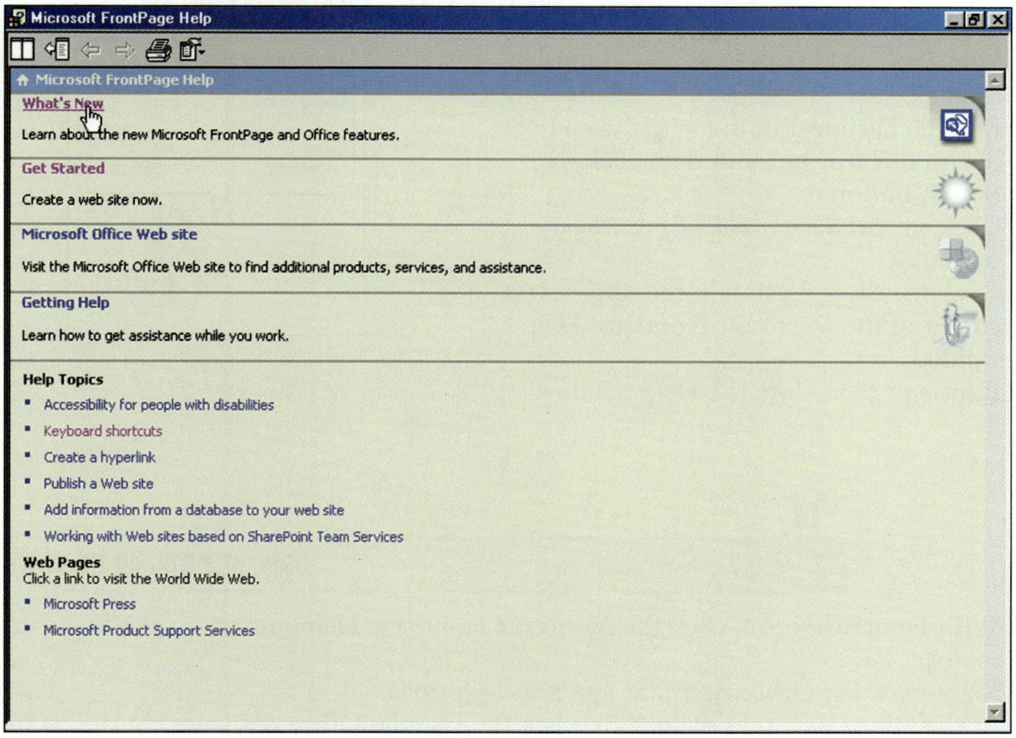

exercise 13 USING THE ASK A QUESTION BOX

1. Open FrontPage.
2. From the Page view, click inside the Ask a Question box.
3. Key **Navigation view** and then press Enter.

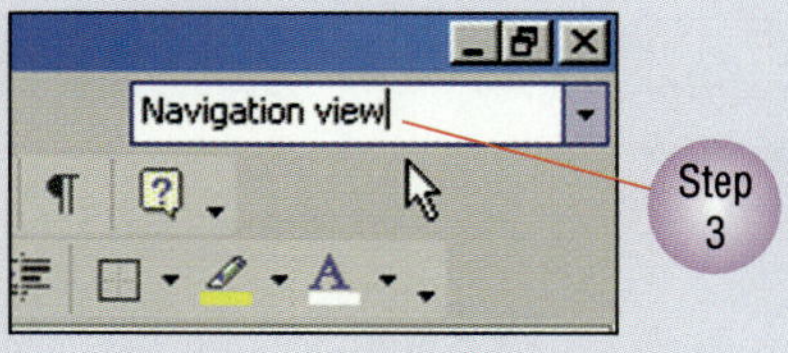

4. Click the *See more* option.
5. Click *Create a navigation structure*.
6. Click the *Show All* link in the upper right corner of the Microsoft FrontPage Help window.
7. Click the Print button on the Help window toolbar.
8. Click OK or press Enter to print the Help topic.
9. Close the Help window.

exercise 14

USING THE OFFICE ASSISTANT

1. With FrontPage open, click the Microsoft FrontPage Help button on the Standard toolbar.
2. Key **Background** in the What would you like to do? text box and then click the Search button.
3. Click the *Set a background for a web page* option.
4. Click the *Show All* link in the upper right corner of the Microsoft FrontPage Help window.
5. Print and then close the Help window.

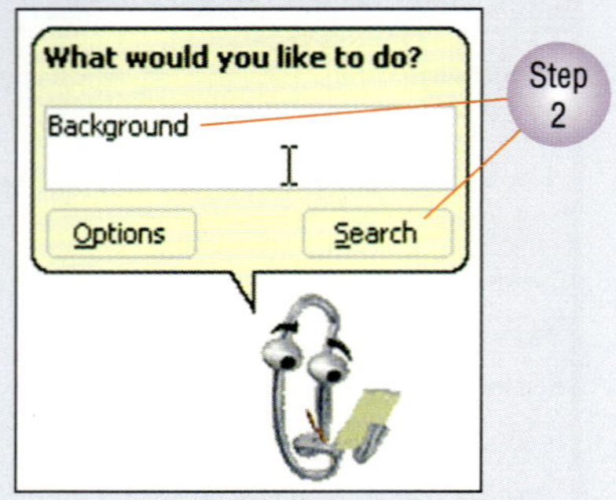

exercise 15

USING HELP WITHOUT THE OFFICE ASSISTANT

1. With FrontPage open, click the Microsoft FrontPage Help button on the Standard toolbar.
2. Right-click the Office Assistant and select Options.
3. At the Office Assistant dialog box, click the Use the Office Assistant check box to remove the check mark.

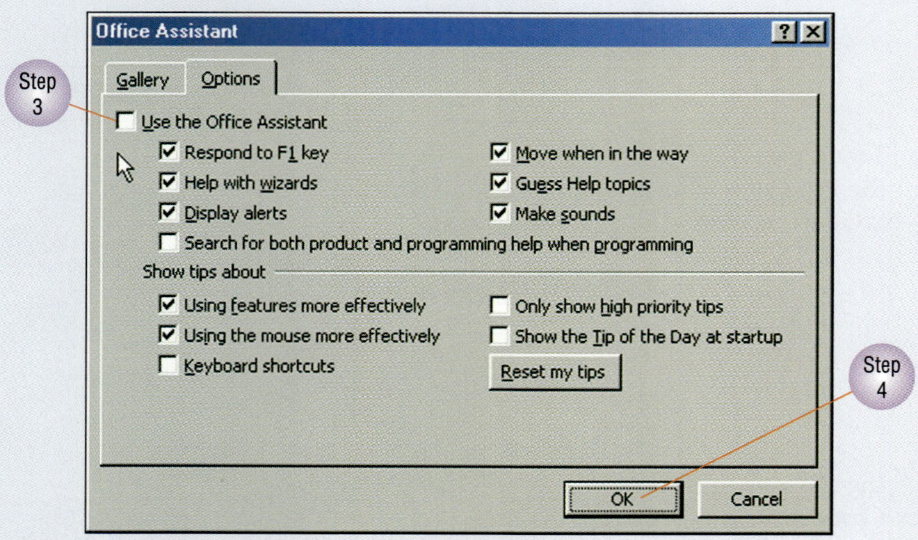

4. Click the OK button or press Enter.
5. Click the Microsoft FrontPage Help button on the Standard toolbar once again. Maximize the Help window, if necessary.
6. Key **graphic** in the What would you like to do? text box and then click the Search button.
7. Click the *Show All* link in the upper right corner of the Microsoft FrontPage Help window.
8. Print and then close the Help window.

Using Help to Investigate the New Features of FrontPage 2002

With each new version of Microsoft Office applications comes a variety of new tools, features, and enhancements. The What's New window in Microsoft FrontPage Help (figure 1.27) introduces many of the new features of FrontPage 2002.

FIGURE 1.27 ***What's New Help Window***

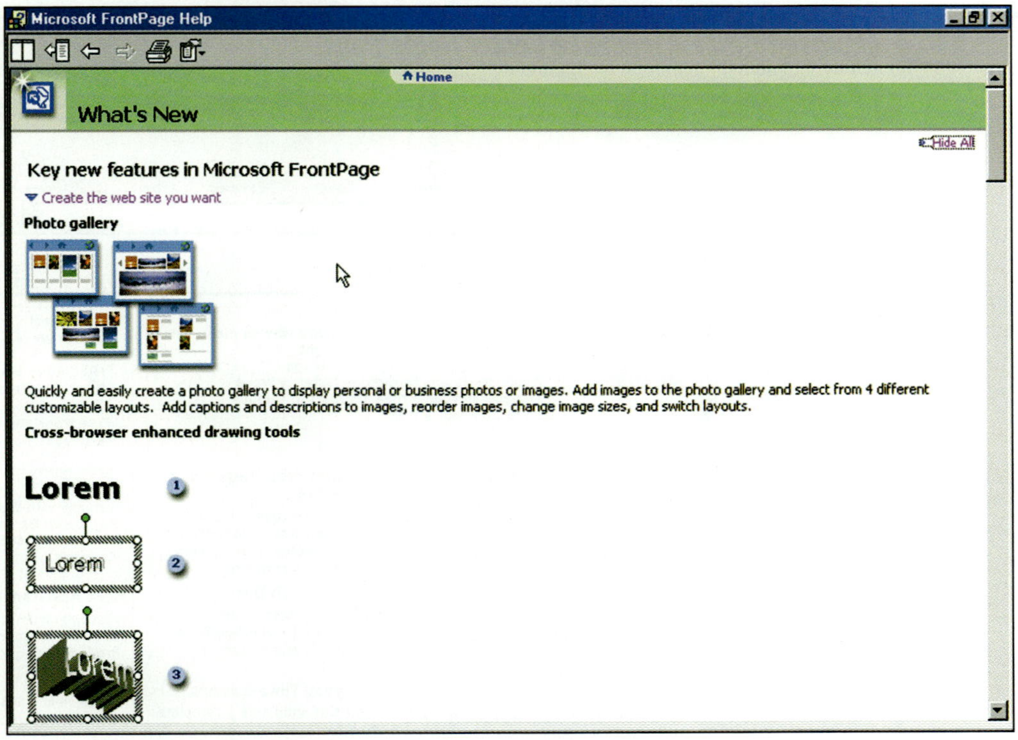

exercise 16 USING HELP TO INVESTIGATE THE NEW FEATURES OF FRONTPAGE 2002

1. With FrontPage open, click the Microsoft FrontPage Help button on the Standard toolbar. Maximize the Help window, if necessary.
2. Click the *What's New* link.
3. Click the *Show All* link.
4. Read through the new features of FrontPage and Microsoft Office. As this topic is lengthy, check with your instructor for printing instructions.
5. Close the Help window.

Step 2

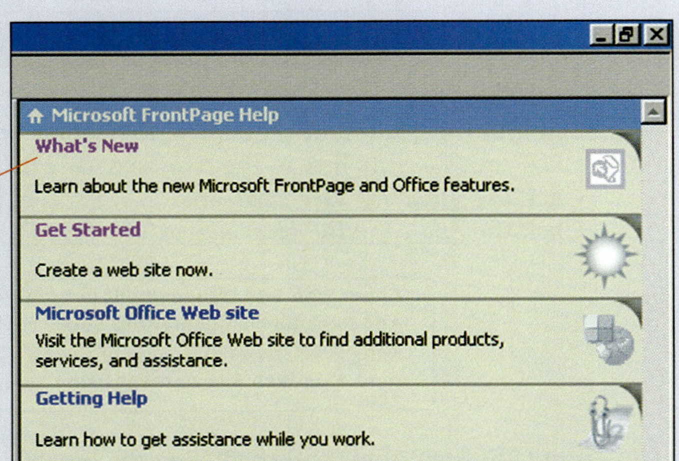

Finding Help on the World Wide Web

In addition to the Help files that come with FrontPage 2002, Microsoft has a Web site called the Microsoft Office Assistance Center (figure 1.28). The Assistance Center has help topics for a variety of Microsoft Office applications as well as links to the Template Gallery and the Design Gallery Live sites. The Assistance Center can be accessed from the Help menu. Help topics that begin with *WEB* not only appear in the Help window, but will also open the topic from the Microsoft Office Assistance Center in a browser window.

FIGURE 1.28 ***Microsoft Office Assistance Center Home Page***

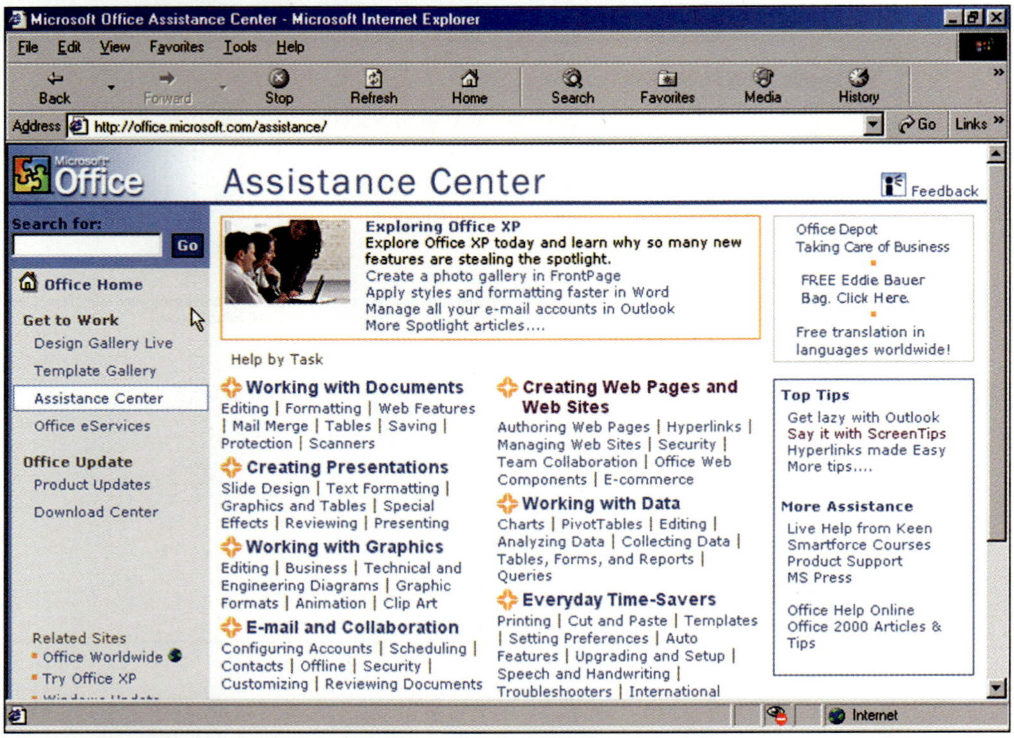

exercise 17

EXPLORING HELP ON THE WEB: THE MICROSOFT OFFICE ASSISTANCE CENTER

1. With FrontPage open, click the Help menu and select Office on the Web.
2. Scroll to the bottom of the Assistance Center home page.
3. Click the *FrontPage* link in the *Assistance By Product* section.
4. Click the *Authoring Web Pages* link.
5. Click the *Add MSNBC Headlines to Your FrontPage 2002 Web Site* link.

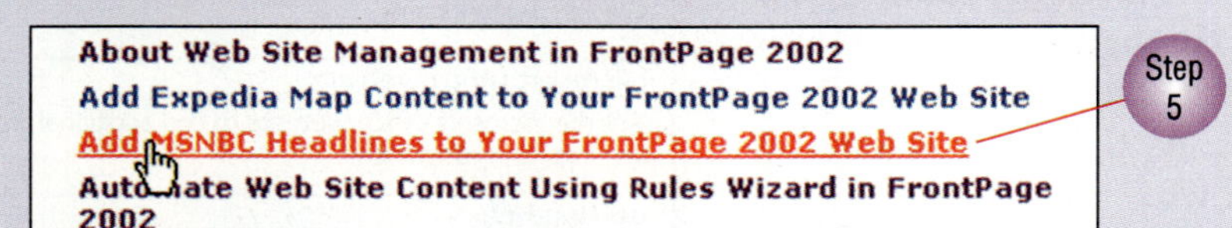

6. Print the Help topic and then close the browser window.

Exploring ScreenTips

ScreenTips give you assistance in describing and/or defining items in the FrontPage window or in dialog boxes. For assistance with understanding menu items, toolbar buttons, or other areas on the FrontPage screen, use the What's This? command in the Help menu. In dialog boxes, you can either right-click a specific area and select What's This?, or use the Help button (?) next to the Close button *(X)* on the dialog box Title bar. ScreenTips can also be applied to hypertext links for viewing in Web browsers. This topic will be explored further in chapter 4.

exercise 18 DEFINING FRONTPAGE TOOLS USING SCREENTIPS

1. With FrontPage open, click Help and then select the What's This? command.
2. Click the Insert Hyperlink button on the Standard toolbar.
3. The definition of *hyperlink* appears. Click anywhere to remove the definition box.
4. Click Help and then click What's This?
5. Click Format and then select Page Transition.
6. The definition of page transition appears. Right-click inside the definition box and select Print Topic.
7. Print the topic.

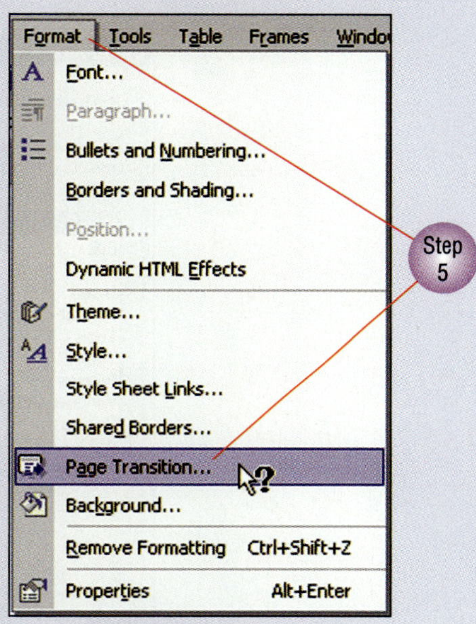

exercise 19 DEFINING A FRONTPAGE DIALOG BOX TASK USING SCREENTIPS

1. With FrontPage open, click Format and select the Background command.
2. At the Page Properties dialog box with the Background tab selected, right-click over the Watermark option and then click the What's This? button.

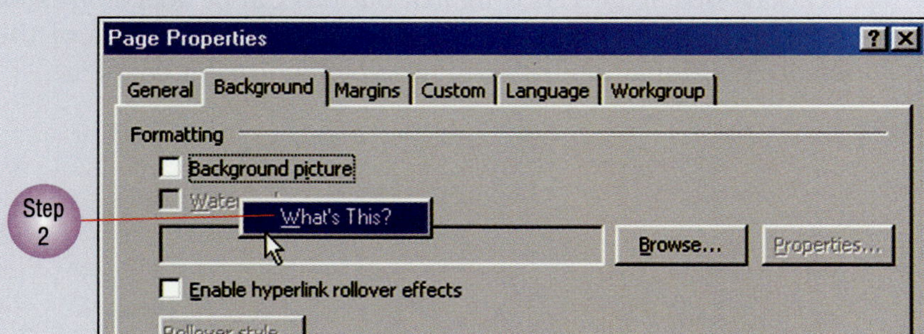

3. Click anywhere to remove the definition box.
4. Close the Page Properties dialog box.

Customizing Menus and Toolbars

Menus are commonplace in all Windows applications. Menu commands can be accessed easily by clicking the menu name. Microsoft FrontPage has a predetermined list of menu items that are displayed when a menu is clicked. To view all commands in a menu, either click the double arrows at the bottom of the menu or double-click the menu name. Menu options can be customized by accessing the View menu, pointing to Toolbars, and then clicking the Customize command. The Customize dialog box is shown in figure 1.29.

FIGURE 1.29 ***Customize Dialog Box***

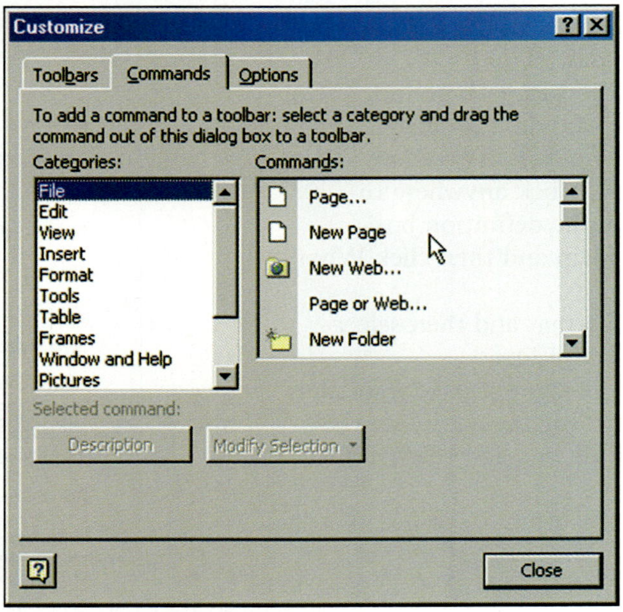

FrontPage includes 12 toolbars, only two of which appear after installation. The Standard toolbar, located just below the Menu bar, contains many of the same buttons as other Microsoft Office applications (see figure 1.30). The Formatting toolbar also contains many buttons that are found in other Microsoft Office applications (see figure 1.31). Toolbar buttons can be added or removed by accessing the Customize dialog box or right-clicking in a blank area of the Menu bar or toolbars. Additional toolbars will be explored in later chapters.

FIGURE 1.30 ***Standard Toolbar Buttons***

Click this button	***Named***	***To do this***
	Create a new normal page	Create a new Web page
	Open	Open an existing page or Web
	Save	Save the current Web page
	Search	Search for text on page
	Publish Web	Publish the current Web to the Internet
	Toggle Pane	Toggle between Folder List and Navigation Pane
	Print	Print the current page or view
	Preview in Browser	Preview the current page in default browser
	Spelling	Check the page for spelling errors
	Cut	Cut selected text or object(s)
	Copy	Copy selected text or object(s)
	Paste	Paste cut or copied text or object(s) from the Clipboard
	Format Painter	Copy formatting from one location to another
	Undo	Undo the last command
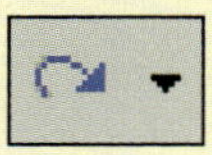	Redo	Redo the last command
	Web Component	Insert Web component
	Insert Table	Insert table into Web page

Continued on next page

	Insert Picture From File	Insert picture from storage media
	Drawing	Open the Drawing toolbar
	Insert Hyperlink	Insert a hyperlink on selected text or object
	Refresh	Refresh the current page or view
	Stop	Stop the page from loading or publishing
¶	Show All	Display nonprinting characters
	Microsoft FrontPage Help	Open the Help feature

FIGURE 1.31 ***Formatting Toolbar Buttons***

Click this button	***Named***	***To do this***
Normal	Style	Format paragraph text style
Times New Roman	Font	Select font from list
3 (12 pt)	Font Size	Select font size from list
B	Bold	Bold text
I	Italic	Italicize text
U	Underline	Underline text
	Align Left	Align paragraph or object to the left margin
	Center	Align paragraph to the center

	Align Right	Align paragraph or object to the right margin
	Justify	Align paragraph text to both left and right margins
	Increase Font Size	Incrementally increase font size
	Decrease Font Size	Incrementally decrease font size
	Numbering	Add numbering to a list of items
	Bullets	Add bullets to a list of items
	Decrease Indent	Decrease the paragraph indent
	Increase Indent	Increase the paragraph indent
	Outside Borders	Format paragraph borders
	Highlight	Highlight text on page
	Font Color	Change font color

Docked and Floating Toolbars

Toolbars can be placed just about anywhere on the FrontPage window. Toolbars can either be docked at the top or bottom of the FrontPage window or floating within the document area (see figure 1.32). To float a toolbar, place your mouse pointer at the far left edge of a menu. Once the mouse pointer turns into a four-sided arrow, click and drag the menu to another location on the screen. To dock a floating toolbar, click anywhere on the Title bar and drag it to the top or bottom of the FrontPage window.

FIGURE

1.32 Floating Toolbar

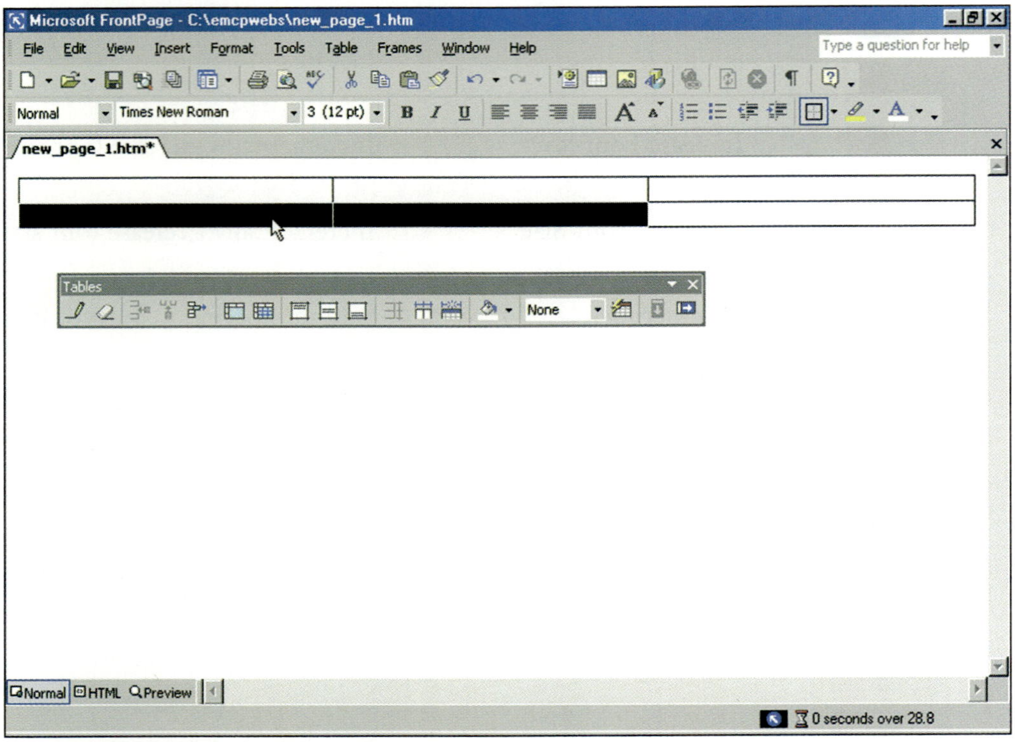

exercise 20

ADDING BUTTONS TO THE STANDARD TOOLBAR

1. With FrontPage open, click View.
2. Point to the Toolbars command and then click Customize.
3. Click the Commands tab in the Customize dialog box.
4. Click *Insert* under Categories.
5. Scroll through the Commands section until you locate the Clip Art command.
6. Click *Clip Art* and drag it to the right of the Insert Picture From File button on the Standard toolbar.
7. To remove the Insert Clip Art button from the toolbar, right-click the toolbar and then click Customize.
8. Click the Insert Clip Art button, drag it off the toolbar, and then release the mouse button.

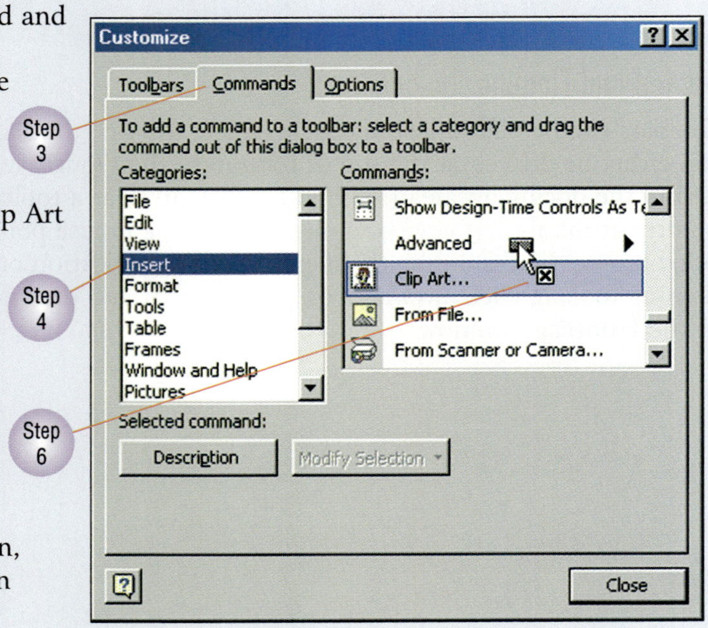

exercise 21 SHOWING FULL MENUS

1. With FrontPage open, right-click an empty area on the toolbars and select the Customize command.
2. At the Customize dialog box with the Options tab selected, click the Always show full menus check box to insert a check mark.

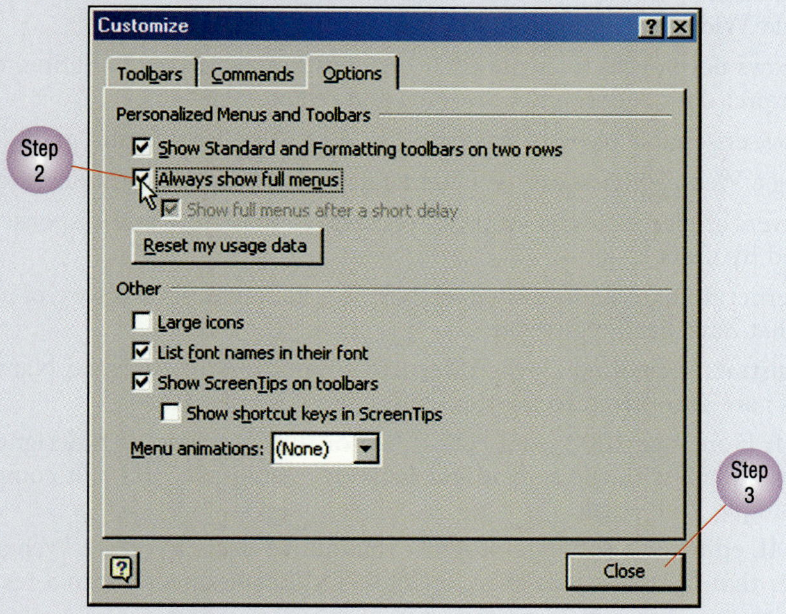

3. Close the Customize dialog box.
4. Click any of the menus to ensure that all menu items appear.
5. To revert to the original, abbreviated menus, repeat steps 1 and 2 above, click the Always show full menus check box to remove the check mark, and then close the Customize dialog box.
6. Close FrontPage.

CHAPTER summary

- The World Wide Web is an interlinked system of computers that supports graphics, multimedia, and text.
- Tim Berners-Lee, at the European Organization for Nuclear Research (CERN), developed the World Wide Web between 1989 and 1990.
- XML allows developers to create their own customizable tags to define, transmit, validate, and interpret data between applications and technologies.
- Web browsers enable users to navigate the Web using textual and graphical hyperlinks.
- Accessing a Web page is as easy as entering its address, the Uniform Resource Locator (URL).
- Web servers are large-storage-capacity computers that store and dispense Web pages as requested by users.
- The Internet domain name system (DNS) is a hierarchical directory of all of the domain names that have been registered.
- Only registrars accredited by the Internet Corporation for Assigned Names and Numbers (ICANN) are authorized to register .com, .net, and .org names.
- Microsoft FrontPage 2002 is an HTML editor that provides Web designers, from beginner to highly skilled, with the canvas and tools to create, save, and edit complex Web sites as well as simple Web pages.
- An HTML editor is a software program that allows users to create Web sites and pages in a manner that is often easier than keying HTML code directly into a text editor.
- The Page view in FrontPage 2002 is the canvas upon which Web pages are created.
- The Folders view is an organized page, graphic, and file structure of your FrontPage Web.
- Pages, graphics, and files in your Web can be analyzed by running reports to list slow pages, unlinked pages, recently added or changed files, broken hyperlinks, component errors, uncompleted tasks, categories of files, and the published status of Web pages, graphics, and files.
- The Navigation view is used primarily to establish the hierarchical structure of a Web site.
- The Hyperlinks view allows Web designers to view exactly how internal and external pages, graphical images, and application documents are hyperlinked within the current Web.
- The Tasks view allows users to determine and assign tasks to specific designers.
- Page tabs are new to FrontPage and allow Web developers to easily switch between open pages.
- New in Microsoft Office XP, the task pane gives users yet another quick access method to frequently used tasks.
- The Office Clipboard, new to FrontPage 2002, allows users to paste content that has been cut or copied from FrontPage as well as other Office applications.
- New in Microsoft Office XP applications is access to the Microsoft Office Tools on the Web site.
- The Office Language bar includes both speech and handwriting recognition tools.
- To utilize the speech recognition tools on the Language bar, click the Microphone button.
- The handwriting recognition tools allow users to convert natural handwriting into text in any Microsoft Office program.

- Additional Microsoft Office highlights, tips, tools, resources, and upgrades can be found at www.microsoft.com/office.
- The official Microsoft FrontPage Web site can be accessed at www.microsoft.com/frontpage.
- The newest Help feature in Microsoft Office XP applications is the Ask a Question box located on the Menu bar.
- The Microsoft Office Assistance Center Web site can be accessed from the Help menu.
- ScreenTips give assistance in describing and/or defining items on the FrontPage window or in dialog boxes.
- Click the What's This? command to describe and/or define items on the FrontPage window or in dialog boxes.
- Menu options and toolbars can be customized by accessing the View menu, pointing to Toolbars, and then clicking the Customize command.
- To float a toolbar, place the mouse pointer at the far left edge of a menu.
- Right-click an empty area of a toolbar, click Customize, and then check the Always show full menus check box to always display all items in each menu.

COMMANDS review

Command	Mouse/Keyboard
Open an existing FrontPage Web	Click File, Open Web
Open Web pages into Page view from Folders view	Double-click the icon or file name
Display or remove Views bar	Click View, Views bar
Toggle between and close the Folder List and Navigation Pane	Click Toggle Pane button's down-pointing triangle
Display the task pane	Click View, Task Pane
Search for documents within FrontPage	Click the Search button on the Standard toolbar
Access the Microsoft Office Tools on the Web site	Click Tools, Tools on the Web
Learn more about Microsoft Office XP	Key **www.microsoft.com/office**
Learn more about Microsoft FrontPage 2002	Key **www.microsoft.com/frontpage**
Ask a natural-language question to solve a FrontPage 2002 problem	Click inside the Ask a Question box and enter your question
Use the Office Assistant to solve a FrontPage 2002 problem	Click the Help button on the Standard toolbar
Use Help on the Web to solve a FrontPage 2002 problem	Click Help, Help on the Web

Add buttons to the toolbar	Click View, point to Toolbars, click Customize, Commands tab
Always show full menus	Click View, point to Toolbars, click Customize, Options tab

CONCEPTS check

Completion: On a blank sheet of paper, indicate the correct term, command, or number for each item.

1. Web pages are primarily created using this coding language.
2. This top-level domain is usually reserved for colleges and universities.
3. Access this Web site to see if your domain name preference is already taken.
4. This view is the canvas upon which Web pages are created and looks very similar to a word processing document.
5. This view is an organized page, graphic, and file structure of your FrontPage Web.
6. This view is used primarily to establish the hierarchical structure of a Web site.
7. These allow users to easily switch between open Web pages in Page view.
8. Click this command on the View menu to display or hide the Views bar.
9. Click this button to locate files in such places as My Computer, Web Folders, and Outlook.
10. Click the Tools on the Web command on this menu to access the Microsoft Office Tools on the Web site.
11. The Office Language bar features these two technologies.
12. Access Help by clicking this button on the Standard toolbar.
13. Click the Help menu and then click Office on the Web to access this Web site.
14. Access the Customize dialog box from this menu to customize menus and toolbars.
15. Floating toolbars can be docked by dragging this.

SKILLS check

Assessment 1

1. Open FrontPage and then open the riversidepark01 FrontPage Web, located in your *Chapter 1* folder.
2. Open the following Web pages into Page view from the Folders view:
   a. Open index.htm.
   b. Open park.htm.
   c. Open zoo.htm.
3. Navigate between and print each Web page.
4. Close FrontPage.

Assessment 2

1. Open FrontPage and then open the riversidepark01 FrontPage Web.
2. Hide the Views bar by using the right-click method.
3. Display the Views bar once again.
4. Display the Views bar in small icons.
5. Return the Views bar to large icons.
6. Hide the Views bar once again.
7. Activate the Folder List.
8. Open the index.htm file in Page view.
9. Activate the Navigation Pane.
10. Open the Riverside Park page in Page View.
11. Hide the Navigation Pane.
12. Close FrontPage.

Assessment 3

1. Access the Basic Search Task Pane and locate a Web page (.htm) file located on your computer system. *(Hint: Use the asterisk (*) wildcard character (*.htm) to list all files that are Web page documents.)*
2. Open any of the files for editing in FrontPage.
3. Print the Web page.
4. Close FrontPage.

Assessment 4

1. Access the Microsoft Office Tools on the Web site from the Tools menu.
2. Link to the Assistance Center.
3. Link to *FrontPage* under *Assistance By Product*.
4. Locate and print the following articles:
   - *Creating Consistent Web Pages with FrontPage 2002*
   - *About Views in FrontPage 2002*
   - *Add MSNBC Headlines to Your FrontPage 2002 Web Site*
   - *View Information About a File or Folder in FrontPage 2002*
   - *About Web Site Management in FrontPage 2002*
5. Close the Web browser.
6. Close FrontPage.

Assessment 5

1. Access the official Microsoft Office Web site at www.microsoft.com/office.
2. From the *Using Office* link submenu, access the Office XP Tips and Tricks Center.
3. View and print one article of interest.
4. Access the FrontPage home page from the *Office Programs* link submenu.
5. Click the *Using FrontPage* link.
6. Click the *Communities* link.
7. Browse the client newsgroup to see what problems other FrontPage users may be experiencing.
8. Close the browser window.

Assessment 6

1. Open FrontPage and access the Customize dialog box.
2. Activate the Large icons feature.
3. Deactivate the Large icons feature.
4. Place the Save All button (File Category) on the Standard toolbar next to the Save button.
5. Remove the Save All button from the toolbar.
6. Close FrontPage.

Assessment 7

1. Use the Ask a Question box to enter a search string to locate information about getting help while you work.
2. Print the Help article (with your instructor's permission).
3. Access the Office Assistant from the Help menu to locate a Help article about creating and designing Web pages.
4. Print the Help article (with your instructor's permission).
5. Disable the Office Assistant from appearing when accessing Help.
6. Access the Contents tab in Microsoft FrontPage Help window.
7. Double-click the *Designing Web Sites* option and then double-click the *Create and Open Web Sites* sub-option.
8. Print the Help topic *WEB: About creating web sites* (with your instructor's permission).
9. At the Index tab, enter **graphic** as a keyword and choose the first article listed—*About using graphics.*
10. Print the Help article (with your instructor's permission).
11. Using the Answer Wizard, locate the article *About formatting text and paragraphs.*
12. Print the Help article (with your instructor's permission).
13. Close the Microsoft FrontPage Help window and then close FrontPage.

CHAPTER 2

PLANNING AND CREATING AN INITIAL FRONTPAGE WEB

PERFORMANCE OBJECTIVES

Upon successful completion of Chapter 2, you will be able to:

- **Establish a FrontPage 2002 Web**
- **Create, name, and rename Web pages in Folders view**
- **Establish a hierarchical site structure in Navigation view**
- **Format Web page backgrounds**
- **Insert, format, edit, and delete text**
- **Use the Spelling Checker and Thesaurus**
- **Format text for fonts, styles, sizes, and colors**
- **Format paragraph alignment, indentations, and line spacing**
- **Preview, print, save, and close FrontPage Web pages**

Chapter 2

When FrontPage 2002 is opened, a blank document displays in the Page view. Unlike documents in other applications such as Word (word processing) and Excel (spreadsheet), it is essential to create the Web page files and hierarchical structure before any content is inserted into the pages. Using an outline and/or site structure diagram, this initial process will be beneficial as you begin inserting content into the pages.

In this chapter you will establish a FrontPage Web and create Web page files for future editing. A hierarchical structure of the site will be created in Navigation view. Various background techniques such as a solid color, tiled image, sidebars, and watermarks will be explored. Text will be inserted and formatted in various fonts, sizes, colors, and styles.

Paragraph formatting in FrontPage is very similar to that in word processing applications. Paragraph alignment can be altered so that text and graphics can appear at the left edge, in the center, or at the right edge of the page. Paragraphs in HTML appear to be double-spaced or to have a blank line between paragraphs. We will explore features that will eliminate this extra spacing. Paragraphs are often indented to emphasize information and to attract a reader's attention by separating the material from the rest of the page.

Establishing a FrontPage 2002 Web

FrontPage Webs can initially be saved onto a disk or published directly to the Web. Publishing to the Web requires that you have an account with an ISP or domain host to host the Web. Instructions in this textbook specify saving to a diskette; however, you may want to save your assignments onto a ZIP, CD-RW, or school file server. Some educational institutions provide Web server space for students. Check with your instructor for the procedure to be followed in your class.

Using a Web Site Wizard

FrontPage 2002 provides you with 10 templates and wizards to help you create your Web presence (see figure 2.1). Templates are preformatted Webs that determine the basic site structure and contain document settings such as headings, text, graphics, and hyperlinks. Wizards ask questions and then use your answers to automatically lay out and format FrontPage Web pages. Once the FrontPage Web has been created through the use of a template, the developer can easily replace the template text and images with content-specific text, graphics, and other elements. Wizards take the developer through a series of specific questions that result in a template-like Web. The end result of a wizard process, therefore, is much more complete than that produced with a template. In either instance, developers can format pages to their own specifications once they are in the Page view. To create a new FrontPage Web, click the *Web Site Templates* link in the New Page or Web Task Pane.

FIGURE 2.1 **Web Template and Wizard Descriptions**

Template/Wizard	Description
One Page Web	Creates a new Web with a single blank page. Automatically creates a blank home page and establishes the page in Navigation view. A common selection for most designers starting from scratch.
Corporate Presence Wizard	Takes you through a series of questions about your company or organization and the content information requirements. Includes a home page, What's New, Products/Services, Table of Contents, Feedback Form, a Search Form page, and even an option for using a FrontPage theme for a Web.
Customer Support Web	For companies to enhance their support services; includes several preformatted Web pages that a typical customer support Web would utilize. The pages are directly linked to a preformatted home page, What's New, FAQ, Bugs, Suggestions, Download, Discussion, and Search pages.

Database Interface Wizard	Creates a new Microsoft Access database within the FrontPage Web. The wizard process allows you to create database form field specifications. The Database Interface pages that can automatically be created for you include a submission form, results page, and even a database editor. You can also password-protect your database editor.
Discussion Web Wizard	For those individuals or organizations who want to create a threaded discussion forum. Members can post articles, read existing articles, and search for specific content within the posted discussions.
Empty Web	Creates a new Web with nothing in it. The Web developer must create all Web pages in the Navigation structure. The perfect start for designing a Web based around frames pages.
Import Web Wizard	Allows FrontPage Web developers to import an existing Web either from the World Wide Web or from files on a storage device. Perfect for backing up Webs and researching existing Webs.
Personal Web	Creates a preformatted Web with a home page, Interests, Photo Album, and a Favorites page.
Project Web	Creates a preformatted Web with a home page, list of project members, a schedule, status reports, an archive of documents and files, and a threaded discussion.
SharePoint-based Team Web Site	Allows companies and organizations to create a team Web site to be accessed through either an intranet or the Internet. Includes an events calendar, a library for shared documents, a task list, contact list, discussion board, announcements, and even surveys. Perfect for groups to store, find, and share information, documents, and Web pages.

Web Site Templates Dialog Box

The command-line text box in the Web Site Templates dialog box (see figure 2.2) indicates where you want your FrontPage Web stored. Saving to the hard drive, for example, would require an address such as c:\emcpwebs. If you were saving directly to the Web, you would key an address such as *http://www.emcp.com*. Before you would be able to publish to a Web server, a dialog box would appear and ask for a user name and password.

All Web pages and files, such as images, must be stored in the same folder *(emcpwebs)* when previewing and publishing the site to the Web. If pages and files are not kept in this folder, also called the root Web, the hyperlinks may not work properly and the images may not appear once the site is published. FrontPage root Web folders will have an icon with a picture of the earth.

Once you click the OK button in the Web Site Templates dialog box, the Create New Web dialog box will appear. This indicates that the Web is being created where specified. Depending on where you store your FrontPage Web, this process should take about 10 to 15 seconds, after which the dialog box will disappear from your screen.

FIGURE 2.2 **Web Site Templates Dialog Box**

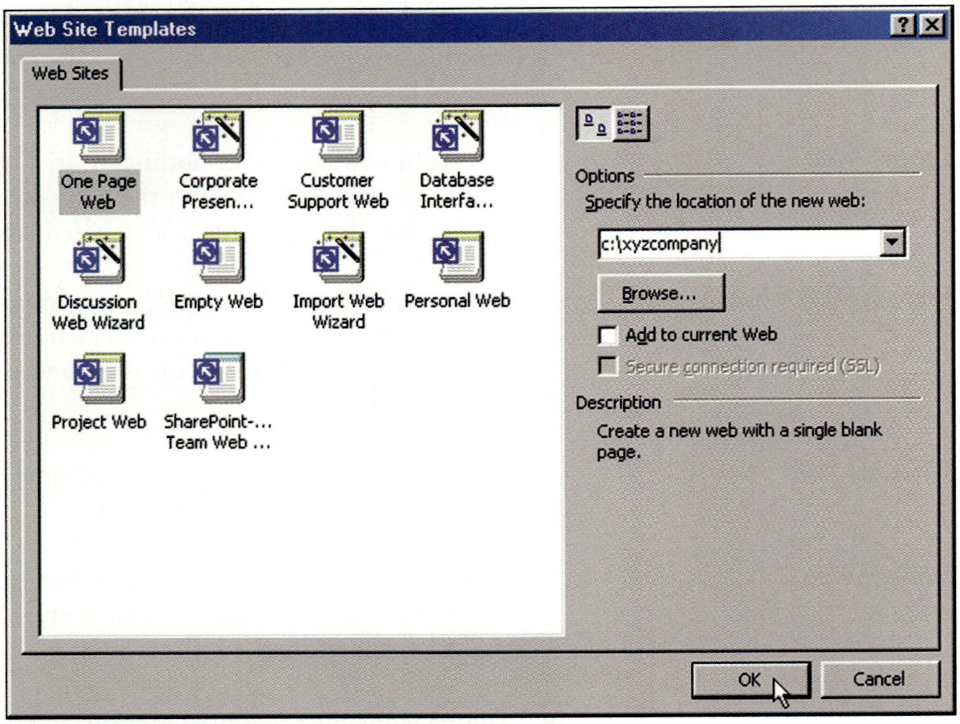

(Note: Before completing computer exercises, delete the Chapter 1 *folder on your disk. Next, download the Chapter 2 data files from the Internet Resource Center to the* Chapter 2 *folder you have created on your disk, and then make* Chapter 2 *the active folder.)*

exercise 1

ESTABLISHING A FRONTPAGE 2002 WEB FROM A WEB SITE TEMPLATE

1. Click the Start button on the Windows taskbar.
2. Point to *Programs* and then click *Microsoft FrontPage*. (This procedure may vary depending on your operating system.)
3. Click the *Web Site Templates* link in the New from template section of the New Page or Web Task Pane.

4. At the WebSite Templates dialog box, select the *One Page Web* icon.

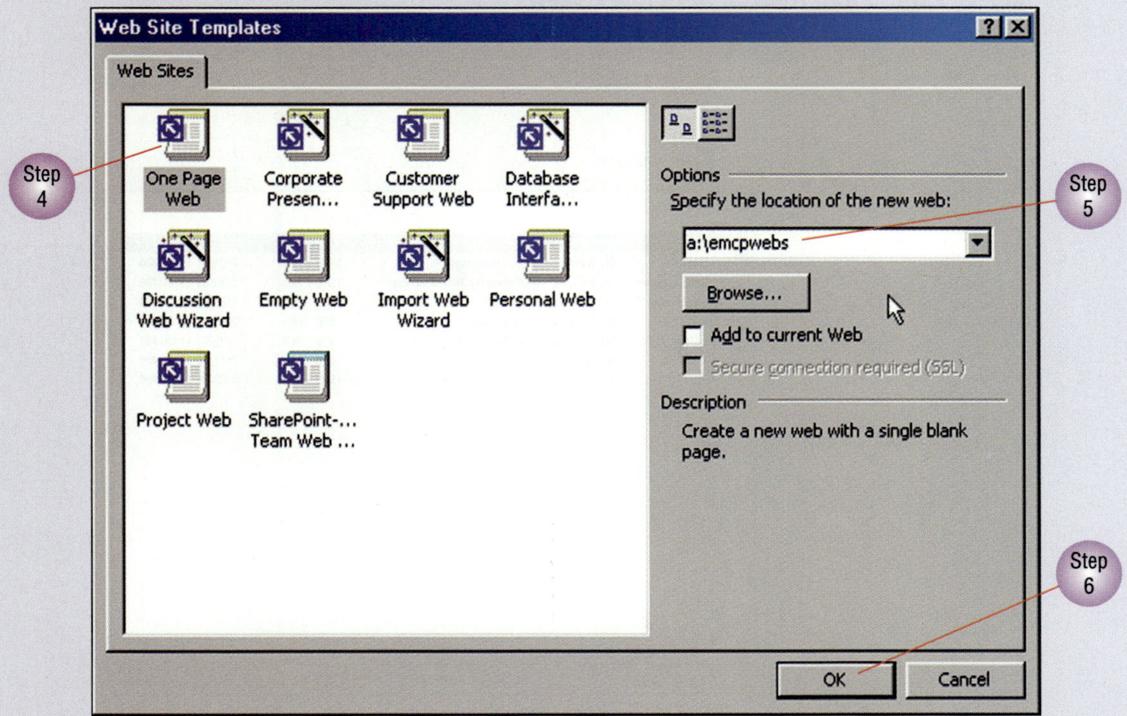

5. Key **a:\emcpwebs** in the Specify the location of the new web text box. *(Note: Check with your instructor for the drive location to which you will be saving your assignments in this textbook.)*
6. Click OK.

Creating, Naming, and Titling Web Pages in Folders View

One of the dynamic aspects of Web sites is that they can be constantly updated with new information, products, and services. It is imperative, however, to have a master plan of the Web site. Preparing a Web site requires much thought and consideration. Essential information must be gathered and organized into an outline or hierarchical structure.

Once you have outlined the content requirements for your Web site, the Folders view allows FrontPage Web developers to create the Web page files and give the pages a file name and title (see figure 2.3). Pages can also be renamed, retitled, and deleted in Folders view. Web pages, folders, and subwebs are organized in alphabetical order.

Web page names should be approximately eight characters in length and in lowercase letters. Title your Web pages in a manner that best describes the content of each page, to help potential visitors find your site by using a search engine or directory. For example, the title *Services* may describe the page well enough to a visitor currently at your site, but *EMCPWebs Web Design Services* may be a better title for those who are searching the Web for Web design services. The page title appears in the Title bar of the browser window.

FIGURE

2.3 Page Files Named in Folders View

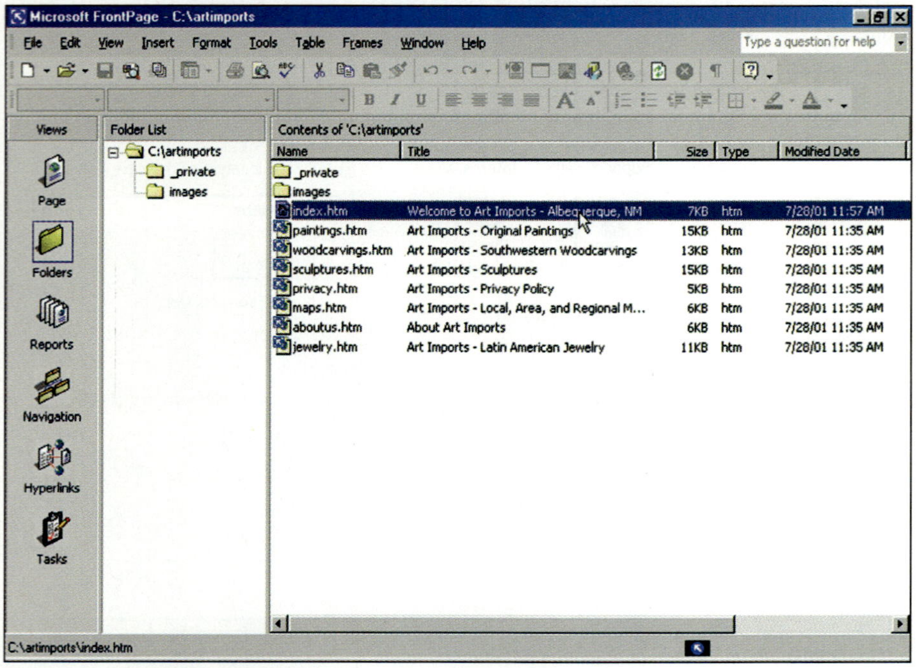

exercise 2

CREATING WEB PAGES IN FOLDERS VIEW

1. With the EMCPWebs FrontPage Web open, click the Folders button on the Views bar. *(Note: If the Views bar is not visible, select the Views Bar command from the View menu.)*
2. Click the Create a new normal page button on the Standard toolbar.
3. Right-click anywhere in an empty area of the Contents pane.
4. Point to New and then click Page.

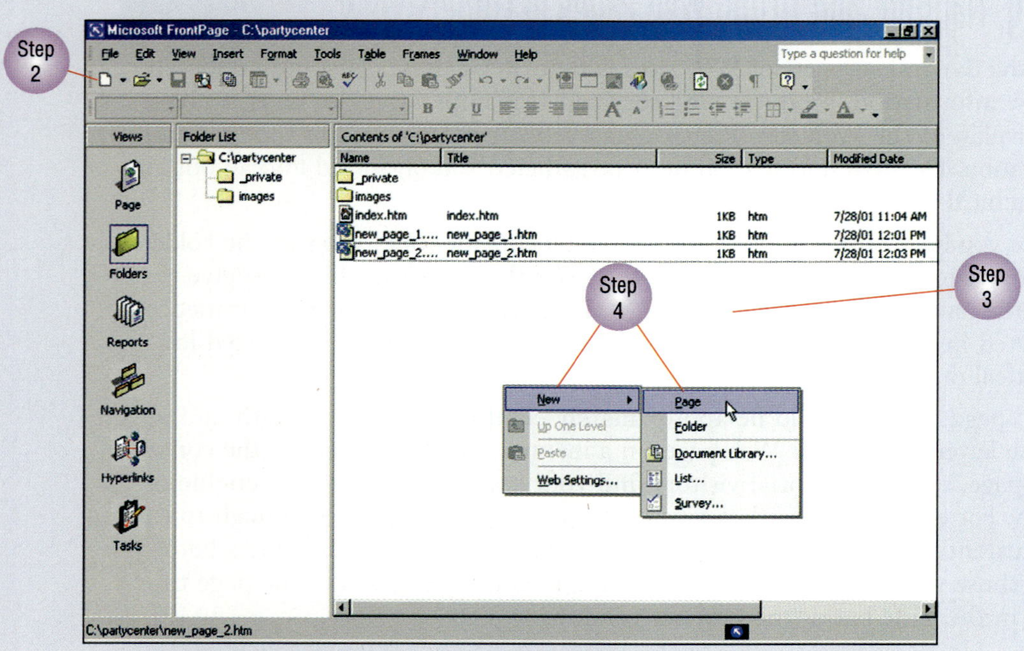

5. Click File, point to New, and then click Page or Web.
6. Click the *Blank Page* link in the New Page or Web Task Pane. The task pane will close.
7. Click the Create a new normal page button on the Standard toolbar seven (7) times for a total of 11 Web page files. *(Note: Microsoft Office applications have multiple ways of accomplishing many common tasks. It is up to you, the developer, to find the most efficient method.)*

exercise 3 NAMING AND TITLING WEB PAGES IN FOLDERS VIEW

1. With EMCPWebs FrontPage Web open in Folders view, click the index.htm home page file.
2. Click *index.htm* again and a box appears around the file name.
3. Press the Tab key and retitle the home page *Welcome to EMCPWebs – Web Design, Graphic Design, and Computer Consulting Services,* and then press the Enter key.
4. Right-click the new_page_1.htm file and select Rename.

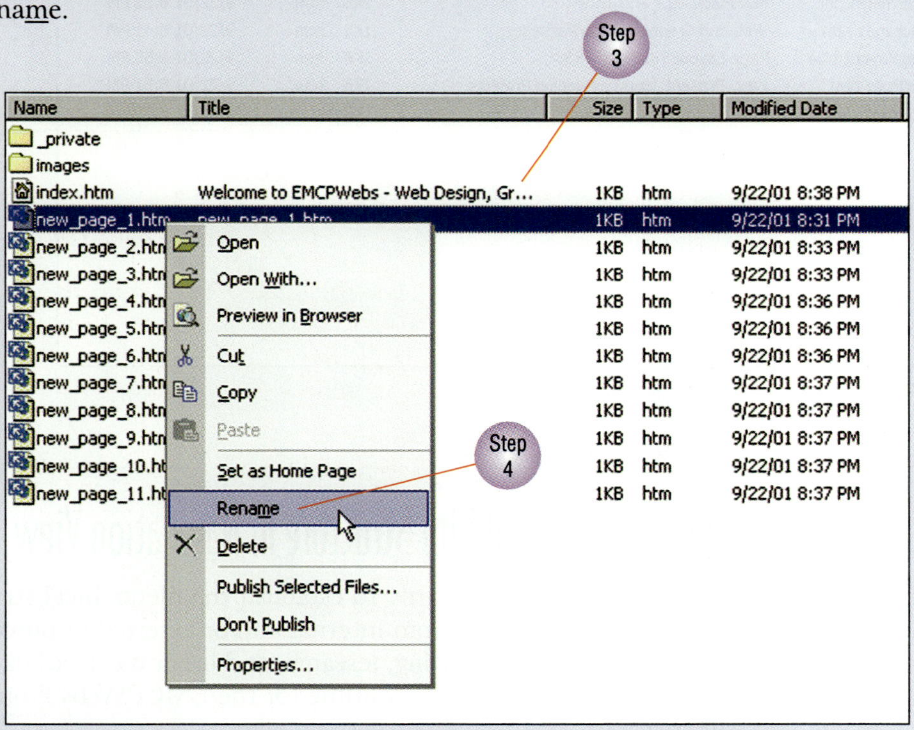

5. Key **aboutus.htm** and press the Tab key.
6. Retitle the Web page *About EMCPWebs* and press Enter.
7. Click the new_page_2.htm file and press the Tab key.
8. Key **packages.htm** and press the Tab key.
9. Retitle the Web page *Web and Graphic Design Packages* and press Shift + Tab.
10. Press the down arrow key on your keyboard.
11. Key **contactus.htm**, press the Tab key, and retitle the page *Contact EMCPWebs*.

12. Rename and retitle the remaining Web pages using the information below:

File Name	***Page Title***
portfolio.htm	*Past, Present, and Developing Projects*
webdesign.htm	*Web Design Tips and Tricks*
html.htm	*HTML Tips and Tricks*
graphics.htm	*Graphics Tips and Tricks*
pagelayout.htm	*Page Layout Tips and Tricks*
multimedia.htm	*Multimedia Tips and Tricks*
frontpage.htm	*FrontPage 2002 Tips and Tricks*

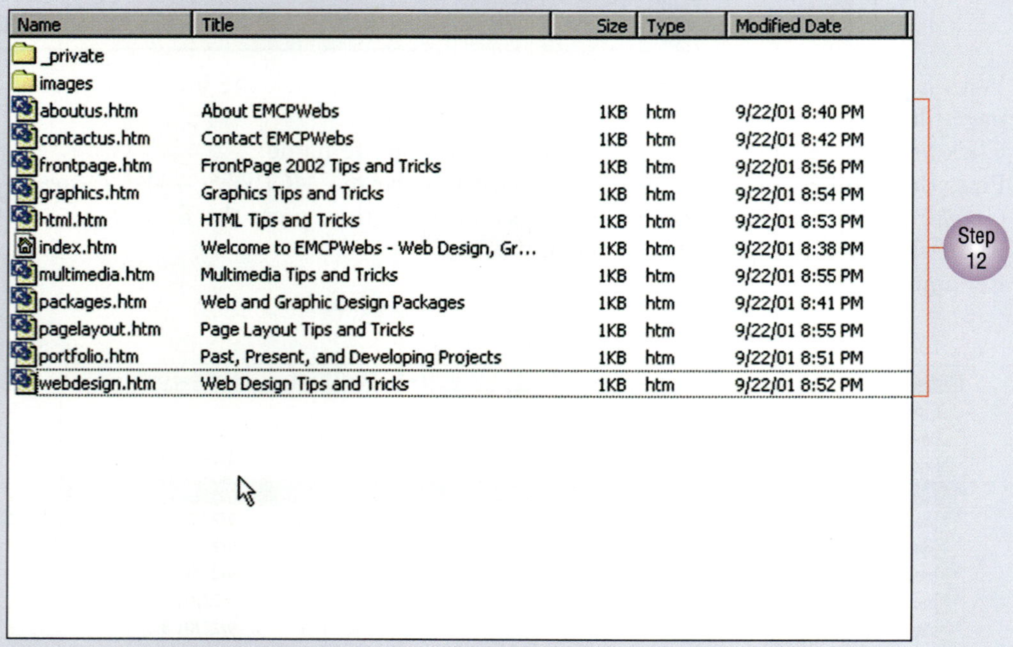

Establishing a Hierarchical Site Structure in Navigation View

The Navigation view is used primarily to establish the hierarchical structure of a Web site. Information gathering from internal and/or external resources can be a challenge. Brainstorming, interviewing, research, and other means of data gathering take time. Figure 2.4 shows a sample outline for the EMCPWebs FrontPage Web site you will create.

FIGURE

2.4 **Drag and Drop Navigation Structure**

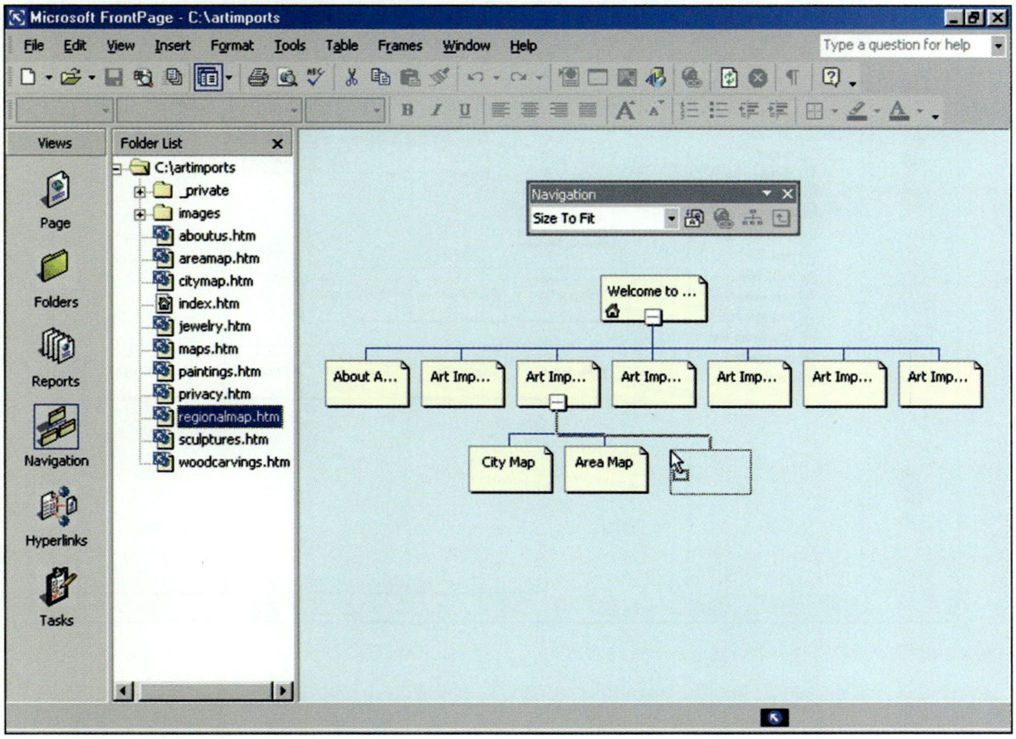

exercise 4 ESTABLISHING A HIERARCHICHAL SITE STRUCTURE IN NAVIGATION VIEW

1. Click the Navigation button on the Views bar.
2. Click the aboutus.htm file in the Folder List and drag it underneath the home page box in the Navigation view.
3. Click the packages.htm file in the Folder List and drag it underneath the home page and to the right of the About Us Web page.
4. Drag the contactus.htm, portfolio.htm, and webdesign.htm files in order underneath the home page.

5. Drag the html.htm, graphics.htm, pagelayout.htm, multimedia.htm, and frontpage.htm files underneath the EMCPWebs – Web Design Tips and Tricks box.

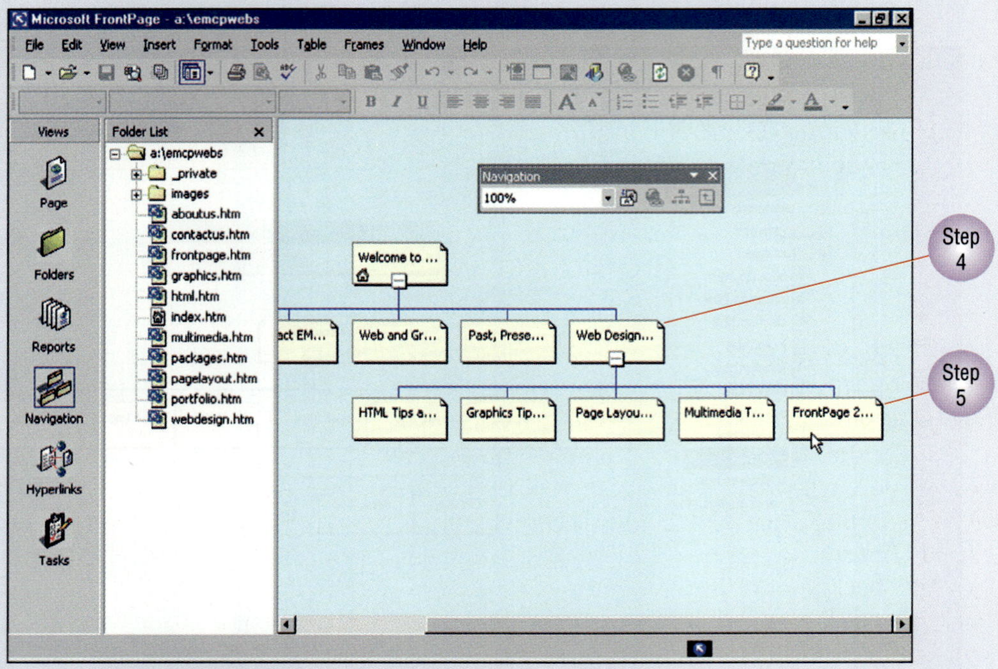

exercise 5

PRINTING THE NAVIGATION STRUCTURE

1. Select *Size To Fit* in the Zoom drop-down list on the Navigation toolbar. *(Note: If the Navigation toolbar is not visible, click View, point to Toolbars, and then click Navigation.)*

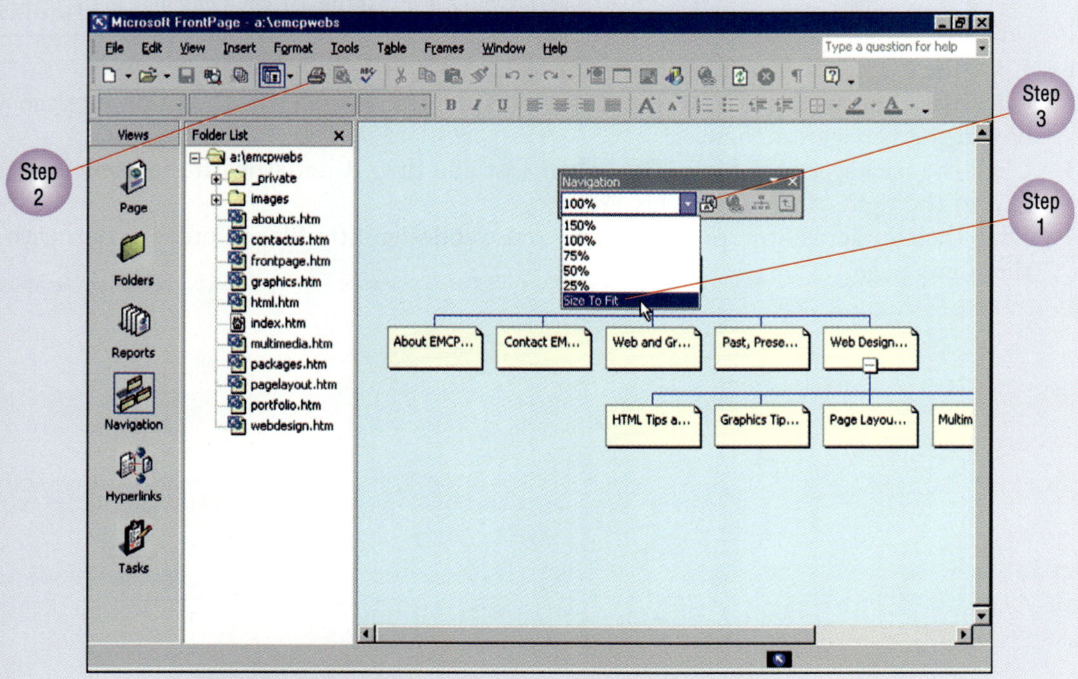

2. Click the Print button on the Standard toolbar.
3. Click the Portrait/Landscape button on the Navigation toolbar to change the orientation to portrait.
4. Click File and then select the Print Preview command.
5. Click the Print button on the Print Preview toolbar.
6. Select the appropriate print settings and then click OK.
7. Right-click inside the Navigation view and click the Portrait/Landscape command to return the navigation orientation to landscape.

Formatting the Background

Your Web page background is dependent on two criteria. The page layout structure is the first criterion. If your page layout requires a sidebar, an image applicable to such an arrangement must be used. The second criterion for background requirements is the theme of the site. If you are developing a Web site that matches your company's color scheme, you will want a background color, texture, or image that matches. In addition to matching a particular color scheme, your background should contrast with textual content for ease of reading. For example, you do not want red text against a black background. In many instances, there is nothing wrong with a plain white background. Figure 2.5 shows various types of images that can be used as Web page backgrounds. *(Note: The background will display on screen, but will not appear in a printout from FrontPage.)*

FIGURE 2.5 ***Comparison of Graphics Used as Web Page Backgrounds***

Image Type		***Description***
Textured Pattern		Commonly used for adding textures and colors to a Web page.
Tiled Image		Commonly used to emphasize an image such as a company logo or a photograph. Too many colors may hinder viewable font color options.
Semitransparent Image		Commonly used to emphasize an image such as a company logo or a photograph. Semitransparent images broaden viewable font color options.

Continued on next page

Tiled Image for Columnar Layouts		Commonly used to segment a Web page with color. Expands options for font colors.
Watermark		Commonly used to emphasize an image such as a company logo or a photograph on a larger scale. As the viewer scrolls through the Web page, the image does not move.

Formatting a Solid-Color Background

To format the background, select the Background command on the Format menu. This takes you directly to the Background tab in the Page Properties dialog box (see figure 2.6). From here you can format the background, default page colors, hyperlink colors, and hyperlink rollover effects that add interest to a Web page. You can also get background information from another page.

FIGURE 2.6 ***Background Tab in Page Properties Dialog Box***

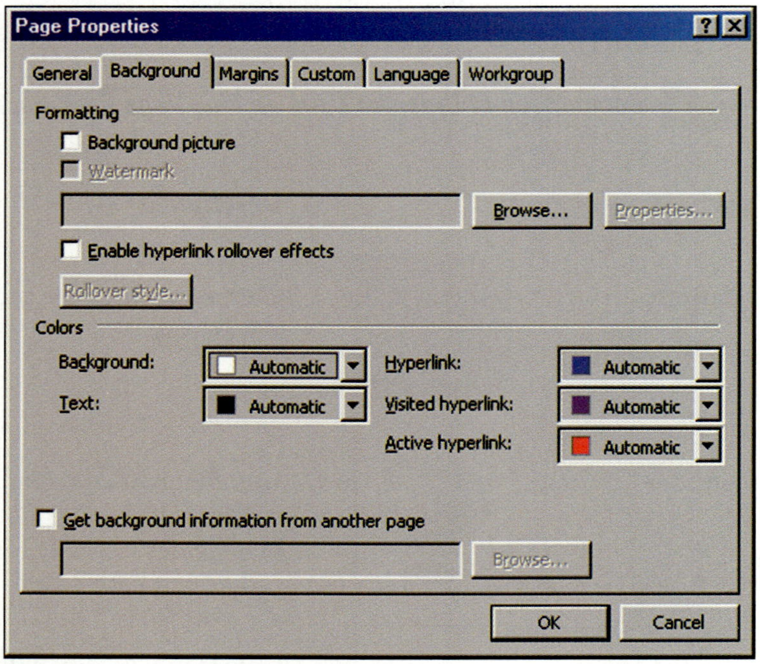

The Background drop-down list box includes the traditional 16-color palette. Selecting the More Colors option will take you to the More Colors dialog box (figure 2.7), which has a hexagonal palette of 127 "Web Safe" colors from which to select. You can also use the Select (eyedropper) button to match the background to a particular graphical image color currently on the Web page. There is also a Custom button that provides a full spectrum of colors and shades.

FIGURE

2.7 More Colors Dialog Box

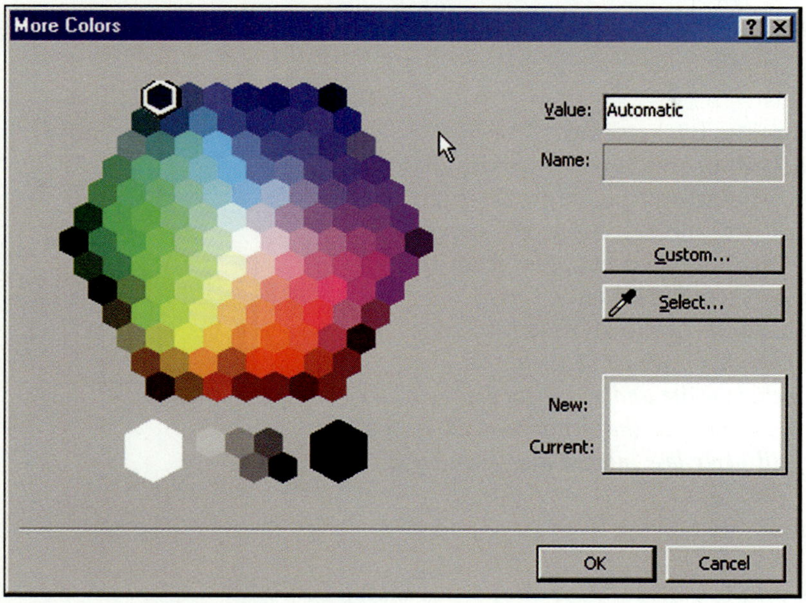

Clicking the Custom button in the More Colors dialog box will open the Color dialog box (figure 2.8). The Color dialog box allows Web developers the flexibility to specify a particular color from the spectrum that may not be located in the More Colors dialog box. Custom colors you have selected can be added to the Custom colors list for later retrieval. Deviating from the "Web Safe" may result in "color dithering" for older monitors and systems set to a low resolution. Dithering converts colors that the monitor cannot display into patterns of two or more colors that closely resemble the original, often resulting in fuzzy colors or images.

FIGURE

2.8 Color Dialog Box

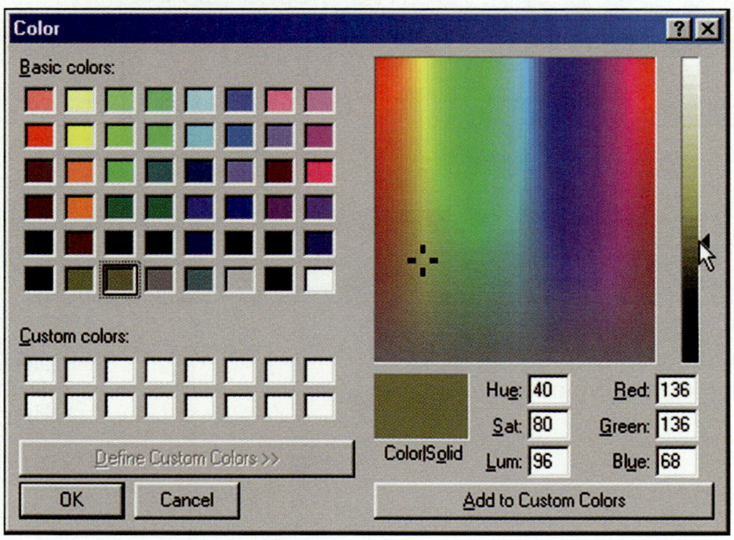

exercise 6

FORMATTING A SOLID-COLOR BACKGROUND

1. With the EMCPWebs FrontPage Web open in Navigation view, double-click *index.htm* in the Folder List.
2. Close the Folder List.
3. Click Format and select Background.
4. At the Background tab of the Page Properties dialog box, click the down-pointing triangle to the right of the Background list box and select More Colors.
5. Select the blue hexagon (fourth hexagon from the left in the second row) and then click OK.

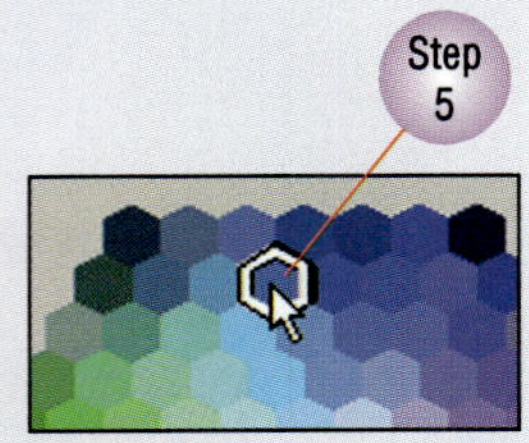

6. Click the OK button once again to return to Page view. *(Hint: Text colors that contrast best with the blue background would include white and very light colors. Make sure your Web pages are easy for the visitor to read. If they are not, the visitor will likely lose interest and move on to another Web site.)*
7. Right-click an empty area of the Web page and then select Page Properties on the pop-up menu.
8. Click the Background tab in the Page Properties dialog box.
9. Click the down-pointing triangle in the Background list box and then click More Colors.
10. Click the Custom button.
11. On the slider scale located on the right side of the Color dialog box, click the arrow and drag it up until the Red, Green, and Blue numbers below the scale read 230, 242, and 255, respectively. *(Note: If you cannot match those numbers precisely using the slider scale, you can key them in the text boxes.)*

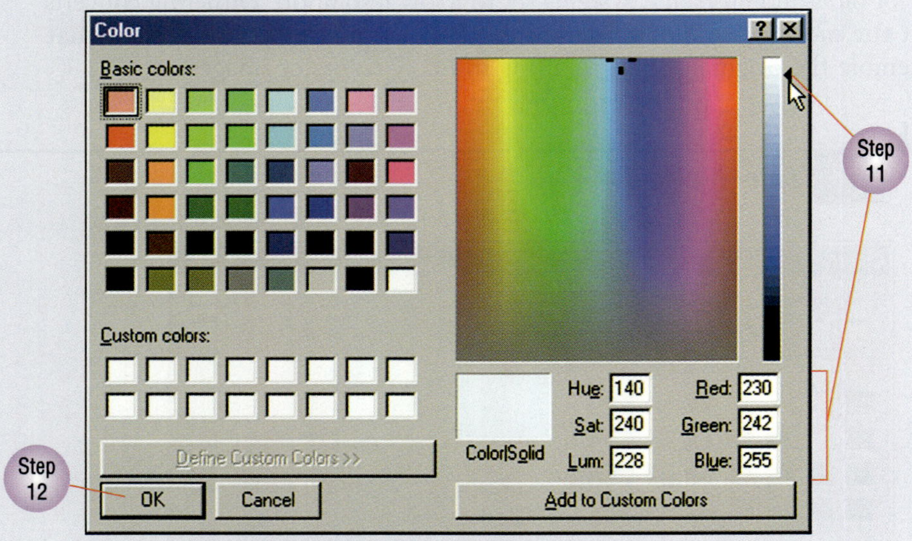

12. Click the OK button on each dialog box to return to the EMCPWebs home page.
13. Click the Save button on the Standard toolbar to save the modifications you have made thus far.

Formatting a Tiled Image Background

An image that is formatted as a Web page background is automatically tiled throughout the page (see figure 2.9). Images are first tiled from left to right and then down the page. Web developers need to be careful with the tiled images that are used. Images with varying contrasts can make it difficult to select a font color that can be easily read throughout the page. Common uses of tiled images are textures and patterns. Textured or patterned backgrounds should appear seamless, and show no abrupt changes in pattern or color.

FIGURE 2.9 ***Tiled Background (a) and Original Image (b)***

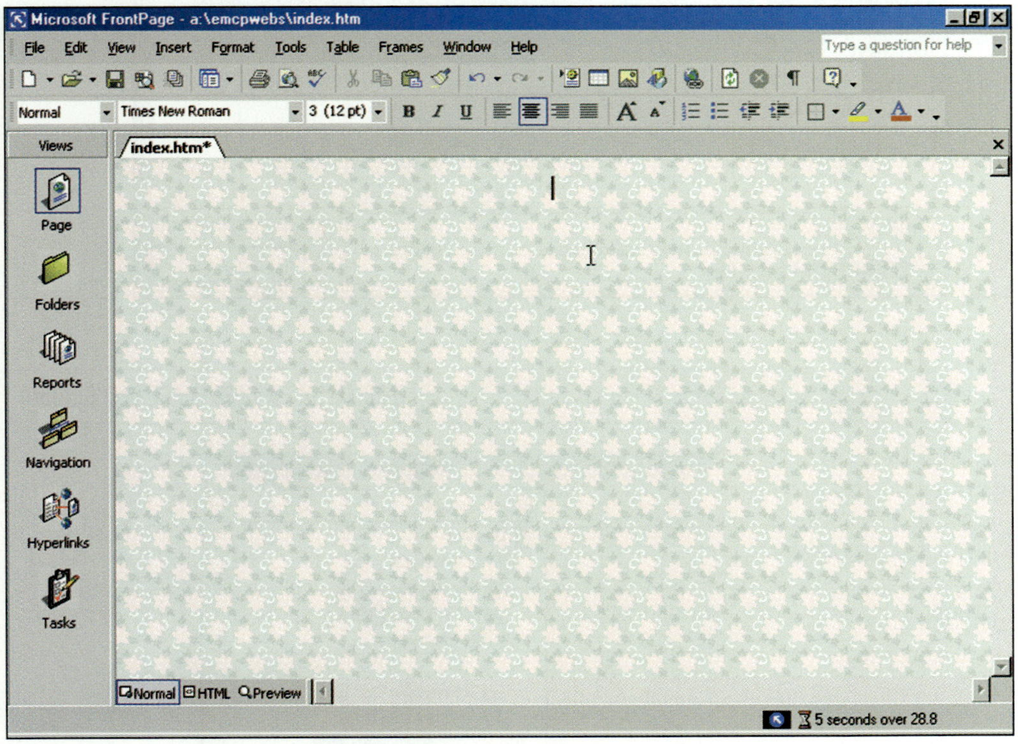

a

b

When browsing for an image to be formatted as the background, you will access the Select Background Picture dialog box (figure 2.10), which looks very similar to the Open, Save As, and (Insert) Picture dialog boxes. Any image already saved on the current Web can be found in the file area of this dialog box. Other images that are to be formatted as the background can be found using either the Look in list box or the buttons on the left side of the dialog box.

FIGURE 2.10 ***Select Background Picture Dialog Box***

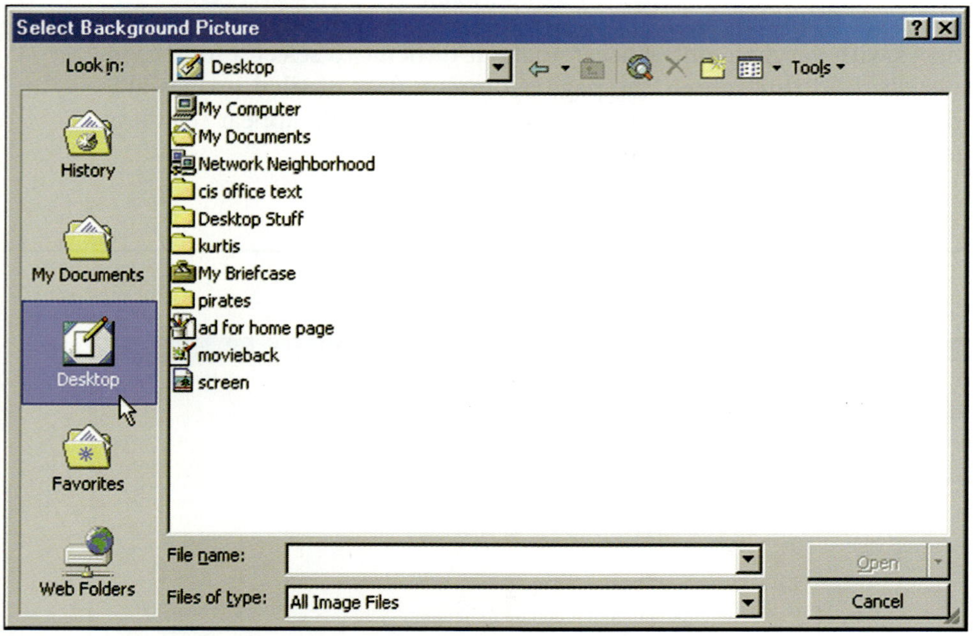

exercise 7

FORMATTING A TILED IMAGE BACKGROUND

1. With the EMCPWebs home page open in Page view, press Alt + O.
2. Press K on the keyboard.
3. In the Page Properties dialog box, click the Browse button in the Formatting section.
4. Locate the *EMCPWebs Images* folder by clicking the down-pointing triangle next to the Look in list box.
5. In the *EMCPWebs Images* folder, click *emcpwebs_back.gif*.
6. Click the OK button on each dialog box to return to the EMCPWebs home page.
7. Click the Save button on the Standard toolbar to save the updated Web page.

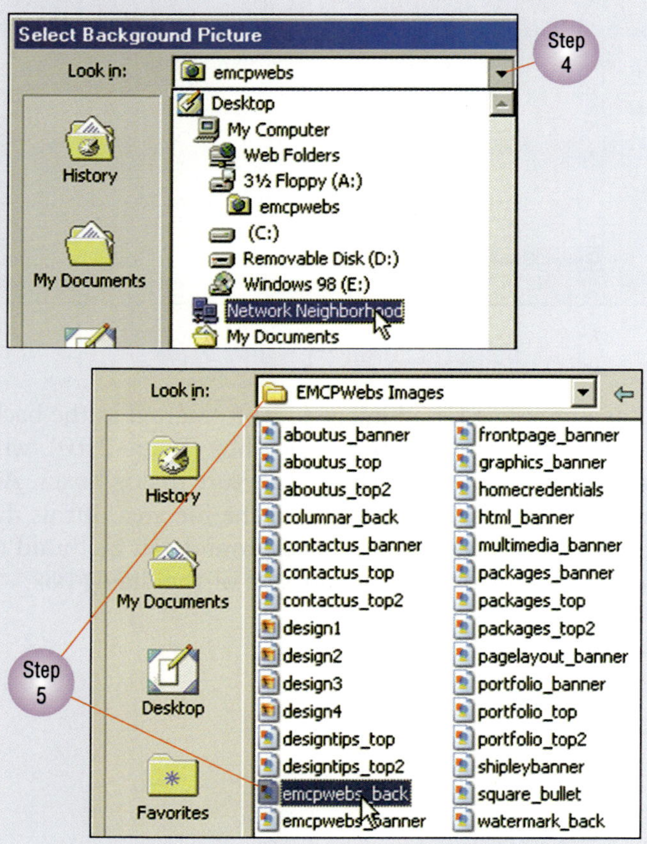

8. When the Save Embedded Files dialog box appears, click the OK button to save the emcpwebs_back.gif file to your FrontPage Web.

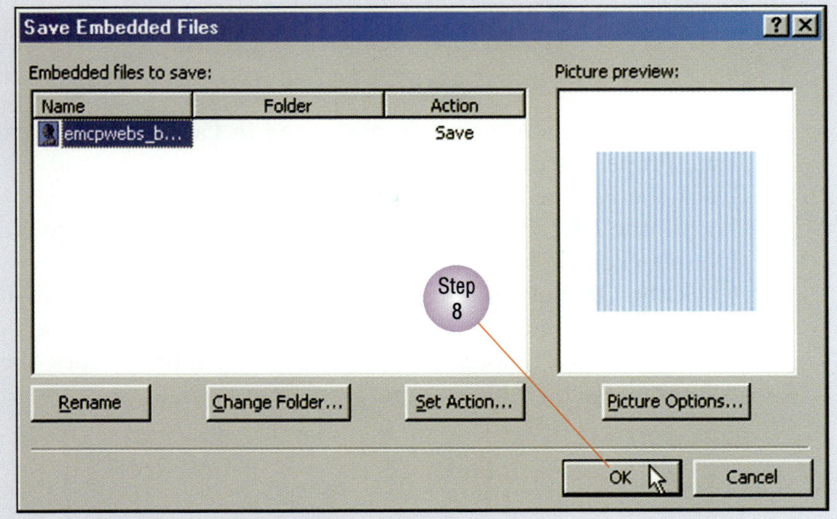

Formatting the Background for Columnar Page Layouts

Web sites with numerous hyperlinks may include a multicolored background designed for a columnar page layout (see figure 2.11). Columnar page layouts are commonly used in Webs today, providing visitors multiple areas on the screen for content. Images that are created for columnar page layout backgrounds are usually short and very wide. In fact, typical image sizes can be as much as 1100 pixels wide and 1 pixel tall. The tiled image is so seamless that the average Web visitor has no idea how it looked when it was originally created in a graphic editing program.

FIGURE 2.11 ***Background Designed for Columnar Page Layout***

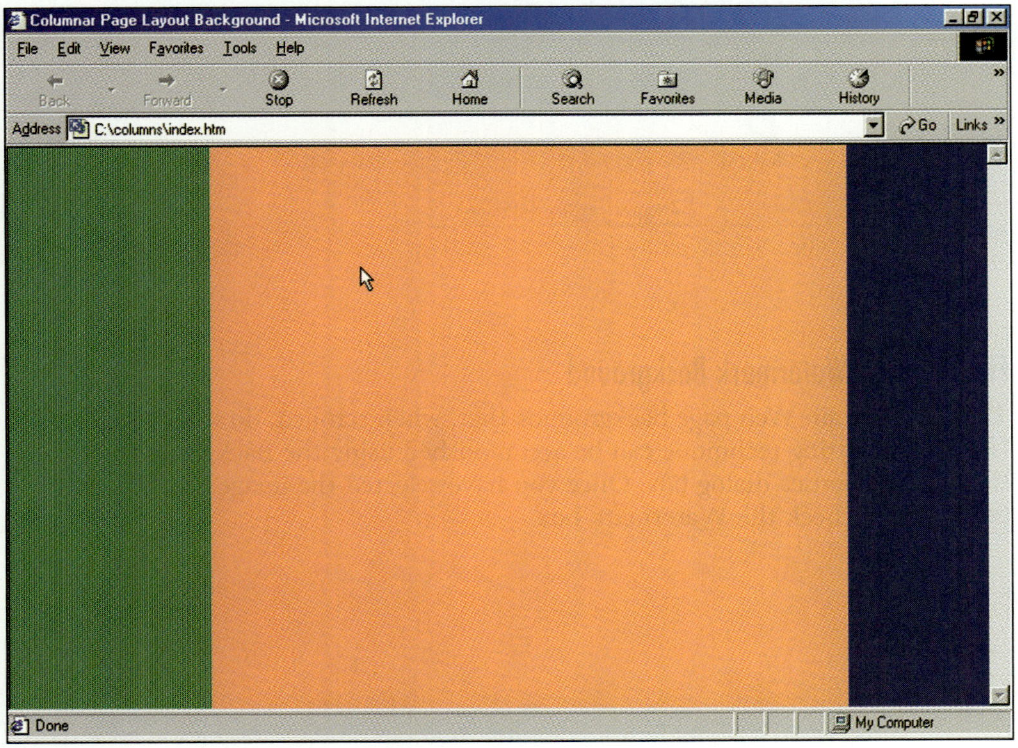

exercise 8

FORMATTING THE BACKGROUND FOR COLUMNAR PAGE LAYOUTS

1. With the EMCPWebs home page open in Page view, access the Background tab of the Page Properties dialog box.
2. Click the Browse button in the Formatting section.
3. Locate the *EMCPWebs Images* folder using the Look in down-pointing triangle.
4. Double-click *columnar_back.gif.*
5. Click the OK button in each dialog box to return to the EMCPWebs home page.
6. Click the Save button on the Standard toolbar to save the updated Web page.
7. When the Save Embedded Files dialog box appears, click the OK button to save the columnar_back.gif file to your FrontPage Web.

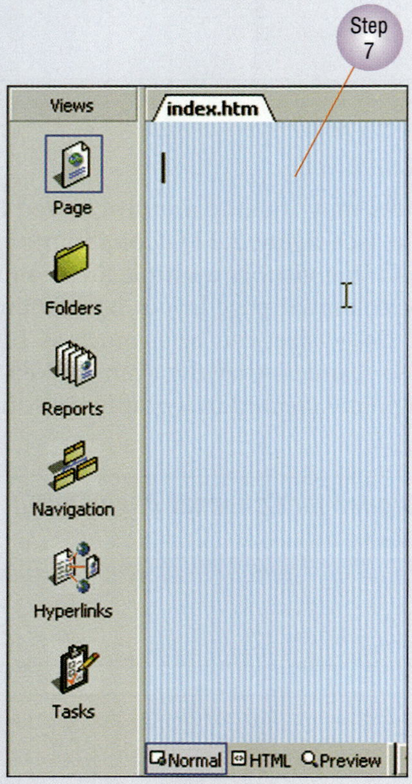

Formatting a Watermark Background

There are certain Web page backgrounds that, when scrolled, do not move. This "fixed" formatting technique can be accomplished using the Background tab of the Page Properties dialog box. Once you have selected the image file for your background, check the Watermark box.

exercise 9

FORMATTING A WATERMARK BACKGROUND

1. With the EMCPWebs home page open in Page view, access the Background tab of the Page Properties dialog box.
2. Click the Browse button in the Formatting section.
3. Locate the *EMCPWebs Images* folder using the Look in down-pointing triangle.
4. Double-click *watermark_back.gif*.
5. In the Formatting section of the Background tab, click in the Watermark check box to insert a check mark.
6. Click the OK button in each dialog box to return to the EMCPWebs home page.

Step 5

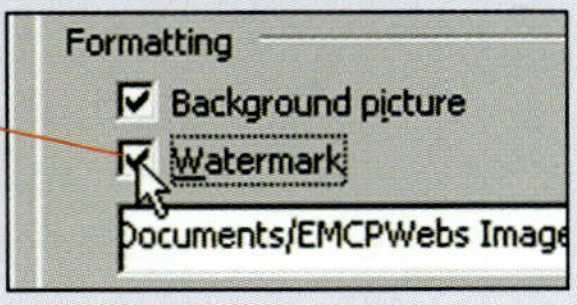

7. Enter the numbers 1 through 15 on separate lines by pressing Enter after each number.
8. Click the Preview tab at the bottom of the Page view and scroll the Web page to test the watermark. *(Note: If your resolution is set to 1024 × 768 or above, you may have to key numbers above 15 to bring up the scroll bar in Preview.)*

Step 7

Step 8

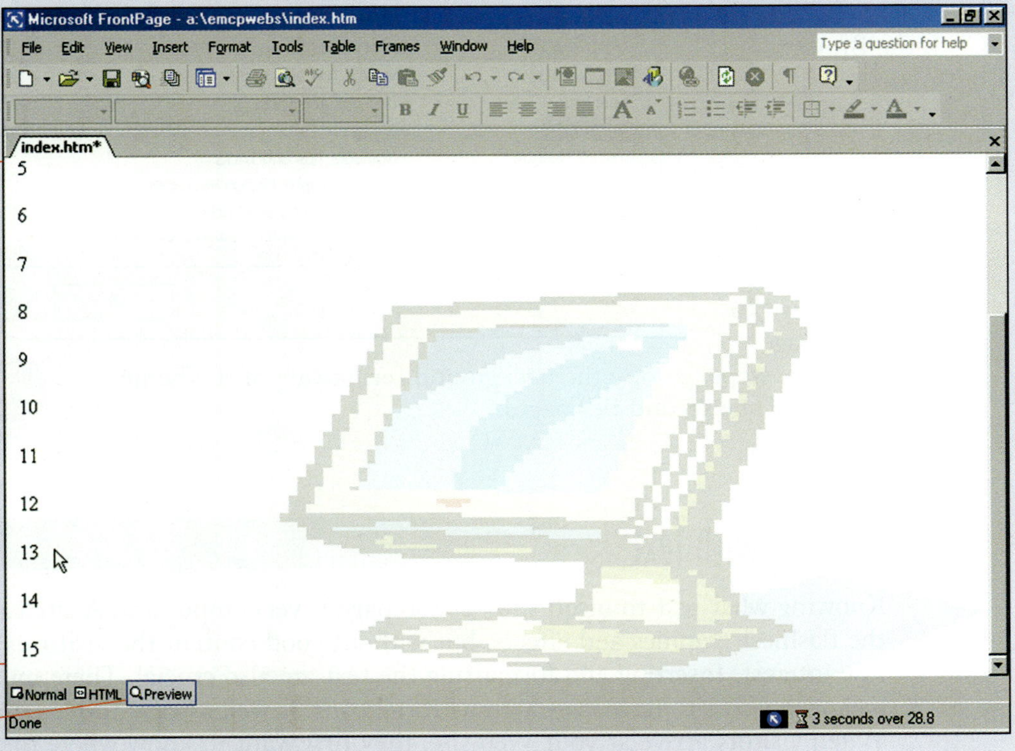

9. Return to *Normal* mode and delete the numbers.
10. Format the background back to emcpwebs_back.gif.
11. Click the Save button on the Standard toolbar to save the updated Web page.

Getting Background Information from Another Page

One of the most important characteristics of a Web presence is its consistency. A consistent background and layout throughout a site will make it easier for visitors to follow the content and navigate the pages. One way to ensure that pages remain consistent within a Web is to use the background formatting of an existing page as the background for all associated pages. The Web pages that get background information from another page will automatically be updated if the associated page background is ever changed.

exercise 10

GETTING BACKGROUND INFORMATION FROM ANOTHER PAGE

1. With the EMCPWebs home page open in Page view, access the Folder List from the Toggle Pane button on the Standard toolbar.
2. Double-click *aboutus.htm*.
3. Access the Background tab of the Page Properties dialog box.
4. Click Get background information from another page to insert a check mark in the check box.
5. Click the Browse button.
6. In the Current Web dialog box, click *index.htm*.
7. Click OK to return to the Page Properties dialog box and then click OK to return to the About Us page.
8. Repeat the above steps to copy the background formatting of the home page to the rest of the second-tier pages.

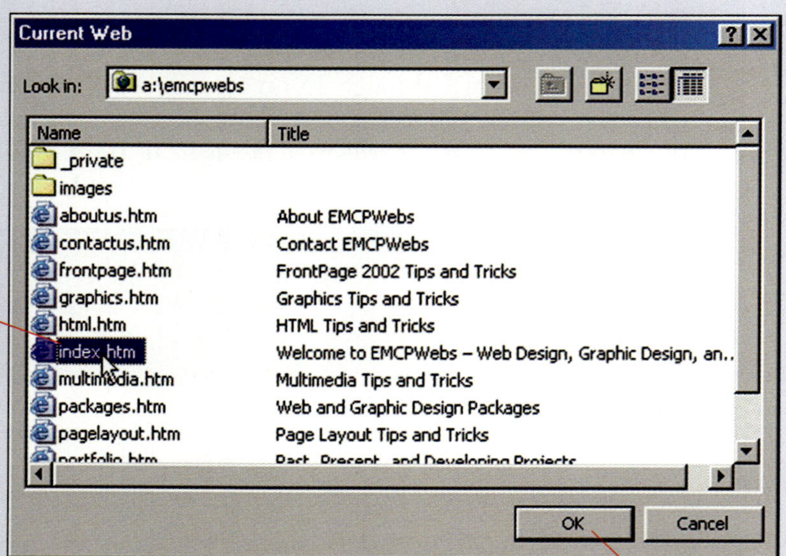

Working with Text

Knowing what text to insert into a Web page is very important. A site can have the flashiest graphics and effects, but without good content the visitor is sure to lose interest. Inserting and formatting the text are also crucial. There must be a balanced effort to have eye-catching formatting as well as easy-to-read content. When visitors arrive at your Web site, they first want to know where they are. Once they have made a conscious determination of their location, they look for content that will direct them where they want to go.

At the top of a typical Web page (see figure 2.12) is a page title or banner. The banner area contains such components as site/page title, subtitle, address, phone numbers, e-mail links, or other identification items. The body area of the Web page is typically the largest and contains the essence of the page. Text, graphics, and hyperlinks that make up the identity of the page are located in the body. The footer area is located at the bottom of the Web page. Common footer components include contact information, navigation text or images, date of last update, author credits, and copyright information.

FIGURE 2.12 *Areas of a Typical Web Page*

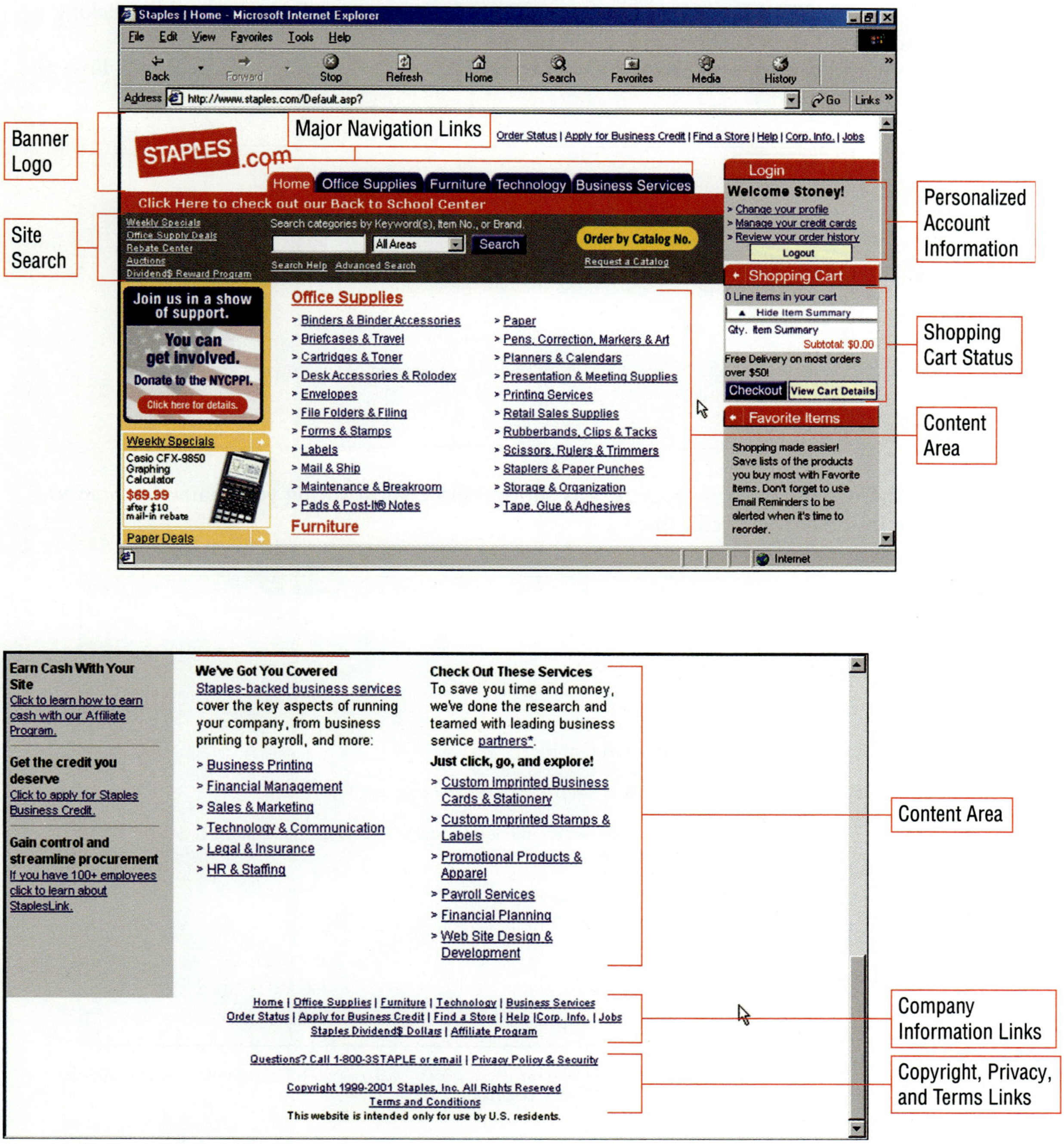

Inserting Web Page Text

When you are writing content for a Web page, remember that the information must come across to the reader in a clear and concise manner. The content must also be complete, accurate, easy to read, and useful. Always keep your audience in mind when constructing the content of the Web site.

exercise 11

INSERTING WEB PAGE TEXT

1. With the EMCPWebs home page open in Page view, return to the home page by clicking Window and then clicking index.htm on the menu.
2. Using the default font, key the text shown below; press the Enter key after each line of text.

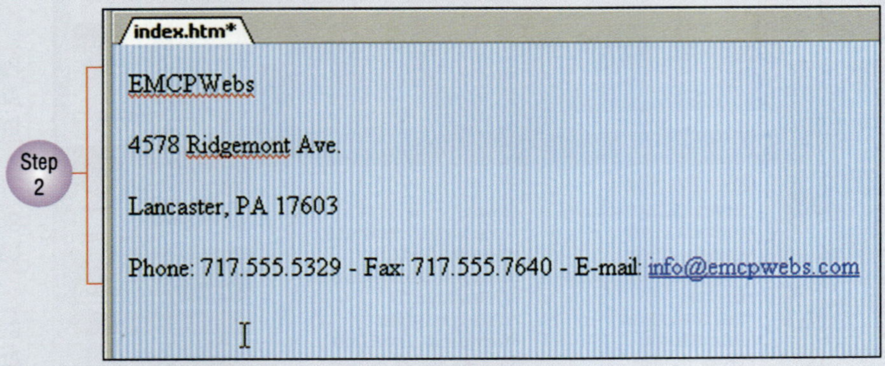

3. Key the remaining home page text as shown below, substituting your name for *Student Name* in the author credit line.

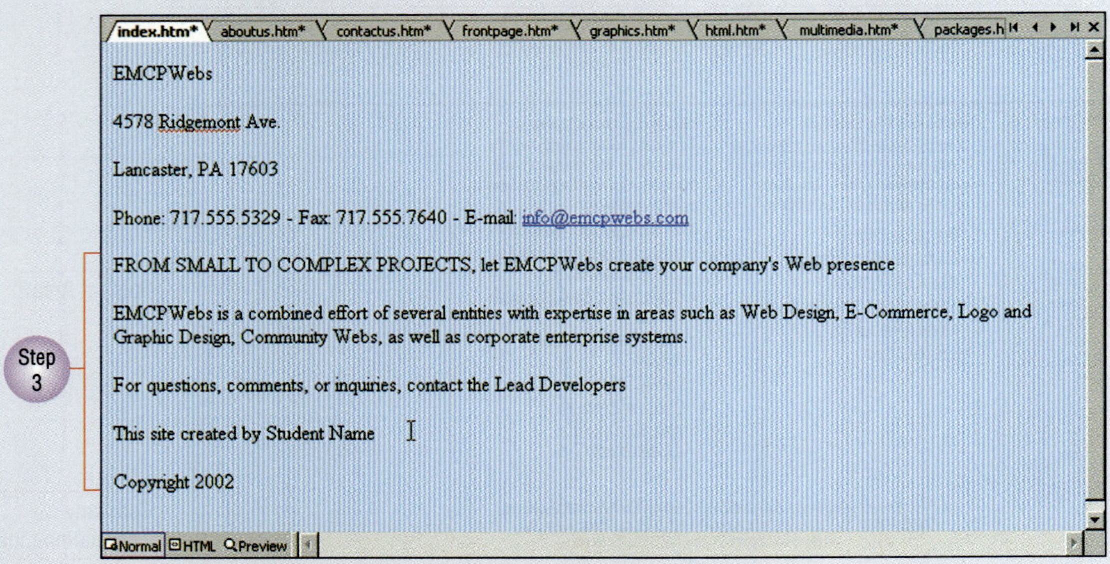

4. Click the Save button on the Standard toolbar.

Using Keyboard Shortcuts to Navigate the Page

Using keyboard shortcuts (see figure 2.13) can make your text entry more efficient and may save time in accomplishing tasks. Common task keyboard shortcuts can be found at the right of commands in menus. In many instances, it is quicker to key a shortcut with your fingers already at the keyboard rather than use the mouse.

FIGURE

2.13 ***Common FrontPage Keyboard Shortcuts***

Keyboard Shortcut	**Description**
End	End of line
Home	Beginning of line
Page Up	Up one screen
Page Down	Down one screen
Ctrl + Home	Beginning of document
Ctrl + End	End of document
Ctrl + S	Save
Ctrl + P	Print
Ctrl + Z	Undo
F1	Help

exercise 12

NAVIGATING A WEB PAGE USING KEYBOARD SHORTCUTS

1. With the EMCPWebs home page open in Page view, press Ctrl + Home to return the insertion point to the beginning of the document.
2. Press the End key to move the insertion point to the end of the first line of text.
3. Press the Enter key once and then key

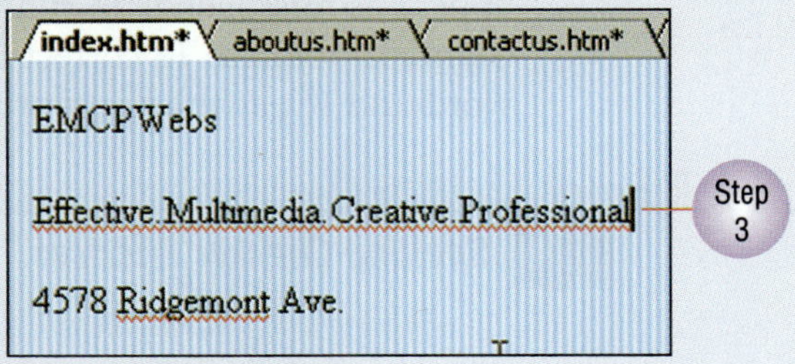

Effective.Multimedia.Creative.Professional

4. Press Ctrl + End to return to the end of the Web page.
5. Position the mouse pointer just after *2002* in the last line of text, press the spacebar once, and then key

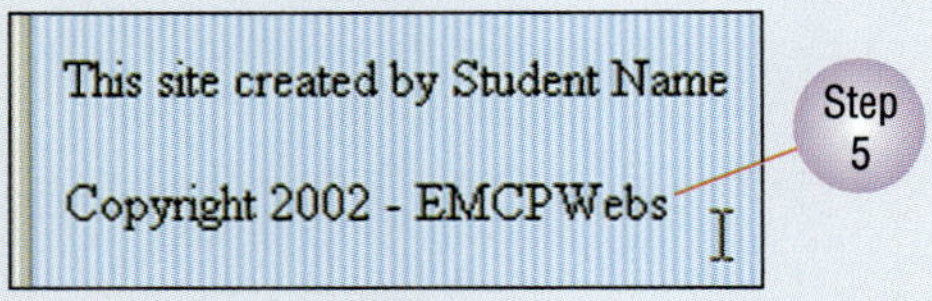

– EMCPWebs

6. Press Ctrl + S to save the updated home page.

Selecting and Replacing Existing Text

There are several tricks you can use to select and replace text and paragraphs. A quick way to highlight a word is to double-click anywhere in the word. Selecting a line of text is as easy as clicking in the left margin. Double-clicking in the left margin will select the entire paragraph.

exercise 13 — REPLACING EXISTING TEXT

1. With the EMCPWebs home page open in Page view, double-click the word *Phone* in the fifth line of text.
2. Key **Voice**.
3. Click in the left margin of the line of text beginning *Effective.Multimedia...* and press the Delete key.
4. Double-click in the left margin of the line of text beginning *EMCPWebs is a combined...* and key the text below, as shown at right.
5. Save the updated home page.

Step 4

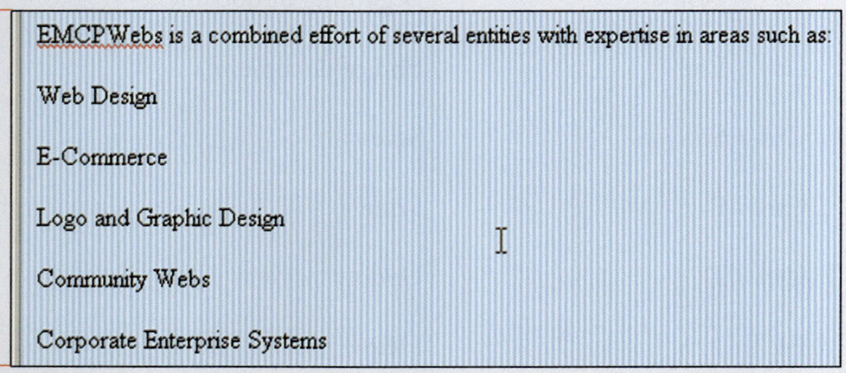

Using the Spelling Checker

By now, you have probably noticed the red wavy lines underneath some of the words on the home page. Words that do not appear in the dictionary will automatically appear as misspelled. To run the Spelling Checker, click the Spelling button on the Standard toolbar. To correct individual words, a quick shortcut is to right-click the word and select the appropriate option (see figure 2.14).

FIGURE 2.14 ***Spelling Checker Shortcut***

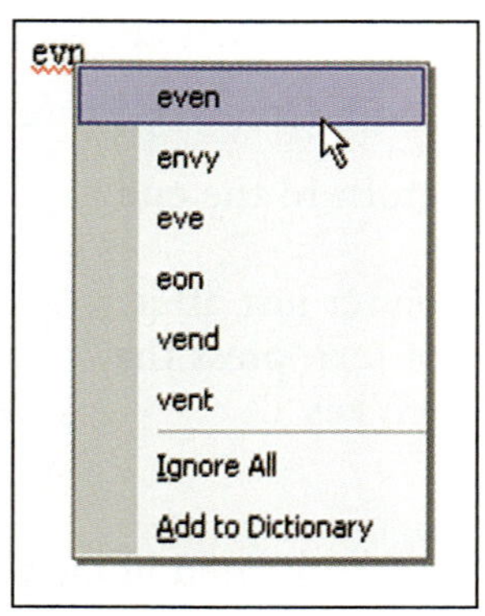

exercise 14

FIXING MISSPELLED WORDS AND ADDING WORDS TO THE DICTIONARY

1. With the EMCPWebs home page open in Page view, place your insertion point after the *m* in *combined*.
2. Press the Backspace key to delete the *m*.
3. Click anywhere outside the now-misspelled word.
4. Right-click the misspelled word, and then select the *combined* option.

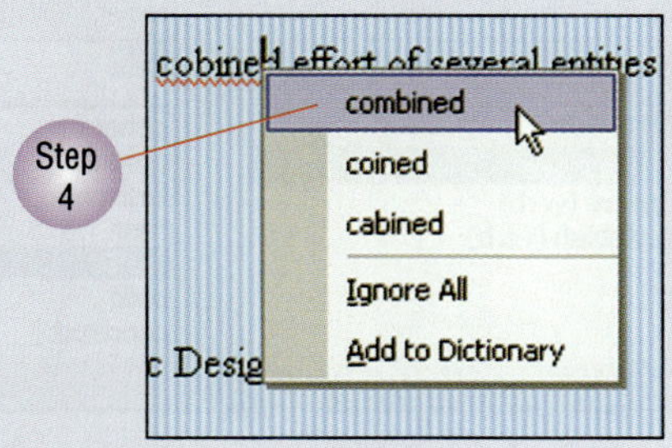

5. Right-click one of the uses of *EMCPWebs*, and then select the *Add to Dictionary* command.

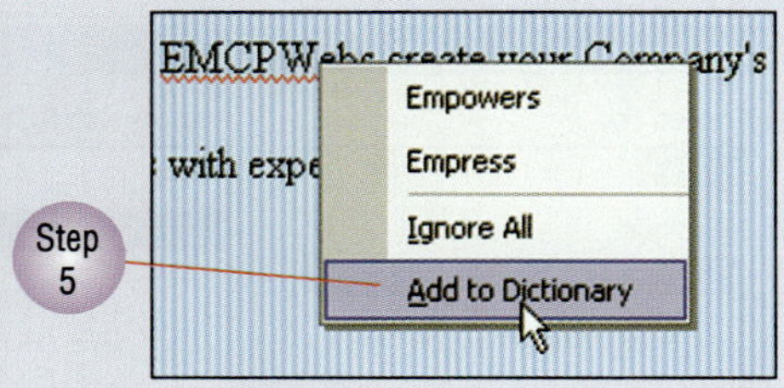

6. Save the updated home page.

Using the Thesaurus

The Thesaurus is a very handy tool for all Web developers. The Thesaurus feature has been a part of Microsoft Office programs for many versions, but it is making its debut FrontPage appearance in FrontPage 2002. To use the Thesaurus, place the insertion point anywhere within a word and select Thesaurus from the Tools menu. Figure 2.15 shows the Thesaurus dialog box.

FIGURE 2.15 **Thesaurus Dialog Box**

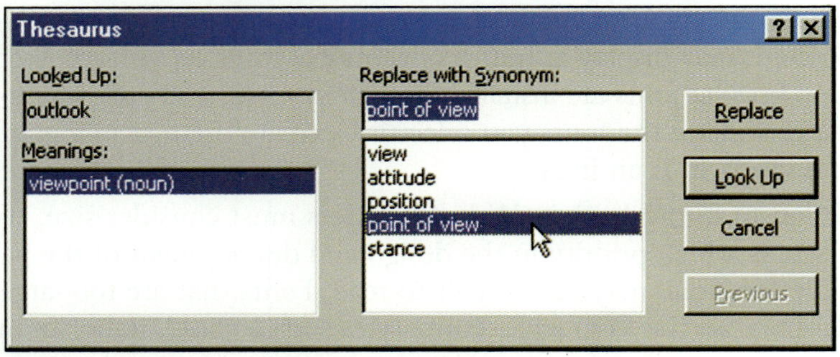

exercise 15 USING THE THESAURUS

1. With the EMCPWebs home page open in Page view, click inside the word *create*.
2. Select the Thesaurus command on the Tools menu.
3. At the Thesaurus dialog box, select the synonym *craft* and then click the Replace button.
4. Click inside the word *entities*.
5. Select the Thesaurus command on the Tools menu.
6. At the Thesaurus dialog box, click the Look Up button.
7. Under Meanings, select *being (noun)*.
8. Select the synonym *individual* and then click the Replace button.
9. Place an *s* at the end of *individual*.
10. Save the updated home page.

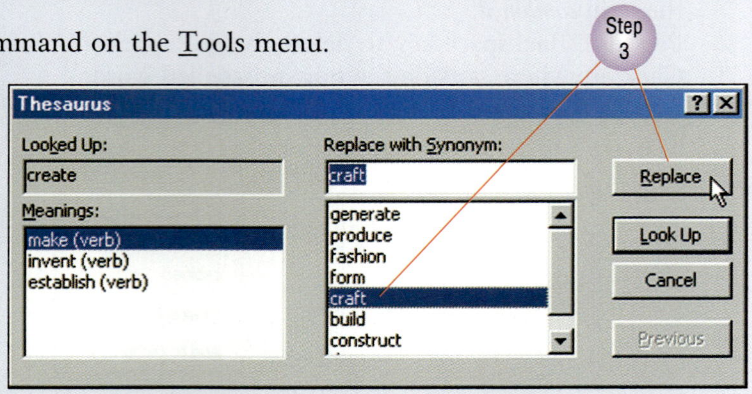

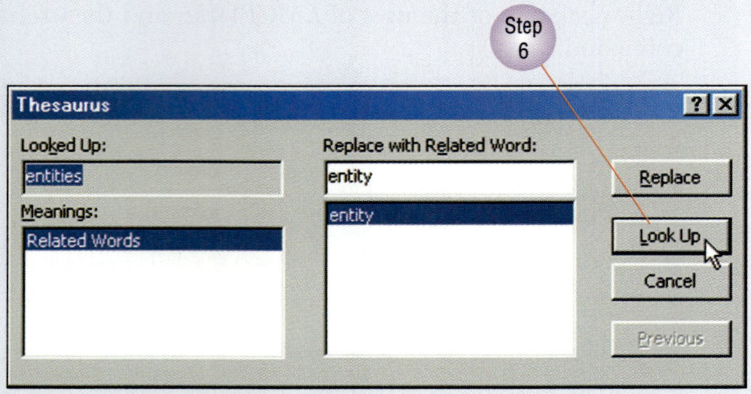

Formatting Text

Text formatting includes changing fonts, styles, sizes, and colors. Text can be formatted either from the Formatting toolbar or from the Font dialog box accessed through the Format menu. The Format Painter button on the Standard toolbar can be used to copy text formatting from one word or block of text to another. The default font in FrontPage is 12-point Times New Roman. To change the default font for FrontPage, click the Tools menu, select the Page Options command, and then click the Default Font tab.

Font choices for Web pages are an important consideration. While most visitors will have fonts such as Arial and Times New Roman, ornate fonts such as Matisse ITC and Bauhaus may display as more conventional fonts on visitors' Web browsers unless those particular fonts are installed on their systems. The only way to guarantee that the visitor will see the fonts you select is to create the text in a graphic editing program and insert it as an image.

In addition to font selection, Web developers must consider size, style, and color. Font size is a high priority in the design and development of the page layout. Fonts that are too small may be difficult to read. Fonts that are too large may take up valuable space on the Web page. Font styles such as bold, italic, and underlined are meant to draw attention to text in the Web page. Use underlined text with caution, as it ordinarily represents hyperlinks. For long text pages, avoid bold and italicized text. Font colors must also contrast with the background for best readability.

exercise 16

USING BUTTONS ON THE FORMATTING TOOLBAR

1. With the EMCPWebs home page open in Page view, select the title *EMCPWebs*.
2. Click the down-pointing triangle in the Font list box on the Formatting toolbar and then click *Verdana*.
3. Click the down-pointing triangle in the Font Size list box and then click *5 (18 pt)*.
4. Click the Bold button on the Formatting toolbar.
5. Click the down-pointing triangle on the Font Color button and then click Navy (the sixth color from the left in the first row).
6. Click to the left of the address line beginning *4578...* and drag down one line.
7. Click the down-pointing triangle on the Font Color button and then click More Colors.
8. Select the hexagon farthest to the left (dark green) in the More Colors dialog box, and then click OK.
9. Select the contact information line (Voice, E-Mail, Fax) and click the Decrease Font Size button once.
10. Select the line of text beginning *FROM SMALL TO...* and format the font color to Purple.
11. On the list of areas of expertise, select from *Web Design* to *Corporate Enterprise Systems*.
12. Click the down-pointing triangle on the Font Color button and then, under Document's Colors, click the dark green color you chose earlier from the More Colors dialog box.
13. With the list still selected, click the Bold button.
14. Double-click your first name in the author credit line and then, without releasing the mouse button, drag to the end of your last name.
15. Click the Bold and Italic buttons on the Formatting toolbar.
16. Save the updated home page.

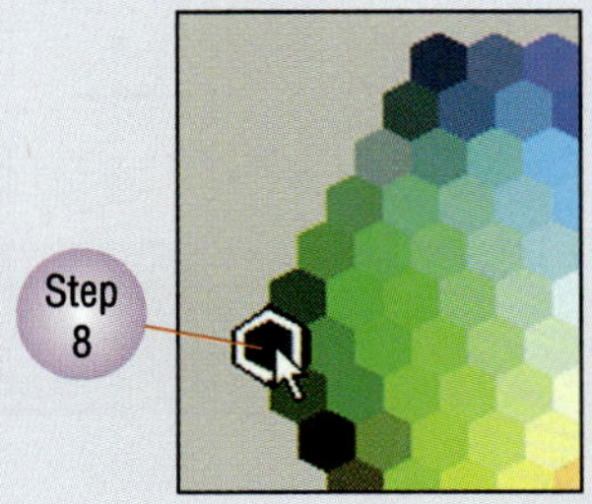

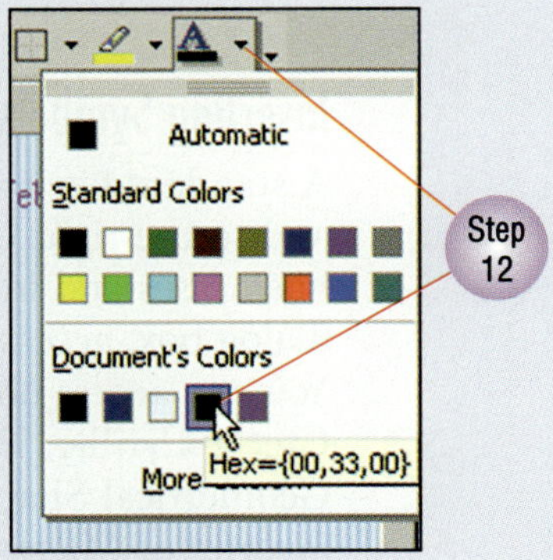

exercise 17 — USING THE FONT DIALOG BOX

1. Press Ctrl + A on the keyboard to select all text on the Web page.
2. Click the Format menu and then click Font.
3. At the Font dialog box, select *Verdana* from the Font list box.

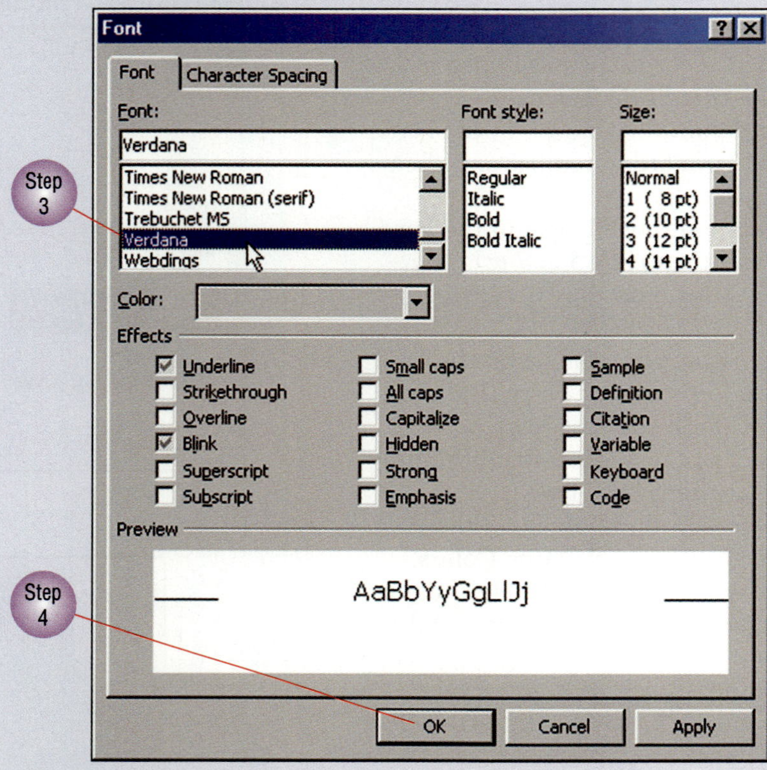

4. Click the OK button.
5. Save the updated home page.

Inserting Symbols

A standard keyboard includes a variety of symbols located above the numbers and to the right of the letters on the alphanumeric keypad. Many symbols that businesses and individuals need are not located on the keyboard. The Symbol dialog box, accessed from the Insert menu, includes an abundance of characters. You can access not only typical characters found on the keyboard, but also Basic Greek, Cyrillic, Hebrew, Arabic, General Punctuation, Mathematical Operators, Geometrical Shapes, Number Forms, and many others (see figure 2.16). Another favorite of Microsoft Office users are Wingdings (figure 2.17). The Wingdings library of symbols has dozens of interesting characters, arrows, designs, and so on.

FIGURE

2.16 ***Symbol Dialog Box (Arial Font)***

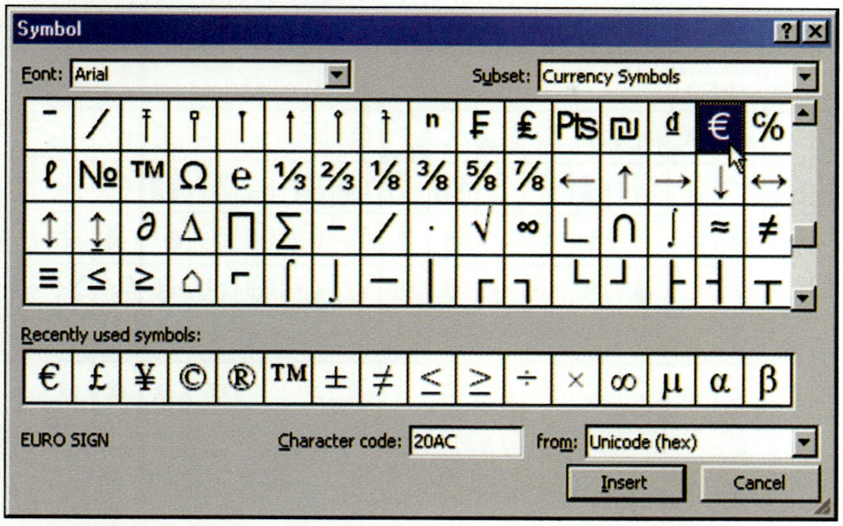

FIGURE

2.17 ***Symbol Dialog Box (Wingdings)***

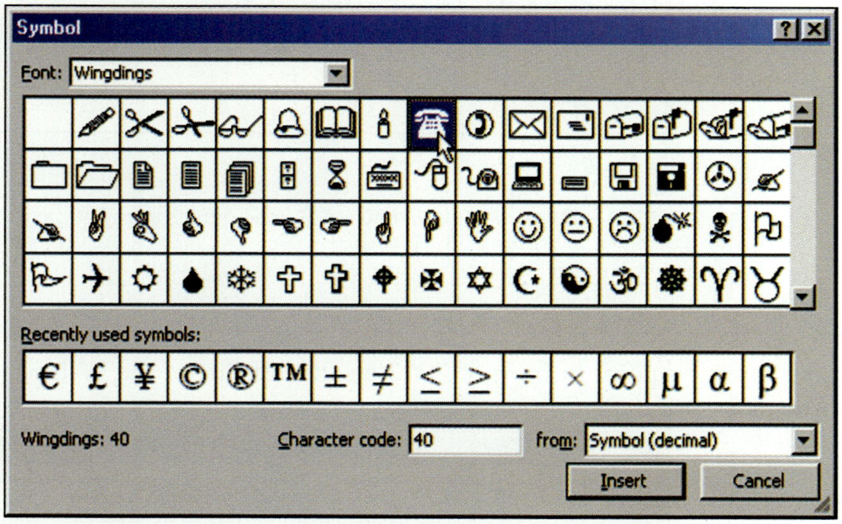

exercise 18

INSERTING SPECIAL SYMBOLS

1. With the EMCPWebs home page open in Page view, place the insertion point at the beginning of the line of text beginning Voice: 717.555....
2. Click the Insert menu and then click Symbol.
3. At the Symbol dialog box, select *Wingdings* from the Font list box.

4. Select the telephone character in the first row.

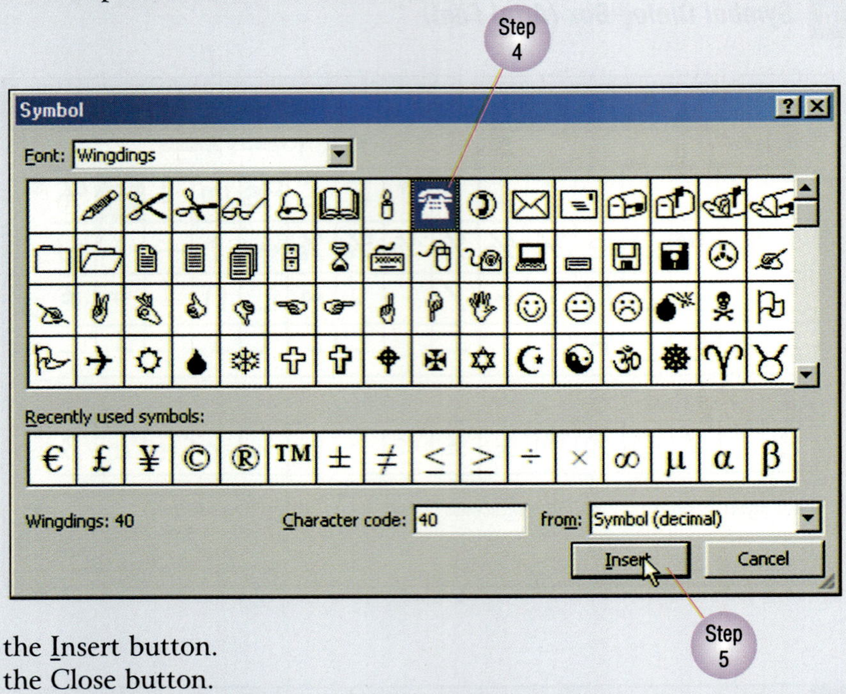

5. Click the Insert button.
6. Click the Close button.
7. Repeat the steps above to place another telephone character in front of *Fax*.
8. Repeat the steps above to place an envelope character in front of *E-mail*.
9. Format the symbol characters to Navy.

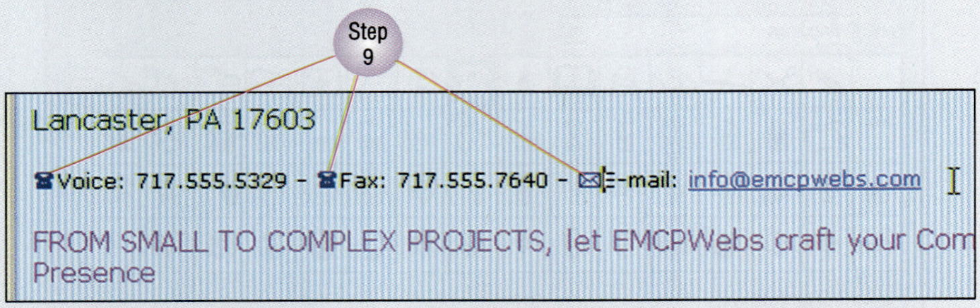

10. Place your insertion point in front of *2002* on the last line of the Web page.
11. Access the Symbol dialog box.
12. Select the copyright (©) symbol.
13. Click the Insert button and then the Close button to return to the home page.
14. Save the updated home page.

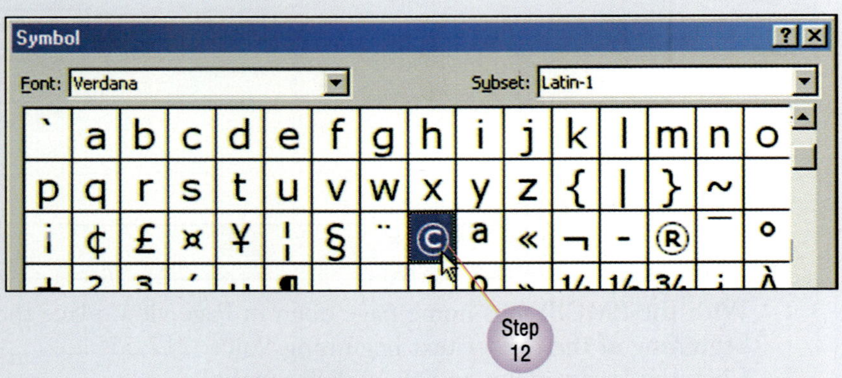

Formatting Paragraphs

Paragraph formatting in FrontPage 2002 is similar to that in word processing applications. Paragraph alignment can be altered so that text and graphics appear at the left edge, in the center, or at the right edge of the page. As you have probably noticed, paragraphs appear to be double-spaced or to have a blank line between lines of text. FrontPage 2002 allows you to format paragraphs without this extra space, giving the appearance of single-spaced text. Paragraphs or lines of text are often indented to attract the reader's attention by separating the material from the rest of the page.

Changing the Alignment of Text in Paragraphs

Paragraph text, by default, is aligned at the left margin on a Web page. Text and graphics can be aligned at center, right, and justified, just as with word processing software. Center-aligned text and objects are located between the edges of the browser window. Right-aligned text and objects are located at the right edge of the browser window. The Justify button aligns text at both the left and the right margins. Paragraph alignment can be accomplished on the Formatting toolbar, using the Paragraph command on the Format menu, or with keyboard shortcuts (see figure 2.18).

FIGURE **2.18** ***Alignment Keyboard Shortcuts***

Alignment	***Keyboard shortcut***
Align left	Ctrl + L
Align center	Ctrl + E
Align right	Ctrl + R

exercise 19 — CHANGING PARAGRAPH ALIGNMENT

1. With the EMCPWebs home page open in Page view, select the first four lines of text on the home page (from *EMCPWebs* through the line beginning *Phone...*).
2. Click the Center button on the Formatting toolbar.
3. Select the last two lines of text on the home page (author credits and copyright notice).
4. Press Ctrl + R on the keyboard to right-align the paragraphs.
5. Save the updated home page.

exercise 20

INDENTING TEXT IN PARAGRAPHS

1. With the EMCPWebs home page open in Page view, select the list of areas of expertise.
2. Click the Increase Indent button on the Formatting toolbar three times.
3. Click the Decrease Indent button on the Formatting toolbar once.
4. Save the updated home page.

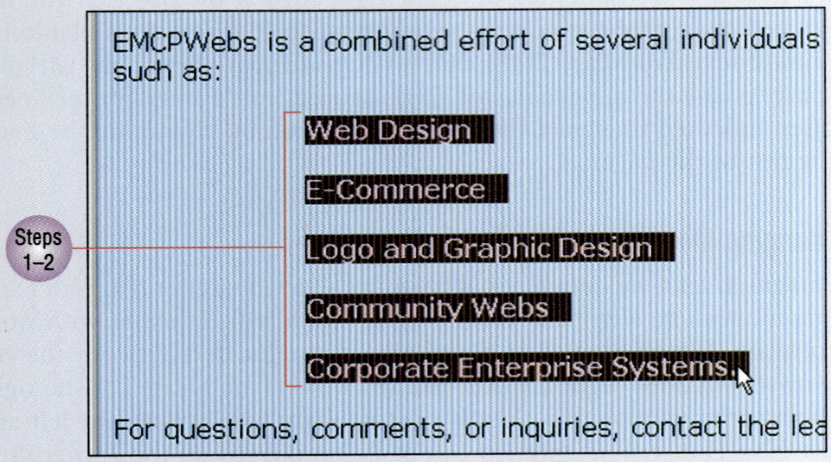

Changing Line Spacing

Each new paragraph in FrontPage gives the appearance of double spacing. To format new paragraphs to appear directly under the previous paragraph, click the Paragraph command on the Format menu. In the Paragraph dialog box, change the Spacing Before and After to zero (0). In addition to changing line spacing, you can insert a line break by pressing Shift + Enter on the keyboard.

exercise 21

CHANGING LINE SPACING

1. With the EMCPWebs home page open in Page view, select the list of areas of expertise.
2. Click the Format menu and select Paragraph.
3. At the Paragraph dialog box, click the up-pointing triangle in the Before text box in the Spacing section so that the text box shows *0*.
4. Click OK.
5. Place the insertion point at the end of the first line of text at the top of the page.

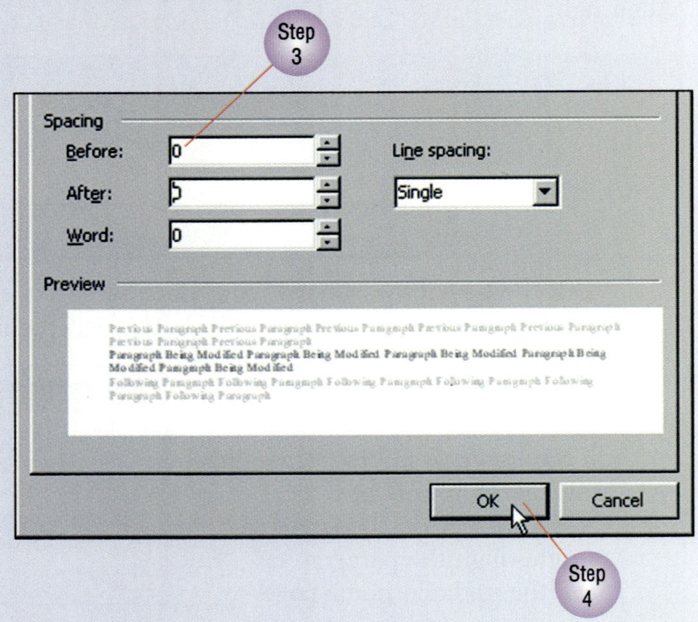

6. Press Delete on the keyboard.
7. Press Shift + Enter to insert a line break.
8. Place the insertion point at the end of the second line of text and press Delete.
9. Insert another line break.
10. Save the updated Web page.

Previewing, Printing, Saving, and Closing a FrontPage Web

The appearance of Web pages as they will display in a browser should be previewed periodically to ensure that the page contents look appropriate. Ordinarily, by this point you would already have previewed several times the Web page you just created. In addition to other considerations, Web page designers must also consider the visitor's window size settings. There are three major window size settings that computer users may be using as they browse the Web: 640 × 480, 800 × 600, and 1024 × 768 pixels. Window size is of great concern when you have large graphics and/or tables with multiple columns. The Preview in Browser command on the File menu allows you to select from various window size settings and browsers to test your Web page. The Preview in Browser button on the Standard toolbar will preview the page with the last specified settings in the Preview in Browser dialog box. The Preview tab in Page view can be used to get a quick preview of your Web page without leaving FrontPage. *(Note: The background will show in the Preview in Browser, but it will not appear when you print the Web page. See your instructor for more information.)*

exercise 22 — PREVIEWING A WEB PAGE

1. With the EMCPWebs home page open in Page view, click the Preview tab at the bottom of the screen.
2. Scroll through the Web page and click the Normal tab.
3. Click File and then click Preview in Browser.

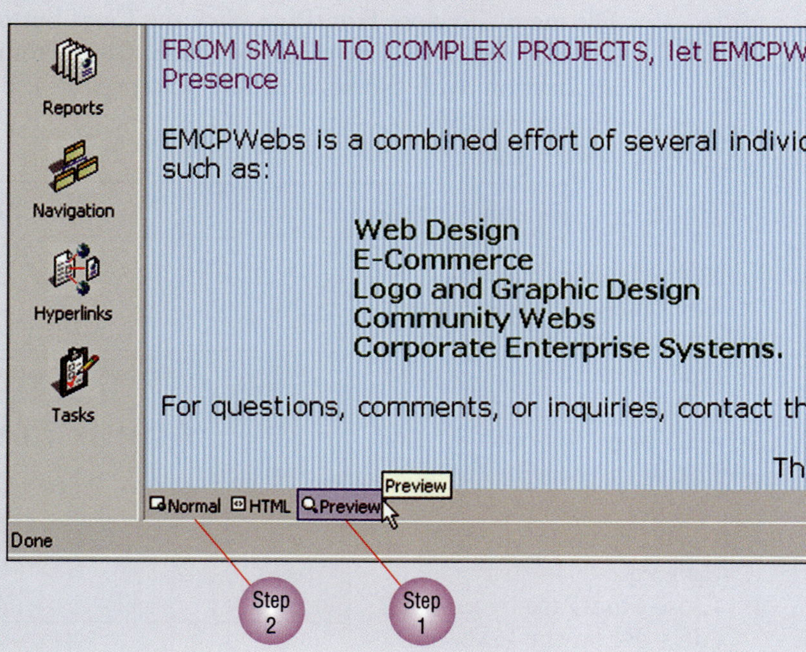

4. At the Preview in Browser dialog box, click the 640 × 480 option under Window size and then click the Preview button.
5. Print this page by clicking the Print button on the Standard toolbar of your Web browser.
6. Close the browser window and return to FrontPage.
7. Preview the home page in other window sizes.

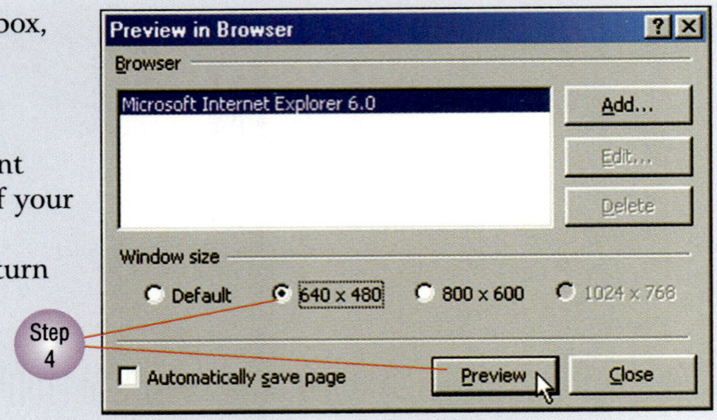

exercise 23 VIEWING AND PRINTING FRONTPAGE WEB PAGES IN PRINT PREVIEW

1. With the EMCPWebs home page open in Page view, click File and then click Print Preview.
2. Click the Zoom In button.
3. Scroll through the Web page.
4. Click the Print button.
5. Click the OK button to close the Print dialog box.
6. Click the Close button in Print Preview to return to Page view.

Making a return to FrontPage 2002 is the Save All feature, which was available in FrontPage 98 but was omitted from FrontPage 2000. Without this feature, each Web page had to be saved individually. Located on the File menu, the Save All command saves all of the open Web pages with a single click. The Save All feature will be used frequently in subsequent chapters.

Web pages can be closed by clicking the Close button *(X)* in the upper right corner of the document window, or by selecting the Close Web command on the File menu. To close FrontPage, click the Close button *(X)* on the Title bar or select the Exit command from the File menu. Close FrontPage, or any other Windows application, with the keyboard by pressing Alt + F4.

exercise 24 USING SAVE ALL TO SAVE MULTIPLE PAGES

1. With the EMCPWebs FrontPage Web open, access the Folders view.
2. Open each second-tier page into Page view and key the Web page title onto the first line of the page in Verdana, 18 points, bold, and Navy.
3. Click File and then click Save All.
4. Close FrontPage by pressing Alt + F4 on the keyboard.

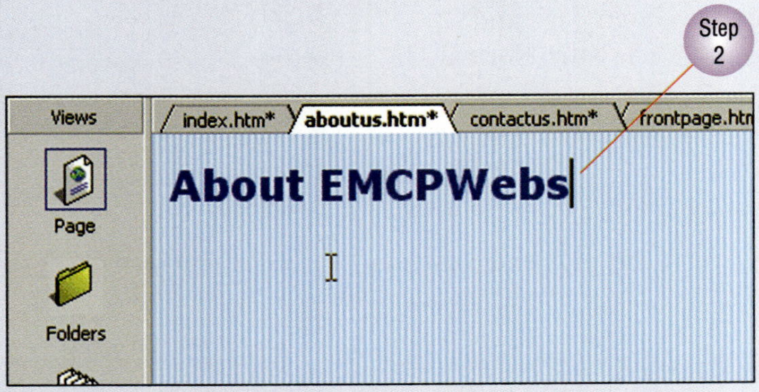

CHAPTER summary

- Publishing to the Web requires that you have an account with an ISP or domain host.
- FrontPage 2002 includes 10 Web site templates to choose from in developing a FrontPage Web.
- The One Page Web template creates a new Web with a single blank page. This is the most common option among FrontPage Web developers.
- The Empty Web Wizard creates a new FrontPage Web with no Web pages being created in the wizard process.
- The root Web is the primary folder for a Web in which all pages, images, and other files must be stored.
- Click the *Web Site Templates* option in the Open Page or Web Task Pane to open the Web Site Templates dialog box.
- Click the Create a new normal page button on the Standard toolbar to create a new Web page.
- Right-click page file names and page titles in Folders view to rename them.
- Drag Web page files from the Folder List to the navigation structure in the Navigation view.
- Click the Print button on the Standard toolbar in Navigation view to print the navigation structure.
- Click Format and then Background to format the Web page background.
- The More Colors dialog box includes a palette of 127 "Web Safe" colors for page backgrounds.
- The Custom button in the More Colors dialog box can be clicked to customize the page background from a full spectrum of colors and shades.
- Click Browse on the Background tab in the Page Properties dialog box to format an image as a page background.
- Check Watermark on the Background tab in the Page Properties dialog box to enable a watermark background image.
- Click Get background information from another page on the Background tab in the Page Properties dialog box to use the background settings of another page for the current page.
- Open Web pages can be accessed from the Window menu.
- Ctrl + Home will establish the insertion point at the beginning of the Web page.
- Ctrl + End will establish the insertion point at the end of the Web page.
- Press Ctrl + S to save the current Web page.
- Press Ctrl + Z to undo the last command.
- Press F1 to open the Help feature.
- Right-click a misspelled word to select from a list of possible suggestions to correct the spelling.
- Correctly spelled words that are underlined with the red wavy line can be added to the dictionary by right-clicking the word and clicking Add to Dictionary.
- Click Tools and then Thesaurus to replace words with a synonym.
- Text can be formatted from the Formatting toolbar and in the Font dialog box accessed from the Format menu.
- Click Insert and then Symbol to insert special characters into a Web page.
- Paragraphs can be formatted from the Formatting toolbar and in the Paragraph dialog box accessed from the Format menu.

- Click the Preview tab to get a quick view of how the page will look on the Web.
- Click the Preview in Browser button on the Standard toolbar to view a Web page in the default browser.
- Click File and then Preview in Browser to select from various window size settings and browsers to test your Web page.
- Click File and then Save All to save all open Web pages.
- The quickest way to close a FrontPage Web is to use the Alt + F4 shortcut.

COMMANDS review

Command	Mouse/Keyboard
Create a new FrontPage Web	Click *Web Site Templates* on the New Page or Web Task Pane
Create a new Web page	Click the Create a new normal page button on the Standard toolbar
Rename a Web page file name	Right-click name, click Rename
Rename a Web page title	Right-click title, click Rename
Set navigation structure in Navigation view	Drag and drop from Folder List
Print navigation structure	Click Print button on Standard toolbar in Navigation view
Format background color	Click Format, Background, Colors
Format background image	Click Format, Background, Browse
Format background watermark	Click Format, Background, Watermark
Get background information from another page	Click Format, Background, Get background information from another page
Establish insertion point at beginning of document	Press Ctrl + Home
Establish insertion point at end of document	Press Ctrl + End
Save the current Web page	Press Ctrl + S
Print the current Web page	Press Ctrl + P
Undo the last command	Press Ctrl + Z
Run the Spelling Checker	Click the Spelling button on the Standard toolbar
Run the Thesaurus	Click Tools, Thesaurus
Change the font	Click Font list box down-pointing triangle on Formatting toolbar

Change the font size	Click Font Size list box down-pointing triangle on Formatting toolbar
Change the font style	Click Bold, Italic, or Underline on the Formatting toolbar
Change the font color	Click Font Color list box down-pointing triangle on Formatting toolbar
Select all text and objects on a Web page	Press Ctrl + A
Insert symbols and special characters	Click Insert, Symbol
Change paragraph alignment	Click Align Left, Center, Align Right, or Justify on the Formatting toolbar
Change paragraph line spacing	Click Format, Paragraph
Quick preview a Web page	Click Preview tab
Preview a Web page in default browser	Click Preview in Browser button on Standard toolbar
Save all open Web pages	Click File, Save All
Close FrontPage 2002	Press Alt + F4

CONCEPTS check

Completion: On a blank sheet of paper, indicate the correct term, command, or number for each item.

1. This Web Site template creates a new FrontPage Web resulting in a blank home page file.
2. Web site files, folders, and subwebs must be contained in this folder.
3. Web page file names can easily be renamed by right-clicking the file name and selecting this command.
4. Perform this action with Web page file icons in the Folder List to establish a hierarchical structure in Navigation view.
5. Select the Background command on this menu to apply colors and images to a Web page background.
6. Click this button in the More Colors dialog box to select from a full spectrum of colors for your Web page background.
7. Formatting a background image with this feature will force the image to remain stationary even when the page is being scrolled.
8. Perform this with the mouse to quickly select a word in the Web page document window.
9. Perform this to select from a list of suggestions for a misspelled word.
10. The Thesaurus feature, located on this menu, assists Web page developers in selecting acronyms for Web page text.
11. Web page text can be formatted using buttons on the Formatting toolbar as well as this dialog box accessed from the Format menu.
12. Symbols and special characters can be added to a document by selecting the Symbols command on this menu.

13. A line break can be inserted into a Web page document by pressing this keyboard shortcut.
14. A Web page can be previewed in your default browser by clicking this button on the Standard toolbar.
15. Use this feature to save all open Web pages at once.

SKILLS check

Assessment 1

1. Open FrontPage and then click *Web Site Templates* on the New Page or Web Task Pane, or click File, point to New, and then click Page or Web.
2. Select the *One Page Web* icon.
3. Save the Web as *trojansports* in your *Chapter 2* folder.
4. Close FrontPage

Assessment 2

1. Open the trojansports FrontPage Web created in assessment 1.
2. Access the Folders view.
3. Retitle the home page *Welcome to Trojan Sports*.
4. Create the following Web page files:

File Name	***Page Title***
football.htm	*Welcome to Trojan Football*
volleyball.htm	*Welcome to Trojan Volleyball*
mensbball.htm	*Welcome to Trojan Men's Basketball*
womensbball.htm	*Welcome to Trojan Women's Basketball*
softball.htm	*Welcome to Trojan Softball*
baseball.htm	*Welcome to Trojan Baseball*
track.htm	*Welcome to Trojan Track and Field*
tennis.htm	*Welcome to Trojan Tennis*
soccer.htm	*Welcome to Trojan Soccer*
fallsports.htm	*Trojan Sports – Fall Sporting News*
springsports.htm	*Trojan Sports – Spring Sporting News*

5. Close FrontPage.

Assessment 3

1. Open the admissions02 FrontPage Web in your *Chapter 2* folder.
2. Access the Navigation view.
3. Make sure the Folder List is open.
4. Create a Navigation structure that matches the following outline.

	Second tier	**Third tier**
Admissions Home		
	Orientation	
	Assessment	
		Testing Center

Second tier	Third tier
Counselors	
	Ruth Thompson
	Greg Butler
Enrollment	
Payment	
	Financial Aid
	Tuition and Fees
	Scholarships
Textbooks	

5. Print the navigation structure.
6. Close FrontPage.

Assessment 4

1. Open FrontPage.
2. Access the Background tab of the Page Properties dialog box and change the background color to Black.
3. Access the Background tab of the Page Properties dialog box again.
4. Access the More Colors dialog box and format the Web page background a light green color.
5. Access the More Colors dialog box again, click the Select button, and use the eyedropper tool to select a color anywhere on the screen.
6. Click OK in each dialog box to return to Page view.
7. Access the More Colors dialog box again and click the Custom button.
8. Experiment with various colors on the color spectrum. Use the slider tool to lighten your selected color.
9. Click the OK button on each dialog box to return to Page view.
10. Close FrontPage without saving any changes.

Assessment 5

1. Open FrontPage.
2. Access the Background tab of the Page Properties dialog box and click the Browse button in the Formatting section.
3. Select the sidebarback.gif file from your *Chapter 2* folder.
4. Return to Page view.
5. Return to the Background tab of the Page Properties dialog box and format the background to textureback.gif.
6. Perform a Preview in Browser.
7. Close FrontPage without saving any changes.

Assessment 6

1. Open FrontPage.
2. Open the watermarktext.htm file from your *Chapter 2* folder.
3. Access the Background tab of the Page Properties dialog box and click the Browse button in the Formatting section.
4. Select the watermarkback.gif file from your *Chapter 2* folder.
5. Enable the Watermark feature.
6. Return to Page view.
7. Perform a Preview in Browser, saving any updates.
8. Close FrontPage.

Assessment 7

1. Open FrontPage and key the following passage in Page view:

   The Internet is full of e-commerce sites offering products and services from vendors across the globe. Community Webs has the experience and vision for developing comprehensive Web sites that are dedicated to community businesses, organizations, and citizens. Community Webs should also attract shoppers and businesses to that area. While not every business needs online shopping, every business should have a Web presence. The potential is great... and your community Web may set a precedent in how businesses should advertise on the Web in your community.

   Among the components of a typical community or chamber of commerce site are:

   Community Structure (city government)

   Economic Indicators (employment, taxes collected, water works, light and power)

   Location and Physical Environment (population and trade area)

   Demographic Profile (population, income, age breakdown, race, education, marital status, occupation, and housing)

   Tourism and Recreation Business and Industry Information
2. Format the first paragraph to Verdana, bold, and Maroon.
3. Format the line of text beginning *Among the components...* to Verdana, 10 points, and italic.
4. Format the list of components to Arial, 10 points, bold, and Navy.
5. Save the Web page as communitywebs.htm in your *Chapter 2* folder.
6. Perform a Preview in Browser.
7. Print the Web page.
8. Close the Web browser and FrontPage.

Assessment 8

1. Open the communitywebs.htm Web page file you created in assessment 7.
2. Format the first paragraph to justified alignment.
3. Format the line of text beginning *Among the components...* to right alignment.
4. Format the list of components to center alignment.
5. Save the updated Web page.
6. Perform a Preview in Browser.
7. Print the Web page.
8. Close the Web browser and FrontPage.

Assessment 9

1. Open the communitywebs.htm Web page file you created in assessments 7 and 8.
2. Place the insertion point anywhere in the first paragraph.
3. Access the Paragraph dialog box.
4. Change the line spacing to Double.
5. Format the list of components to a spacing of zero (0) before and after each paragraph.
6. Save the updated Web page.
7. Preview and print the Web page in your browser.
8. Close the Web browser and FrontPage.

CHAPTER 3

WORKING WITH GRAPHICS AND PHOTO GALLERIES

PERFORMANCE OBJECTIVES

Upon successful completion of chapter 3, you will be able to:

- **Open existing FrontPage Webs and pages**
- **Differentiate between GIF and JPEG image file formats**
- **Insert clip art and pictures**
- **Alter and enhance graphics in FrontPage 2002**
- **Insert drawing objects from the Drawing toolbar**
- **Create a FrontPage Photo Gallery**

Chapter 3 IRC

Two of the most recognized benefits of the World Wide Web are the ability to view graphical images and the ability to hyperlink to other documents either on the current Web site or on sites around the world. Common graphical elements of a Web page include company logos, photographs, illustrations, diagrams, animations, image hyperlinks, image maps, cartoons, and advertisements. One of the best visual marketing tools employed by many companies for customer recognition is their logo. Photographs of products, facilities, and personnel are often essential in gaining a response from customers or interested visitors. Animations are attention-getting graphics frequently used for advertisements and anecdotes.

Images are also utilized as hyperlinks. An image that has multiple hyperlinks is called an image map and can present an excellent visual enhancement to a Web page. Whatever layout structure you design, keep your audience in mind as visitors to your site will have varying connection speeds. Furthermore, too many graphics and animations may overwhelm the visitor.

New to FrontPage 2002 are the enhanced drawing tools and a Photo Gallery Web component. Drawing tools consist of shapes, drop shadows, WordArt, and text boxes. These tools should sound familiar if you use other Microsoft Office applications. The Photo Gallery is perfect for displaying photographs in a variety of customizable layouts.

Opening Existing Webs and Pages

FrontPage 2002 allows you to manage many Web sites that are either located on your computer system or have already been published to a Web server. Once FrontPage 2002 has been installed on your computer system, a *Web Folders* folder is created for you. Web sites that have been published to the World Wide Web are automatically placed in *Web Folders* for ease of access. FrontPage Webs that are stored on disk cannot be accessed from *Web Folders* and must be accessed from the hard drive or floppy disk. Web pages can also be edited by clicking the Edit with Microsoft FrontPage button on the Internet Explorer toolbar (see figure 3.1).

FIGURE 3.1 **Edit with Microsoft FrontPage Button in Internet Explorer**

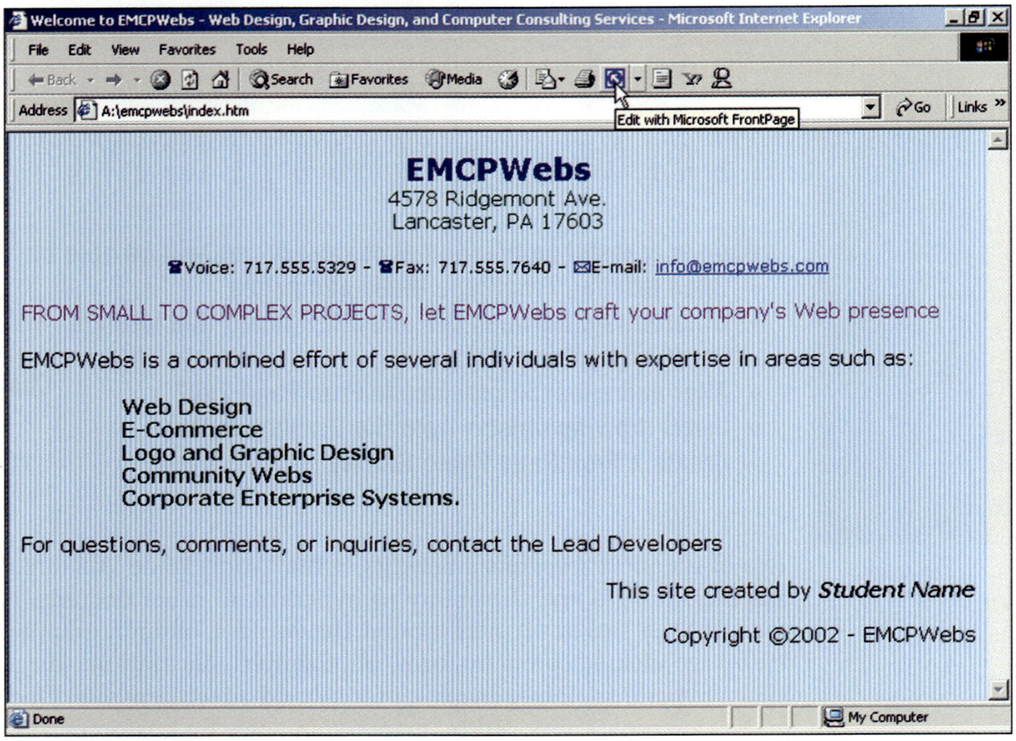

Preventing FrontPage from Opening the Last Edited Web

By default, FrontPage 2002 will open the last edited Web. Often, however, the last edited Web is not the Web you want to work on. To disable this feature, access the Tools menu and then select the Options command. With the General tab of the Options dialog box selected, remove the check mark from the Open last Web automatically when FrontPage starts option.

(Note: Before completing computer exercises, delete the Chapter 2 *folder on your disk. Next, download the Chapter 3 data files from the Internet Resource Center to the* Chapter 3 *folder you have created on your disk, and then make* Chapter 3 *the active folder.)*

exercise 1

PREVENTING FRONTPAGE FROM OPENING THE LAST EDITED WEB

1. Click the Start button on the Windows taskbar.
2. Point to *Programs* and then click *Microsoft FrontPage*.
3. With FrontPage 2002 open, click the Tools menu and select Options.
4. Remove the check mark from the Open last Web automatically when FrontPage starts option.
5. Close FrontPage.

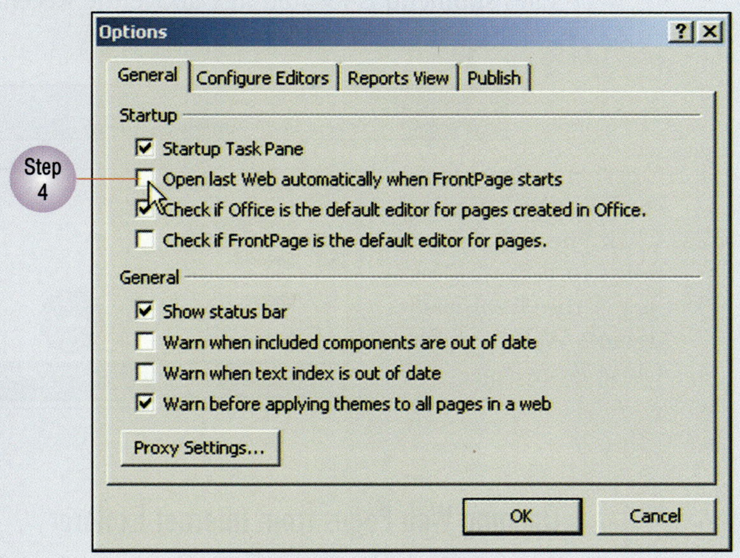

Opening Recent FrontPage 2002 Webs

Recent Webs can be quickly accessed from the File menu by pointing to Recent Webs and then clicking the appropriate Web title. FrontPage Webs not located in the Recent Webs submenu can be accessed from the Open Web command on the File menu, or by selecting the Open Web command from the Standard toolbar.

exercise 2

OPENING A RECENT WEB

1. Open FrontPage from the *Programs* submenu.
2. Click File and then point to Recent Webs.
3. Select the *A:\emcpwebs* FrontPage Web. *(Note: If you are at a different computer system than you used when working on chapter 2, your FrontPage Web will not appear on the Recent Webs submenu. If you did not complete chapter 2, your instructor can provide you with a completed copy of the chapter project.)*
4. Click the Navigation view button.
5. Double-click the EMCPWebs home page.
6. Close FrontPage.

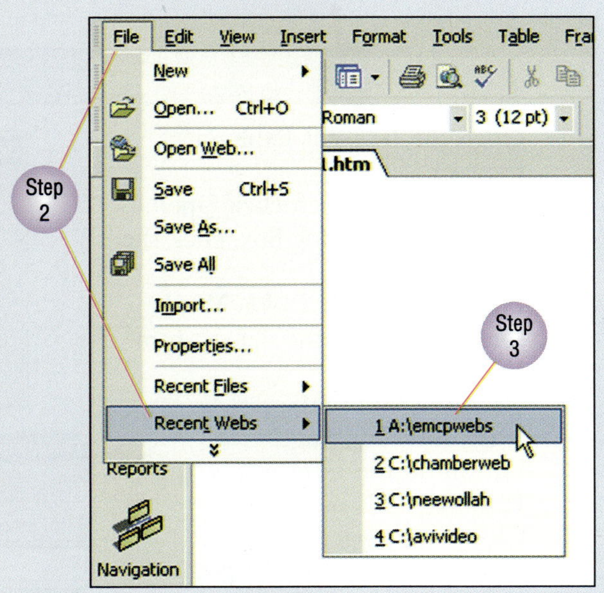

Opening Recent Web Page Files

In addition to opening recent Webs, you can use the File menu to open recent Web pages that may or may not be associated with FrontPage Webs. The Recent Files submenu is located just above the Recent Webs command.

exercise 3

OPENING RECENT FILES

1. Open FrontPage from the *Programs* submenu.
2. Click File and then point to Recent Files.
3. Select the *A:\emcpwebs* default Web page file.
4. Close FrontPage.

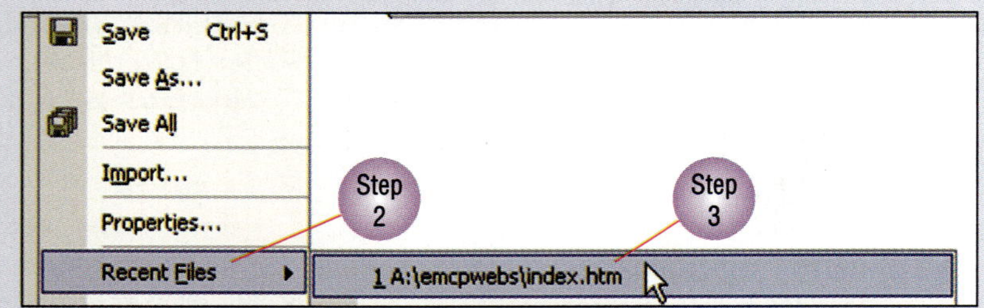

Opening Web Pages from Internet Explorer

A common task among FrontPage designers is to edit Web pages that they are browsing or testing in their browser. For example, a visitor browsing your site may send you an e-mail message indicating an error on a particular Web page. Before editing the page in FrontPage, you visit the specific page in question and notice there is an error. Simply click the Edit with Microsoft FrontPage button on the Internet Explorer toolbar, and you will be able to edit that Web page and then quickly save the changes. On a disk-based Web, the Web page will open in FrontPage without prompting. A FrontPage Web stored on a Web server will require a user name and password to open pages for editing. This topic will be explored further in chapter 9. Since HTML is an open-source code, novice to advanced developers can easily observe how other developers have designed and coded their Web pages.

exercise 4

OPENING WEB PAGES FROM INTERNET EXPLORER

1. Open the Internet Explorer browser.
2. Click File and then click Open.
3. At the Open dialog box, click the Browse button.
4. Locate your *EMCPWebs* Web folder and open the default.htm home page file.
5. Click the Edit with Microsoft FrontPage button on the Internet Explorer toolbar.
6. Close FrontPage.

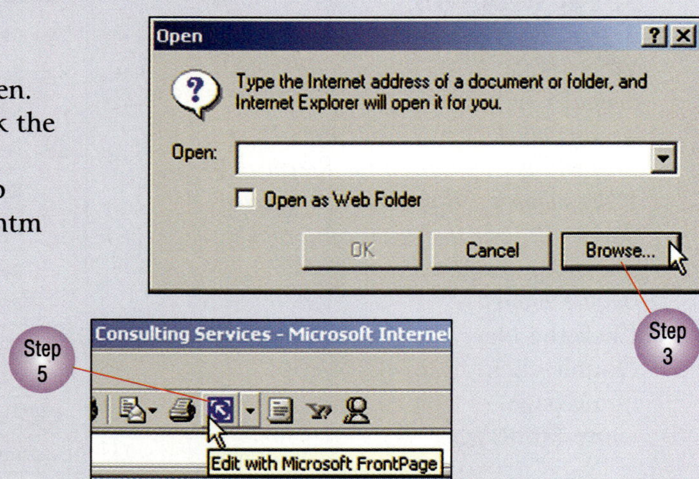

Exploring Web Graphic Fundamentals

The widespread attraction of the World Wide Web has been its ability to transmit and display graphical images on the computer screen. Digital cameras, color scanners, and graphic editing software programs have all contributed to the increased use of graphics on the Web. Web graphics can consist of photos, figures, artwork, text, and special effects. Graphical images can also be used for bullets, navigation buttons, and borders.

As new computer hardware and software technology standards are introduced, many companies attempt to make their technology the standard. Computer graphic technology is no different. Graphic qualities and compatibilities vary greatly. Figure 3.2 describes several of the most popular graphic formats.

FIGURE 3.2 ***Common Image Format Types and Descriptions***

Image Format	***Description***
GIF	Graphics Interchange Format (GIF) formatted images can contain up to 256 colors. One color of a GIF graphic can be made transparent. This feature is perfect for allowing the Web page background to surround the image itself without excess "white space."
JPEG or JPG	Joint Photographic Experts Group (JPEG) formatted images can contain up to 16.7 million colors and are commonly used for photorealistic pictures. JPEG picture file sizes can be decreased by increasing the compression percentage using a graphic editing software program. Increasing the compression, however, decreases the quality of the image.
PNG	The Portable Network Graphics (PNG) format is an alternative to GIF and JPEG that supports transparency for pictures containing thousands or millions of colors. Some older Web browsers may not be able to display PNG pictures without a special plug-in.
BMP	The Windows bitmap (BMP) format is a standard file format for Windows Paint files. The quality is high, and it is a good format for desktop publishing and digital photographs. BMP-formatted graphics should never be used for the Web, however, as the files are very large.
TIFF or TIF	The Tagged Image File Format (TIFF) is a high-quality format used for graphics and photographs that can be read by either PC or Macintosh platform computers.
EPS	The Encapsulated Post Script (EPS) format is another high-quality image type commonly seen in illustration and layout software programs.

Using GIF Images

The Graphics Interchange Format (GIF) is best suited for line art, grayscale images (see figure 3-3), and images with 256 or fewer colors. A variation of the GIF is the animated GIF. Animated GIFs, commonplace in Web sites today, may have two or more frames of action that resemble motion, encompass multiple-image advertisements, or add special effects. GIF animations are often used to draw the visitor's attention to an item as well as to add movement to the page. The image standard for GIF animations is GIF89A. The number 89 comes from 1989, the year in which the GIF standard was established. The A refers to the ability of the image to animate.

FIGURE 3.3 ***Grayscale Image Comparison***

GIF Format 14.6 KB   JPEG Format 19.2 KB

Have you ever noticed that on some Web pages the images appear instantly on the screen in fuzzy focus and then slowly transform into a finished image? These images have been interlaced. Interlaced GIF files build a low-resolution image that develops into a defined image as the file is downloading, whereas noninterlaced images load pixel-by-pixel until the entire image is finally visible (see figure 3.4). This fuzzy preview effect does not load the image faster than the standard noninterlaced image. It does, however, give the visitor a sense of accomplishment and something to look at as the image becomes more visible. Images must be interlaced in the graphics editing software program.

FIGURE 3.4 ***Noninterlaced vs. Interlaced Image***

Noninterlaced   Interlaced

Using JPEG Images

The Joint Photographic Experts Group (JPEG) format is often used when high-quality images such as photographs and colorful drawings are to be included in a Web page. JPEG-formatted graphics also allow designers to compress images to smaller file sizes (see figure 3.5).

FIGURE 3.5 ***JPEG Format Compression Rates and File Sizes***

40.9 KB, 0% Compression   8.0 KB, 40% Compression   2.88 KB, 90% Compression

File sizes of your graphics will depend to a large extent on the number of colors displayed in the image. A black-and-white cartoon saved in GIF format will probably be smaller than if it were saved in JPEG format. JPEG graphics are 24-bit, as opposed to 8-bit GIF images. Photographic images with more than 256 colors stored in GIF format will likely be larger in file size than JPEG because GIF supports fewer colors. In addition to a potential larger file size, the image may not be as crisp as the same image saved in JPEG format. The better graphic editing software programs of today allow users to specify the file format and compression rate to get the best quality picture for the smallest file size (see figure 3.6).

FIGURE 3.6 ***Color Photograph File Format Comparison***

GIF Format 44 KB   JPEG Format 19.6 KB

Before creating and/or inserting graphics into a Web page, follow these guidelines:

- Use thumbnail images for linking to larger and higher quality images.
- Use alternative text for those visitors whose browsers do not have graphic capabilities enabled.
- Since images are the culprit of long load times, keep page load time at 30 or fewer seconds for 28.8Kbps modems, if possible.
- Use GIF animations sparingly to emphasize content on the page.

Inserting Clip Art and Pictures

New to Microsoft Office applications is the Insert Clip Art Task Pane. Key a descriptive keyword in the Search text: text box and click the Search button to search for a clip art image that meets your criteria. Use the Other Search Options to narrow your search results. The *Clips Online* hyperlink at the bottom of the task pane will take you to the Microsoft Office Design Gallery Live Web site (see figure 3.7) for literally thousands of clip art images and photographs. Images from file can also be inserted by clicking the Insert Picture From File button on the Standard toolbar.

FIGURE 3.7 ***Microsoft Office Design Gallery Live Web Site***

exercise 5 INSERTING CLIP ART FROM THE INSERT CLIP ART TASK PANE

1. Open the EMCPWebs FrontPage Web and then open the home page into Page view.
2. Place the insertion point at the beginning of the document.
3. Click Insert, point to Picture, and then select the Clip Art command.
4. At the Insert Clip Art Task Pane, enter the keyword **computer** into the Search text: text box and then click the Search button.
5. Locate and point to the clip art shown below.
6. Click the down-pointing triangle that appears next to the illustration and click *Insert* on the pop-up menu.
7. Close the Insert Clip Art Task Pane.
8. Click the Save button on the Standard toolbar.
9. Click OK in the Save Embedded Files dialog box to save the computer image to the *Images* folder.

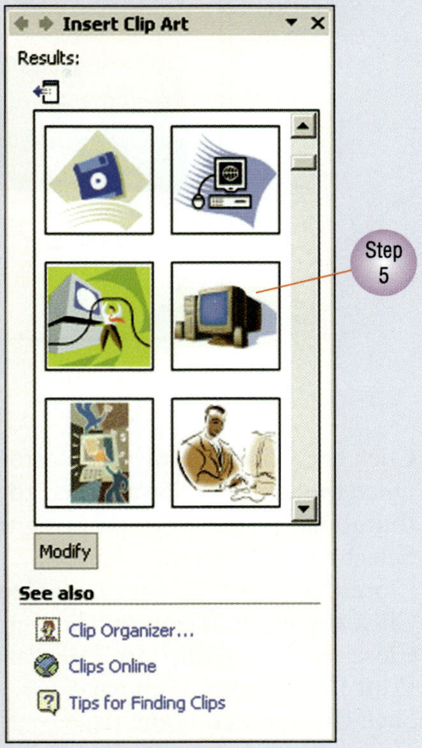

Inserting Clip Art from the World Wide Web

In addition to the clip art on your computer system, the *Clips Online* hyperlink on the Insert Clip Art Task Pane will take you directly to the Microsoft Office Design Gallery Live Web site. From here, you can search for everything from clip art to photos to sounds to GIF animations.

exercise 6 INSERTING CLIPS FROM THE MICROSOFT OFFICE DESIGN GALLERY LIVE WEB SITE

1. With the EMCPWebs home page open in Page view, place the insertion point at the end of the voice/fax/e-mail line of text and press Enter.
2. With the Insert Clip Art Task Pane open, click the *Clips Online* hyperlink.
3. At the Microsoft Office Design Gallery Live Web site, key **City** in the Search for text box.
4. Select *Photos* in the Results should be drop-down menu and click the Go button.

5. Locate the photo shown below.

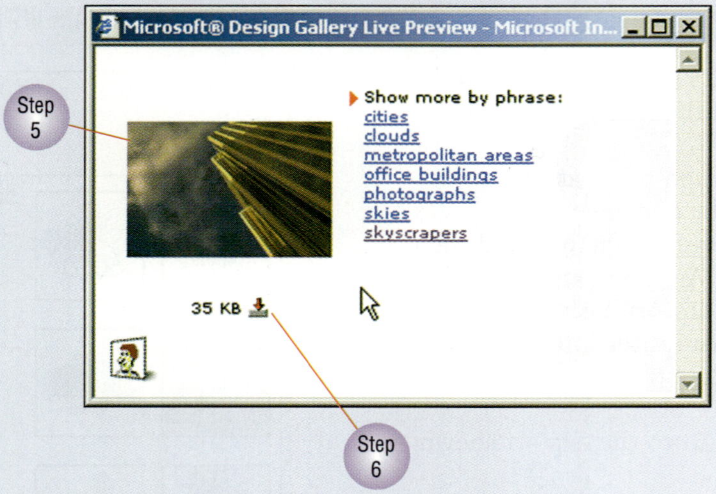

6. Click the Click to Download arrow image.
7. Once the image is downloaded to the Microsoft Clip Organizer, click on the thumbnail image down-pointing triangle.
8. Select the Copy command.
9. Close the Microsoft Clip Organizer.
10. Click the Paste button on the Standard toolbar.
11. Close the Insert Clip Art Task Pane.
12. Print the updated Web page.
13. Save the updated home page.

Inserting Images from File

Although the availability of previously created graphics and photos can be useful, most individuals and organizations need to be able to insert their own graphics, photos, and Web elements. Images that are typically inserted from a file are either public domain clip art/photos or images that were created specifically for the organization to be used in that organization's documents and/or Web pages. It is very important to the Web designer, and to the organization, that the graphics on the Web site positively reflect the look and image of the company. Logos, photos, slogans, and other identifiable characteristics of an organization should be carefully integrated into the Web. If the primary color scheme of a business is red, white, and blue, the Web site should utilize this same scheme.

Several software programs exist for users who create Web-oriented graphics. Most of these software programs include features to optimize images for quality and file size. In selecting a graphic editing software program, look for the following features and capabilities:

- The ability to save in GIF and JPEG formats
- The ability to apply image effects such as artistic and color enhancements, and textures
- The ability to scan images directly onto canvas
- The ability to insert digital camera pictures

exercise 7

INSERTING PICTURES FROM FILE

1. With the EMCPWebs home page (index.htm) open, highlight the title, address, and contact information.

2. Click the Insert Picture From File button on the Standard toolbar.
3. At the Select File dialog box, click the down-pointing triangle in the Look in list box.
4. Locate the *EMCPWebs Images* folder you have downloaded, and then select that folder.
5. Select the *emcpwebsbanner.gif* file and then click OK.

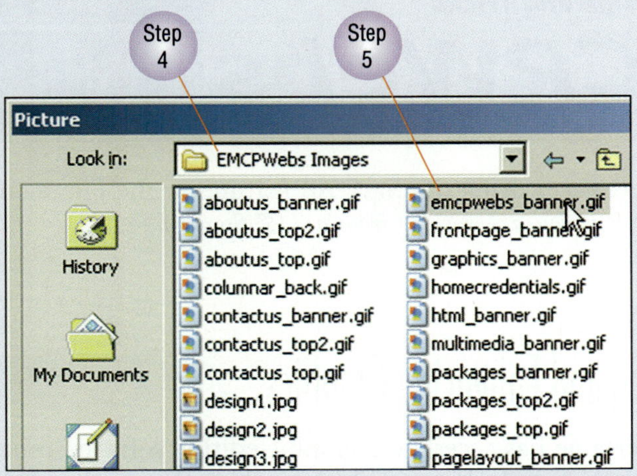

6. Place the insertion point after the banner image and press Enter once.
7. Click the Save button on the Standard toolbar and then click OK in the Save Embedded Files dialog box.
8. From the Navigation or Folders view window, open the About EMCPWebs (aboutus.htm) file into Page view.
9. Select the text and repeat steps 2–5 to insert the aboutus_banner.gif image file into the Web page.
10. Click the Center button on the Formatting toolbar.

11. Insert the remaining banner logo images in their respective pages.

12. Save the updated pages using the Save All feature on the File menu. *(Note: This may take several minutes if you are working from a 3½" floppy.)*

Altering and Enhancing Graphics

Not everyone has access to a graphic editing software program. Web designers who insert images and photographs into FrontPage may need to crop and resize the images from time to time, especially if a graphic doesn't fit well on the page, so FrontPage includes some features that perform editing functions that would be contained in a separate program. Cropping is basically cutting away edges of the photograph or image that are not needed. Resizing an image may be necessary if the image is large and needs to be reduced to fit properly on the page. Resampling an image will match the file size to the image size, thus reducing the download time. This feature may reduce the need to compress the image in a graphic editing program.

exercise 8

CROPPING AN IMAGE

1. With the EMCPWebs home page (index.htm) open, scroll down the Web page until the photograph of the building is completely visible.
2. Click the image to select it. The Pictures toolbar will appear at the bottom of the FrontPage window.
3. Click the Crop button on the Pictures toolbar.
4. Click and drag the sizing handles of the dotted crop line to match the figure below.

5. Click the Crop button on the Pictures toolbar once again to crop the image.
6. Save the updated home page.

exercise 9

RESIZING AND RESAMPLING AN IMAGE

1. With the EMCPWebs home page (index.htm) open, scroll down the Web page until the photograph of the building is completely visible.
2. Double-click the building image to open the Picture Properties dialog box.
3. Click the Specify size check box in the Size area to insert a check mark.

4. Key **250** in the Height spin box and make sure the in pixels option button is selected.
5. Click the OK button to return to the home page.
6. Select the image once again.
7. Click the Resample button on the Pictures toolbar. *(Note: This should reduce the Estimated Time to Download to about 18 seconds. Any time an image is resized, the original image file size is not automatically altered. Thus, resampling an image matches the image size with the file size and ultimately the time to download the image.)*

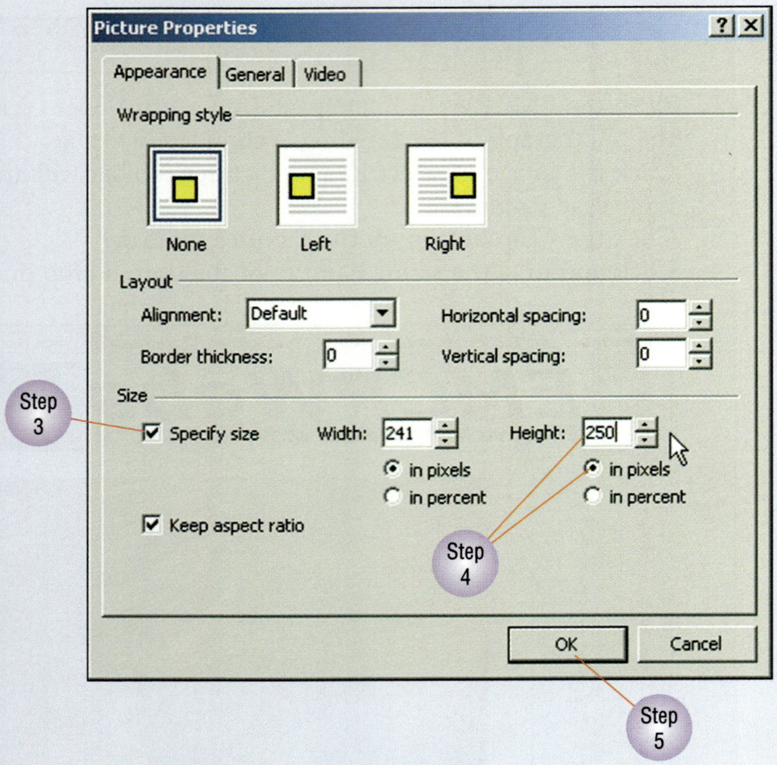

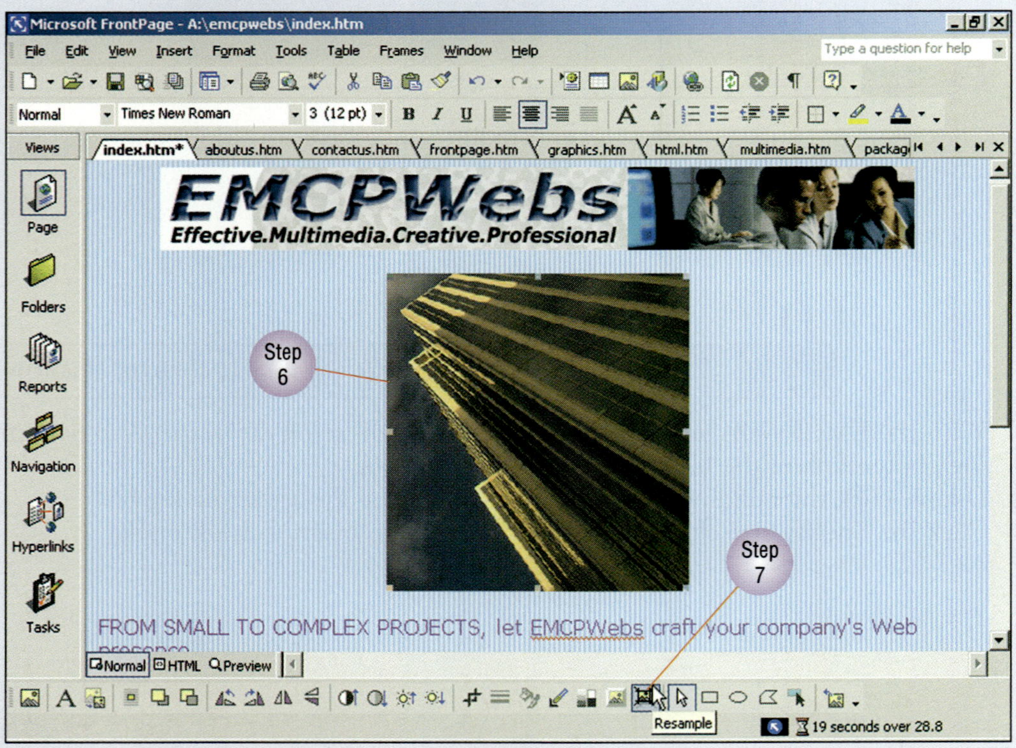

Setting Transparent Color to Images

Typical graphic editing software programs have a white canvas upon which to create and/or edit graphics. The ability to delete the "white space" background of a graphic can give the image a more subtle look by "fitting" in with the background. In addition, images without the surrounding white color will look more three-dimensional if a shadow has been applied. Some images, however, cannot be made transparent very easily. For example, images that have a speckled texture are nearly impossible to make fully transparent.

exercise 10

SETTING TRANSPARENT COLOR TO IMAGES

1. Press Ctrl + Home on the keyboard in the EMCPWebs home page to return to the top of the page.
2. Click anywhere on the EMCPWebs banner image.
3. Click the Set Transparent Color button on the Pictures toolbar.
4. Click a white area of the banner image (left side of image).

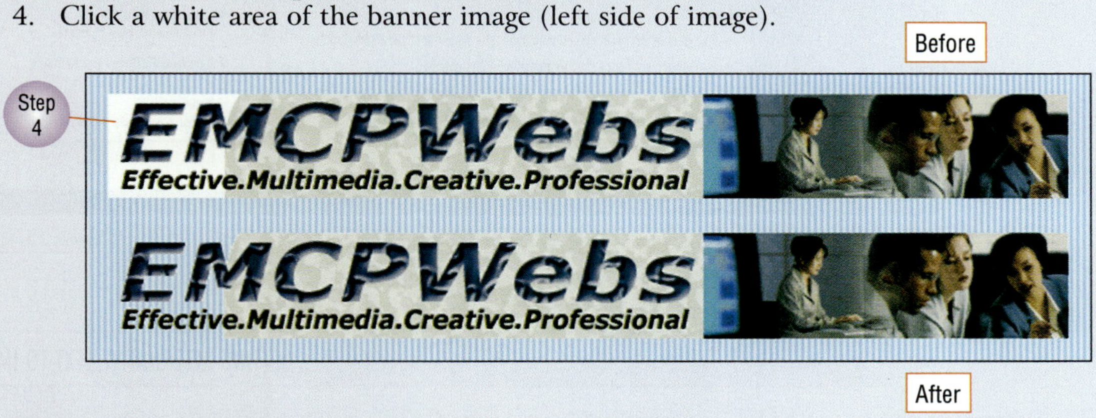

5. Follow the same steps to set the transparent color for each of the second-tier banner images.

Setting Alternative Text to Images

Alternative text (alt text) (see figure 3.8) is text displayed in place of a graphic that cannot be displayed in the browser window. Newer browsers can view most graphics that Web designers publish on their pages. However, some individuals may have an option in their browser settings to hide pictures for quicker downloads. Another reason designers may use alt text can be to create a message for viewers as they hover over an image.

FIGURE

3.8 *Web Page Image Alternative Text*

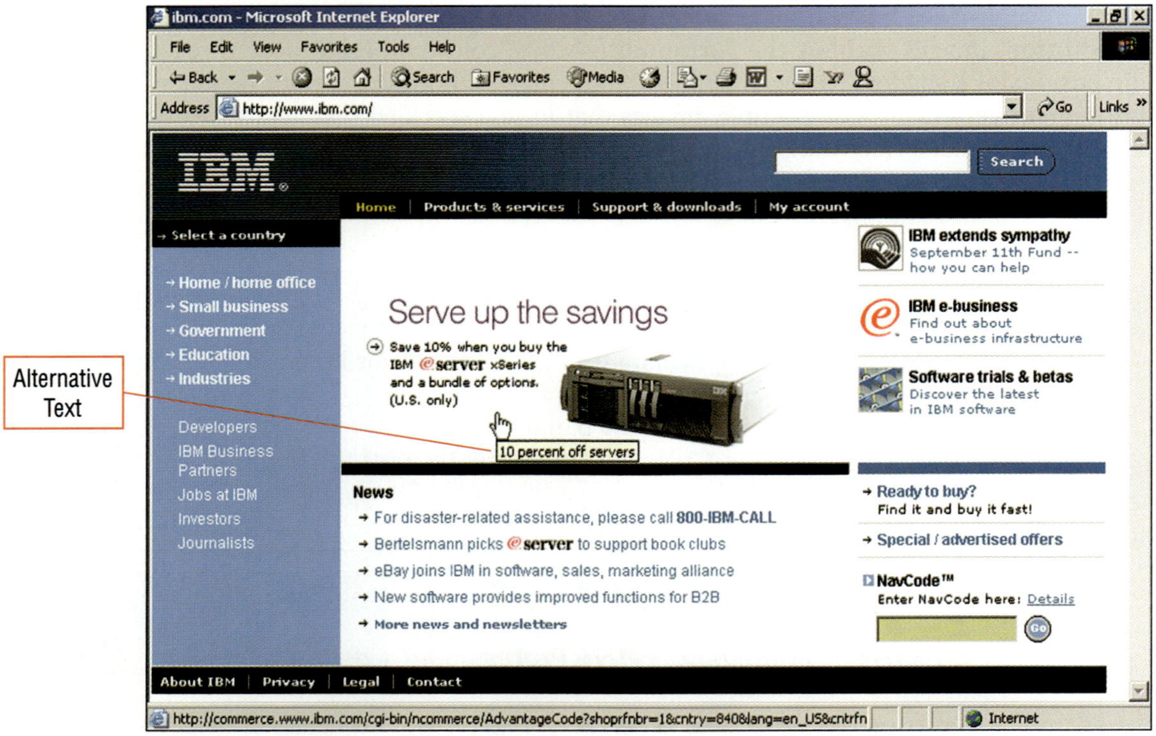

exercise 11

SETTING ALTERNATIVE TEXT TO IMAGES

1. Return to the EMCPWebs home page in Page view.
2. With the banner image selected, press Alt + Enter to open the Picture Properties dialog box.
3. Click the General tab.
4. Place the insertion point in the Text box in the Alternative representations section and then key: **Welcome to EMCPWebs - Effective.Multimedia. Creative.Professional**
5. Click the OK button to return to the Page view.

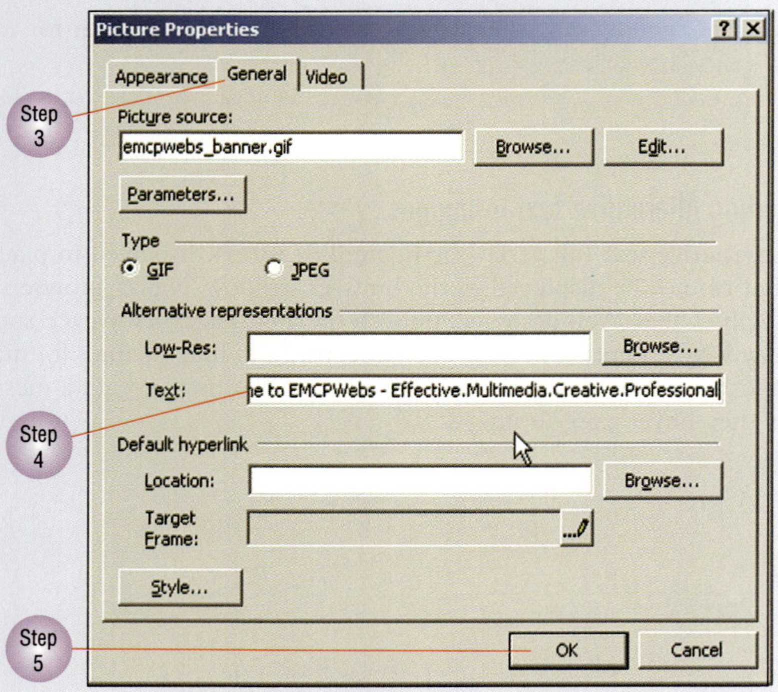

6. Save the updated Web pages and the updated images using the Save All feature on the File menu. *(Note: This may take several minutes if you are working from a 3½" floppy.)*
7. Return to the EMCPWebs home page and click the Preview in Browser button on the Standard toolbar.
8. Hover your mouse pointer over the banner image.
9. Close the Web browser.

Wrapping Text around Images

Many of the current Web design principles come from desktop publishing. Having the ability to wrap text around images is a must for those Web designers with print page layout designs. Text can be wrapped around an image and aligned at either the left or right. To wrap text around a graphic, select the graphic and then click either the Align Left or Align Right button on the Formatting toolbar. The amount of white space between the graphic and the text can be changed in the Appearance tab of the Picture Properties dialog box. Enter the number of pixels to space in the Horizontal and Vertical spacing text boxes. Figure 3.9 shows a news article with text wrapped around an image.

FIGURE 3.9 ***Example of Major Tech News Site with Image Wrapping***

exercise 12

WRAPPING TEXT AROUND IMAGES

1. With the EMCPWebs home page (index.htm) open, scroll down the Web page until the photograph of the building is completely visible.
2. Click the image of the building and drag it to the left of the text beginning *FROM SMALL TO COMPLEX PROJECTS.*

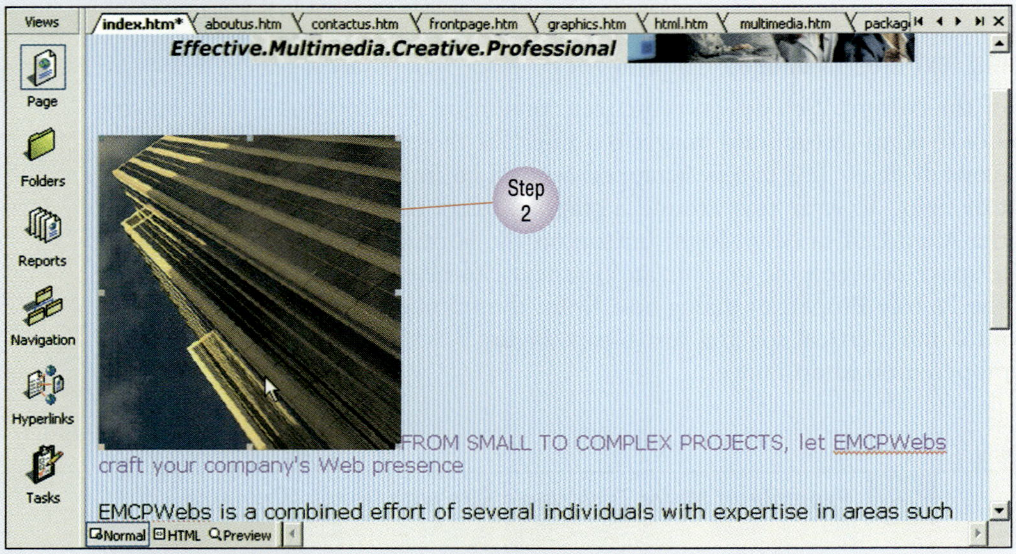

3. Click the Align Right button on the Formatting toolbar.
4. Save the updated home page.

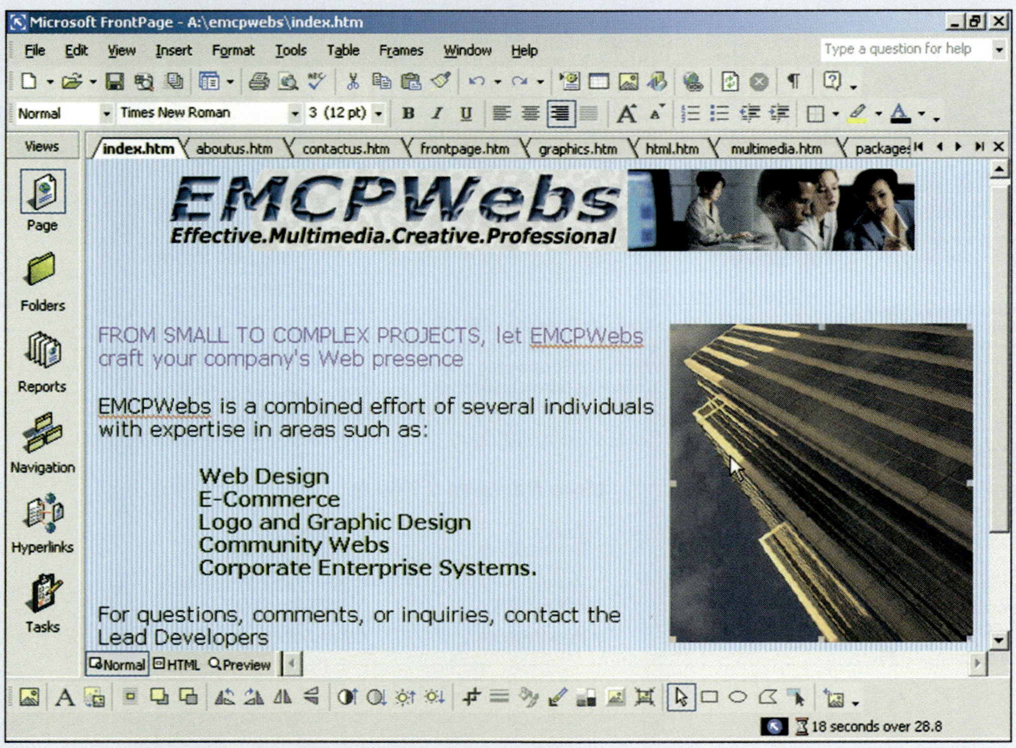

Formatting Graphics Using the Pictures Toolbar

In addition to the image manipulation features you have already discovered, FrontPage has several other effects you can apply to enhance your pictures. Images can be rotated or flipped for better positioning on the page or just for an interesting effect. Dark photographs can be brightened and light photos can be darkened for better contrast. Color photos can be formatted into a black-and-white (grayscale) image. The Wash Out button will cause the image to appear faded.

Although there is no substitute for a full-blown graphic editing software program, the Pictures toolbar (figure 3.10) has a number of image manipulation features. The Pictures toolbar can be accessed from the Toolbars submenu on the View menu, but it will automatically dock itself at the bottom of the Page view window anytime an image is selected in the window.

FIGURE 3.10 ***Pictures Toolbar Buttons***

Click this button	***Named***	***To do this***
	Insert Picture From File	Insert a picture from a storage medium
	Text	Insert text onto an image
	AutoThumbnail	Create a thumbnail image of a picture
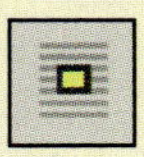	Position Absolutely	Position an image absolutely on a page
	Bring Forward	Bring an image forward
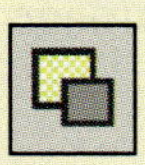	Send Backward	Send an image backward
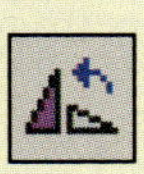	Rotate Left	Rotate an image to the left
	Rotate Right	Rotate an image to the right
	Flip Horizontal	Flip an image horizontally
	Flip Vertical	Flip an image vertically

Continued on next page

More Contrast	Increase contrast
Less Contrast	Decrease contrast
More Brightness	Increase brightness
Less Brightness	Decrease brightness
Crop	Crop an image
Line Style	Format line border style
Format Picture	Format the selected picture
Set Transparent Color	Set the transparent color of an image
Color	Format the color of selected image
Bevel	Bevel selected image
Resample	Optimize resized image
Select	Select an image
Rectangular Hotspot	Insert a rectangular hotspot on an image
Circular Hotspot	Insert a circular hotspot on an image
Polygonal Hotspot	Insert a polygonal hotspot on an image
Highlight Hotspots	Highlight all hotspots on selected images
Restore	Restore Pictures toolbar defaults

exercise 13

ROTATING AN IMAGE

1. With the EMCPWebs home page (index.htm) open, scroll down the Web page until the photograph of the building is completely visible.
2. Select the image of the building.
3. Click the Flip Horizontal button on the Pictures toolbar. This will rotate the graphic so that the building is facing the other direction. *(Note: The Flip Horizontal tool may not be very practical with photographic images; however, navigation arrows and other basic shapes can be rotated and flipped in any direction to serve a specific purpose on the Web page.)*

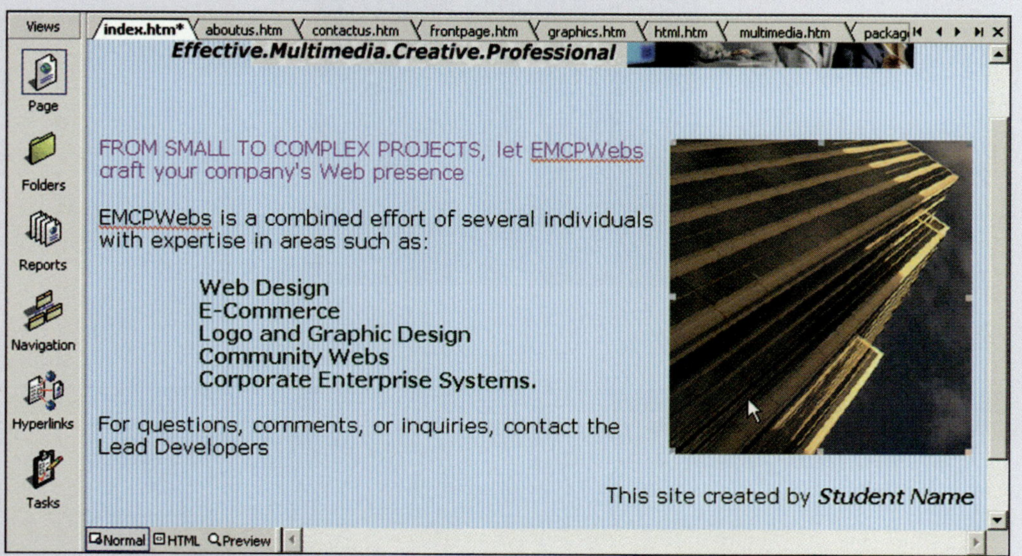

exercise 14

ALTERING THE BRIGHTNESS OF AN IMAGE

1. With the EMCPWebs home page open, select the building image.
2. Click the More Brightness button five times.

3. Click the Less Brightness button seven times.
4. Save the updated home page.

exercise 15

FORMATTING AN IMAGE TO GRAYSCALE

1. With the EMCPWebs home page open, select the building image.
2. Click the Color button on the Pictures toolbar.
3. Select the Grayscale command.

4. Save the updated home page.

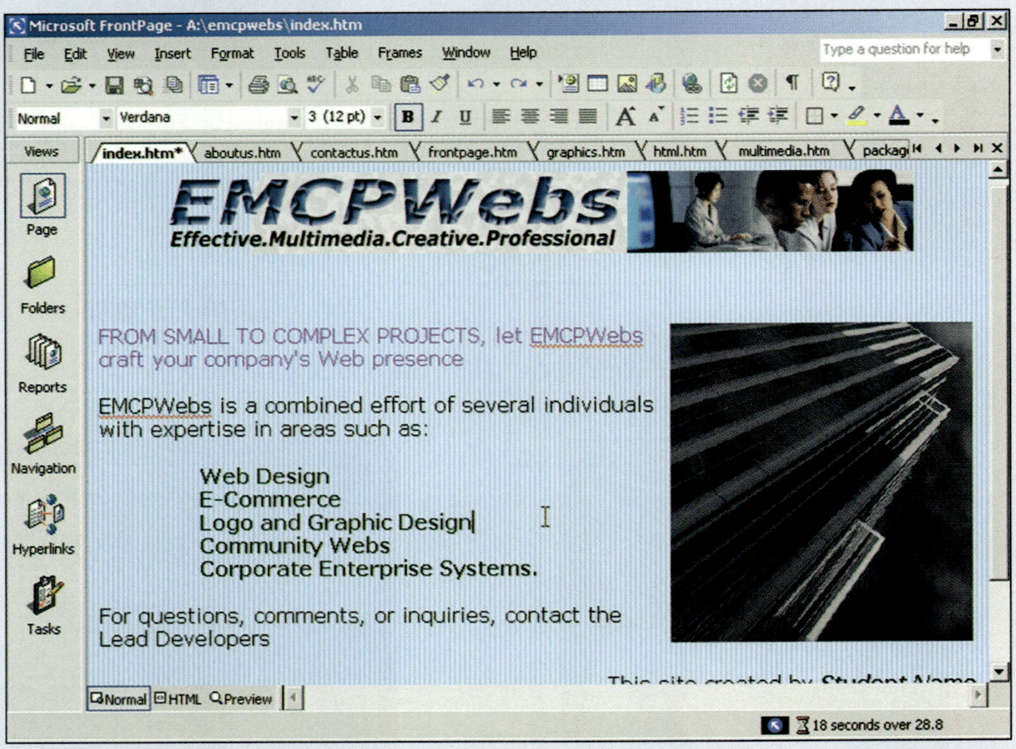

exercise 16

WASHING OUT AN IMAGE

1. With the EMCPWebs home page open, select the building image.
2. Click the Color button on the Pictures toolbar.
3. Select the Wash Out command.
4. Click the Undo button on the Standard toolbar.

The Undo button will undo your last command, such as inserting, formatting, and deleting text and images. FrontPage 2002 retains the last 30 commands you have performed. This feature is especially handy if you have made a mistake or are just trying out new possibilities in your Web pages.

Any image that is to have text placed on it using the text tool must be converted to GIF. A dialog box will appear indicating that the picture will be converted to GIF and that the number of colors in the image may be reduced and the file size may be larger than the original.

exercise 17

ADDING TEXT TO AN IMAGE

1. With the EMCPWebs home page open, select the building image.
2. Click the Text button on the Pictures toolbar.
3. A box area will appear in the center of the image. Key the following text:

   MEMBERSHIPS:
   Association of Web Professionals
   International Webmasters Assn.

   CERTIFICATIONS:
   MOUS - FrontPage 2002
   Master CIW Designer
   Adobe Cert. Expert - PhotoShop

4. With the text box still selected, click the down-pointing triangle next to Font Color on the Formatting toolbar and then select White.
5. Change the font to Verdana.
6. Change the font size to 10 points.
7. Click the Align Right button on the Formatting toolbar.
8. Resize the text box to match the position of text in the illustration by dragging the sizing handles and text box around the image.
9. Print the updated Web page.
10. Save the updated Web page.

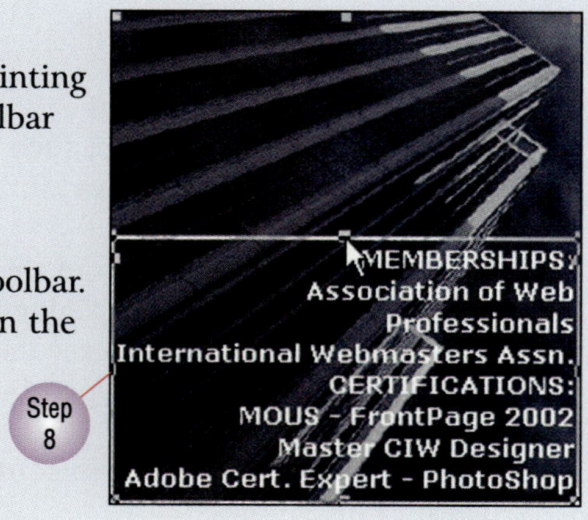

Assigning a Program to Edit Image Files

Just because an image is placed on a Web page does not mean that the image can no longer be edited. It may still require some tweaking. The Configure Editors tab in the Options dialog box allows designers to assign programs installed on the computer system to edit the images inserted into Web pages. The Options dialog box can be accessed by selecting the Options command from the Tools menu.

Before completing the following exercise, refer to your instructor for the preferred image editing program installed on the institution's computer systems. *(Some possibilities might be Microsoft PhotoDraw, Adobe PhotoShop, Macromedia Fireworks, CorelDraw, or JASC PaintShop Pro.)*

exercise 18 CONFIGURING FRONTPAGE TO OPEN A GRAPHIC EDITING PROGRAM FOR IMAGE EDITING

1. With the EMCPWebs home page open in Page view, click the Tools menu.
2. Select the Options command.
3. Click the Configure Editors tab in the Options dialog box.

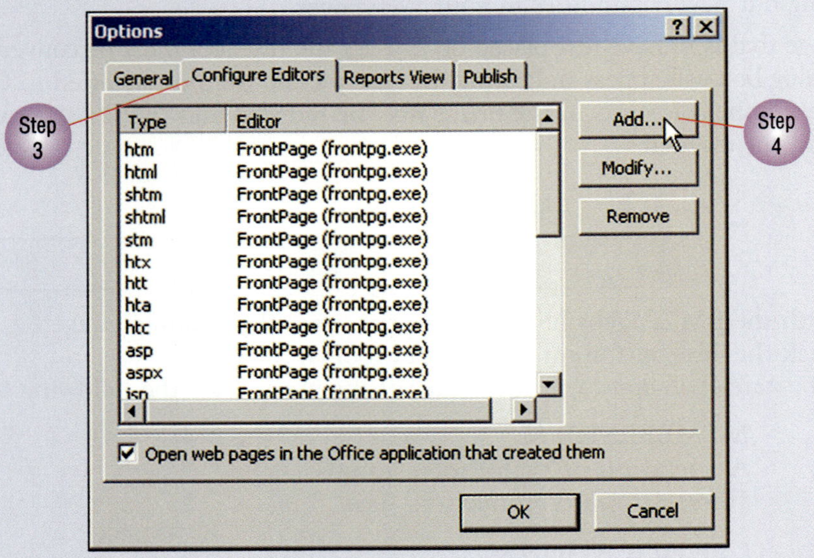

4. Click the Add button.
5. At the Add Editor Association dialog box, key **gif** for File type and key a graphic editing software program installed on your system, such as **Microsoft PhotoDraw**, for the Editor name.
6. Click the Browse button in the Add Editor Association dialog box
7. Locate the appropriate executable file for the graphic editing program used to edit graphics and click the Open button.
8. Click the OK button.
9. Perform the same steps to configure your graphic editing program for editing JPEG (.jpg) image files.

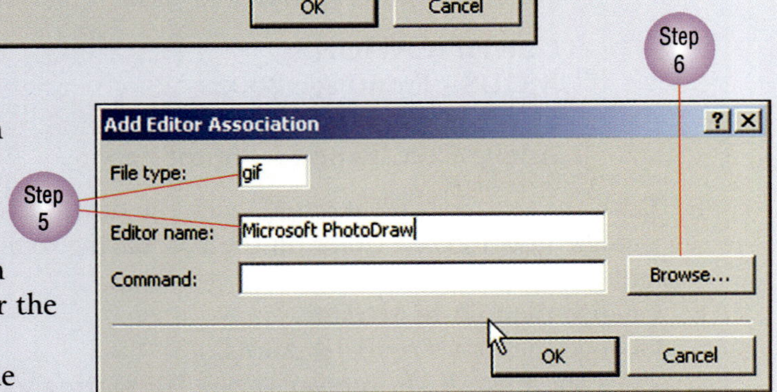

10. Return to the EMCPWebs home page in Page view.
11. Double-click the home page banner image.
12. Click the General tab.
13. Click the Edit button.

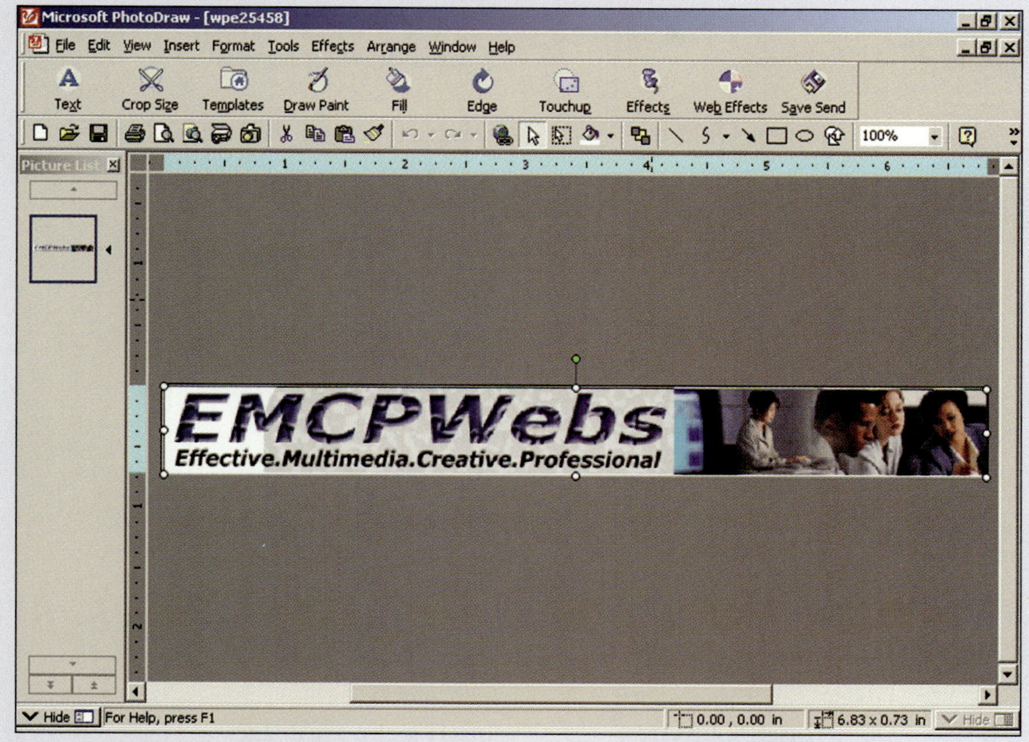

14. Close Microsoft PhotoDraw.
15. Close FrontPage and save any changes.

Inserting Drawing Objects from the Drawing Toolbar

The Drawing toolbar in Microsoft FrontPage (see figure 3.11) is very similar to the Drawing toolbars in Microsoft Word and PowerPoint. The AutoShapes tool includes various line, arrow, star, callout, and other object shapes. There are individual Line, Arrow, Rectangle, and Oval buttons on the Drawing toolbar. Text can be placed anywhere on the Web page by using the Text Box tool. WordArt, a traditional Microsoft feature, can now be inserted into FrontPage Web pages. Clip art and images from files can be inserted from this toolbar as well. The Fill Color tool is used to fill shapes with color, patterns, gradients, or textures. The Line Color tool is used to change the color of lines and shape outlines. Line formatting such as styles, weight, dashed, and color can be applied to lines and shape outlines. Various arrow styles are available for effect. Shadow effects at various angles can be used for three-dimensional effects. There is even a 3-D Style tool that includes various 3-D shape effects.

FIGURE

3.11 Drawing Toolbar Buttons

Click this button	Named	To do this
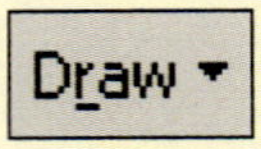	Draw	Format drawing objects
	Select Objects	Select objects on the screen
	AutoShapes	Insert AutoShapes
	Line	Insert a line
	Arrow	Insert an arrow
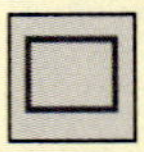	Rectangle	Insert a rectangle
	Oval	Insert an oval
	Text Box	Insert a text box
	Insert WordArt	Insert WordArt
	Insert Clip Art	Insert a clip art image
	Insert Picture From File	Insert picture from storage media
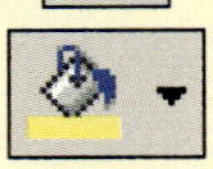	Fill Color	Fill selected object with color
	Line Color	Format line color
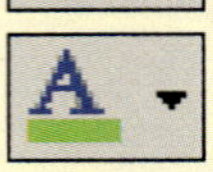	Font Color	Change font color
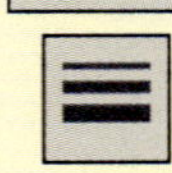	Line Style	Format line style
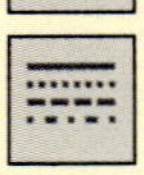	Dash Style	Format dash style
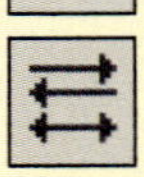	Arrow Style	Format arrow style
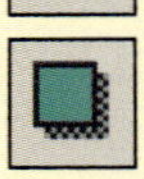	Shadow Style	Apply a shadow effect to an object
	3-D Style	Apply a 3-D effect to an object

exercise 19

INSERTING AND FORMATTING AUTOSHAPE IMAGES

1. Open the EMCPWebs FrontPage Web.
2. Open the Contact EMCPWebs (contactus.htm) Web page from the Folders or Navigation view.
3. Place the insertion point below the banner image.
4. Press the Enter key 10 times.
5. Scroll up to the top of the Web page.
6. Click the Drawing button on the Standard toolbar.
7. Click the AutoShapes button on the Drawing toolbar.
8. Point to Basic Shapes and then click the Rounded Rectangle shape.
9. Draw the rounded rectangle.

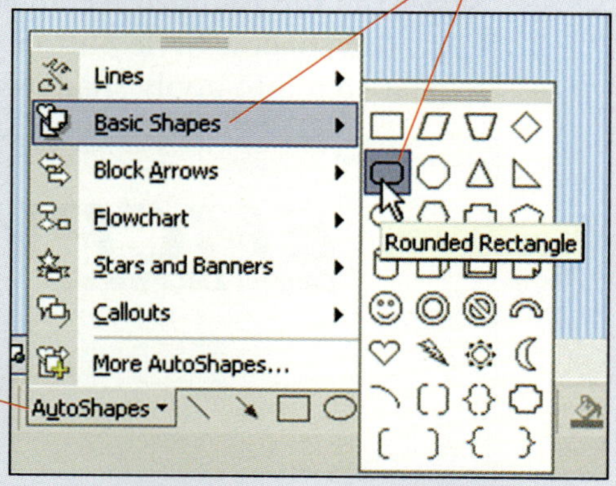

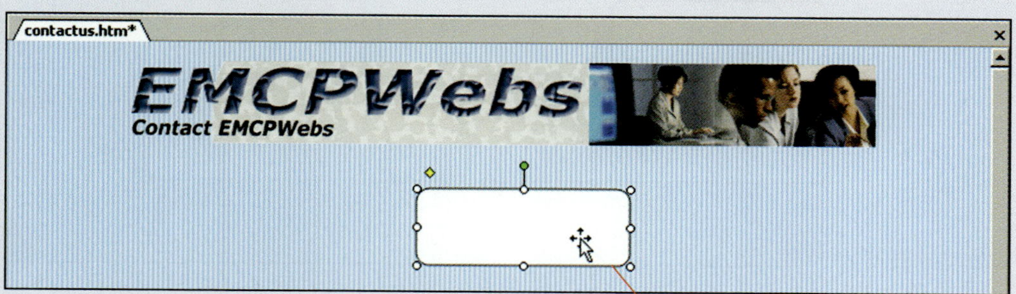

10. Double-click the rounded rectangle and format the size of the box to 60 × 170 pixels.
11. Right-click the rectangle shape and select the Copy command.
12. Click the Paste button on the Standard toolbar three times.
13. Click and drag the new rounded rectangle boxes to match the illustration.

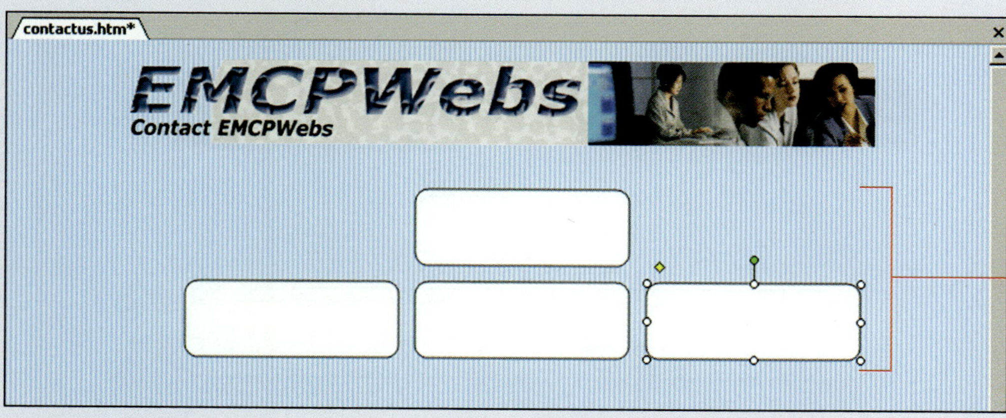

14. Create a new rounded rectangle shape measuring 60 × 540 pixels and center it under the three boxes.
15. Save the updated Contact EMCPWebs page.

exercise 20

APPLYING SHADOW STYLES TO SHAPES

1. Open the Contact EMCPWebs (contactus.htm) Web page from the Folders or Navigation view.
2. Select the top rounded rectangle shape.
3. Click the Shadow Style button on the Drawing toolbar and then select Shadow Style 4.
4. Repeat step 3 to apply shadows to the remaining rounded rectangle shapes.

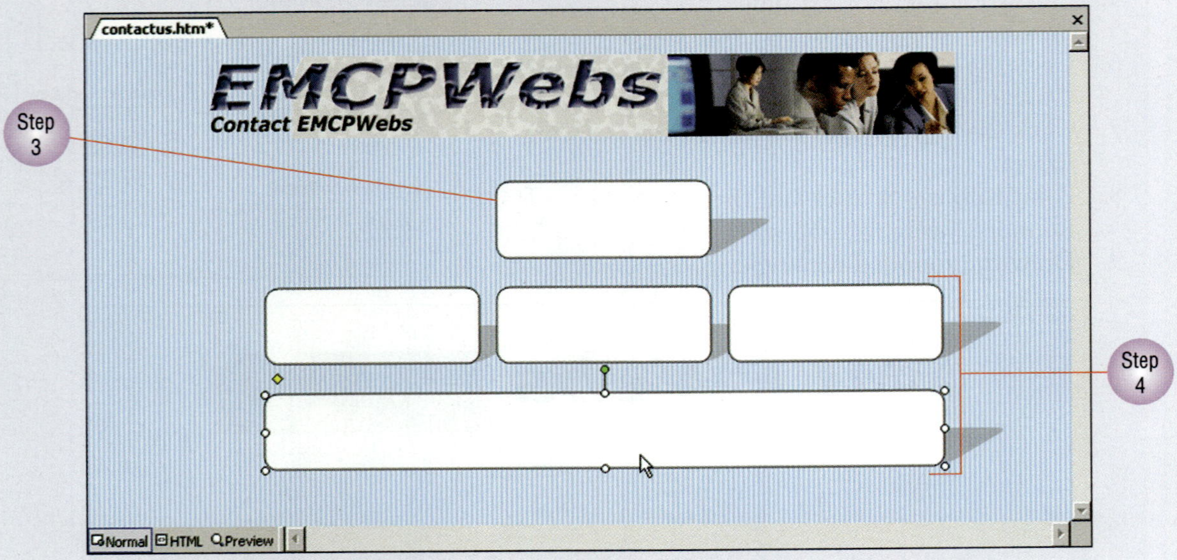

exercise 21

DRAWING LINES AND ARROWS

1. With the Contact EMCPWebs (contactus.htm) Web page open, click the Line tool on the Drawing toolbar.
2. Draw lines to connect the rounded rectangle boxes, as shown in the illustration.

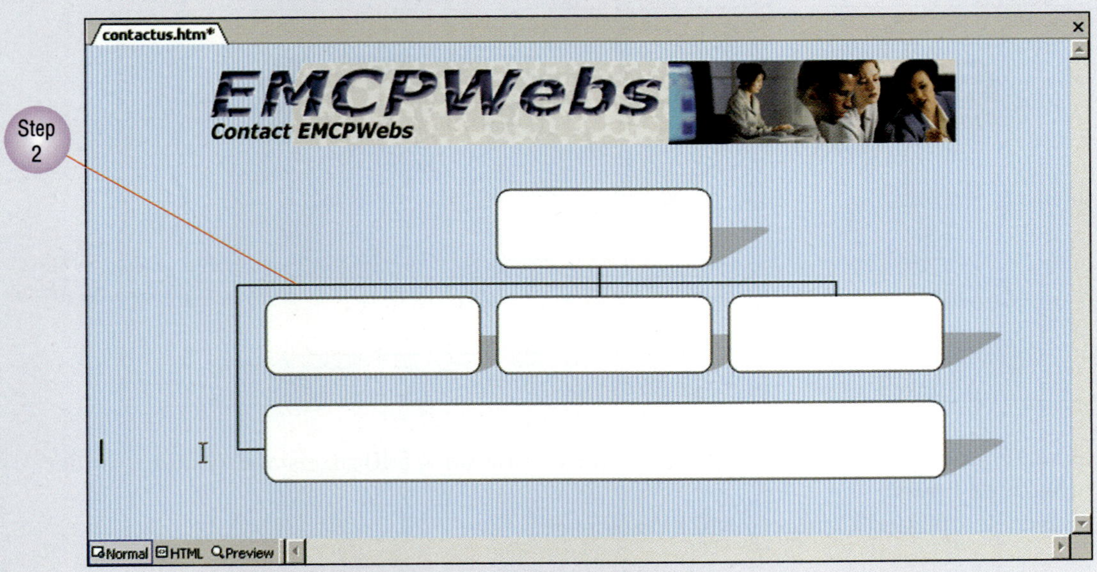

3. Using the Line tool and the Arrow tool, draw lines that match the illustration below.
4. Double-click the vertical line you just drew.
5. At the AutoFormat dialog box with the Colors and Lines tab selected, in the Line section, click the down-pointing triangle in the Dashed list box and then select the Square Dot option.
6. Click the OK button.
7. Click the Line Style button on the Drawing toolbar.
8. Select the 4½ pt option.
9. Repeat steps 4–8 to apply the same formatting effects to the horizontal arrow.
10. Save the updated Contact EMCPWebs page.

exercise 22 FILLING SHAPES WITH COLOR

1. With the Contact EMCPWebs (contactus.htm) Web page open, click the top rounded rectangle box.
2. Click the down-pointing triangle next to the Fill Color button on the Drawing toolbar.

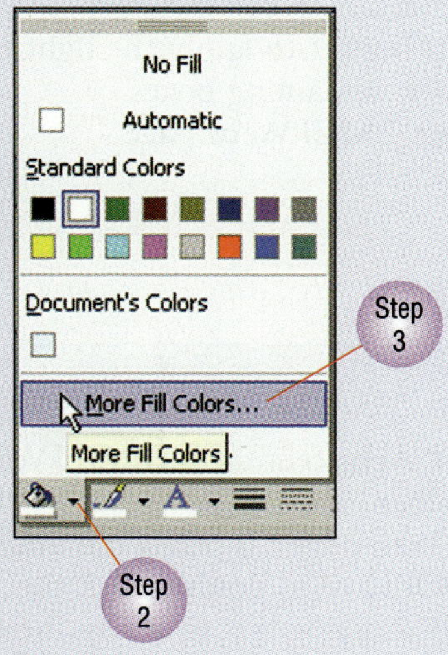

3. Select the More Fill Colors option.

4. At the More Colors dialog box, click the Select button.

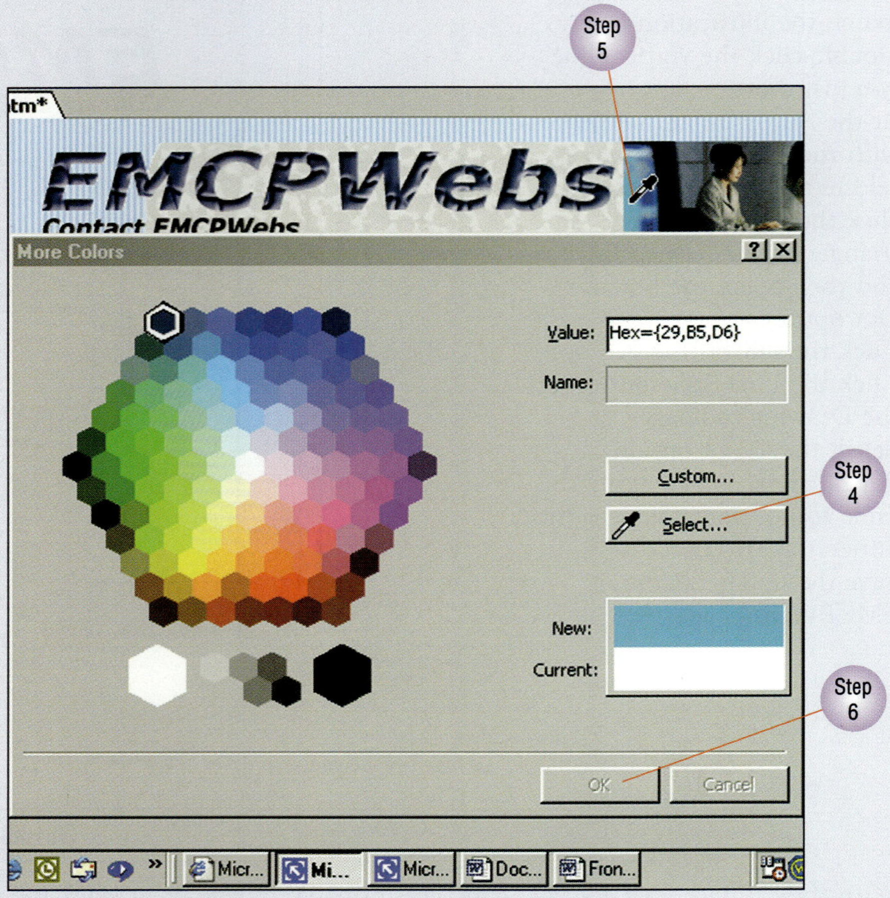

5. Click the light blue part of the television screen on the banner image.
6. Click the OK button.
7. Select the next rounded rectangle box.
8. Click the Fill Color paint bucket to apply the light blue fill.
9. Repeat steps 7–8 to fill the remaining boxes.
10. Save the updated Contact EMCPWebs page.

exercise 23

INSERTING TEXT BOXES

1. With the Contact EMCPWebs (contactus.htm) Web page open, click the Text Box tool on the Drawing toolbar.
2. Draw a text box on the Web page 60 pixels tall and 170 pixels wide in an empty area below the banner. You will have to double-click the text box and then click the Size tab in the Format Text Box dialog box to verify the measurements.
3. Key **Drew Shipley,** in the text box.
4. Press Shift + Enter to insert a line break.
5. Key **Owner & CEO**.

6. Format the two lines of text to Verdana, 12 points, bold, White, and center aligned.
7. Double-click the text box boundary.
8. At the Format Text Box dialog box with the Colors and Lines tab selected, select the No Fill option on the Fill Color drop-down menu.
9. Select the No Line option on the Line Color drop-down menu and then click OK.

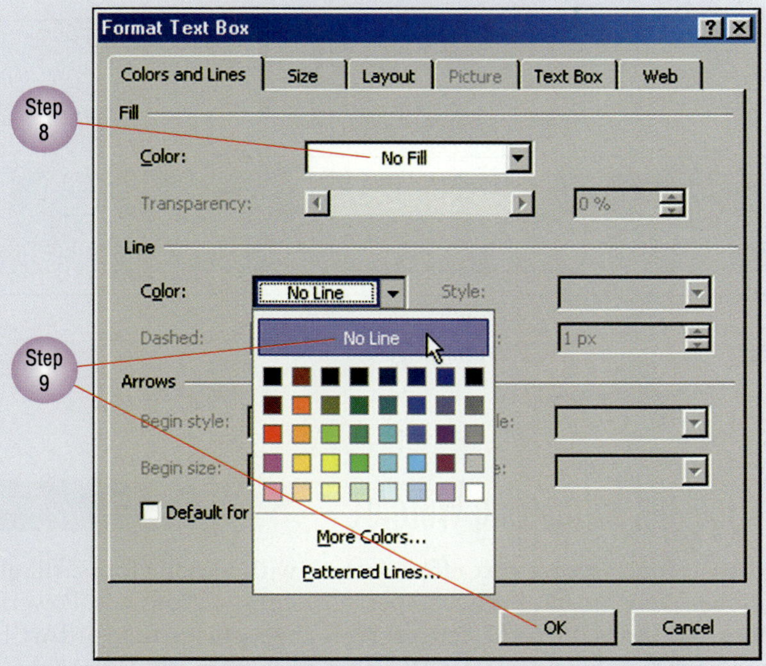

10. Select the text box boundary and use the arrow keys to position the box over the top rounded rectangle box.

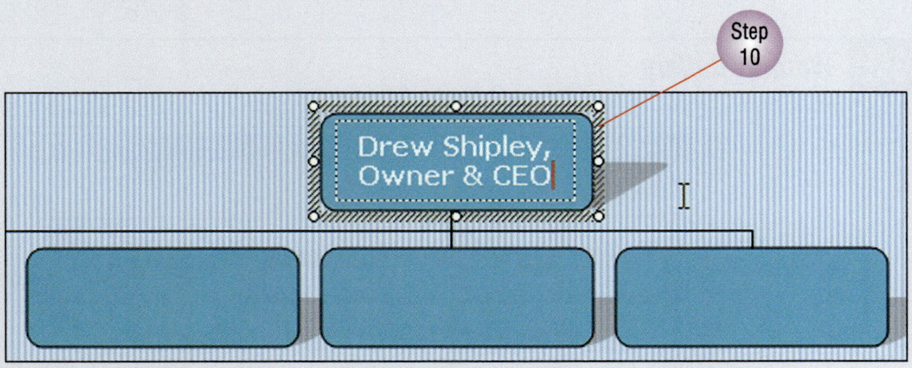

11. Repeat steps 2–10 to create and format text boxes for the following employees, and to position them over the three remaining small rounded rectangles:

    Peter Downey, Programmer
    Rob Caballero, Graphic Designer
    Bernard Brown, Layout Design

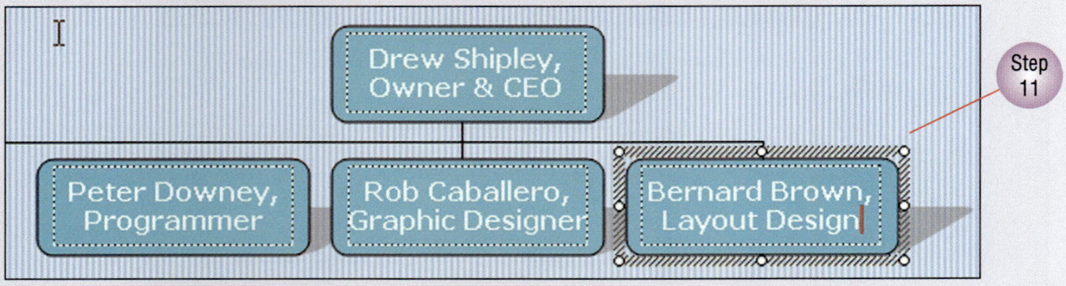

12. Save the updated Contact EMCPWebs page.

Inserting and Formatting WordArt

WordArt is a decorative text effect feature with various fonts, fill effects, and text directions. WordArt has been a staple in Microsoft Word and PowerPoint for several versions. To insert WordArt into a Web page, click the WordArt button on the Drawing toolbar. Next, select a WordArt style from the WordArt Gallery (figure 3.12). Finally, enter your text in the Edit WordArt Text dialog box and click OK. (Figure 3.13 identifies buttons on the WordArt toolbar.)

FIGURE 3.12 ***WordArt Gallery***

FIGURE 3.13 WordArt Toolbar Buttons

Click this button	Named	To do this
	Insert WordArt	Insert WordArt
Edit Text...	Edit Text	Edit WordArt text
	WordArt Gallery	Select a different WordArt style
	Format WordArt	Format the WordArt image
	WordArt Shape	Alter the WordArt shape
	WordArt Same Letter Heights	Make all characters same height
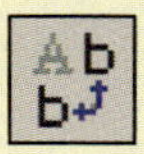	WordArt Vertical Text	Make WordArt text appear vertical
	WordArt Alignment	Change WordArt alignment
	WordArt Character Spacing	Change WordArt spacing between characters

exercise 24

INSERTING AND FORMATTNG WORDART

1. With the Contact EMCPWebs (contactus.htm) Web page open, click the WordArt button on the Drawing toolbar.
2. Select the second WordArt style from the left in the second row.

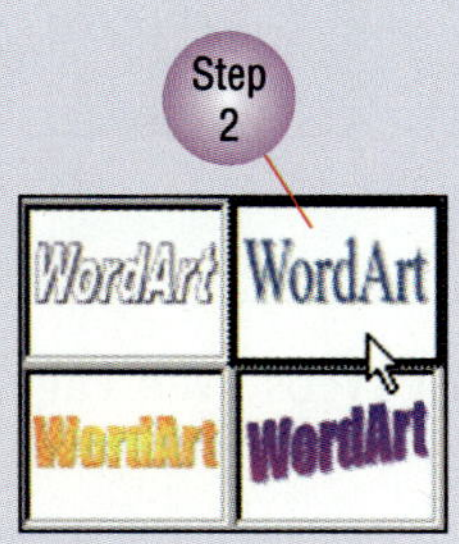

3. Click the OK button.
4. Key **Support Staff** in the Edit WordArt Text dialog box and then click OK.

5. With the WordArt text selected in Page view, click the Format WordArt button on the WordArt toolbar.
6. Click the Layout tab in the Format WordArt dialog box.
7. Select the Absolute Positioning Style and click OK.

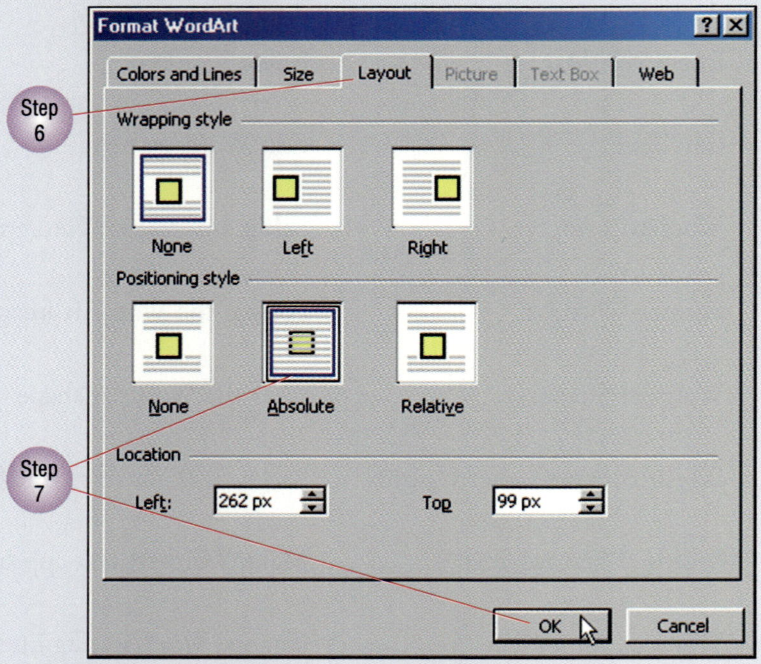

8. Move and resize the WordArt text to match the illustration below.

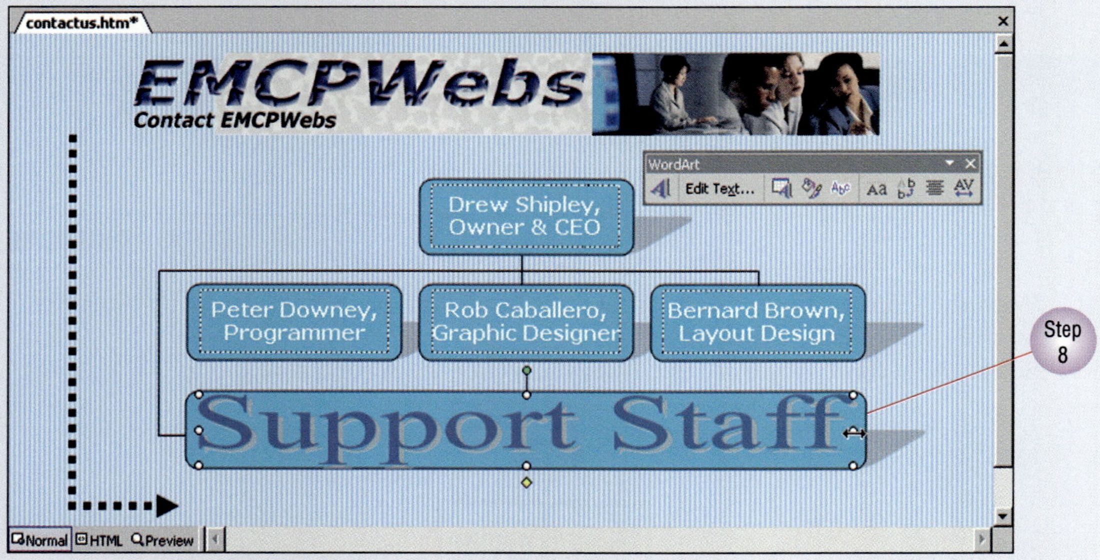

9. Print the updated Contact EMCPWebs Web Page.
10. Save the updated Contact EMCPWebs Web page.

Creating a Photo Gallery

Organizations and individuals alike view the World Wide Web as an opportunity to showcase photographs. Businesses often publish photographs of products, employees, and facilities. Individuals utilize the Web to publish photographs of family members, vacations, birthday parties, weddings, and other occasions. A FrontPage Photo Gallery is a Web page that contains a collection of photographs arranged in various layout designs. The layout designs consist of thumbnail images that open to a larger image for viewing. This photo album approach is an excellent addition to FrontPage 2002. Figure 3.14 illustrates the four Photo Gallery layout designs available in FrontPage.

FIGURE 3.14 **_Photo Gallery Layout Designs_**

Horizontal Layout

Montage Layout

Vertical Layout

Slide Show Layout

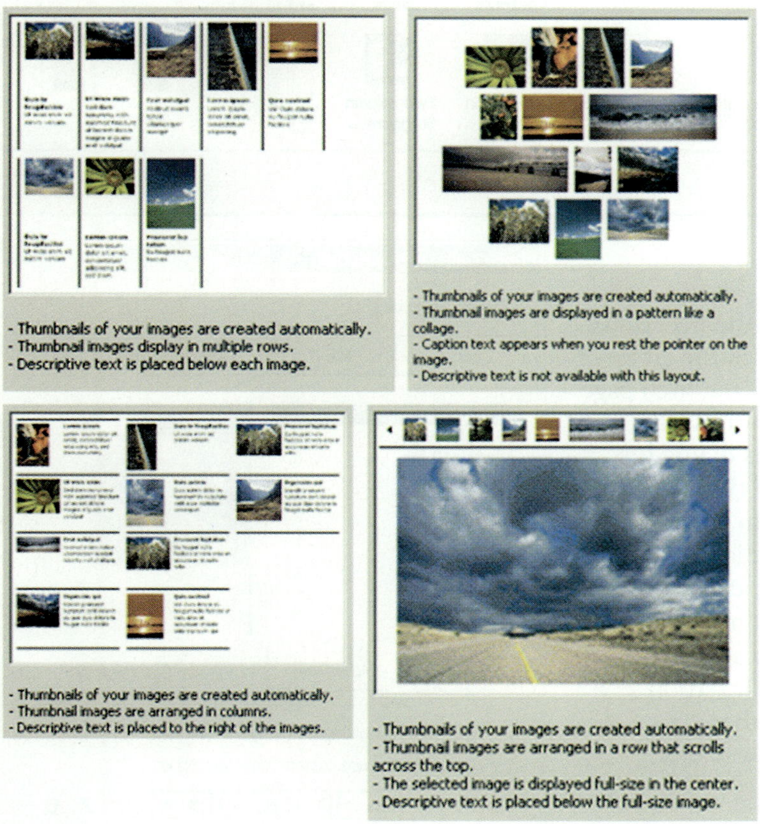

exercise 25 — CREATING A PHOTO GALLERY

1. Open the EMCPWebs FrontPage Web.
2. Click File, point to New, and then select the Page or Web command.
3. At the New Page or Web Task Pane, click the *Page Templates* link.

4. Select the *Photo Gallery* icon in the Page Templates dialog box.

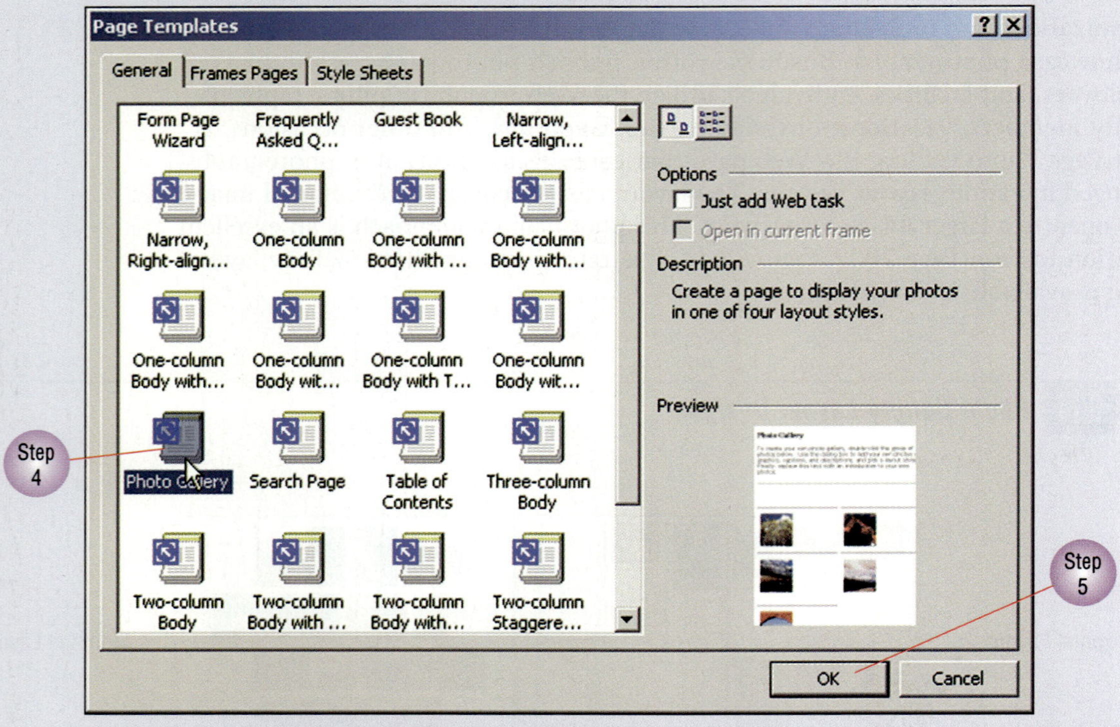

5. Click OK.
6. Following the Comment instructions, double-click the group of photos on the Web page.
7. In the Photo Gallery Properties dialog box, using the five sample pictures in the Photo Gallery, click the Override and use custom font formatting option to select it.
8. Place the insertion point in the Caption text box.

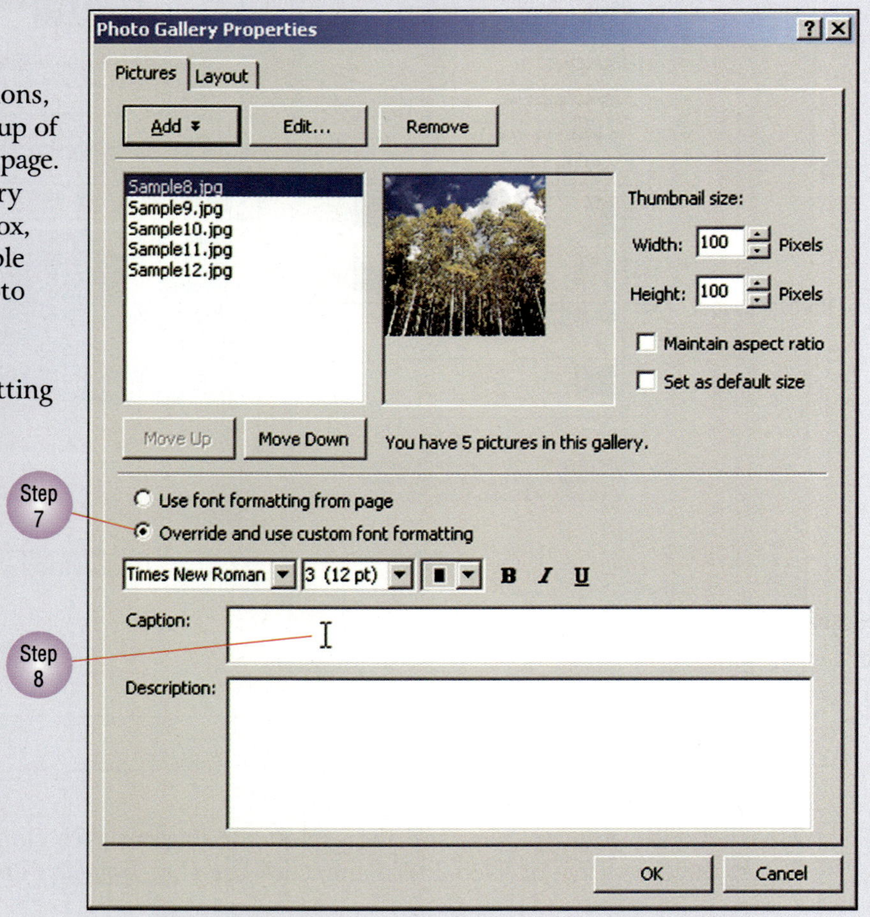

9. Key the information below to enter captions and descriptions for the five photographs. Click the file name to access each caption and description.

Image Title	*Caption*	*Description*
Sample8.jpg	**Aspen Trees**	**A wonderful view of the treetops**
Sample9.jpg	**Canyon View**	**A late-afternoon photograph of the canyon**
Sample10.jpg	**River Bottom**	**A cool day's hike in the mountains**
Sample11.jpg	**Spectacular Mount**	**A majestic shot overlooking the river**
Sample12.jpg	**Desert Southwest**	**A picturesque view in the middle of nowhere**

10. Format all captions to to Verdana, 12 points, and bold.
11. Format all descriptions to to Verdana and 10 points.
12. Click the OK button to generate the Photo Gallery.
13. Select the Comment component and press the Delete key twice.
14. Delete the horizontal line and any extra spaces between the page title and Photo Gallery component.
15. Click the Preview in Browser button on the Standard toolbar.
16. When prompted, save the updated Web page as photo_gallery.htm.
17. Test the Photo Gallery by clicking the thumbnail images.

Step 17

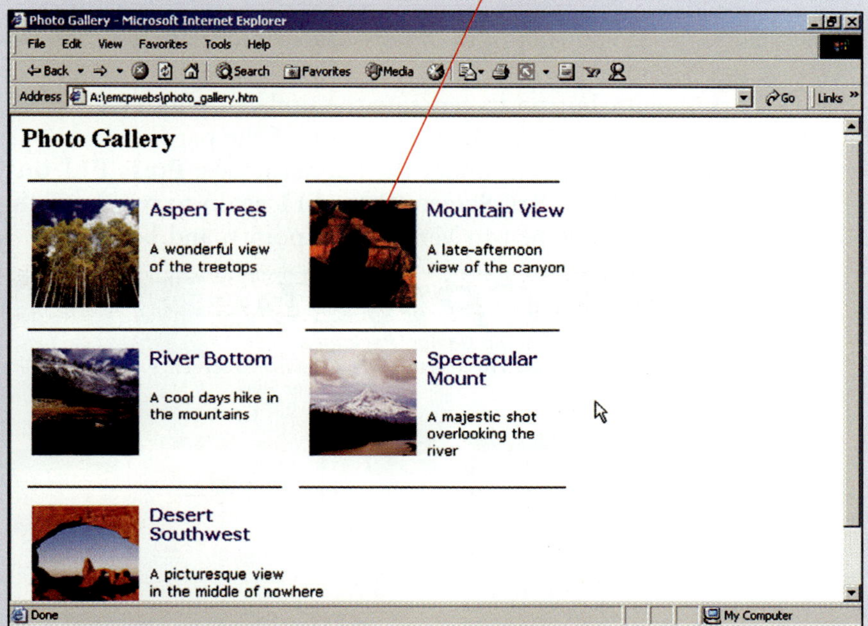

18. Print the Photo Gallery Web page in your browser window.

exercise 26

CREATING A SLIDE SHOW PHOTO GALLERY

1. Open the Web and Graphic Design Packages (packages.htm) file from either the Folders or Navigation view.
2. Place the insertion point after the banner image and then press the Enter key.
3. Click Insert, point to Picture, and then select the New Photo Gallery command.
4. At the Photo Gallery Properties dialog box with the Pictures tab selected, click the Add button.
5. Select the Pictures from Files command.
6. At the File Open dialog box, click the down-pointing triangle next to the Look in list box, locate the *EMCPWebs Images* folder you have downloaded, and then select that folder.

7. Select the design1.jpg file and then click Open.
8. Repeat steps 4–7 to add the following image files: design2.jpg, design3.jpg, and design4.jpg. *(Note: The images may not be part of any design packages, but the Web sites represented are excellent resources for information technology news.)*

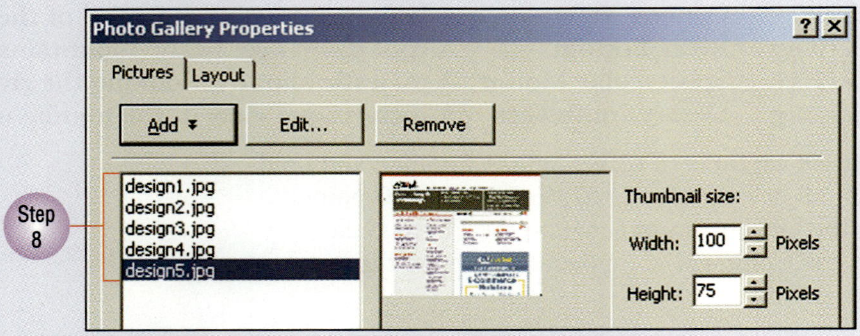

9. Click the Layout tab in the Photo Gallery Properties dialog box.
10. Click *Slide Show*.
11. Click the OK button to generate the updated photo gallery.
12. Select the *Photo Gallery* text at the top of the page.
13. Key the following text under the banner image: **Press F11 on your keyboard to view this Web page in Full Screen. Press F11 again to return to the normal browser view.**
14. Format the above text to Verdana, 10 points, and bold.

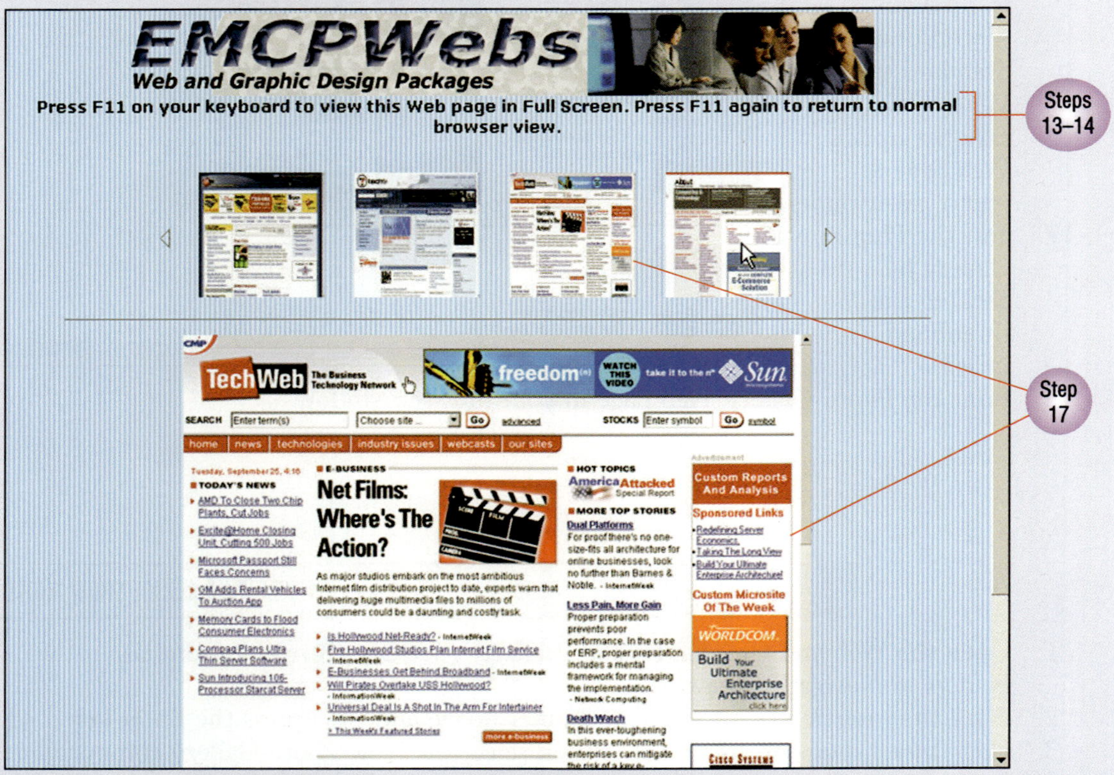

15. Click the Preview in Browser button on the Standard toolbar and save the updated Web page as prompted.

16. Once in your browser, press F11 to toggle to *Full Screen* mode.
17. Click on each of the thumbnails to test the Photo Gallery.
18. Print the Photo Gallery Web page.
19. Press F11 once again to return to the normal browser view.
20. Close your browser window.
21. Close FrontPage, saving any unsaved EMCPWebs Web pages.

exercise 27

UPDATING THE NAVIGATION VIEW

1. Open the EMCPWebs FrontPage Web.
2. Access the Navigation view.
3. Drag the newly created Photo Gallery file (photo_gallery.htm) in the Folder List underneath the About EMCPWebs box in the Navigation window.

CHAPTER summary

- FrontPage 2002 will automatically open the last edited Web.
- To prevent FrontPage from opening the last edited Web, access the Tools menu, select the Options command, and then uncheck Open last Web automatically when FrontPage starts.
- Open a recently edited Web quickly by clicking File, pointing to Recent Webs, and then clicking the Web you wish to open.
- Open an existing FrontPage Web not located in the Recent Webs submenu by selecting the Open Web command on the File menu.
- Open a recently edited Web page quickly by clicking File, pointing to Recent Files, and then clicking the specific page you wish to edit.
- Open a FrontPage Web directly from Internet Explorer by clicking the Edit with Microsoft FrontPage button on the toolbar.
- GIF-formatted images can contain up to 256 colors.
- JPEG-formatted images can contain up to 16.7 million colors and are commonly used for photographic pictures.
- JPEG-formatted images can be compressed by percentage to decrease Web page download time.
- The higher JPEG-formatted images are compressed, the lower the image quality will be.

COMMANDS review

Command	Mouse/Keyboard
Prevent FrontPage from opening last edited Web	Click Tools, Options, Open last Web automatically when FrontPage starts
Open recent Web	Click File, point to Recent Webs, click desired Web
Open recent file	Click File, point to Recent Files, click desired title
Open Web page from Internet Explorer	Click Edit with Microsoft FrontPage button on the Internet Explorer toolbar
Insert clip art	Click Insert, point to Picture, click Clip Art
Insert clips from Design Gallery Live Web site	Click *Clips Online* hyperlink on Insert Clip Art Task Pane
Insert picture from file	Click Insert Picture From File button on Standard toolbar
Crop an image	Select image, click Crop button on Pictures toolbar
Resize an image	Drag the image sizing handles; or double-click image, click Specify size
Resample an image	Select image, click Resample button on Pictures toolbar
Set transparent color to an image	Select image, click Set transparent Color button on Pictures toolbar, click solid color on image
Set alternate text to an image	Double-click image, General tab
Wrap text around image	Select image, click Align Left or Align Right button on Formatting toolbar
Rotate an image	Select image, click Rotate button on Pictures toolbar
Increase brightness of an image	Select image, click More Brightness button on Pictures toolbar
Decrease brightness of an image	Select image, click Less Brightness button on Pictures toolbar
Format an image to grayscale	Select image, click Color button on Pictures toolbar, click Grayscale
Wash out an image	Select image, click Color button on Pictures toolbar, click Wash Out
Add text to an image	Select image, click Text button on Picture toolbar
Configure image editor	Click Tools, Options, Configure Editors tab
Insert an AutoShape image	Click AutoShapes button on Drawing toolbar
Apply shadow styles	Click Shadow Style button on Drawing toolbar
Draw lines and arrows	Click Line or Arrow tool on Drawing toolbar

Fill shapes with color	Select shape, click Fill Color button on Pictures toolbar
Insert a text box	Click Text Box tool on Drawing toolbar
Insert WordArt	Click WordArt button on Drawing toolbar
Create a Photo Gallery page	Click File, New, Page or Web, Photo Gallery

CONCEPTS check

Completion: On a blank sheet of paper, indicate the correct term, command, or number for each item.

1. Recent FrontPage Webs and files can be quickly accessed by first clicking this menu.
2. Web pages in Internet Explorer can be edited by clicking this toolbar button.
3. This image file format is best for images with 256 colors or less.
4. This image file format is best for photorealistic pictures and can be compressed to reduce file size.
5. Clip art can be inserted into a Web page from this task pane.
6. Click this link in FrontPage to access the Microsoft Office Design Gallery Live Web site.
7. This toolbar automatically becomes visible each time an image is selected.
8. Perform this to cut away portions of an image.
9. Once an image is resized in FrontPage, click this button on the Pictures toolbar to compress the image to reduce file size and download time.
10. Click this button and then select a region on an image to remove that color and show the background.
11. Text displayed in place of a graphic that cannot be displayed in the browser window or that pops up a ScreenTip as the mouse hovers over an image is called this.
12. To wrap text around the right side of an image, you must click this button.
13. This toolbar includes many different graphic and illustration buttons as well as AutoShapes.
14. This Microsoft feature creates decorative text effect images.
15. This FrontPage feature contains a collection of photographs arranged in various layout designs.

SKILLS check

Assessment 1

1. Open Microsoft Internet Explorer.
2. Access in turn three Web sites of your choice and click the Edit with Microsoft FrontPage button on the toolbar.
3. Observe the WYSIWYG (What You See Is What You Get) design layout of how the Web pages may have been created in an HTML editor.
4. Print each of the Web pages.
5. Close FrontPage without saving any changes.

Assessment 2

1. Open FrontPage.
2. Click Insert, point to Picture, and then select Clip Art.
3. Search for a clip art image of a car.
4. Insert one of the clip art images into Page view.
5. Close FrontPage without saving any changes.

Assessment 3

1. Open FrontPage.
2. Click the Insert Picture From File button on the Standard toolbar.
3. Insert the picture1.jpg image from the *Pictures* folder in your *Chapter 3* folder in Page view.
4. Save the Web page as myschoolsplash.htm in your *Chapter 3* folder.
5. Preview the Web page in your default browser.
6. Print the Web page.

Assessment 4

1. Open FrontPage.
2. Open the mycity FrontPage Web in your *Chapter 3* folder.
3. Open the My City Home page in Page view.
4. Double-click the Home image button.
5. Click the General tab.
6. Key the alternative text **Take Me Home**.
7. Key the following alternative text representations to the remaining navigation images:

Button	***Alternative Text***
The City	**Find out more about our city**
Our Community	**Enjoy stories and photographs of our city**
Commerce	**Our city has a wide variety of commercial activity**
Business & Industry	**Career opportunities abound in our city**
Entertainment	**Things to do and see in our city**
Lodging	**From hotels to bed and breakfasts**
Restaurants	**From fast-food to five star . . . Enjoy!**

8. Save the changes.
9. Perform a Preview in Browser and test the alt text representations.

Assessment 5

1. Open the mycity FrontPage Web.
2. Open the My City Home page in Page view.
3. Select the photograph of the city.
4. Crop the black car out of the image.
5. Save the updated home page.
6. Print the Web page.

Assessment 6

1. Open the mycity FrontPage Web.
2. Open the My City Home page in Page view.
3. Select the photograph of the city.
4. Double-click the image.
5. Change the size of the image to 200 pixels tall.
6. Click the Resample button.
7. Save the updated home page.

Assessment 7

1. Open the mycity FrontPage Web.
2. Open the My City Home page in Page view.
3. Select the banner image.
4. Click the Set Transparent Color button on the Pictures toolbar.
5. Click anywhere on the yellow background of the image.
6. Save the updated home page.
7. Print the Web page.

Assessment 8

1. Open the mycity FrontPage Web.
2. Open the My City Home page in Page view.
3. Select the image of the city.
4. Click the Align Left button on the Formatting toolbar.
5. Drag the image so that it is even with the city introduction paragraph text.
6. Save the updated home page.
7. Print the Web page.

Assessment 9

1. Open FrontPage.
2. Create the following objects using the Drawing toolbar:

Drawing Toolbar Object	*Formatting Description*
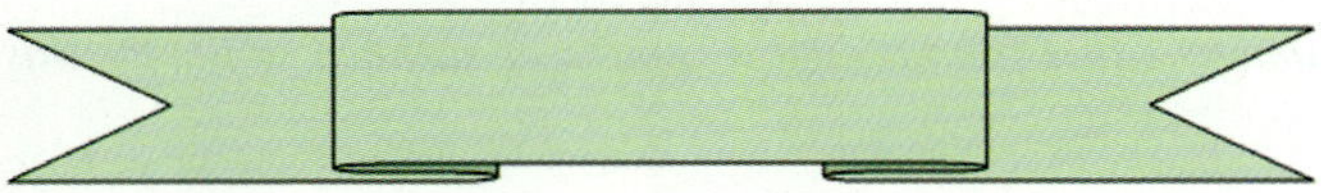	light green fill color
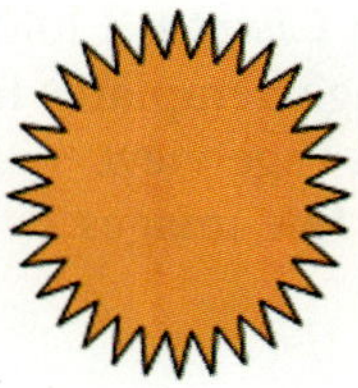	orange fill color
	yellow fill color

Company Picnic	Arial Black, 18 points, no fill color, no line color
May 21, 2002	Arial, 12 points, bold, no fill color, no line color

3. Arrange the objects as shown below using the Order command on the Draw pop-up menu.

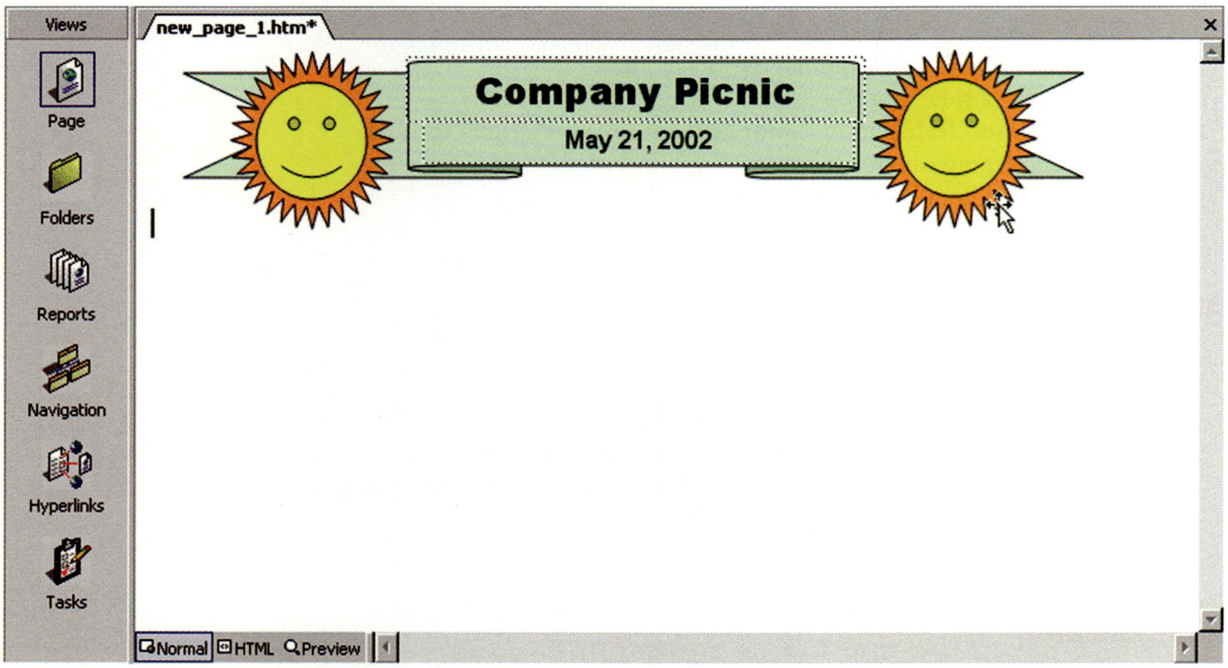

4. Save the Web page as picnic.htm with the Page Title *Company Picnic - AutoShapes*.

Assessment 10

(Note: You will need your own photographic images either from a digital camera or scanned to file for this assessment activity.)

1. Open FrontPage.
2. Create a new Empty Web titled *familyphotos* in your *Chapter 3* folder.
3. Create a new Photo Gallery Web page using the Page Templates feature.
4. Double-click the Photo Gallery Web component in Page view.
5. Remove the sample images and add a minimum of five images.
6. Format the layout to Slide Show.
7. Save the Web page as index.htm.
8. Perform a Preview in Browser and view your picture slide show.
9. Close FrontPage.

CHAPTER 4

CREATING AND CUSTOMIZING HYPERLINKS

PERFORMANCE OBJECTIVES

Upon successful completion of chapter 4, you will be able to:

- **Create a hypertext navigation bar**
- **Create bookmark hyperlinks**
- **Create hyperlinks automatically**
- **Create e-mail hyperlinks**
- **Remove hyperlinks**
- **Delete Web pages and files**
- **Format and insert a hyperlink on an image**
- **Create link bars**
- **Insert a hotspot hyperlink on an image**
- **Hyperlink to a new document**
- **Hyperlink to an external Web site**
- **Set hyperlinks to open in a new window**
- **Use the AutoThumbnail feature**
- **Test and verify hyperlinks**
- **Modify hypertext**

Chapter 4 IRC

While creating the graphics for a Web site can be very time consuming, one of the easiest aspects of Web page development is creating the hyperlinks. There are three major types of hyperlinks. The most common hyperlink uses text and images to navigate from one location or page to another. The default hyperlink for FrontPage Web page text is blue and underlined; after the site has been visited, the hyperlink color turns purple. While entire images can be hyperlinked, an image may have multiple hyperlinked regions that link to various Web pages and content. These multiple-region hyperlinks are called hotspots.

The second common use for hyperlinks is to download files and programs. Hyperlinks to Microsoft Word and PowerPoint files are typical at educational as well as business sites. If visitors do not have the application that the files are associated with, many applications have free downloadable viewers for installation onto their system. Software developers often provide links to their applications for testing and trial purposes.

A third use of hyperlinking is for e-mail. An e-mail hyperlink will automatically open the default e-mail program installed on the user's computer system, such as Microsoft Outlook. FrontPage 2002 has a new feature that allows designers to assign subject line text to e-mail hyperlinks. For Webmasters who may have e-mail hyperlinks to themselves on various pages and Webs, specifying the subject line can be beneficial for purposes of filing e-mails into the appropriate folder and replying to the sender promptly.

Creating Hypertext Links

The most common use of hyperlinks is to navigate from page to page on the World Wide Web. If your Web site has numerous links to other pages within the site (see, for example, figure 4.1), it is important to consider several navigation techniques when designing the Web pages:

- Avoid dead ends; provide appropriate and consistent navigation links throughout the site.
- Always provide a hyperlink to the home page.
- Hyperlinks should clearly state where they are taking the visitor.
- Do not link to unrecognizable or long addresses. Following are examples of address links to use and to avoid:
  - Good: EMCPWebs Home
  - Acceptable: www.emcpwebs.com
  - Unacceptable: www.emcpwebs.com/users/b/software/downloads.htm

Navigational efficiency is the cornerstone of a good Web site. Effective linkages between pages on a Web not only make a site look more professional, but will also help your visitors move from page to page without becoming frustrated. Navigation bars can be a series of hypertext links, image buttons, or a single graphic image with multiple hotspot links.

FIGURE 4.1 ***Hyperlink Intensive ESPN Home Page***

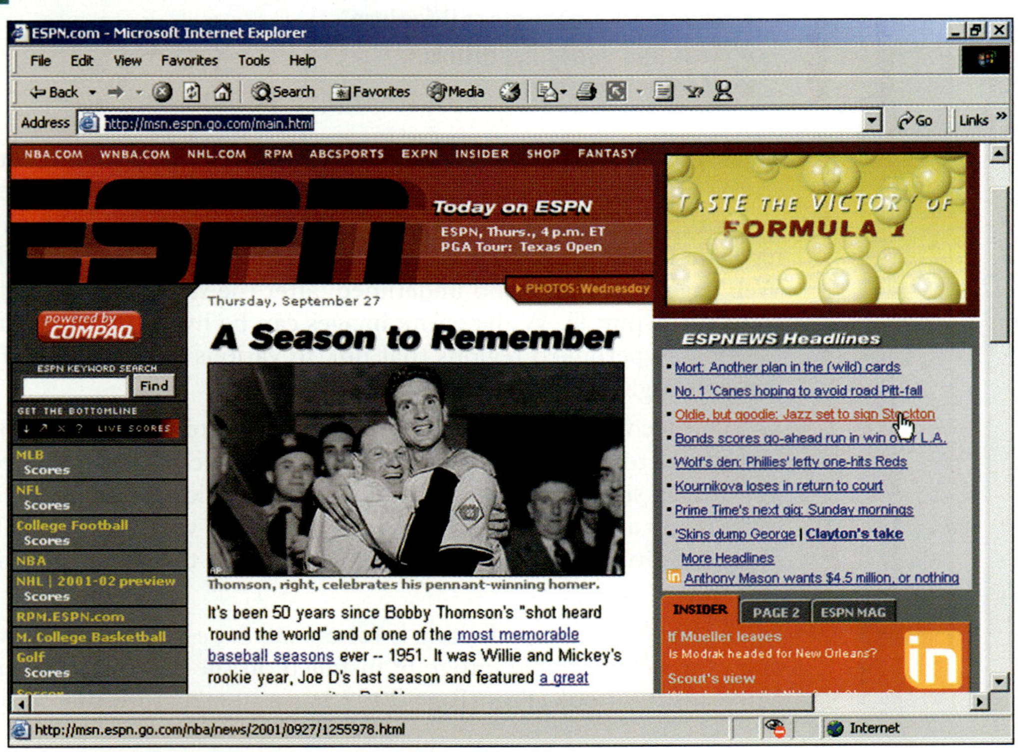

(Note: Before completing chapter exercises, delete the Chapter 3 *folder on your disk. Next, download the Chapter 4 data files from the Internet Resource Center to the* Chapter 4 *folder you have created on your disk, and then make* Chapter 4 *the active folder.)*

exercise 1

CREATING A TEXT NAVIGATION BAR

1. Open FrontPage from the *Programs* submenu.
2. Click the Open Web button on the Standard toolbar.
3. Open the EMCPWebs FrontPage Web.
4. Access the Folders view.
5. Open the EMCPWebs home page (index.htm) in Page view.
6. Place the insertion point after the line of text ending *contact the lead developers*.
7. Press the Enter key and click the Center button on the Formatting toolbar.
8. Enter the following navigation bar text formatted to Verdana 10 points. *(Note: The vertical character separating the text links, sometimes referred to as the "pipe," is located just above the Enter key and can be inserted by pressing Shift + the backslash key.)*

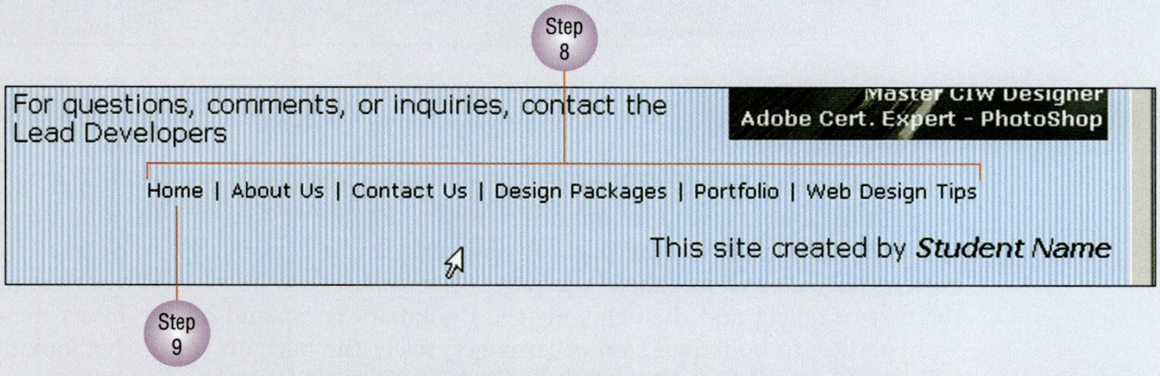

9. Double-click the word *Home* on the newly created navigation bar to select the entire word.
10. Click the Insert Hyperlink button on the Standard toolbar.
11. Click *index.htm (open)*.

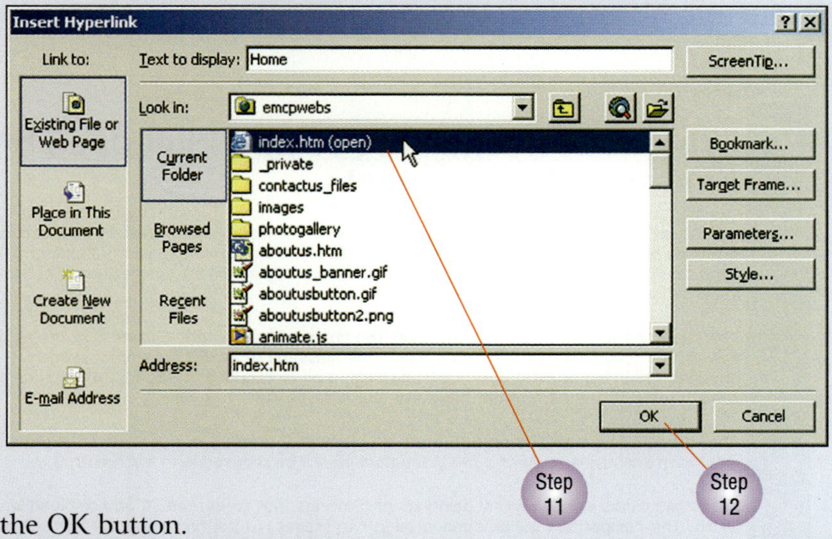

12. Click the OK button.
13. Repeat steps 9–12 for the About Us, Contact Us, Design Packages, Portfolio, and Web Design Tips navigation links.

14. Press the Ctrl + S keyboard shortcut to save the updated home page.
15. Perform a Preview in Browser and print the home page.
16. Test your text navigation bar hyperlinks.

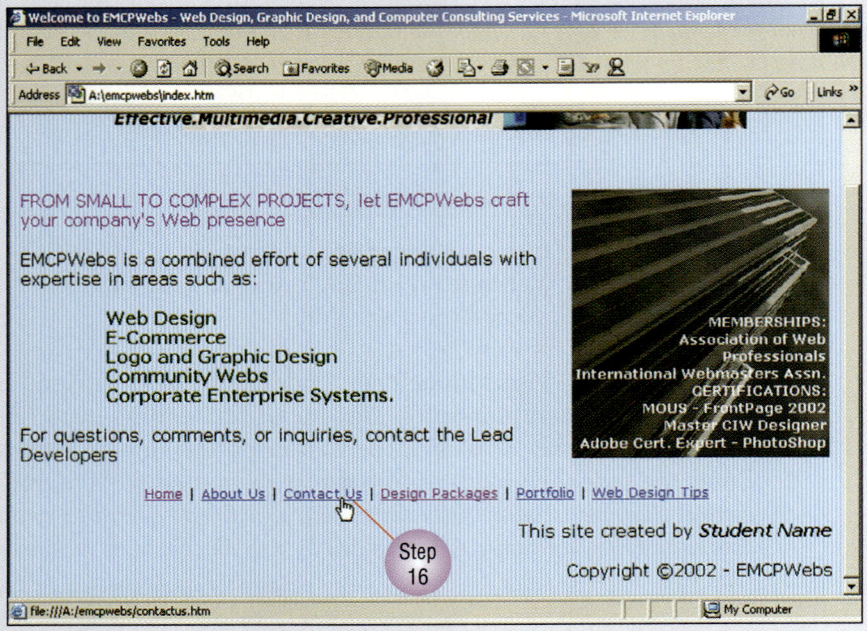

Creating Bookmark Hyperlinks

A bookmark is a specified location on a Web page that serves as a hyperlink destination. Bookmark links are often used in a table of contents to jump down to a specific location on the page. Bookmarks can be hyperlinked to or from the current page as well as other Web pages. Bookmarks can be created by selecting the text or object and then clicking the Bookmark command on the Insert menu. To hyperlink to bookmarks on other pages, select the page on which the bookmark is located in the Insert Hyperlink dialog box and then click the Bookmark button. Bookmarks are identified by a dotted line under the text (see figure 4.2).

FIGURE 4.2 *Text with Bookmark*

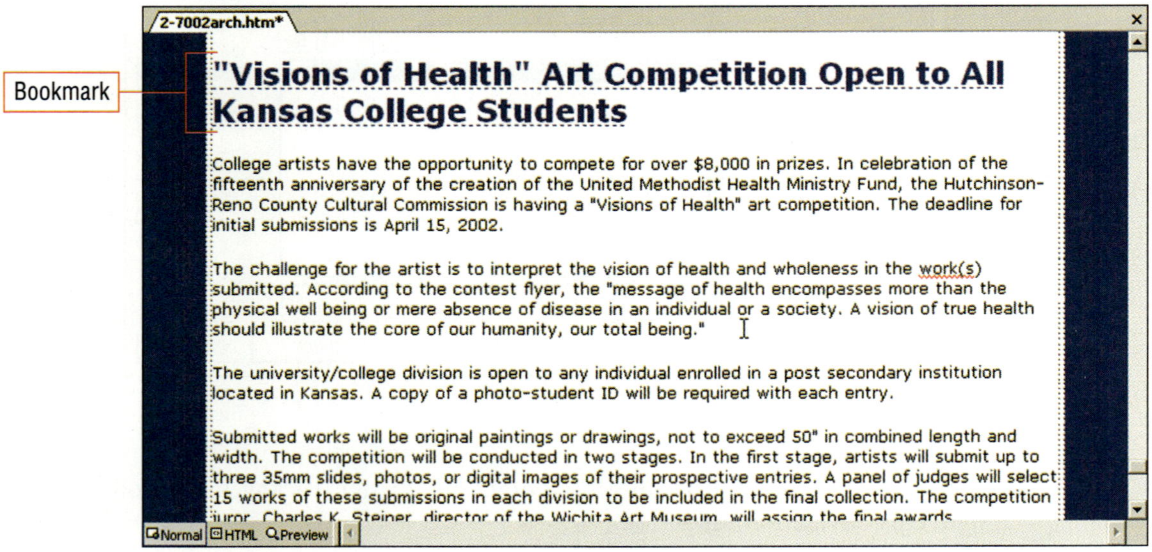

exercise 2

INSERTING BOOKMARKS

1. Open the EMCPWebs home page in Page view.
2. Hold down the Ctrl key and click the *About Us* hypertext link.
3. Place the insertion point one line below the banner image.
4. Click the Align Left button on the Formatting toolbar.
5. Format the font to Verdana 10 points.
6. Key the list as shown in the illustration.

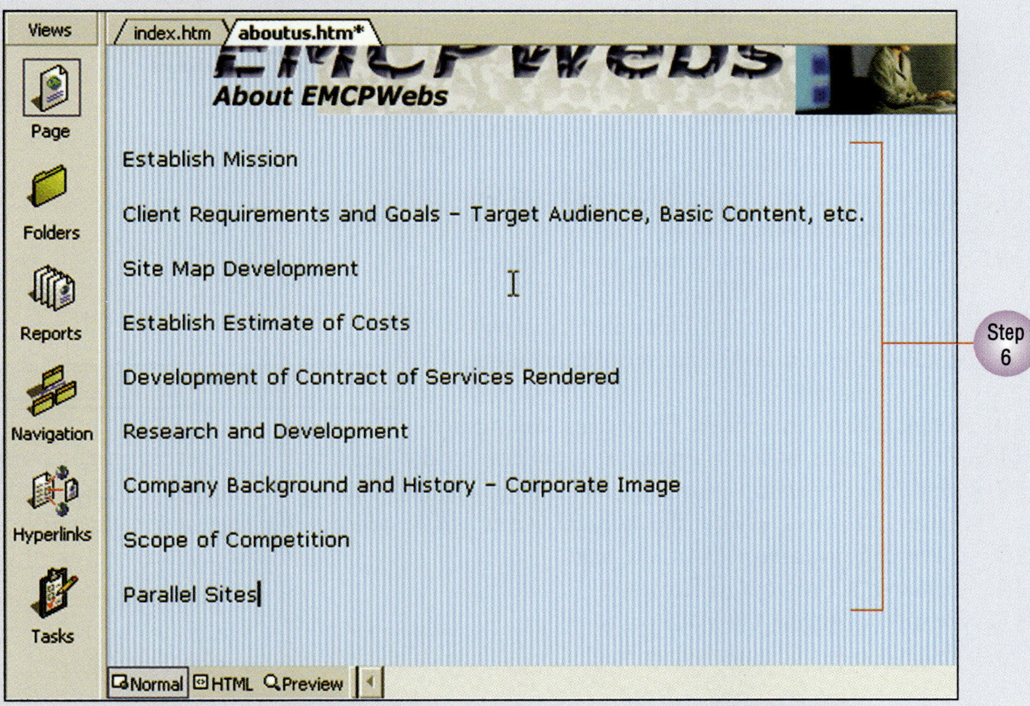

7. Select and format the line of text *Establish Mission* to 12 points, bold, and Navy.
8. With the text *Establish Mission* still selected, click Insert and then click Bookmark.
9. In the Bookmark dialog box, notice that *Establish Mission* appears in the Bookmark name text box. Click the OK button.
10. Repeat steps 7–9 to insert a bookmark for Research and Development.
11. Save the updated home page.

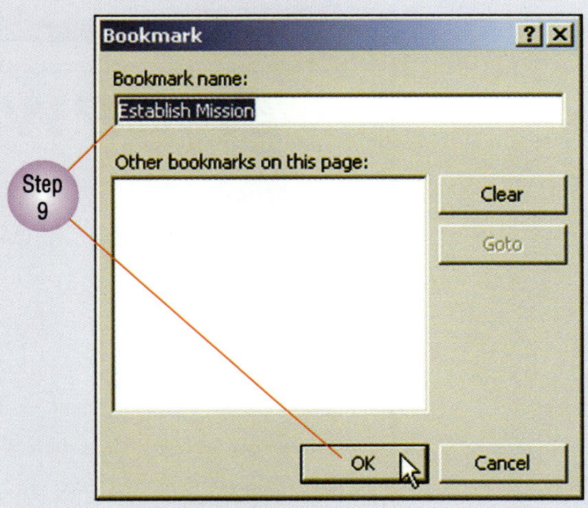

exercise 3

CREATING HYPERLINKS TO BOOKMARKS

1. Open the EMCPWebs About Us Web page in Page view.
2. Place the insertion point after the banner image and then press Enter.
3. Click the Align Left button on the Formatting toolbar.
4. Format the font to Verdana, 12 points, bold, and Navy.
5. Key the following list:

   Establish Mission
   Research and Development
   Preliminary Design
   Prototype
   Site Launch

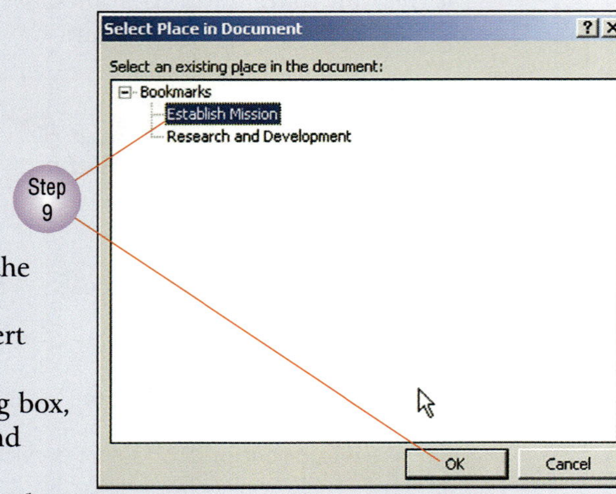

6. Select the text *Establish Mission*.
7. Click the Insert Hyperlink button on the Standard toolbar.
8. Click the Bookmark button in the Insert Hyperlink dialog box.
9. At the Select Place in Document dialog box, click the *Establish Mission* bookmark and then click OK.
10. Click OK in the Insert Hyperlink dialog box.
11. Repeat steps 6–10 to create a hyperlink to the Research and Development bookmark.
12. Place the insertion point below the text *Parallel Sites* at the bottom of the page and press Enter 10 times. *(Note: The remaining text will be added to the page in the upcoming chapters.)*
13. Save the updated About Us page.
14. Perform a Preview in Browser.
15. Print the About Us Web page.
16. Test your bookmark hyperlinks.

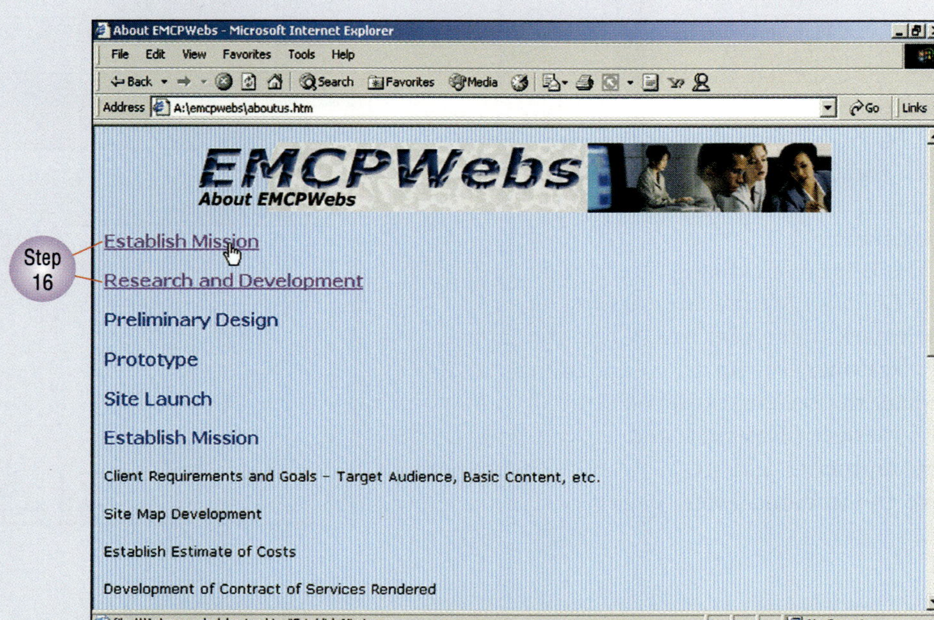

exercise 4

CREATING AN AUTOMATIC HYPERLINK

1. Open the EMCPWebs home page in Page view.
2. Press Ctrl + End on the keyboard.
3. Key your personal e-mail address and then press Enter.
4. Key your personal Web site address and then press Enter. *(Note: If you do not have a personal Web site, enter the URL of a favorite site.)*
5. Save the updated home page.
6. Perform a Preview in Browser.
7. Print the EMCPWebs home page.

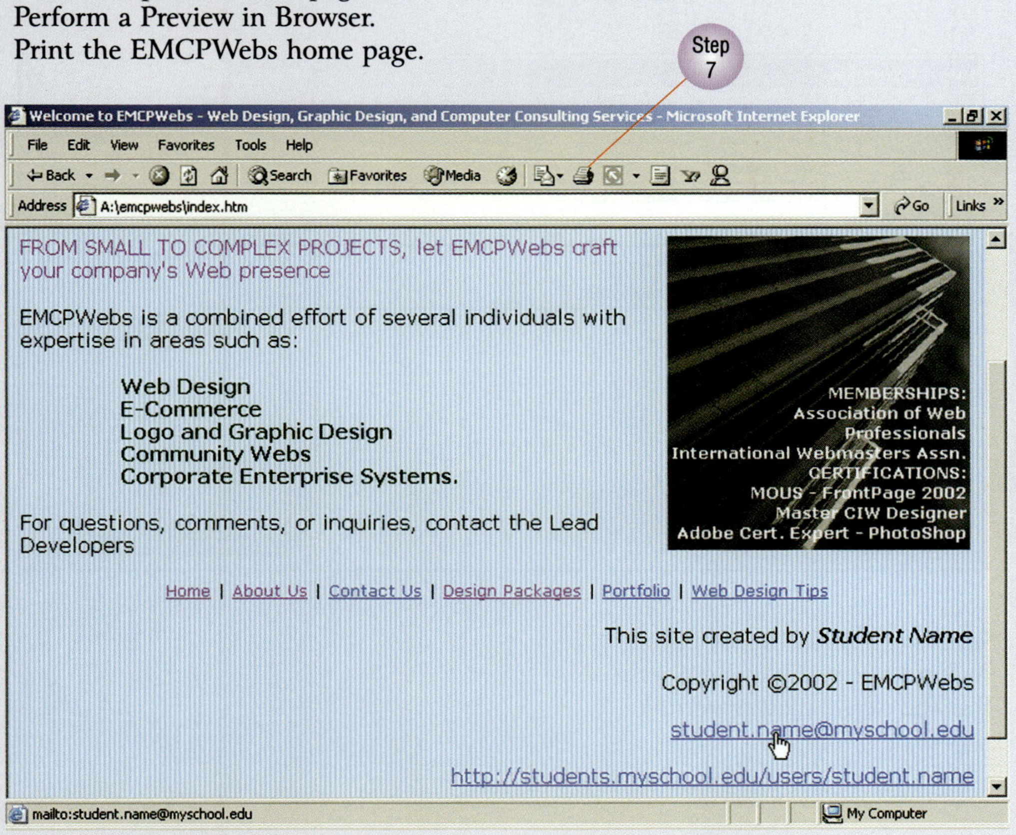

8. Test your hyperlinks.

Creating E-Mail Hyperlinks

While some developers set up an e-mail address to automatically create a hyperlink, most will display the person, position, or group name on the page and list the actual address in the Insert Hyperlink dialog box. FrontPage 2002 has a new feature that allows designers to add subject line text automatically for the visitor. This is especially handy for Webmasters who monitor multiple pages or sites of varying topics.

exercise 5

CREATING E-MAIL HYPERLINKS WITH A BUILT-IN SUBJECT

1. Open the EMCPWebs home page in Page view.
2. Double-click the word *Developers* in the contact line.
3. Click the Insert Hyperlink button on the Standard toolbar.
4. At the Insert Hyperlink dialog box, click E-mail Address in the Link to area.
5. In the E-mail address text box, key **developers@emcpwebs.com**.
6. In the Subject text box, key **EMCPWebs Site Inquiry** and then click OK.

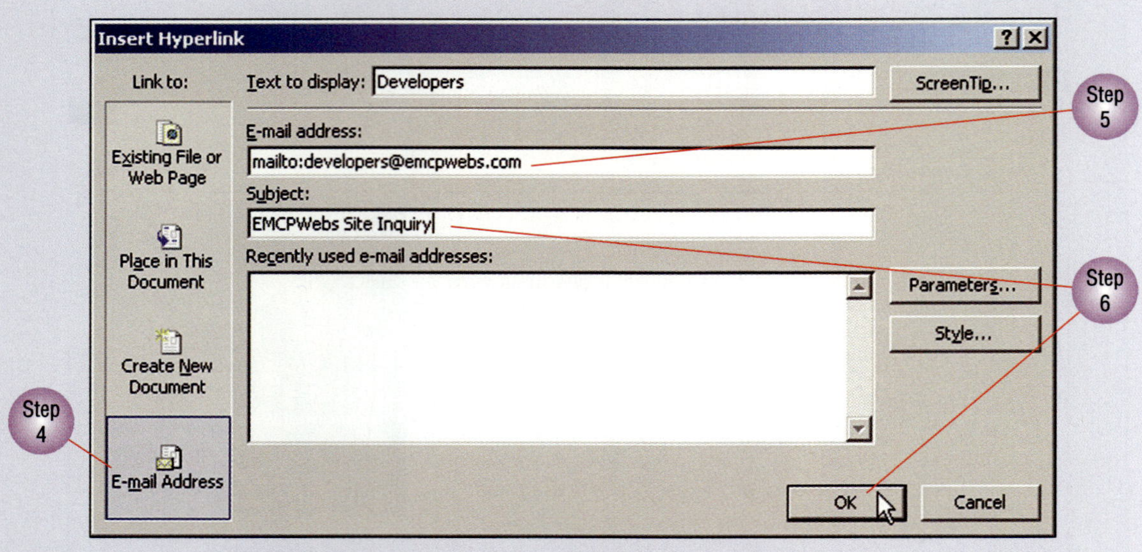

7. Save the updated home page.
8. Perform a Preview in Browser.
9. Test the new e-mail hyperlink.

Removing Hyperlinks

Hyperlinks may need to be changed occasionally as a result of updated domains or page file names. Rarely do you need to completely remove a hyperlink. Nevertheless, these occasions do arise from time to time. To remove a hyperlink, select the text or image that has a hyperlink on it and click the Insert Hyperlink button on the Standard toolbar. Next, click the Remove Link button in the Edit Hyperlink dialog box and then click OK.

exercise 6

REMOVING HYPERLINKS

1. Open the EMCPWebs home page (index.htm) in Page view.
2. Double-click the *Home* hypertext link below the Membership/Certification image.
3. Click the Insert Hyperlink button on the Standard toolbar.
4. In the Edit Hyperlink dialog box, click the Remove Link button.

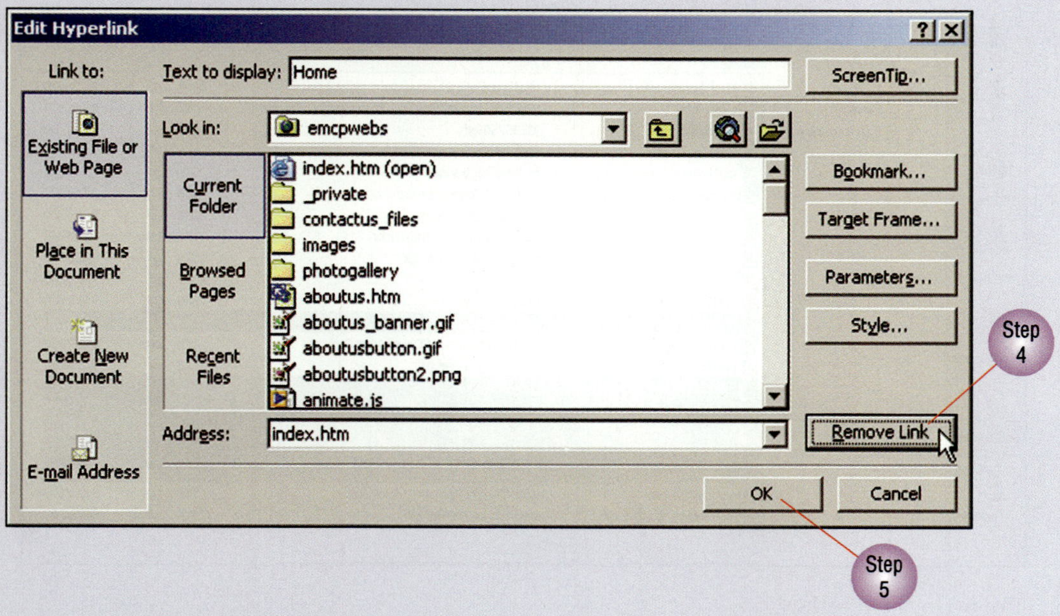

5. Click OK.
6. Save the updated home page.

Deleting FrontPage Web Pages and Files

As a result of experimenting with and creating new Web sites, your hard drive will quickly fill up with Web sites that you no longer need. The Folders view is the best location to delete files and folders from the current Web. There are several ways to delete folders and files. One way to delete items in Folders view is to right-click the item and select the Delete command. Another way is to select the icon and press the Delete key on the keyboard. A third way to delete an item is to select the Delete command on the Edit menu. To select multiple files in succession in the Folders view, select the first file, hold down the Shift key, and then select the last file. To select multiple files in nonadjacent locations in Folders view, hold down the Ctrl key while clicking each file you want selected.

exercise 7

DELETING FRONTPAGE WEB PAGES AND FILES

1. Open the EMCPWebs FrontPage Web.
2. Access the Folders view.
3. Select the Sample10.jpg file in the Contents pane of the Folders view.
4. Hold down the Shift key and click *Sample9.jpg*.
5. Hold down the Ctrl key and click *photo_gallery.htm*.

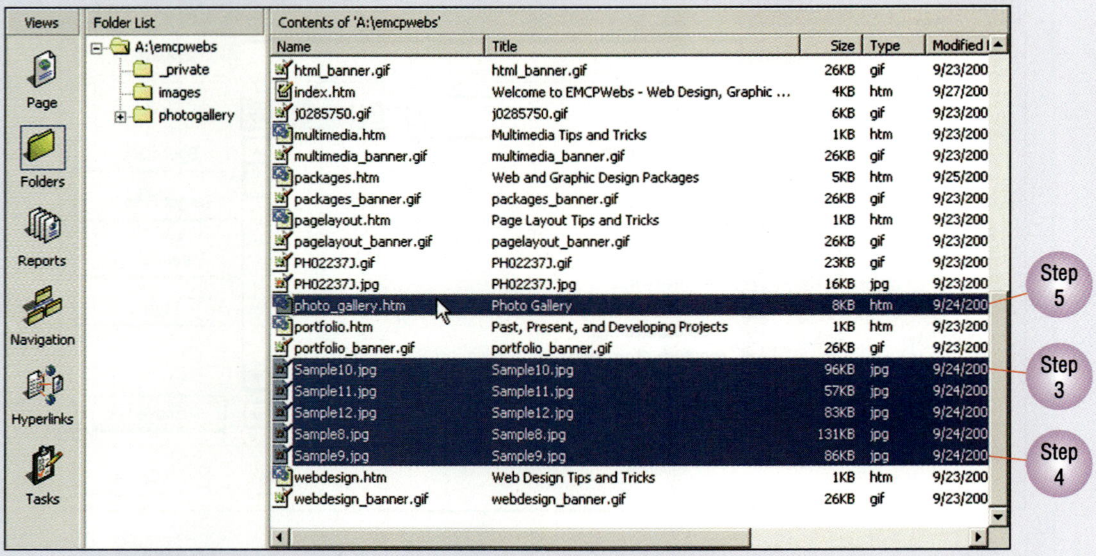

6. Press the Delete key.
7. Click the Yes to All button in the Confirm Delete dialog box.

Creating Image Hyperlinks

The most common types of image hyperlinks are navigation buttons and banner ads. To hyperlink an image, select the image and click the Insert Hyperlink button on the Standard toolbar. Depending on your page layout design and space limitations, you may insert multiple hyperlinks on a single image. These hyperlink regions are called hotspots. As broadband technology becomes more widely available, the use of graphics in Web pages will become even more prevalent. The ability to create hotspot links on images gives Web graphic designers the opportunity to make Web pages more attractive as well as more interactive.

An image that has multiple hyperlinks is often called an image map. Another common use of hyperlinks on images is to link smaller thumbnail images to larger and more detailed images. Thumbnails are common for displaying images on a Web page without causing long download times (see figure 4.3). The visitor can click the thumbnail and a larger image will open in a new window.

FIGURE

4.3 *Image Hyperlink Intensive Sony Home Page*

exercise 8

INSERTING A HYPERLINK ON AN IMAGE

1. Access in your browser the Web page http://www.microsoft.com/frontpage/logo.htm.

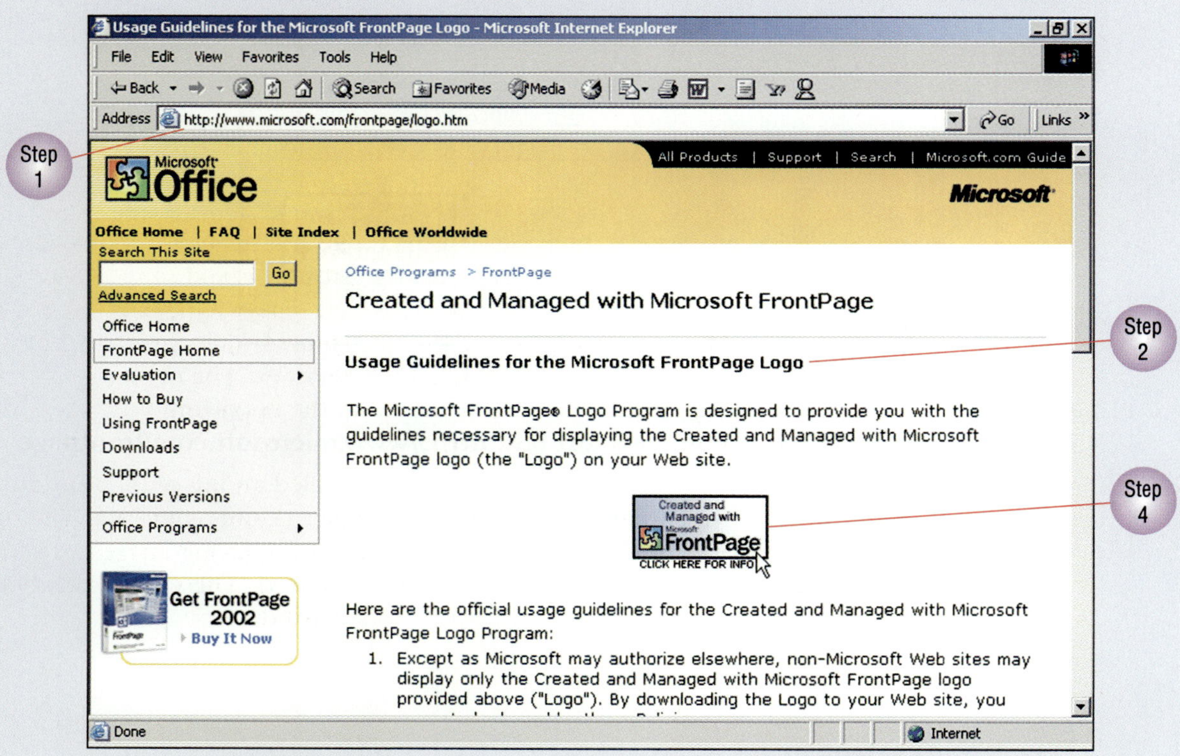

2. Read through the Usage Guidelines.
3. Return to the top of the Web page.
4. Right-click the Created and Managed with Microsoft FrontPage logo image.
5. Select the Save Picture As command.

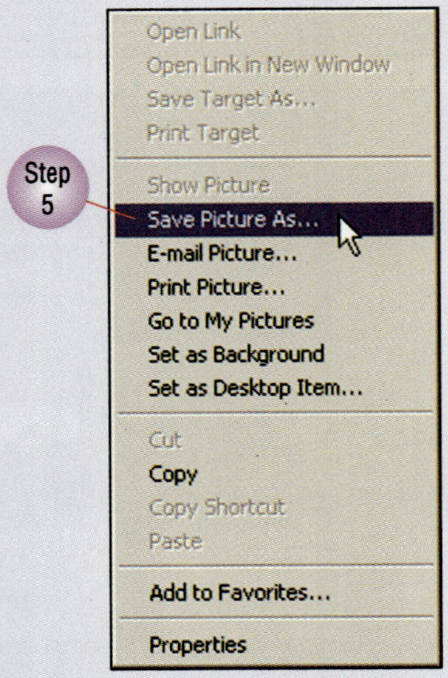

6. Save the image to your *Chapter 4* folder.
7. Return to FrontPage and the EMCPWebs home page in Page view.
8. Press Ctrl + End to place the insertion point at the bottom of the home page. Ensure that you are on the line just below the last line of text.
9. Click Insert Picture From File on the Standard toolbar and click *createdwFP.gif*.
10. Select the image you just inserted and click the Insert Hyperlink button on the Standard toolbar.

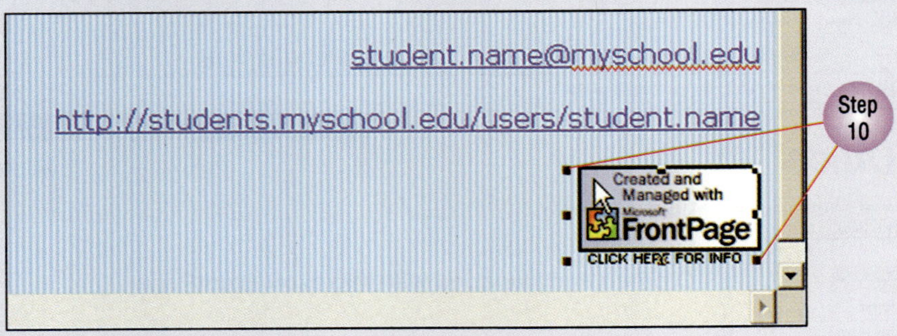

11. Click the *Existing File or Web Page* icon.
12. Key the following URL in the Address text box: **http://www.microsoft.com/frontpage**.
13. Save the updated home page.
14. Perform a Preview in Browser and test the hyperlink.
15. Print the updated home page.

exercise 9

CREATING AN IMAGE NAVIGATION BAR

1. Open the EMCPWebs home page in Page view.
2. From the View menu, remove the check mark in front of Views Bar.
3. Place the insertion point on a blank line under the home page banner.
4. Click the Insert Picture From File button on the Standard toolbar.
5. From your *EMCPWebs Images* folder, click the aboutusbutton.gif image.
6. Insert the following button images on the same line as the aboutusbutton.gif image: contactbutton, packagesbutton, portfoliobutton, and webtipsbutton.

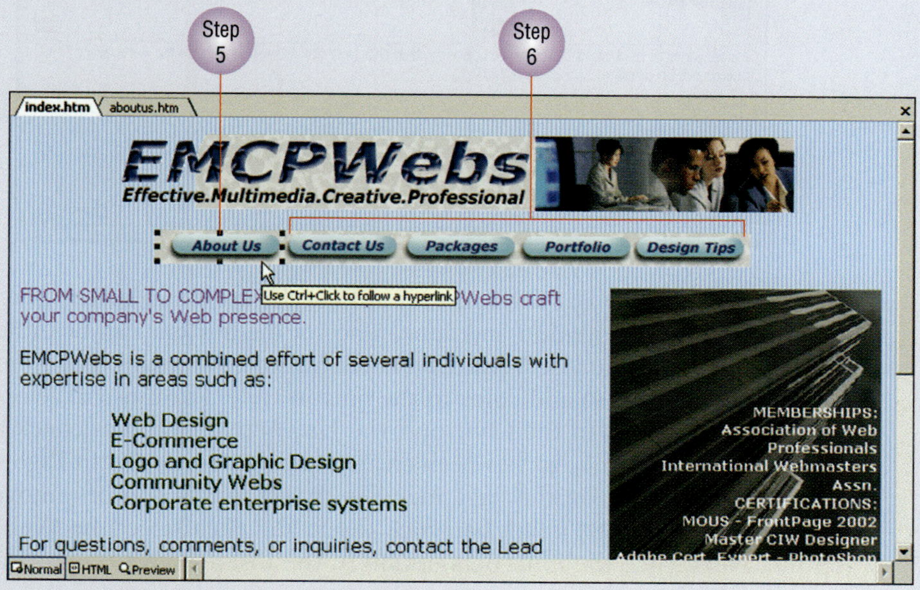

7. Click the About Us image button and then click the Set Transparent Color button on the Pictures toolbar.
8. Click on a white area of the image.
9. Repeat steps 7 and 8 to remove the white space from the remaining image buttons.
10. Select the About Us button and then click the Insert Hyperlink button on the Standard toolbar.
11. Select the aboutus.htm file in the Current Folder and then click OK.
12. Repeat steps 10 and 11 to create hyperlinks to the remaining images.
13. Save the updated home page.
14. Perform a Preview in Browser and test the hyperlinks.

Creating Link Bars

A FrontPage link bar is a preformatted set of hyperlinks used for navigating a Web site. A FrontPage link bar can be either a set of preformatted images or text. There are three types of link bars you can specify for your site (see figure 4.4). The first type of link bar is the *Bar with custom links*. With a custom link bar, developers have full control of the pages added to the bar, the graphic style of the buttons, and the horizontal or vertical position of the buttons. The second type of link bar, *Bar with back and next links,* uses your navigation structure to determine which page will be linked to when the Back or Next button is clicked. The third type, *Bar based on navigation structure,* uses the Navigation view structure of your Web site and the page titles of the pages to create the relative buttons.

FIGURE 4.4 **Link Bar Web Component Types**

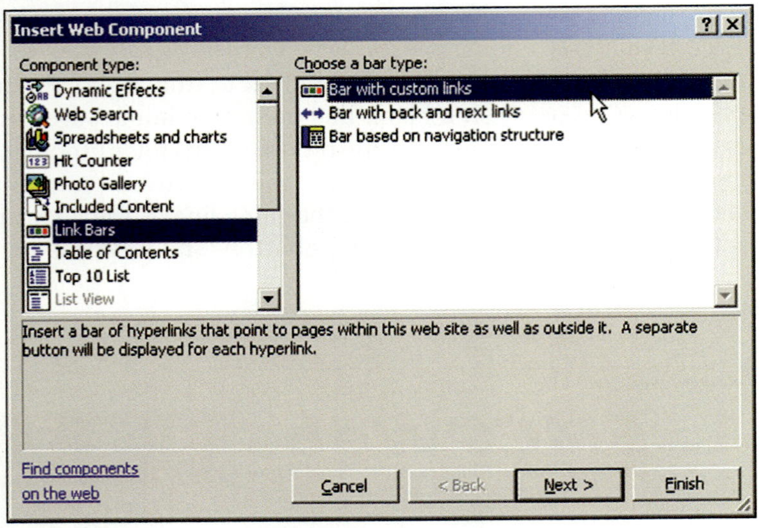

When using the Bar with custom links style, users can specify the button style they prefer. The orientation and appearance of the buttons can be either horizontal or vertical. Select the Use Vivid Colors check box in the Link Bar Properties dialog box (see figure 4.5) to add color to the button style. For those developers who like to add hover effects to their buttons, the Use Active Graphics check box can be selected. Once the link bar has been created and can be viewed in Page view, the link bar Web component in the page includes an *add link* to add or remove hyperlinks from the bar. To insert a link bar, click Insert and then select the Web Component option. Next, click the Link Bars option in the Insert Web Component dialog box, and proceed from there.

FIGURE 4.5 **Link Bar Properties Dialog Box**

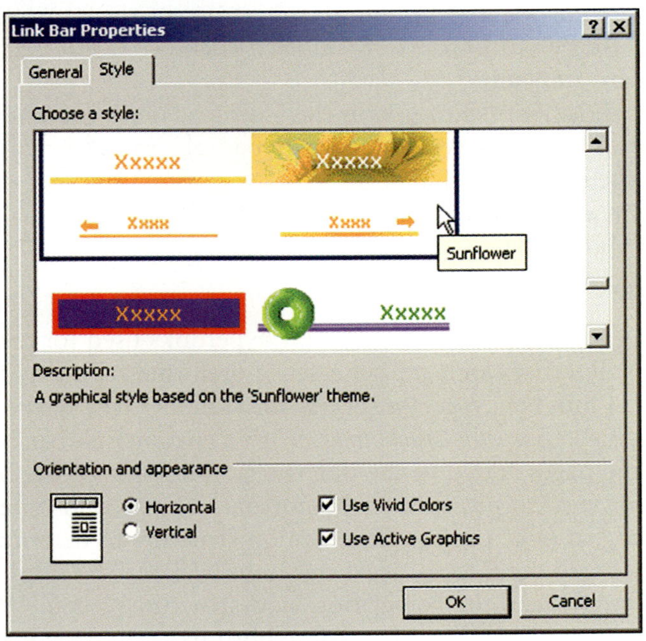

exercise 10

CREATING A FRONTPAGE LINK BAR

1. Open the EMCPWebs home page in Page view.
2. Click in the left margin beside the image navigation bar below the banner image.
3. Click Insert and select *Web Component*.
4. At the Insert Web Component dialog box, select *Link Bars* in the Component type drop-down list box.
5. Ensure that the *Bar with custom links* type is selected and then click the Next button.
6. Select the Pixel bar style.
7. Click the Next button.
8. Select the horizontal orientation.
9. Click the Finish button.
10. At the Create New Link Bar dialog box, key **EMCPWebs Link Bar** in the Name text box and then click OK.
11. At the Link Bar properties dialog box with the General tab selected, select *EMCPWebs Link Bar* in the Choose existing text box.
12. Add the following Web page links using the Add Link button: *aboutus.htm, contactus.htm, packages.htm, portfolio.htm,* and *webdesign.htm.*
13. Insert a check mark in the Home page check box under Additional links.
14. Click the OK button to return to Page view.
15. Save the updated home page.
16. Perform a Preview in Browser and test the hyperlinks.
17. Print the home page in your browser.

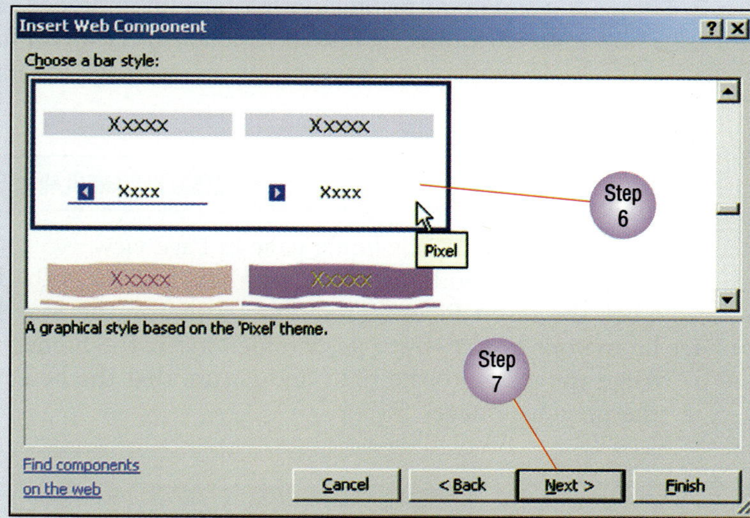

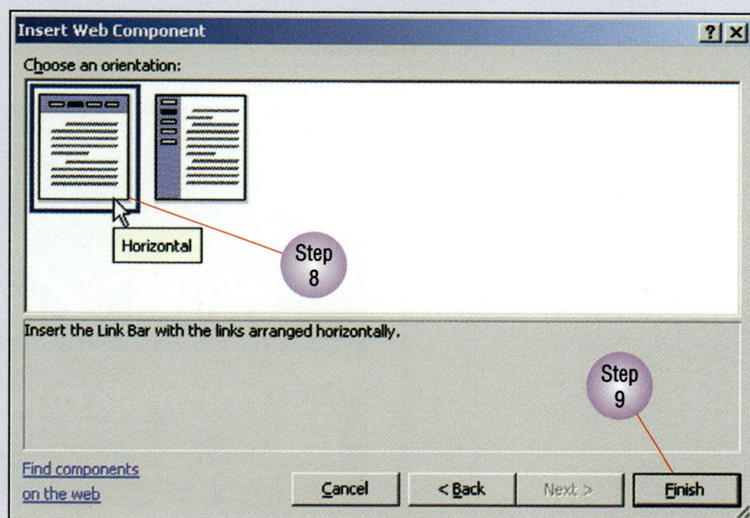

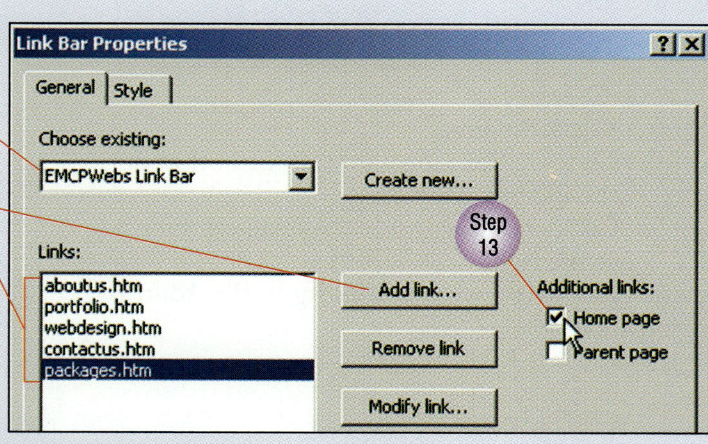

Creating Hotspot Hyperlinks on Images

The Pictures toolbar includes three options for inserting hotspot hyperlinks onto an image. The Rectangular Hotspot allows developers to insert hotspots that match a square or rectangular pattern on an image. The Circular Hotspot allows visitors to click directly onto a circular object on an image. The Polygonal Hotspot allows developers to trace objects on an image to create precise hyperlinks.

exercise 11 — CREATING RECTANGULAR AND CIRCULAR HOTSPOT HYPERLINKS ON AN IMAGE

1. Open the EMCPWebs home page in Page view.
2. Select the city building image with text and press the Delete key.
3. Click the Insert Picture From File button on the Standard toolbar.
4. From your *EMCPWebs Images* folder, insert the homecredentials.gif image.
5. Align the image to the right and ensure that the new image is in the same location as the previous image.

6. Select the image.
7. Click the Rectangular Hotspot button on the Pictures toolbar.
8. Click and drag inside the image as shown at the right.
9. Key **http://www.a-w-p.org** in the Address text box.
10. Click the OK button.

11. Repeat steps 7–10 to apply hotspot hyperlinks to the sites below:

Web Site Name	*URL*
International Webmasters Assn.	**http://www.iwanet.org**
MOUS – FrontPage 2002	**http://www.mous.net**
Master CIW Designer	**http://www.ciwcertified.com/**
Adobe Cert. Expert – PhotoShop	**http://partners.adobe.com/asn/training/aceprogram.html**

12. With the image still selected, click the Circular Hotspot button on the Pictures toolbar.
13. Click in the center of the EMC/Paradigm logo and drag outward until the entire logo is outlined by the circular hotspot.
14. Key **http://www.mous.net** in the Address text box:
15. Save the updated home page.
16. Perform a Preview in Browser.
17. Test each of the hotspot hyperlinks.

Step 13

Not all image regions to which you want to apply hotspot hyperlinks are rectangular or round. The Polygonal Hotspot button allows you to click and drag around an image item to create precise hotspot links.

exercise 12

CREATING POLYGONAL HOTSPOT HYPERLINKS ON AN IMAGE

1. Open the EMCPWebs home page in Page view.
2. Select the home page banner image.
3. Click the Polygonal Hotspot button on the Pictures toolbar.
4. Click on any corner of the *W* on the banner image, drag to the next corner, and release the mouse button.
5. Continue to drag and release the mouse until you have completely outlined the *W*.
6. Key a URL of your choice in the Address text box.
7. Save the updated home page.
8. Perform a Preview in Browser and test your new hyperlink.

Step 5

Step 4

Hyperlinking to a New Document

Although it is best to create Web pages and title the pages in Folders view, there are times when creating new page documents from a hyperlink is the most efficient method of building site content. Click the Insert Hyperlink button on the Standard toolbar, then click Create New Document in the Insert Hyperlink dialog box. Key the document name in the Name of new document text box. You can check whether to edit the new Web page document now or later depending on the option selected in the When to edit section.

exercise 13

HYPERLINKING TO A NEW DOCUMENT

1. Open the Contact EMCPWebs (contactus.htm) Web page in Page view.
2. Select the *Drew Shipley, Owner & CEO* text box.
3. Click the Insert Hyperlink button.
4. Click the Create New Document button in the Insert Hyperlink dialog box.
5. Key **drew_shipley** in the Name of new document text box.
6. Ensure that the Edit the new document now option is selected, and then click OK.

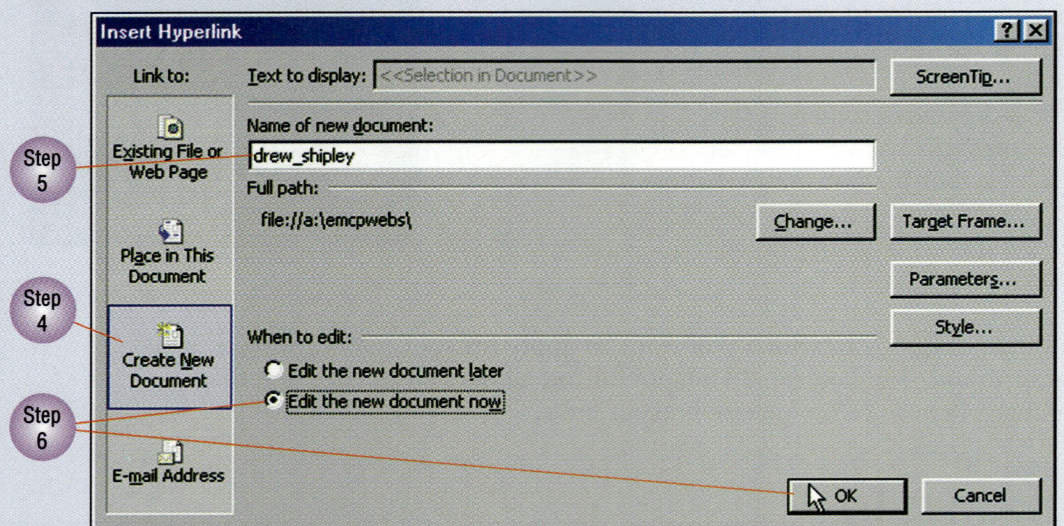

7. Click the Center button on the Formatting toolbar.
8. Insert the shipleybanner.gif image into the Web page.
9. Format the background to match the EMCPWebs home page.
10. Set the white space on the banner image to transparent by clicking the Set Transparent Color button on the Pictures toolbar and then clicking a white spot on the banner image.

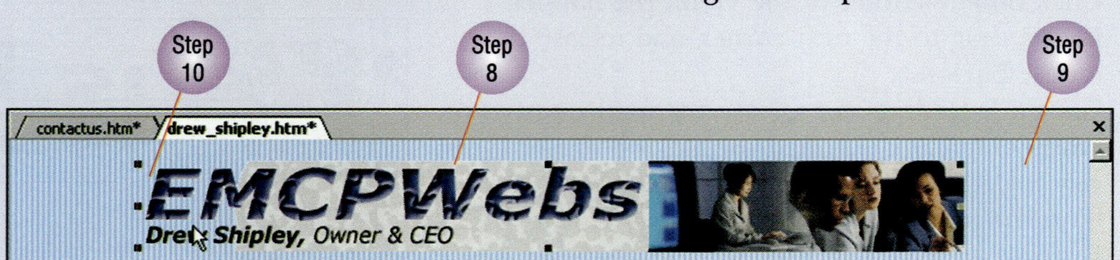

11. Save the updated drew_shipley.htm Web page.
12. Repeat steps 2 through 11 to create hyperlinks to the following documents:

Partner	*File Name*	*Banner Image*
Peter Downey, Programmer	peter_downey	downeybanner.gif
Rob Caballero, Graphic Designer	rob_caballero	caballerobanner.gif
Bernard Brown, Layout Design	bernard_brown	brownbanner.gif
Support Staff	support_staff	staffbanner.gif

13. Click File and then click Save All.

Customizing, Navigating, and Verifying Hyperlinks

Hyperlinks, by default, open in the same browser window. Sometimes, however, it is a good idea to format a hyperlink to open in a new browser window. This will allow visitors to browse the Web page content and close the window without affecting the parent page. The AutoThumbnail feature falls somewhere in between a graphic and a hyperlink feature. The AutoThumbnail button on the Pictures toolbar reduces an inserted picture to a smaller image. This smaller image can then be clicked in a browser window to open the larger original in a new window.

Before a FrontPage Web is published to the World Wide Web, the hyperlinks should be tested and verified. Even if the current hyperlinks are verified, Web sites can change domain names and pages may change file names. It is a good idea to verify the hyperlinks of a Web at least once a month.

Setting Hyperlinks to Open in a New Window

The ability to set hyperlinks to open in a new window (see figure 4.6) offers Web developers the flexibility to keep the current Web page open and visible. Typical Web pages that developers would have open in a new window include pages to external Web sites and internal pages that do not fit inside the normal flow of the site. Examples may include special events, news and information, or even advertisements for goods and services.

FIGURE 4.6 ***Sample Web Page Opening in a New Window***

SETTING HYPERLINKS TO OPEN IN A NEW WINDOW

1. Open the EMCPWebs home page (index.htm) in Page view.
2. Scroll down the page until the homecredentials.gif image is visible.
3. Double-click the circular hotspot on the EMC/Paradigm logo.
4. Click the Target Frame button in the Edit Hyperlink dialog box.

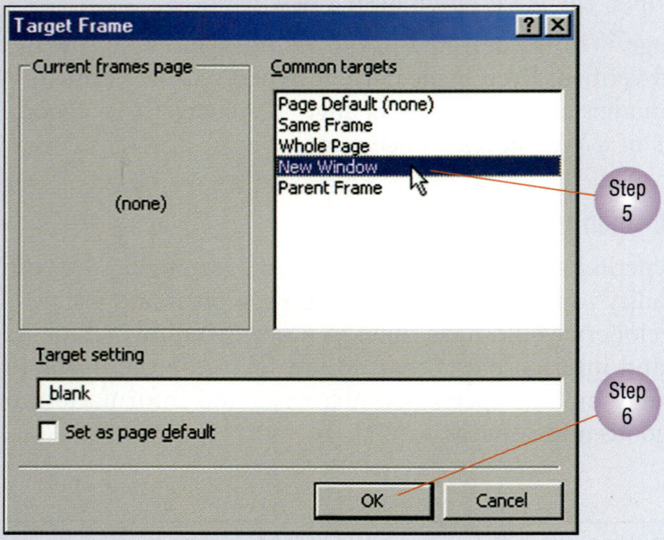

5. Select New Window in the Common targets section of the Target Frame dialog box.
6. Click the OK button in each dialog box to return to Page view.
7. Repeat steps 2-6 to set the hotspot hyperlinks to open in a new window.
8. Save the updated home page.
9. Perform a Preview in Browser and test your hyperlinks.

Using the AutoThumbnail Feature

Thumbnails can be defined as miniature displays of images or pages that are opened in full view on a different Web page. Thumbnail images allow you to view many images on the screen without taking up valuable screen space and download time. Once an image is inserted into Page view, click the Auto Thumbnail button on the Pictures toolbar. FrontPage will create a second smaller image file that will be saved into the root Web folder. Thumbnail image settings can be altered by clicking Tools, selecting Page Options, and then clicking the AutoThumbnail tab (see figure 4.7).

FIGURE

4.7 AutoThumbnail Tab in Page Options

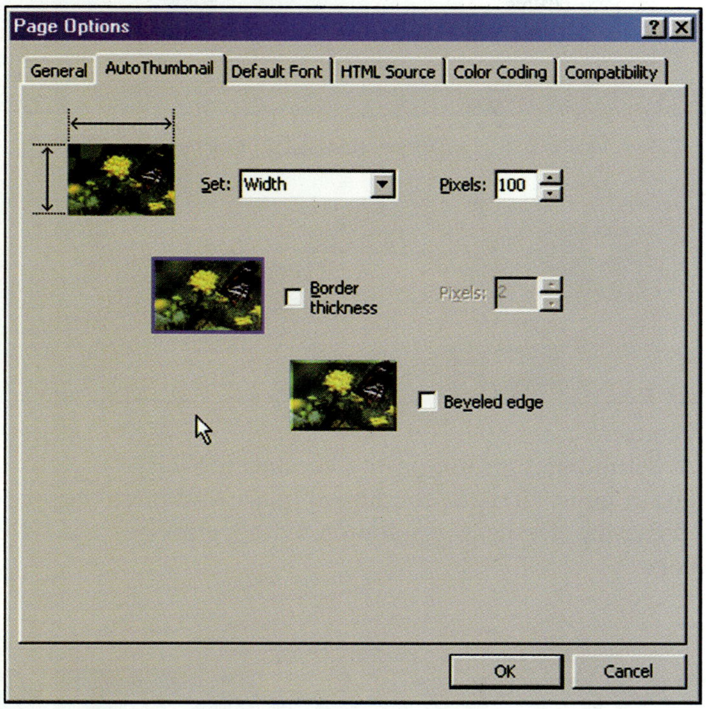

exercise 15

USIJNG THE AUTOTHUMBNAIL FEATURE

1. Open the Past, Present, and Developing Projects (portfolio.htm) file in Page view.
2. Place the insertion point one line below the banner image.
3. Click the Center button on the Formatting toolbar.
4. Click the Insert Picture From File button on the Standard toolbar.
5. Select the Design1.jpg image in the *emcpwebs root Web* folder.
6. Click the Insert button.

7. Select the inserted image.
8. Click Tools, select Page Options, and then click the AutoThumbnail tab.
9. Set Width to 150 Pixels.

Step 9

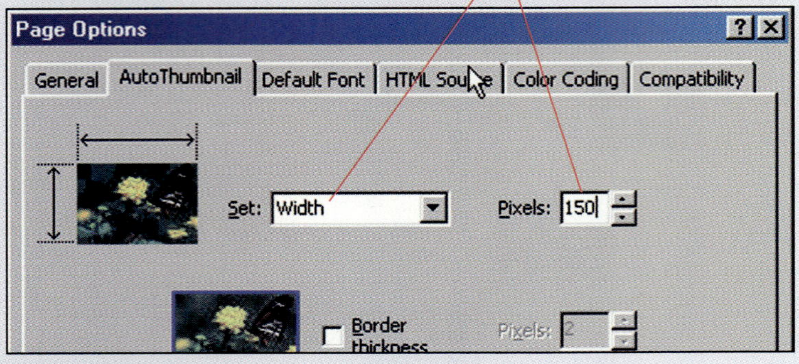

10. Click the OK button.
11. Click the Auto Thumbnail button on the Pictures toolbar.
12. Place the insertion point after the thumbnail image and press the spacebar three times.
13. Insert the Design2.jpg, Design3.jpg, and Design4.jpg images and set each one as a thumbnail image.

Step 13

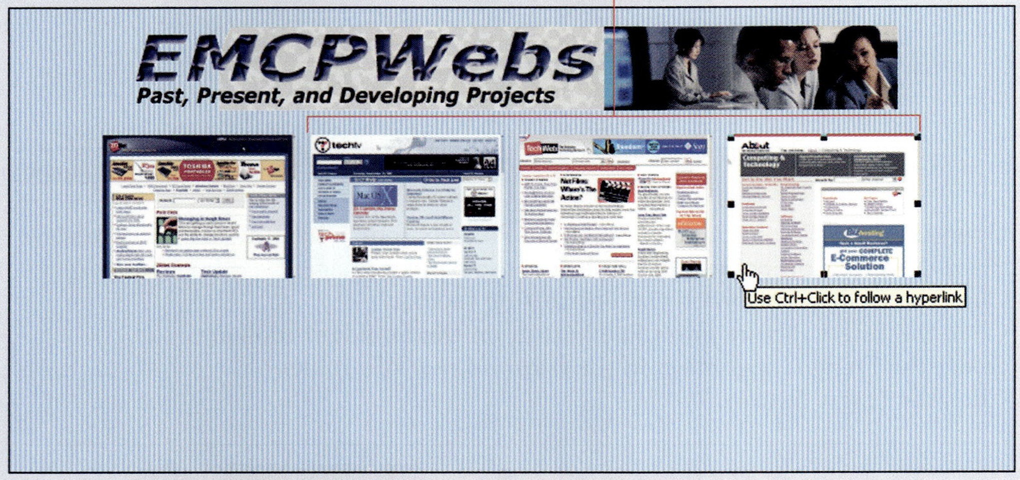

14. Save the updated portfolio page.
15. Perform a Preview in Browser and test your thumbnail hyperlinks.
16. Print the Web page in your browser.

Testing Hyperlinks in Page View

Hyperlinks can be tested not only in *Preview* mode or a browser, but also within Page view. By hovering over text or image hyperlinks and pressing the Ctrl key, developers can navigate from page to page. If there is a hyperlink that is incorrect or no longer exists, an alert dialog box will pop up with a Server error message. Developers can also right-click a text or image hyperlink and select the Follow Hyperlink command.

exercise 16

TESTING HYPERLINKS IN PAGE VIEW

1. Open the EMCPWebs home page (index.htm) in Page view.
2. Hold down the Ctrl key and click the *Master CIW Designer* hotspot hyperlink.
3. View the CIWCertified home page as it would have been designed in an HTML editor.

Step 4

4. Close the CIWCertified Web page.
5. Select the Save All command on the File menu.
6. Close each of the open Web pages in Page view.

exercise 17

UPDATING PAGE TITLES AND NAVIGATION VIEW

1. Open the EMCPWebs FrontPage Web and click the Folders view.
2. Right-click the drew_shipley.htm file and select the Rename command.
3. Press the Tab key.
4. Key **Drew Shipley, Owner & CEO** as the page title.
5. Repeat steps 2 through 4 for Peter Downey, Programmer; Rob Caballero, Graphic Designer; Bernard Brown, Layout Design; and EMCPWebs Support Staff.

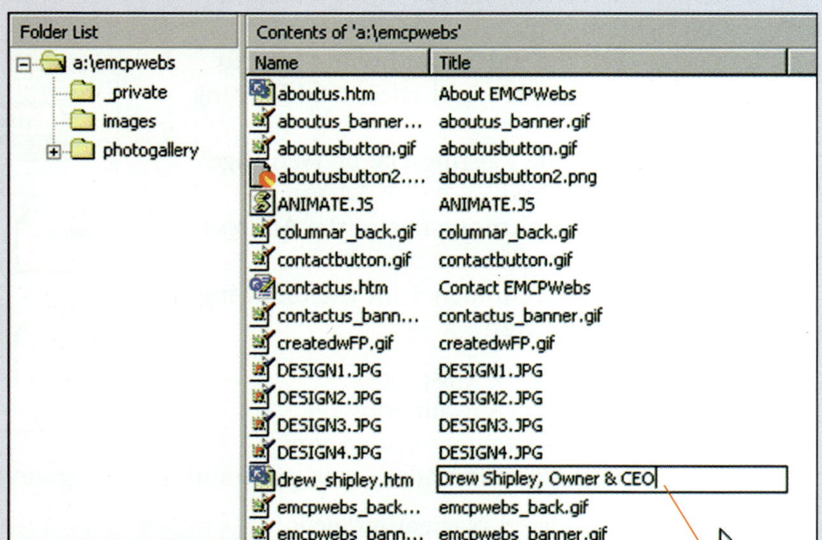

Step 4

6. Click the Navigation button.
7. Click the drew_shipley.htm file in the Folder List and drag it under the Contact EMCPWebs box in Navigation view.

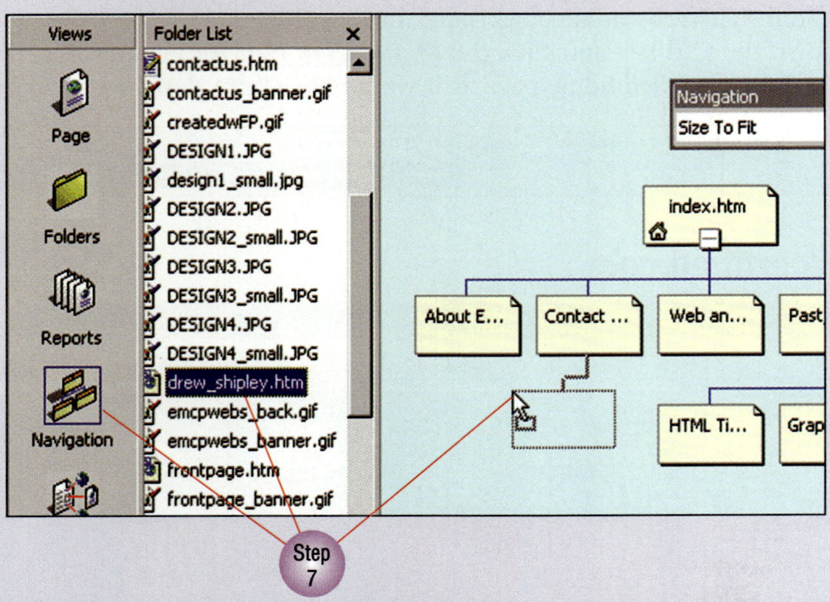

8. Drag the following files under the Contact EMCPWebs box in Navigation view: peter_downey.htm, rob_caballero.htm, bernard_brown.htm, and support_staff.htm.

exercise 18

CREATING EXTERNAL HYPERLINK ASSOCIATIONS IN NAVIGATION VIEW

1. Open the EMCPWebs FrontPage Web in Navigation view.
2. Right-click the index.htm home page box in Navigation view and select Add Existing Page.
3. Ensure that the Existing File or Web Page button is selected.
4. Key **http://www.mous.net** in the Address text box.
5. Repeat steps 2 through 4 for the following external Web sites:

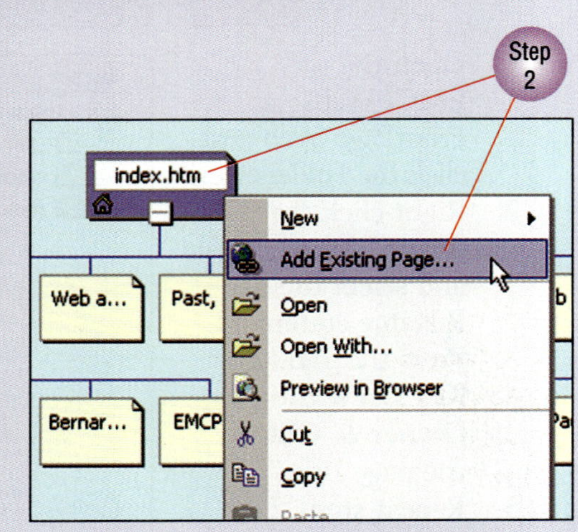

- http://www.a-w-p.org
- http://www.iwanet.org
- http://www.ciwcertified.com
- http://partners.adobe.com/asn/training/aceprogram.html

6. Print the updated Navigation view.

Verifying Hyperlinks

As Web sites become more complex over time, the potential for hyperlinks to be *broken* increases. The occurrences in which hyperlinks may become broken include Web pages that are deleted, renamed, or moved to another location. If you are managing your Web in FrontPage, pages that are moved or renamed will prompt the author to update the hyperlink associations so that they will not be broken. When Web pages are deleted from a FrontPage Web, however, it is imperative to remove dead links from your pages. The Broken hyperlinks feature in the Reports view gives those who manage FrontPage Webs a helpful tool for fixing dead links. Hyperlinks can be verified in the Broken hyperlinks summary in the Reports view.

exercise 19 — VERIFYING HYPERLINKS

1. With the EMCPWebs home page open, click the homecredentials.jpg image.
2. Double-click the EMC/Paradigm logo hotspot hyperlink.
3. Change the Web address to http://www.mous.nett.
4. Click the OK button.
5. Double-click the *About Us* hypertext link.
6. Click the Insert Hyperlink button on the Standard toolbar.
7. Change the Web address to about.htm.
8. Click the OK button.
9. Click the Reports view button.
10. Click the *Unverified hyperlinks* icon in the Site Summary.

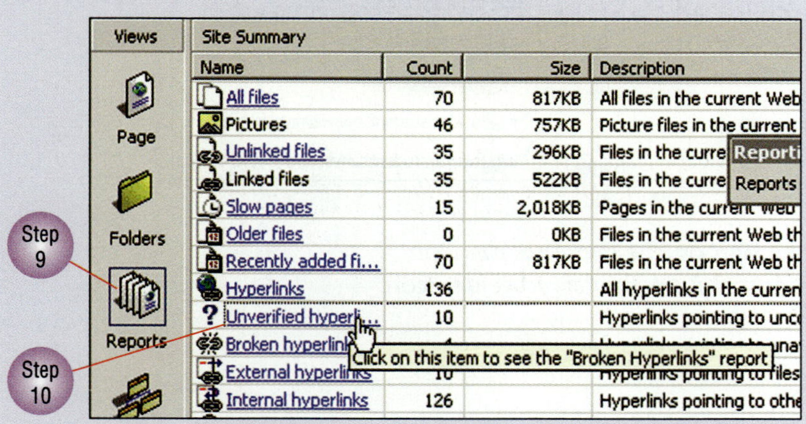

11. Click the Yes button to verify the hyperlinks.
12. Right-click the *http://www.mous.nett* broken hyperlink.
13. Select the Edit Hyperlink command.
14. Delete the extra *t* in *.nett* and click the Replace button.
15. Repeat steps 12 and 13 and replace about.htm with aboutus.htm.

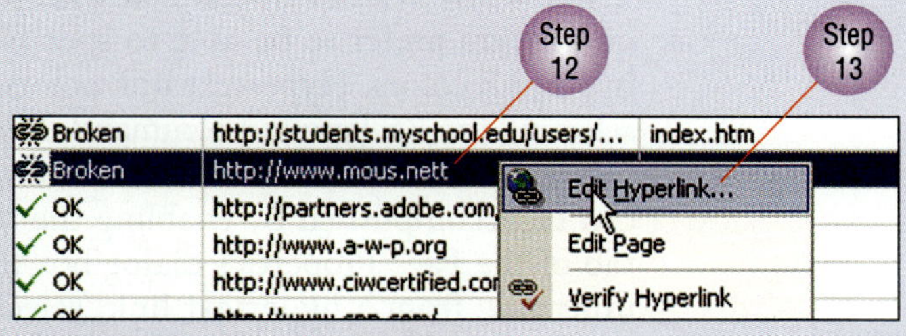

Observing the Hyperlinks View

The Hyperlinks view allows developers to view exactly how internal and external pages, graphical images, and application documents are hyperlinked within the current Web. Any broken hyperlinks that need to be fixed or deleted can be easily seen as well. The default starting point for Hyperlinks view is the home page. The Hyperlinks view is similar to the Navigation view; however, the Hyperlinks view shows all links on a given page and does not discern among levels, or hierarchy, as does the Navigation view. Any Web page that has hyperlinks or is associated with another page (e.g., *Get background information from another page*) will have a plus sign (+) on the icon. The plus sign can be clicked to expand the view of that page to view hyperlink associations, when it will change to a minus sign (-). To collapse a page, click the minus sign.

exercise 20 — OBSERVING THE HYPERLINKS VIEW

1. With the EMCPWebs FrontPage Web open, click the Hyperlinks view button.
2. Notice that the hyperlink for the student personal home page appears broken. This is because the Web page does not exist.

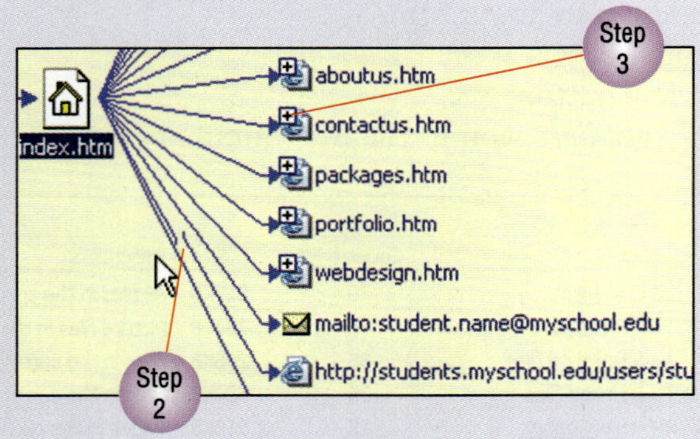

3. Click the plus sign on the *contactus.htm* icon.
4. Click the minus sign on the *contactus.htm* icon.

Modifying Hypertext Links

While many visitors are familiar with the standard blue and purple hypertext links, developers prefer to be able to specify hyperlink, visited hyperlink, and active hyperlink colors. Hypertext link colors can be changed by clicking Format and selecting the Background command. In addition to changing colors, many developers like to remove the underline style from hypertext links as they are hovered. This can be accomplished by enabling the hyperlink rollover effects in the Background tab of the Page Properties dialog box (see figure 4.8). To completely remove the underline from a hypertext link, select the text and right-click, select the Font command, and then remove the check mark next to Underline in the Effects section of the Font dialog box.

FIGURE 4.8 ***Altered Hyperlink Colors and the Rollover Style Button***

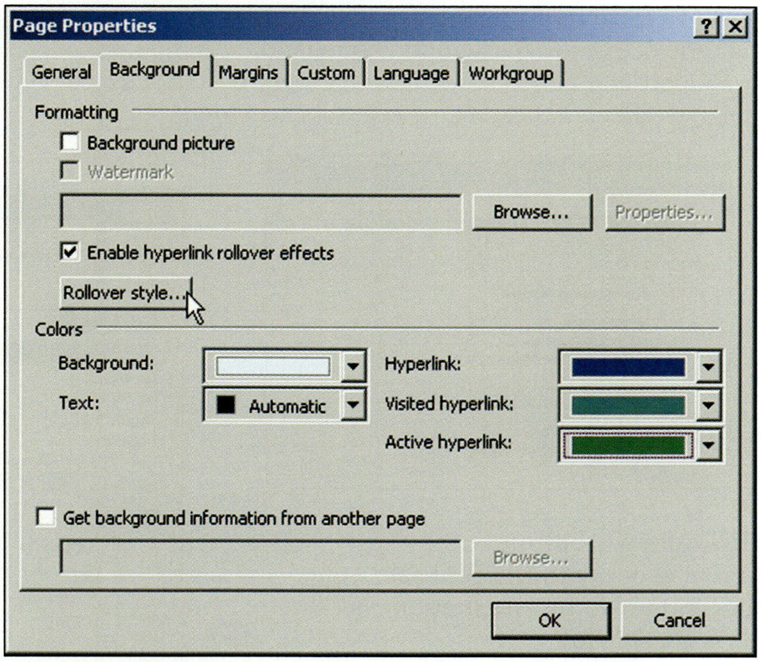

exercise 21 CHANGING HYPERLINK TEXT COLOR

1. Open the EMCPWebs home page (index.htm) from the Folder List.
2. Hide the Views bar by right-clicking the Views bar and selecting Hide Views Bar.
3. Click Format and select the Background command.
4. In the Page Properties dialog box with the Background tab selected, change the Hyperlink color to Green, Visited hyperlink color to Red, and the Active hyperlink color to Yellow.

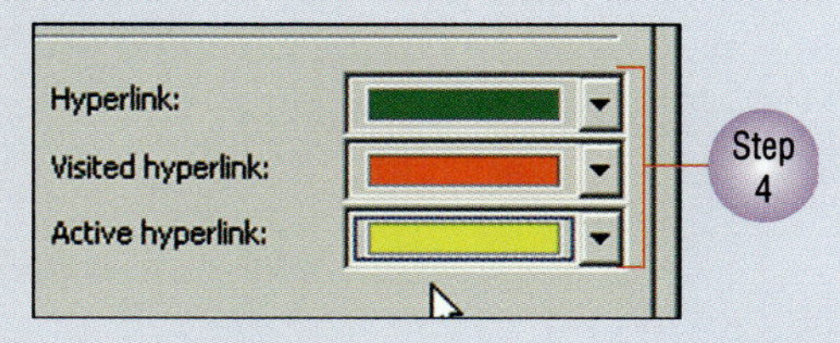

5. Save the updated home page.
6. Perform a Preview in Browser to test the hypertext links.

exercise 22

ENABLING ROLLOVER EFFECTS TO REMOVE THE UNDERLINE

1. Open the EMCPWebs home page (index.htm) in Page view.
2. Click Format and select the Background command.
3. At the Page Properties dialog box with the background tab selected, click in the Enable hyperlink rollover effects check box to insert a check mark.

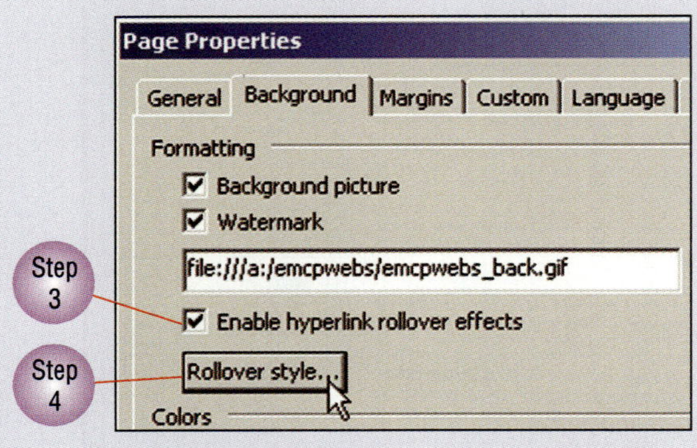

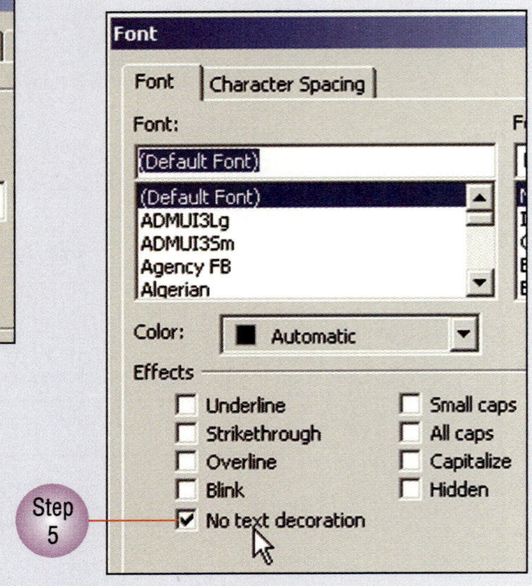

4. Click the Rollover style button.
5. At the Font dialog box with the Font tab selected, click in the No text decoration check box to insert a check mark.
6. Click the OK button in each dialog box to return to Page view.
7. Click the Preview tab at the bottom of the Page view window.
8. Test the hyperlink effects.

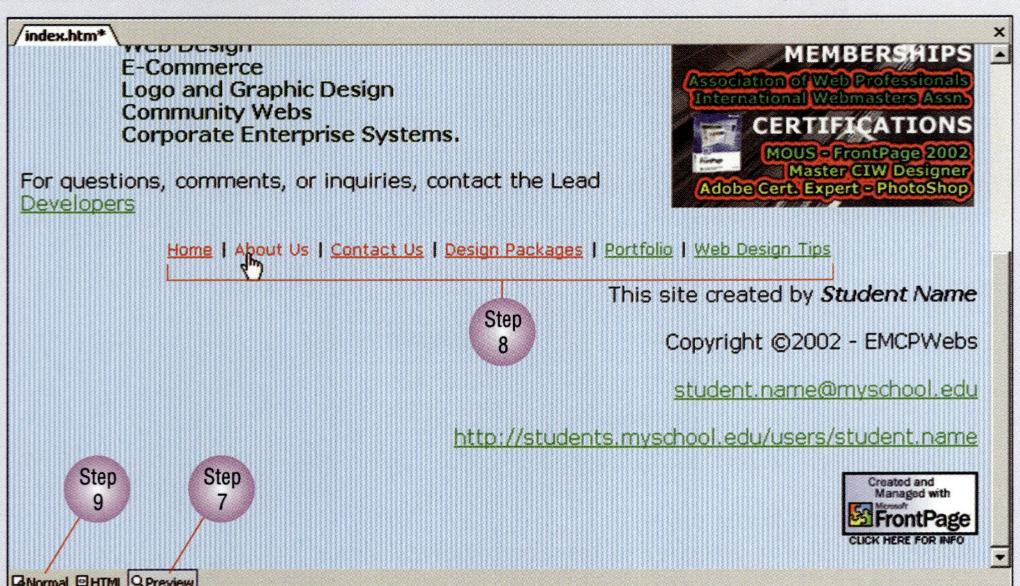

9. Click the Normal tab to return to Page view.
10. Save the updated home page.

exercise 23

REMOVING THE UNDERLINE COMPLETELY FROM HYPERLINKS

1. Open the EMCPWebs home page (index.htm) in Page view.
2. Select the lines of text from *Web Design* through your e-mail address.
3. Right-click anywhere in the selected text.
4. Select the Font command.
5. At the Font dialog box with the Font tab selected, remove the check mark for Underline in the Effects section.
6. Click the OK button.
7. Click the Preview tab at the bottom of the Page view window.

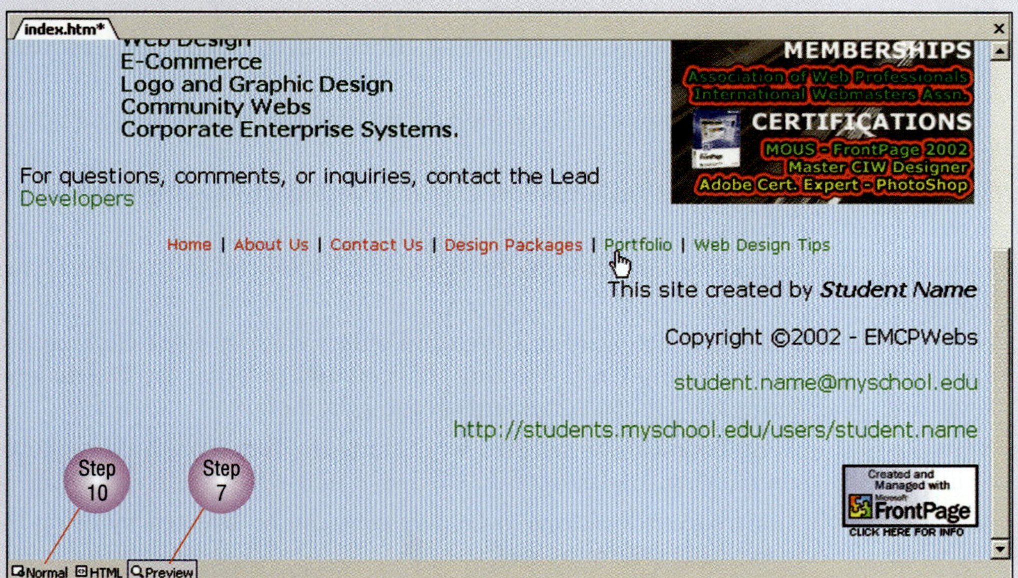

8. Test the hyperlink effects.
9. Print the home page.
10. Click the Normal tab to return to Page view.
11. Save the updated home page and exit FrontPage.

CHAPTER summary

- The three major uses of hyperlinks are to navigate from one location to another; to download files and programs; and to access an e-mail program.
- The pipe key (Shift + \) is often used to separate hypertext links.
- Select an object or text and click the Insert Hyperlink button on the Standard toolbar to initiate the hyperlink process.
- A bookmark is a specified location on a Web page that serves as a hyperlink destination.
- Bookmarks can be inserted by clicking the Insert menu and selecting Bookmark.
- Automatic hyperlinks can be created by keying either a URL or an e-mail address directly into a Web page in Page view.
- Hyperlinks to e-mail addresses can be created by clicking the E-mail Address button in the Insert Hyperlink dialog box.
- Built-in subject lines can be formatted for e-mail hyperlinks by keying the subject in the Insert Hyperlink dialog box.
- Hyperlinks can be removed by clicking the Remove Link button in the Edit Hyperlink dialog box.
- Files and folders can be deleted from a Web in Folders view by right-clicking the item and selecting the Delete command; selecting the icon and pressing the Delete key on the keyboard; or selecting the Delete command on the Edit menu.
- Multiple files in succession can be selected by clicking the first icon, holding down the Shift key, and then clicking the last icon in the list.
- Multiple files in nonadjacent locations in Folders view can be selected by using the Ctrl key while clicking each file you want selected.
- To hyperlink an image, select the image and click the Insert Hyperlink button on the Standard toolbar.
- A FrontPage link bar is a preformatted set of hyperlinks used for navigating a Web site.
- To insert a FrontPage link bar, click the Insert menu and select the Web Component option.
- Hotspot hyperlinks are applied to specific regions of an image to allow for multiple hyperlinks on one image.
- The three hotspot hyperlink shapes are Rectangular Hotspot, Circular Hotspot, and Polygonal Hotspot.
- Clicking the Create New Document button in the Insert Hyperlink dialog box will create a new blank page linked from a hyperlink.
- Hyperlinks can be opened in a new browser window by clicking the Target Frame button in the Edit Hyperlink dialog box and selecting the New Window target.
- Thumbnails are miniature displays of images or pages that are opened in full view on a different Web page.
- Images can be formatted to thumbnails by selecting the image and clicking the AutoThumbnail button on the Pictures toolbar.
- Thumbnail image settings can be altered by clicking the Tools menu, selecting Page Options, and then clicking the AutoThumbnail tab.

- Pages can be navigated using hyperlinks in Page view by holding down the Ctrl key and clicking the hyperlink.
- Pages can also be navigated in Page view by right-clicking a hyperlinked object or text and selecting the Follow Hyperlink command.
- External hyperlink associations can be applied to the Navigation view by right-clicking the appropriate Web page box and selecting the Add Existing Page command.
- Hyperlinks can be verified by selecting the Unverified hyperlinks command in the Site Summary window of the Reports view.
- The Broken hyperlinks feature in the Reports view gives those who manage FrontPage Webs a helpful tool for fixing dead links.
- The Hyperlinks view allows developers to view exactly how internal and external pages, graphical images, and application documents are hyperlinked within the current Web.
- Hyperlink, Visited hyperlink, and Active hyperlink colors can be formatted in the Background tab of the Page Properties dialog box.
- The underline in hypertext link rollovers can be removed by clicking the Rollover style button in the Background tab of the Page Properties dialog box and then clicking the No text decoration check box.
- The underline in hypertext links can be completely removed by selecting the text, right-clicking the selected text, clicking the Font command, and removing the check mark before Underline in the Effects section.

COMMANDS review

Command	Mouse/Keyboard
Create a hypertext link	Select text, click Insert Hyperlink on Standard toolbar
Create a bookmark	Select text or object, click Insert, Bookmark
Hyperlink to a bookmark	Select text or object, click Insert Hyperlink, click Bookmark, select bookmark
Create an automatic hyperlink	Key URL or e-mail address and press spacebar or Enter key
Create an e-mail hyperlink	Select text or object, click Insert Hyperlink, click E-mail Address
Remove a hyperlink	Select hyperlink, click Insert Hyperlink, click Remove Link
Delete a Web page from Folders view	Right-click file icon, press Delete key; or select file icon, press Delete key; or select file icon, click Edit, Delete
Insert a FrontPage link bar	Click Insert, Web Component, Link Bars

Create a hotspot hyperlink on an image	Select image, click Rectangular, Circular, or Polygonal Hotspot on Pictures toolbar
Hyperlink to a new document	Select text or object, click Insert Hyperlink, Create New Document
Set hyperlinks to open in a new window	Select text or object, click Insert Hyperlink, Target Frame, New Window
Create a thumbnail link to an image	Select image, click AutoThumbnail on Pictures toolbar
Navigate hyperlinked pages in Page view	Right-click hyperlink, click Follow Hyperlink; press Ctrl + hyperlink
Create external hyperlink associations	Right-click box, click Add Existing Page
Verify hyperlinks	Click Reports, Unverified hyperlinks, Yes
Fix broken hyperlinks	Right-click broken hyperlink, click Edit Hyperlink
Change hypertext link color	Click Format, Background
Remove underline on hypertext link rollover	Click Format, Background, Enable hyperlink rollover effects, click Rollover style, click No text decoration
Completely remove underline from a hyperlink	Select text, click Format, Font, uncheck Underline

CONCEPTS check

Completion: On a blank sheet of paper, indicate the correct term, command, or number for each item.

1. This character is often used to separate hypertext links and can be inserted by pressing Shift + \.
2. To create a hyperlink, select the text or object to be hyperlinked and click this button on the Standard toolbar.
3. Bookmarks can be formatted by selecting the text or object and selecting the Bookmark command on this menu.
4. Automatic hyperlinks can be applied to URLs and this type of address by pressing the spacebar, Enter key, or Tab key.
5. E-mail hyperlinks can be applied to text and images by selecting this button in the Insert Hyperlink dialog box.
6. Hyperlinks can be removed by selecting the hyperlinked object and clicking this button in the Edit Hyperlink dialog box.

7. Use this key while you click to select multiple files in nonadjacent locations in Folders view.
8. Applying multiple hyperlinks to an image is accomplished using these three types of hotspots.
9. An image that has multiple hyperlink regions is called this.
10. This Web component is a preformatted set of hyperlinks with varying colors and styles used for site navigation.
11. Hyperlinking to a new blank document can be accomplished by selecting this command in the Insert Hyperlink dialog box.
12. Hyperlinks can be formatted to open in a new browser window by selecting this command in the Target Frame dialog box.
13. These are miniature displays of images or pages that are opened in full view on a different Web page.
14. Broken hyperlinks can be identified by running this report in the Site Summary window of the Reports view.
15. Hypertext, visited, and active links can be changed to various colors by accessing the Background tab in this dialog box.

SKILLS check

Assessment 1

1. Open the craftfest04 FrontPage Web in your *Chapter 4* folder.
2. Open the CraftFest home page (index.htm) in Page view.
3. Place the insertion point after the banner image and press Enter.
4. Enter the following navigation bar text:

   Home | Events | Craft Vendors | Food Vendors | Contests | Carnival Info

5. Create hyperlinks to each of the CraftFest Web pages.
6. Save the updated Web page.
7. Test the hyperlinks in your browser.
8. Print the CraftFest home page.

Assessment 2

1. Open the craftfest04 FrontPage Web in your *Chapter 4* folder.
2. Open the CraftFest Craft Vendors (crafts.htm) Web page in Page view.
3. Scroll down the page until you can view the *Wood Crafts* heading and list.
4. Select the *Wood Crafts* heading and insert a bookmark.
5. Insert a bookmark on the remaining headings.
6. Scroll back to the top of the Web page.
7. Create hyperlinks from the table of contents to the corresponding bookmarks on the page.
8. Test the bookmark hyperlinks in your browser.

Assessment 3

1. Open the craftfest04 FrontPage Web in your *Chapter 4* folder.
2. Open the CraftFest home page (index.htm) in Page view.
3. Select the *Contact Webmaster* text at the bottom of the Web page.
4. Create an e-mail hyperlink to your e-mail address.
5. Key the subject **Craft Fair Home Page Inquiry**.
6. Save the updated Web page.
7. Test the hyperlink in your browser.
8. Print the Web page.

Assessment 4

1. Open the technews04 FrontPage Web in your *Chapter 4* folder.
2. Open the Tech News home page (home.htm) in Page view.
3. Create a custom link bar under the banner image with the *Bold Stripes* bar style.
4. Arrange the link bar horizontally.
5. Name the link bar Tech News Links.
6. Hyperlink to the following pages:

Text to display	***Page/Address***
Classifieds	classifieds.htm
Sports	sports.htm
Weather	weather.htm
Education	education.htm
Lifestyle	lifestyle.htm
CNN	http://www.cnn.com

7. Use Vivid Colors and Active Graphics.
8. Save the updated Tech News home page.
9. Perform a Preview in Browser.
10. Print the Tech News home page.
11. Test the link bar hyperlinks.

Assessment 5

1. Open the technews04 FrontPage Web in your *Chapter 4* folder.
2. Open the Tech News home page (index.htm) in Page view.
3. If you completed assessment 4, remove the FrontPage link bar from the Web page.
4. Insert the following image buttons under the banner image:

   classifieds.gif
   sports.gif
   weather.gif
   education.gif
   lifestyle.gif
   cnn.gif

5. Hyperlink them to their appropriate pages.
6. Save the updated Tech News home page.
7. Perform a Preview in Browser.
8. Print the Tech News home page.
9. Test the hyperlinks.

Assessment 6

1. Open the technews04 FrontPage Web in your *Chapter 4* folder.
2. Open the Tech News splash page (index.htm) in Page view.
3. Using assessments 4 and 5 as a guide, create hotspot hyperlinks to the Web pages identified on the splash image.
4. Save the updated Tech News home page.
5. Perform a Preview in Browser.
6. Print the Tech News splash page.
7. Test the hyperlinks.

Assessment 7

1. Open the technews04 FrontPage Web in your *Chapter 4* folder.
2. Open the Tech News splash page (index.htm) in Page view.
3. If you have not completed assessment 6, create a hotspot hyperlink on the CNN Interactive text.
4. Change the target frame for the hyperlink to New Window.
5. Save the updated Tech News home page.
6. Perform a Preview in Browser.
7. Test the hyperlink.

Assessment 8

1. Open the technews04 FrontPage Web in your *Chapter 4* folder.
2. Open the Tech News Archive page (archive.htm) in Page view.
3. Place the insertion point under the navigation link bar.
4. Insert the v1i1.jpg image.
5. Format the image to a thumbnail using the AutoThumbnail feature.
6. Place the following images, in thumbnail, next to the above image, with all images appearing on the same line when finished: v1i2.jpg, v1i3.jpg, and v1i4.jpg.
7. Save the updated Tech News Archive page.
8. Perform a Preview in Browser.
9. Print the Tech News Archive page.
10. Test the thumbnail hyperlinks.

Assessment 9

1. Open the europetour04 FrontPage Web in your *Chapter 4* folder.
2. Access the Reports view and run a report on the unverified hyperlinks.
3. Fix all broken hyperlinks.
4. Open the home page (index.htm) in Page view.
5. Perform a Preview in Browser.
6. Test the hyperlinks.

Assessment 10

1. Open the europetour04 FrontPage Web in your *Chapter 4* folder.
2. Open the Europe Tour home page (index.htm) in Page view.
3. Format the hyperlinks to the following colors:

Hyperlink	Teal
Visited hyperlink	Red
Active hyperlink	Light Green

4. Enable the hyperlink rollover effects to remove the underline as the hypertext link is being hovered over.
5. Save the updated Europe Tour home page.
6. Perform a Preview in Browser.
7. Test the hyperlink rollover effects.
8. Exit FrontPage.

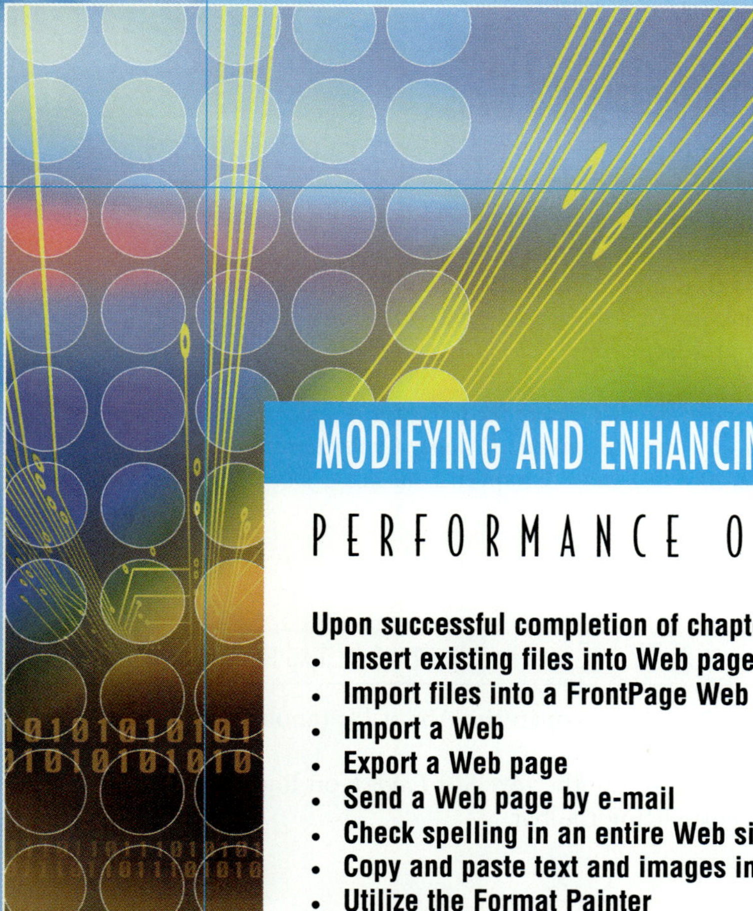

CHAPTER 5

MODIFYING AND ENHANCING FRONTPAGE WEBS AND PAGES

PERFORMANCE OBJECTIVES

Upon successful completion of chapter 5, you will be able to:

- **Insert existing files into Web pages**
- **Import files into a FrontPage Web**
- **Import a Web**
- **Export a Web page**
- **Send a Web page by e-mail**
- **Check spelling in an entire Web site**
- **Copy and paste text and images into a Web page**
- **Utilize the Format Painter**
- **Use the Find and Replace feature**
- **Modify paragraph elements**
- **Apply and format numbering and bullets**
- **Subscribe to Microsoft newsletters**

Chapter 5 IRC

This chapter will focus primarily on many common tasks involving existing documents and Webs, text, and images. These tasks, while varied, are important to the effectiveness of creating FrontPage Webs. As in previous chapters, if you have worked in other Microsoft Office applications, many of the tasks in this chapter may be familiar to you. The first section of this chapter covers topics relating to existing documents and FrontPage Webs. You will insert existing Microsoft Office files into Web pages. In addition to inserting files, you will import a PowerPoint file into your FrontPage Web and create a hyperlink to the file. You will also import a PowerPoint presentation saved in HTML format.

The second section of this chapter covers text features, many of which are common to the other Office programs, such as Copy and Paste and Undo. Other text features covered in this chapter include using the Format Painter, formatting paragraphs, applying bullets and numbering, finding and replacing text, and inserting the date and time Web components. Although graphic and image manipulation activities were covered in chapters 2 and 3, this chapter introduces the Microsoft Office Clipboard for pasting images. The Office Clipboard is new to FrontPage 2002 and allows users to copy multiple items that can be pasted.

Working with Existing Documents and Webs

Inserting Existing Files into Web Pages

The ability to insert existing files into a Web page allows users to quickly incorporate information from other Web sites, word processing documents, spreadsheet files, and other software applications that may involve text, graphics, and tables. Workers in different locations can collaborate by developing parts of projects and then inserting their files into Web pages at a later time.

(Note: Before completing computer exercises, delete the Chapter 4 *folder on your disk. Next, download the Chapter 5 data files from the Internet Resource Center to the* Chapter 5 *folder you have created on your disk, and then make* Chapter 5 *the active folder.)*

exercise 1

INSERTING EXISTING FILES INTO A WEB PAGE

1. Open the EMCPWebs FrontPage Web and then open the About Us (aboutus.htm) Web page.
2. Place the insertion point on a blank line below the text *Site Launch* on line seven and click the Align Left button on the Formatting toolbar.
3. Click Insert and then click File.

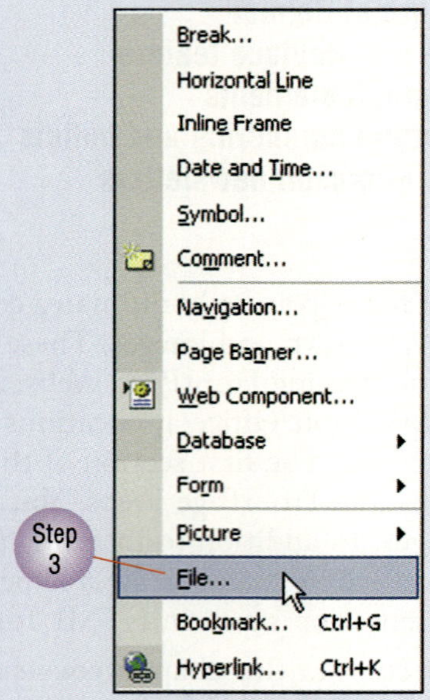

4. At the Select File dialog box, locate and open the *EMCPWebs Files* folder.
5. In the Files of type drop-down list, click *Word 97-2002 (*.doc)*.

6. Select the aboutus.doc file.
7. Click the Open button.

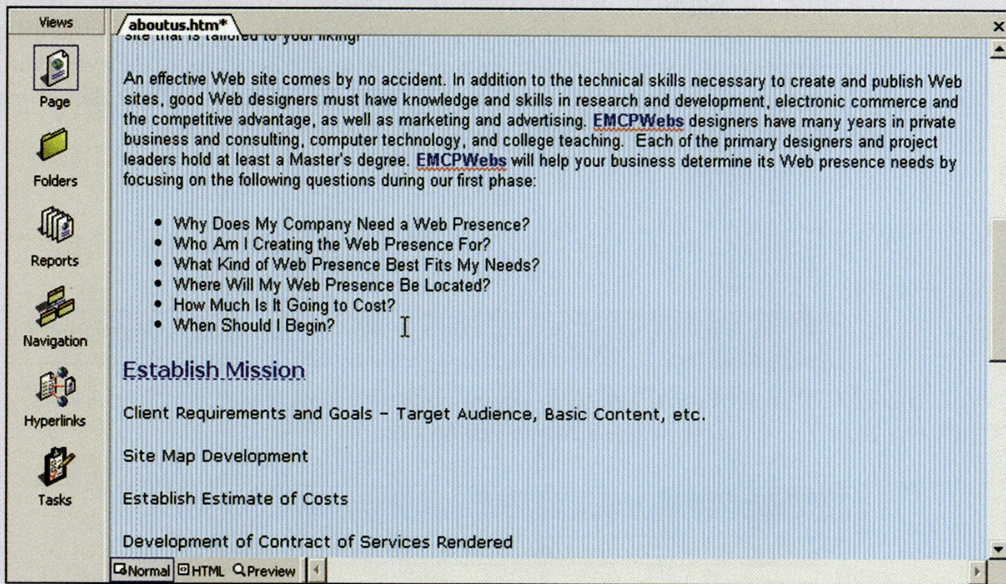

8. Place the insertion point one line below the *Parallel Sites* list item at the bottom of the Web page.
9. Click Insert and then click File once again.
10. At the Select File dialog box, ensure that the HTML Files (*.htm, *.html) Files of type option is selected.
11. Select the phases.htm file and click the Open button.

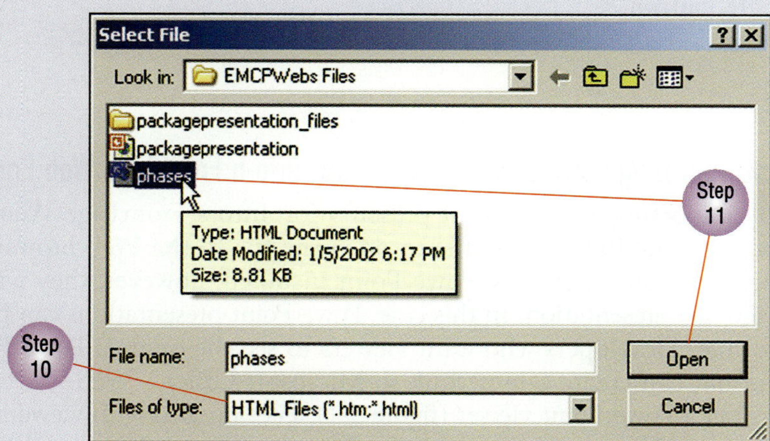

12. Save the updates for the About Us page.
13. Perform a Preview in Browser.
14. Print the Web page.

Importing and Inserting PowerPoint Presentations

PowerPoint presentations are an excellent tool for communicating information in a slide show format. Many companies have existing PowerPoint presentations to communicate information about products, services, procedures, facilities, and other important aspects of their business. Many educators use PowerPoint almost exclusively as their preferred delivery format. FrontPage 2002 makes it especially easy to incorporate PowerPoint presentations into Web pages.

exercise 2

IMPORTING A POWERPOINT PRESENTATION

1. With the EMCPWebs FrontPage Web open, click File and then click Import.
2. Click the Add File button in the Import dialog box.

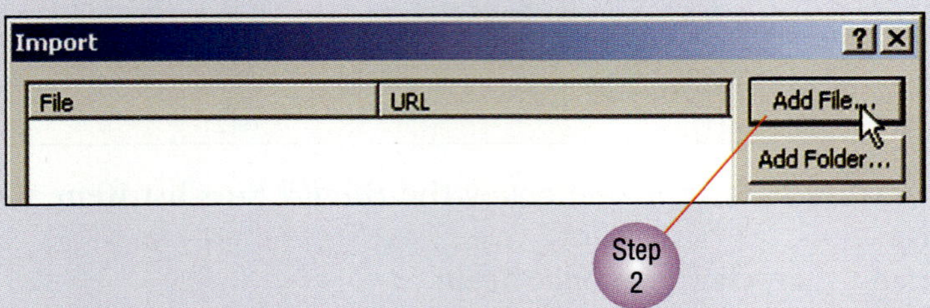

3. Locate and select the packagepresentation.ppt file in the *EMCPWebs Files* folder.
4. Click the Open button in the Add File to Import List dialog box.
5. Click the OK button.

Incorporating PowerPoint Presentations into a FrontPage Web Page

By importing a PowerPoint presentation into a FrontPage Web, developers can create hyperlinks to the file to open the file in the Web browser. If the target audience does not have PowerPoint installed, however, they will not be able to view the presentation. In this case, PowerPoint presentations can be saved in HTML format. Developers who want viewers to see the original PowerPoint presentation format can create a hyperlink to Microsoft Office's Web site to download and install a PowerPoint viewer (figure 5.1). Files opened with viewers cannot be edited, however. Viewers are available for Microsoft Word, Excel, and PowerPoint.

FIGURE

5.1 PowerPoint Viewer Download Page

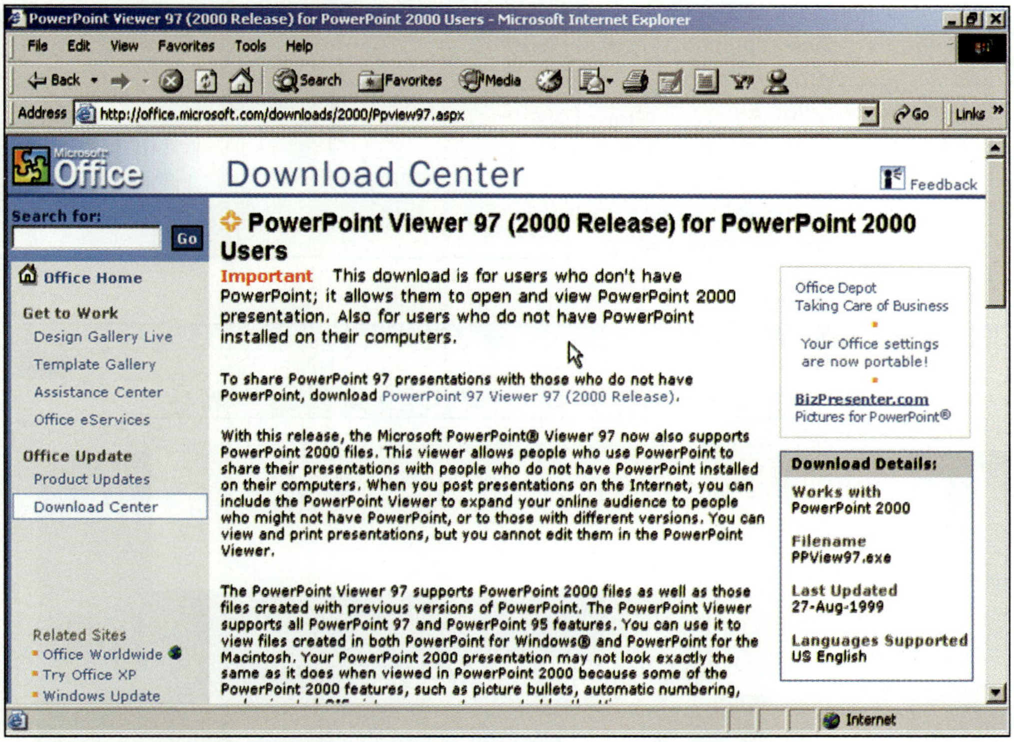

exercise 3

HYPERLINKING TO A POWERPOINT PRESENTATION

1. Open the EMCPWebs FrontPage Web and then open the Web and Graphic Design Packages (packages.htm) Web page.
2. Place the insertion point one line below the Photo Gallery Web component.
3. Key the text **View Our Presentation** and format to Verdana, 18 points, bold.
4. Create a hyperlink to the packagepresentation.ppt file.

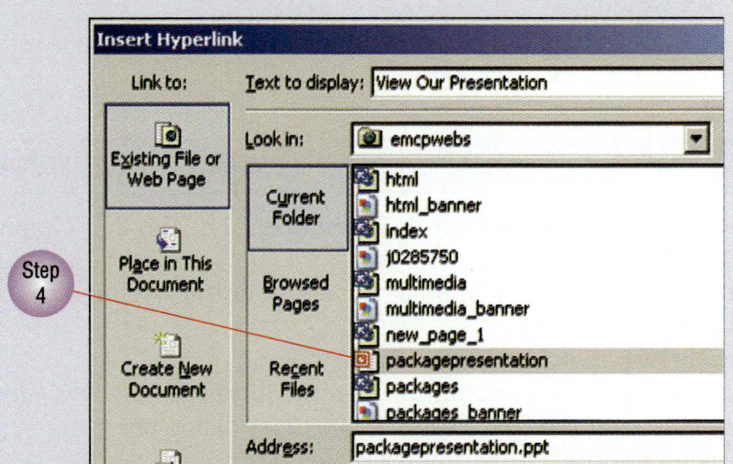

5. Save the updated packages.htm Web page.
6. Perform a Preview in Browser.
7. Test the hyperlink. *(Note: You will not be able to view the presentation if your computer system does not have Microsoft PowerPoint installed.)*
8. Click the Open button in the File Download dialog box.
9. Run through the presentation in Internet Explorer.

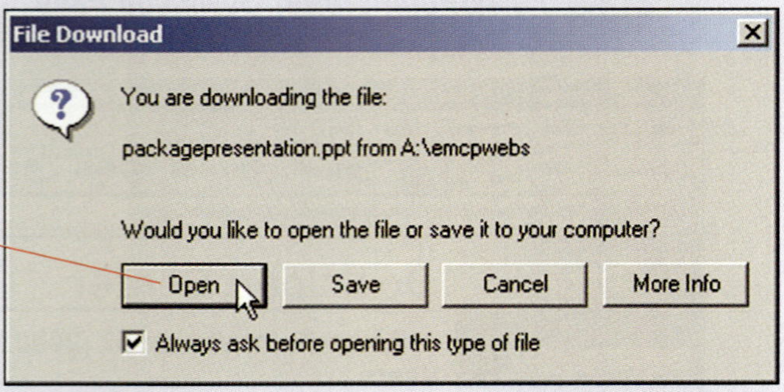

Step 8

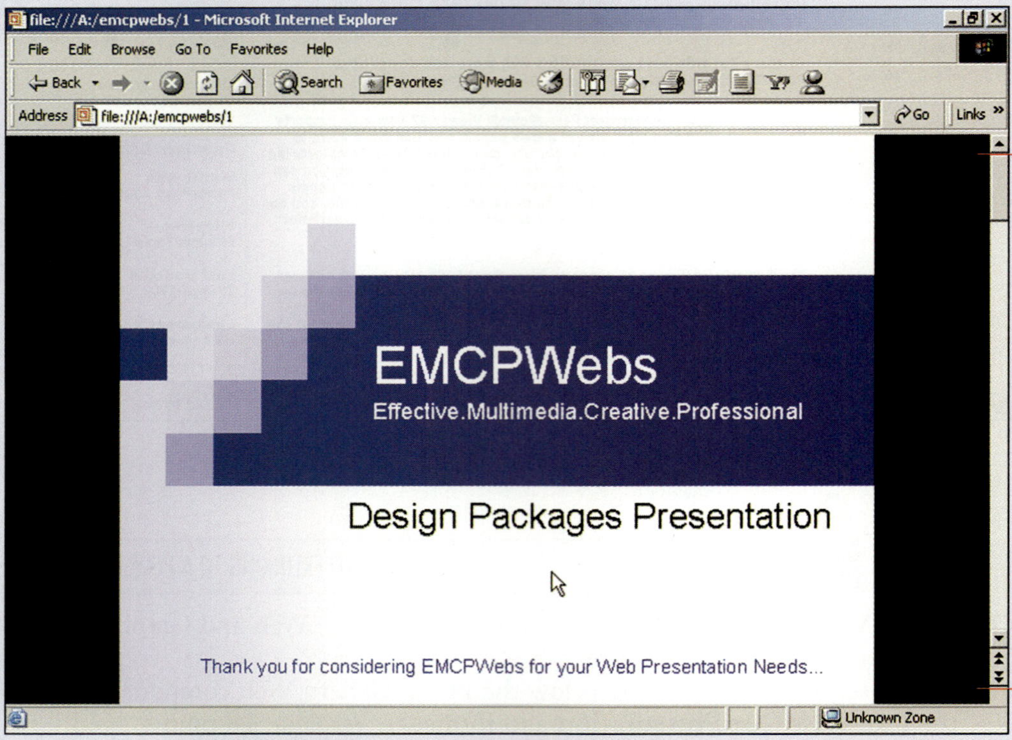

Step 9

10. Close the browser window.

exercise 4 INSERTING A POWERPOINT PRESENTATION FROMATTED IN HTML

1. Open the EMCPWebs FrontPage Web and then open the Web and Graphic Design Packages (packages.htm) Web page.
2. Delete all text, the Photo Gallery, and the hyperlink on the Web page.
3. Click File and then click Import.
4. Click the Add File button in the Import dialog box.
5. Locate and select the packagepresentation.htm file in the *EMCPWebs Files* folder.
6. Click the Open button in the Add File to Import List dialog box.
7. Click the Add Folder button in the Import dialog box.

8. Select the *packagepresentation_files* folder and click the Open button.

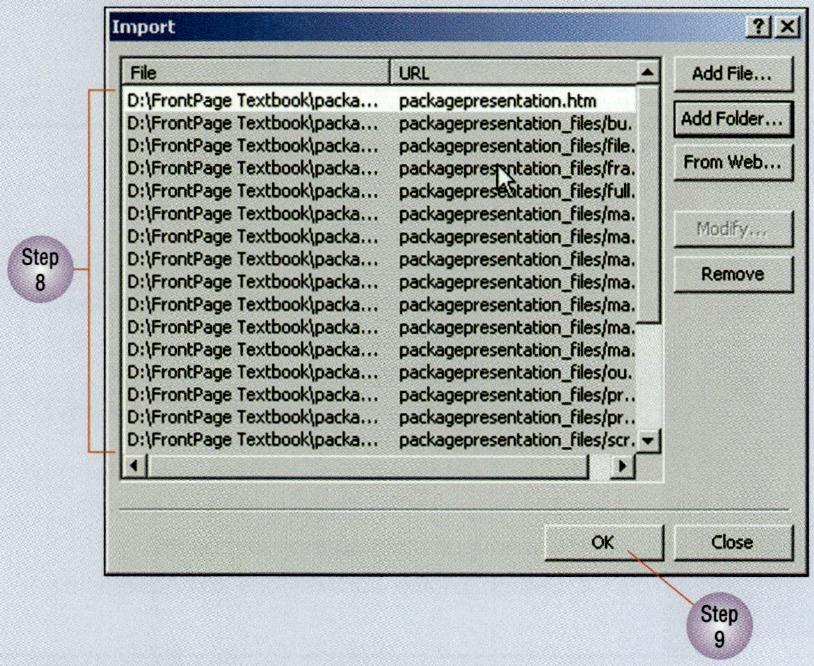

9. Click the OK button.
10. Place the insertion point one line below the banner image.
11. Click Insert and then click File.
12. Select the packagepresentation.htm file in the *EMCPWebs Files* folder.
13. Click the Open button.
14. Save the updated Packages page.
15. Perform a Preview in Browser.
16. Click the click *here* link.

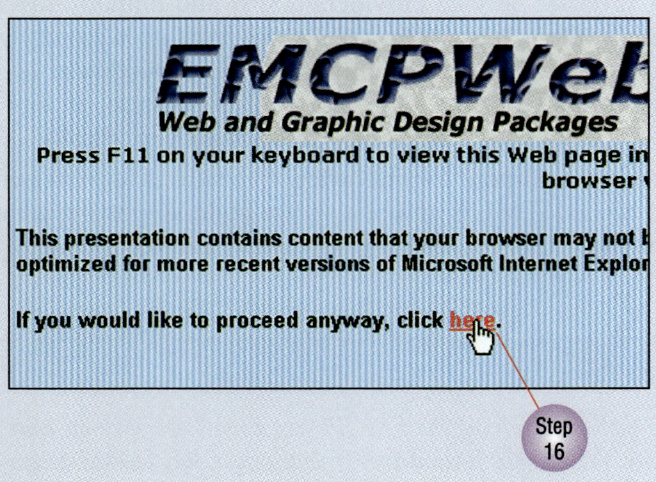

17. Run through the HTML formatted PowerPoint presentation.

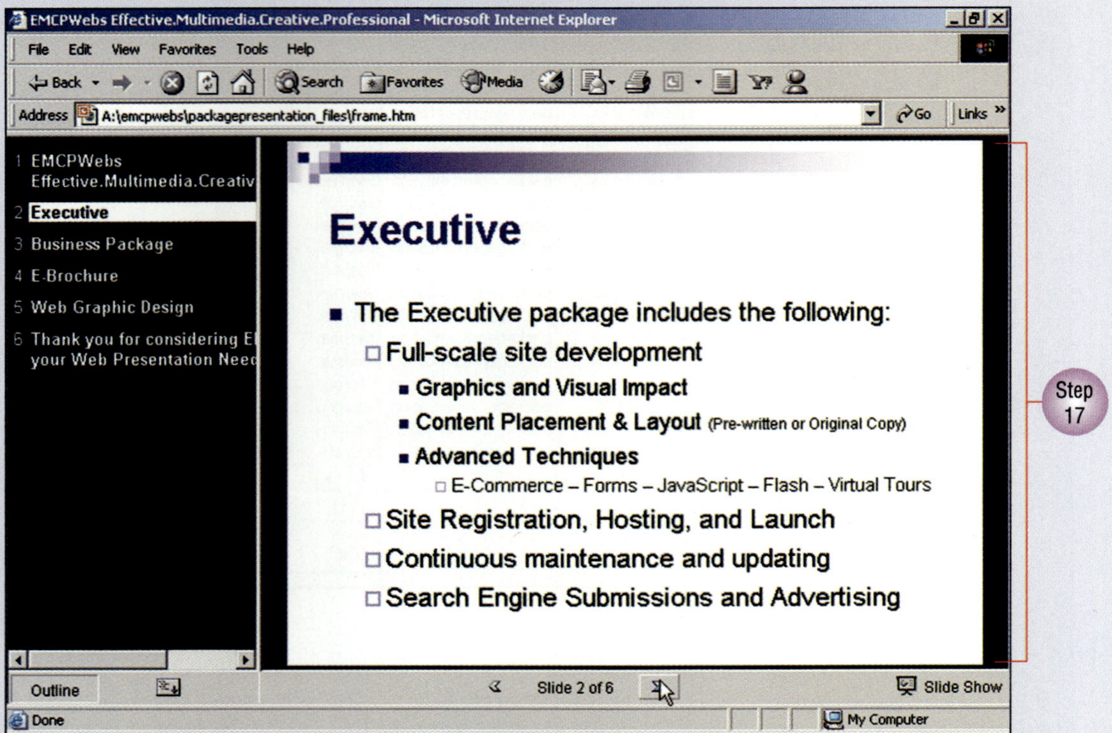

18. Close the Web browser.

Importing a Web Site

Importing a Web site into an existing FrontPage Web can serve a couple of purposes. Importing a Web from a Web server can serve as a backup of a Web site. While most Internet Service Providers (ISPs) and domain hosts back up their servers routinely, there are situations in which Web sites strangely disappear. In addition, ISPs and domain hosting companies can be purchased by other companies, merge with another company, or even go out of business. In any of the above cases, it is very important to make your own backups periodically.

Another purpose for importing Web sites is for observing and testing other Web sites. Since HTML is an open source code, importing someone else's Web site is an excellent tool for learning new tricks and technologies.

exercise 5 IMPORTING A WEB SITE FOR BACKUP PURPOSES

(Note: This exercise involves importing the EMCPWebs FrontPage Web on your student disk into an EMCPWebs FrontPage Web on the hard drive. If your school has blocked access to the hard drive or does not allow students to save files to the hard drive, you may opt to save to a Zip drive or CD-RW if available. Please contact your instructor for further instructions.)

1. Open a new session of FrontPage.
2. Click the <u>*Web Site Templates*</u> option in the New Page or Web Task Pane.
3. At the Web Site Templates dialog box, select the *Import Web Wizard* icon.

4. In the Specify the location of the new web text box, key **c:\emcpwebs**.

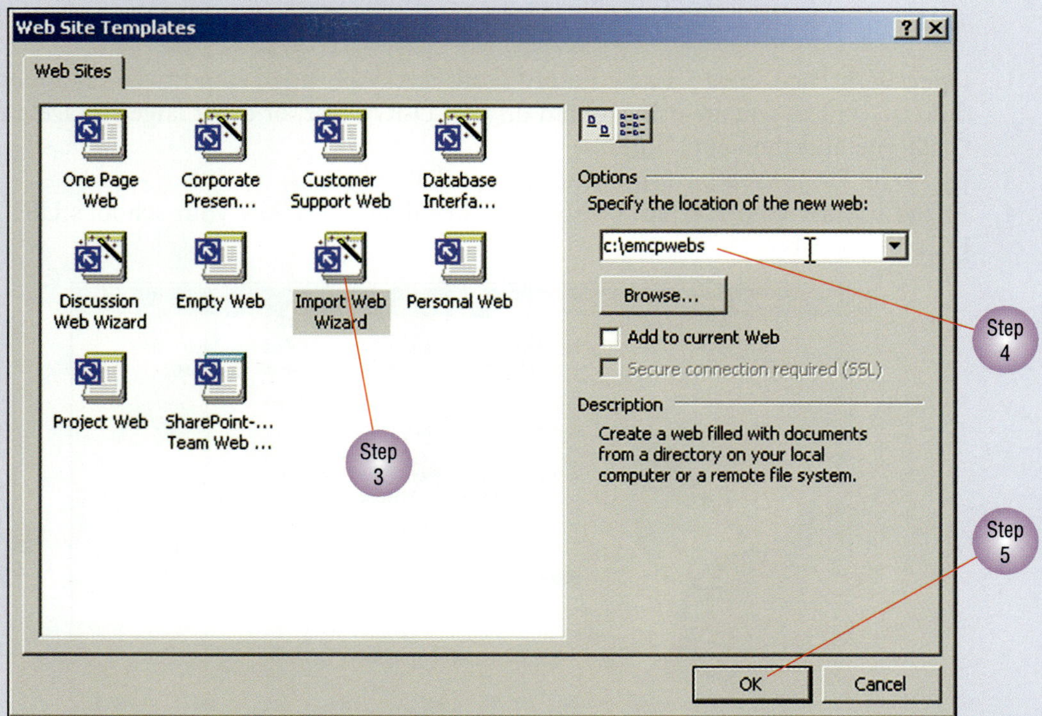

5. Click the OK button.
6. At the Import Web Wizard – Choose Source dialog box, select the From a source directory of files on a local computer or network option.
7. Key **a:\emcpwebs** in the Location text box.
8. Click the Include subfolders check box to insert a check mark.
9. Click the Next button.
10. Click the Next button in the Import Web Wizard – Edit File List dialog box.
11. Click the Finish button.
12. Open the EMCPWebs home page in Page view.
13. Perform a Preview in Browser and test the hyperlinks. *(Note: Notice that the pages open much faster from the hard drive than they do from the disk. All exercise screen images in the textbook from this point on will show the hard drive [C:] on the title bar, views, and dialog boxes, rather than the floppy [A:].)*
14. Close the Web browser and FrontPage.

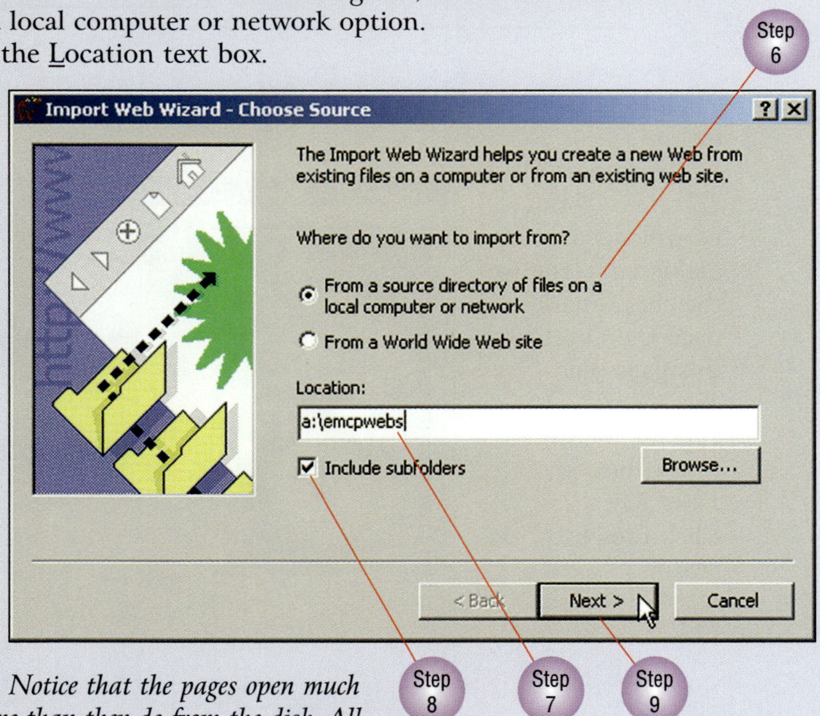

exercise 6

IMPORTING A WEB FOR TESTING PURPOSES

1. Open FrontPage, create a new Empty FrontPage Web titled importweb on a blank diskette (unless you are using a hard drive, CD-RW disc, or other large storage medium).
2. Click File and then click Import.
3. Click the From Web button in the Import dialog box.
4. At the Import Web Wizard – Choose Source dialog box, key your school's URL in the Location text box.

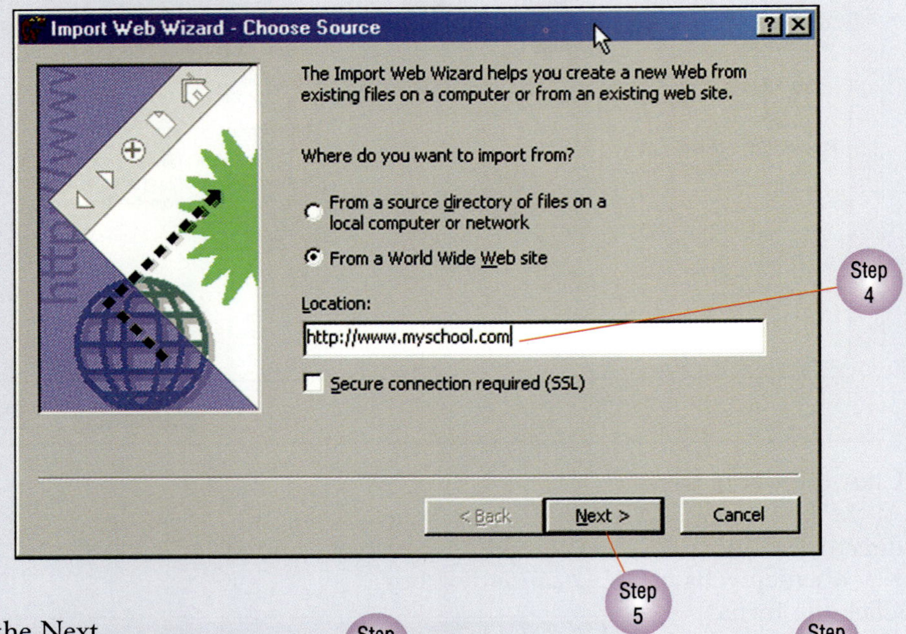

5. Click the Next button.
6. At the Import Web Wizard – Choose Download Amount dialog box, remove the check mark from the Limit to this page plus check box.
7. Change the Limit to text box to 1000 KB.
8. Click the Next button.

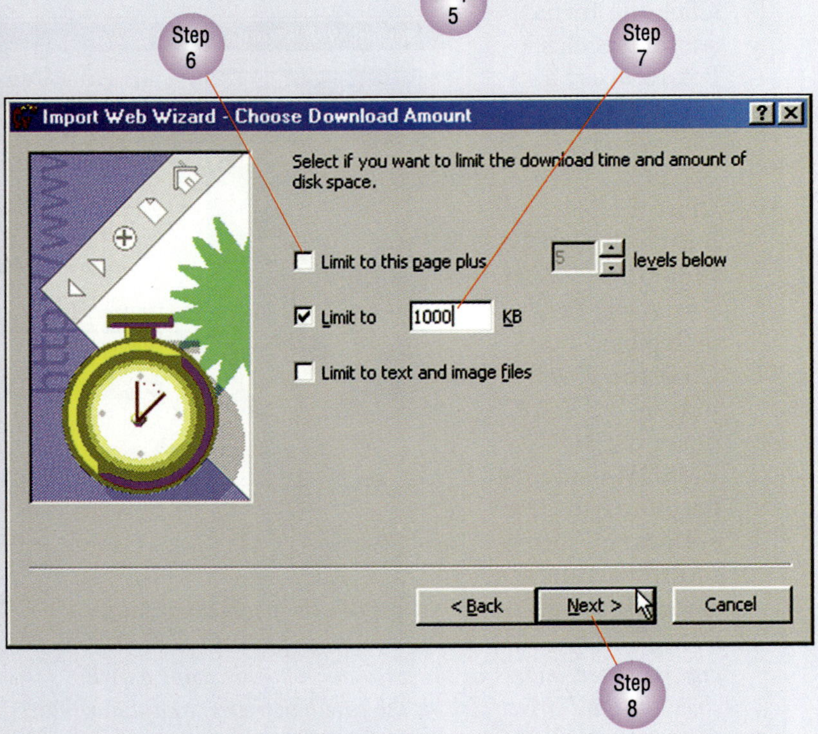

9. Click the Finish button. The Import Web Progress process may take one to several minutes depending on your connection speed.
10. When the Import Web has reached the size limit specified, click the OK button on the Import Web Wizard dialog box.
11. Click Folders view to observe the file and folder naming and titling scheme.
12. Open the home page in Page view.
13. Perform a Preview in Browser.
14. Close the Web browser.

Exporting a Web Page

Individual files in a FrontPage Web can be exported to a storage medium for keeping an original copy of a Web page or file as well as for backup purposes. Keeping an original copy of a Web page can be very useful if you are testing a new layout design and later decide that it doesn't look as good as you had hoped! You can then easily import the original file to replace the existing file.

exercise 7

EXPORTING A WEB PAGE

1. Open the importweb FrontPage Web and access the Folders view.
2. Select the home page file in the Contents window.
3. Click File and then click Export.
4. Export the file to your storage medium.
5. From the My Computer window, check to see if the file is there.

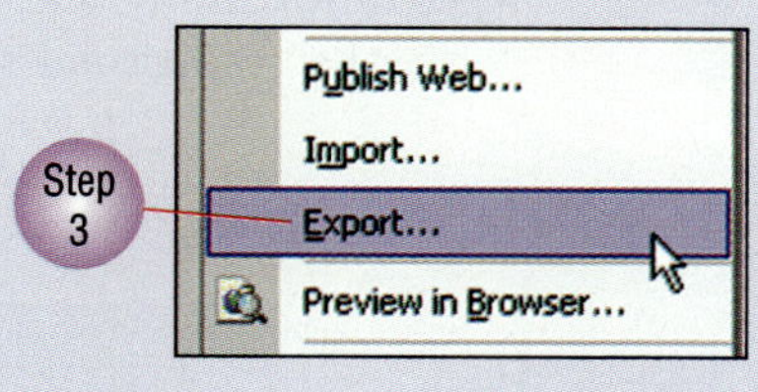

Sending Web Pages by E-Mail

The Send command on the File menu is a quick way to send Web page content to another department, person, or group of people for review or editing purposes. When you are ready, click File and then click Send. This will automatically open your default e-mail program with the Web page as the message.

exercise 8

SENDING WEB PAGES BY E-MAIL

(Note: This exercise uses Microsoft Outlook. Use your default e-mail program. If you do not have an e-mail program installed on your computer, you may have to skip this exercise.)

1. Open the home page file of the importweb FrontPage Web.
2. Click File and then click Send.

3. In Outlook, key your personal e-mail address with a subject of Home Page.

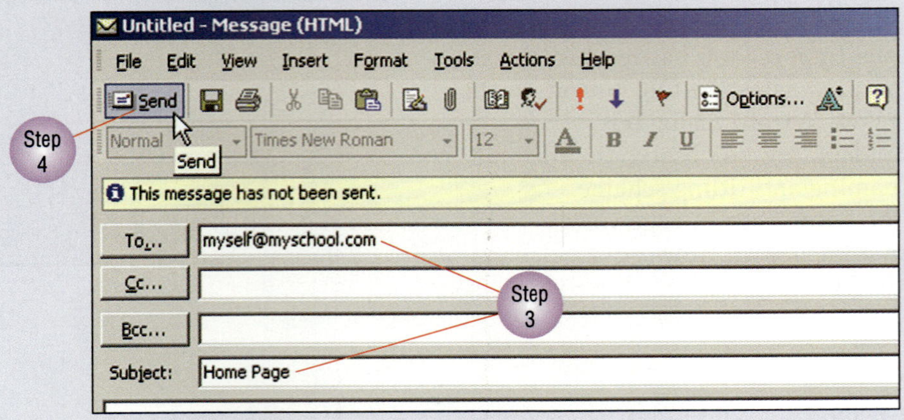

4. Click the Send button.

Checking Spelling in an Entire Web Site

Even with automatic spelling and grammar checkers, it is a good idea to run the Spelling feature for the entire Web periodically. To run the Entire Web Spelling feature, first access any view other than Page view. Next, click the Spelling button on the Standard toolbar. Click the Entire web option in the Spelling dialog box and then click Start. On the task list, double-click to access each page and run the traditional spelling checker feature.

exercise 9 — CHECKING SPELLING IN AN ENTIRE WEB SITE

1. Open the importweb FrontPage Web and access the Folders view.
2. Click the Spelling button on the Standard toolbar.
3. Click the Entire web option.

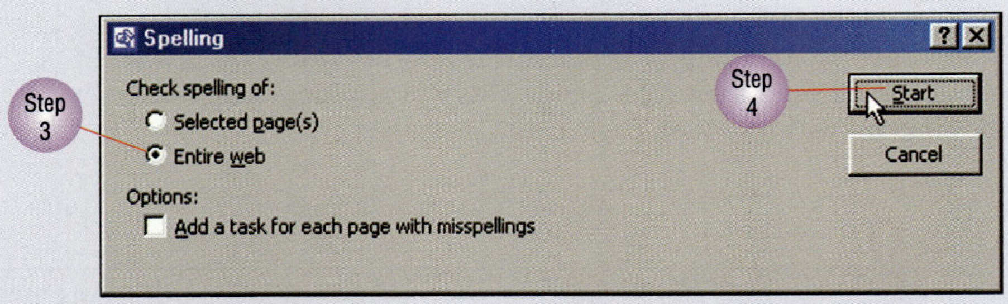

4. Click the Start button.

5. Double-click the first page in the list.
6. Check each page in the Spelling dialog box, either clicking the Ignore button for each alleged misspelled word or correcting the misspelling.

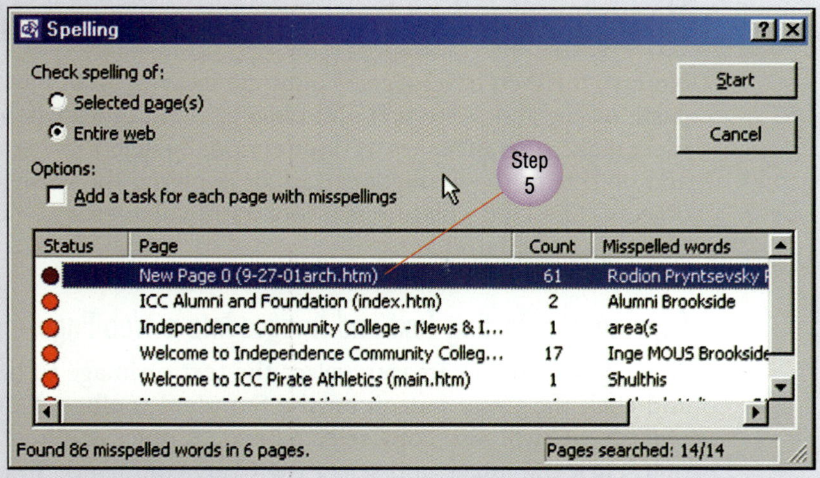

7. At the Continue with the next page? dialog box, click the Next Page button.
8. When you have finished checking all pages, click the Back to List button in the Finished checking all pages dialog box.
9. Close the Spelling window.

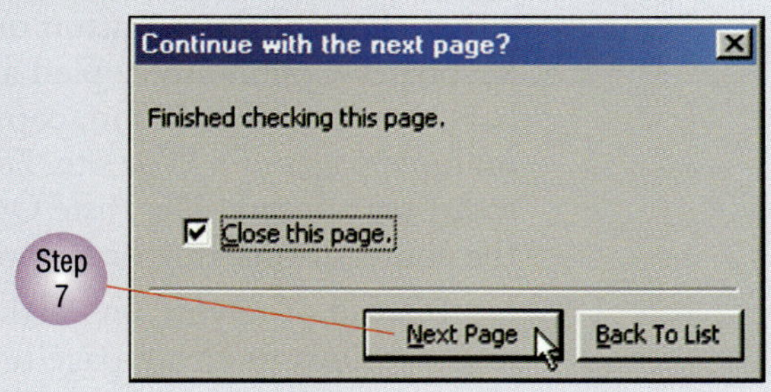

Enabling the Indexing Service

When the Indexing Service is enabled, the files on your computer are indexed and maintained so you can perform faster searches. The Indexing Service runs when your system is idle and searches My Computer, Microsoft Outlook folders, and My Network Places. Without the Indexing Service enabled, searches to the above locations are conducted on a search-by-search basis and take up valuable time.

exercise 10

ENABLING THE INDEXING SERVICE

1. With FrontPage open, click the Search button on the Standard toolbar.
2. Click the *Search options* link in the Basic Search Task Pane.
3. Click the Yes, enable Indexing Service and run when my computer is idle option.
4. Click the OK button.
5. Close FrontPage.

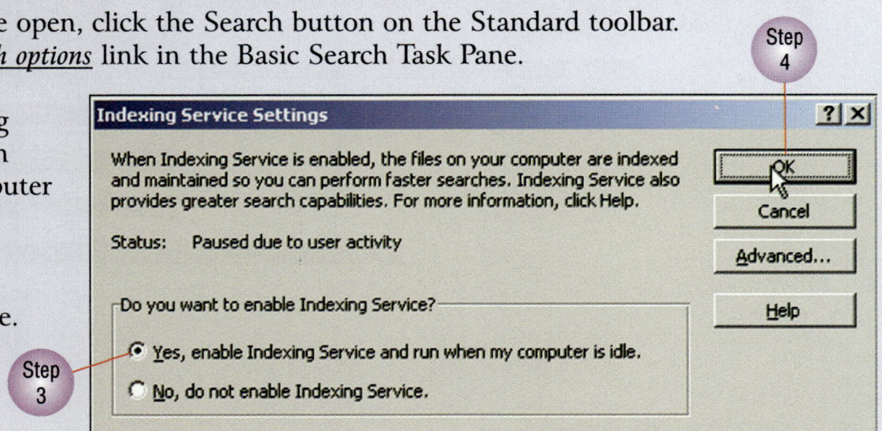

Modifying Web Page Text

No task for Web developers is more time-saving than having the ability to copy and paste or cut and paste text and objects. Sometimes when working in a document, users make such mistakes as unintentionally deleting text and objects, inserting text and objects in the wrong location, or applying the wrong formatting to text and objects. The Undo feature is a tool with which every Microsoft Office application user should be familiar.

Copying and Pasting Text and Images into a Web Page

To copy text and/or images, select the text or image to be copied with the mouse and click the Copy button on the Standard toolbar. A quick keyboard shortcut of Ctrl + C will also copy selected text. A quick method for copying images is to right-click the image and select the Copy command. To paste copied or cut text, either click the Paste button on the Standard toolbar or press Ctrl + V on the keyboard. Commonly copied and pasted text includes hypertext navigation link bars, contact information, copyright information, and other information found on multiple pages of a Web site. Each time text is pasted in Page view, the Paste Options smart tag appears. The Paste Options smart tag provides the opportunity for keeping the source formatting or keeping only the text.

Instead of relying on pasting images and text into multiple pages, it may be less laborious to create page templates that can be applied to Web pages as the Web grows. Page templates will be explored further in chapter 10.

exercise 11

COPYING AND PASTING TEXT AND IMAGES

1. Open the EMCPWebs FrontPage Web and then the home page (index.htm) in Page view.
2. Scroll down and select the hypertext links through the *Created and Managed with Microsoft FrontPage* image link.

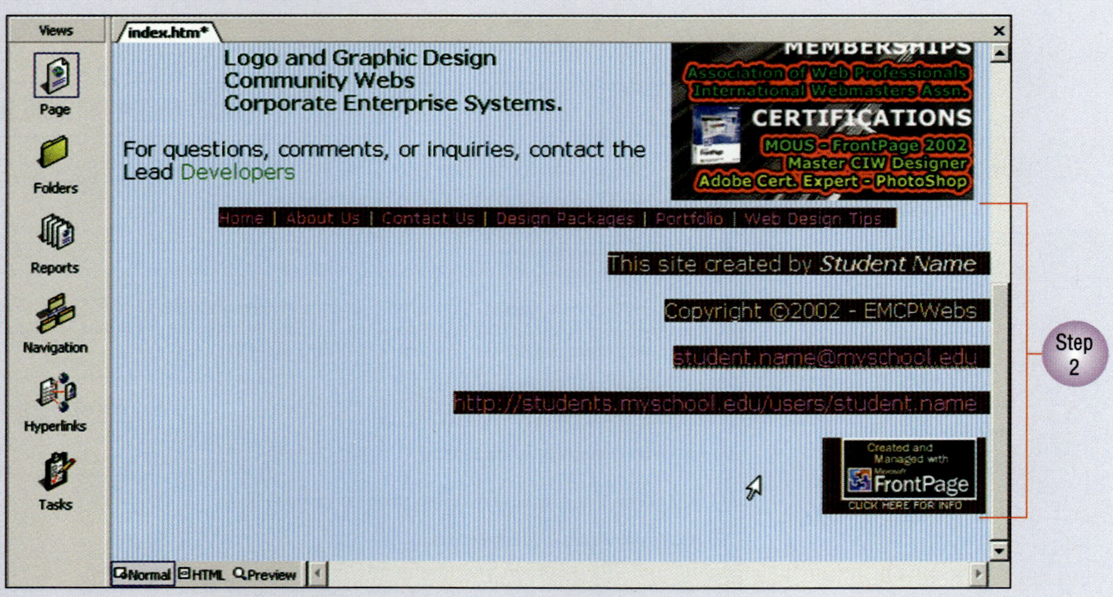

3. Click the Copy button on the Standard toolbar.
4. Open the aboutus.htm page in page view.
5. Place the insertion point one line below the last line of text on the page.
6. Click the Paste button on the Standard toolbar.
7. Open the remaining EMCPWeb pages and paste the selection on each page using the Ctrl + V paste keyboard shortcut.
8. Click the Save All command in the File menu to save the updated pages.

exercise 12

COPYING, PASTING, AND MODIFYING LINK BAR WEB COMPONENTS

1. Open the EMCPWebs FrontPage Web and then the home page (index.htm) in Page view.
2. Right-click anywhere on the link bar Web component and then click Copy.

3. Open the aboutus.htm Web page in Page view.
4. Place the insertion point on a blank line under the banner image.
5. Click the Paste button on the Standard toolbar.
6. Perform the same task as in steps 2-5 to copy and paste link bars to the remaining second-tier pages contactus.htm, packages.htm, portfolio.htm, and webdesign.htm.
7. Click Save All in the File menu.
8. Close all open Web pages.

Using Format Painter

Format Painter allows developers to copy text formatting and apply it to text located elsewhere. Text formatting characteristics that are copied include fonts, font sizes, font styles (e.g., bold, italic, underline), and font colors. Format Painter has been a feature of Microsoft Office applications for several versions. To apply formatting from one text to another, place the insertion point anywhere in the text where you want to copy the formatting, click the Format Painter button on the Standard toolbar, and select the text to which you want the formatting to be applied. To apply formatting multiple times, double-click the Format Painter button before applying the paintbrush.

exercise 13

USING THE FORMAT PAINTER

1. Open the aboutus.htm Web page in Page view.
2. Scroll down to the *Establish Mission* bookmark.
3. Format the text to 14 points and Gray.
4. With the text still selected, double-click the Format Painter button on the Standard toolbar.
5. Select the remaining four headings *(Research and Development, Preliminary Design, Prototype,* and *Launch).*

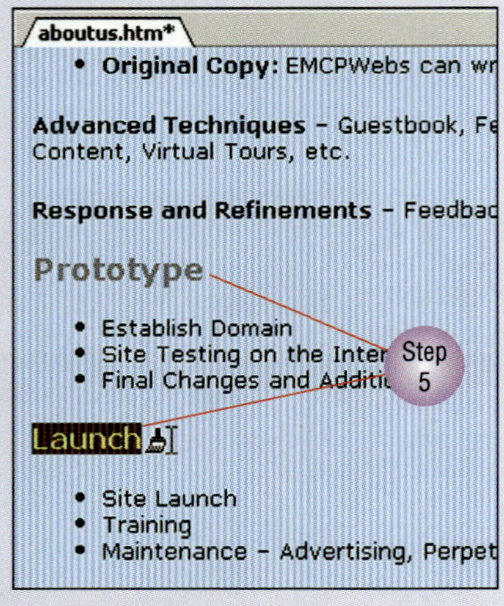

6. Click the Format Painter button to toggle the feature.
7. Save the updated aboutus.htm Web page.

Finding and Replacing Text

The Find and Replace feature is used to locate specific text and replace it with other text. One example of this feature would be substituting abbreviations for commonly used phrases during the initial text entry phase, and then later replacing the abbreviations with the full text. Another example would be changing references to an employee or customer whose name has changed because of marriage. To replace text, click Edit and select the Replace command.

exercise 14

FINDING AND REPLACING TEXT

1. Open the aboutus.htm Web page in Page view.
2. Click Edit and then click Replace.
3. At the Find and Replace dialog box, key **EMCPWebs** in the Find what text box.
4. Key **Our Company** in the Replace with text box.
5. Click the Replace All button.
6. Click the Close button in the upper right corner of the Find and Replace dialog box.

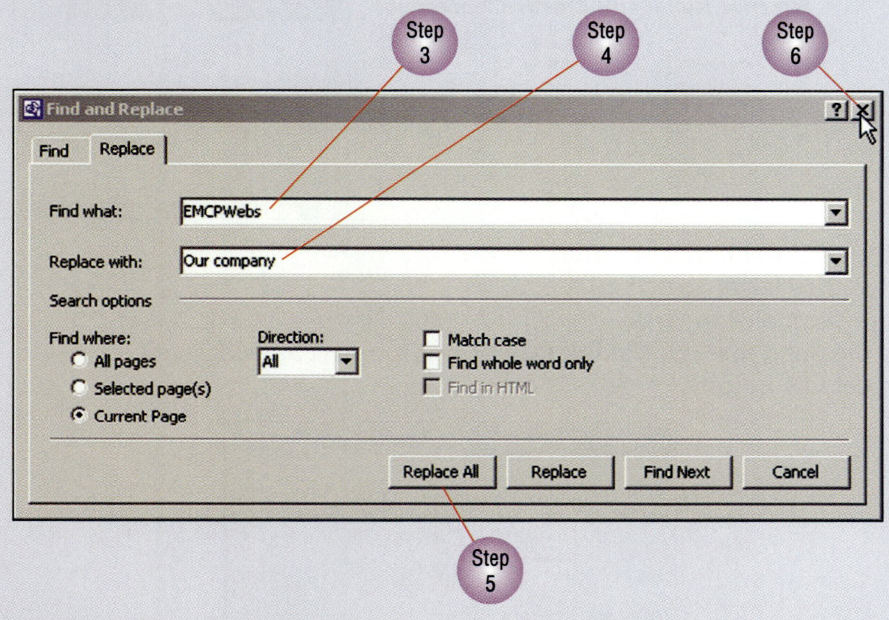

7. Scroll through the Web page and view the changes.
8. Click the Undo button on the Standard toolbar.

Working with Paragraphs

Many common paragraph formatting tasks have already been performed in previous chapters. This section will introduce you to horizontal rules, line spacing, numbering, and bullets.

Inserting Horizontal Rules

Horizontal rules, or lines, can be inserted to separate text or add an accent to your page. Horizontal rules can be inserted by clicking Insert and selecting the Horizontal Line command. A horizontal rule can be formatted by double-clicking the line in Page view and making adjustments in the Horizontal Line Properties dialog box. If you have applied a FrontPage theme to your Web, any inserted horizontal rule will adhere to the theme.

exercise 15

INSERTING HORIZONTAL RULES

1. Open the EMCPWebs home page in Page view.
2. Place the insertion point to the right of the link bar.
3. Click Insert and then click Horizontal Line.

4. Double-click the horizontal rule.
5. Change the Height to 1 Pixel.
6. Change the Color to Gray.
7. Click the Solid line (no shading) check box to insert a check mark.
8. Click the OK button.

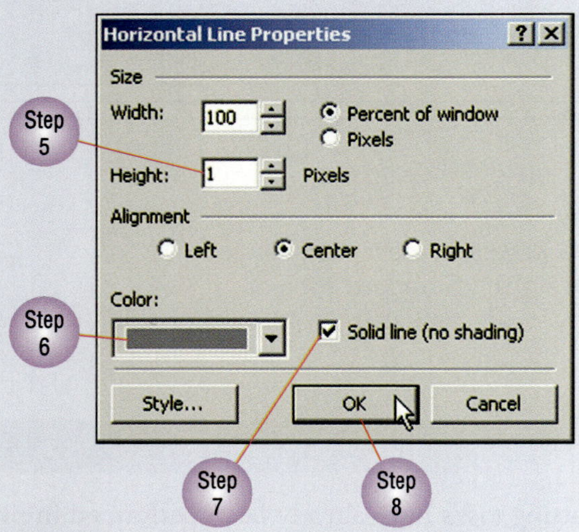

9. Right-click the horizontal line and select the Copy command.
10. Access each of the other EMCPWebs Web pages, place the insertion point to the right of the link bar, and press Ctrl + V to paste the horizontal rule into the remaining Web pages.
11. Click Save All on the File menu.

Formatting Line Spacing

Each new paragraph in a Web page has extra spacing between lines of text, giving the appearance of double spacing before and after paragraphs. To format paragraphs with a single-spaced appearance, access the Paragraph dialog box from the Format menu. In the Paragraph dialog box, change the Before and After Spacing to zero.

FORMATTING LINE SPACING

1. Open the EMCPWebs home page in Page view.
2. Scroll down the page and select the lines of text shown below.

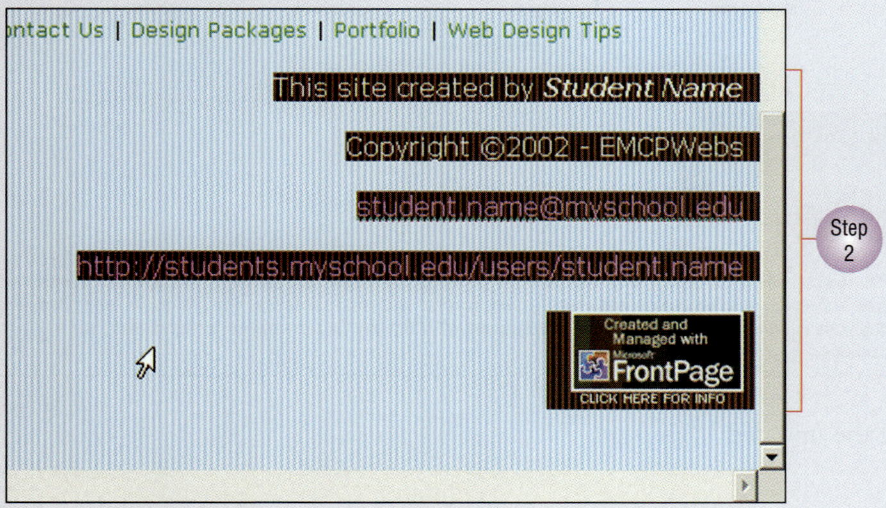

3. Click Format and then click Paragraph.
4. At the Paragraph dialog box, click the up-pointing triangle once in the Before text box of the Spacing section so that the number in the text box is *0*.
5. Click the up-pointing triangle once in the After text box of the Spacing section so that the number in the text box is *0*.
6. Click the OK button.
7. With the lines of text still highlighted, click the Copy button on the Standard toolbar.

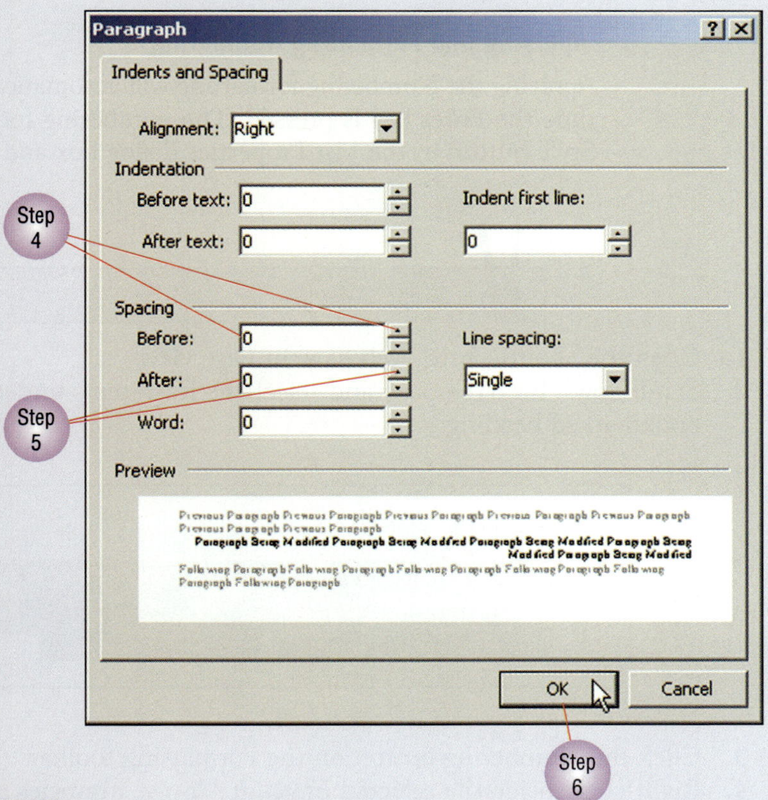

8. Save the updated home page.
9. Open the aboutus.htm Web page in Page view.
10. Select the same lines of text and press Ctrl + V.
11. Repeat step 10 to replace the lines of text on the remaining Web pages.

12. Return to the aboutus.htm Web page.
13. Select the five hyperlinks below the link bar.
14. Repeat steps 3–6 to remove the extra spacing between the lines.

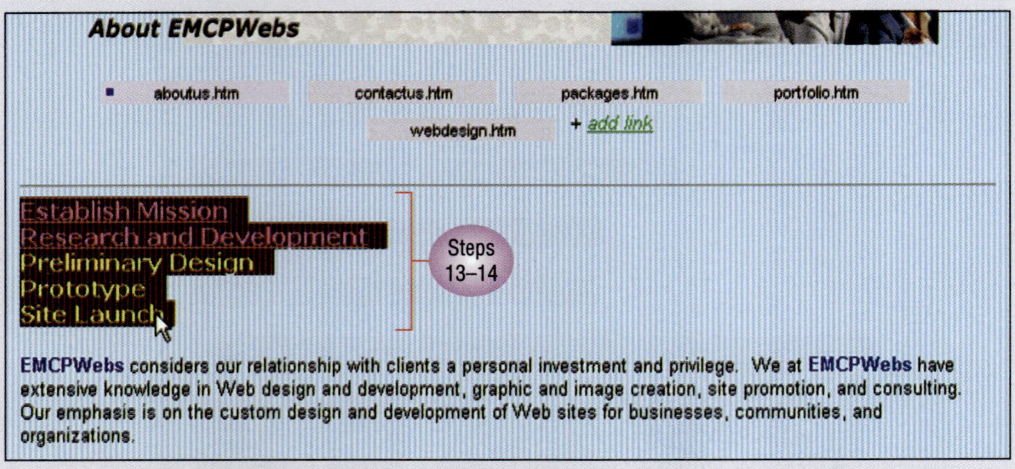

15. Save the updated Web page.

Applying and Formatting Numbering

Applying the Numbering formatting will automatically number an entry in a list each time the Enter key is pressed. The numbering font can be altered by clicking the Style button in the List Properties dialog box and then selecting Format and Font.

exercise 17 APPLYING AND FORMATTING NUMBERING

1. Open the aboutus.htm Web page in Page view.
2. Scroll down the Web page and select the four items under the *Establish Mission* bookmarked heading.

3. Click the Numbering button on the Formatting toolbar.
4. Right-click inside the selected *Establish Mission* strategies and click List Properties on the pop-up menu.
5. Click the Style button in the List Properties dialog box.
6. Click the Format button and select *Font* on the drop-down list.

7. At the Font dialog box, format the Numbering font to Verdana and 10 points.
8. Click the OK button in each dialog box to return to Page view.
9. Save the updated Web page.

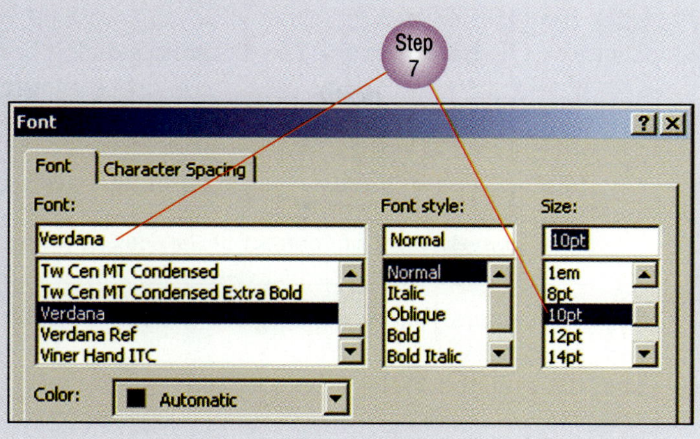

Applying and Formatting Bullets

Bulleted lists are set by default with a small black circle preceding the text. In addition, the line spacing is reduced to single-spaced and the bullets are automatically indented. Bullets can be changed to other symbols such as squares and empty circles. Images can be substituted for the plain bullets by accessing the Bullets and Numbering dialog box. Bullets can be applied using the Bullets button on the Formatting toolbar.

exercise 18

APPLYING BULLETS

1. Open the aboutus.htm Web page in Page view.
2. Scroll down the Web page and select the three items under the *Research and Development* bookmarked heading.
3. Click the Bullets button on the Standard toolbar.

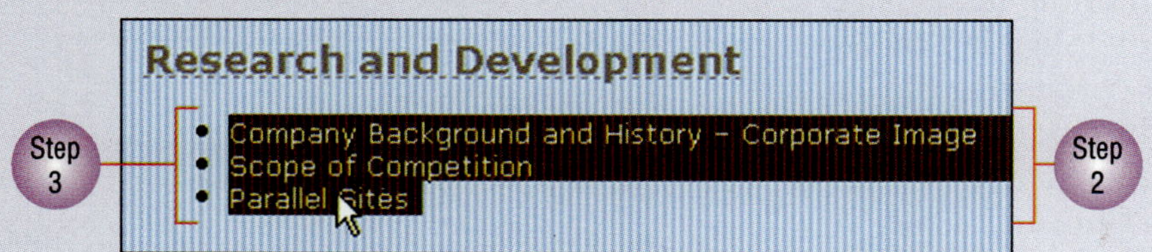

4. Save the updated Web page.

exercise 19

FORMATTING BULLETS

1. Open the aboutus.htm Web page in Page view.
2. Scroll down the Web page and select the four *Establish Mission* numbered items.
3. Right-click in the selected area and click the List Properties command.
4. At the List Properties dialog box, click the Picture Bullets tab.
5. Click the Browse button.
6. Select the square_bullet.gif image file in the *EMCPWebs Images* folder.

7. Click the Open button.
8. Click the OK button in the List Properties dialog box.

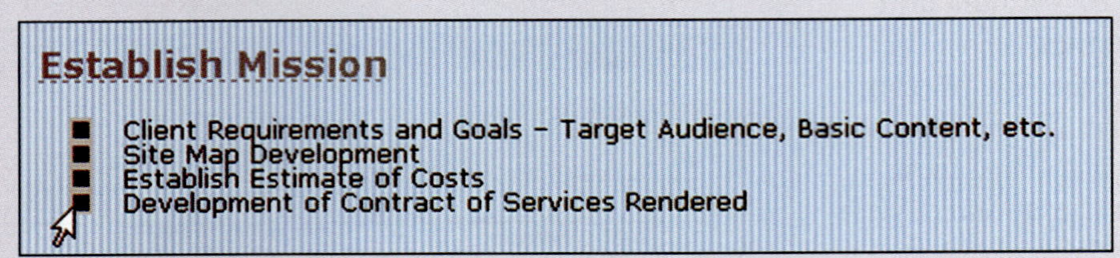

9. Apply the square_bullet.gif image to the rest of the bulleted items on the aboutus.htm Web page.
10. Save the updated Web page.

Inserting the Date and Time Web Component

The date and time Web component can be inserted into a page to let visitors know how recently the page contents have been created or edited. This is especially important for time-sensitive information. For example, individuals conducting research on a current topic need to know when the information was posted.

exercise 20

INSERTING THE DATE AND TIME WEB COMPONENT

1. Open the EMCPWebs home page in Page view.
2. Press Ctrl + End to position the insertion point at the bottom of the home page.
3. Click the Align left button on the Formatting toolbar.
4. Click Insert and then click Date and Time.
5. At the Date and Time dialog box, select the format shown at the right from the Date format drop-down list.
6. Click the OK button.
7. Select the inserted date and time Web component.
8. Format the text to Verdana, 12 points, bold.
9. Save the updated home page.
10. Perform a Preview in Browser and print the Web page.

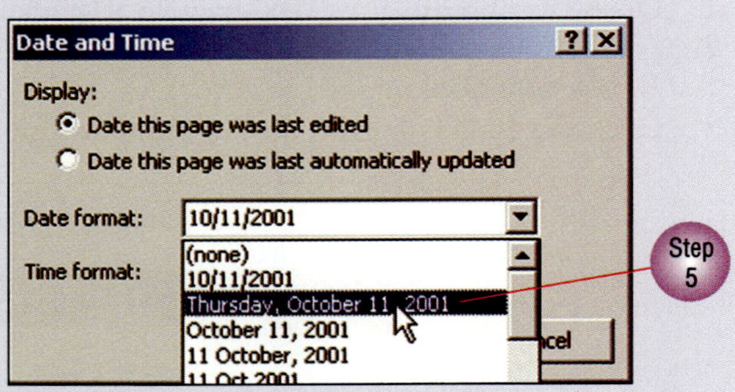

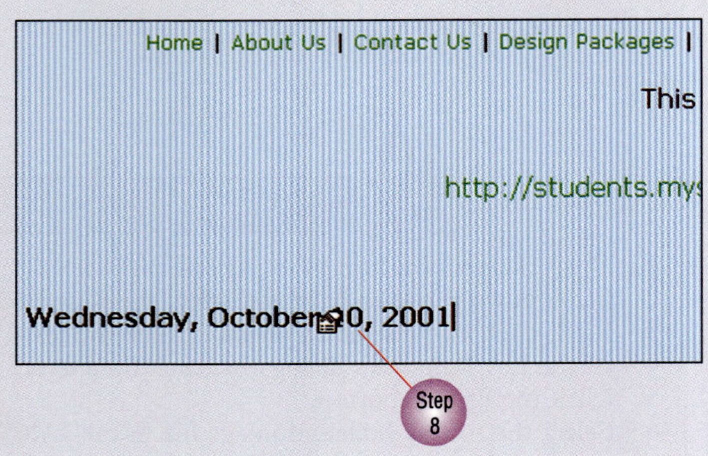

Copying and Pasting Images

Images such as logos, banners, and banner ads are often seen on multiple pages. A common practice is to insert an image on one page, copy the image, and paste it onto one or more pages on the Web site. The quickest way to copy an image is to right-click the image and select the Copy command.

The Microsoft Office Clipboard gives Microsoft Office users the capability of copying more than just one item onto the clipboard. Whether you copy a single character or an entire page, or one image or a selection of images, 24 items can be copied to the Office Clipboard. To copy items to the Office Clipboard, the Office Clipboard Task Pane must be open in any of the Microsoft Office applications. In addition to copying, items that are cut are also placed on the Office Clipboard. To paste an item from the Office Clipboard, just click the object. To delete an item from the Office Clipboard, click the down-pointing triangle on the thumbnail and select Delete.

exercise 21

COPYING AND PASTING IMAGES FROM THE WEB

1. Open the EMCPWebs home page in Page view.
2. Open your Web browser.
3. Access www.emcp.com.
4. Right-click the EMCParadigm logo image and then click Copy.

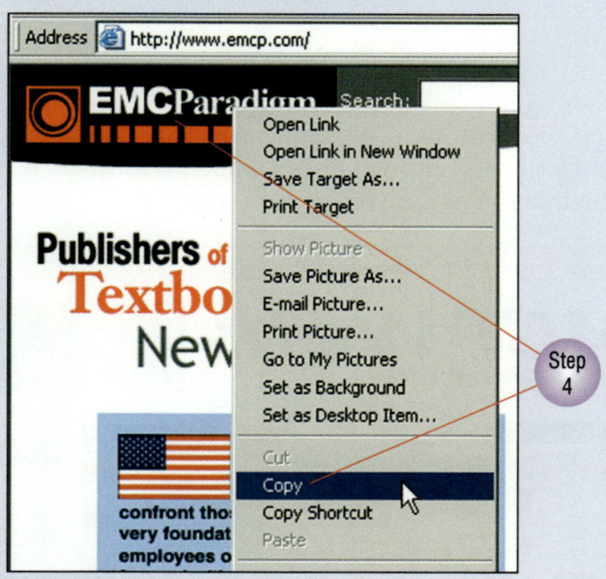

5. Return to the EMCPWebs home page.
6. Press Ctrl + End to place the insertion point at the end of the Web page.
7. Click the Align Left button on the Formatting toolbar.
8. Press Ctrl + V to paste the image.
9. Save the updated home page.

exercise 22

PASTING IMAGES FROM THE OFFICE CLIPBOARD

1. Open the portfolio.htm Web page in Page view.
2. Click Edit and then click Office Clipboard.
3. Right-click the ZDNet thumbnail image and then click Copy.
4. Select the next thumbnail image and press Ctrl + C on the keyboard.
5. Copy the remaining two thumbnail images.

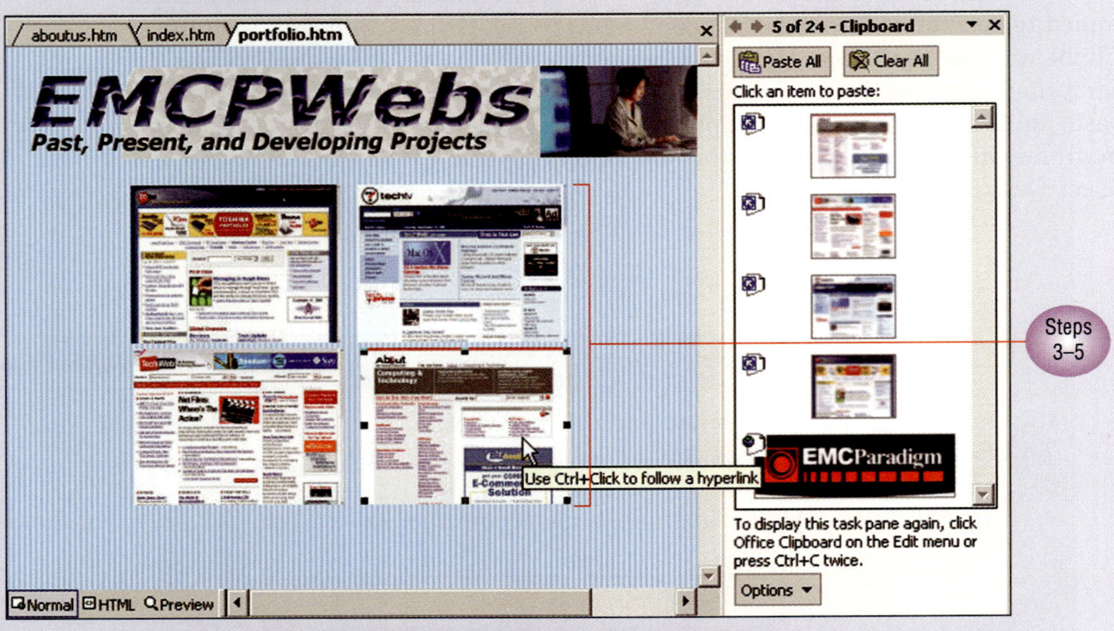

6. Open the webdesign.htm Web page in Page view.
7. Place the insertion point after the banner image and press Enter.
8. Click the TechNet image on the Office Clipboard to insert it in the Web page.
9. Insert the remaining Web page images in the page.

10. Close the Office Clipboard Task Pane.

exercise 23

REMOVING ITEMS FROM THE OFFICE CLIPBOARD

1. With the webdesign.htm Web page open in Page view, open the Office Clipboard Task Pane.
2. Click the down-pointing triangle that appears when you hover over each image on the Office Clipboard and then click Delete.

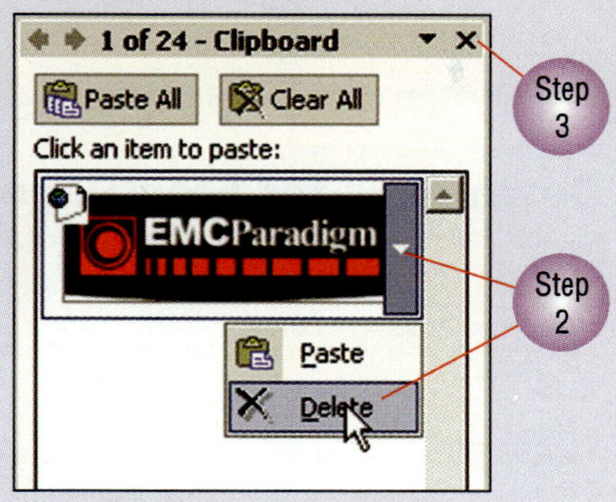

3. Close the Office Clipboard Task Pane.

exercise 24

PERFORMING MULTIPLE UNDOS

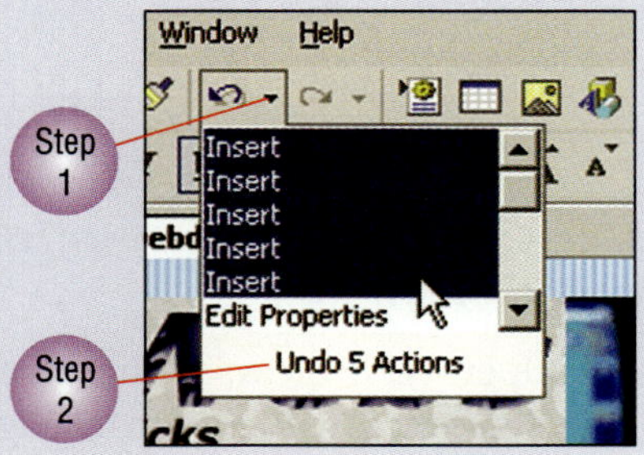

1. With the portfolio.htm Web page open, click the down-pointing triangle on the Undo button.
2. Move your mouse pointer down the drop-down list and then select the bottommost Insert option to undo your actions in the preceding exercises.
3. Close the portfolio.htm and webdesign.htm Web pages without saving any changes.
4. Close FrontPage.

Additional FrontPage 2002 Enhancement Resources

With new developments, add-ins, plug-ins, and product updates becoming available periodically, FrontPage Web developers need to keep abreast of current resources. Microsoft has several links on its Downloads for FrontPage Users Web site (see figure 5.2). The FrontPage Download Center includes security updates, HTML Tools, third-party add-ins, and more. The FrontPage Server Extensions can be downloaded from here. The FrontPage Add-in Center allows FrontPage developers to download add-ins created by third-party companies and developers as well as to submit custom plug-ins.

FIGURE

5.2 Downloads for FrontPage Users

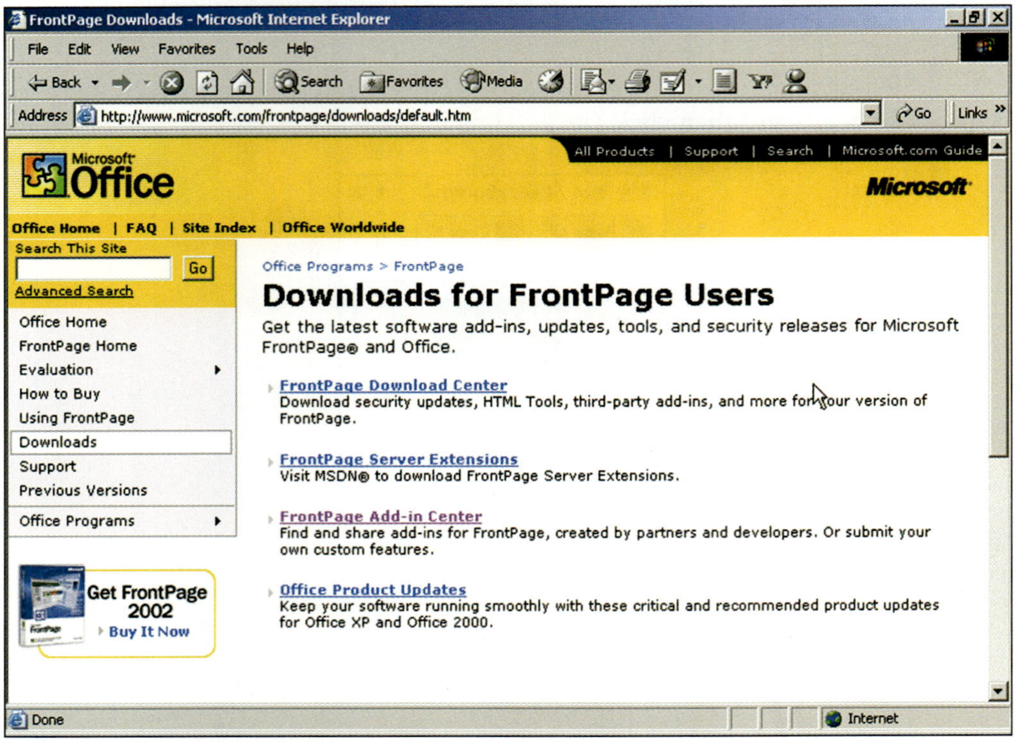

exercise 25 SUBSCRIBING TO THE MICROSOFT PRONTPAGE BULLETIN

(Note: Check with your instructor before performing this exercise. Your school may not want you to execute these activities.)

1. Open your browser and access the official Microsoft FrontPage home page at www.microsoft.com/frontpage.
2. Scroll to the bottom of the Web page and click the <u>*Get the latest news and tips – sign up for the* FrontPage Bulletin</u> link.

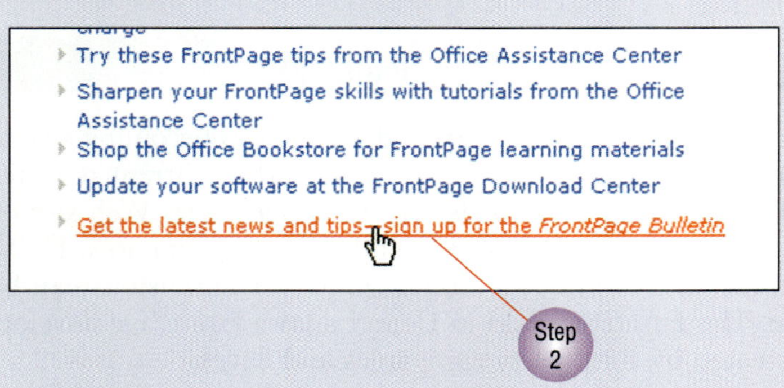

3. Read through the subscription information and click the Register button at the bottom of the Subscribe to E-mail News About Office Web page.
4. If you already have a Microsoft Passport, click the *Sign In* link; otherwise, click the *Get a Passport* link. *(Note: Steps 5–8 show the process for creating a Microsoft Passport Account and then signing up for the newsletter.)*

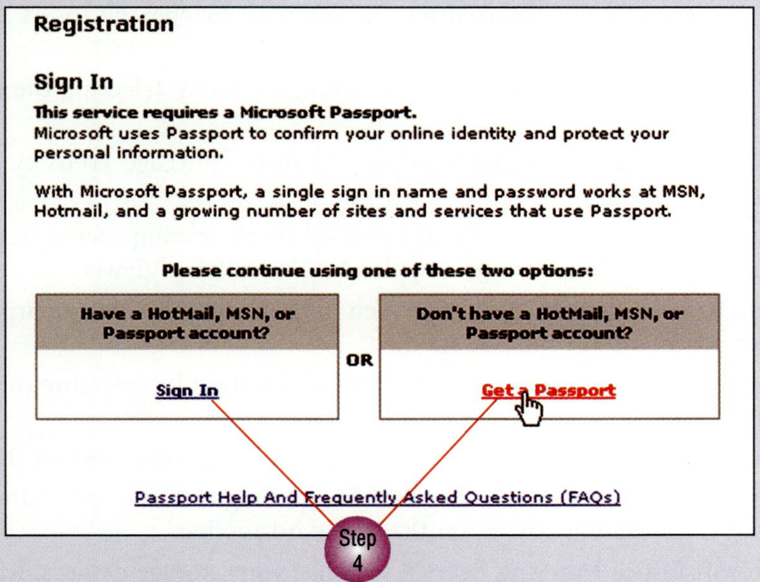

5. Key your registration information in the Registration form and then click the Submit button.
6. Continue through the registration process as directed.
7. At the Choose Your Newsletters Web page, click inside the Microsoft FrontPage Bulletin check box to insert a check mark.
8. Click the Update button. *(Note: The* FrontPage Bulletin *will arrive in your e-mail Inbox each month.)*

CHAPTER summary

- Files from such applications as Microsoft Word, Excel, and PowerPoint as well as other HTML documents can be inserted into a Web page by clicking Insert and then selecting the File command.
- Files can be imported into the current FrontPage Web by selecting the Import command on the Insert menu.
- PowerPoint presentations can be incorporated into FrontPage Webs by hyperlinking to the .ppt or .htm file.
- Visitors who do not have PowerPoint installed on their computer system can be directed to Microsoft Office's Web site to download a PowerPoint Viewer.
- A Web can be imported into an open Web for backup and testing purposes by selecting the Import command on the File menu
- A Web page can be exported to another storage location by selecting the Export command on the File menu.
- Web pages can be sent by e-mail by selecting the Send command on the File menu.
- An entire FrontPage Web can be checked for spelling errors by accessing the Folders view and clicking the Spelling button on the Standard toolbar.
- The Microsoft Office Indexing Service searches your storage devices, Microsoft Outlook folders, and My Network Places while your system is idle to make searches much quicker.
- Text, images, and other objects can be copied by selecting the item and clicking the Copy button on the Standard toolbar; pressing Ctrl + C on the keyboard; right-clicking the item and selecting Copy; or selecting the Copy command on the Edit menu.
- Text, images, and other objects can be pasted into a Web page by clicking the Paste button on the Standard toolbar; pressing Ctrl + V on the keyboard; right-clicking the location to be pasted and selecting the Paste command; or selecting the Paste command on the Edit menu.
- The Format Painter feature allows developers to copy text formatting and apply the formatting to text located elsewhere.
- To apply the Format Painter feature to multiple text locations, first double-click the Format Painter button on the Standard toolbar.
- The Find and Replace feature, located on the Edit menu, can be used to find specific text within a Web page and to replace that text with other text.
- Horizontal rules can be inserted from the Insert menu to separate text or add accent to a Web page.
- Extra space between paragraphs can be removed by accessing the Paragraph dialog box from the Format menu and keying *0* in the Before and After text boxes in the Spacing section.
- Numbers and bullets can be applied to paragraph text by clicking the Numbering or Bullets buttons on the Formatting toolbar.
- Bullets and numbering can be formatted by selecting the text and then accessing the Bullets and Numbering dialog box from the Format menu.
- The date and time Web component can be inserted from the Insert menu to let visitors know how recently the page contents have been created or edited.

- The Microsoft Office Clipboard gives Microsoft Office users the capability of copying up to 24 items for pasting at a different location or a later time.
- To insert copied text or other items, click the thumbnail box in the Office Clipboard Task Pane.
- Items can be removed from the Office Clipboard by clicking the down-pointing triangle on the clipboard object and selecting the Delete command.

COMMANDS review

Command	Mouse/Keyboard
Insert an existing file into a Web page	Click Insert, File
Import a file into a FrontPage Web	Click File, Import, click Add File, select file, click Open button
Import a folder into a FrontPage Web	Click File, Import, click Add Folder, select file, click Open button
Import a Web	Click File, Import, click Import Web Wizard
Export a Web page	Click File, Export
Send Web page by e-mail	Click File, Send
Check the spelling of an entire document	Click Folders view, click Spelling button on Standard toolbar
Enable the Indexing Service	Click Search button on Standard toolbar, click *Search options* link, click Yes, enable Indexing Service and run when my computer is idle
Copy text or objects to the Office Clipboard	Select the text or object and: press Ctrl + C; click the Copy button on the Standard toolbar; right-click and select Copy; or select Copy from Edit menu
Paste text or objects onto a Web page	Press Ctrl + V; click the Paste button on the Standard toolbar; right-click and select Paste; or select Paste from Edit menu
Apply formatting using the Format Painter	Select text, click Format Painter button on Standard toolbar, click text on Web page
Find text on a Web page	Click Edit, Find
Replace text on a Web page	Click Edit, Replace
Insert a horizontal rule	Click Insert, Horizontal Line
Format line spacing	Click Format, Paragraph
Apply numbering to a list	Click Numbering button on Formatting toolbar
Apply bullets to a list	Click Bullets button on Formatting toolbar

Format bullets and numbering	Click Format, Bullets and Numbering
Insert the date and time Web component	Click Insert, Date and Time
Open the Office Clipboard Task Pane	Click Edit, Office Clipboard

CONCEPTS check

Completion: On a blank sheet of paper, indicate the correct term, command, or number for each item.

1. To place an existing file into a Web page, select the File command on this menu.
2. To import a Web, select this icon in the Web Site Templates dialog box.
3. Sending a Web page by e-mail can be accomplished by clicking the File menu and then this command.
4. Developers must be in any view except this view to check for spelling errors of an entire Web.
5. Enabling this will assist Microsoft Office users who use the Basic Search Task Pane by searching the hard drive and other locations while the computer system is idle.
6. Use this keyboard shortcut to copy text to the Clipboard.
7. This feature allows users to copy text formatting from one location and apply it to text in other locations.
8. To replace text, click this menu and select the Replace command.
9. These can be inserted onto Web pages to separate text or add an accent to a page.
10. Key this number in the Before and After text boxes of the Spacing section to remove extra spacing between paragraphs.
11. Bullets and numbering can be altered in this dialog box.
12. The date on which your Web page was last edited can automatically be updated by inserting this Web component.
13. The Office Clipboard Task Pane can be opened from this menu.
14. Multiple commands can be undone by performing this.
15. FrontPage Web developers can receive monthly tips, tricks, and news by subscribing to this newsletter.

SKILLS check

Assessment 1

1. Open FrontPage.
2. Insert the webpage.htm file from your *Chapter 5* folder in Page view.
3. Place the insertion point on a blank line under the last line of text.
4. Insert the webpage2.doc file from your *Chapter 5* folder in Page view.
5. Select the bulleted list of clothes and insert the spreadsheet.xls file in its place.
6. Save the page as clothingstore.htm in your *Chapter 5* folder.
7. Print the Web page.
8. Close FrontPage.

Assessment 2

1. Open FrontPage.
2. Create a new One Page FrontPage Web titled testpresentation.
3. Import the testpresentation.htm file and the *testpresentation_files* folder into the FrontPage Web.
4. Key the text **View Presentation** on the home page and create a link to the testpresentation.htm file.
5. Save the updated home page.
6. Perform a Preview in Browser and test the PowerPoint presentation.
7. Print the presentation.
8. Close your Web browser.
9. Close FrontPage.

Assessment 3

1. Open FrontPage.
2. Create a new Empty FrontPage Web titled assessimport.
3. Access the Web site www.coolhomepages.com.
4. Locate a Web site that has a design that you like.
5. Return to FrontPage and import the Web with a limit of 500KB.
6. Explore the Web pages in Page view.
7. Print the home page.
8. Explore the HTML code in the HTML view.
9. Close FrontPage.

Assessment 4

1. Open FrontPage.
2. Open the assessimport FrontPage Web created in assessment 3 in Folders view.
3. Run the Spelling feature and check the spelling of the imported Web.
4. Save any changes to the updated pages.
5. Close FrontPage.

Assessment 5

1. Open FrontPage.
2. Open the assessment05.htm file from your *Chapter 5* folder in Page view.
3. Select the entire page.
4. Format the Web page content to *0* spacing before and after paragraphs.
5. Save the updated Web page.
6. Print the Web page.
7. Close FrontPage.

Assessment 6

1. Open FrontPage.
2. Open the assessment06.htm file from your *Chapter 5* folder in Page view.
3. Use the Format Painter to copy the formatting from the first paragraph heading and text to the three paragraphs below it.
4. Save the updated Web page.
5. Print the Web page.
6. Close FrontPage.

Assessment 7

1. Open FrontPage.
2. Open the assessment07.htm file from your *Chapter 5* folder in Page view.
3. Locate all text with the name *fox* and replace with *cat*.
4. Save the updated home page.
5. Print the Web page.
6. Close FrontPage.

Assessment 8

1. Open FrontPage.
2. Open the assessment08.htm file from your *Chapter 5* folder in Page view.
3. Apply bullets to each of the lines beginning with *The quick brown fox*.
4. Apply and format numbering in Arial, 10 points, and Red to the first bulleted list.
5. Apply the fox_bullet.gif image to the bulleted lines of text.
6. Save the updated Web page.
7. Print the Web page.
8. Close FrontPage.

Assessment 9

1. Open FrontPage.
2. Open the assessment08.htm file from your *Chapter 5* folder in Page view.
3. Open the Office Clipboard Task Pane.
4. Copy the two images to the Clipboard.
5. Copy the paragraph text to the Clipboard.
6. Access www.nytimes.com and copy the headline image to the Clipboard.
7. Paste each of the items onto a new Web page.
8. Close the Web page without saving any changes.
9. Delete all items from the Office Clipboard Task Pane.
10. Close FrontPage.

Assessment 10

1. Access www.microsoft.com/frontpage.
2. Access the FrontPage Download Center by clicking the link in the Build Better Websites section at the bottom of the Web page.
3. Select the FrontPage 2002/XP version.
4. Select all three types of downloads and update the list.
5. Explore the various downloads for Microsoft FrontPage 2002/XP.
6. Close your Web browser.

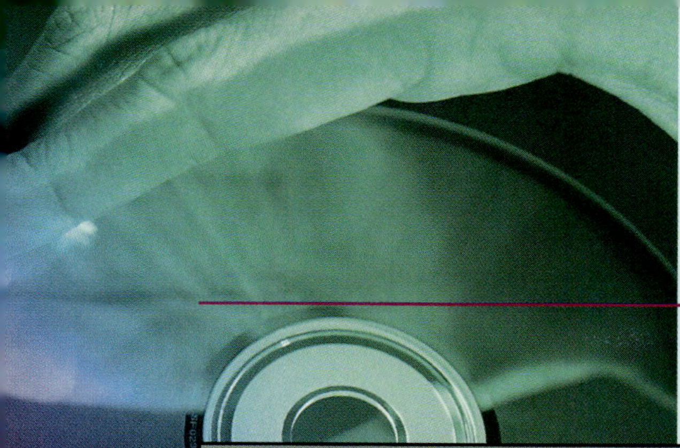

UNIT 1 PERFORMANCE ASSESSMENTS

Creating, Modifying, and Enhancing FrontPage Webs and Pages

ASSESSING Proficiency

Unit 1 IRC

In this unit, you have explored the basic concepts of Microsoft FrontPage 2002, including investigating FrontPage 2002 components; planning and creating an Initial FrontPage Web; working with graphics and photo galleries; creating and customizing hyperlinks; modifying and enhancing FrontPage Webs and pages; and working with tables, borders, themes, and publishing basics.

(Note: Before completing unit assessments, delete the Chapter 5 *folder on your disk. Next, download the Unit 1 data files from the Internet Resource Center to the* Unit 1 *folder you have created on your disk, and then make* Unit 1 *the active folder.)*

Assessment 1

1. On your preferred storage device, create a One Page Web titled cityrecweb.
2. In Folders view, title the home page *City Recreation Web*.
3. Create the following Web page files in Folders view:

File Name	***Title***
aboutus.htm	*About the City Recreation Center*
activities.htm	*Current City Rec Activities*
calendar.htm	*City Rec Calendar of Activities and Games*
athletics.htm	*Current City Rec Athletic Programs*
soccer.htm	*City Rec Soccer Leagues*
football.htm	*City Rec Football Leagues*
basketball.htm	*City Rec Basketball Leagues*
baseball.htm	*City Rec Baseball Leagues*
softball.htm	*City Rec Softball Leagues*
cancellations.htm	*City Rec Activity and Game Cancellations*

4. Organize the above Web page files into the following hierarchical structure in Navigation view:

First Tier	***Second Tier***	***Third Tier***
index.htm		
	aboutus.htm	
	activities.htm	
	calendar.htm	
	athletics.htm	
		soccer.htm
		football.htm
		basketball.htm

First Tier	Second Tier	Third Tier
		baseball.htm
		softball.htm
	cancellations.htm	

5. Print the Navigation view.

Assessment 2

1. Open the cityrecweb FrontPage Web.
2. Research the following information from your local city recreation center. *(Note: If your city does not have a recreation center, locate a recreation facility on the Web from which to obtain the information.)*
   - Mission statement
   - Center hours
   - Staff members
   - Contact information
3. Enter an appropriate page title for the home page in Page view.
4. Format the page title to Arial, 14 points, bold, and Purple.
5. Enter the *Mission Statement* heading in Arial, 12 points, and bold.
6. Key the mission statement below the heading and format the text to Arial, 10 points.
7. Enter and format the *Center Hours, Staff Members,* and *Contact Information* headings and text to match the mission statement.
8. Enter your first and last name at the bottom of the home page.
9. Save the updated home page.
10. Perform a Preview in Browser and print the Web page.

Assessment 3

1. Open the cityrecweb FrontPage Web.
2. Open the home page in Page view.
3. Center align the page title.
4. Indent each of the paragraphs of text below the *Mission Statement, Center Hours, Staff Members,* and *Contact Information* headings.
5. Apply bullets to each of the staff member names.
6. Format the entire Web page line spacing to 0 before and after each line of text.
7. Save the updated home page.
8. Perform a Preview in Browser and print the Web page.

Assessment 4

1. Create a One Page Web titled newssources.
2. Title the home page *My Favorite News Sources*.
3. Insert the newsbanner.gif file from your *Unit 1* folder in the first line in Page view.
4. Center align the image.
5. Use the Clips Online tool to locate, download, and insert the following *news* GIF animation clip one line below the banner.

6. Use the Clips Online tool to locate, download, and insert the following *newspaper (Photo)* clip one line below the newspaper GIF animation.

7. Resize the photographic image to 175 pixels wide.
8. Resample the image.
9. Crop the image so that the pole behind and to the right of the woman is no longer visible.
10. Save the updated home page.
11. Perform a Preview in Browser and print the Web page.

Assessment 5

1. Open the newssources FrontPage Web created in assessment 4.
2. Enter the following news category headings below the photographic image, aligned at the left margin: *National and Global; Weather; Business and Financial; Sports;* and *Computing.*
3. Search the Internet, ask your instructor and classmates, and use any other resource to locate at least three news Web sites that fit the above categories. *(Some examples would include CNN.com, The Weather Channel, Webfn.com, Fox Sports, and About.com: Computing & Technology.)*
4. Enter the official Web site names under the category headings in a font, size, style, and color of your choice.
5. Create hyperlinks to those Web sites.
6. Key your first and last name at the bottom of the Web page and create an e-mail hyperlink on it.
7. Insert the newsnavbar.gif image file from your *Unit 1* folder one line below the banner image.
8. Create rectangular hotspot hyperlinks to the Web sites listed on the image.

Web Site	***URL***
CNN Interactive	http://www.cnn.com
Weather Channel	http://www.weather.com
Webfn	http://www.webfn.com
Fox Sports	http://www.foxsports.com
About.com: Computing	http://www.about.com/compute/

9. Format all hyperlinks to open in a new browser window when clicked.
10. Save the updated home page.
11. Perform a Preview in Browser and test each of the hyperlinks.
12. Print the newssources home page.

Assessment 6

1. Create a One Page Web titled photogallery.
2. Obtain photographs of yourself, family, vacation, or other event in order to create a photo gallery. *(Note: Film prints will have to be scanned and saved. Ask your instructor for instructions on using scanners and/or digital camera photographs. Most scanners and digital cameras optimize images for best quality; therefore, the image and file size may both be quite large. Optimizing your photographs to fit in*

a browser window and compressing the files to download faster can be accomplished with specialized image editing software. While image optimization is not directly related to FrontPage, it is directly related to effective Web publishing. Refer to your instructor for further instructions.)

3. Insert a Photo Gallery Web component using one of the four gallery layout options.
4. Add a minimum of ten images to your photo gallery.
5. Add appropriate captions and descriptions to the images.
6. Save the updated home page.
7. Perform a Preview in Browser and test each of the image thumbnails.
8. Print the photo gallery home page.

Assessment 7

1. In a blank Web page in Page view, insert a 3-column × 5-row table.
2. Key the following cell references in the table cells:

A1	B1	C1
A2	B2	C2
A3	B3	C3
A4	B4	C4
A5	B5	C5

3. Insert a new row between rows 3 and 4.
4. Insert a new column between columns B and C.
5. Distribute all table columns evenly.
6. Merge the four cells A1 through C1 and delete the letters and numbers.
7. Split cell C2 into three columns.
8. Set the Border size to 0 for the table properties.
9. Format a Navy, 2-point border on the bottom border of the first row in the table.
10. Format the background color for cells A2 through C5 to Gray.
11. Save the Web page onto your preferred storage device.
12. Perform a Preview in Browser and print.

Assessment 8

1. Open the photogallery Web created in assessment 6.
2. Apply the Blank FrontPage theme to all Web pages.
3. Insert a picture Page Banner with text of your choice at the top of the page.
4. Insert a Navigation Link Bar with custom links, also with the Blank theme.
5. Choose the horizontal orientation.
6. Add links to three of your favorite images.
7. You may wish to modify the links to display a description of the image on the button, as opposed to a file name.
8. Modify the banner text to Red.
9. Modify the body and all heading text to Verdana.
10. Save the updated Web page.
11. Perform a Preview in Browser and print.

WRITING Activities

Activity 1

Content is crucial in the publishing industry. Even with the most impressive graphics, visitors will not stay long if the content is not clear and meaningful. It is equally essential to avoid spelling and grammatical errors; proofread your work carefully.

Access the Web site http://webdesign.about.com/cs/content/and prepare a two-page summary of your findings regarding Web content, using a minimum of three articles linked to the site.

Activity 2

Prepare a three-paragraph report about why you took this course. Deliberately misspell at least two words, make at least two sentences grammatically incorrect, and replace at least two words with others that make absolutely no sense. With the guidance of your instructor, exchange your paper with another student. Proofread the other student's paper, correcting all spelling and grammatical errors.

INTERNET Project

Use a search engine of your choosing to look for information on firms that specialize in Web design and development. Locate companies of varying complexity and create a Web page with links to the Web sites.

Save the Web page as webdesignfirms.htm.

JOB Study

Creating a Knowledge Base FrontPage Web

As a Web designer at a major corporation, you realize that there are many techniques used to create Web pages. Whether the subject is the use of color or DHTML, you would like to create for reference a Web site archiving as many tips, tricks, and articles relating to Web design as you can. You must research the Web for articles relating to a variety of categories. The categorical Web pages will contain hyperlinks to the Web pages of the specific articles. You must create a home page that introduces the Knowledge Base Web and include appropriate textual formatting and images. Depending on your skill level, you may want to experiment with such image creation programs as Adobe PhotoShop or Macromedia Fireworks for your page banners and navigation buttons.

Your Knowledge Base Web should contain at least five major categories. One example category could be FrontPage Tips and Tricks. All Web pages must be consistent in layout design and formatting. Test your FrontPage Web for errors.

For those who have CD Rewritable (CD-RW) drives, you may want to move or copy your FrontPage Knowledge Base Web to a CD-RW disc. To make the home page open automatically when you insert the CD into the drive, you will need to create an autorun.inf file and place it on the CD-RW disc. To create the file, perform the following steps:

1. In Notepad, key the following text:

   [autorun]
   open=start index.htm

2. Save the document as autorun.inf on your CD-RW disc.

FRONTPAGE

UNIT 2: CUSTOMIZING FRONTPAGE WEBS AND PAGES AND WORKING WITH ADVANCED CONCEPTS

Working with Tables, Borders, Themes, and Publishing Basics

Customizing Tables and Publishing FrontPage Webs and Web Pages

Working with FrontPage Components, Plug-Ins, and Frames

Working with Languages, Scripts, and Styles

Working with Forms and Databases, and Managing and Analyzing FrontPage Webs

CHAPTER 6

WORKING WITH TABLES, BORDERS, THEMES, AND PUBLISHING BASICS

PERFORMANCE OBJECTIVES

Upon successful completion of chapter 6, you will be able to:

- **Create simple tables**
- **Insert or draw tables in a Web page**
- **Convert text to a table**
- **Insert and delete columns and rows**
- **Merge and split table cells**
- **Apply and format borders and shading**
- **Apply and modify FrontPage themes**
- **Insert page banners and navigation bars**
- **Apply shared borders**
- **Define and describe FrontPage server extensions**
- **Publish a FrontPage Web to a Web server with FrontPage server extensions**
- **Publish a FrontPage Web to a Web server without FrontPage server extensions**

Chapter 6 IRC

Traditionally, tables are a series of horizontal rows and vertical columns used for organizing text and numbers. The rectangular boxes in a table are called cells. Text, by default, is aligned at the left of a cell. Text and objects, by default, are aligned in the horizontal middle of a cell; however, they can be formatted to align at the top, middle, or bottom of a given cell. This flexibility can be helpful for positioning items specifically where you want them on the Web page. FrontPage gives Web developers the necessary tools to insert, delete, merge, and split columns and rows.

Even without the use of tables, FrontPage users can apply borders and shading to paragraphs. Borders can surround or be placed in any combination (e.g., above, below, left, or right) relative to the line or paragraph. Lines or paragraphs can be shaded with color or have a picture placed behind the text.

FrontPage themes are basically Web site templates that have preformatted design elements such as page banners, navigation buttons, bullets, fonts, background images, and other image and text elements. Themes can be applied to an entire Web or a single page; they can be altered by selecting the Theme command on the Format menu. Shared borders are areas at the top, bottom, left, and right of some or all of the pages in a Web site. Users can update the content on every page by updating it in only one place. This can ultimately save time that might be spent editing each page and also provides design consistency for the pages.

Publishing a Web basically involves copying each of the files on your FrontPage Web to a Web server. A Web server may be part of an intranet in which only company personnel can access the Web pages, or it may be connected to the World Wide Web. To publish a FrontPage Web to a Web server, click the Publish Web button on the Standard toolbar.

Creating Simple Tables

Simple tables are frequently used in Web pages to organize and present text and images in a structured setting (see figure 6.1). Tables can be inserted into a Web page using the Insert Table button on the Standard toolbar, through the Table menu, or by using the Draw Table feature on the Tables toolbar. Tables, by default, have a border pixel size of 1 and browser window width of 100 percent.

FIGURE 6.1 ***A Simple HTML Table***

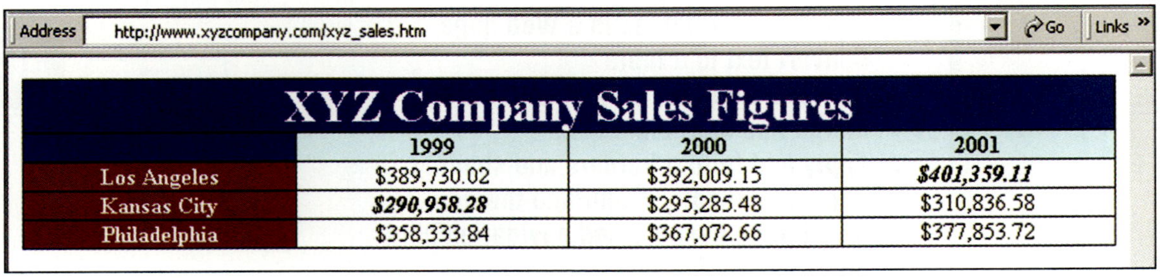

XYZ Company Sales Figures			
	1999	2000	2001
Los Angeles	$389,730.02	$392,009.15	***$401,359.11***
Kansas City	***$290,958.28***	$295,285.48	$310,836.58
Philadelphia	$358,333.84	$367,072.66	$377,853.72

Creating a Simple Table with the Insert Table Button

To insert a table using the Insert Table button, click Insert Table on the Standard toolbar and drag the mouse down and to the right until you have selected the necessary number of rows and columns.

(Note: Before completing computer exercises, delete the Unit 1 *folder on your disk. Next, download the Chapter 6 data files from the Internet Resource Center to the* Chapter 6 *folder you have created on your disk, and then make* Chapter 6 *the active folder.)*

exercise 1

CREATING A SIMPLE TABLE WITH THE INSERT TABLE BUTTON

1. Open FrontPage and the EMCPWebs FrontPage Web.
2. Open the webdesign.htm file in Page view.
3. Place the insertion point on a blank line below the links bar.
4. Click the Insert Table button on the Standard toolbar and then drag the mouse to the right and down until you have selected a 2 by 5 table (2 rows deep, 5 columns wide).
5. With the insertion point in the first cell, key the heading **FrontPage** and then press the Tab key to move to the next cell.

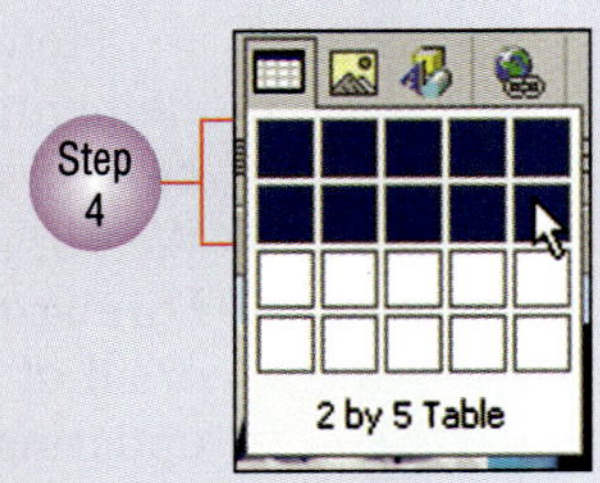

6. Key the following cell contents, pressing the Tab key after each to move to the next cell:

Cell	*Contents*
2	**Graphics**
3	**HTML**
4	**Multimedia**
5	**Web Design**

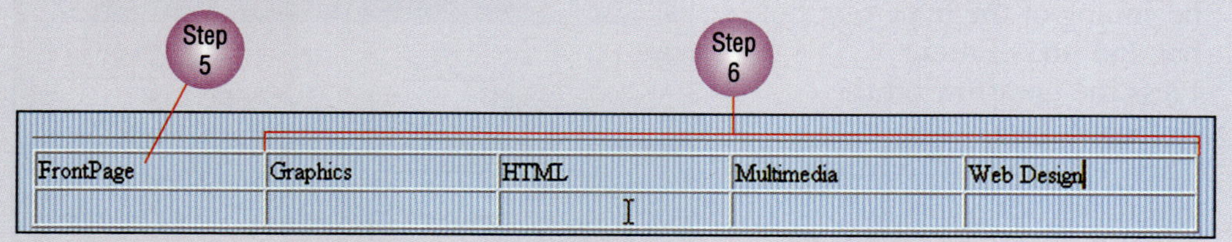

7. Select all cells in the table and format the font to Verdana, 10 points.
8. Select the *FrontPage* text heading in the first cell and click the Insert Hyperlink button on the Standard toolbar.
9. Create a hyperlink to the frontpage.htm file in the EMCPWebs FrontPage Web.
10. Create a hyperlink from the remaining first-row headings to the appropriate pages in the EMCPWebs FrontPage Web.
11. Key the following contents in the second row of cells and create a hyperlink to each one, formatting each to open in a new window:

    Official Microsoft FrontPage Web Site
    http://www.microsoft.com/frontpage
    About.com - Graphic Software
    http://graphicssoft.about.com
    Webmonkey - HTML Basics
    http://hotwired.lycos.com/webmonkey/authoring/html_basics/
    Webmonkey - Multimedia
    http://hotwired.lycos.com/webmonkey/multimedia/
    About.com - Design Tips and Guidelines
    http://webdesign.about.com/cs/designtips/

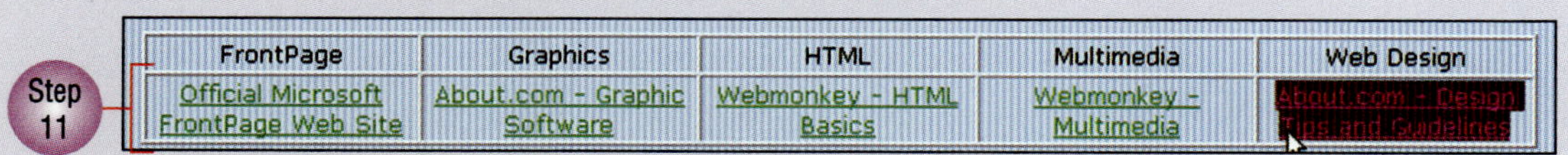

12. Press Ctrl + S to save the updated Web page.
13. Click the Preview in Browser button and print the Web page.
14. Test each of the Web Design Tips and Tricks links.

Creating a Simple Table at the Insert Table Dialog Box

The Insert Table dialog box can be accessed by clicking Table, pointing to Insert, and then clicking Table. Once in the Insert Table dialog box, developers can determine the number of rows and columns, format the layout, and modify the style of the new table.

exercise 2

CREATING A SIMPLE TABLE AT THE INSERT TABLE DIALOG BOX

1. Open the EMCPWebs home page (index.htm) in Page view.
2. Place the insertion point at the beginning of the hypertext link bar and press Enter.
3. Press the up arrow on the keyboard once.
4. Click Table, point to Insert, and then click Table.
5. At the Insert Table dialog box, key **3** Rows and **2** Columns in the Size section.
6. Click the OK button.
7. Select all cells in the table and click the Center alignment button.
8. Select the text link bar and drag it into the first cell.

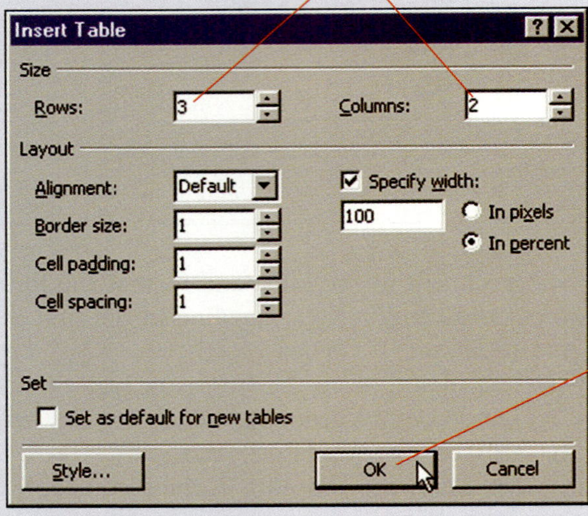

9. Drag the remaining text and Microsoft FrontPage logo image into the cells as shown in the illustration.

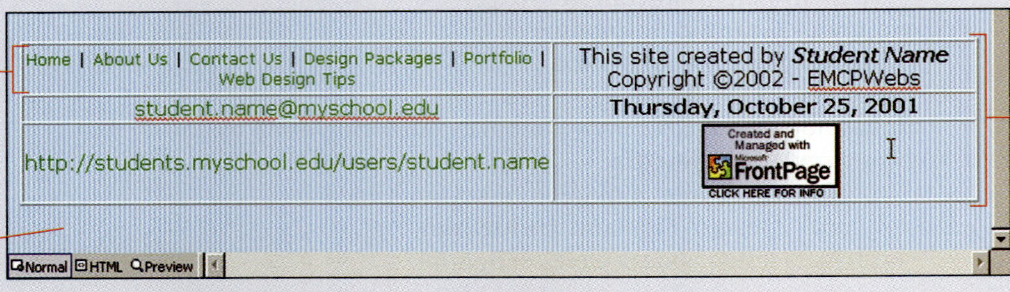

10. Delete any extra blank lines of text at the bottom of the Web page.
11. Save the updated Web page.
12. Perform a Preview in Browser and print the Web page.

Creating a Simple Table Using the Draw Table Feature

Using the Draw Table feature, quick and simple tables can easily be drawn into Web pages. Additional rows and columns can also be inserted into the tables, depending on your specific requirements. Because of the freehand nature of the Draw Table feature, it is recommended that the table content not depend on specific cell and table height and width requirements. The Draw Table feature is located on the Tables toolbar (figure 6.2), which can be accessed from the View menu.

FIGURE

6.2 ***Tables Toolbar***

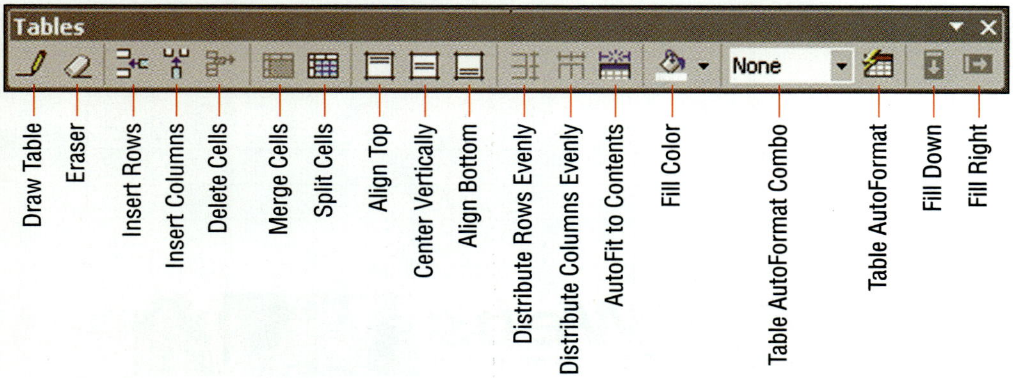

exercise 3

CREATING A SIMPLE TABLE USING THE DRAW TABLE FEATURE

1. Open the EMCPWebs home page (index.htm) in Page view.
2. Place the insertion point at the beginning of the Web page by pressing Ctrl + Home.
3. Press the Enter key and then the up arrow key.
4. Click View, point to Toolbars, and then click Tables.
5. Click the Draw Table button on the Tables toolbar.
6. Click and drag on the Web page to draw a simple one-row, single-column table.

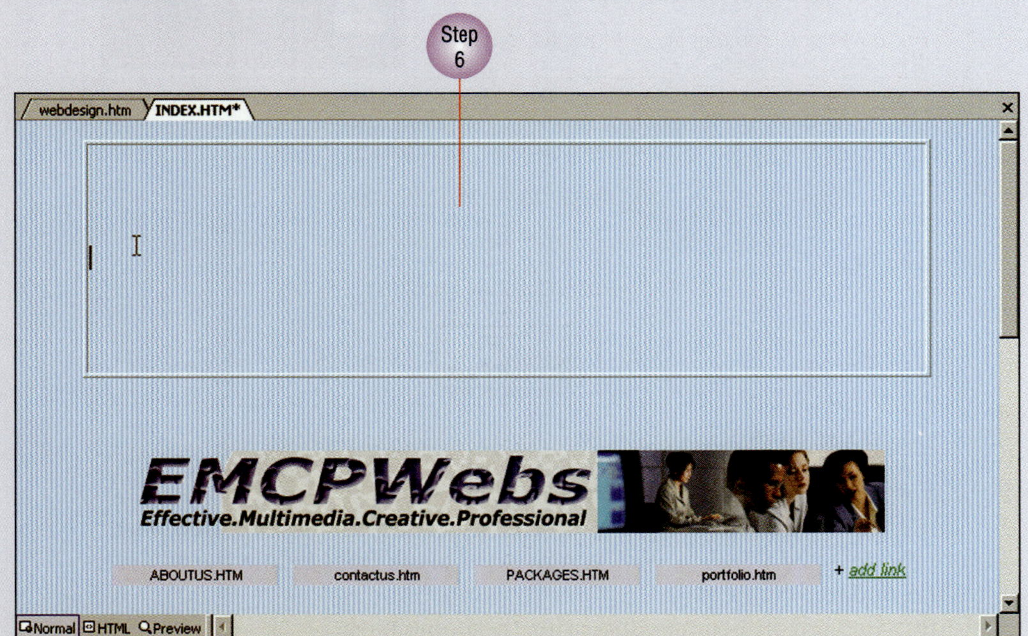

7. Click toward the left table border and drag to the right table border to create a second row for the table.

8. Draw in the remaining columns and rows as shown below.

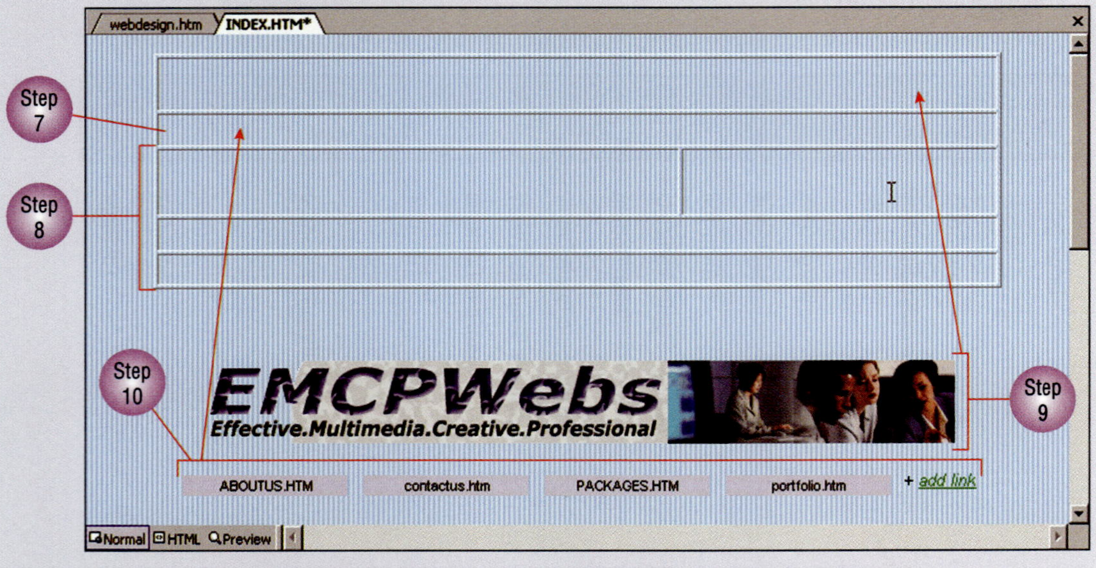

9. Click the banner image and drag it into the top row of the new table.
10. Select the link bar Web component and drag it into the second row.
11. Select the homecredentials.gif image and drag it into the right column of row three.
12. With the image still selected, click the Align Right button on the Formatting toolbar.
13. Select, drag, and align the remaining text and image as shown below.

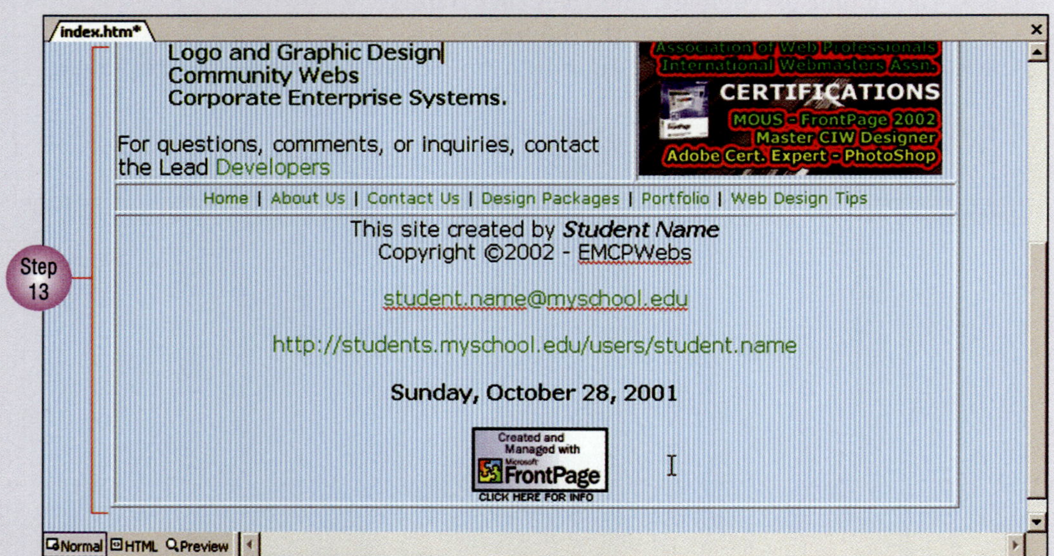

14. Format all text in the bottom row to 10 points.
15. Select the empty table and horizontal rule at the bottom of the Web page.
16. Delete the selected items as well as any extra blank lines below the table.
17. Save the updated home page.
18. Perform a Preview in Browser and print the home page.
19. Close the Web browser and FrontPage.

Converting Text to a Table

Text that is to be converted into table format must have character separators (e.g., paragraph marks, tabs, commas, or other characters) to differentiate between rows and columns. While not the most common method of table creation, there are times when this feature is very useful. School Web developers, for example, may receive a team roster created in Microsoft Word utilizing tabs to organize player information. Tabs do not work the same in HTML as they do in word processing programs. Developers can open the roster in Word, remove excess tab stops, insert the text into FrontPage, and then convert the text into a table format. Text can be converted into table format by clicking Table, pointing to Convert, and then clicking Text to Table. Figure 6.3 shows text before and after being converted to table format.

FIGURE 6.3 ***Converting Text to a Table (Before and After)***

-1999-2000-2001

Los Angeles-$389,730.02-$392,009.15-***$401,359.11***

Kansas City-*$290,958.28-*$295,285.48-$310,836.58

Philadelphia-$358,333.84-$367,072.66-$377,853.72

Original Text

	1999	**2000**	**2001**
Los Angeles	$389,730.02	$392,009.15	***$401,359.11***
Kansas City	***$290,958.28***	$295,285.48	$310,836.58
Philadelphia	$358,333.84	$367,072.66	$377,853.72

Converted to Table

exercise 4 CONVERTING TEXT TO A TABLE

1. Open FrontPage.
2. In a blank page in Page view, click Insert and then click File.
3. Open the team_roster.doc file in your *Chapter 6* folder.

4. Select each line of text.

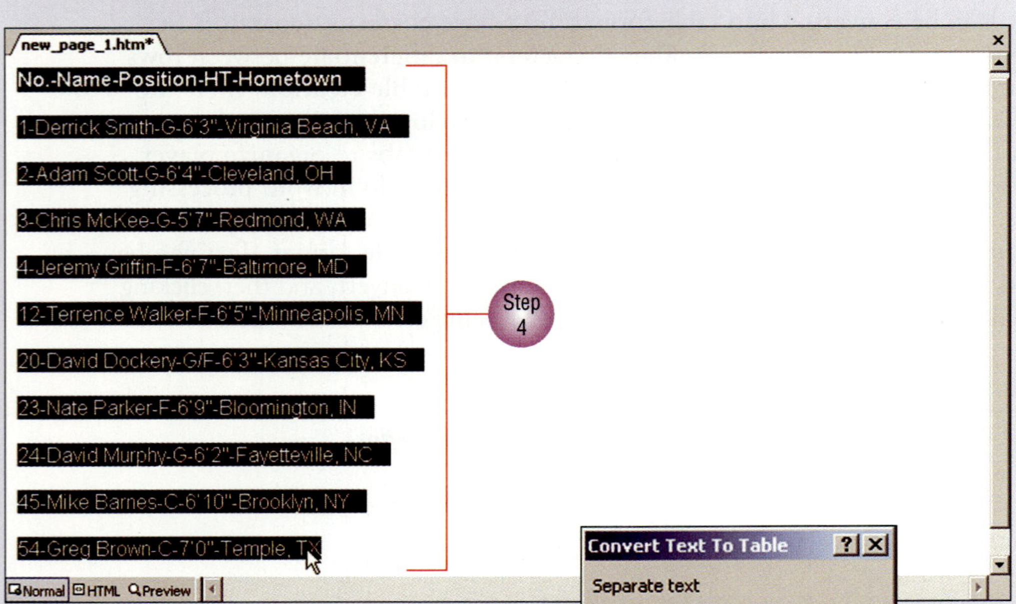

5. Click Table, point to Convert, and then click Text to Table.
6. At the Convert Text To Table dialog box, select the Other option and then key the minus sign (-) in the text box.
7. Click the OK button.
8. Click and drag the column borders to match the illustration below.

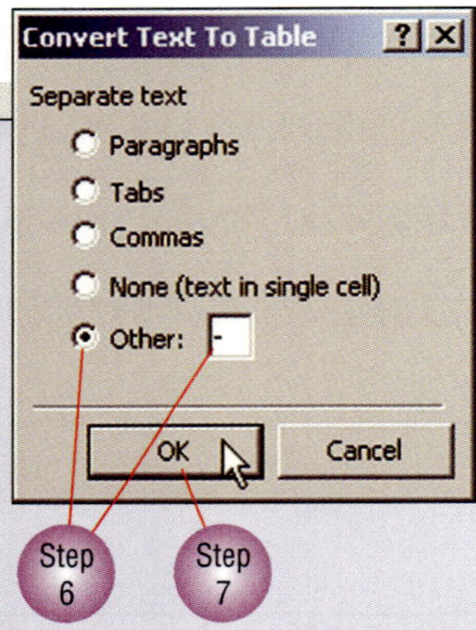

No	Name	Position	HT	Hometown
1	Derrick Smith	G	6'3"	Virginia Beach, VA
2	Adam Scott	G	6'4"	Cleveland, OH
4	Chris McKee	G	5'7"	Redmond, WA
8	Jeremy Griffin	F	6'5"	Baltimore, MD
12	Terrence Walker	F	6'5"	Minneapolis, MN
20	David Dockery	G/F	6'3"	Kansas City, KS
23	Nate Parker	F	6'9"	Bloomington, IN
24	David Murphy	G	6'2"	Fayetteville, NC
45	Mike Barnes	C	6'10"	Brooklyn, NY
54	Greg Brown	C	7'0"	Temple, TX

9. Print the Web page.
10. Close and save the Web page in your *Chapter* 6 folder as team_roster.htm, with the title *2002 Basketball Team Roster*.

Inserting and Deleting Columns and Rows

No matter how thoroughly you plan your tables, there are going to be times when rows and columns need to be added. If you own a company and have a Web page of clients or products, you will probably want to add to that as often as possible. Rows and columns can easily be added or deleted through the Table menu or by right-clicking inside the table and selecting the option from the shortcut menu. Rows and columns can also be added using the buttons on the Tables toolbar. To delete a column or row using the Tables toolbar, select each cell in the row or column and click the Delete Cells button. A quick method of inserting a row at the bottom of a table is to press the Tab key.

exercise 5 — INSERTING ROWS

1. Open the team_roster.htm file.
2. Place the insertion point after the text in the rightmost column of the bottom row of the table.
3. Press the Tab key.
4. Open the Tables toolbar, if it is not already open.
5. Place the insertion point anywhere in the *Chris McKee* row.
6. Click the Insert Rows button on the Tables toolbar. (A new row will be inserted above the *Chris McKee* row.)
7. Key the player information for Bobby Berry in the new row.

Step 7

2	Adam Scott	G	6'4"	Cleveland, OH
3	Bobby Berry	G/F	6'5"	Washington, DC
4	Chris McKee	G	5'7"	Redmond, WA

8. Right-click anywhere in the *Terrence Walker* row.
9. Click the Insert Rows command.
10. Place the insertion point anywhere in the *David Murphy* row.
11. Click Table, point to Insert, and then click Rows or Columns.
12. At the Insert Rows or Columns dialog box, key **2** in the Number of rows spinner box.
13. Select the Below selection option.
14. Click the OK button.

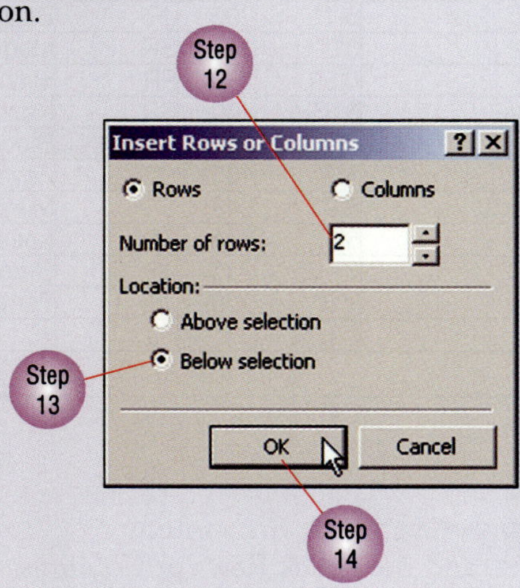

15. Enter the remaining player information into the new rows as shown below.

team_roster.htm*

No.	Name	Position	HT	Hometown
1	Derrick Smith	G	6'3"	Virginia Beach, VA
2	Adam Scott	G	6'4"	Cleveland, OH
3	Bobby Berry	G/F	6'5"	Washington, DC
4	Chris McKee	G	5'7"	Redmond, WA
8	Jeremy Griffin	F	6'7"	Baltimore, MD
10	Alvin Titus	G	6'0"	Modesto, CA
12	Terrence Walker	F	6'5"	Minneapolis, MN
20	David Dockery	G/F	6'3"	Kansas City, KS
23	Nate Parker	F	6'9"	Bloomington, IN
25	David Murphy	G	6'2"	Fayetteville, NC
26	Sasha Petryovski	F	6'9"	Minsk, Belarus
33	Kareem Murphy	F	6'8"	Los Angeles, CA
45	Mike Barnes	C	6'10"	Brooklyn, NY
54	Greg Brown	C	7'0"	Temple, TX

Step 15

16. Save the updated Web page.

exercise 6

INSERTING COLUMNS

1. Open the team_roster.htm file.
2. Place the insertion point anywhere in the last column.
3. Click the Insert Columns button on the Tables toolbar.
4. Right-click inside the newly inserted column and then click Insert Columns.
5. Key the *WT* and *Class* text into the columns as shown.

team_roster.htm*

No.	Name	Position	HT	WT	Class	Hometown
1	Derrick Smith	G	6'3"	178	JR	Virginia Beach, VA
2	Adam Scott	G	6'4"	189	SO	Cleveland, OH
3	Bobby Berry	G/F	6'5"	210	SR	Washington, DC
4	Chris McKee	G	5'7"	140	JR	Redmond, WA
8	Jeremy Griffin	F	6'7"	200	JR	Baltimore, MD
10	Alvin Titus	G	6'0"	177	SR	Modesto, CA
12	Terrence Walker	F	6'5"	190	FR	Minneapolis, MN
20	David Dockery	G/F	6'3"	200	SR	Kansas City, KS
23	Nate Parker	F	6'9"	230	SR	Bloomington, IN
25	David Murphy	G	6'2"	185	SO	Fayetteville, NC
26	Sasha Petryovski	F	6'9"	248	SO	Minsk, Belarus
33	Kareem Murphy	F	6'8"	225	FR	Los Angeles, CA
45	Mike Barnes	C	6'10"	235	JR	Brooklyn, NY
54	Greg Brown	C	7'0"	250	JR	Temple, TX

Step 6

Step 5

6. Place the insertion point anywhere in the first column.
7. Click Table, point to Insert, and then click Rows or Columns.

8. At the Insert Rows or Columns dialog box, select the Columns option.
9. Select Left of selection in the Location section.
10. Click the OK button.
11. Save the updated Web page.

exercise 7

DELETING ROWS

1. Open the team_roster.htm file.
2. Select each cell in the empty row at the bottom of the page.
3. Click the Delete Cells button on the Tables toolbar.
4. Click the Undo button on the Standard toolbar.
5. Select the row once again.
6. Right-click inside the selection and select the Delete Cells command.
7. Click the Undo button on the Standard toolbar.

exercise 8

DELETING COLUMNS

1. Open the team_roster.htm file.
2. Place your mouse pointer on the border of the top cell in the empty column and click.
3. Right-click anywhere inside the highlighted area and select Delete Cells.
4. Click the Undo button on the Standard toolbar.
5. Print the updated Web page.

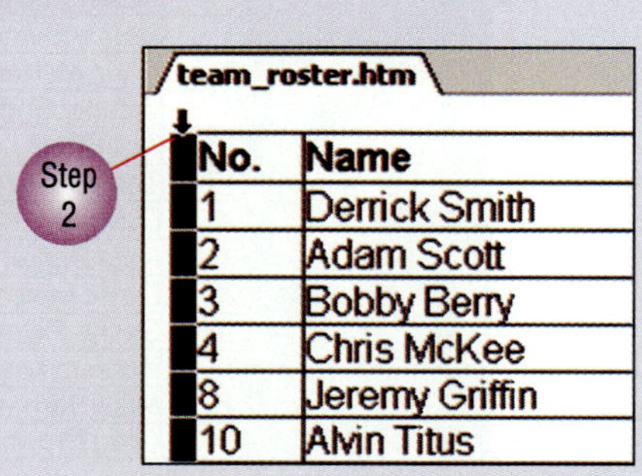

Merging and Splitting Table Cells

The addition of columns and rows may be appropriate for certain tables. Other table structures, however, are already designed to the appropriate dimensions. Merging cells is the combining of multiple cells to make one cell. Cells can be split into rows or columns. Merging and splitting cells gives designers the ability to add additional cells and delete unnecessary cells without disrupting the overall structure of the table.

exercise 9 — MERGING CELLS

1. Open the team_roster.htm file.
2. Select each of the cells in the bottom row.
3. Click the Merge Cells button on the Tables toolbar.

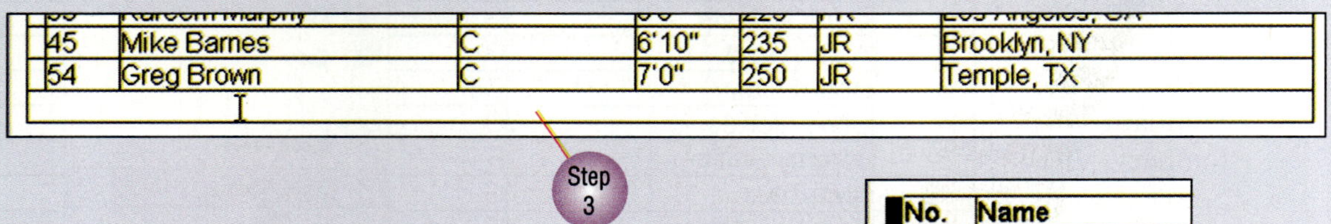

4. Select the cells in the first column.
5. Right-click anywhere inside the selection and then click Merge Cells.
6. Insert the basketball_side.jpg image from your *Chapter 6* folder into the merged column.
7. Resize the columns to match the illustration.
8. Save the updated Web page.

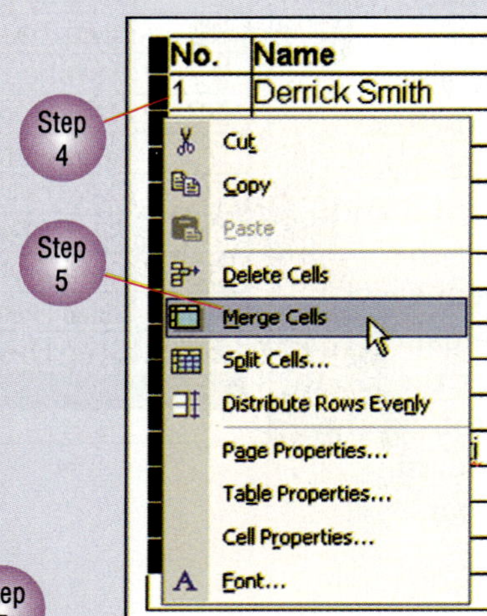

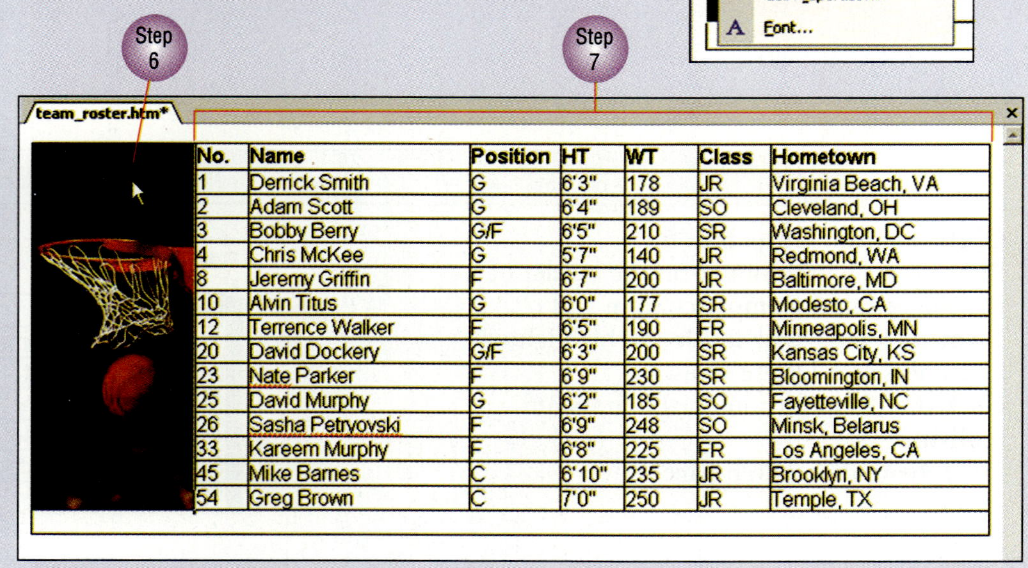

9. Print the Web page.

exercise 10

SPLITTING CELLS INTO COLUMNS

1. Open the team_roster.htm file.
2. Place the insertion point in the bottom row of the table.
3. Click the Split Cells button on the Tables toolbar.
4. At the Split Cells dialog box, ensure that the Split into columns option is selected and that the Number of columns is set to *2*. Click OK.
5. Key and format **Probable Starters in Bold** in the new left column, and **Head Coach - Jim Moore** in the new right column.
6. Apply bold to the coach's probable starters, as shown below.

7. Save the updated Web page.

exercise 11

SPLITTING CELLS INTO ROWS

1. Open the team_roster.htm file.
2. Right-click in the *Head Coach* cell and select Split Cells.

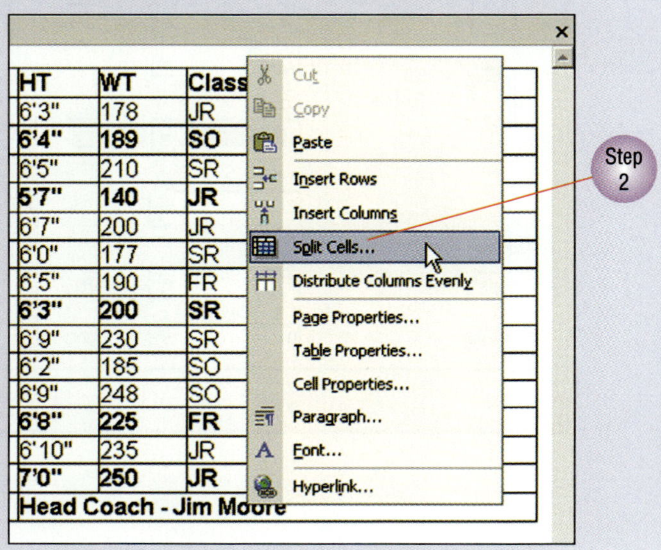

3. At the Split Cells dialog box, select Split into rows and set Number of rows to *2*. Click OK.
4. Remove the bold formatting.
5. Key **Assistant Coach - Mike Davis** in the new row.
6. Save the updated Web page.
7. Perform a Preview in Browser.
8. Print the Web page.

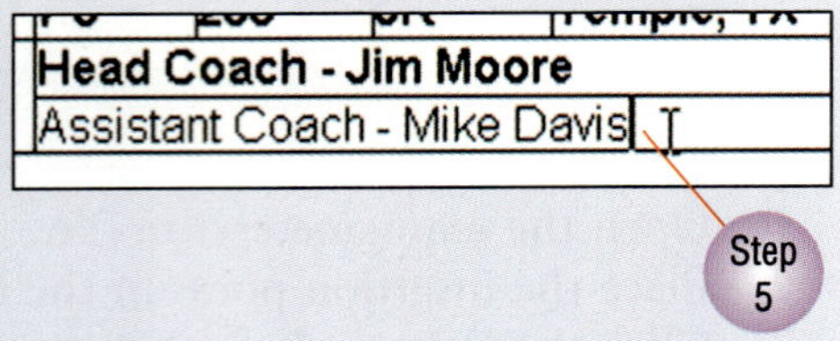

Applying and Formatting Borders and Shading

Borders and shading can be formatted for paragraph text to emphasize the content as well as to give paragraphs a tabled look. The ability to apply border and shading effects to paragraphs is common to word processing documents. Borders can surround or be placed in any combination (e.g., above, below, left, or right) relative to the line or paragraph. Various line styles are available and users can apply custom colors, widths, and padding to the lines. Shading effects can consist of pictures as well as colors. The Borders and Shading dialog box (figure 6.4) can be accessed from the Format menu.

FIGURE 6.4 ***Borders and Shading Dialog Box***

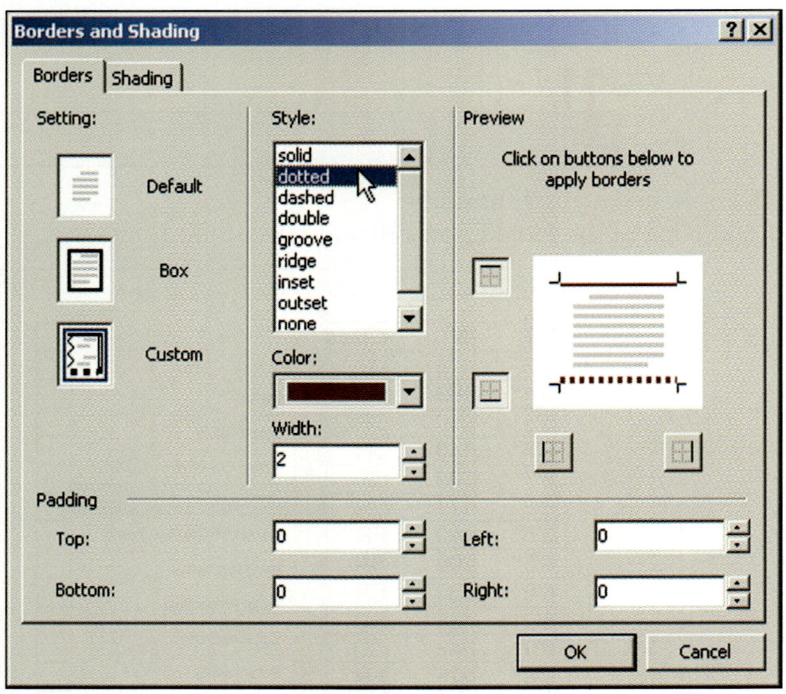

exercise 12

APPLYING BORDERS TO A PARAGRAPH

1. Open the employment.htm file from your *Chapter 6* folder.
2. Place the insertion point in the *EMCPWebs* Web page title.
3. Click the Outside Borders button on the Formatting toolbar.
4. Click the border sizing handle and drag it to match the illustration below.

5. Save the updated Web page.

exercise 13

FORMATTING BORDER STYLE, COLORS, AND WIDTH

1. Open the employment.htm file.
2. Place the insertion point anywhere in the bordered lines of text.
3. Click Format and then click Borders and Shading.
4. At the Borders and Shading dialog box with the Borders tab selected, click *solid* in the Style section.
5. In the Color section, select Teal.
6. Key **3** in the Width spin box.
7. In the Preview section, set a border at the top, left, and right.
8. In the Style section, click *double* for the border at the bottom.
9. Click the OK button.
10. Save the updated Web page.

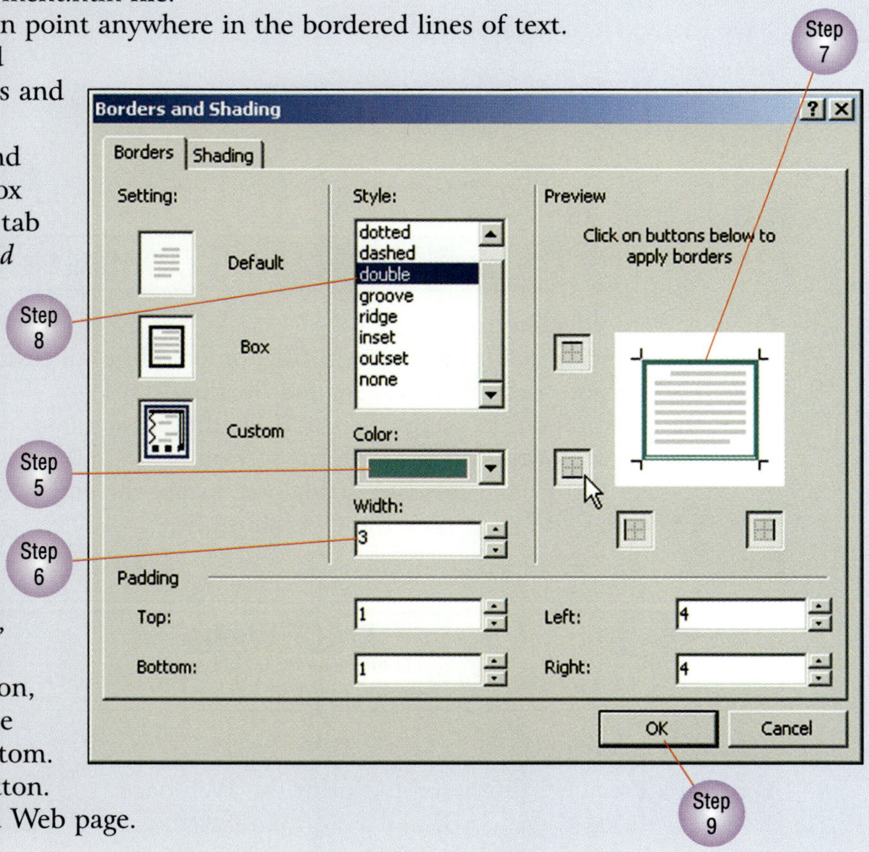

exercise 14

APPLYING BACKGROUND COLOR FILLS

1. Open the employment.htm file.
2. Place the insertion point anywhere in the bordered lines of text.
3. Click Format and then click Borders and Shading.
4. Click the Shading tab in the Borders and Shading dialog box.
5. Select Silver on the Background color drop-down menu.

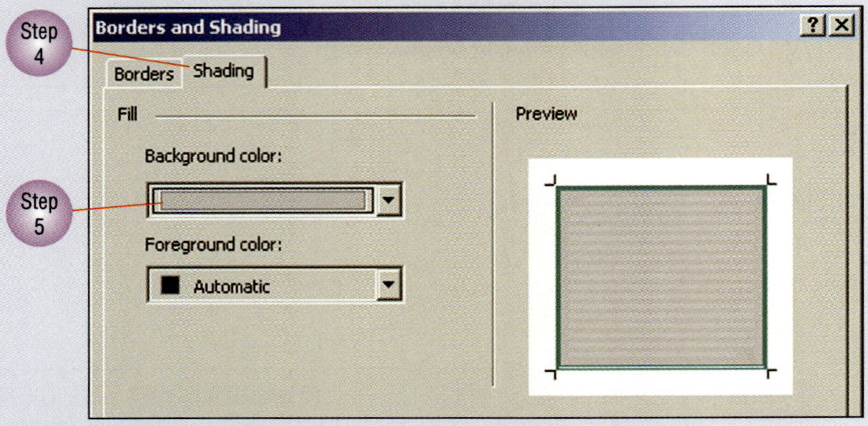

6. Click the OK button.
7. Save the updated Web page.

exercise 15

APPLYING AND FORMATTING BACKGROUND PICTURES

1. Open the employment.htm file.
2. Place the insertion point anywhere in the bordered lines of text.
3. Click Format and then click Borders and Shading.
4. Click the Shading tab in the Borders and Shading dialog box.
5. Click the Browse button in the Patterns section.
6. At the Select Picture Background dialog box, locate the emcpworkers.gif image in your *Chapter 6* folder and then click the Open button.
7. Click the OK button.

8. Save the updated Web page.
9. Perform a Preview in Browser and print the Web page.

Applying and Modifying FrontPage Themes and Shared Borders

FrontPage themes are collections of eye-catching design elements and color schemes that can be applied to Web pages. Applying a theme to your Web site or page is a quick and easy way to add interesting graphics, colors, and styles to a FrontPage Web, as shown in figure 6.5. Color effects that are associated with themes can be added to body text, headings, hyperlinks, page banner text, table borders, and page backgrounds. Theme graphic elements include page banners, navigation buttons, bullets, horizontal lines (rules), and even backgrounds. Theme style examples include fonts and font sizes. Themes can be applied to just one page or to all pages in a FrontPage Web. To format and test different themes for your FrontPage Web, click Format and then click Theme.

FIGURE 6.5 ***Sample Theme Applied to a FrontPage Web***

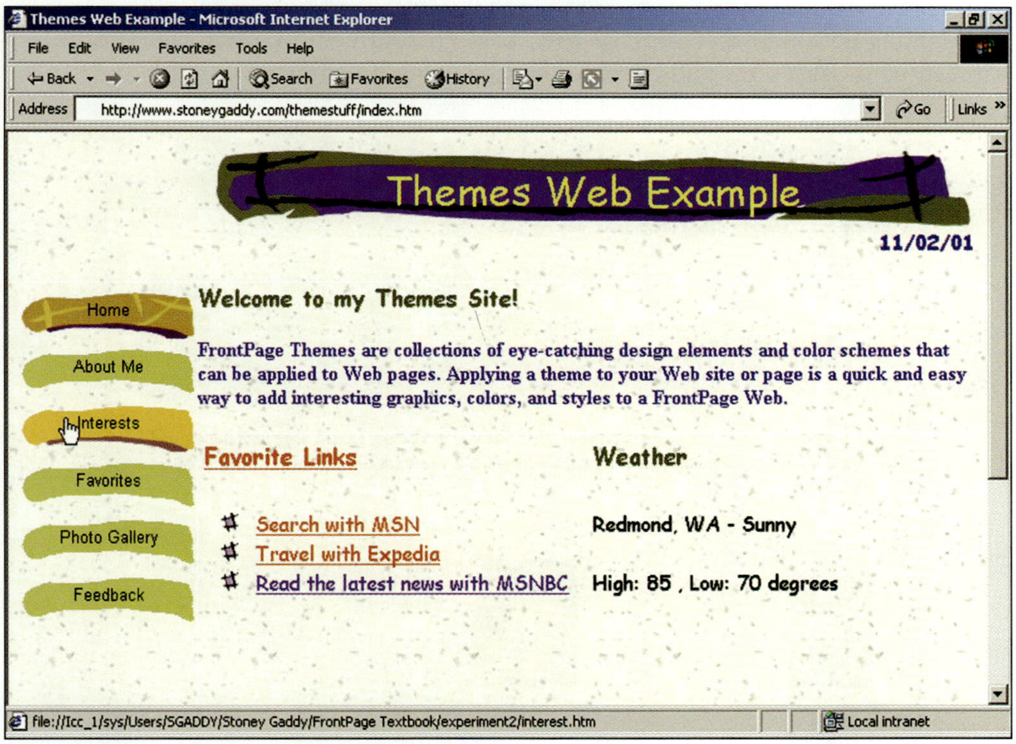

exercise 16 APPLYING A FRONTPAGE THEME TO A FRONTPAGE WEB

1. Copy the personalweb FrontPage Web from your *Chapter 6* folder onto your preferred storage medium.
2. Click File and then click Open Web.
3. At the Open Web dialog box, open the personalweb FrontPage Web from your storage medium.

4. Click the Folders view to verify that your personalweb FrontPage Web files match the illustration.

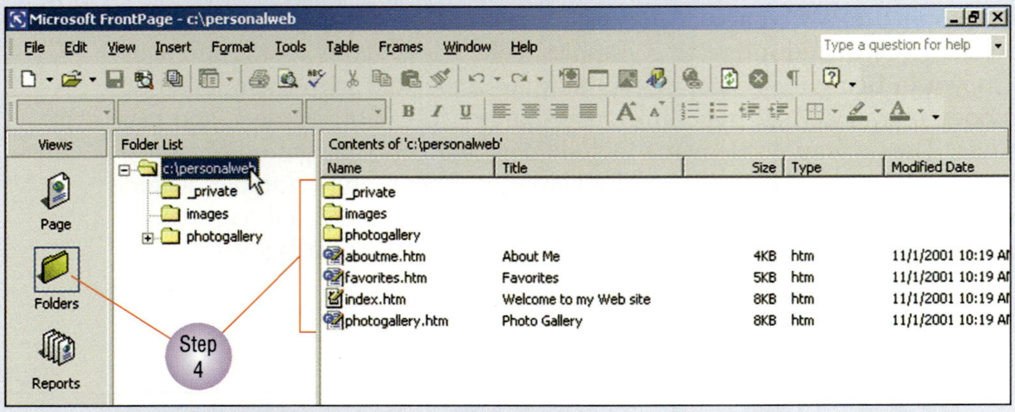

5. Open the personalweb (index.htm) home page in Page view and observe the appearance of the home page.
6. Open the remaining personalweb FrontPage Web pages (aboutme.htm, photogallery.htm, and favorites.htm) in Page view and observe their current appearance.

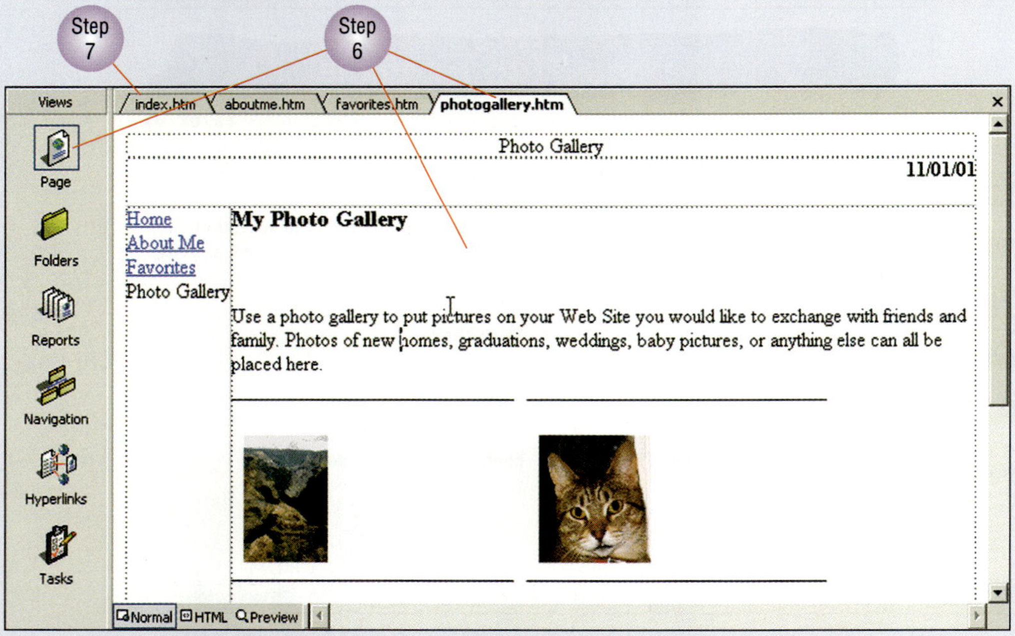

7. Return to the home page.
8. Click Format and then click Theme.

9. At the Themes dialog box, ensure that the All pages option is selected.
10. Click *Profile* in the theme list box.
11. Click the Vivid colors check box to insert a check mark.
12. Ensure that the Active graphics and Background picture check boxes are checked.
13. Click the OK button.
14. Read and click the Yes button on the Microsoft FrontPage Alert box.
15. Click each of the page tabs to view the updated look for the second-tier pages.

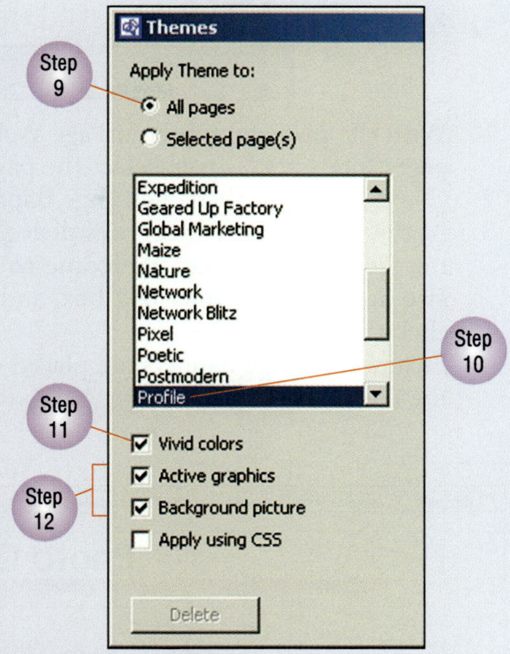

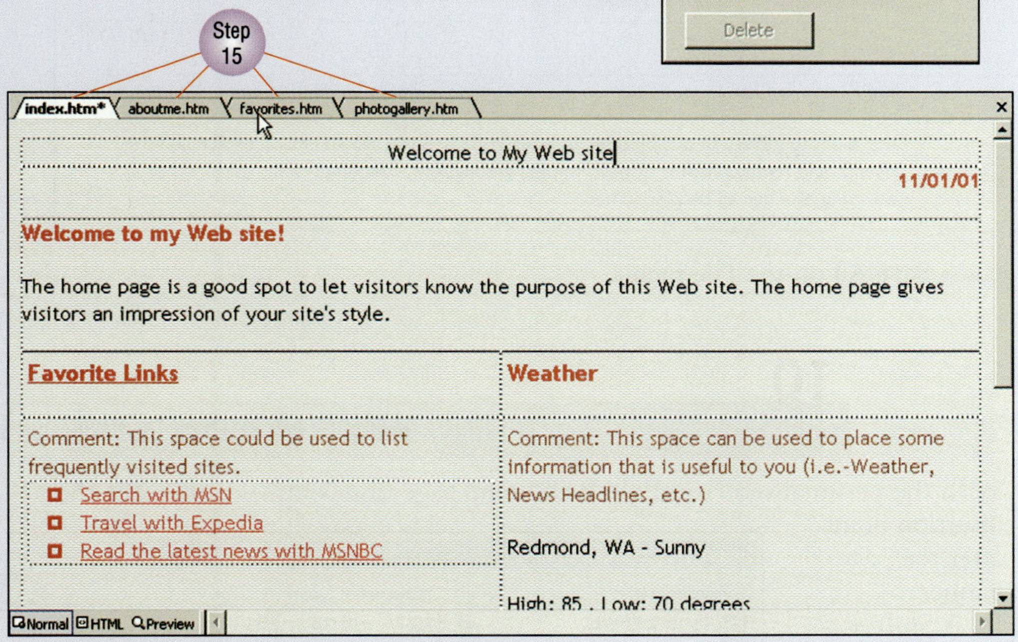

Inserting Page Banners and Navigation Bars

Page banners are a graphic element applied to the page or Web that matches the applied FrontPage theme. Navigation bars, or link bars, are also graphic hyperlink elements that match the current FrontPage theme. If a FrontPage theme has not been applied to the page, page banners and navigation bars display in text. In addition to the theme requirement, users must have a navigation structure established in the Navigation view. The text in the page banner and link bar is directly reflected by the page titles entered in the Navigation view.

exercise 17

INSERTING PAGE BANNERS

1. With the personalweb FrontPage Web home page (index.htm) open, select the page title text.
2. Click Insert and then click Page Banner.
3. At the Page Banner Properties dialog box, select the Picture option, key **Welcome to my Web site** in the Page banner text box, and then click the OK button.
4. Ensure that page banners are placed on the remaining pages.

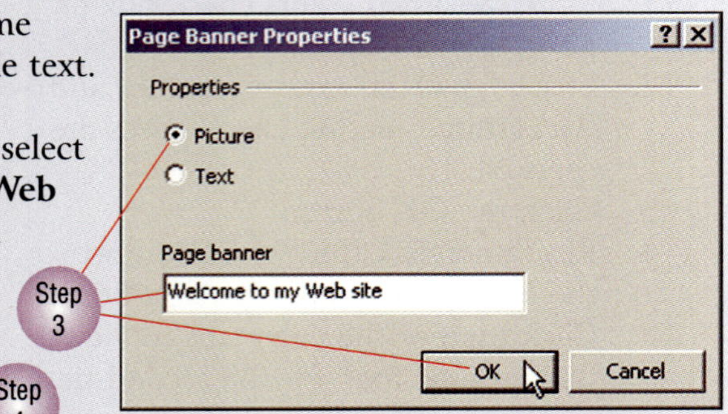

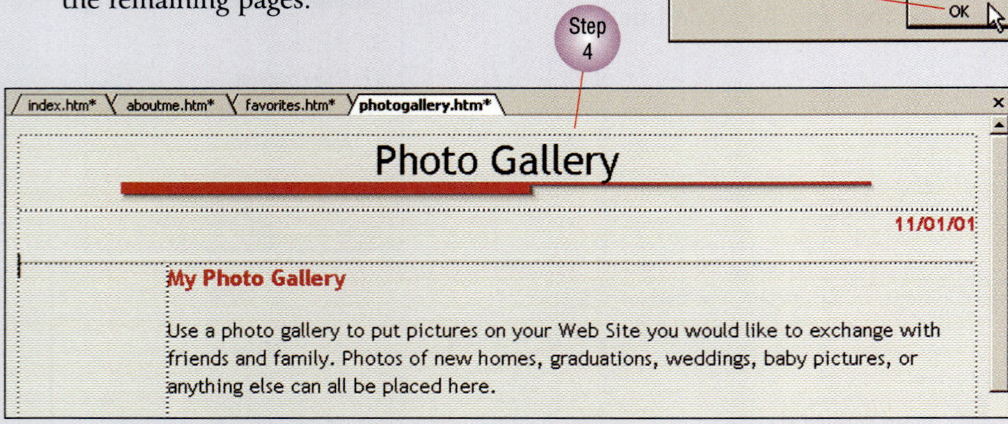

5. Click Save All on the File menu.

exercise 18

INSERTING A NAVIGATION BAR BASED ON THE NAVIGATION STRUCTURE

1. With the personalweb FrontPage Web home page (index.htm) open, place the insertion point after the page banner.
2. Press Shift + Enter to insert a line break.
3. Click Insert and then click Navigation.
4. In the Insert Web Component dialog box, click *Bar based on navigation structure* in the Choose a bar type section.
5. Click the Next button.

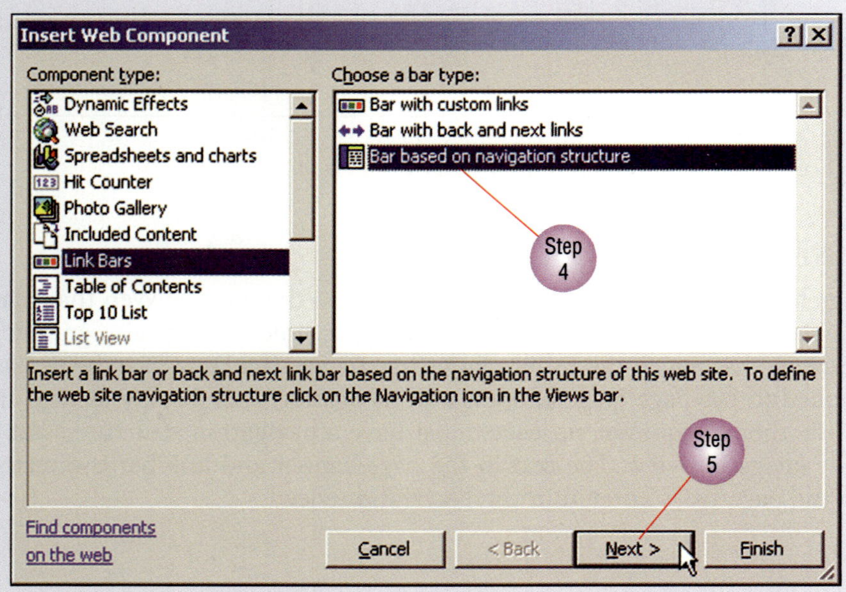

6. Scroll down and select *A graphical style based on the 'Profile' theme.*
7. Click the Next button.
8. Select the Horizontal orientation.
9. Click the Finish button.
10. At the Link Bar Properties dialog box, select the Child level option.

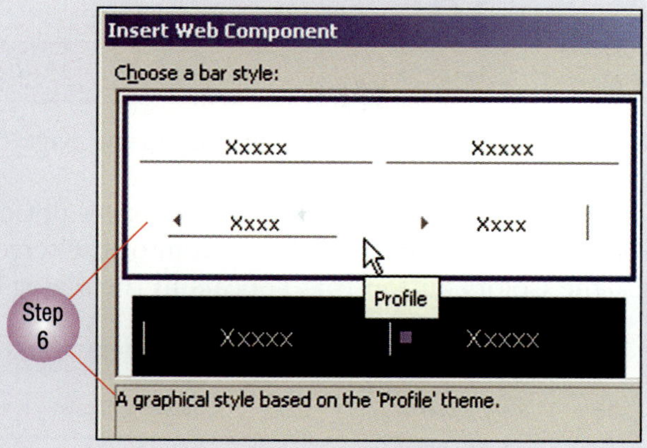

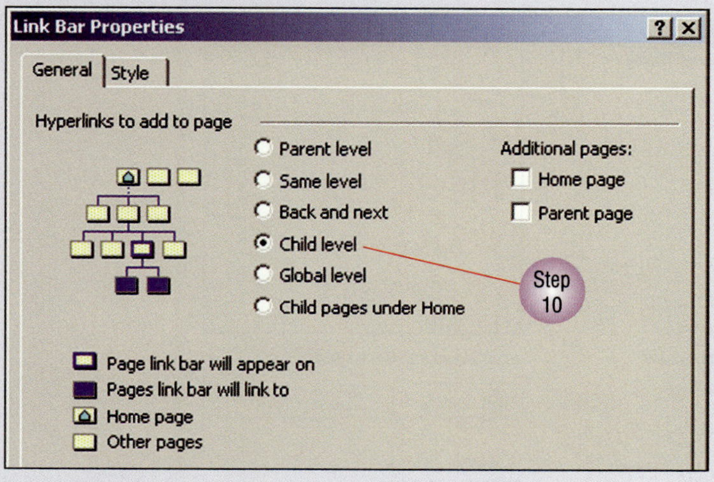

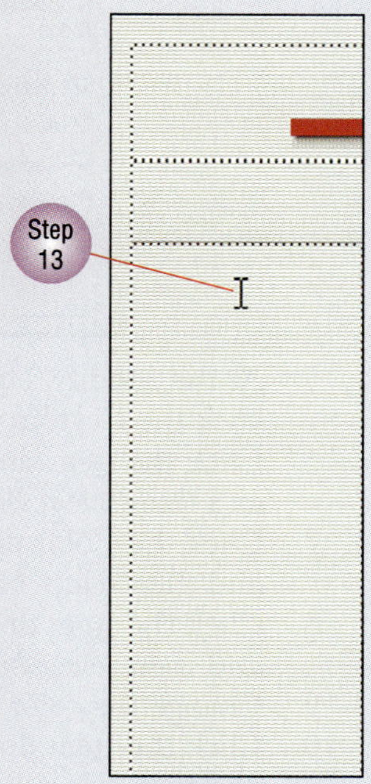

11. Click the OK button.
12. Access the About Me Web page.
13. Place the insertion point in the empty cell at the left of the page.
14. Repeat steps 3–11, substituting Vertical orientation in step 8 and Back and next in step 10, and providing a link back to the home page for each of the second-tier pages.
15. Click Save All on the File menu.
16. Return to the home page and perform a Preview in Browser to test the hyperlinks.

Modifying Theme Colors, Graphics, and Text

Although FrontPage may make page design a simple task with the use of themes, developers still need to be able to modify fonts, colors, backgrounds, hyperlinks, and even banner text. To modify theme elements, access the Themes dialog box from the Format menu and then click the Modify button. This will show the details of what can be modified. You can then click the Colors, Graphics, or Text buttons to open the Modify Theme dialog box.

exercise 19

MODIFYING THEME COLORS

1. With the personalweb FrontPage Web home page (index.htm) open, click Format and then click Theme.
2. At the Themes dialog box, click the All pages option.
3. Click the Modify button at the bottom of the screen.
4. Click the Colors button that appears in the dialog box.

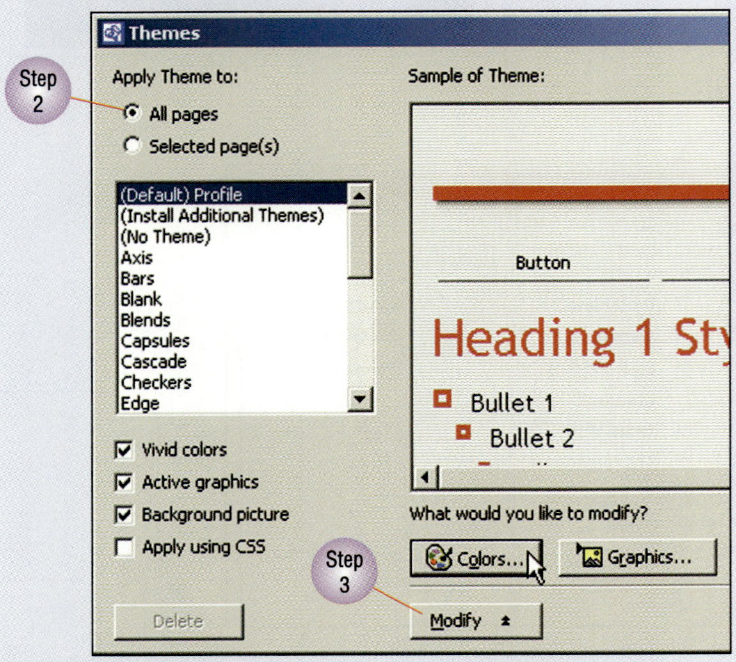

5. At the Modify Theme dialog box, click the Custom tab.
6. Click the Item drop-down menu and then select *Banner Text*.
7. Click the Color drop-down menu and then select Navy.
8. Click the Item drop-down menu and then select *Navigation Text*.
9. Change the color to Navy.
10. Click the Item drop-down menu and then select *Body*.
11. Change the color to Navy.
12. Click the OK button.
13. At the Themes dialog box, click the Save As button.
14. At the Save Theme dialog box, key **Profile Modification** in the Enter new theme title text box.
15. Click the OK button.
16. Click the Yes button in the Microsoft FrontPage Alert dialog box.

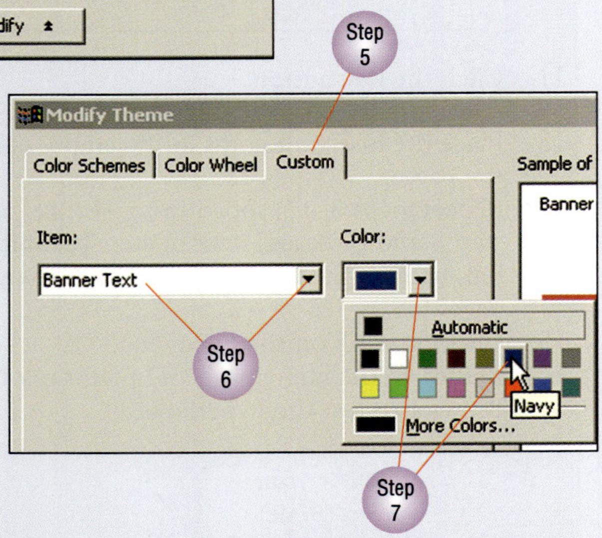

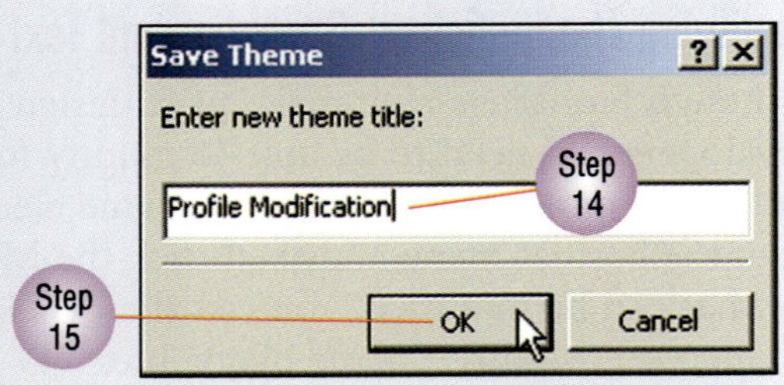

exercise 20

MODIFYING THEME GRAPHICS

1. With the personalweb FrontPage Web home page (index.htm) open, click Format and then click Theme.
2. At the Themes dialog box, click the Modify button.
3. Click the Graphics button that appears in the dialog box.
4. At the Modify Theme dialog box, click the Item drop-down menu and then select *Banner*.
5. Click the Font tab.
6. Change the font to Times New Roman.
7. Change the style to bold.
8. Click the Picture tab in the dialog box.
9. Click the Browse button.
10. Locate and open the profileback.gif image from your *Chapter 6* folder.
11. Click the OK button in each dialog box to return to Page view.
12. Click Yes when prompted to save changes to the Profile Modification theme.
13. Save any unsaved Web page.

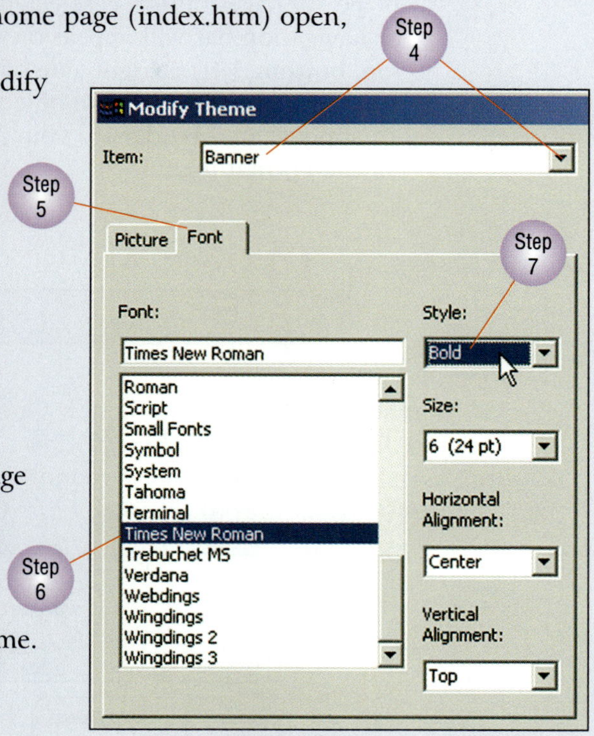

exercise 21

MODIFYING THEME TEXT

1. With the personalweb FrontPage Web home page (index.htm) open, click Format and then click Theme.
2. At the Themes dialog box, click the Modify button.
3. Click the Text button that appears in the dialog box.
4. At the Modify Theme dialog box, change the body font to Verdana.
5. Change each of the six heading fonts to Century Gothic.
6. Click the OK button in each dialog box to return to Page view.
7. Click Yes when prompted to save changes to the Profile Modification theme.
8. Replace the filler text, comments, hyperlinks, and Photo Gallery photos with your own information, hyperlinks, and photos.
9. Click Save All on the File menu.
10. Perform a Preview in Browser and print each of the personalweb FrontPage Web pages.

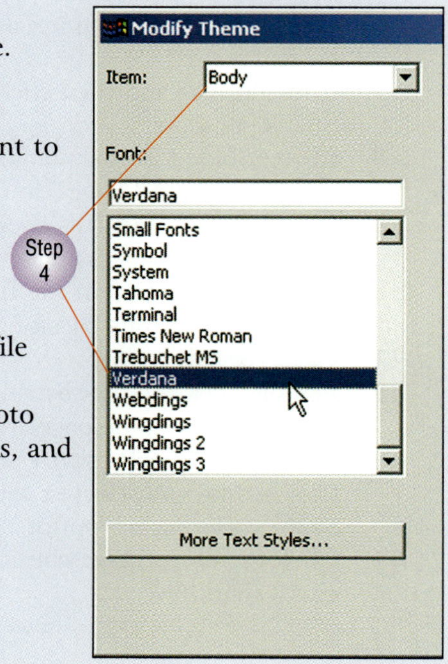

Applying Shared Borders

Shared borders are areas in a Web page in which a page banner and/or navigation bar can be inserted once and then updated as the visitor navigates the Web site. If the All pages option is selected when applying shared borders, the page banner or navigation bar will appear on each page. Shared borders can be inserted at the top, bottom, left, or right side of a Web page. Shared borders may be an easier alternative to inserting the objects separately in each page and to using frames. To apply shared borders to your Web page, select the Shared Borders command on the Format menu.

exercise 22

APPLYING SHARED BORDERS

1. Open FrontPage.
2. On your storage device, create a new One Page FrontPage Web titled sharedborders.
3. Title the home page (index.htm) *Welcome to the Home Page*.
4. In Navigation view, create four second-tier pages.
5. Change the page titles to *Favorites, Photo Gallery, Personal,* and *Resume*.

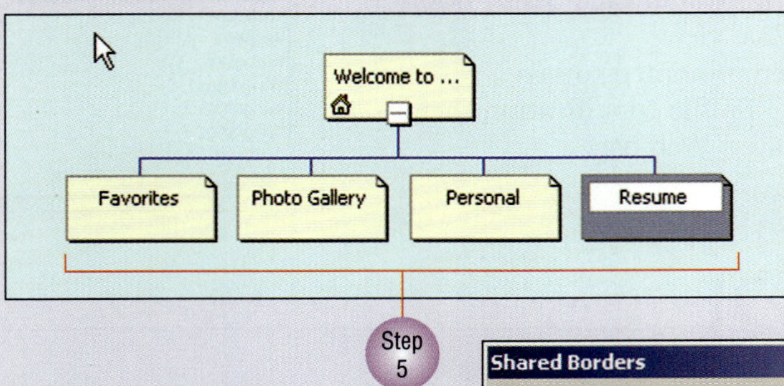

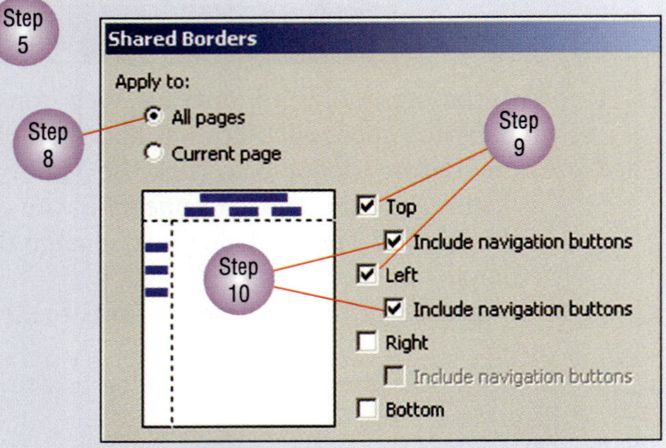

6. Open the Home page in Page view.
7. Click Format and then click Shared Borders.
8. At the Shared Borders dialog box, click the All pages option.
9. Click the Top and Left check boxes to insert check marks.
10. Insert check marks in the Include navigation buttons check boxes.
11. Click the OK button.
12. Double-click the link bar in the left shared border of the home page.
13. At the Link Bar Properties dialog box with the General tab selected, click the Child pages under Home option.
14. Click the Home page check box to insert a check mark.

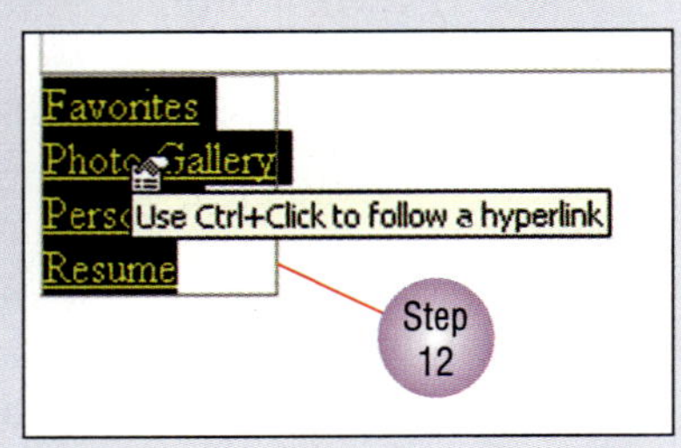

15. Click the Style tab.
16. Click *A graphical style based on the 'Nature' theme.*
17. Click the Use Vivid Colors and Use Active Graphics check boxes to insert check marks.
18. Click the OK button.
19. At the home page, double-click *[Edit the properties for this link bar to display hyperlinks here].*
20. At the Link Bar Properties dialog box with the General tab selected, click the Child pages under Home option.
21. Click the Home page check box to insert a check mark.
22. Click the Style tab.
23. Select the Brackets HTML style.
24. Click the OK button to return to Page view.
25. Apply the Nature theme to all Web pages.
26. Save all Web pages and perform a Preview in Browser to test the hypertext and graphic links.

Step 15

Step 16

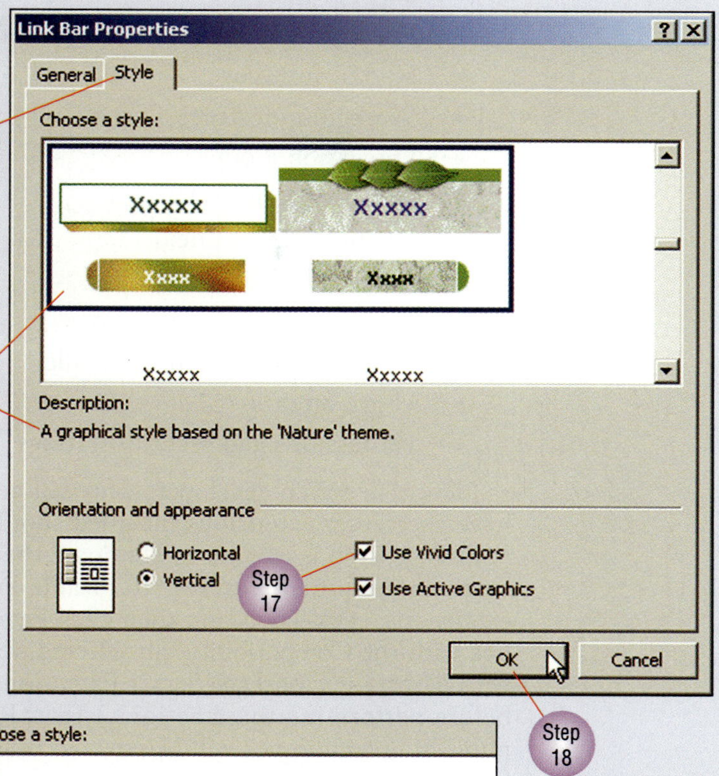

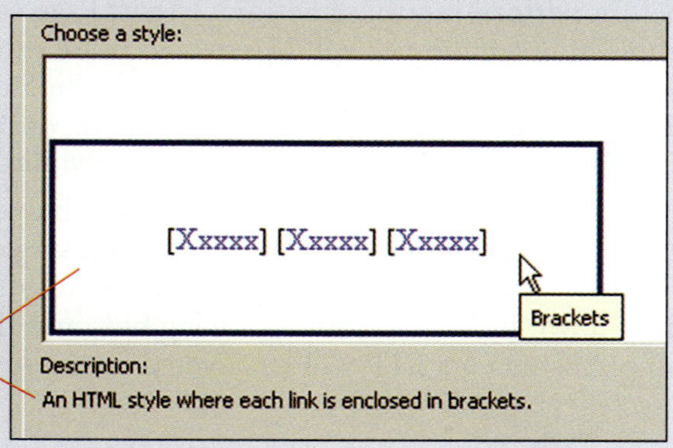

Step 23

Exploring FrontPage Publishing Basics

Publishing to a host Web server can take different processes and require that certain components be installed on the server. FrontPage Webs can be published to servers with or without FrontPage server extensions.

FrontPage server extensions are a set of programs and scripts that are installed on Web servers. The server extensions allow ease of authoring, such as opening, editing, and saving FrontPage Web pages without using a File Transfer Protocol (FTP) program to upload pages to a server. While FrontPage extensions are not required to create and publish pages to the World Wide Web, they are required for the following features:

- Confirmation fields
- Web search
- Hit counter
- Table of contents based on categories

- Top 10 lists
- Password protection for the _private folder
- Nested subwebs
- Workgroup features
- Discussion groups
- User Registration Wizard
- File upload form field
- Custom link bars
- Database Interface Wizard
- Send to Database form handler
- Usage reports
- Permissions and security settings

FrontPage Web developers who will be publishing to Web servers that do not have the server extensions installed should take certain precautions before the FrontPage Web is created to eliminate the possibility of adding FrontPage server extension-required features. To disable FrontPage features that require server extensions, click Tools and then click Page Options. At the Page Options dialog box with the Compatibility tab selected, remove the check mark from the Enabled with Microsoft FrontPage Server Extensions check box. (Check with your instructor before performing these actions.) FrontPage server extensions and advanced publishing techniques will be covered more extensively in chapter 7. FrontPage forms are actually designed to work with the FrontPage server extensions; however, developers can format the form handler to work on any Web server. Forms and FrontPage extensions will be covered in chapter 8.

To publish a FrontPage Web or a Web-based page, click the Publish Web button on the Standard toolbar. To save a single page to a Web server via FTP, click the Save button on the Standard toolbar, select *FTP Locations* in the Save in drop-down list in the Save As dialog box, and then click the FTP location. More on publishing via FTP will be covered in chapter 7.

exercise 23

PUBLISHING TO A SERVER WITH FRONTPAGE EXTENSIONS

(Note: To complete this exercise you must have access to a Web server with FrontPage extensions installed as well as authorized permission to publish. Ask your instructor for school-specific Web publishing instructions. If you are not able to complete this activity, please read through the steps.)

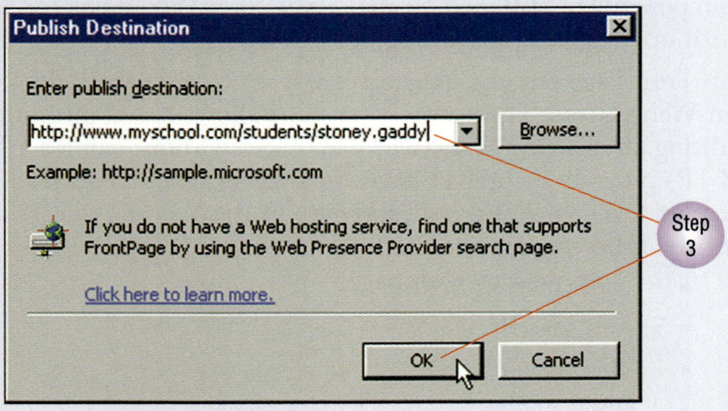

1. Open your personalweb FrontPage Web.
2. Click the Publish Web button on the Standard toolbar.
3. At the Publish Destination dialog box, key the Web address that your instructor has provided and then click OK.

4. At the Enter Network Password dialog box, key your user name and your network password and then click OK.
5. At the Publish Web dialog box, click the Publish button.
6. At the confirmation of successful publication, click the *Click here to view your published web site* link.
7. View your published Web site. Test the hyperlinks.
8. Exit FrontPage.

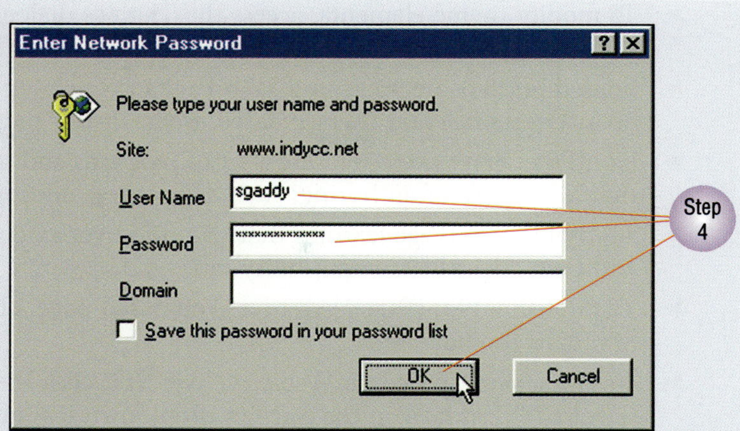

CHAPTER summary

- Tables are frequently used in Web pages to organize and present text and images in a structured setting.
- Tables inserted into a Web page have a border pixel size of 1 and a browser window width of 100 percent.
- Text can be converted into table format by clicking the Table menu, pointing to Convert, and then clicking the Text to Table command.
- Text that is to be converted into table format must have character separators (e.g., paragraph marks, tabs, commas, or other characters) to differentiate between rows and columns.
- Rows and columns can be inserted or deleted by accessing the Table menu; right-clicking inside the table; or using the buttons on the Tables toolbar.
- Rows can be added to the end of a table by pressing the Tab key.
- Merging cells is the combining of multiple cells to make one cell.
- Splitting cells divide the current cell into rows or columns.
- Borders and shading can be formatted to paragraph text for emphasizing the content as well as give paragraphs a tabled look.
- FrontPage themes are collections of eye-catching design elements and color schemes that can be applied to Web pages.
- Page banners are graphic elements applied to the page or Web that match the applied FrontPage theme.
- Navigation bars, or link bars, are graphic hyperlink elements that match the current FrontPage theme.

- To modify theme elements, access the Themes dialog box from the Format menu and then click the Modify button.
- Shared borders are areas in a Web Page in which a page banner and/or navigation bar can be inserted once and then updated as the visitor navigates the Web site.
- FrontPage server extensions are a set of programs and scripts that are installed on Web servers that allow ease of authoring, such as opening, editing, and saving FrontPage Web pages.
- To disable FrontPage features that require server extensions, click Tools, click Page Options, and then click the Compatibility tab.
- To publish a FrontPage Web or a Web-based page, click the Publish Web button on the Standard toolbar.
- To save a single page to a Web server via FTP, click the Save button on the Standard toolbar, select *FTP Locations* in the Save in drop-down list, and then click the FTP location in the Save As dialog box.

COMMANDS review

Command	Mouse/Keyboard
Insert a table	Click Table, Insert, Table; or click and drag the Insert Table button on the Standard toolbar
Draw a table	Click Draw Table button on the Tables toolbar
Convert text to a table	Select text, click Table, Convert, Text to Table
Insert a column	Click Table, Insert, Rows or Columns; or click the Insert Columns button on Tables toolbar; or right-click in table, click Insert Columns
Insert a row	Click Table, Insert, Rows or Columns; or click the Insert Rows button on Tables toolbar; or right-click in table, click Insert Rows
Delete a row or column	Select each cell in the row or column and then (1) click Delete Cells button on Tables toolbar; (2) click Table, Delete Cells; (3) right-click, Delete Cells
Merge cells	Select cells to merge and then (1) click Merge Cells button on Tables toolbar; (2) click Table, Merge Cells; (3) right-click, Merge Cells
Split cells	Click Split Cells button on Tables toolbar; or click Table, Split Cells; or right-click, Split Cells
Apply a border to a paragraph	Click Borders button on Formatting toolbar
Format border style, colors, and/or width	Click Format, Borders and Shading
Format line shading	Click Format, Borders and Shading
Apply a FrontPage theme	Click Format, Theme

Insert a page banner	Click Insert, Page Banner
Insert a navigation bar	Click Insert, Navigation
Modify theme colors, graphics, or text	Click Format, Theme
Apply shared borders	Click Format, Shared Borders
Publish a FrontPage Web	Click Publish Web button on the Standard toolbar; or click File, Publish Web

CONCEPTS check

Completion: On a blank sheet of paper, indicate the correct term, command, or number for each item.

1. Tables, by default, have a width of this amount.
2. A table can be drawn into a Web page by first clicking this button on the Tables toolbar.
3. Text that is to be converted into table format must have these to differentiate between rows and columns.
4. A row can be added to the bottom of a table by pressing this key on the keyboard.
5. Rows or columns can be deleted by clicking this button on the Tables toolbar.
6. This is the process of combining multiple cells into one.
7. Click this button to divide a cell into multiple cells.
8. Borders can be applied to a paragraph and formatted in this dialog box.
9. These are collections of eye-catching design elements and color schemes that can be applied to Web pages.
10. FrontPage themes can be applied to a Web or individual pages through this menu.
11. Theme colors, graphics, and text can be altered by clicking this button in the Themes dialog box.
12. Page banners can be added to FrontPage Web pages through this menu.
13. These must be installed on a Web server in order for the full FrontPage publishing capabilities as well as the component and form features to work properly.
14. Select this tab in the Page Options dialog box to enable or disable Web features.
15. FrontPage Webs can be published using this transfer method if FrontPage extensions have not been installed on the destination server.

SKILLS check

Assessment 1

1. Open FrontPage.
2. In a blank Web page in Page view, create the table shown in the illustration.

Time	Days	Class Number	Class	Location	Instructor
8:00-8:50	MWF	BIO 1005	General Biology	BIO234	Daniels
9:00-9:50	MWF	MAT 1003	College Algebra	MSC104	Leonard
9:30-10:50	TR	COM 1003	Speech I	FIN308	Dryer

3. Drag the second-column borders as necessary.
4. Use the Distribute Columns evenly feature for columns 2 through 6.
5. Save the Web page as semester_sched.htm with the title *Fall Semester Schedule*.
6. Perform a Preview in Browser and print the Web page.

Assessment 2

1. In a blank Web page in Page view, create the table in the illustration.

<table>
<tr><td colspan="2">ABC Clothing Company</td></tr>
<tr><td>Men's, Women's, and Children's Shirts</td><td rowspan="2"></td></tr>
<tr><td>All t-shirts are 100% cotton. Sizes include XS to XXX. Customized lettering and numbering can be added to t-shirts upon request.</td></tr>
</table>

2. Insert an appropriate picture from the Clip Organizer or the Design Gallery Live Web site into the blank table cell.
3. All text is Times New Roman and 10 points. Format the text using appropriate font styles, colors, and alignment.
4. Save the Web page as clothing.htm with the title of *ABC Clothing Company – T-Shirt*.
5. Perform a Preview in Browser and print the Web page.

Assessment 3

1. Open a blank Web page in Page view.
2. Insert the sales_summary.htm file into the Web page.
3. Convert the inserted text to a table using Tabs as the separator.
4. Format the table as shown in the illustration using the Classic 4 Table AutoFormat.

	Quarter 1	Quarter 2	Quarter 3	Quarter 4	TOTALS
New York	$341,942.59	$356,975.80	$359,002.57	$368,100.32	$1,426,021.28
Texas	$384,556.09	$390,005.41	$397,674.22	$409,772.44	$1,582,008.16
California	$467,798.28	$470,076.83	$474,773.95	$481,033.10	$3,008,029.44
TOTALS	$1,194,296.96	$1,217,058.04	$1,231,450.74	$1,258,905.86	$6,016,058.88

5. Save the Web page as sales_table.htm with the page title *Sales Summary*.
6. Perform a Preview in Browser and print the Web page.

Assessment 4

1. Open the course_roster.htm file from your *Chapter 6* folder.
2. Insert a new column between the *Last Name* and *Percentage* columns using the Tables toolbar.
3. Insert a new column between the *Last Name* column and new column using the right-click shortcut.
4. Insert another new column between the other two new columns using the Table menu.

5. Delete one of the new columns using the Tables toolbar.
6. Key the information in the new columns as shown below:

Absences	Grade
1	A
2	B
5	D
0	A
3	B
2	C

7. Save the updated Web page.
8. Perform a Preview in Browser and print the Web page.

Assessment 5

1. Open the course_roster.htm Web page file updated in assessment 4.
2. Add a new row to the bottom of the table using the Tab key.
3. Key the following student record into the cells:

07	07	Joe	Rogers	1	B	87

4. Add a row underneath the *Sarah Hutchins* record using the Tables toolbar.
5. Add another row below the new row using the right-click shortcut.
6. Add another row under using the Tables menu.
7. Delete one of the rows using the right-click shortcut.
8. Key the following records in the two new rows:

08	08	William	Sanders	3	C	79
09	09	Rosa	Phillips	0	A	94

9. Save the updated Web page.
10. Perform a Preview in Browser and print the Web page.

Assessment 6

1. Open a new blank Web page in Page view.
2. Insert a one-cell table.
3. Use the Merge Cells and Split Cells commands on the Tables toolbar or the right-click shortcut to create the table below.

<table>
<tr><td colspan="5">22 – Jenny Hanchett</td></tr>
<tr><td colspan="2">5'8"</td><td colspan="2">Shawnee Mission
High School</td><td rowspan="3">Insert Photo Here

jhanchett.jpg</td></tr>
<tr><td>AB</td><td>R</td><td>H</td><td>RBI</td></tr>
<tr><td>89</td><td>24</td><td>38</td><td>26</td></tr>
</table>

4. Select the *Insert Photo Here* filler text and insert the jhanchett.jpg picture from your *Chapter 6* folder into that cell.
5. Save the Web page as jhanchett.htm with the title *Jenny Hanchett Softball Stats*.
6. Save the updated Web page.
7. Perform a Preview in Browser and print the Web page.

Assessment 7

1. Open a new blank Web page in Page view.
2. Using your resume as a guide, create a Web page based on your resume.
3. Format your name, biographical/demographical information, and the resume headings.
4. Apply a colored border around your name.
5. Fill the bordered paragraph with a light color.
6. Apply shading to the resume headings.
7. Save your resume Web page as myresume.htm with the title *[Student Name's] Resume,* substituting your name for *Student Name*.
8. Perform a Preview in Browser and print the Web page.

Assessment 8

1. Create a new One Page Web titled *resume* in your storage device.
2. At the home page (index.htm), insert the myresume.htm Web page created in assessment 7.
3. Format your name to Heading 1.
4. Format the resume headings to Heading 3.
5. Format the remaining resume items as you see fit.
6. Format the page to the Cascade theme.
7. Save the updated Web page.
8. Perform a Preview in Browser and print the Web page.

Assessment 9

1. Open the resume FrontPage Web home page (index.htm) in Page view.
2. Select your name at the top of the Web page and replace it with a page banner image with your name as the text.
3. Add the following Web pages to Folders view:

File Name	***Page Title***
philosophy.htm	*Philosophy of [Your Major]*
references.htm	*Professional References*

4. Add the above Web page to the navigation structure.
5. Create a navigation bar on the home page to the philosophy.htm and references.htm Web pages.
6. Save the updated Web page.
7. Perform a Preview in Browser and print the Web page.
8. Exit FrontPage.

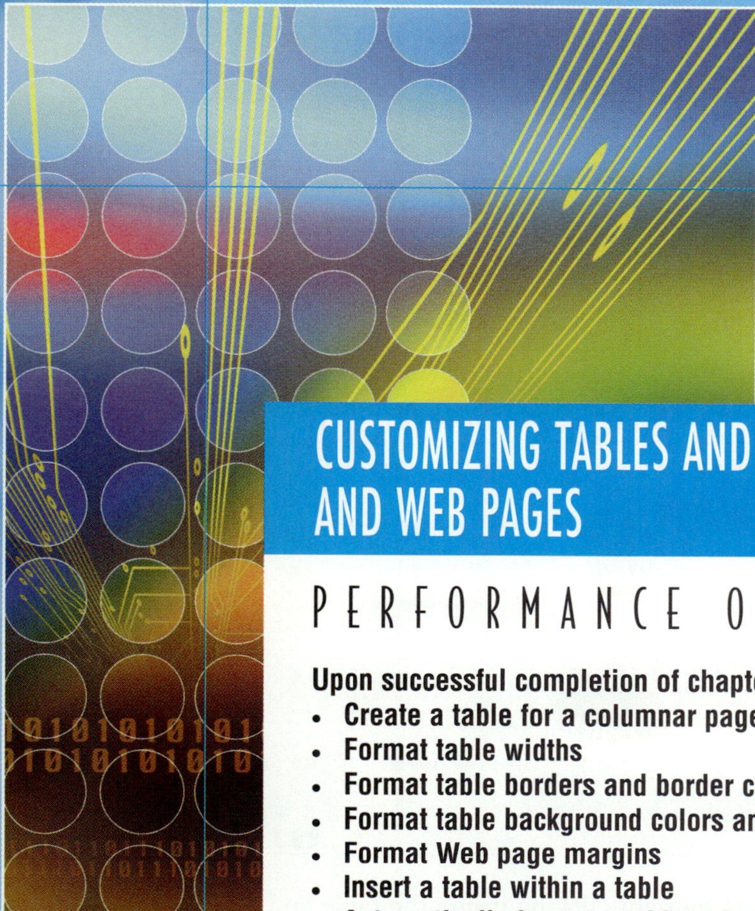

CHAPTER 7

CUSTOMIZING TABLES AND PUBLISHING FRONTPAGE WEBS AND WEB PAGES

PERFORMANCE OBJECTIVES

Upon successful completion of chapter 7, you will be able to:

- **Create a table for a columnar page layout**
- **Format table widths**
- **Format table borders and border colors**
- **Format table background colors and pictures**
- **Format Web page margins**
- **Insert a table within a table**
- **Automatically format a table using the Table AutoFormat feature**
- **Format cells and cell properties**
- **Format cell background colors and pictures**
- **Understand the purpose of Web server platforms and software**
- **Test browser compatibility features**
- **Publish or not publish specified pages and files**
- **Publish to a Web server that does not have FrontPage server extensions installed**
- **Create a backup of a Web site using the Publish Web feature**

Chapter 7

Formatting Table Properties

Most of today's professional Web sites are based on a columnar format (see figure 7.1). The HTML language does not support the columnar paragraphs created in word processing and desktop publishing software programs to which we have become accustomed in professional publications. Web designers, therefore, must be very inventive to design layouts that are appealing and easy to navigate.

Table properties are often altered to specific widths and heights to reflect table content. Tables can be formatted by pixel size or percent of browser window size. Tables, by default, are formatted at 100 percent of the browser window. Actually, tables do not extend from the left edge of the browser window to the right. FrontPage sets page margins to approximately 20 pixels on all four sides. Top and left margins can be set to zero (0) in the Page Properties dialog box. Web designers who format tables by pixel must be aware of their intended audience. A high percentage of users have their monitors set to 800 × 600 pixels. Furthermore, the scroll bar is approximately 20 pixels wide.

FIGURE 7.1 ***Sample Web Site Based on a Table Structure***

Tables can be formatted by right-clicking inside the table and selecting the Table Properties command or by clicking Table, pointing to Table Properties, and clicking Table. The table properties that can be formatted in the Table Properties dialog box (figure 7.2) include table alignment, cell padding, cell spacing, border size, table width, table height, border color, background color, and background picture.

FIGURE 7.2 ***Table Properties Dialog Box***

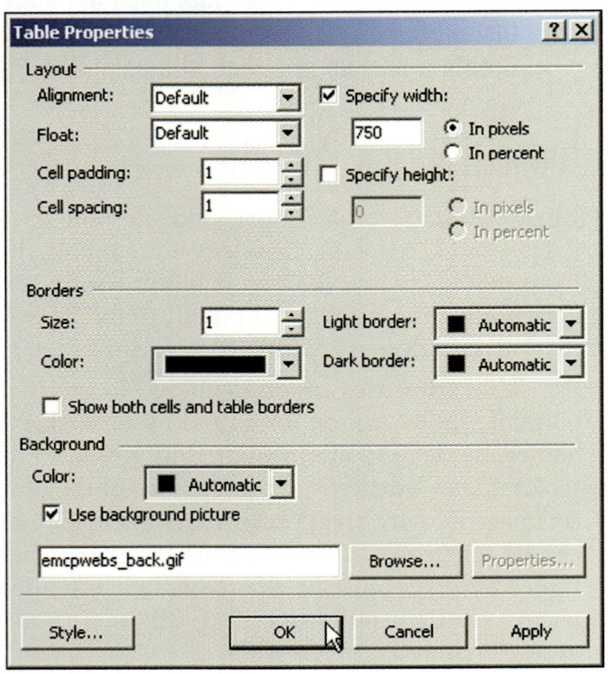

(Note: Before completing computer exercises, delete the Chapter 6 *folder on your disk. Next, download the Chapter 7 data files from the Internet Resource Center to the* Chapter 7 *folder you have created on your disk, and then make* Chapter 7 *the active folder.)*

exercise 1

CREATING A TABLE FOR A COLUMNAR PAGE LAYOUT

1. Open FrontPage and the EMCPWebs FrontPage Web.
2. Click the Create a new normal page button on the Standard toolbar.
3. Using the Insert Table button on the Standard toolbar, click and drag a table that has three columns and six rows.
4. Merge the three cells in the top row to create one cell.
5. Merge the second and third column cells of the second row.
6. Split the middle cell of row three into two rows.
7. Merge the second and third column cells of the fourth row.
8. Merge the second and third column cells of the fifth row.

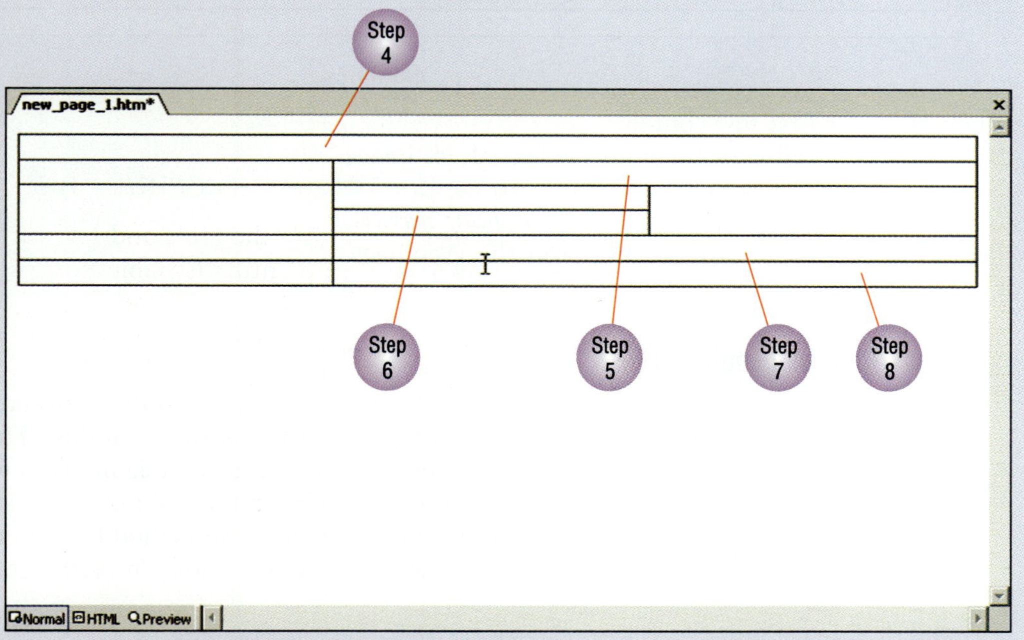

9. Open the home page (index.htm) in Page view.

10. Copy the necessary text and objects from the home page and paste them into the new Web page as shown.

11. Right align the first row contents.
12. Right align the cell with the homecredentials.gif image.
13. Save the Web page as index-new.htm with the title *Welcome to EMCPWebs – Web Design, Graphic Design, and Computer Consulting Services.*
14. Perform a Preview in Browser and print the Web page.

Formatting Table Widths

Table widths can be formatted in pixels or by percentage. Tables formatted by percentage will automatically adjust to the size of the browser window. This may work well for some design layouts, but not all. Formatting a table in pixels will help ensure that your text and objects are placed in specific locations within a table structure regardless of browser size or monitor settings. The quickest method for altering table properties is to right-click inside the table and select the Table Properties command.

exercise 2

FORMATTING TABLE WIDTHS

1. Open the index-new.htm page in Page view.
2. Right-click inside the table and select the Table Properties command.
3. Key **657** in the Specify width text box in the Table Properties dialog box.
4. Click the In pixels option.
5. Click the OK button.
6. Save the updated Web page.

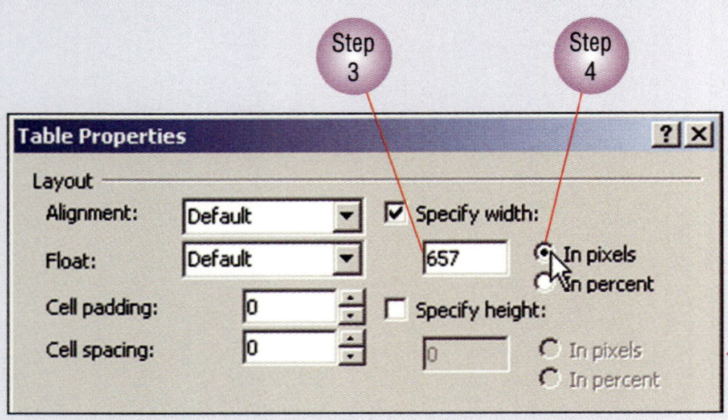

Altering Table Cell Padding and Spacing

Cell padding is the spacing between the text and the cell borders. Cell spacing is the spacing between each cell. A common setting for tables designed for page layouts is 0 (zero) for both cell padding and cell spacing. To alter cell padding or spacing, access the Table Properties dialog box.

exercise 3 — ALTERING CELL PADDING AND SPACING

1. Open the index-new.htm page in Page view.
2. Right-click inside the table and select the Table Properties command.
3. At the Table Properties dialog box, ensure that *0* (zero) is inserted in both the Cell padding and Cell spacing text boxes.
4. Save the updated Web page.

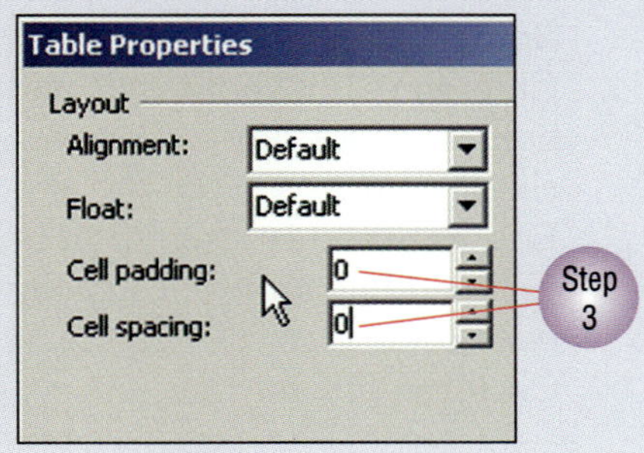

Formatting Table Borders and Border Colors

Depending on the purpose of a table, borders can be visible to emphasize content or invisible to emphasize placement. Borders can be formatted in the Table Properties dialog box. Borders formatted to a size of 0 pixels will appear as dotted lines in FrontPage but will not be visible in a browser window.

exercise 4 — FORMATTING TABLE BORDERS AND BORDER COLORS

1. Open the index-new.htm page in Page view.
2. Right-click inside the table and select the Table Properties command.
3. At the Table Properties dialog box, key **6** in the Size text box under Borders.
4. Click the Light border down-pointing triangle and then select More Colors.
5. At the More Colors dialog box, click the Select button and then click anywhere on the image of the television.
6. Click the OK button.
7. At the Table Properties dialog box, click the Dark border down-pointing triangle and then select *Navy*.
8. Click the Show both cells and table borders check box to insert a check mark.

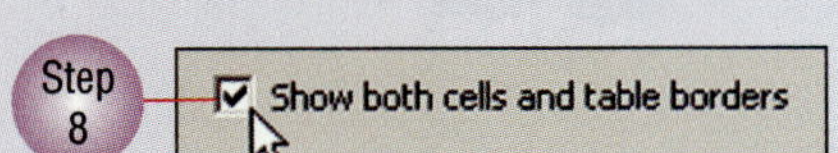

9. Click the OK button.
10. Save the updated Web page.
11. Perform a Preview in Browser and print the Web page.

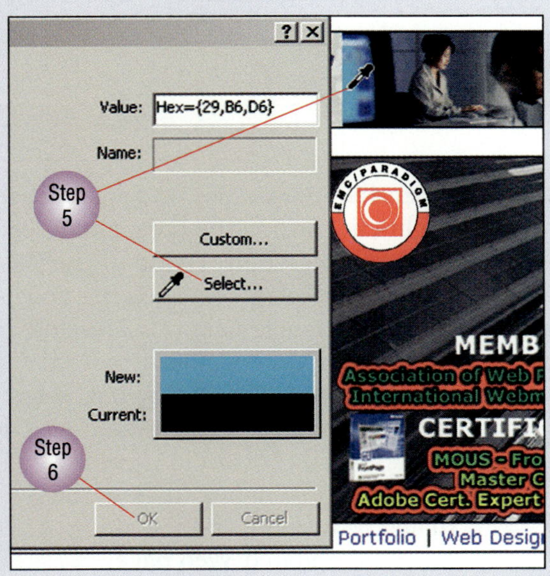

exercise 5

REMOVING TABLE BORDERS

1. Open the index-new.htm page in Page view.
2. Right-click inside the table and select the Table Properties command.
3. At the Table Properties dialog box, key **0** in the Size text box under Borders.
4. Click the Show both cells and table borders check box to remove the check mark.
5. Ensure that *0* is inserted in both the Cell padding and Cell spacing text boxes.
6. Click the OK button.

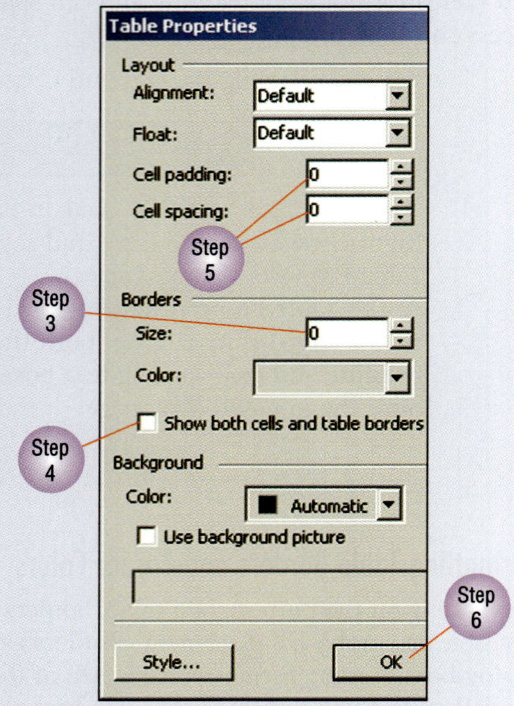

Formatting Table Background Colors and Pictures

Table background colors are often formatted to contrast with the Web page background and emphasize table content. Dark table backgrounds require light-colored text. Table background colors can be formatted in the Table Properties dialog box. Web developers who want textures and patterns formatted in a table background can do so in the Table Properties dialog box as well.

exercise 6

FORMATTING TABLE BACKGROUND COLOR

1. Open the index-new.htm page in Page view.
2. Right-click inside the table and select the Table Properties command.
3. In the Background section of the Table Properties dialog box, click the down-pointing triangle next to Color and then select More Colors.
4. At the More Colors dialog box, select the light gray color and then click OK.
5. Click the OK button in the Table Properties dialog box to close the dialog box.
6. Save the updated Web page.

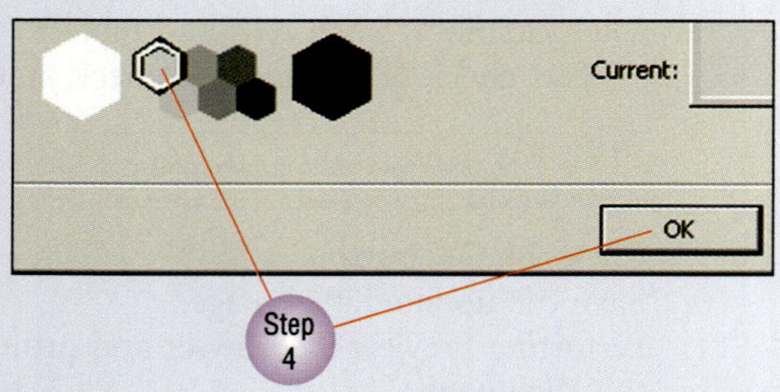

exercise 7

FORMATTING A TABLE BACKGROUND PICTURE

1. Open the index-new.htm page in Page view.
2. Return to the Table Properties dialog box.
3. Format the table Background Color to Automatic.
4. Click the Browse button in the Background section.
5. Select the emcpwebs_back.gif image and then click the Open button.
6. Click the OK button.

7. Save the updated Web page.
8. Perform a Preview in Browser and print the Web page.

Formatting Web Page Margins

Web pages, by default, have empty spacing at the top and left. This spacing is typically removed for table-based Web pages. To remove the margins, click Format, select Background, and then click the Margins tab in the Page Properties dialog box. Next, key **0** pixels in the Specify top margin and Specify left margin text boxes. The Page Properties dialog box can also be accessed by clicking File and selecting Properties.

exercise 8

FORMATTING WEB PAGE MARGINS

1. Open the index-new.htm page in Page view.
2. Remove the empcwebs_back.gif image from the table properties.
3. Click Format and then click Background.
4. At the Page Properties dialog box, click the Margins tab.
5. Specify top and left margins at 0.
6. Click the Background tab.
7. Click the Browse button in the Formatting section.
8. Locate and select the columnar_back.gif image and then click the Open button.

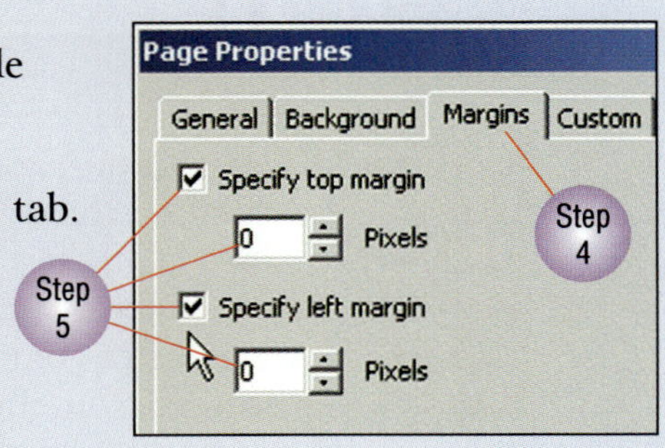

9. Click the OK button.
10. Click and drag the border between the first and second columns to the position shown.

Step 9

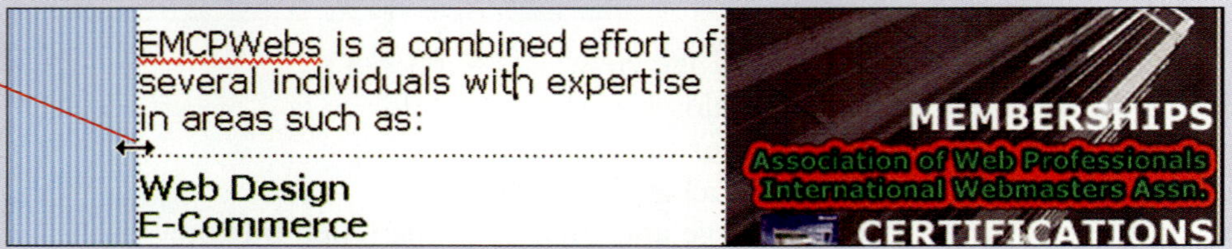

11. Delete the word *Web* from the *Web Design Tips* navigation text link at the bottom of the table.
12. Save the updated Web page.

Inserting a Table within a Table (Nested Table)

Table cells that are merged or split to create additional cells within a table are bound to the rest of the table. This lack of flexibility in cell height and width can make it difficult to design a precise Web page layout scheme. Inserting a table into a cell of an existing table gives the designer additional flexibility for the table(s) and the content requirements of that table. A multiple row or column table, therefore, can be inserted into a single cell (see figure 7.3) and formatted to different height or width specifications without affecting the cell properties of the original table.

FIGURE 7.3 ***A Table Inserted within a Table Cell (Nested Table)***

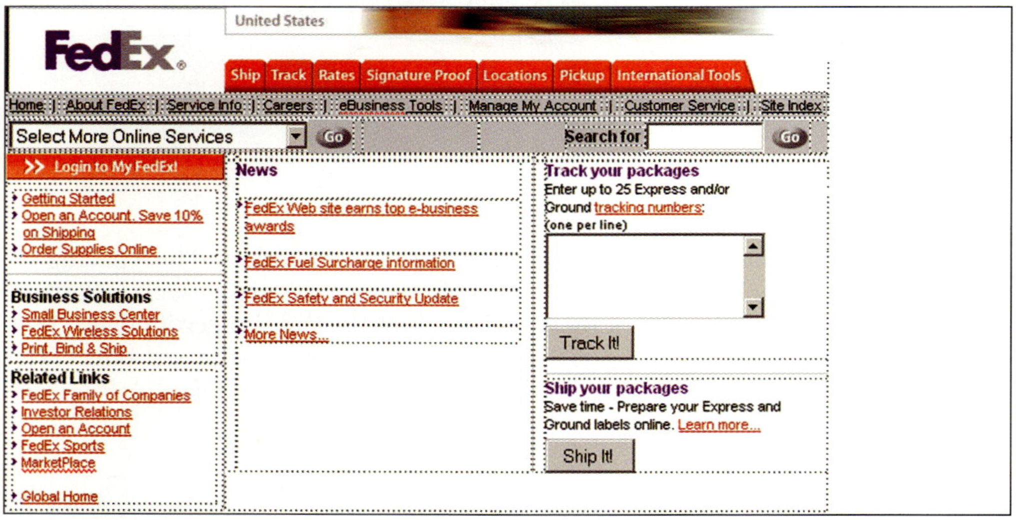

exercise 9 INSERTING A NESTED TABLE

1. Open the index-new.htm page in Page view.
2. Merge the second and third column cells in the last row of the table.
3. Place the insertion point in the right column, bottom row of the table.
4. Create a 2 by 2 table (2 columns × 2 rows) using the Insert Table button on the Standard toolbar.
5. Right-click inside the new table and select the Table Properties command.

Step 4

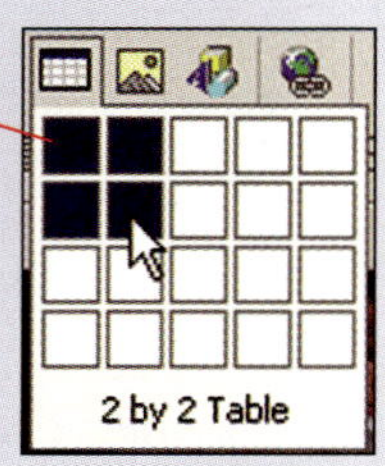

6. Change the border size to 0 and click the OK button.
7. Merge the top two cells of the first row.
8. Copy the necessary home page text and object to match the illustration below.

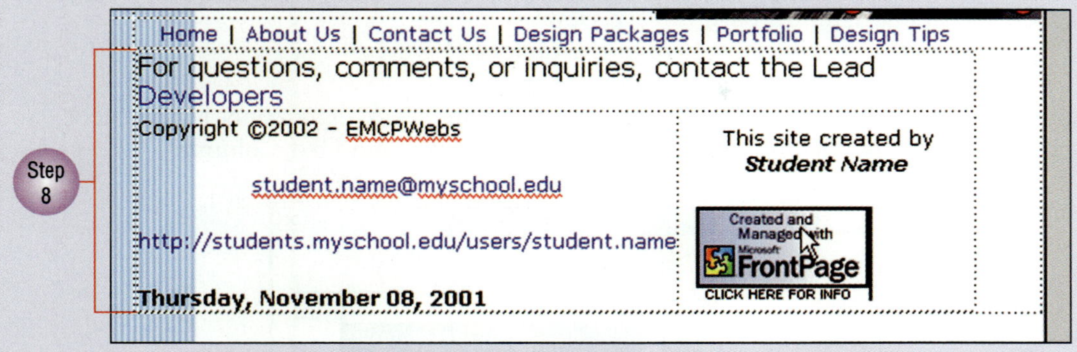

9. Save the updated Web page.

Automatically Formatting a Table Using Table AutoFormat

The Table AutoFormat feature has numerous preformatted table designs, as shown in figure 7.4. Features include border colors, background colors, font styles, sizes, and colors, and an AutoFit option. Table AutoFormat designs can be applied by selecting the Table AutoFormat command on the Table menu.

FIGURE 7.4 ***Table AutoFormat Dialog Box***

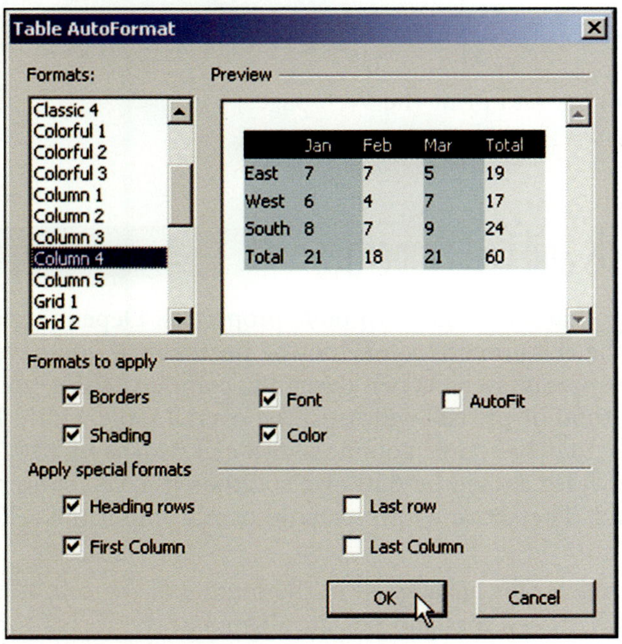

exercise 10 — USING TABLE AUTOFORMAT

1. Open the webdesign.htm page in Page view.
2. Place the insertion point anywhere in the table.
3. Click Table and then click Table AutoFormat.
4. Select the *Classic 3* format and ensure that there are check marks only in the check boxes for Borders, Shading, Font, Color, Heading rows, and First Column.

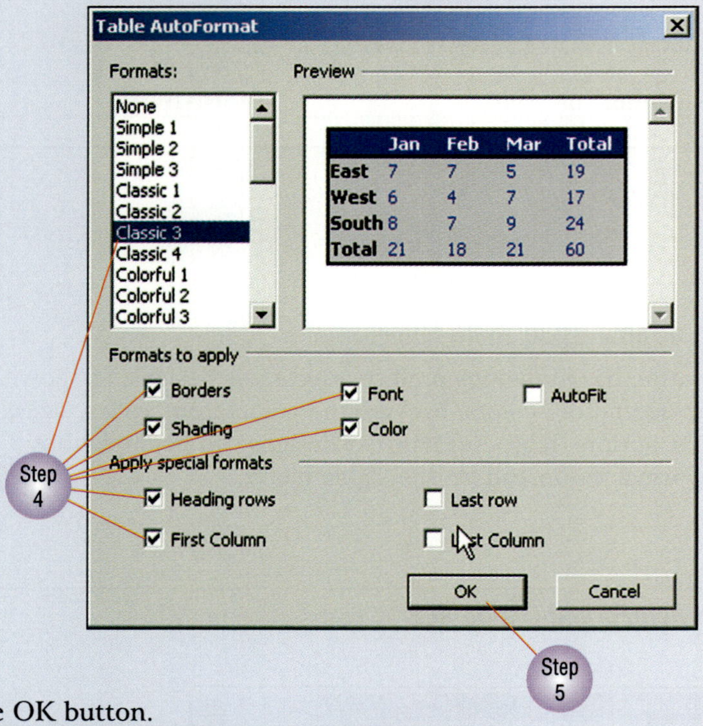

5. Click the OK button.
6. Save the updated Web page.
7. Perform a Preview in Browser and print the Web page.

Formatting Cells and Cell Properties

Cell properties go hand-in-hand with table properties. Depending on your specific needs, altering the cell properties may not be necessary if you have adjusted your table properties appropriately. When designing complex tables, you will need to match the pixel total of the cell widths to the overall table width. For example, if you have a table that has three columns with cell widths of 150, 250, and 250 pixels, the table width should be 650 pixels. Otherwise, cell contents may not line up as they should. The above width scenario works only if the cell spacing is set to 0!

By default, cell content is aligned in the middle of the cell. In most instances, Web developers want cell text and objects aligned at the top of the cell. To format vertical cell alignment and other cell properties, access the Cell Properties dialog box and select *Top* in the Vertical alignment list box.

exercise 11 FORMATTING CELL WIDTH

1. Open the index-new.htm page in Page view.
2. Format the *For questions, comments,...* text to 10 points.
3. Format the line spacing for each line of text in the bottom cell to 0 on both the Before text and After text boxes in the Spacing section of the Paragraph dialog box.
4. Center align all contents in the cells of the embedded table.
5. Insert an extra space between your Web address and the time stamp.

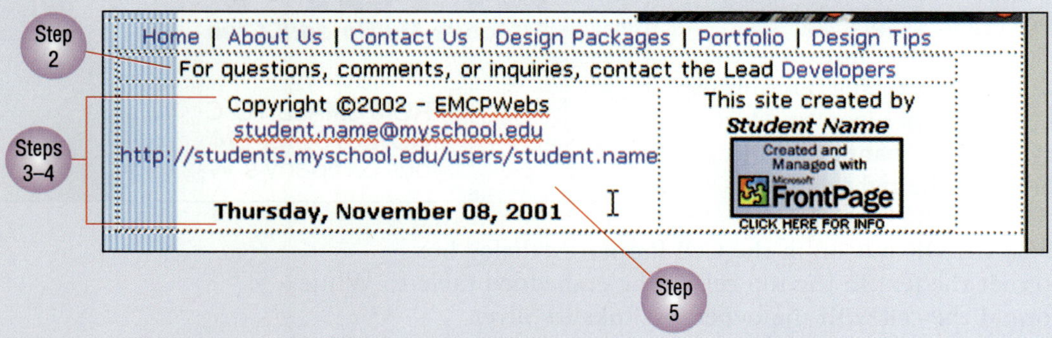

6. Right-click inside the top cell of the embedded table and select Cell Properties.
7. Specify the width to 527 pixels.
8. Format the left column cell in the second row to 377 pixels.
9. Format the right column cell in the second row to 150 pixels.

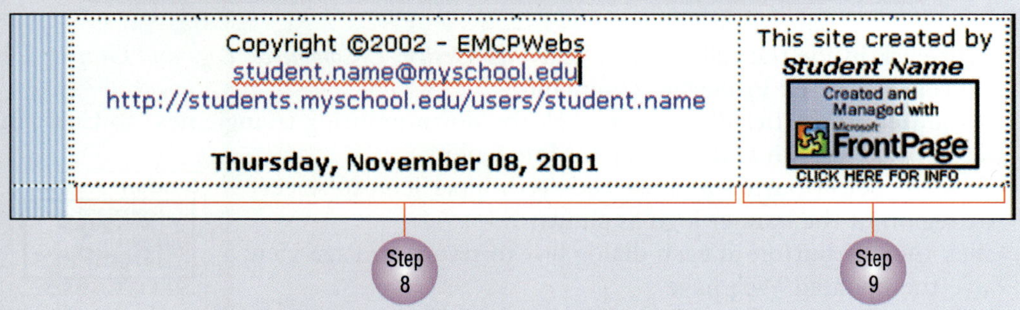

10. Format the table width properties to 527 pixels.
11. Save the updated Web page.

Formatting Cell Background Colors and Pictures

Having the ability to format cell backgrounds gives developers one more option when it comes to background formatting. The Web page, table, and cells can all be formatted with colors, textures, and pictures to add additional dimensions to a Web page. To format cell backgrounds, access the Cell Properties dialog box.

exercise 12

FORMATTING CELL BACKGROUND COLOR

1. Open the index-new.htm page in Page view.
2. Right-click inside the top cell of the embedded table and click Cell Properties.
3. At the Cell Properties dialog box, click the down-pointing triangle next to Color in the Background section and then click More Colors.
4. Click the Select button in the More Colors dialog box and use the eyedropper icon to select the region of the banner logo as shown at the right.

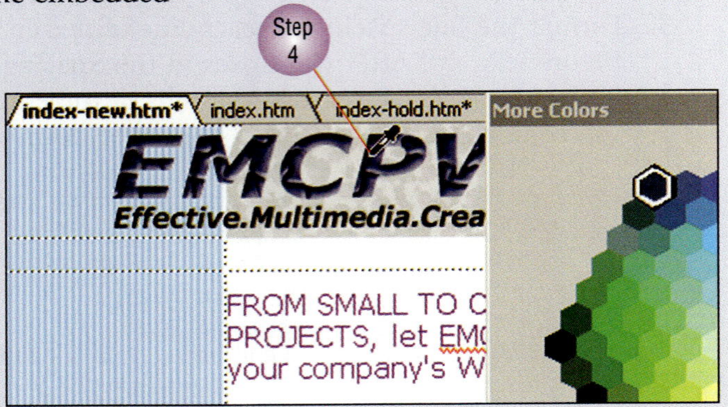

5. Click the OK button.
6. Click the OK button in the Cell Properties dialog box.
7. Format the text in the top cell of the embedded table to White.
8. Format the cell with the hypertext links to Silver.

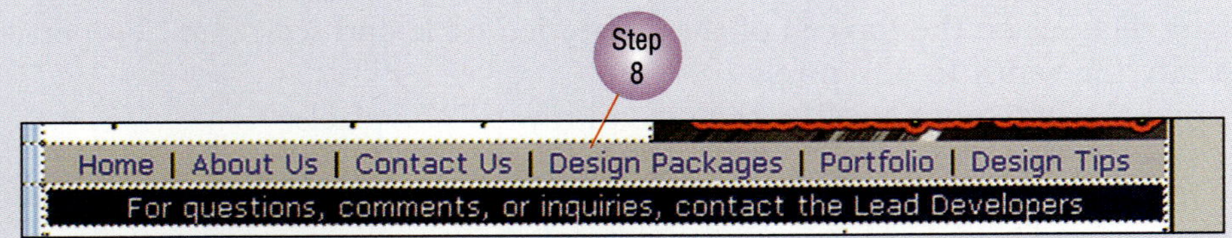

9. Right-click inside the cell with the text *Web Design, E-Commerce, Logo and Graphic Design* and select the Cell Properties command.
10. At the Cell Properties dialog box, click the down-pointing triangle next to Color in the Background section and then click More Colors.
11. Click the Select button and use the eyedropper icon to select the region of the banner logo as shown.

12. Click the OK button in each dialog box to return to Page view.
13. Save the updated Web page.
14. Perform a Preview in Browser and print the Web page.

exercise 13

FORMATTING A CELL BACKGROUND PICTURE

1. Open the index-new.htm page in Page view.
2. Right-click inside the cell that includes your name and the *Created and Managed with…* image and then click Cell Properties.
3. Click the Browse button in the Background section of the Cell Properties dialog box.

4. Locate and open the emcpwebs_back.gif image.
5. Click the OK button (results are as shown at the right).
6. Save the updated Web page.

Placing a Border on a Cell Boundary

Borders are a useful way to separate cells and emphasize cell content. While table borders affect all cells in the table, formatting individual cell borders is a practical feature required by novice to professional Web developers. Cell borders can be formatted to various colors, sizes, and styles. To format cell borders, access the Cell Properties dialog box and click the Style button. Click the Format button at the bottom of the Modify Style dialog box and then click *Border* on the drop-down menu.

exercise 14 APPLYING AND FORMATTING CELL BORDERS

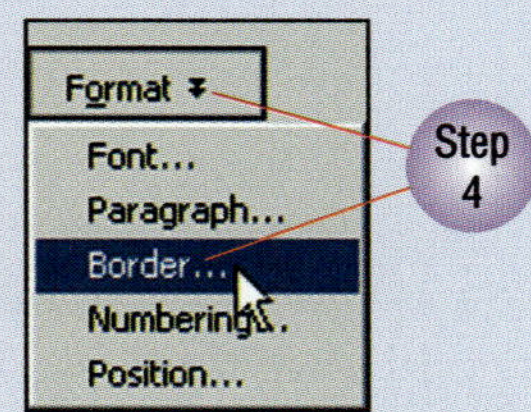

1. Open the index-new.htm page in Page view.
2. Right-click inside the cell with the text *Web Design, E-Commerce, Logo and Graphic Design* and select the Cell Properties command.
3. Click the Style button in the Cell Properties dialog box.
4. Click the Format button in the Modify Style dialog box and then click Border.
5. At the Borders and Shading dialog box, under Color, select Red.
6. Key **1** in the Width text box.
7. In the Preview area, click the buttons to apply the border at the top and bottom.

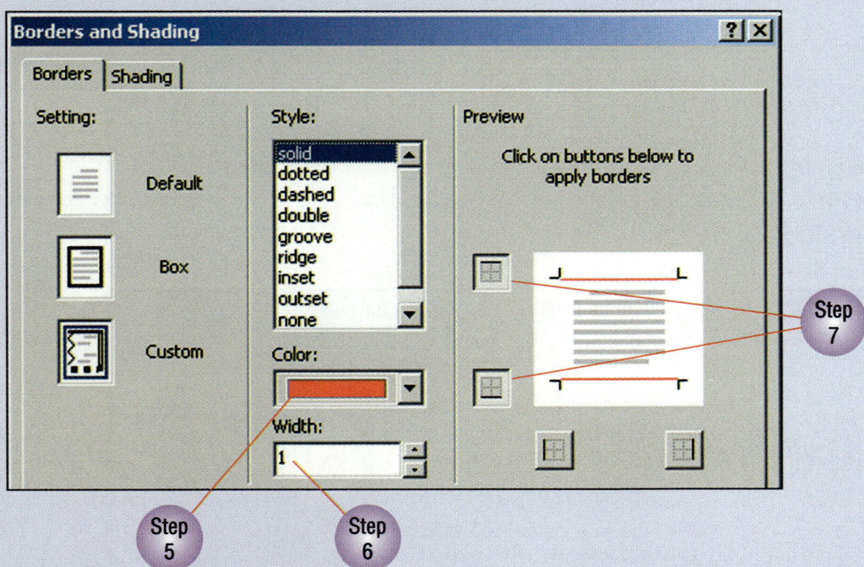

8. Click OK in each dialog box to return to Page view.

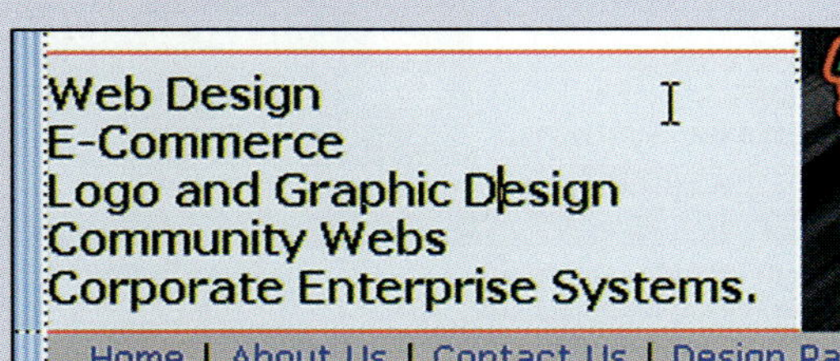

9. Save the updated Web page.
10. Perform a Preview in Browser and print the Web page.

exercise 15

APPLYING THE FINISHING TOUCHES TO THE NEW HOME PAGE

1. Open the index-new.htm page in Page view.
2. Place the insertion point in the second column of the second row below the Web page banner.
3. Insert the following images into the cell: aboutusbutton.gif, contactusbutton.gif, packagesbutton.gif, portfoliobutton.gif, and designtipsbutton.gif.

Step 3

4. Format the background of the top table cell of the Web page to emcpwebs_back.gif.
5. Format the background of the first cell in the second row below the Web page banner to White.
6. Click Insert and then click Date and Time.
7. At the Date and Time dialog box, select the options shown in the illustration.
8. Format the date component to Verdana, 12 points, and bold.

Step 7

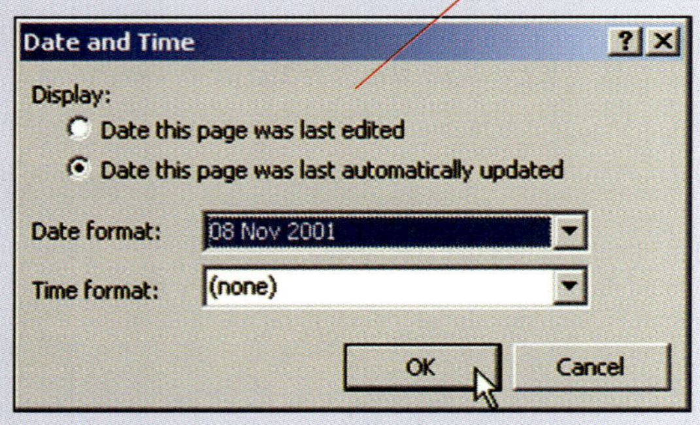

Step 8

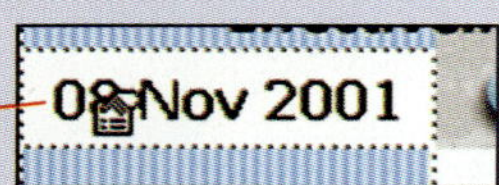

9. Save the updated Web page.
10. Perform a Preview in Browser and print the Web page.

Automatically Formatting Cell Widths to Match Contents

While many table and cell properties are preformatted prior to entering content, some cell content is too small to command wide cell widths. The AutoFit to Contents button on the Tables toolbar will conform the cells to match the cell content.

exercise 16 AUTOMATICALLY FORMATTING CELL WIDTHS TO MATCH CONTENTS

1. Open the webdesign.htm page in Page view.
2. Dock the Tables toolbar below the Formatting toolbar, if it is not already positioned there.
3. Place the insertion point anywhere in the table.
4. Click the AutoFit to Contents button on the Tables toolbar.

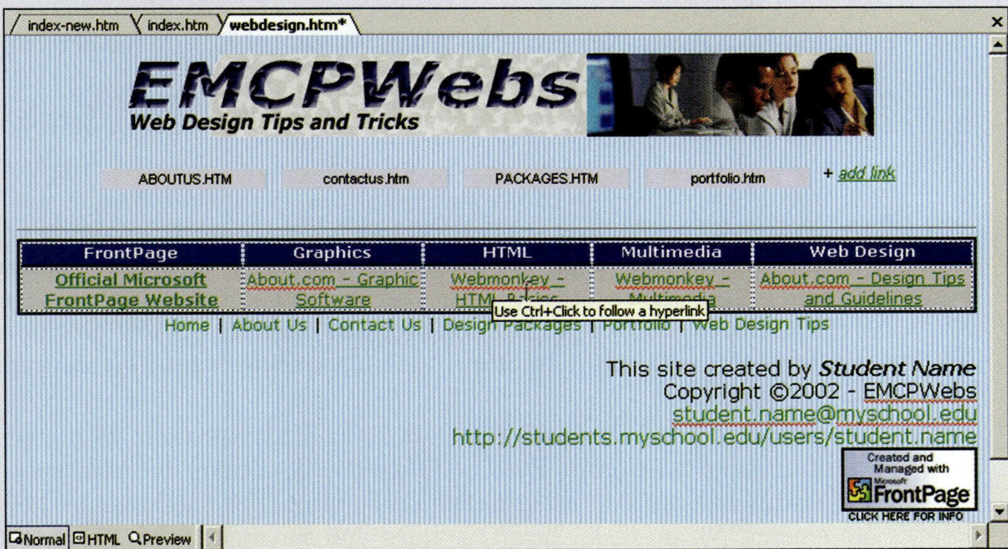

5. Save the updated Web page.
6. Perform a Preview in Browser and print the Web page.

Publishing FrontPage Webs and Web Pages

Publishing FrontPage Webs and pages can be the most intimidating part of the Web development process. Most Web designers are not experts in server software and servicing. When publishing a Web site to the World Wide Web, you must have a place to store your Web folder and files that the whole world can access. This storage location is typically not the computer system on which you created the Web and pages. Companies often either have a Web server set up for the company Web site or lease space on a Web server through an Internet Service Provider (ISP) or domain host. These topics were discussed briefly in chapter 1.

Exploring Web Server Functions

A Web server can be simply defined as a computer system that dispenses Web pages to a viewer's browser. The Web server must have installed not only an operating system but also Web server software. The Web server software program that best supports the Microsoft FrontPage server extensions is Microsoft Internet Information Services (IIS). Other server software that works with FrontPage includes the UNIX operating system and the Netscape and Apache Web server programs.

Although not all companies or ISPs have or want FrontPage server extensions installed on their servers, it is still possible to publish a FrontPage Web to almost any Web server. As you may recall from chapter 6, certain FrontPage Web components do not work unless the FrontPage server extensions are installed. Make sure your company or ISP has the extensions installed on its system if you plan to utilize any of these components.

In addition to FrontPage server extensions on a server, users can utilize the Microsoft Personal Web Server (PWS). The PWS is designed to allow users to test Webs and the various FrontPage Web components on a local computer prior to publishing to a server. Refer to your Windows manual for any further instructions.

Exploring Microsoft Internet Information Services (IIS) Web Server Software

Microsoft's IIS software is intended for building and administering Web sites. Microsoft IIS is a common choice for companies and ISPs to handle and monitor Web sites, files, traffic, and application processing. With IIS, Web developers can create active server pages (ASPs) and ActiveX controls that are located and processed on the server rather than the user's computer. In addition, developers can create Internet Server Application Program Interface (ISAPI) programs, similar to CGI (Common Gateway Interface) scripts that request and get data from Web sites and databases.

If you are running Microsoft Windows 2000 or XP, Microsoft IIS can be installed by first accessing the Control Panel and then double-clicking the *Add/Remove Programs* icon. Next, select the Internet Information Services (IIS) check box in the Windows Components Wizard dialog box. One thing you may need to be aware of if you are using Windows 2000 is that clicking the Details button in the Wizard includes the FrontPage 2000 Server Extensions option. Since you are using FrontPage 2002, do not select this option; install the 2002 server extensions separately. Refer to your Windows manual for any further instructions. (Check with your instructor before performing any of these actions.)

Testing Browser Compatibility

What are those features that work only with the FrontPage server extensions? What if my company uses only Netscape Navigator? What about Web TV? In a perfect world, every Web technology would work exactly as it should in any browser. Unfortunately, standardization is almost impossible as people and companies continue to develop entertaining and page-enhancing technologies. FrontPage 2002 has a browser, server, and technology compatibility feature that is located on the Tools menu. Keep in mind when designing a Web site that using this method is only a start. The best practice is to test your Web page(s) in the various browsers.

exercise 17

TESTING BROWSER COMPATIBILITY

1. Open FrontPage 2002, if it is not already open.
2. Click Tools and then click Page Options.
3. At the Page Options dialog box, click the Compatibility tab.
4. Select *Netscape Navigator only* from the Browsers drop-down menu.
5. Click the OK button.
6. Click Insert and then click Web Component.
7. At the Inseert Web Component dialog box, note that the *Marquee* component in the *Dynamic Effects* category is ghosted, or dimmed, and cannot be selected.

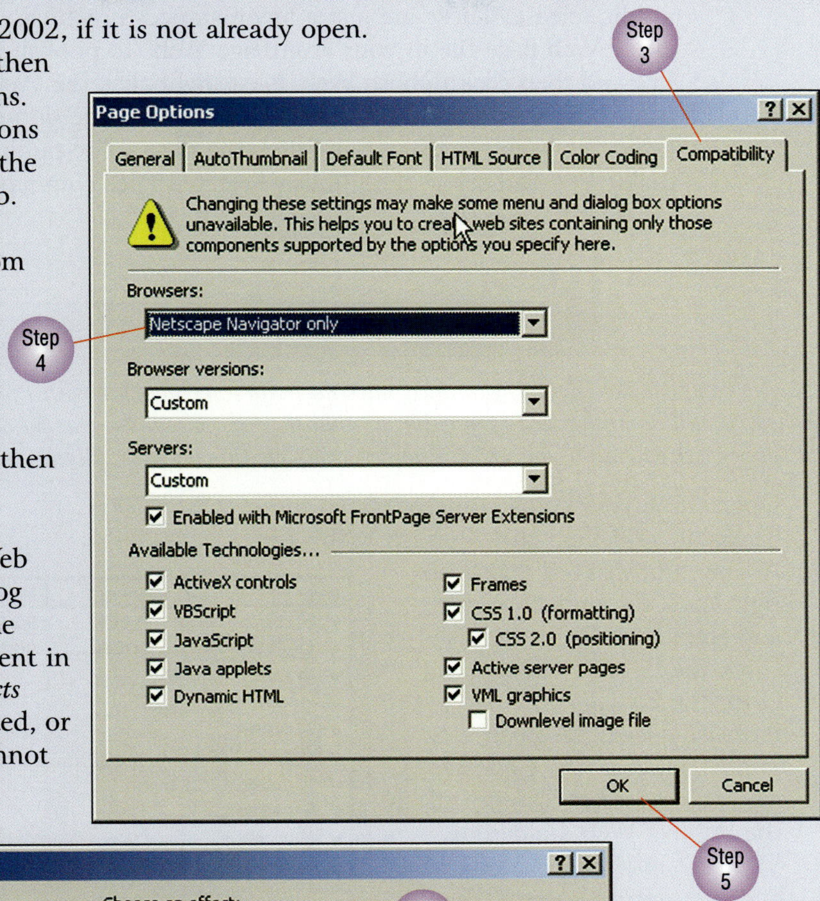

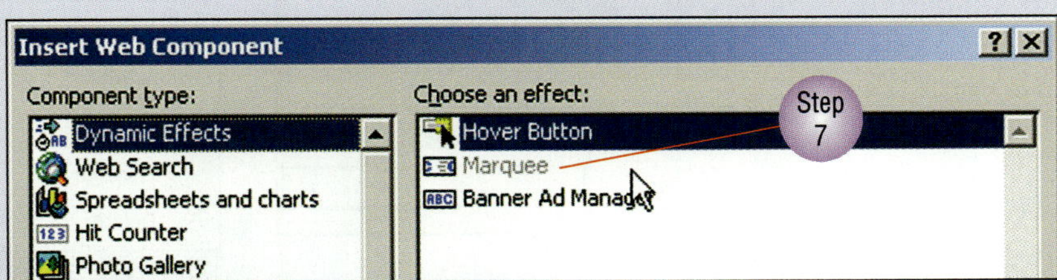

8. Return to the Compatibility tab in the Page Options dialog box.
9. Select *Both Internet Explorer and Navigator* from the Browsers drop-down menu.
10. Click the Enabled with Microsoft FrontPage Server Extensions check box to remove the check mark and disable the settings.
11. Click the OK button.
12. Click Insert and note that the Page Banner and Navigation Bar commands are not available from the menu.
13. Return to the Compatibility tab in the Page Options dialog box and restore the check mark to the Enabled with Microsoft FrontPage Server Extensions check box.

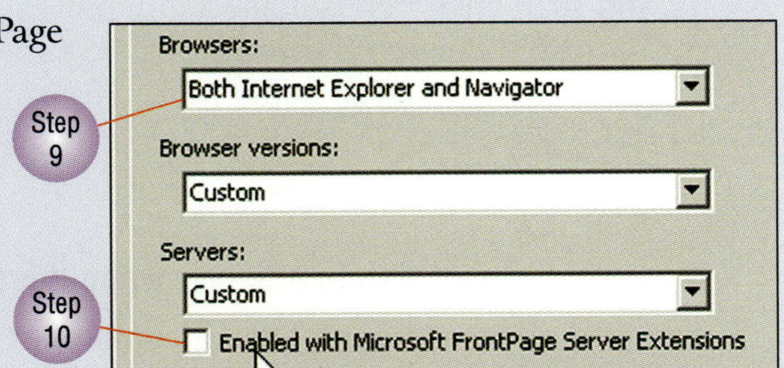

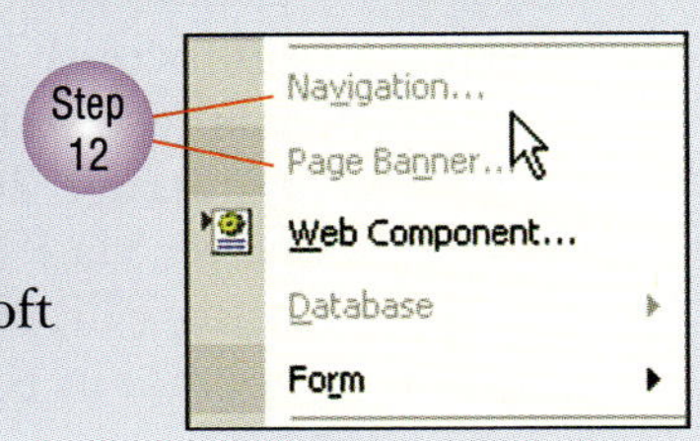

Publishing Only the Pages You Want

In chapter 6, you published an entire FrontPage Web to a Web server. Web pages within a FrontPage Web may be under construction, incomplete, or not ready for public release. These are just a few instances in which you do not want to publish every Web page file in your FrontPage Web. To publish individual pages, first click File and then click Publish Web. Next, right-click the Web page files that you do not want published and select Don't Publish from the pop-up menu. To publish only a specific Web page file, right-click the page to be published in the Publish Web dialog box and select the Publish Selected Files command.

exercise 18 PUBLISHING SELECTED PAGES

(Note: To complete exercise 18, you must have access to a Web server with FrontPage server extensions installed as well as authorized permission to publish. Ask your instructor for school-specific Web publishing instructions. If you are not able to complete this activity, please read through the steps.)

1. Open the EMCPWebs FrontPage Web in FrontPage 2002.
2. Click File and then click Publish Web.
3. At the Publish Web dialog box, right-click the index.htm file and then click Don't Publish.
4. Click the Publish button.
5. Once the EMCPWebs FrontPage Web has been published, click the *Click here to view your published Website* link in the Publish Web dialog box.
6. View the unchanged home page and then return to FrontPage.
7. Click File and then click Publish Web.
8. At the Publish Web dialog box, right-click the index.htm file and then click Publish Selected Files.
9. Perform a Preview in Browser to view the most recent update of the home page.

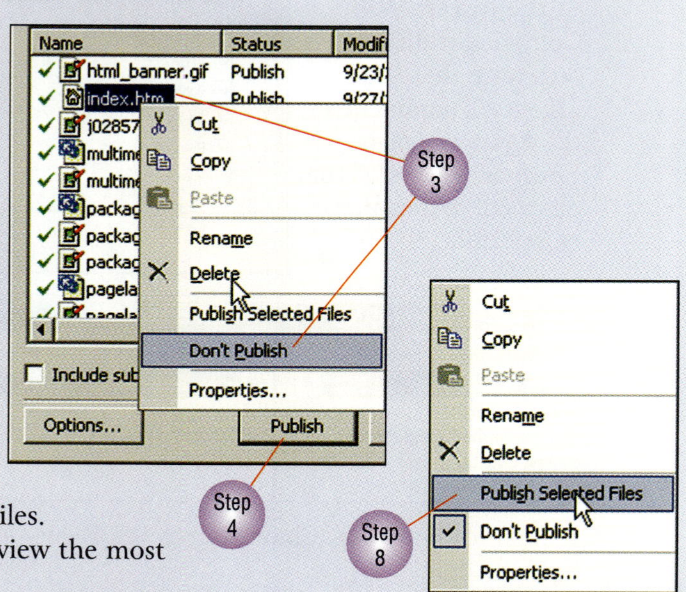

Publishing to a Server without FrontPage Server Extensions

Even though not all companies and ISPs have the Microsoft FrontPage server extensions installed on their Web server(s), most server software allows file transfer protocol (FTP) access for publishing pages and files. (Figure 7.5 shows the alert you receive if you try to publish to a server without FrontPage server extensions.) FrontPage 2002 has the ability to publish Web pages and other files to a Web server via FTP. When you are ready to publish a FrontPage Web to a Web server using FTP, click the Publish Web button on the Standard toolbar and key the FTP address in the Publish Destination dialog box.

FIGURE 7.5 ***Alert Dialog Box***

As long as the Web server to which you are publishing has FrontPage server extensions installed, only those pages that have changed since the last update will be published.

exercise 19

PUBLISHING TO A SERVER WITHOUT FRONTPAGE SERVER EXTENSIONS

(Note: To complete exercise 19, you must have access to a Web server with FTP access and authorized permission to publish. Ask your instructor for school-specific Web publishing instructions. If you are not able to complete this activity, please read through the steps.)

1. Using FrontPage, create on your storage device a personal FrontPage Web titled *electronicportfolio* that you can use to promote yourself, your skills, and your resume to the world. Include at least the following:
   - biographical information
   - resume-oriented information (skills, experience, education, etc.)
   - hobbies and interests
2. Import the following portfolio-oriented files into your FrontPage Web:
   - resume
   - exemplary research papers, writing samples, etc.
   - scanned and digital photographs of projects, artwork, performances, etc.
3. Keep the following aspects of Web design and structure in mind as you design and create your personal Web site:
   - navigation structure
   - table structure layout design
   - background (image, color, texture, or watermark)
   - personal photos (scanned or digital)
   - image map (use Hotspot hyperlinks)
   - page banners (located on each page)
   - navigation links to other pages and files
   - e-mail hyperlink
   - copyright information
   - date of last update
   - textual content properly formatted (e.g., fonts, sizes, colors)

4. Once you are finished, click the Publish Web button on the Standard toolbar.
5. Key the FTP address in the Publish Destination dialog box.

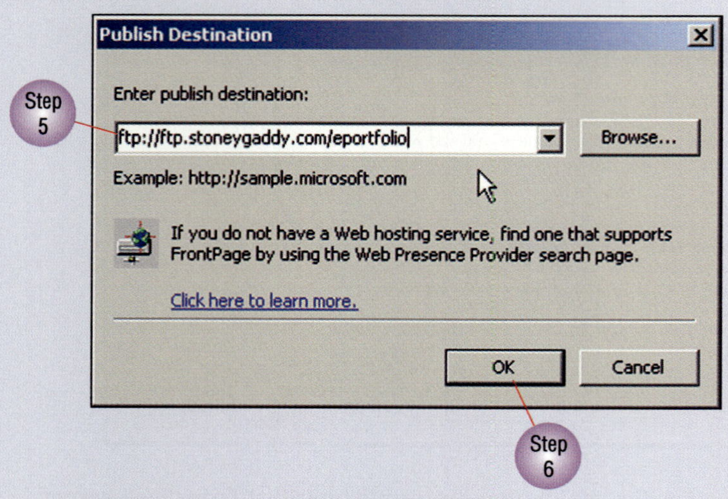

6. Click the OK button.
7. Key your user name and password in the Name and Password Required dialog box.

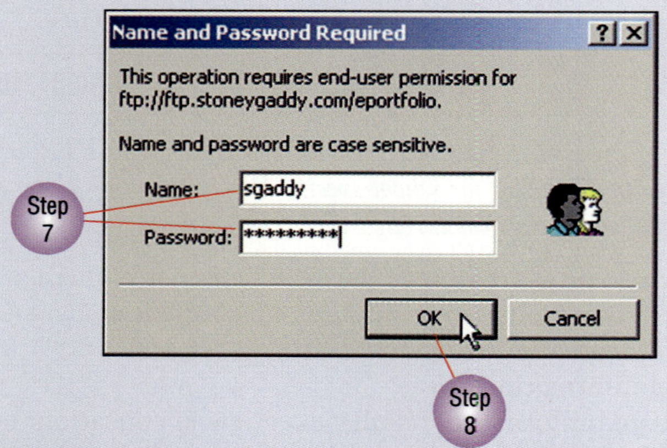

8. Click the OK button.
9. Click OK when asked if you want to create a Web.

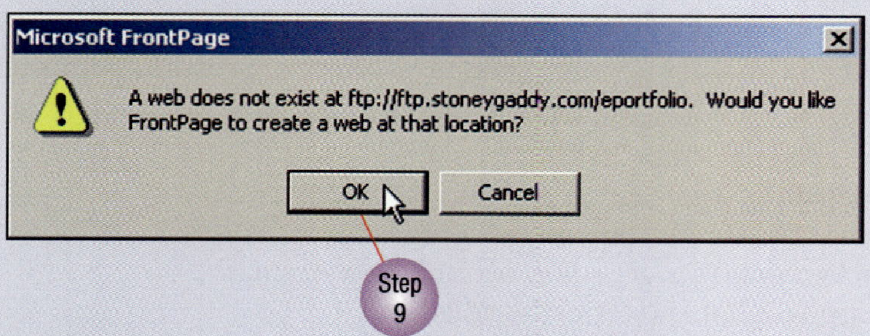

10. Click the Publish button in the Publish Web dialog box.
11. View your published eportfolio.
12. Exit FrontPage.

Publishing to a Different Server or Location (Making a Backup)

There are several different ways to make a backup of your FrontPage Web. Using the Publish Web feature, you can create a backup not only onto a disk, but also onto a Web server. To make a backup copy of your FrontPage Web on a floppy disk, follow these steps:

1. Open your eportfolio Web into FrontPage.
2. Click File and then click Publish Web.
3. Click the Change button in the Publish Web dialog box.
4. Insert a blank diskette into the floppy drive and then key the copy destination **a:\eportfolio**.
5. Click the OK button in each of the next two dialog boxes.
6. Click the Publish button.

CHAPTER summary

- Tables, by default, are formatted to 100 percent of the browser window.
- Table widths can be formatted in pixels or by percent.
- Table properties can easily be formatted by right-clicking inside the table and selecting the Table Properties command.
- Cell padding is the spacing between the text and the cell borders.
- Cell spacing is the spacing between each cell.
- Set border sizes to 0 pixels to make cell borders invisible in Web browsers.
- Table backgrounds can be formatted to colors and images in the Table Properties dialog box.
- Web pages have a 20-pixel margin at the top and left by default and can be altered by clicking the Format menu and selecting the Background command.
- Tables inserted into a cell of an existing table give designers flexibility in cell height and width specifications without affecting the cell properties of the original table.
- The Table AutoFormat feature, located on the Table menu, can be used to quickly format tables.
- Table AutoFormat features include border colors, background colors, font styles, sizes, and colors, and an AutoFit option.
- Cell widths should correspond to the original table's width.
- Cell contents are aligned in the vertical middle of the cell by default.
- Cells can be formatted by right-clicking inside the table and selecting the Cell Properties command.
- Cell backgrounds can be formatted to colors and images in the Cell Properties dialog box.
- Cell borders can be formatted to various colors, sizes, and styles to separate cells and emphasize cell contents.

- Cell width can conform to the contents by clicking the AutoFit to Contents button on the Tables toolbar.
- FrontPage Webs must be stored on a Web server for the entire world to access them.
- A Web server is basically a computer system that dispenses Web pages to a viewer's browser.
- The Microsoft Internet Information Services (IIS) Web server software best supports the FrontPage server extensions.
- Microsoft IIS is a common choice for companies and ISPs to handle and monitor Web sites, files, traffic, and application processing.
- Microsoft IIS can be installed by first accessing the Control Panel and then double-clicking the *Add/Remove Programs* icon in either the Windows 2000 or XP operating system.
- FrontPage 2002 has a browser, server, and technology compatibility feature that can be accessed by clicking the Tools menu, Page Options, and then clicking the Compatibility tab.
- Individual Web pages can be set to not publish by right-clicking the file in the Publish Web dialog box and selecting the Don't Publish command.
- To publish only a specific Web page file, right-click the page to be published in the Publish Web dialog box and select the Publish Selected Files command.
- FrontPage 2002 has the ability to publish Web pages and other files to a Web server via FTP.

COMMANDS review

Command	Mouse/Keyboard
Format table width	Right-click inside table, select Table Properties, Specify width
Alter table cell padding	Click Table Properties, Cell padding
Alter table cell spacing	Click Table Properties, Cell spacing
Format table border color	Click Table Properties, Color
Remove table borders	Click Table Properties, Borders Size
Format table background	Click Table Properties, Background
Format Web page margins	Click Format, Background
Apply Table AutoFormat	Click Table, Table AutoFormat
Format cell width	Right-click inside table, select Cell Properties, Specify width
Format cell background	Right-click inside table, select Cell Properties, Background
Format cell borders	Right-click inside table, select Cell Properties, click Style button, click Format, Border
Format cell width to match contents	Click AutoFit to Contents button on Tables toolbar

Test browser compatibility	Click Tools, Page Options, Compatibility tab
Exclude pages from being published	Click File, Publish Web, right-click the file, select Don't Publish
Publish only selected Web pages	Click File, Publish Web, right-click the file, select Publish Selected File
Publish to a server using FTP	Click Publish Web button on Standard toolbar, key FTP address, key user name and password, click Publish button

CONCEPTS check

Completion: On a blank sheet of paper, indicate the correct term, command, or number for each item.

1. Tables are formatted to this width by default.
2. The spacing between the text and the cell borders can be formatted by altering this in the Table Properties dialog box.
3. The spacing between each table cell can be formatted by altering this in the Table Properties dialog box.
4. Table borders can be made invisible in browser windows by formatting table borders to this size.
5. Web page margins can be altered in this dialog box.
6. Web page margins are approximately this many pixels on the top and left.
7. Use this feature to quickly format a table with various border colors, background colors, and font styles, sizes, and colors.
8. The quickest method for accessing either the Table Properties or Cell Properties dialog box is to perform this shortcut.
9. Vertical cell alignment is set to this by default.
10. To apply individual borders to a cell, first click this button in the Cell Properties dialog box.
11. Click this button on the Tables toolbar to automatically conform table cell widths to match the contents.
12. This Web server software program best supports Microsoft FrontPage server extensions.
13. Select this right-click command to omit files from being published.
14. Select this right-click command to publish only specific files.
15. While not all servers have FrontPage server extensions installed, most servers allow you to publish pages using this method.

SKILLS check

Assessment 1

1. In FrontPage, create the 4 × 4 table as shown below.

Banner Logo	Merge with Cell 1-1	Banner Ad	Contact Info
Headline News, Weather, Business of the Week, Sports, Classifieds, Archives, The Staff, Contact Us	News Headline	Merge with Cell 2-2	Your Opinion
Hit Counter	Sports Headline	Around the Town Headline	Merge with cell 4-4
Date of Last Update	Text Navigation Bar	Copyright Information	Merge with cell 3-4

2. Merge cells 1-1 and 1-2 in the first row of the table.
3. Delete the *Merge with Cell 1-1* text in the merged cell.
4. Delete any extra blank spaces and center align the *Banner Logo* text in the cell.
5. Merge cells 2-2 and 2-3 in the second row of the table.
6. Delete the *Merge with Cell 2-2* text and any blank spaces.
7. Merge cells 3-4 and 4-4 in the last column of the table.
8. Delete all text in that cell and key **Current Temperature**.
9. Split cell 2-1 into 8 rows.
10. Move each news heading into an individual cell as shown below.

<table>
<tr><td colspan="2">Banner Logo</td><td>Banner Ad</td><td>Contact Info</td></tr>
<tr><td>Headline News</td><td colspan="2" rowspan="8">News Headline</td><td rowspan="8">Your Opinion</td></tr>
<tr><td>Weather</td></tr>
<tr><td>Business of the Week</td></tr>
<tr><td>Sports</td></tr>
<tr><td>Classifieds</td></tr>
<tr><td>Archives</td></tr>
<tr><td>The Staff</td></tr>
<tr><td>Contact Us</td></tr>
<tr><td>Hit Counter</td><td>Sports Headline</td><td>Around the Town Headline</td><td rowspan="2">Current Temperature</td></tr>
<tr><td>Date of Last Update</td><td>Text Navigation Bar</td><td>Copyright Information</td></tr>
</table>

11. Save the Web page as newstemplate.htm with the title *Community News Template*.
12. Print a copy of the Web page in your browser.

Assessment 2

1. Open the newstemplate.htm file created in assessment 1.
2. Format a Maroon border that surrounds each cell of the table.
3. Format a 3-pixel Green border that surrounds the table.
4. Save the updated Web page.
5. Print the Web page in your browser.

Assessment 3

1. Open the conference.htm file from your *Chapter 7* folder.
2. Format the table background a Light Green color.
3. Format the table background with the conference.gif image located in your *Chapter 7* folder.
4. Save the updated Web page.
5. Print the Web page in your browser.

Assessment 4

1. Create a table and cell arrangement to match the illustration below.

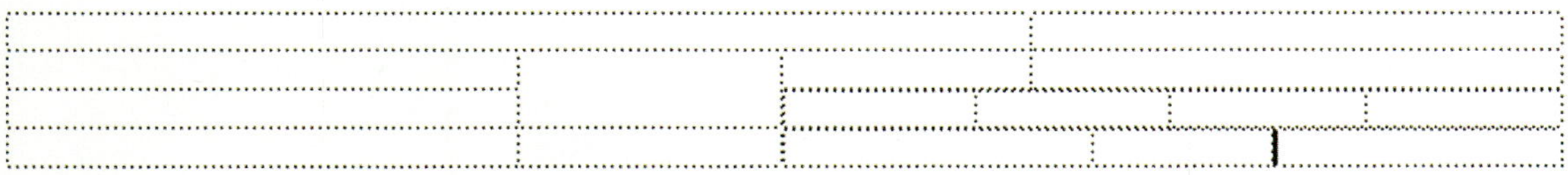

2. Format the bounding table with a Navy border and Light Blue cell shading.
3. Format the first embedded table with a Maroon border and Pink shading.
4. Format the second embedded table with a Green border and Light Green shading.
5. Save the Web page as embeddedtable.htm with the title *Table with a Table.*
6. Print the Web page in your browser.

Assessment 5

1. Create a table that contains your semester schedule.
2. Include *Class Title, Cr. Hrs., Days, Time, Room No.,* and *Instructor* as your column headings.
3. Format the table using a Table AutoFormat of your choice.
4. Save the Web page as schedule.htm with the title *2002 [or 2003] Fall [or Spring] Schedule.*
5. Print the Web page in your browser.

Assessment 6

1. Open the schedule.htm file created in assessment 5.
2. Using at least three different formats (color, width, style), apply your own cell border scheme to the table.
3. Using at least two different colors, apply your own cell shading scheme to the table.
4. Save the updated table.
5. Print the Web page in your browser.

Assessment 7

1. Open the schedule.htm file created in assessment 5 and modified in assessment 6.
2. Format the cell widths to match the table contents.
3. Save the updated table.
4. Print the Web page in your browser.

Assessment 8

1. Create a Web site based on an area of interest at your school. Examples could be clubs, organizations, campus news, admissions, athletics, and so on.
2. Create an outline of the content needed for the Web site.
3. Create a hierarchical Web page structure in Navigation view.
4. Use parallel sites on the Internet, campus resources, brainstorming techniques, and other sources to design and create your Web.
5. Publish the FrontPage Web to your school or other Web server. Check with your instructor for trademark, copyright, and other publishing guidelines and policies.

CHAPTER 8

WORKING WITH FRONTPAGE COMPONENTS, PLUG-INS, AND FRAMES

PERFORMANCE OBJECTIVES

Upon successful completion of chapter 8, you will be able to:

- **Insert dynamic effect components**
- **Insert a hit counter, table of contents, and a top 10 list**
- **Insert MSNBC and other Microsoft components**
- **Insert included content such as page includes and pages and pictures based on a schedule**
- **Insert and customize advanced controls such as Macromedia Flash animations and Windows Media Player videos**
- **Insert an inline frame into a Web page**
- **Create a FrontPage Web based around a frames page**
- **Create a frames page using a wizard**
- **Format frame contents and properties**
- **Target frames to open in various frames**

Chapter 8 IRC

FrontPage 2002 has several Web page enhancement features called Web components. Web component types include dynamic effects, photo gallery, link bars, MSNBC components, and advanced controls. Common FrontPage components include hover buttons, marquees, the banner ad manager, hit counters, tables of contents, and top 10 lists. Hover buttons are customizable hyperlinks in which designers can alter color effects and sounds, and even set images to change as the mouse hovers over the button. Marquees are scrolling text banners that typically include announcements and welcome messages. Hit counters keep track of the number of hits (visits) the Web page has received. In this chapter, you will incorporate various Web components into the EMCPWebs FrontPage Web.

FrontPage 2002 is the first version of the program that includes automatic content feed components. Automatic Web content feeds for FrontPage 2002 come from MSNBC (an Internet and broadcast partnership between Microsoft and NBC) and include headlines from business, living and travel, news, sports, technology, and weather. Another component new to FrontPage 2002 is the ability to insert Expedia maps into Web pages. This chapter will also explore the Search the Web with MSN Web component and a stock quote search component.

In many Web sites, identical content is located on multiple pages. Examples of identical page content can include hyperlinks, copyright information, and special announcements. FrontPage 2002 has a Web component feature called page includes that allows developers to insert existing Web page files into another Web page document. Other included content in this chapter comprises pages and pictures based on schedule. With these, Web developers can create birthday announcements, holiday greetings, and other special announcements in advance to be displayed at later specified times.

Inserting FrontPage Web Components

Inserting a Scrolling Marquee

The marquee component is an area of text that animates across the Web page. Marquees are often inserted into Web pages to attract attention to special announcements and to welcome visitors to the Web page. To insert a scrolling marquee, click Insert and then click Web Component. The Marquee effect is located in the Dynamic Effects category. Marquee effects that can be applied include text direction, speed, scroll behavior, size, background color, and the ability to occur once, multiple times, or continuously. The marquee component will not work in Netscape Navigator and displays as regular text on the page.

(Note: Before completing computer exercises, delete the Chapter 7 *folder on your disk Next, download the* Chapter 8 *data files from the Internet Resource Center to the* Chapter 8 *folder you have created on your disk, and then make* Chapter 8 *the active folder.)*

exercise 1

INSERTING A SCROLLNG MARQUEE

1. Drag the *emcpwebs* folder from your *Chapter 8* folder onto your storage device.
2. When prompted, click the Yes to All button in the Confirm Folder Replace dialog box.
3. Open the EMCPWebs FrontPage Web.
4. Open the home page (index.htm) in Page view.
5. Place the insertion point in cell 2-3.
6. Click Insert and then click Web Component.
7. At the Insert Web Component dialog box, ensure that the *Dynamic Effects* component type is selected, and then select the *Marquee* effect.

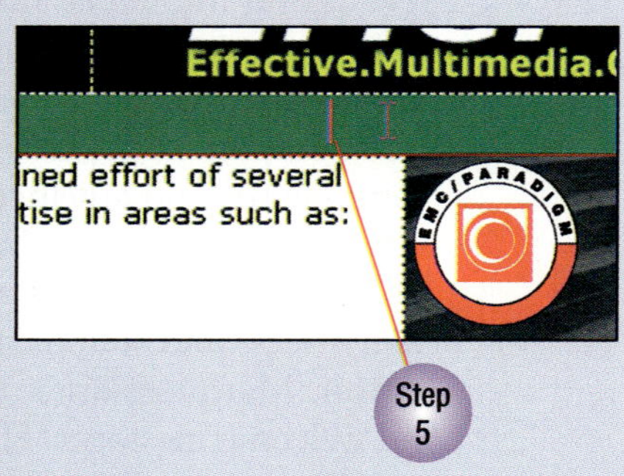

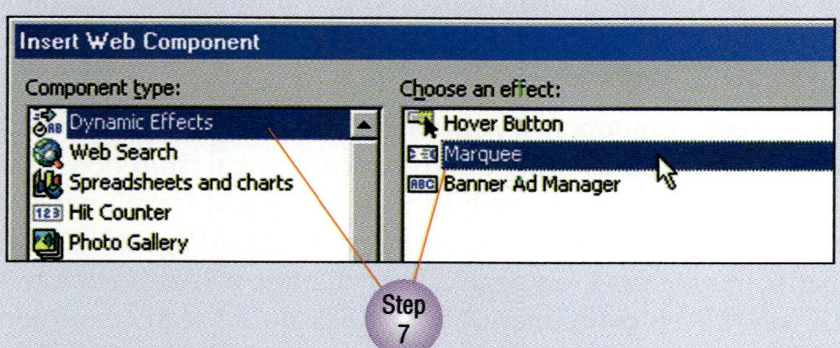

8. Click the Finish button.

9. Key **Attend our Booth at the Web Developer Expo in Los Angeles** in the text box in the Marquee Properties dialog box.
10. Ensure that the width of the marquee is set to 100 percent.
11. Click the OK button.
12. Select the marquee component in the Web page.
13. Using the Formatting toolbar, format the font to Verdana, 10 points, bold, and White.

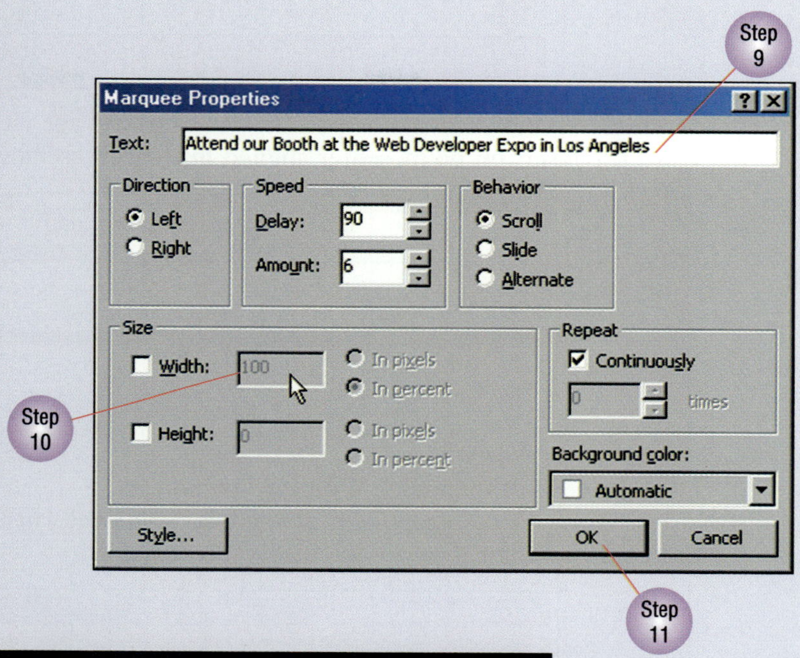

14. Save the updated Web page and perform a Preview in Browser.
15. Return to FrontPage and double-click the marquee component.
16. At the Marquee Properties dialog box, change the Behavior to Slide.
17. Click the OK button.
18. Save the updated Web page and perform a Preview in Browser.
19. Print the Web page.

Inserting a Hit Counter

A Web page hit counter displays the number of times the Web page has been accessed. Since hit counters register each time the page has been accessed, this does not accurately represent the actual number of visitors to the Web page. They are, however, an excellent way to gauge site or page activity. There are five hit counter image styles to choose from. Web developers can also create their own images or download custom images from various Web sites. Hit counters can be inserted into a Web page from the Web Component dialog box. Hit counters will not work unless or until the Web page has been published to a Web server running the FrontPage server extensions.

exercise 2

INSERTING A HIT COUNTER

1. Open the EMCPWebs home page (index.htm) in Page view.
2. Place the insertion point center aligned in the cell as shown.

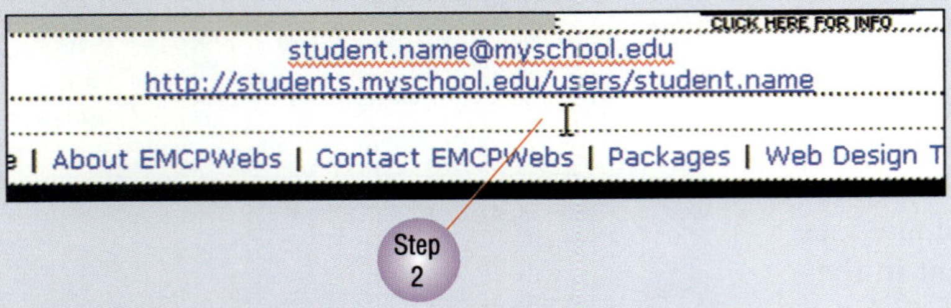

3. Click Insert and then click Web Component.
4. At the Insert Web Component dialog box, select the *Hit Counter* component type.
5. Select the counter style shown in the illustration.

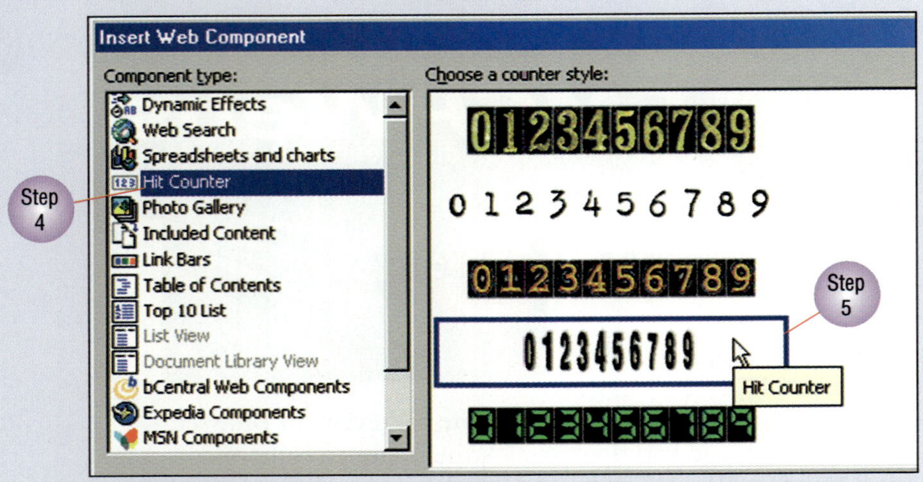

6. Click the Finish button.
7. Click the OK button.
8. Save the updated Web page. *(Note: The illustration below shows the hit counter inserted in the above steps as it would look on the Web running on a server that has the FrontPage server extensions installed.)*

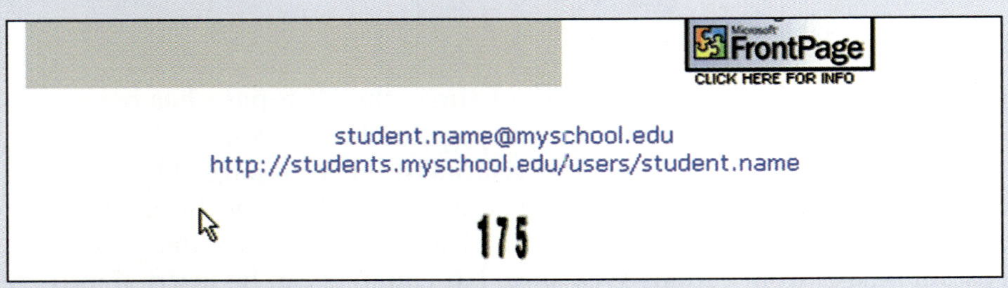

9. Perform a Preview in Browser.

Inserting a Table of Contents

The table of contents component creates an outline of your FrontPage Web pages. In essence, the table of contents feature creates a site map with hyperlinks to the various Web pages and even files within the FrontPage Web. The Web page hyperlinks are based on the page titles.

exercise 3

INSERTING A TABLE OF CONTENTS

1. Ensure that the EMCPWebs FrontPage Web is open.
2. Open the toc.htm Web page in Page view.
3. With the insertion point in the blank cell under the page heading, click Insert and then click Web Component.
4. At the Insert Web Component dialog box, select the *Table of Contents* component type.
5. Select the *For This Web Site* option.

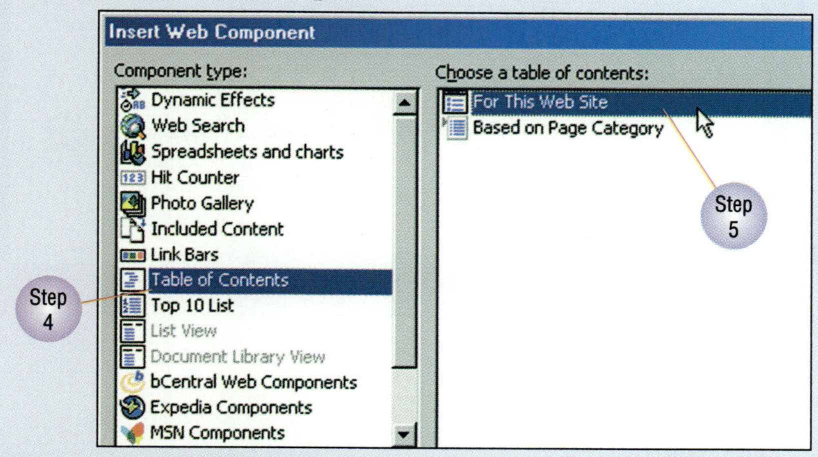

6. Click the Finish button.
7. At the Table of Contents Properties dialog box, ensure that the EMCPWebs home page (index.htm) is the starting point for the table of contents.

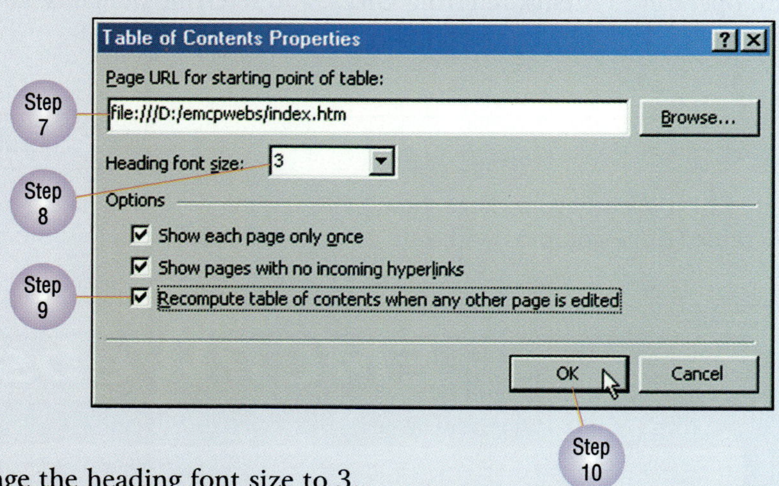

8. Change the heading font size to 3.
9. Click the Recompute table of contents when any other page is edited check box to insert a check mark.
10. Click the OK button.

11. Save the updated Web page.
13. Perform a Preview in Browser (see illustration below) and print the table of contents.

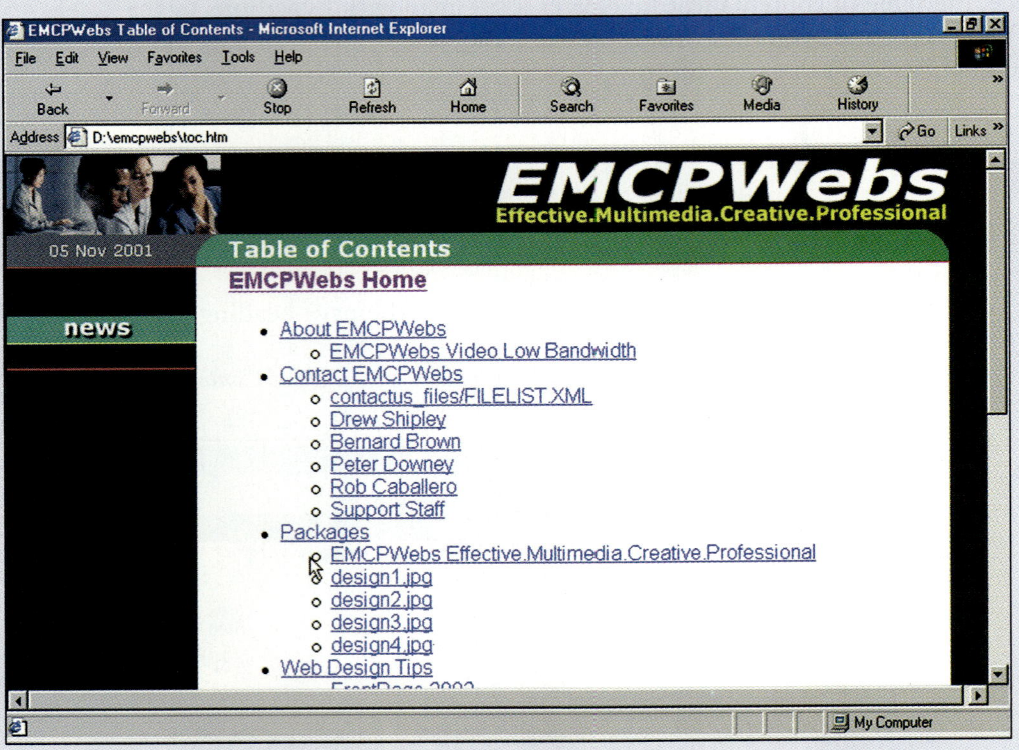

Inserting a Top 10 List

The top 10 list Web component creates hyperlinks to the top 10 most visited pages on your Web site. There are several different top 10 categories, including visited pages, operating systems, referring URLs, and referring domains.

exercise 4

INSERTING A TOP 10 LIST

1. Open the topten.htm Web page in Page view.
2. Insert a 3 × 1 table (three columns with one row) one blank line below the page heading.

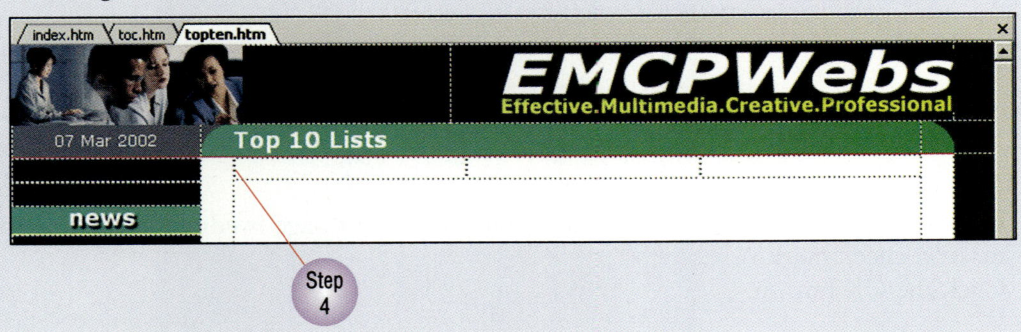

3. Ensure that the table border properties, cell padding, and cell spacing have been set to 0.
4. Place the insertion point in the first cell of the table, click Insert, and then click Web Component.

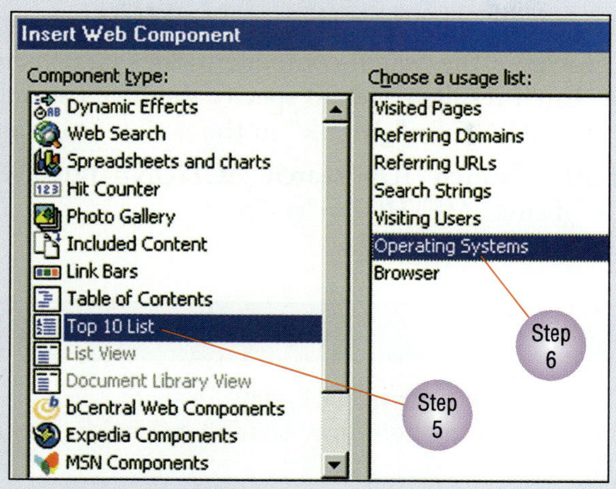

5. At the Insert Web Component dialog box, select the *Top 10 List* component type.
6. Select the *Operating Systems* usage list.
7. Click the Finish button.
8. Click the OK button in the Top 10 List Properties dialog box.
9. Place the insertion point in the second cell of the table and repeat steps 2-8 to insert the *Visited Pages* top 10 list component.
10. Place the insertion point in the third cell of the table and repeat steps 2-8 to insert the *Browsers* top 10 list component.
11. Select the three original cells of the top 10 lists and click the AutoFit to Contents button on the Tables toolbar.
12. Save the updated Web page.
13. Print the Web page from Page view (see illustration below). *(Note: Top 10 Lists will work only on a server that has the FrontPage server extensions installed.)*

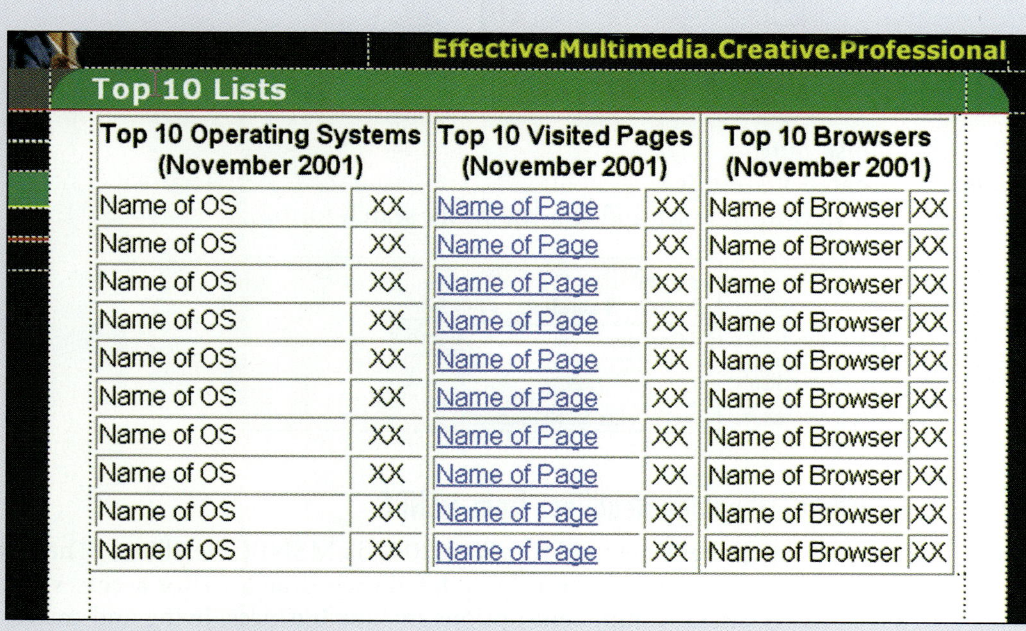

Inserting Microsoft and MSNBC Components

Inserting an MSN Search Component

The MSN search component gives visitors an added option in searching for Web content. However, the search component does take visitors away from your site to the MSN search results page. To specify the MSN search page to open in a new window, key **TARGET="_blank"** in the action script as shown below:

<form NAME="search" ID="search" ACTION="http://search.msn.com/results.asp" TARGET="_blank" METHOD="get">

exercise 5

INSERTING AN MSN SEARCH COMPONENT

1. Open the EMCPWebs home page in page view.
2. Place the insertion point in the light gray shaded cell below the *Lead Developers* e-mail hyperlink.
3. Click Insert and then click Web Component.
4. At the Insert Web Component dialog box, select the *MSN Components* component type.
5. Select the *Search the Web with MSN* component option.

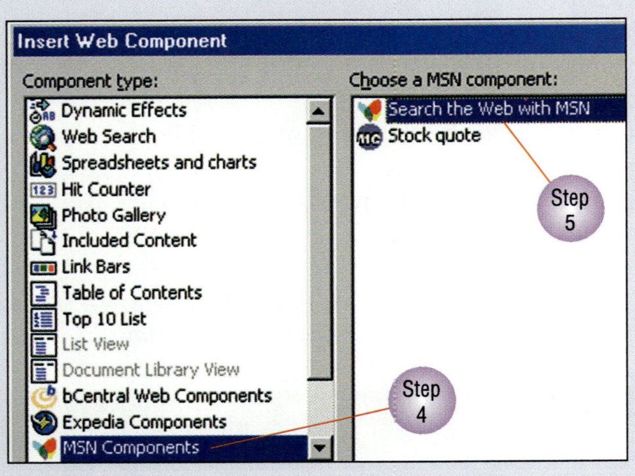

6. Click the Finish button.
7. Save the updated Web page.
8. Perform a Preview in Browser and test the MSN search form.

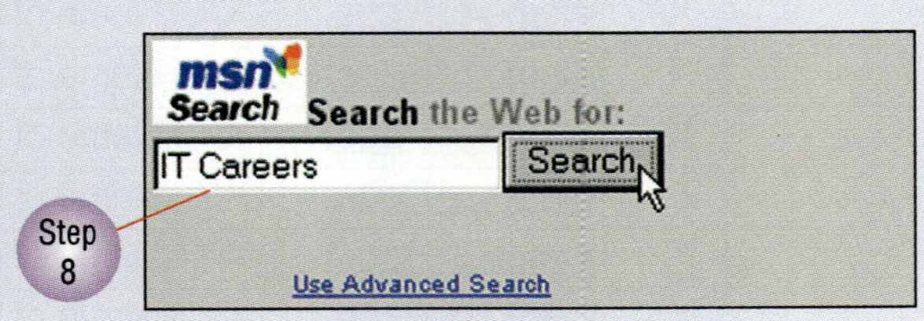

Inserting Technology Headlines from MSNBC

Another component new to FrontPage 2002 is MSNBC headlines. The news headlines, or feeds, are constantly updated each time a visitor accesses the Web page. The headline component options include business, living and travel, news, sports (see figure 8.1), technology, and weather.

FIGURE 8.1 **Sports Headlines from MSNBC**

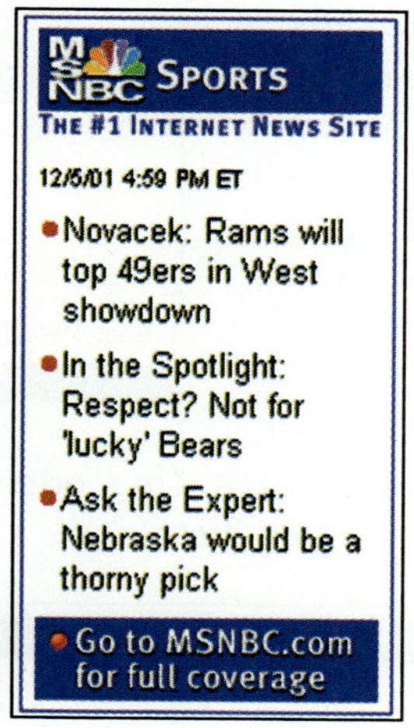

exercise 6

INSERTING TECHNOLOGY HEADLINES FROM MSNBC

1. Open the EMCPWebs home page in page view.
2. Place the insertion point in the cell below the red border, as the inserted Web component is shown in the illustration at the right.
3. Click Insert and then click Web Component.
4. At the Insert Web Component dialog box, select the *MSNBC Components* component type.
5. Select the *Technology Headlines from MSNBC* component option.
6. Click the Finish button.
7. Save the updated Web page.

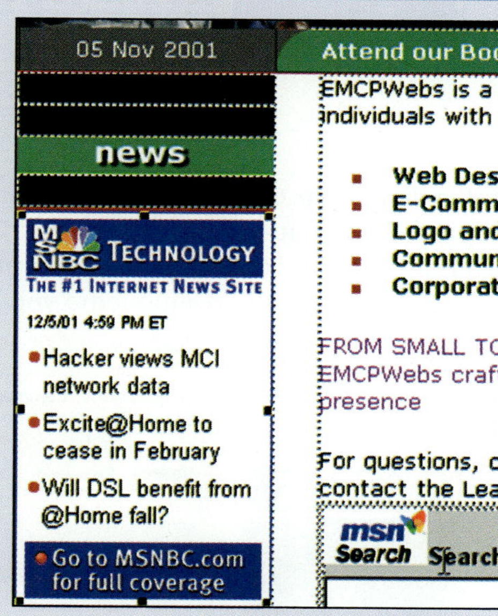

Inserting Weather Information from MSNBC

You do not have to be the local news station to have weather information on your Web site. In addition to the current temperature, the MSNBC weather component offers wind and humidity factors as well as next-day forecasts.

exercise 7

INSERTING WEATHER INFORMATION FROM MSNBC

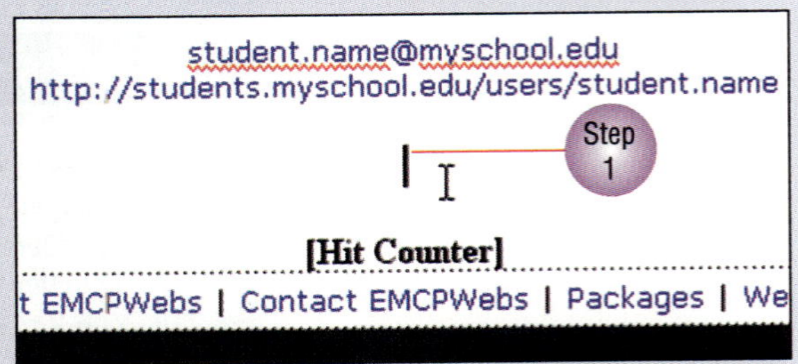

1. Place the insertion point in the cell above the hit counter, click Insert, click Web Component, and select the *MSNBC Components* component type in the Insert Web Component dialog box.
2. Select the *Weather forecast from MSNBC* component option.
3. Click the Finish button.
4. At the Weather forecast from MSNBC Properties dialog box, key your five-digit Zip Code in the Search for a city by name or U.S. ZIP code text box and then click Next.

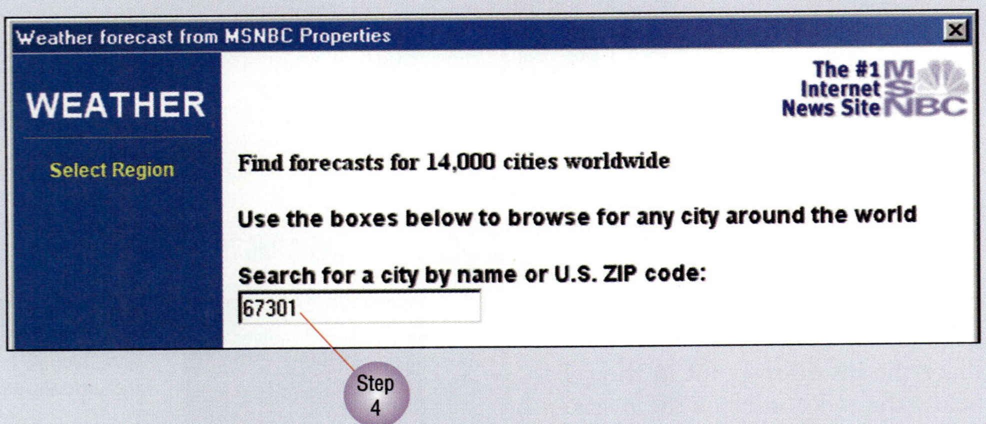

5. Confirm your city and then click Finish.
6. Save the updated home page.
7. Perform a Preview in Browser and print the home page. The illustration below shows the three MSNBC components you have inserted into the home page.

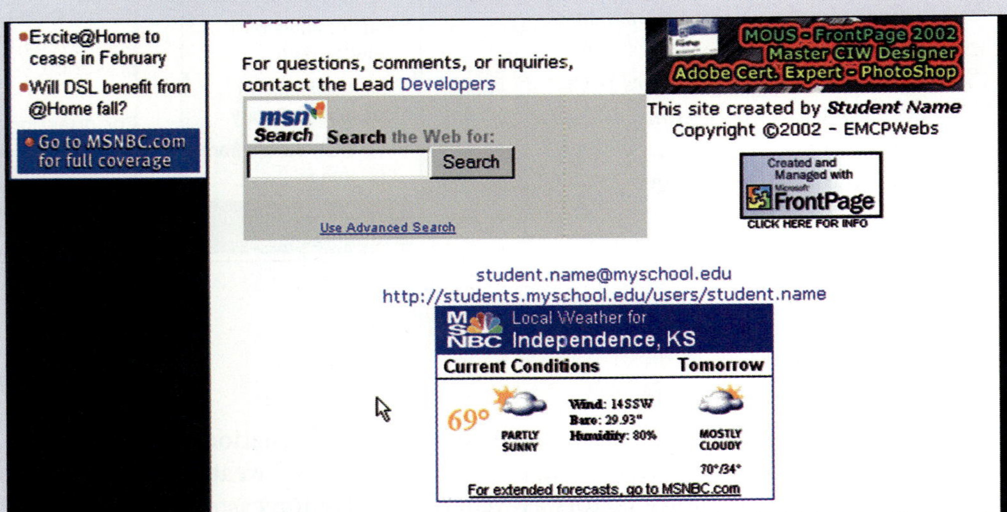

Inserting a Static Map from Expedia

While your address may be sufficient in most instances, providing a map can be of additional assistance to prospective customers or visitors to your Web site. Users can insert an Expedia map based on either an address or a place, such as a city. Once the map is inserted into the Web page and published, visitors wanting additional map information or needing to zoom in to a street-level view can click the map and link to expedia.com.

exercise 8

INSERTING A STATIC MAP FROM EXPEDIA

1. Open the map.htm Web page in Page view and place the insertion point in the empty cell below the heading.
2. Click Insert and then click Web Component.
3. At the Insert Web Component dialog box, select the *Expedia Components* component type.
4. Select the *Static map* component option
5. Click the Finish button.
6. Click the Next button in the first Static map Properties dialog box.
7. At the next Static map Properties dialog box, key a street address, city, state, and Zip Code in the text boxes.

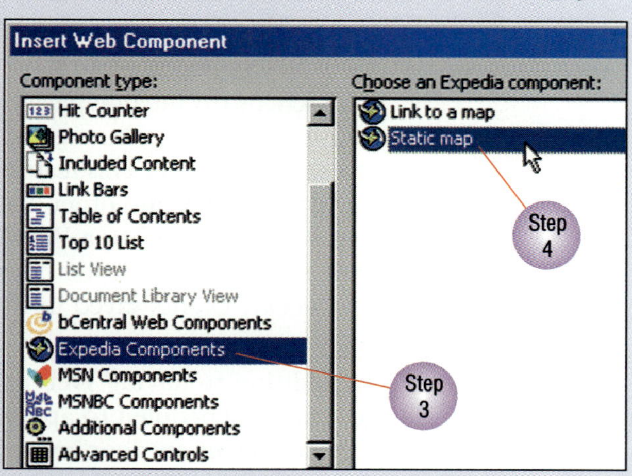

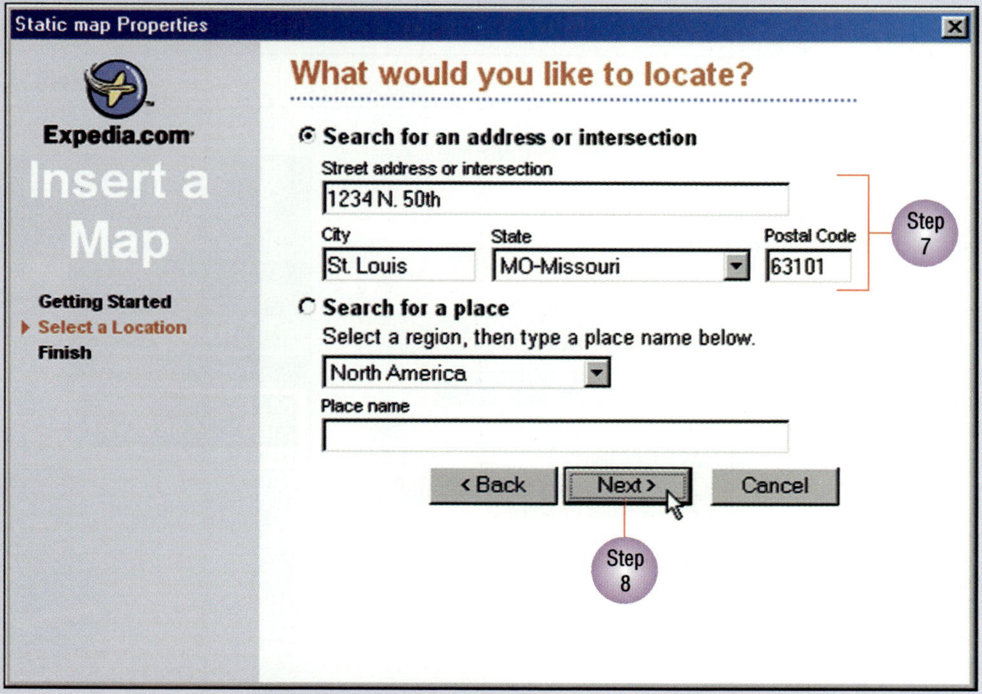

8. Click the Next button.

9. Click the Finish button.
10. Save the updated Web page.
11. Perform a Preview in Browser and print the home page.

Inserting Included Content

The page include component gives Web developers an excellent opportunity to create a single Web page with repetitive content—such as hyperlinks, copyright information, and special announcements—and insert it into another Web page. Unlike shared borders, page includes can be inserted anywhere on the page. Unlike frames (covered later in this chapter), page includes are integrated into the existing Web page; therefore, printing a Web page doesn't require additional selections in the Print dialog box of the Web browser.

The scheduled include page component not only inserts an existing Web page into another Web page, but also can be scheduled to appear from a specified starting date to an ending date. This feature can be used to display announcements, greetings, holiday decorations, and other content at predetermined times. Thus, dynamic Web content can be applied to a Web page in advance. One example of the use of this component is a school master calendar. The master calendar content can be broken up into weekly events saved in the FrontPage Web to be changed every Sunday at midnight.

In addition to having Web pages change within a page include component, images can be scheduled to appear and change. For example, it may be a clever idea to include an outdoor image of a facility or location based on the season (e.g., snowy cityscape in the winter, sunny cityscape in the summer).

exercise 9

INSERTING PAGE INCLUDES

1. Open the EMCPWebs home page in page view.
2. Place the insertion point in cell 3-1.
3. Click Insert and then click Web Component.
4. At the Insert Web Component dialog box, select the *Included Content* component type.

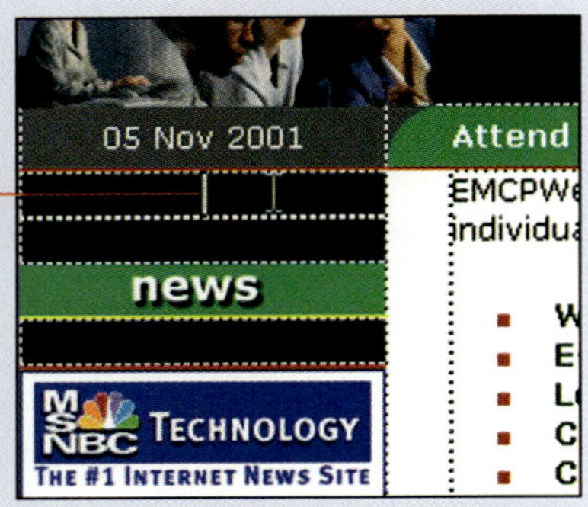

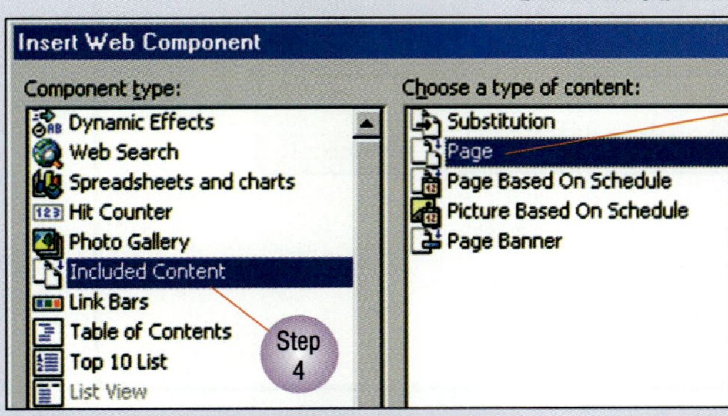

5. Select the *Page* component option.

6. Click the Finish button.
7. At the Include Page Properties dialog box, click the Browse button.

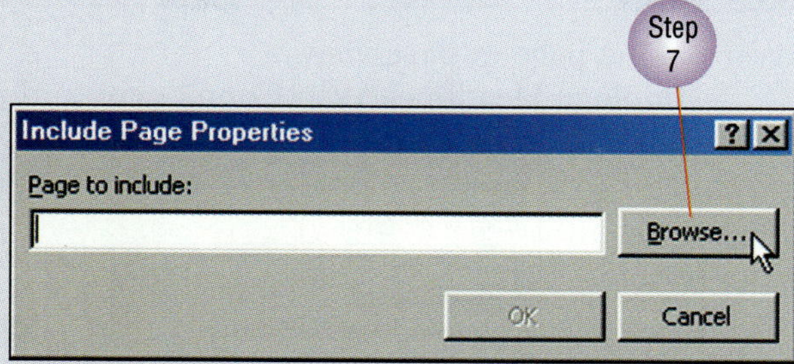

8. Select the links.htm file and then click OK.

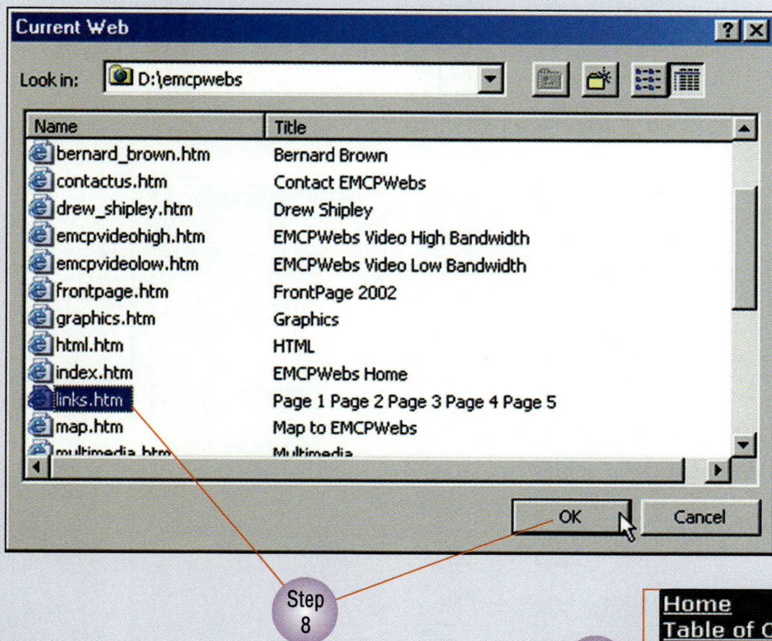

9. Click the OK button to return to Page view.
10. Delete any extra spacing below the page include component in the cell.
11. Repeat steps 2-10 to include the links.htm Web page file in each of the other Web pages in the EMCPWebs FrontPage Web.
12. Repeat steps 2-10 to include the news.htm Web page file.
13. Save the updated home page.
14. Perform a Preview in Browser and print the home page.

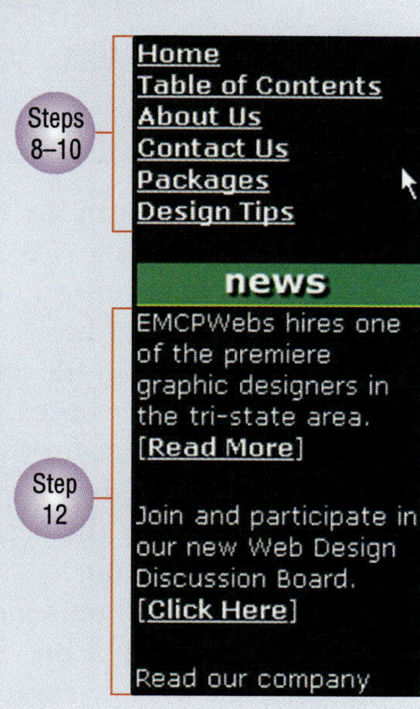

exercise 10

INSERTING PAGE BASED ON SCHEDULE

1. Open the EMCPWebs home page in page view.
2. Select the MSNBC Technology Headlines Web Component and press the Delete key.
3. Click Insert and then click Web Component.
4. At the Insert Web Component dialog box, select the *Included Content* component type.
5. Select the *Page Based On Schedule* content type.
6. Click the Finish button.
7. At the Scheduled Include Page Properties dialog box, click the Browse button next to the During the scheduled time text box.

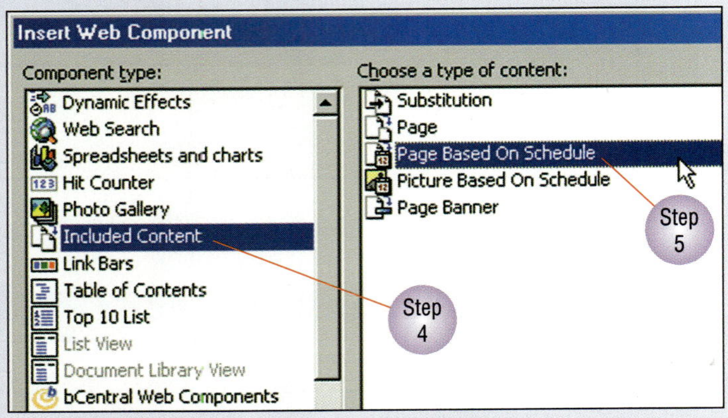

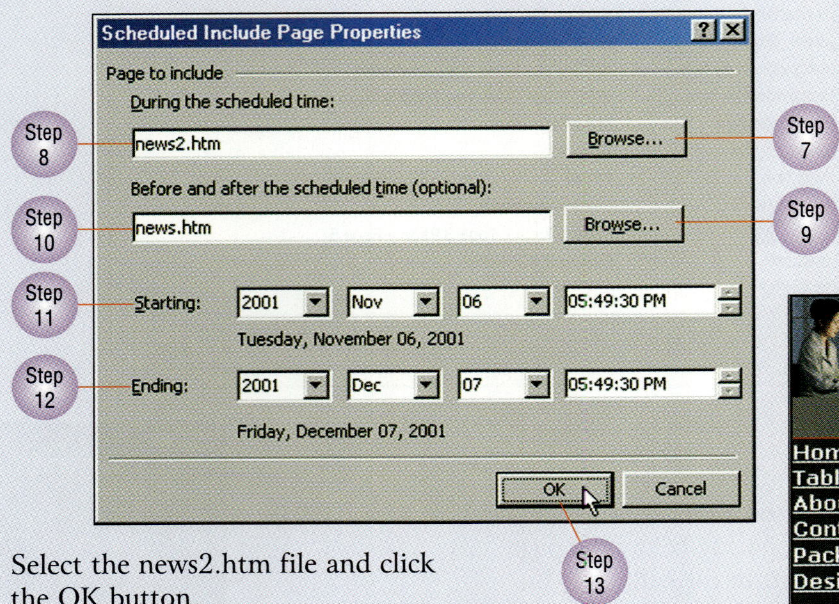

8. Select the news2.htm file and click the OK button.
9. Click the Browse button next to the Before and after the scheduled time text box.
10. Select the news.htm file and click the OK button.
11. In the Starting text boxes, enter the date of your next Web design class set for the beginning of class.
12. In the Ending text boxes, enter the date of the following Web design class set for the beginning of class.
13. Click the OK button.
14. Save the updated home page.
15. Perform a Preview in Browser at your next class meeting and test the page include component.
16. Print the Web page.

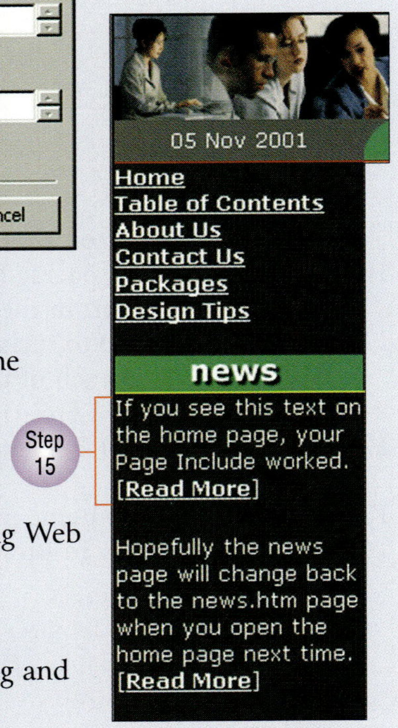

exercise 11 INSERTING PICTURE BASED ON SCHEDULE

1. Open the EMCPWebs home page in page view.
2. Place the insertion point to the right of the home page banner.
3. Click Insert and then click Web Component.
4. At the Insert Web Component dialog box, select the *Included Content* component type.
5. Select the *Picture Based On Schedule* content type.
6. Click the Finish button.
7. At the Scheduled Picture Properties dialog box, click the Browse button next to the During the scheduled time text box.
8. Select the summer.gif image file and click the OK button.
9. In the Starting text boxes, enter the date of your next Web design class set for the beginning of class.
10. In the Ending text boxes, enter the date of the following Web design class set for the beginning of class.
11. Click the OK button.
12. Save the updated home page.
13. Perform a Preview in Browser at your next class meeting and test the page include component.

Step 7

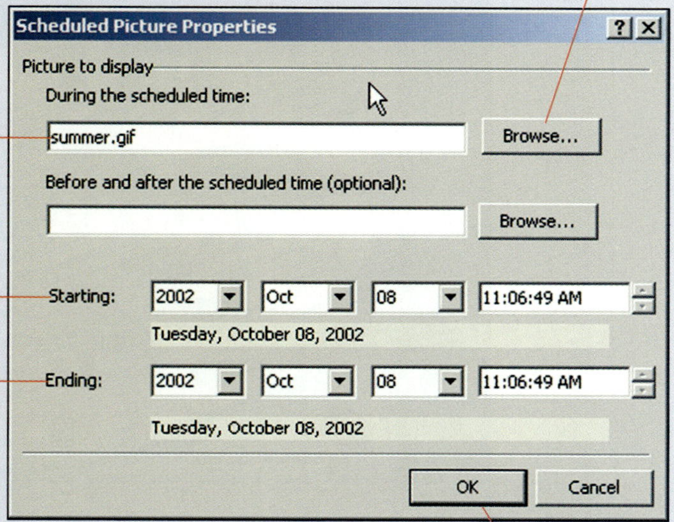

Step 8

Step 9

Step 10

Step 11

Step 13

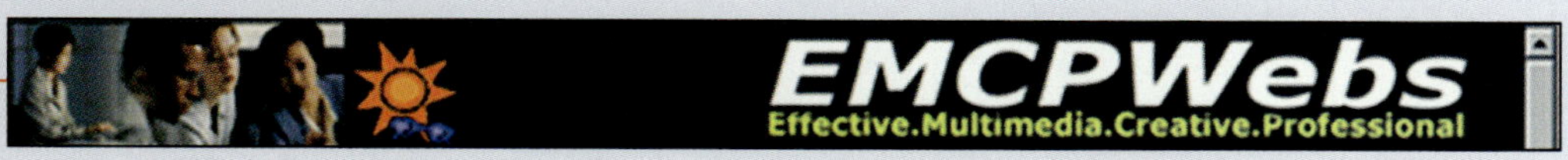

14. Print the Web page.
15. Return to the EMCPWebs home page in Page view and delete the summer.gif include.

Inserting Advanced Controls

Two of the most common advanced control plug-ins Web designers incorporate into their Web sites are Macromedia Flash animations (figure 8.2) and video clips in either Microsoft Windows Media Player format (AVI) or RealPlayer format (RAM) (figure 8.3). RealPlayer ActiveX controls can be added to the control list by double-clicking the ActiveX control option in the Web Component dialog box and then clicking the Customize button. The name of the RealPlayer control is RealPlayer G2 Control. As more homes and businesses incorporate high-speed Internet access into their everyday lives, the more advanced and lively Web sites will become. FrontPage 2002 works well with Macromedia Flash and audio/video content in either Windows Media or RealPlayer format.

FIGURE 8.2 **Web Page with Macromedia Flash (Disney.com)**

FIGURE 8.3 **Web Page with Windows Media Component (WebFN)**

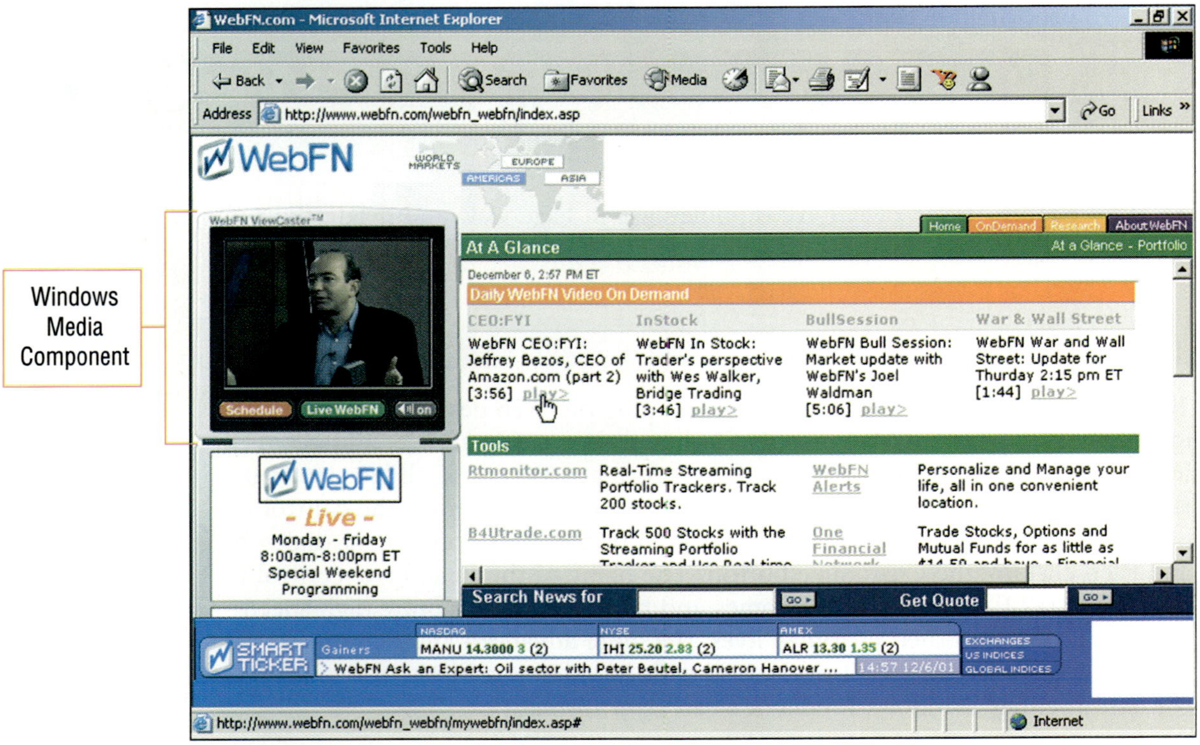

Inserting a Macromedia Flash Animation

Macromedia Flash content can be inserted into a Web page in one of two ways—as a plug-in (figure 8.4) or as an ActiveX control (figure 8.5). Flash files inserted as ActiveX controls will actually appear animated in Page view. The drawback to this is that the Flash animation will not work in Netscape Navigator. For Flash content to work in both Internet Explorer and Netscape, the file must be inserted as a plug-in.

FIGURE 8.4 ***Flash Animation Inserted as a Plug-In***

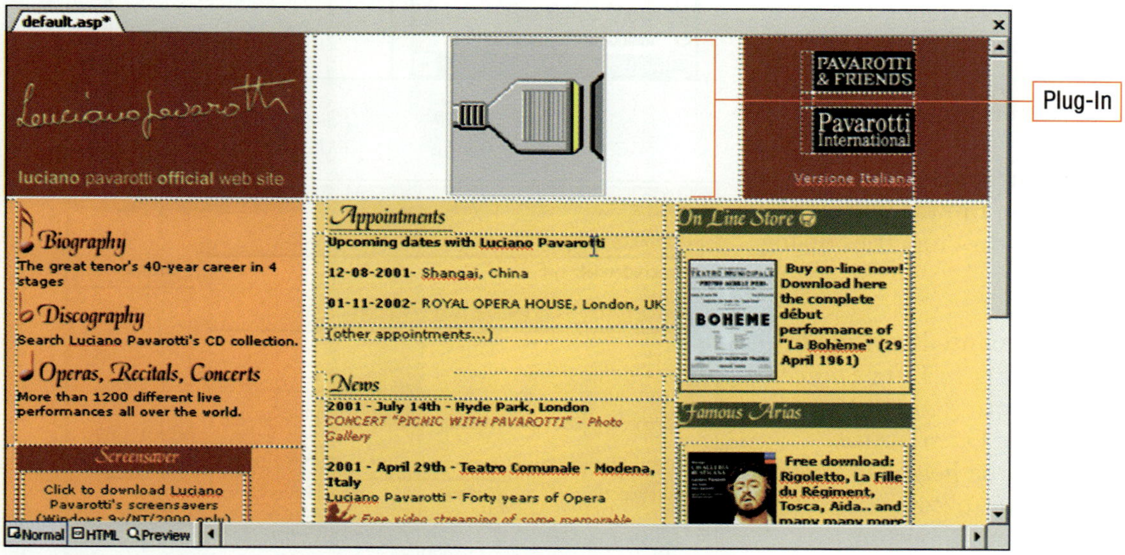

FIGURE 8.5 ***Flash Animation Inserted as an ActiveX Control***

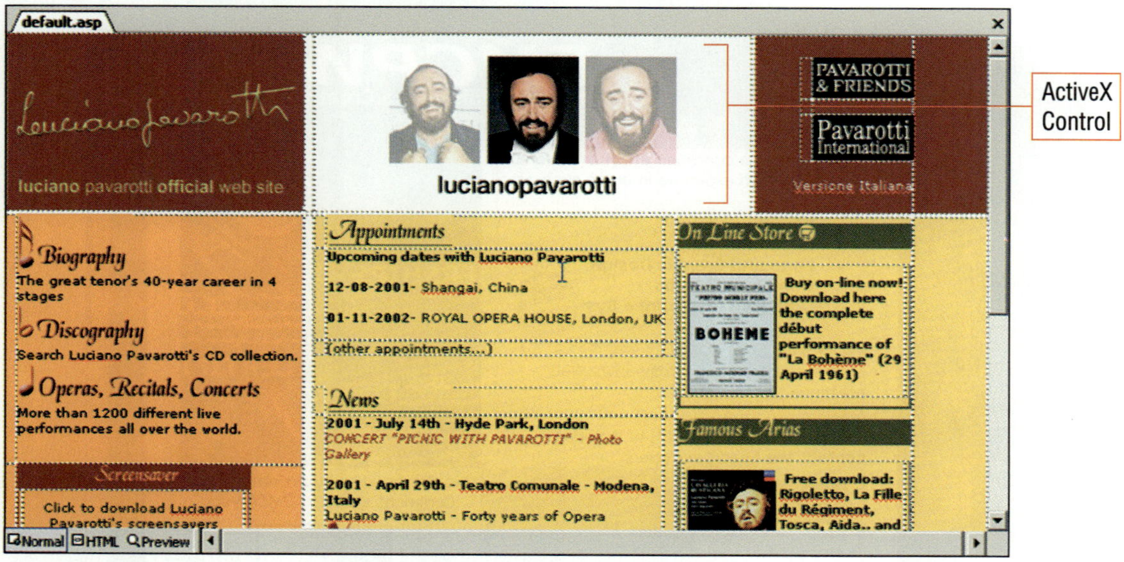

exercise 12

INSERTING A MACROMEDIA FLASH ANIMATION

1. Open the EMCPWebs home page in page view.
2. Select the homecredentials.gif image and press the Delete key.
3. Click Insert and then click Web Component.
4. At the Insert Web Component dialog box, select the *Advanced Controls* component type.
5. Select the *Plug-In* control option.
6. Click the Finish button.
7. Click the Browse button in the Plug-In Properties dialog box.
8. Select the homecredentials.swf file in the Select Plug-In Data Source dialog box.
9. Click the Open button.
10. Change the height to 250 and the width to 240.
11. Click the OK button.
12. Save the updated home page.
13. Perform a Preview in Browser and print the home page.

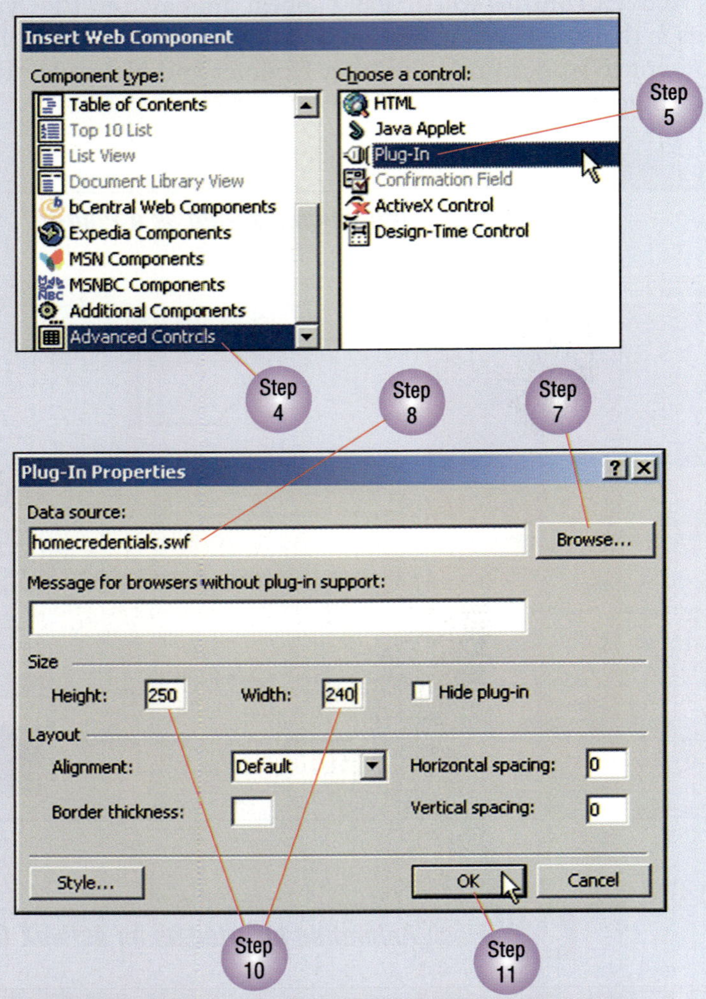

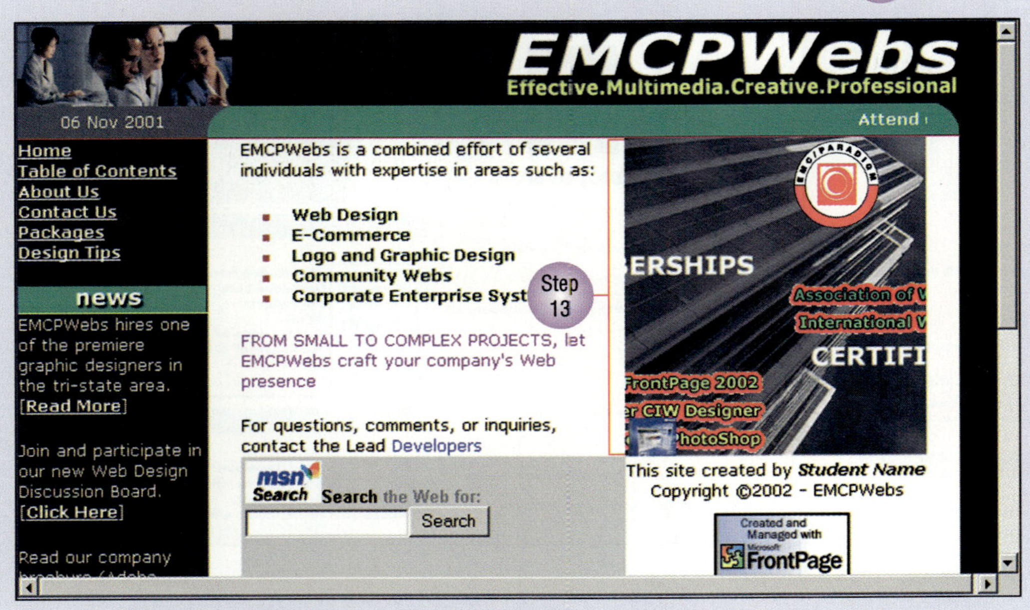

Inserting Videos for the Windows Media Player

The easiest method of inserting a video is to click Insert, point to Picture, and then click the Video command. Once published, the video will play as soon as the Web page is opened (or sometime thereafter if it is large file) (figure 8.6). If you want to add Windows Media Player controls such as Play, Pause, Stop, and Volume to the video, you will have to insert the video as an ActiveX control (figure 8.7). As with Macromedia Flash content, ActiveX content will not work in Netscape.

FIGURE 8.6 ***Video Inserted as a Picture from the Insert Menu***

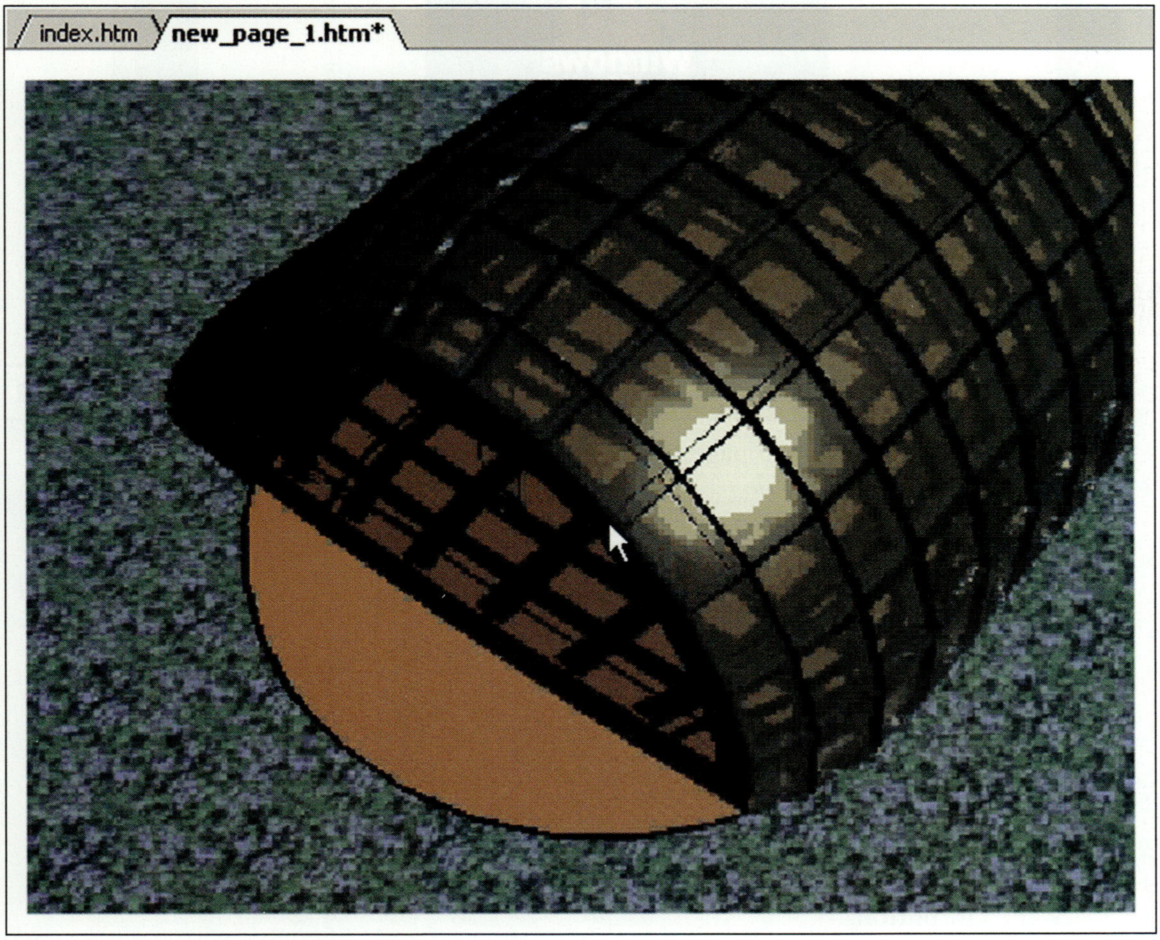

FIGURE 8.7 *Video Inserted as an ActiveX Control*

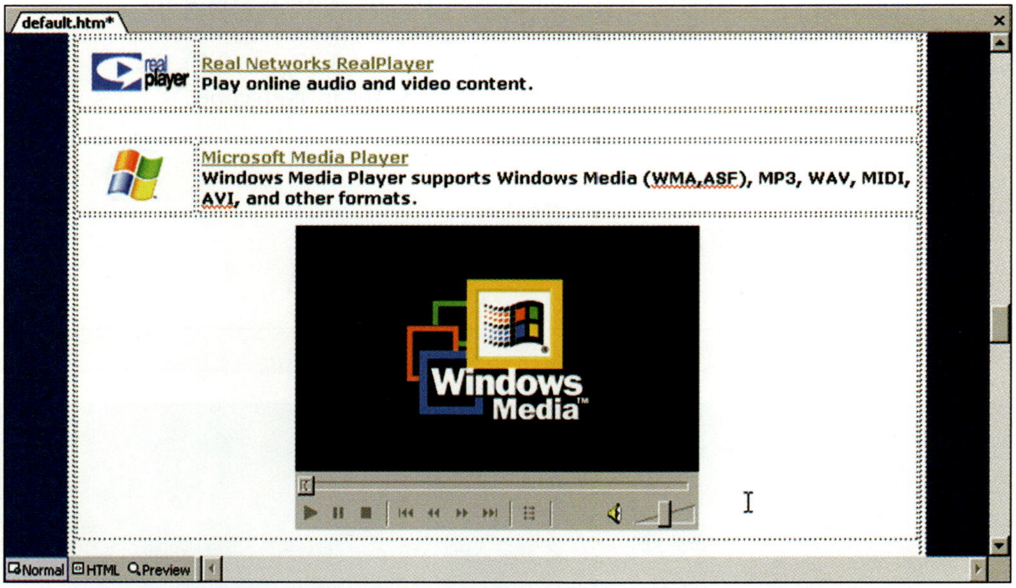

exercise 13

INSERTING A VIDEO FOR THE WINDOWS MEDIA PLAYER

1. Open the packages.htm Web page in Page view.
2. Select the text *Low Bandwidth*.

3. Click the Insert Hyperlink button on the Standard toolbar.
4. Select the emcpvideolow.htm file in the Current Folder List.
5. Click the OK button.
6. Open the emcpvideolow.htm Web page in Page view.
7. Place the insertion point in the blank cell as shown.
8. Click Insert and then click Web Components.
9. At the Insert Web Component dialog box, select the *Advanced Controls* component type and the *Plug-in* control option.
10. Click the Finish button.

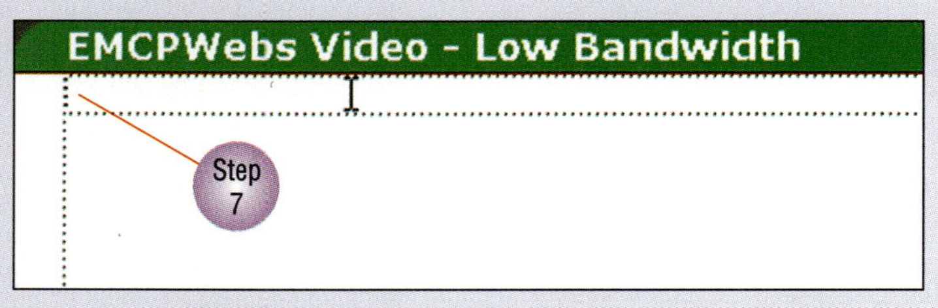

11. Click the Browse button in the Plug-in Properties dialog box.

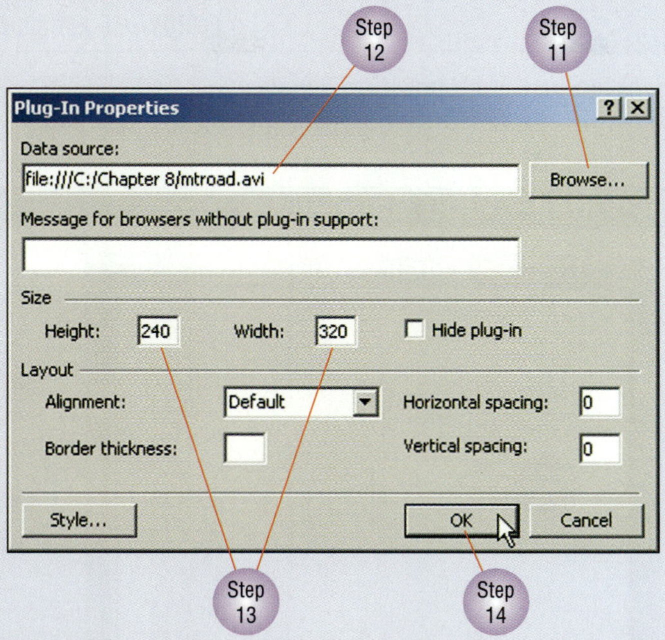

12. Locate and insert the mtroad.avi file from your *Chapter 8* folder.
13. Change the height to 240 and the width to 320.
14. Click the OK button.
15. Save the updated Web page.
16. Perform a Preview in Browser to view the video clip.

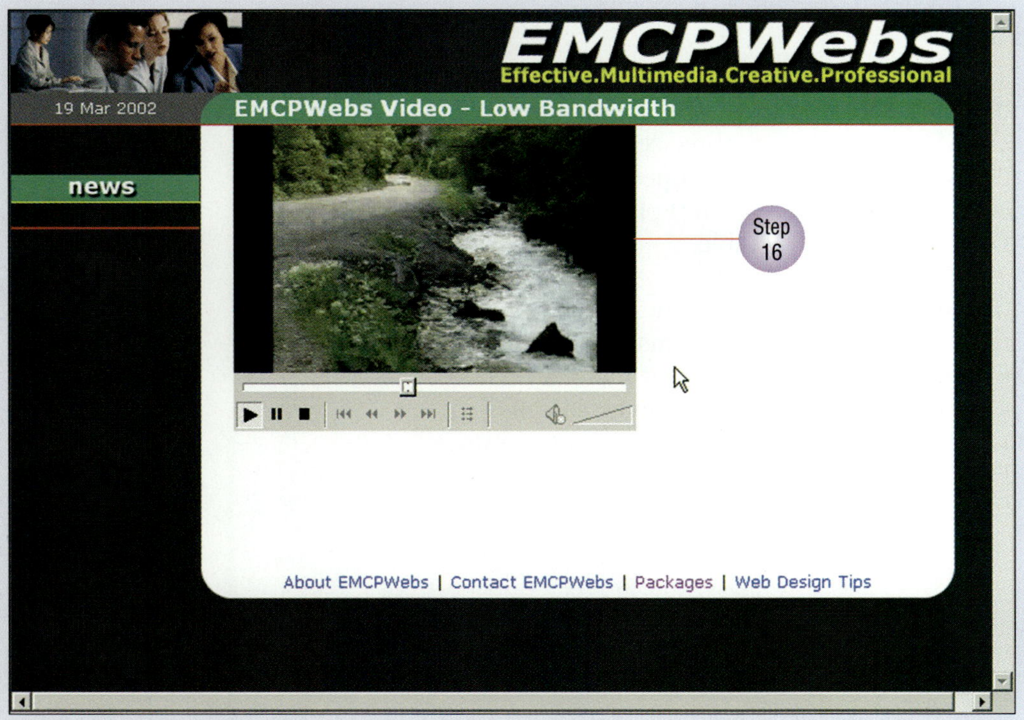

17. Print the Web page.

exercise 14

CUSTOMIZING A WINDOWS MEDIA PLAYER VIDEO

1. Open the emcpvideohigh.htm Web page in Page view.
2. Create the table shown in the illustration by completing the following steps:

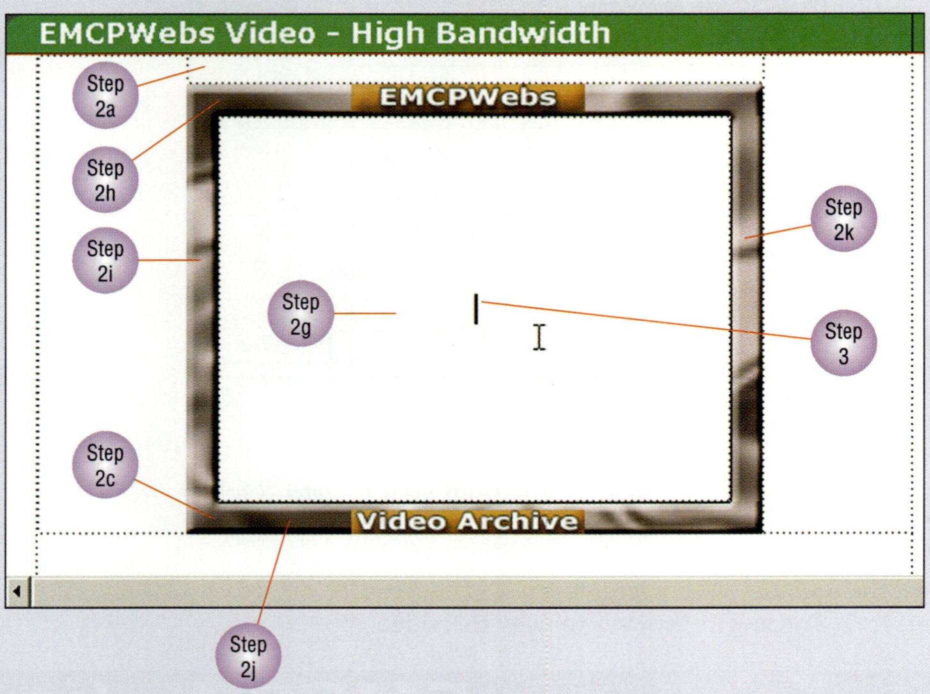

   a. Insert a 3 × 4 table.
   b. Merge the top three cells.
   c. Merge the bottom three cells.
   d. Set the table border properties to 0.
   e. Format the table to 360 pixels wide.
   f. Center align the table.
   g. Center align cell 3-2.
   h. Insert the topframe.gif image in cell 2-1.
   i. Insert the leftframe.gif image in cell 3-1.
   j. Insert the bottomframe.gif image in cell 4-1.
   k. Insert the rightframe.gif image in cell 3-3.
3. Drag the Windows Media Player control into cell 3-2.
4. Double-click the Windows Media Player control.
5. Save the updated Web page.

6. Perform a Preview in browser and print the Web page.

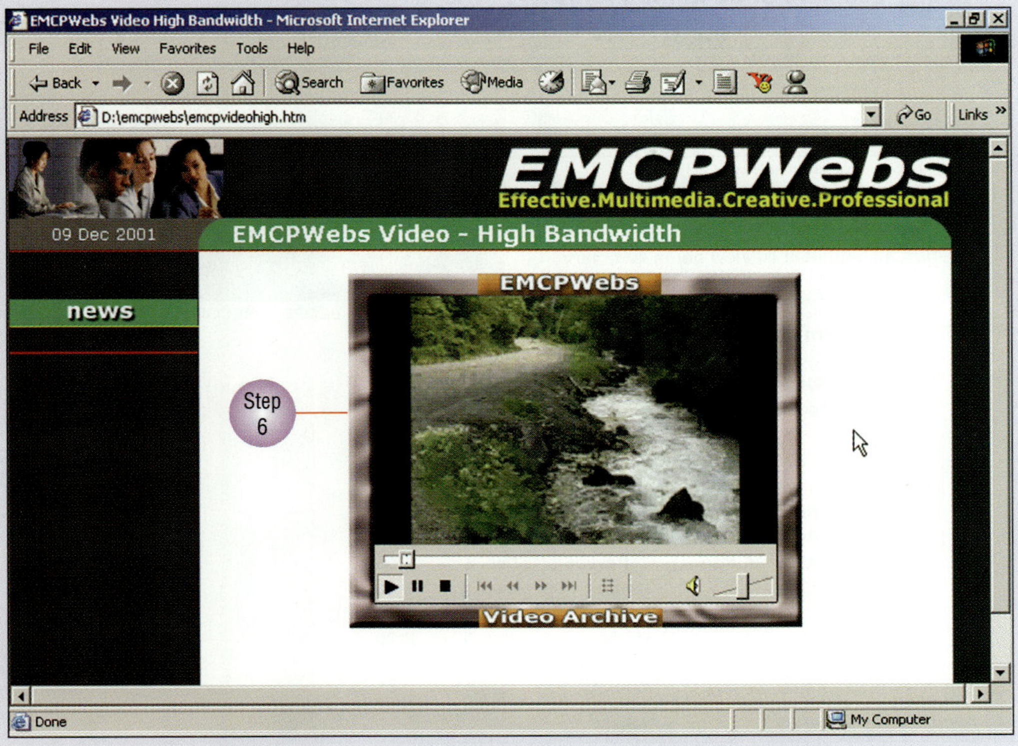

Working with Frames

Frame Web pages divide a visitor's browser window into two or more separate Web pages. Each frame can be scrolled and viewed independently. The entire Web page that is made up of multiple frames is called a *frames page*. The hyperlinks to frames are typically targeted to open in a specific area of the frames page. This *target frame* is ordinarily consistent with the hyperlinks of the frames page. For example, a series of navigation links in a header frame would each open in the main frame for consistency and ease of navigation.

In addition to frames pages and Web page frames, FrontPage 2002 has a new feature that allows developers to insert *inline frames*. An inline frame is basically a Web page that can be inserted anywhere within a Web page, including table cells. Unlike page includes, inline frames can include scroll bars. Therefore, inline frames can fit a large amount of Web page content in a relatively small space.

Inserting Inline Frames

Inline frames, or floating frames, work with browser versions beginning with Internet Explorer 3.0 and Netscape 6.0. To insert an inline frame (figure 8.8), click Insert and then click Inline Frame. To configure an inserted inline frame, click the Set Initial Page button to apply an existing Web page to the frame, or click the New Page button to create the inline frame content from scratch. Double-click the frame boundary to open the Inline Frame Properties dialog box. From the Inline Frame Properties dialog box, users can format frame size, margins, alignment, scroll bars, and alternative text.

FIGURE

8.8 ***Example of an Inline Frame***

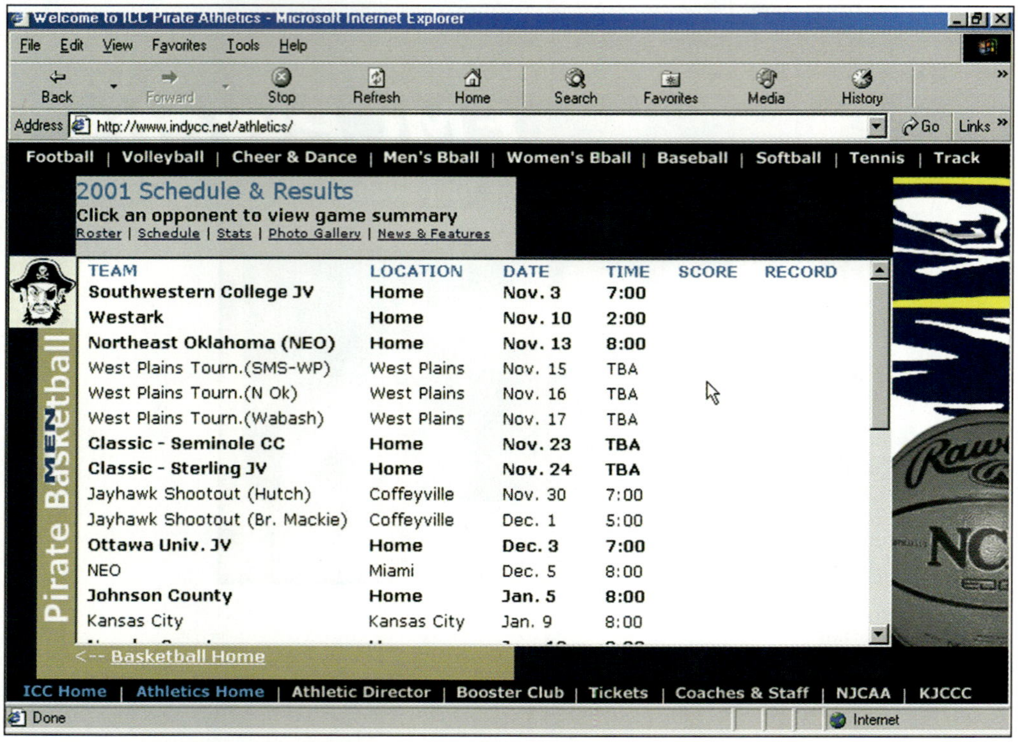

exercise 15

INSERTING INLINE FRAMES

1. Open the index.htm Web page in Page view.
2. Replace the filler e-mail and Web address with your address information.
3. Place the insertion point on a blank line above your e-mail address.
4. Click Insert and then click Inline Frame.
5. Double-click on a gray area of the inline frame to open the Inline Frame Properties dialog box.

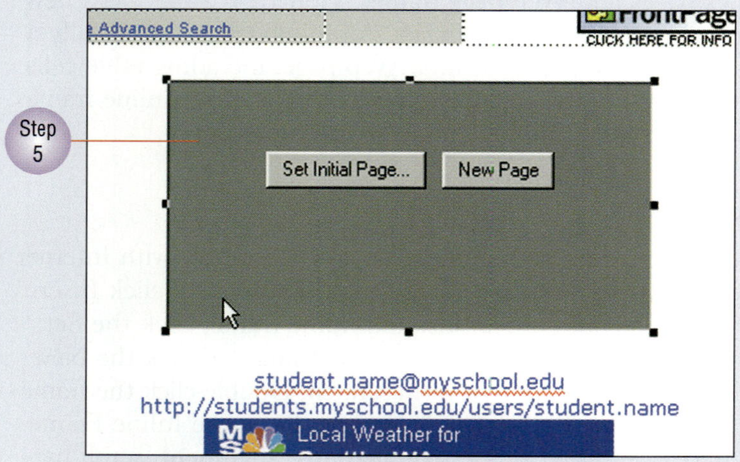

6. Under Frame size, click the Width check box to insert a check mark and then change the width to 100 percent.
7. Under Margins, change the width and height to 1 pixel each.
8. Click the OK button.

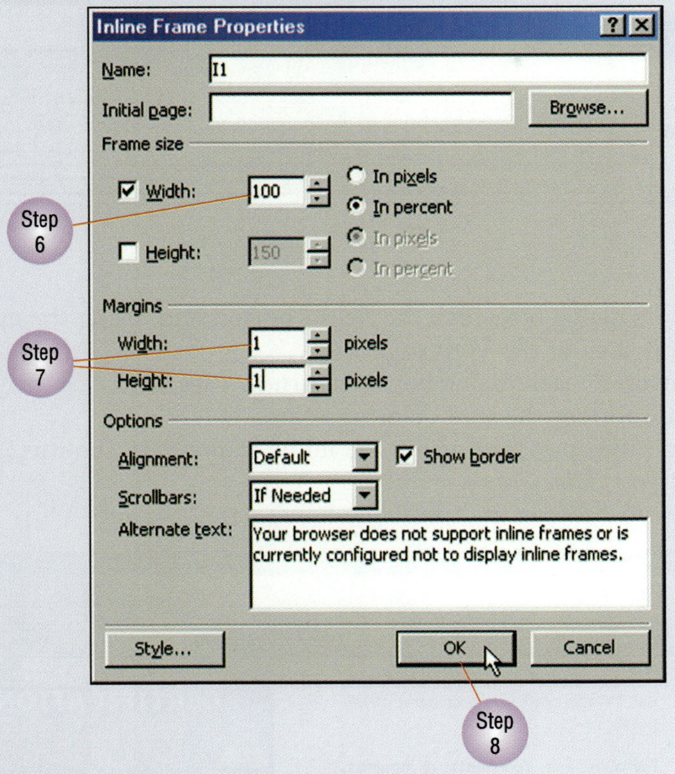

9. Click the New Page button in the inline frame.
10. Open the aboutus.htm Web page in Page view.
11. Copy the first two paragraphs of the text.
12. Return to the index.htm Web page.
13. Paste the text into the inline frame.

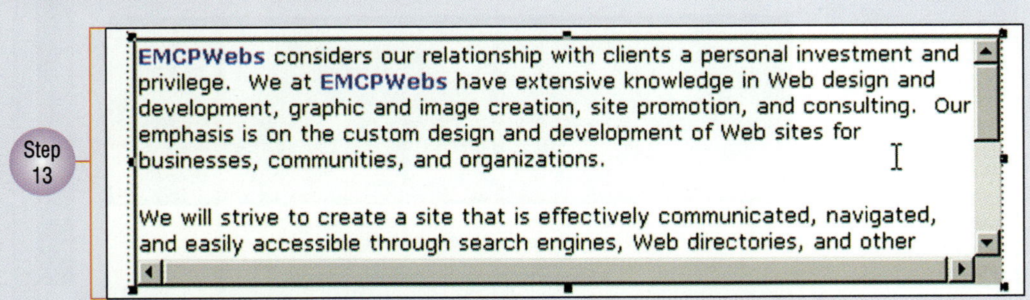

14. Right-click inside the frame and click Page Properties on the pop-up menu.
15. At the Page Properties dialog box with the Background tab selected, click the Background drop-down menu.
16. Select the More Colors option.

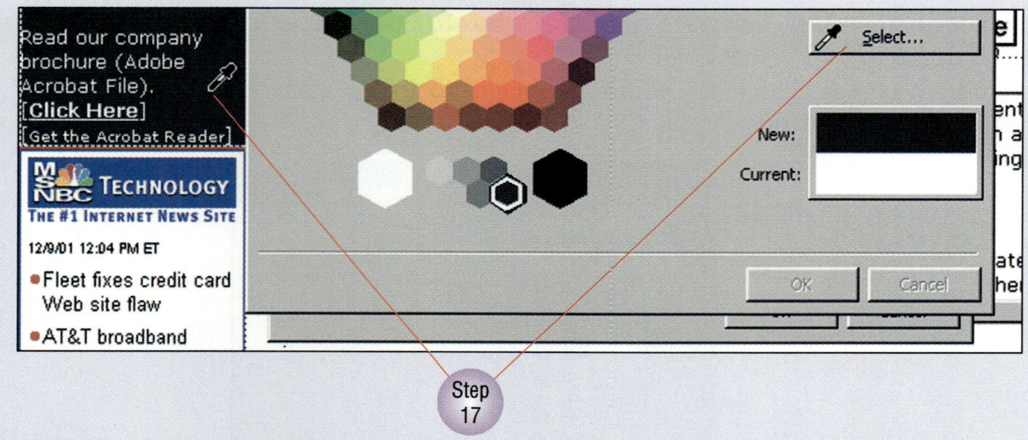

17. At the More Colors dialog box, click the Select button and, using the eyedropper icon, click in a dark gray area of the Web page.
18. Click the OK button in each dialog box to return to Page view.
19. Press Ctrl + A and format the font color to White.
20. Save the updated home page and name the inline frame page aboutus2.htm, with the page title *EMCPWebs Inline Frame*.
21. Perform a Preview in Browser and print the home page.

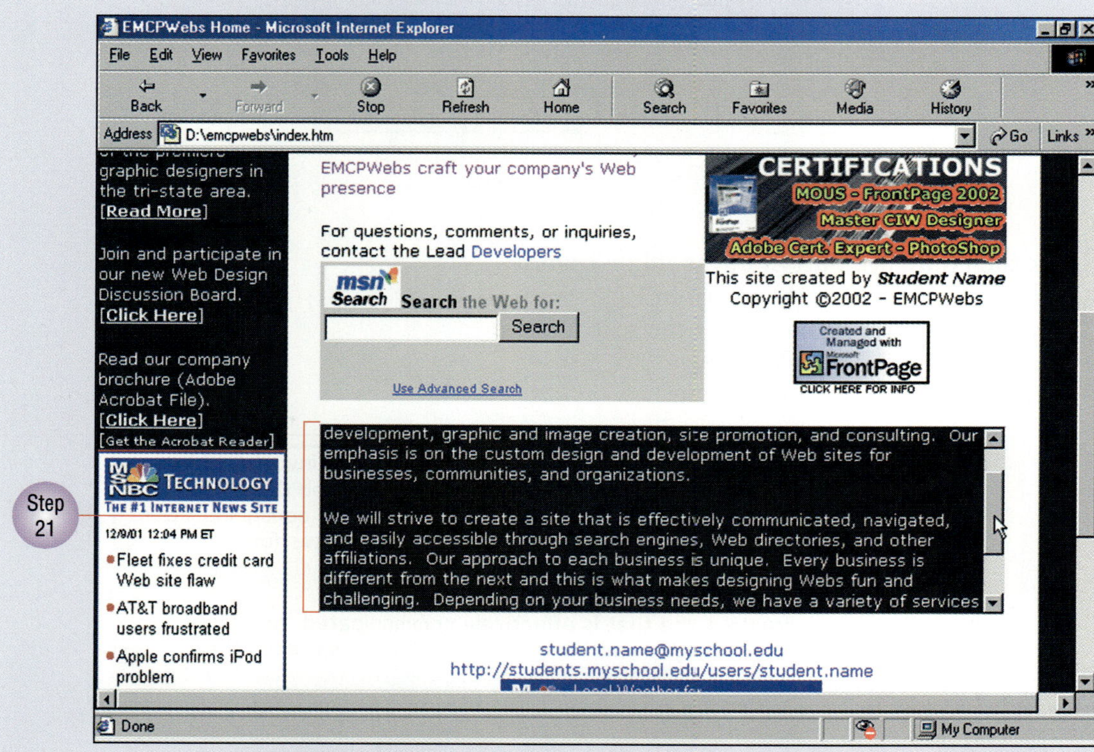

Creating a New Frames Page Using a Wizard

A frames page surrounds a set of Web pages that are displayed in the browser. The frames page serves as the command center and determines what other Web pages to open in the browser window and the frame sizes in which the Web pages are displayed. If your Web site is based around a framed environment, you will want to save your frames page as index.htm or default.htm.

exercise 16

CREATING A NEW FRAMES PAGE USING A WIZARD

1. Click File, point to New, and then click Page or Web.
2. Click *Web Site Templates* on the New Page or Web Task Pane.
3. At the Web Site Templates dialog box, click the *Empty Web* icon and then key **__:\framesweb** (substituting your preferred drive location letter for the underscore) in the Specify the location of the new web text box.
4. Click the OK button.
5. Click File, point to New, and then click Page or Web.
6. Click *Page Templates* on the task pane.
7. Click the Frames Pages tab in the Page Templates dialog box.
8. Click the *Header* icon.

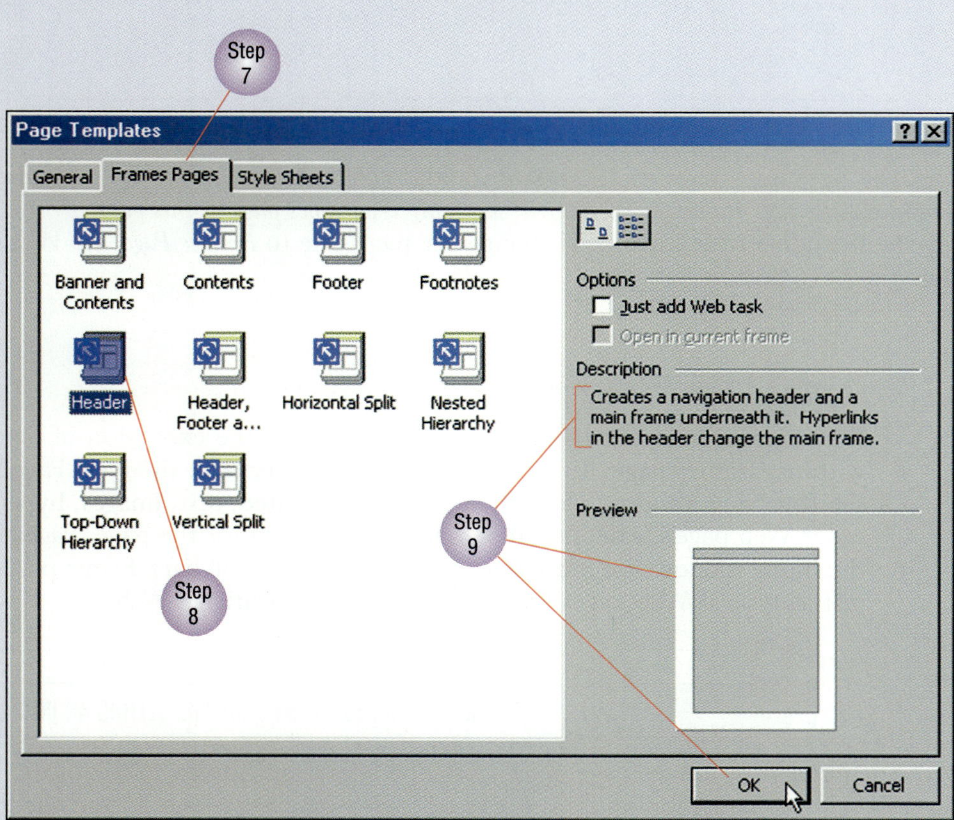

9. Read the Description of the Header frame option, view the Preview to see how the frames pages will be configured (see the illustration on page 292), and then click the OK button.

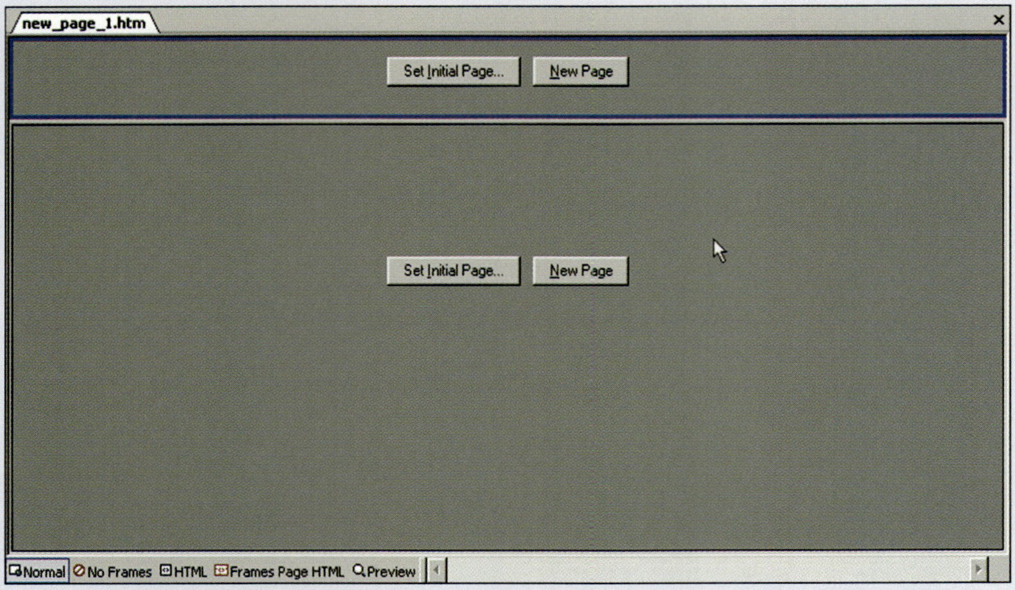

10. Click the Save button on the Standard toolbar. *(Note: Although there are two frames associated with your frames page, you will save only the frames page at this point.)*
11. Key the file name **index.htm** and change the page title to *Frames Page Test Web.*
12. Click the Save button.

Creating a New Frame Page

Frame pages are your basic Web page files, with the exception of being placed within a frames page. To create a new frame page, click the New Page button in the Page view window. Once the new page is created, text, images, hyperlinks, and other Web page elements can be added as required for the page. Pages larger than the frame window size must be formatted to show scroll bars. Frame pages are saved just as typical Web pages are saved within the FrontPage Web.

exercise 17 CREATING A NEW FRAME PAGE AND SETTING AN INITIAL FRAME PAGE

1. With the index.htm frames page open, click the New Page button in the header frame.
2. Center align the paragraph and insert the emcpwebsbanner.gif image from the *EMCPWebs Images* folder on your storage device into the header frame.

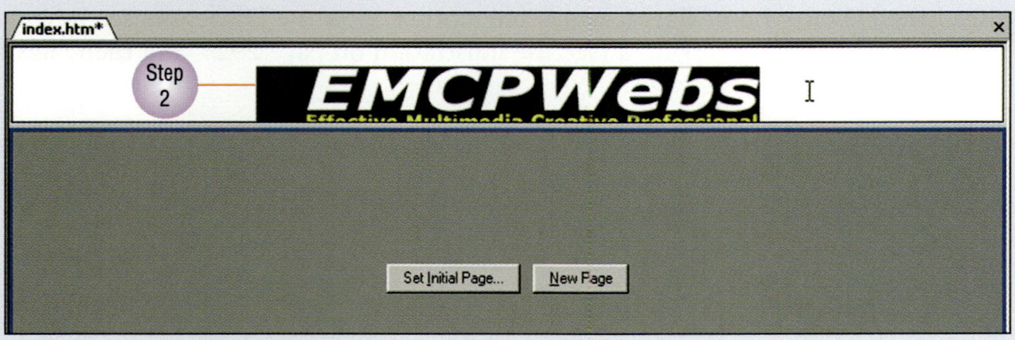

3. Import the aboutus.htm Web page file from the emcpwebs FrontPage Web into the framesweb Web.
4. Open the aboutus.htm page in Page view.
5. Copy the About Us text from *Establish Mission* to *...outside of the Internet*.

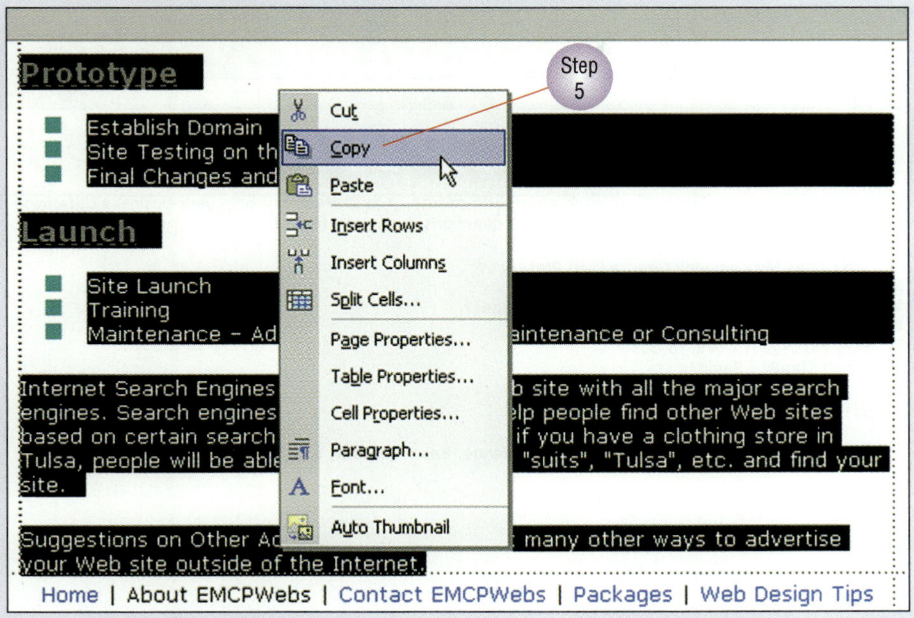

6. Return to the framesweb FrontPage Web.
7. Click the Create a new normal page button on the Standard toolbar.
8. Paste the text into the empty Web page.
9. Save the Web page as mainframe.htm with the title *About EMCPWebs*.
10. Save the header frame as headerframe.htm with the title *Header Frame*.
11. Return to the index.htm page and click the Set Initial Page button in the main frame.
12. At the Insert Hyperlink dialog box, select *mainframe.htm* in the Current Folder list box and click OK.

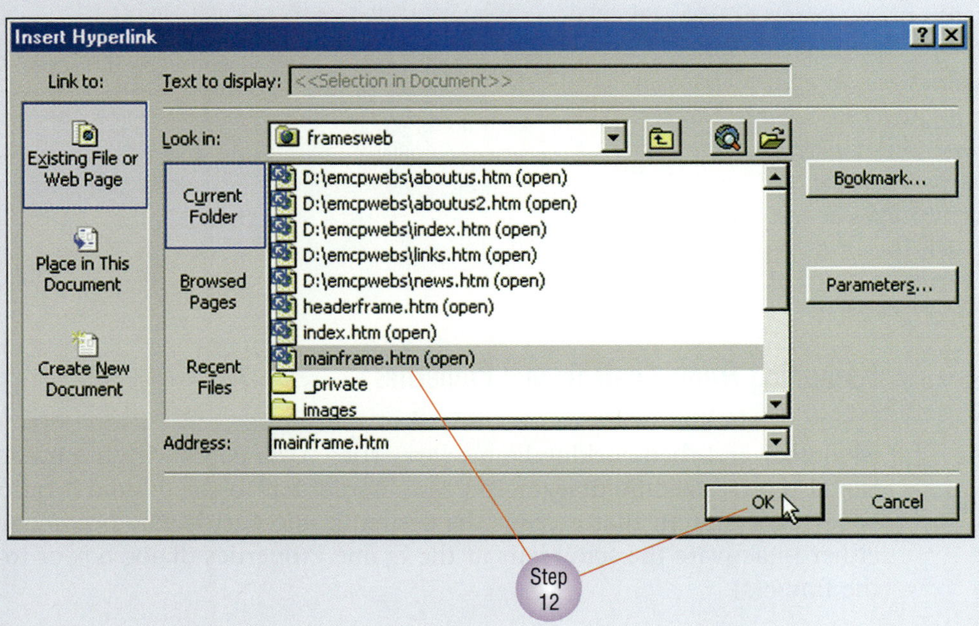

13. Click the Save button on the Standard toolbar.
14. Save the header frame as headerframe.htm with the page title *Header Frame*.
15. Perform a Preview in Browser.

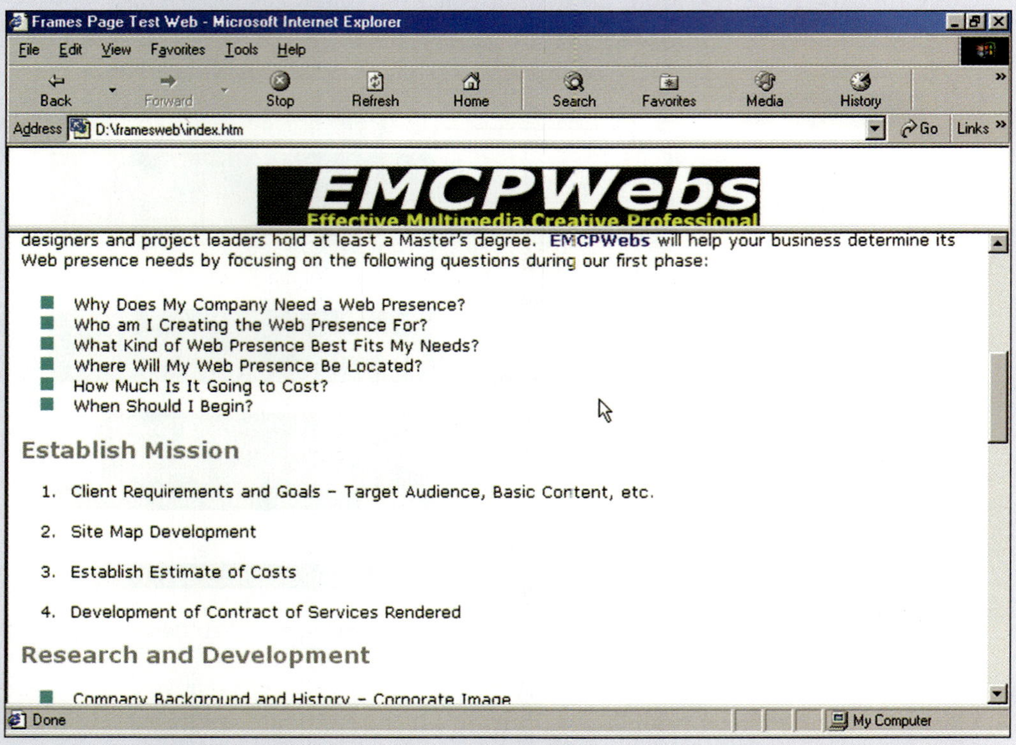

16. Click File and then click Print.
17. At the Print dialog box in Internet Explorer, under Print frames, select the As laid out on screen option. *(Note: Keep in mind that visitors to a framed environment must perform this command to print a Web page as it appears on their browser. Otherwise, only the main frame will print.)*
18. Click the Print button.

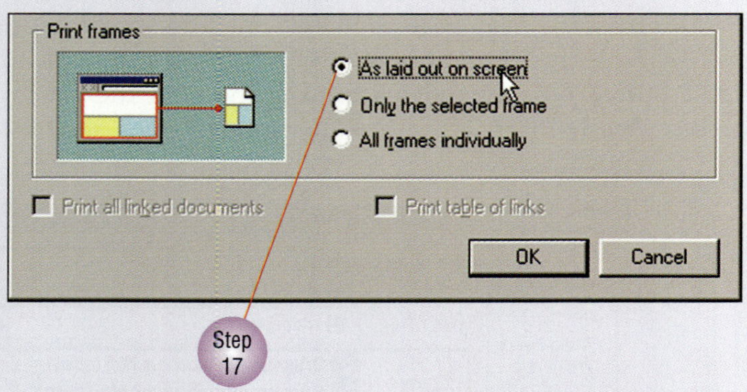

Formatting Frame Contents and Properties

Frame height and width can be resized to specific sizes by clicking Frames on the Menu bar and then clicking Frame Properties. Web pages within a frames page can also be resized by dragging the gray border bar to the desired location. For pages with content that exceeds the desired frame size, it may become necessary either to activate the scroll bars at the Frame Properties dialog box or to resize the frame(s).

1. With the framesweb FrontPage Web open, place the mouse pointer on the gray horizontal border that separates the header frame and the main frame.
2. Click and drag the frame border so that it is placed just under the EMCPWebs banner image.

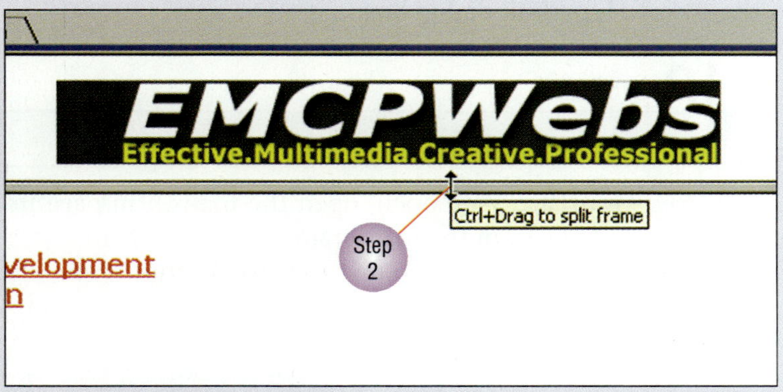

3. Click anywhere inside the header frame.
4. Click Frames and then click Frame Properties.
5. At the Frame Properties dialog box, change the frame height to 100 pixels.
6. Click the Frames Page button.
7. At the Page Properties dialog box with the Frames tab selected, click inside the Show Borders check box to remove the check mark and remove the gray border from the frames pages.
8. Click the OK button in each dialog box to return to the frames pages.
9. Right-click inside the mainframe frame and select Frame Properties.
10. At the Frame Properties dialog box, under Options, click *If Needed* in the Show scrollbars drop-down list.
11. Click OK in each dialog box to return to the frames pages.
12. Save the updated Web pages.
13. Perform a Preview in Browser.
14. Print the Web page as laid out on the screen.

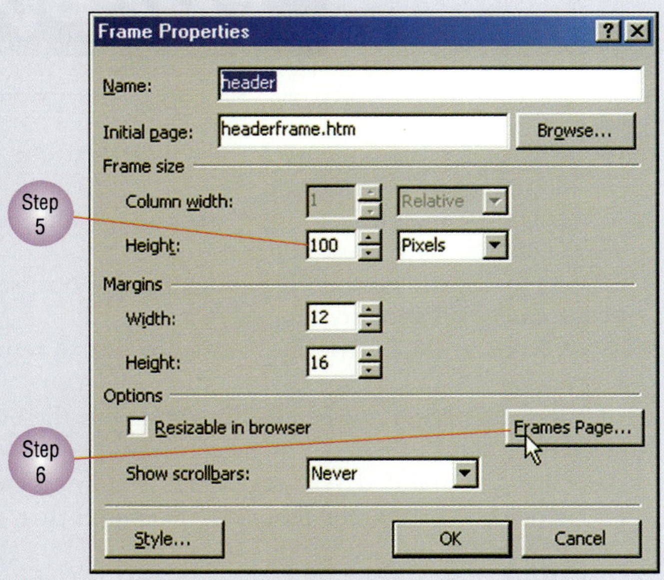

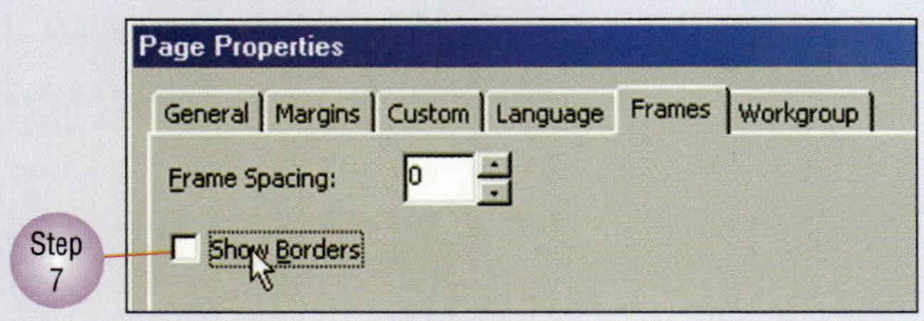

Targeting Frames

When working in a frames environment, it is essential to plan the target frames in which hyperlinks open. The default target frame is the main frame. The Same Frame common target will open the hyperlinked Web in the same frame. Typical Web pages you would target to Whole Page would be the home page of a frames pages Web and external Web sites. The New Window target is commonly used when linking to external Web sites or internal pages that fit outside the normal flow of the Web site. To change hyperlink targets, click the Target Frame button in the Insert Hyperlink dialog box.

exercise 19 TARGETING FRAMES

1. With the framesweb FrontPage Web open, open the index.htm page in Page view.
2. Cut the bookmark hyperlinks from the main frame and paste them into the header frame.
3. Remove the bold formatting, format the text font to 10 points, and arrange the hypertext links to match the illustration, using the pipe symbol (|) on your keyboard to separate the links.

4. Right-click the *Establish Mission* hypertext link and select the Hyperlink Properties command.
5. Click the mainframe.htm file in the Current Folder list box.
6. Click the Bookmark button.
7. At the Select Place in Document dialog box, select the *Establish Mission* bookmark.
8. Click the OK button in each dialog box to return to Page view.
9. Repeat steps 4–8 to create hyperlinks to the bookmarks in the main frame from the header frame.

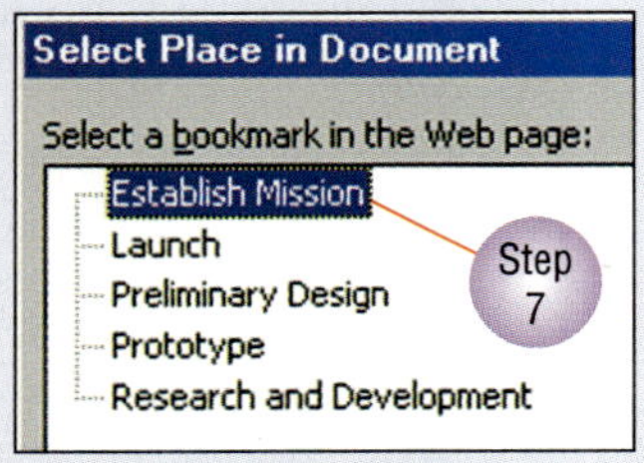

10. Save the updated Web pages and perform a Preview in Browser to test the hyperlinks.
11. Open the emcpwebs FrontPage Web and then open the webdesign.htm Web page in Page view.
12. Right-click the *Official Microsoft FrontPage Website* hyperlink and select Hyperlink Properties.
13. At the Hyperlink Properties dialog box, click the Target Frame button.
14. At the Target Frame dialog box, select the *New Window* option under Common targets.
15. Click the OK button in each dialog box to return to Page view.
16. Repeat steps 12–15 to set the target frame for the remaining four hyperlinks in the Web Design Tips and Tricks page.
17. Save the updated Web page.
18. Perform a Preview in Browser and test the hyperlinks.

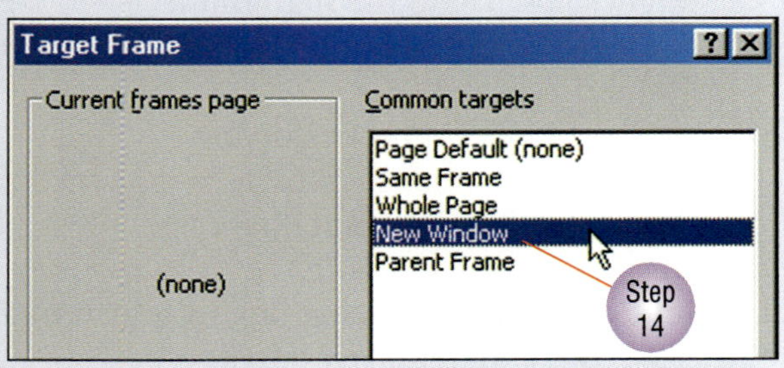

CHAPTER summary

- A marquee is text that scrolls across a Web page.
- Scrolling marquees are often inserted into Web pages to attract attention to special announcements and to welcome visitors to the Web page.
- The marquee component will not scroll in Netscape; it appears as regular text.
- A hit counter can be inserted onto a Web page to count the number of times the Web page has been accessed.
- Users can either choose from five different counter image styles or apply custom images to match the design scheme of the Web page.
- Hit counters will work only if the FrontPage server extensions have been installed on the Web server.
- The table of contents component creates a complete listing, with hyperlinks, of the Web pages and files within the FrontPage Web.
- The top 10 list component creates hyperlinks to the top 10 listings of such categories as visited pages, operating systems, referring URLs, and referring domains.
- The MSN search component can be inserted into a Web page to give visitors an option to search the Internet.
- News feeds from MSNBC in such categories as business, living and travel, news, sports, technology, and weather can be incorporated into a Web page.
- MSNBC headline component news feeds inserted into Web pages are updated each time a visitor accesses the Web page.
- An Expedia map component can be configured to display a specific address location or a place such as a city and inserted into a Web page.
- The page include component can be used to insert an existing Web page into a current Web page.
- Not only do page includes ensure consistency, but they also allow developers to change content of an included Web page once and apply it to other pages that have the inserted page include.
- The pages based on schedule component can be configured to appear from a starting date to an ending date and is typically used to display announcements, greetings, and other content.
- The picture based on schedule component can be scheduled to appear and change at specified times.
- Videos created in the AVI format are designed to open in the Microsoft Windows Media Player by default.
- Videos created in RAM format are designed to open in RealPlayer by default.
- Macromedia Flash files can be inserted into a Web page as either a plug-in or an ActiveX control.
- ActiveX controls do not work properly in Netscape browsers.
- Videos can be inserted into a Web page either as a picture using the Insert menu or as an ActiveX control in the Web Components dialog box.
- Frame Web pages divide the browser into two or more separate Web pages.

- The original Web page that is made up of multiple Web pages is called the frames page.
- An inline frame allows a separate Web page to be inserted within the current Web page.
- Inline frames can be formatted to specific heights and widths to meet design requirements and still have a scroll bar if the frame content exceeds the frame properties.
- Individual frames can be resized by dragging the frame border in Page view.
- Frame borders can be removed by changing the border size to 0 in the Frame Properties dialog box.
- Target frames play an important role when working with hyperlinks in a framed environment.
- The default target frame is the main frame.
- The New Window target frame is commonly used in nonframe pages to open hyperlinks in a new browser window.

COMMANDS review

Command	Mouse/Keyboard
Insert a scrolling marquee	Click Insert, Web Component, Dynamic Effects
Insert a hit counter	Click Insert, Web Component, Hit Counter
Insert a table of contents	Click Insert, Web Component, Table of Contents
Insert a top 10 list	Click Insert, Web Component, Top 10 List
Insert an MSN search component	Click Insert, Web Component, MSN Components
Insert an MSNBC headline component	Click Insert, Web Component, MSNBC Components
Insert weather information from MSNBC	Click Insert, Web Component, MSNBC Components
Insert an Expedia map	Click Insert, Web Component, Expedia Components
Insert a page include	Click Insert, Web Component, Included Content
Insert page based on schedule	Click Insert, Web Component, Included Content
Insert picture based on schedule	Click Insert, Web Component, Included Content
Insert a Macromedia Flash file (plug-in/ActiveX)	Click Insert, Web Component, Advanced Controls
Insert an autoplay video	Click Insert, Picture, Video

Insert a video with play/pause controls	Click Insert, Web Component, Advanced Controls, ActiveX Control
Insert an inline frame	Click Insert, Inline Frame
Create a new frames page	Click File, New, Page or Web, *Page Templates*, Frames Page tab
Resize a frame border	Drag frame border to appropriate location
Alter frame properties	Click Frames, Frame Properties
Remove borders from a frame	Click Frames, Frame Properties, Frames Page button, Show Borders check box
Target hyperlinks to open in specific frames	Click Insert Hyperlink button on Standard toolbar, Target Frame button

CONCEPTS check

Completion: On a blank sheet of paper, indicate the correct term, symbol, or command for each item.

1. This component creates an area of text that scrolls text across a Web page.
2. This FrontPage component keeps track of the number of times a Web page has been accessed.
3. This FrontPage component creates a listing of and links to all Web pages and files located in the Web.
4. Insert this code string into the Action script of the MSN search component to have the search results open in a new window.
5. MSNBC headline feed components include these six options.
6. Visitors clicking the map component in their browser will be hyperlinked to this Web site.
7. Use this feature to display Web pages at specified times based on the date.
8. Use this feature to display pictures at specified times based on the date.
9. This common animation media can be inserted as a plug-in or ActiveX control.
10. Files of this type are best suited for Microsoft Media Player video controls.
11. Select this control to insert RealPlayer videos into your Web page.
12. These types of controls will not work in Netscape browsers.
13. Insert these to display a Web page file in the current Web page while at the same time providing a scroll bar for exceeding content.
14. The original Web page that is made up of multiple pages is called this.
15. Select this option in the Page Properties dialog box to remove borders from a frame page.

SKILLS check

Assessment 1

1. Open the ch8assess FrontPage Web.
2. Open the index.htm page in Page view.
3. Insert a marquee as directed on the page with the following text: *Print this Web page and receive an additional 10% off your next purchase.*
4. Format the marquee to repeat only twice.
5. Format the marquee to match the cell width properties.
6. Format the font to Arial, 10 points, and bold.
7. Format the background to match the cell background properties.
8. Perform a Preview in browser and print.

Assessment 2

1. Open the ch8assess FrontPage Web.
2. Create a new Web page titled toc.htm with the title *Table of Contents*.
3. Key the page title **Table of Contents** with formatting of your choice.
4. Insert a table of contents component.
5. Save the updated Web page.
6. Perform a Preview in browser and print.

Assessment 3

1. Open the ch8assess FrontPage Web.
2. Open the index.htm page in Page view.
3. Place the insertion point in the cell with the text *Living and travel* as directed on the page.
4. Insert a Living and travel headlines component into the home page.
5. Place the insertion point in the *Weather* cell as directed on the page.
6. Insert a weather forecast component into the home page.
7. Save the updated Web page.
8. Perform a Preview in browser and print.

Assessment 4

1. Open the ch8assess FrontPage Web.
2. Open the index.htm page in Page view.
3. Place the insertion point in the *Expedia Map* cell as directed on the page.
4. Insert a map using your school's address.
5. Save the updated Web page.
6. Perform a Preview in browser and print.

Assessment 5

1. Open the ch8assess FrontPage Web.
2. Open the index.htm page in Page view.
3. Place the insertion point in the *Page Include* cell as directed on the page.
4. Insert the links.htm Web page as a page include.
5. Save the updated Web page.
6. Print the Web page in your browser.
7. Add a hyperlink to CNN.com on the links.htm Web page and save.
8. Refresh the home page in your browser.
9. Print the Web page in your browser.

Assessment 6

1. Open the ch8assess FrontPage Web.
2. Open the index.htm page in Page view.
3. Place the insertion point in the *Flash Animation* cell as directed on the page.
4. Insert the Flash animation file intro.swf as a plug-in with the dimensions of 225 pixels wide by 200 pixels tall.
5. Save the updated Web page.
6. Preview the Web page.
7. Delete the inserted plug-in and insert the intro.swf file as a Windows Media Player ActiveX control.
8. Preview the Web page in your browser and print.

Assessment 7

1. Open the ch8assess FrontPage Web.
2. Open the index.htm page in Page view.
3. Place the insertion point in the *Video Clip* cell as directed on the page.
4. Insert the NewYork.avi file in the cell.
5. Preview the Web page in your browser.
6. Delete the inserted video and insert the NewYork.avi file as an ActiveX control with the play/pause controls.

Assessment 8

1. Using the guidelines below, create a frame-based Web as a photo gallery of your family, vacation, a special event, or another subject of your choice.
   - Use the Banner and Contents frame template.
   - Use a FrontPage theme for the Web.
   - Insert a page banner in the header frame.
   - Insert your photographic images (10) into individual Web pages (10).
   - Key a page title and caption for each photo page.
   - Establish the hierarchical structure in Navigation view.
   - Create a vertical link bar in the side frame to the photo pages.
   - Using tables, create thumbnail hyperlinks to the image pages.
2. Preview the Web pages and print the home page and at least one photo page.

Assessment 9

1. Open the photo gallery Web created in assessment 8.
2. Create hypertext links to the photos in header frame.
3. Target the header frame links to the main frame.
4. Create a hyperlink to USAToday.com in the side pane that opens in the whole browser window and not a frame.
5. Test the hyperlinks in your browser.
6. Format the *USAToday.com* link to open in a new browser window.

CHAPTER 9

WORKING WITH LANGUAGES, SCRIPTS, AND STYLES

PERFORMANCE OBJECTIVES

Upon successful completion of chapter 9, you will be able to:

- **View HTML code in Page view**
- **Alter HTML color code options**
- **Format text fonts, sizes, styles, and color in HTML**
- **Format paragraph breaks, alignment, bullets, and numbering in HTML**
- **Insert images and hyperlinks in HTML**
- **Create and format tables in HTML**
- **Use meta tags to provide search engines with significant data about a Web site**
- **Use the REFRESH meta tag to create an automatic slide show**
- **Add meta data to HTML code in the Page Properties dialog box**
- **Adjust spacing of lines of code by using the Reformat HTML feature**
- **Apply XML formatting rules to lines of HTML code**
- **Apply DHTML page load and transition effects**
- **Apply DHTML effects to a Web page slide show**
- **Apply mouse over effects to hyperlinks**
- **Apply JavaScript effects to a Web page**
- **Apply styles using Cascading Style Sheets (CSS), embedded styles, and inline styles**

Chapter 9 IRC

Hypertext Markup Language, or HTML, is an authoring language used to create Web pages for the World Wide Web. HTML is basically a text-based coding scheme that can be created using any text editing program. Microsoft Office documents created in programs such as Word and Excel can be saved as Web pages to be published to the Web. Programs such as Notepad are often used by code enthusiasts to create Web pages. For most businesses, however, developing Web sites and pages using strictly a text coding environment is not very time efficient. While FrontPage takes a great deal of the coding out of the picture, it is often an advantage to be able to access the HTML view to enter code as necessary. Advanced Web designers will find themselves in HTML view entering meta tags, inserting DHTML tags and JavaScripting, or just because they enjoy the challenge of HTML.

Exploring HTML Fundamentals

To this point, your Web design experience has involved a What You See Is What You Get (WYSIWYG) environment. Before there were HTML editors such as FrontPage, Web designers had to enter the HTML code directly into a text editor and save the text file as an HTML document. While FrontPage users at any level of expertise can design professional sites without entering HTML code, having knowledge and expertise of HTML elements and tags is beneficial for enhancing a Web site.

(Note: Many of the HTML tags in this chapter are in ALL CAPS for emphasis. HTML tags can be entered in either upper- or lowercase, and they will be shown in both styles.)

Basic HTML Tags

HTML tags basically instruct the encompassing text how to be displayed in the browser. An HTML tag is surrounded by a less than (<) and a greater than (>) sign. HTML tags must be closed after the content element to end the tag properties before the next Web page element is entered. An end tag is identical in structure to the start tag except that it has a forward slash (/) before the tag name (e.g., </TITLE>). There are four basic tags essential to every Web page:

<html></html>

<head></head>

<title></title>

<body></body>

HTML Tag

At the top of each HTML document you will see the **<HTML>** tag. This tag is read by the browser and indicates that the document is an HTML document. The end </HTML> tag is located at the bottom of the document.

Head Tag

The <HEAD> tag contains such elements as:

- Web page title: <title>Web Page Title</title>
- background information: <bgcolor= #182166> or <body background= file.gif>
- meta tag elements: <meta name="description" content="Welcome to XYZ Company!">
- DHTML and JavaScripts: <script language="JavaScript">
- Web page styles: <style> <!— a:hover {text-decoration: none} </style>

Title Tag

The **<TITLE>** tag must be entered within the <HEAD> tag and is the title of your Web page, just as you enter the page title in the Save As dialog box in FrontPage. The Web page <TITLE> appears on the title bar of the browser window.

Body Tag

The <BODY> tag encompasses the actual content of your Web page. Some of the elements included in the body are headings from largest <H1> through smallest <H6>, paragraphs <P>, bulleted lists <UL>, numbered lists <OL>, horizontal rules <HR>, hyperlinks <a href=http://www.webaddress.com>, and images <img src=filename.jpg>.

The most basic HTML document would look something like this:

```
<HTML>
<HEAD>
<TITLE>Welcome to XYZ Company!</TITLE>
</HEAD>
<BODY>
   Under Construction!</BODY>
<HTML>
```

Viewing HTML Tags in Page View

Why not have the best of both worlds? The Reveal Tags feature, accessed from the View menu, can be enabled to display HTML tags in Page view (see figure 9.1). Hover over a reveal tag to view additional information about the tag and its properties. The reveal tag feature is similar to the Show/Hide ¶ feature in Microsoft Word, in which paragraphs, spaces, tabs, and other nonprinting characters can be seen. In FrontPage, however, double-clicking a tag will open the properties dialog box for that specific tag. This is an especially handy tool for quickly formatting text, paragraphs, and other content.

FIGURE 9.1 ***Reveal Tags Enabled in FrontPage 2002***

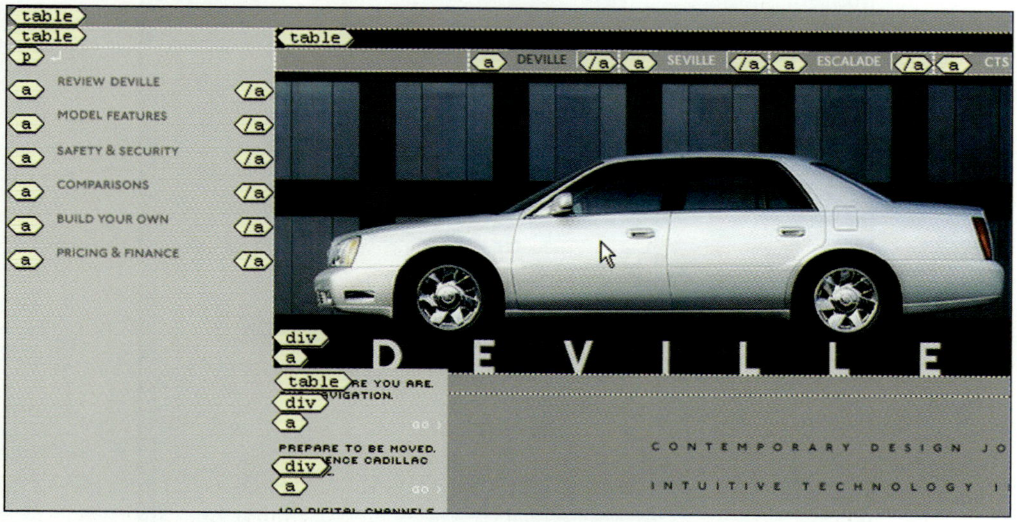

(Note: Before completing computer exercises, delete the Chapter 8 *folder on your disk. Next, download the Chapter 9 data files from the Internet Resource Center to the* Chapter 9 *folder you have created on your disk, and then make* Chapter 9 *the active folder.)*

exercise 1

VIEWING REVEAL TAGS IN PAGE VIEW

1. Open the EMCPWebs FrontPage Web in FrontPage.
2. Open the index.htm Web page in Page view.
3. Click View and then click Reveal Tags.
4. Double-click the font tag as shown at the right.
5. Format the font to match the light green color already used on the Web page.
6. Disable the Reveal Tags feature.

Step 4

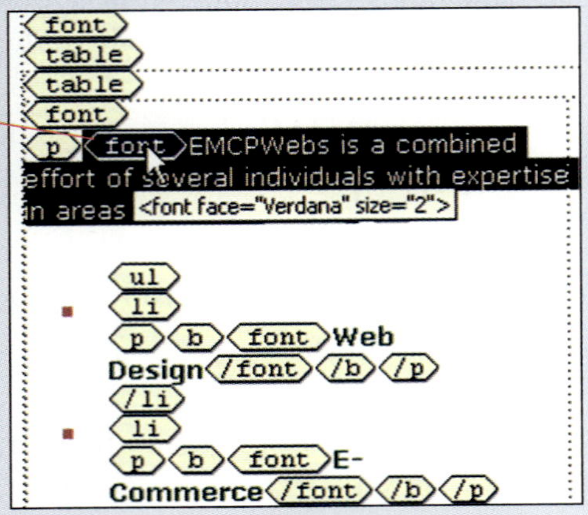

Exploring the HTML View

The HTML view is used to manually code HTML, styles, and scripts. HTML tags, attributes, comments, scripts, and normal text are color coded in HTML view to make coding easier. To quickly edit code in HTML view, highlight the component in Page view and click the HTML button. This will automatically highlight the code in HTML view, thus keeping you from hunting for the code. By default, normal text is black, tags are blue, comments are gray, and scripts are red. To alter HTML view coding colors, click Tools, click Page Options, and then click the Color Coding tab in the Page Options dialog box (see figure 9.2).

FIGURE 9.2 ***Color Coding Options for HTML View***

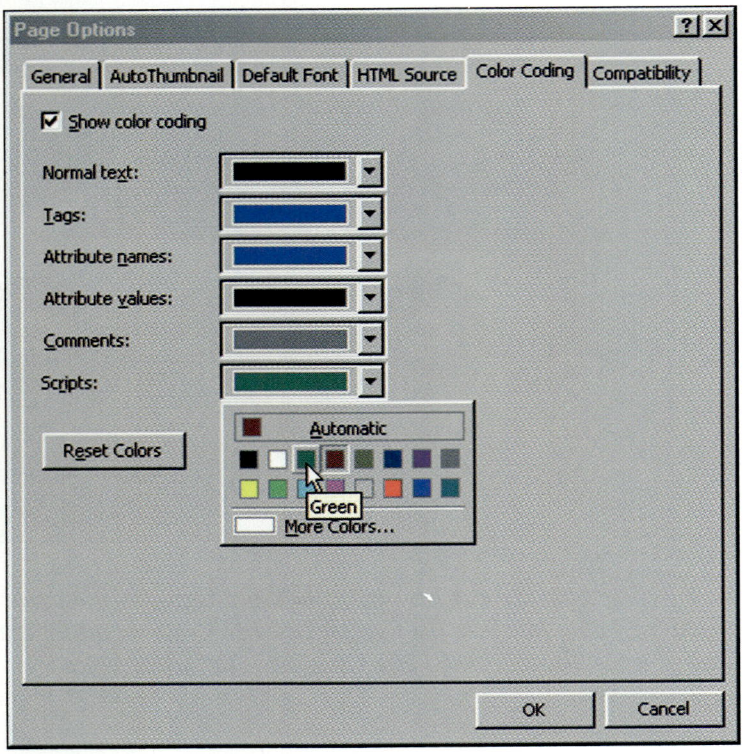

exercise 2

EXPLORING THE HTML VIEW

1. Open the EMCPWebs home page in Page view.
2. Click the HTML button at the bottom of the screen.

3. Scroll through the code.
4. Print the HTML code.
5. Click the Normal button to return to Normal view.

exercise 3

VIEWING THE COLOR CODING IN HTML VIEW

1. Open the EMCPWebs home page in HTML view.
2. Click Tools and then click Page Options.
3. At the Page Options dialog box, click the Color Coding tab.
4. Change the Tags color to Green.
5. View the color change in HTML view.
6. Reset the default Tags color.

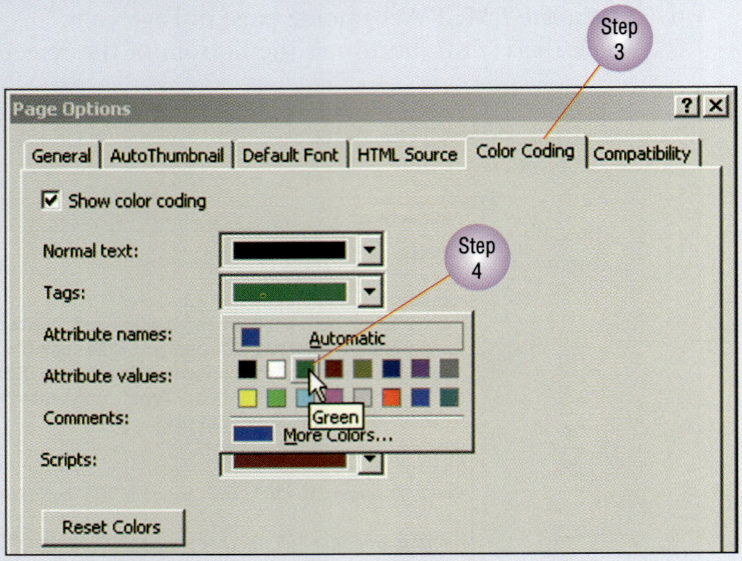

Formatting Text in HTML View

Text, or character, formatting consists of fonts, font sizes, bold, italic, underline, and color. Key the tag **<FONT FACE="Arial">** to format text to the Arial font. Font size can be formatted to 18 points by keying the tag **<FONT SIZE="5">** or **<FONT STYLE="font-size: 18pt">**. Font sizes can be formatted as headings or by specific size. Below is a table of font sizes and their relative heading equivalents.

Font Size	Heading Size
8	1
10	2
12	3
14	4
18	5
24	6
36	7

Bold <B>, Italic <I>, and Underline <U> tags can be applied to text in multiple combinations. Closing tags must appear in the reverse order as applied before the text, as shown below:

```
<p><b><i><u>This text is bolded, italicized, and
    underlined.</u></i></b></p>
```

Font color <FONT COLOR="#918CDF"> is specified using a hexadecimal color coding scheme. If there is one area of Web design that no one should have to memorize, it would be the hexadecimal code for font colors. In addition to using FrontPage for applying font color, there are posters available that designers can hang around the office for color reference (see figure 9.3).

FIGURE 9.3 ***References for HTML Font Color Coding***

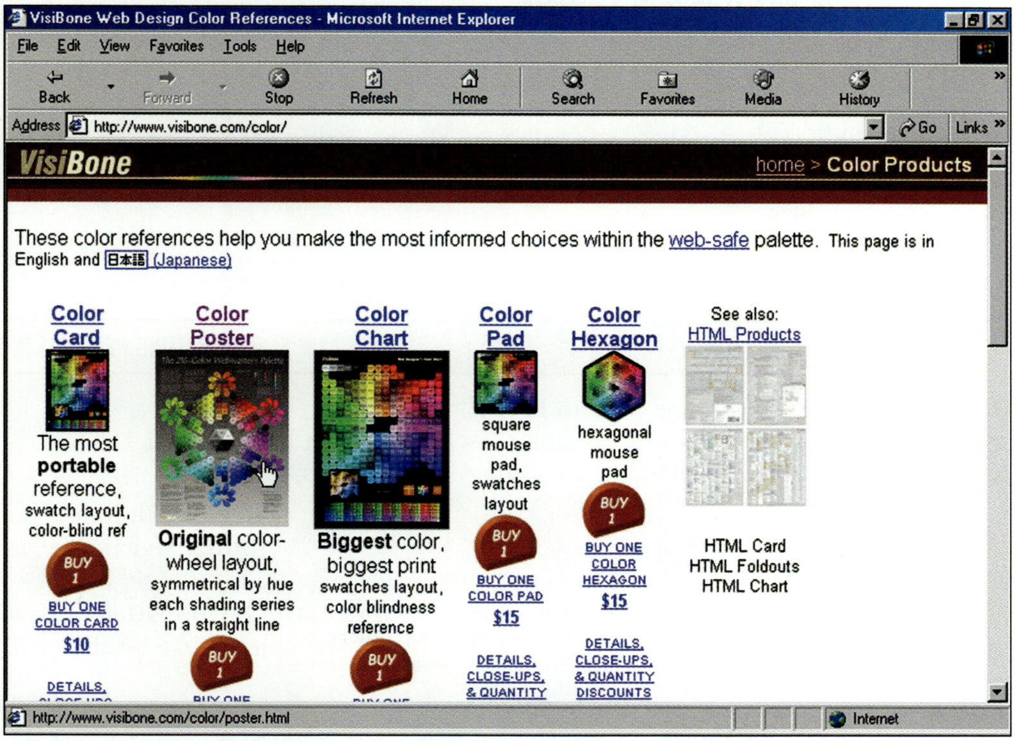

exercise 4 FORMATTING TEXT IN HTML VIEW

1. With the EMCPWebs FrontPage Web open, click the Create a new normal page button.
2. In Page view, key the text shown in the illustration.
3. Click the HTML button.
4. Key the bold **<b>** tag before and after the text *Welcome to My Web Page*.
5. Key the italic **<i>** tag before and after the same text.

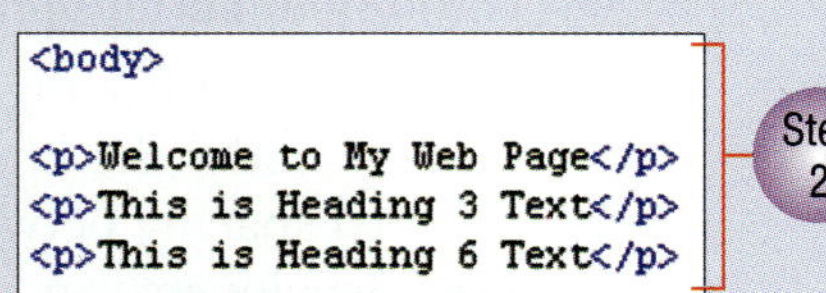

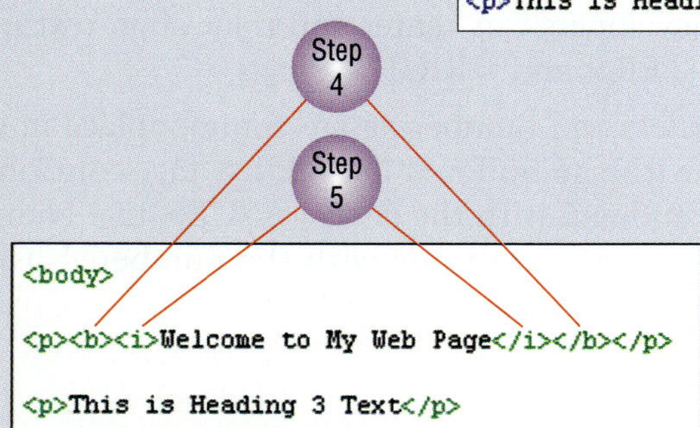

6. Key the tag **<font color="#000080">** before the tag on line 13. *(Note: When you place the insertion point in a line of text, or press the Enter key at the end of a line, the line number will appear at the bottom of the screen.)*
7. Close the font color tag </font>.

Step 6 Step 7

```
<p><font color="#000080">Welcome to My Web Page</p></font>
<p>This is Heading 3 Text</p>
<p>This is Heading 6 Text</p>
```

8. Return to Page view and view the updated text.
9. Save the Web page as htmlpractice.htm with the page title *HTML Practice Web Page*.

exercise 5

FORMATTING HEADINGS IN HTML VIEW

1. Open the EMCPWebs home page in HTML view.
2. Key the Heading 3 **<H3>** and Heading 6 **<H6>** tags in lines 14 and 15.
3. Close the Heading 3 **</H3>** and Heading 6 **</H6>** tags.

Step 2 Step 3

```
<p><h3>This is Heading 3 Text</h3></p>
<p><h6>This is Heading 6 Text</h6></p>
```

4. Return to Page view and view the updated text.
5. Save the updated Web page.

Formatting Paragraphs in HTML View

The Break <BR> tag can be used to insert a line break and force text to be placed directly under the line. It is always a better solution to format the paragraphs to zero (0) spacing between lines, but the break command can be a quick solution. Web developers can center and right align text in the browser window using the <CENTER> and <RIGHT> tags.

Bullets and numbering are commonplace in many Web pages. Bulleted lists begin with the bulleted list <UL> tag, continue with the bulleted list <LI> items, and end with the closing </UL> tag. Numbered lists begin with the ordered list <OL> tag, continue with the numbered list <LI> items, and end with the closing </OL> tag.

exercise 6

FORMATTING PARAGRAPHS IN HTML VIEW

1. Open the htmlpractice.htm Web page in HTML view.
2. Key the paragraph text in Lines 16 through 19 as shown.

Step 2

```
<p><h6>This is Heading 6 Text</h6>
<p>Below is a bulleted list:</p>
<p>Item 1</p>
<p>Item 2</p>
<p>Item 3</p>

</body>
```

3. Key the paragraph text and the break **
** tag in lines 20 and 21 as shown.
4. Return to Page view and view the updated text.
5. Return to HTML view.
6. Key the center alignment tag **<h3 align="center">** in line 14.

Step 3

```
<p>Item 3</p>
<p>A line break forces text<br>
to the next line</p>

</body>
```

Step 6

```
<p><font color="#000080">Welcome to My Web Page</p></font>
<p><h3 align="center">This is Heading 3 Text</h3></p>
<p><h6>This is Heading 6 Text</h6>
```

7. Return to Page view and view the updated text.
8. Save the updated Web page.

exercise 7

FORMATTING BULLETS AND NUMBERING IN HTML VIEW

1. Open the htmlpractice.htm Web page in HTML view.
2. Key the bulleted list **<ul>** and **<li>** tags in lines 17 through 21.

Step 2

```
<p>Below is a bulleted list:</p>
<ul>
   <p><li>Item 1</li></p>
   <p><li>Item 2</li></p>
   <p><li>Item 3</li></p>
</ul>
<p>A line break forces text<br>
```

3. Key the code and text to create a numbered list beginning on line 22.
4. Return to Page view and view the updated text.
5. Save the updated Web page.
6. Perform a Preview in Browser and print the Web page.

Step 3

```
</ul>
<p>Below is a numbered list:</p>
<ol>
   <p><li>Item A</li></p>
   <p><li>Item B</li></p>
   <p><li>Item C</li></p>
</ol>
<p>A line break forces text<br>
```

Inserting Images and Hyperlinks in HTML View

Images can be inserted into a Web page using the <IMG> tag. The SRC attribute is required to identify the source location of the image. The ALT attribute (alt= "Alternative text here") is a common attribute applied to images that appears on the image as the visitor hovers over the image. Other common attributes include WIDTH and HEIGHT (width="117" height="58"). Below is a complete code entry for an image with no border, alternative text, a width of 150, and a height of 300:

```
<img border="0" src="filename.gif" alt="Alternative text here"
    width="150" height="300">
```

exercise 8 — INSERTING IMAGES AND HYPERLINKS IN HTML VIEW

1. Open the htmlpractice.htm Web page in HTML view.
2. Key the **<img src= "emcpwebs_banner.gif"** tag in line 13.

Step 2

```
<body>

<p><img src="emcpwebs_banner.gif"</p width="400" height="50">
<p><font color="#000080">Welcome to My Web Page</p></font>
```

3. Key the hyperlink **<a href="http://www.cnn.com"> CNN Interactive</a>** tag in line 31.

Step 3

```
to the next line</p>
<p><a href="http://www.cnn.com"> CNN Interactive</a></p>

</body>
```

4. Return to Page view and view the updated text.
5. Save the updated Web page.

Creating Tables in HTML View

Spend time creating complex tables in HTML and you will appreciate the ability of editors such as FrontPage. Table attributes, rows, columns, text, and other content must be surrounded by the <TABLE> tag. The table row <TR> tag is used to create rows, and the table column <TD> tag is used to create multiple columns. Common table attributes include ALIGN, BORDER, CELLPADDING, CELLSPACING, and WIDTH.

exercise 9

CREATING TABLES IN HTML VIEW

1. Open the htmlpractice.htm Web page in HTML view.
2. Key the table **<TABLE>**, row **<TR>**, and column **<TD>** tags as well as text in cells 13 through 19.

```
<body>

<table width="100%">
  <tr>
    <td>Cell 1-1</td>
    <td>Cell 1-2</td>
    <td>Cell 1-3</td>
  </tr>
</table>

<p><img src="emcpwebs_banner.gif"</p width="400" height="50">
```

Step 2

3. View the table in Page view.
4. Add the row and column text to the table as shown.

```
<table width="100%">
  <tr>
    <td>Cell 1-1</td>
    <td>Cell 1-2</td>
    <td>Cell 1-3</td>
  </tr>
    <tr>
    <td>Cell 2-1</td>
    <td>Cell 2-2</td>
    <td>Cell 2-3</td>
  </tr>
  <tr>
    <td>Cell 3-1</td>
    <td>Cell 3-2</td>
    <td>Cell 3-3</td>
  </tr>
</table>
```

Step 4

5. View the table in Page view.
6. Format the table background color <BGCOLOR> to Navy Blue by adding the tag shown in the illustration.

Step 6

```
<body>

<table width="100%"bgcolor="#000080">
  <tr>
```

7. View the table in Page view.
8. Format the top three cell backgrounds <BGCOLOR> in the table to Red by adding the tags shown.

Step 8

```
<body>

<table width="100%"bgcolor="#000080">
  <tr>
    <td bgcolor="#FF0000">Cell 1-1</td>
    <td bgcolor="#FF0000">Cell 1-2</td>
    <td bgcolor="#FF0000">Cell 1-3</td>
  </tr>
```

9. View the table in Page view.

10. Format the font color <FONT COLOR="#FFFFFF"> of all cell text to White by adding the tags shown. *(Note: You may want to exercise your copy and paste skills.)*

Step 10

```
<table width="100%"bgcolor="#000080">
  <tr>
    <td bgcolor="#FF0000"><font color="#FFFFFF">Cell 1-1</font></td>
    <td bgcolor="#FF0000"><font color="#FFFFFF">Cell 1-2</font></td>
    <td bgcolor="#FF0000"><font color="#FFFFFF">Cell 1-3</font></td>
  </tr>
    <tr>
    <td><font color="#FFFFFF">Cell 2-1</font></td>
    <td><font color="#FFFFFF">Cell 2-2</font></td>
    <td><font color="#FFFFFF">Cell 2-3</font></td>
  </tr>
  <tr>
    <td><font color="#FFFFFF">Cell 3-1</font></td>
    <td><font color="#FFFFFF">Cell 3-2</font></td>
    <td><font color="#FFFFFF">Cell 3-3</font></td>
  </tr>
</table>
```

11. View the table in Page view.

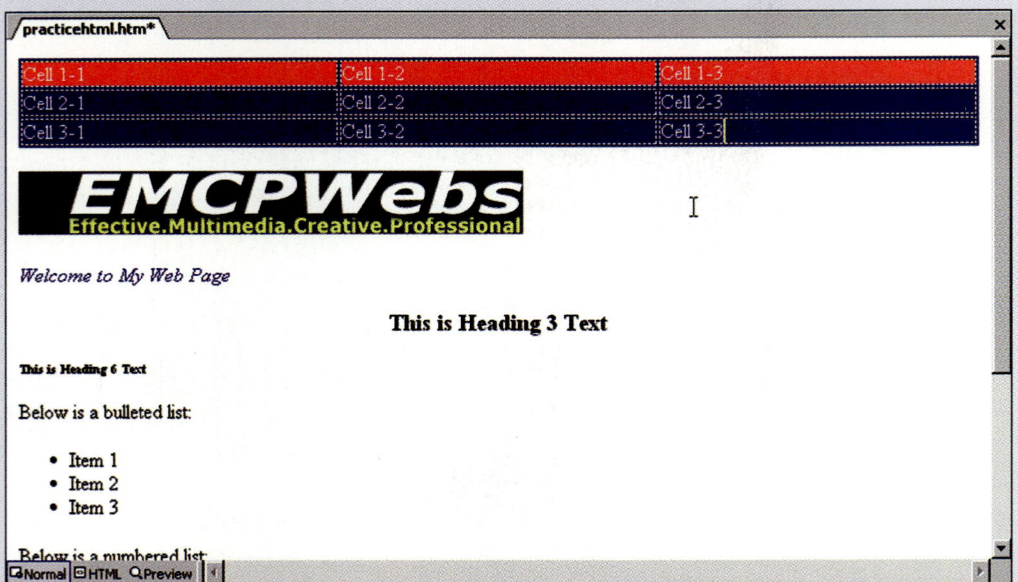

12. Save the updated Web page.
13. Perform a Preview in Browser and print the Web page.
14. Return to the htmlpractice.htm Web page in HTML view and print the code.

Inserting Meta Data into HTML

Meta tags provide useful information to search engines and are placed in the <HEAD> of an HTML document. Meta tags are not seen by visitors on the Web page itself, but can be viewed in the HTML source. The most common meta tags used by search engines are the DESCRIPTION and KEYWORDS tags. The description meta tag is used by search engines not only for indexing content but also on the search results page for describing content (figure 9.4). The keywords meta tag is used to improve search engine rankings. The REFRESH meta tag forces the page to load a specific Web page after a specified amount of time. This may be useful to create a slide show of Web pages as well as automatically access a new Web page if the Web page reference no longer exists.

FIGURE 9.4 ***Page Descriptions on Search Engine Results Page***

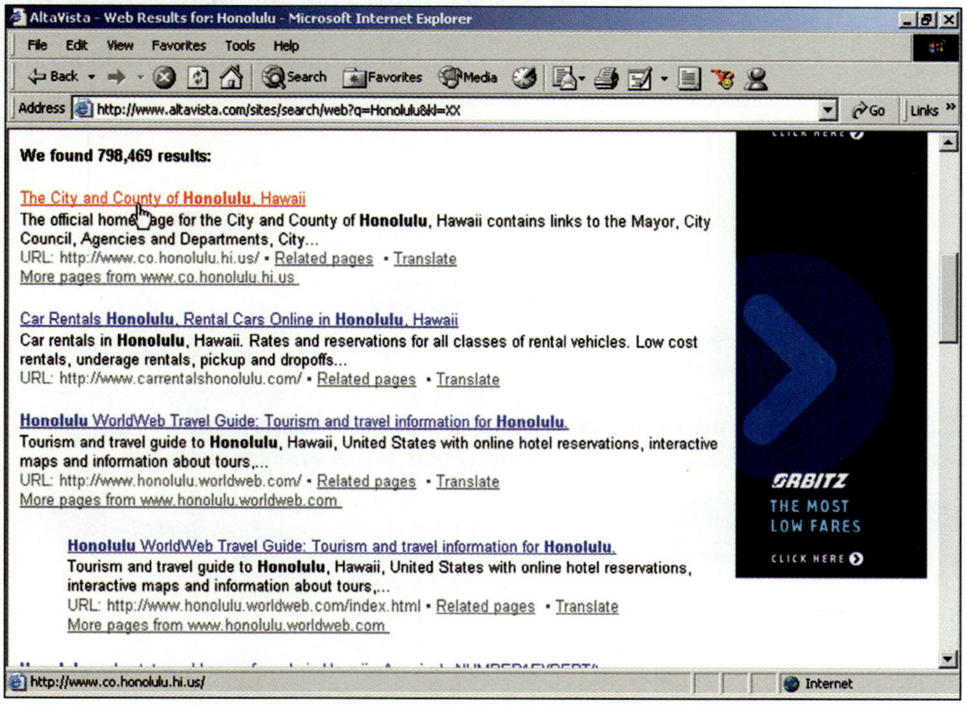

exercise 10 INSERTING THE DESCRIPTION AND KEYWORDS META TAGS INTO HTML

1. Open the EMCPWebs home page (index.htm) in HTML view.
2. Place the insertion point after the tag <meta name="GENERATOR" content="Microsoft FrontPage 5.0"> and press the Enter key.
3. Key the following DESCRIPTION meta data in line 6: **<meta name="description" content="Welcome to EMCPWebs Web Design Services: Effective.Multimedia. Creative.Professional. Your Web Design and Development Specialist">**
4. Press the Enter key once again and key the following KEYWORDS meta data in line 7: **<meta name="keywords" content="Web Design, developer, Web site, HTML, e-commerce, FrontPage, PhotoShop, multimedia, graphics, logo, video, corporate, enterprise, systems, Association of Web Professions, International Webmasters Association, CIW, Certified Internet Webmaster">**

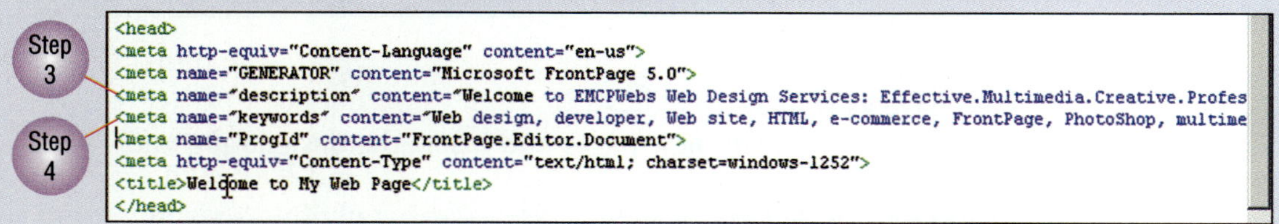

5. Save the updated home page.

exercise 11

CREATING AN AUTOMATIC SLIDE SHOW USING THE REFRESH META TAG

1. Open the EMCPWebs packages.htm Web page in Page view.
2. Place the insertion point after the Photo Gallery Web component and press the Tab key to insert another row in the table.
3. Key the text **View the Slide Show** in the cell and press the Center button on the Formatting toolbar.
4. Select the keyed text and click the Insert Hyperlink button on the Standard toolbar.

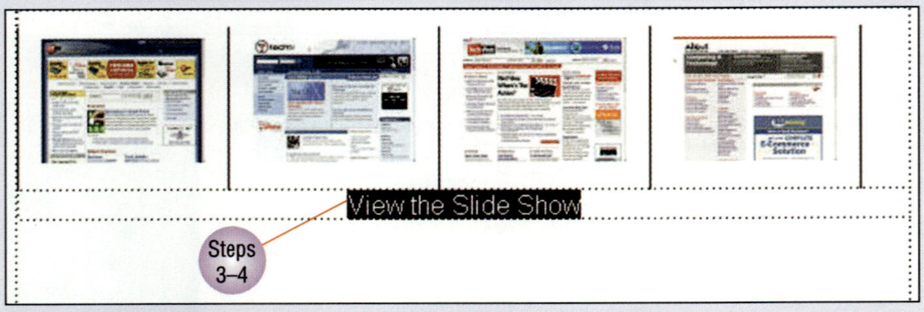

5. At the Insert Hyperlink dialog box, click Create New Document.
6. Key **slide1** in the Name of new document text box and then click OK.

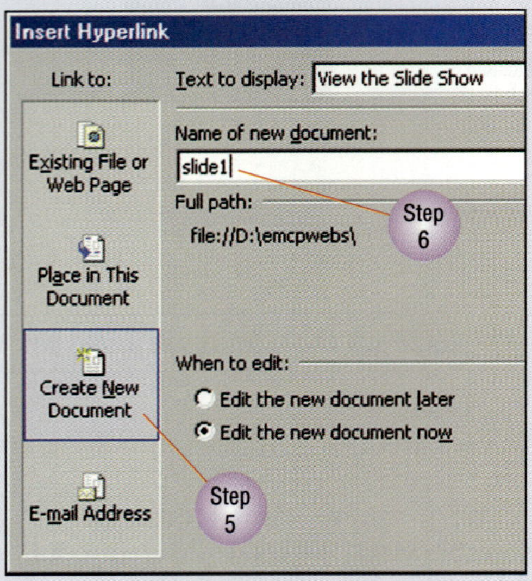

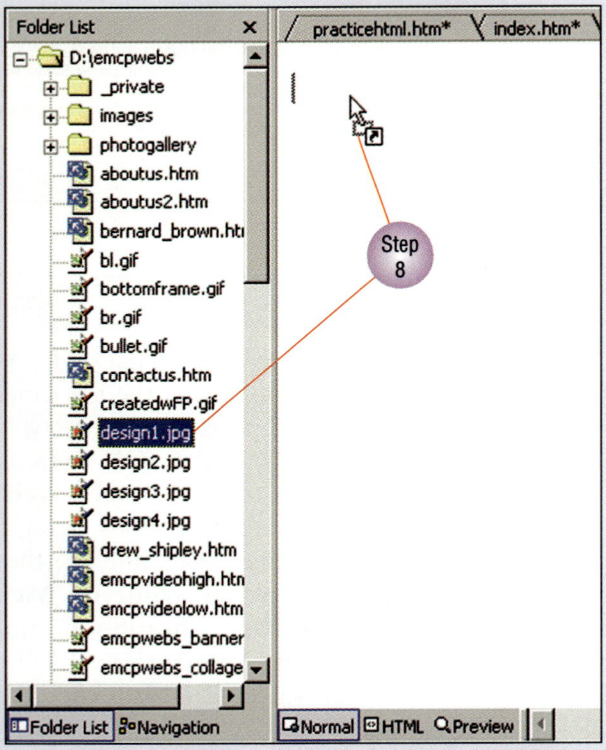

7. Click the Toggle Pane button on the Standard toolbar.
8. Click *design1.jpg* in the Folder List and drag it into the Web page in Page view.
9. Click the Create a new normal page button on the Standard toolbar.
10. Drag design2.jpg into the new page.
11. Save the new Web page as slide2.
12. Repeat steps 9 through 11 to create new pages and insert the design3.jpg and design4.jpg image files.
13. Open the slide1.htm page in HTML view.

14. Place the insertion point after the tag <meta name="GENERATOR" content="Microsoft FrontPage 5.0"> and press the Enter key.
15. Key the following REFRESH meta data in line 5: **<meta http-equiv="refresh" content="10; url=slide2.htm">**
16. Repeat steps 14 and 15 to apply the REFRESH meta data to the following pages:

Web Page	*REFRESH Meta Data*
slide2.htm	**<meta http-equiv="refresh" content="10; url=slide3.htm">**
slide3.htm	**<meta http-equiv="refresh" content="10; url=slide4.htm">**
slide4.htm	**<meta http-equiv="refresh" content="10; url=packages.htm">**

17. Click File and then click Save All.
18. Open the packages.htm page in Page view.
19. Perform a Preview in Browser and test the automatic slide show.

Adding Meta Data in Page Properties

In addition to adding meta data in HTML view, developers can add meta data to Web pages in the Page Properties dialog box. To perform this, click File and then Properties, select the Custom tab in the Page Properties dialog box, and then click the Add button in the User variables section.

exercise 12

ADDING META DATA IN PAGE PROPERTIES

1. Open the EMCPWebs home page (index.htm) in Page view.
2. Click File and then click Properties.
3. At the Page Properties dialog box, click the Custom tab.
4. Click the Add button in the User variables section.

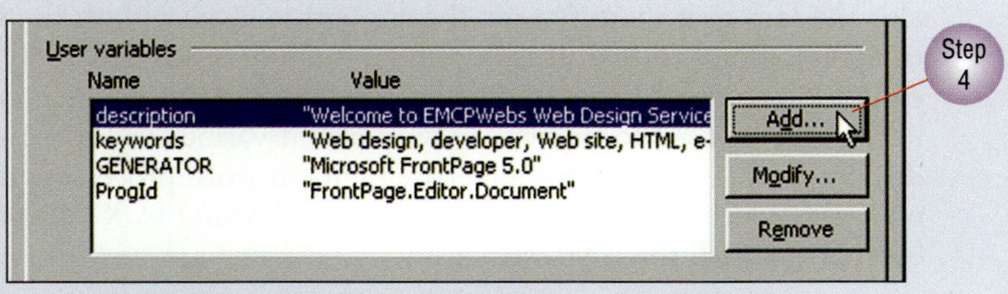

5. Key the **copyright** meta data in the Name text box in the User Meta Variable dialog box.
6. Press the Tab key and key **2002 - EMCPWebs** in the Value text box, and then click OK.

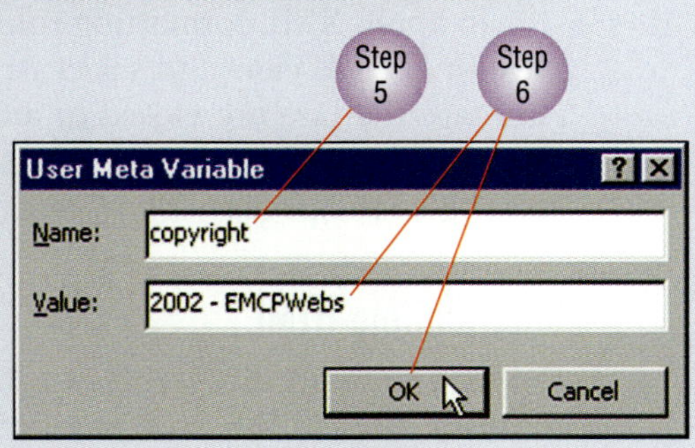

7. At the Page Properties dialog box, confirm that *copyright* has been added to the Name list box in the System variables section, and then click OK to return to Page view.

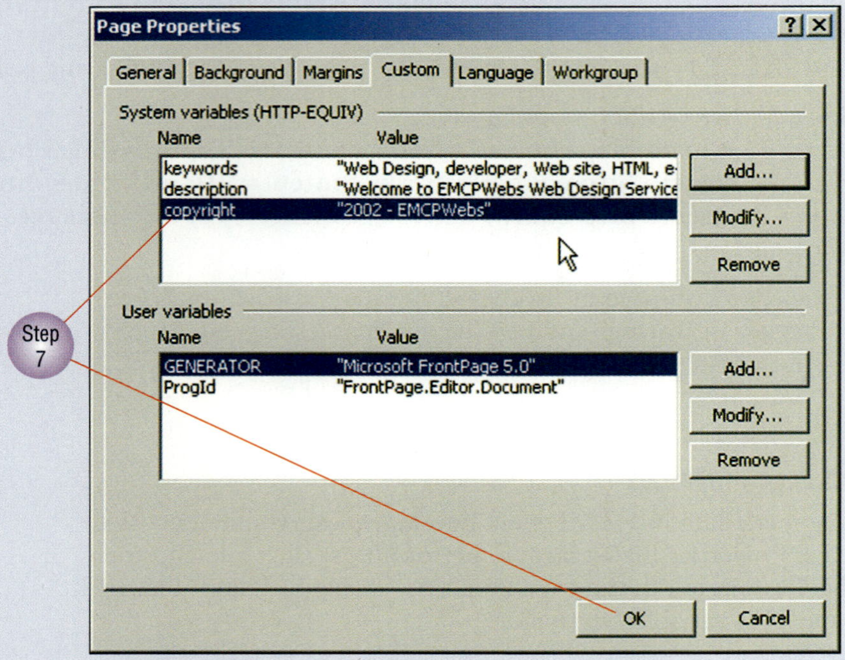

8. Return to HTML view.
9. Print the HTML code.

Formatting in XML

Extensible Markup Language, or XML, is a document markup language used for defining structured information. An XML document shows not only the content, but also the tags that identify how the content is displayed on the screen. In addition to applying tags to text, it is becoming more necessary to apply tags to the actual content. The tagged content can then be used in other contexts. For example, an item could be used for inventory purposes at various levels of the supply chain, for display on a Web page, for advertisements in word processing documents, and so on. While entire textbooks and courses are devoted to XML, we will apply rules compatible with the XML structure.

To apply XML formatting rules to a Web page, right-click anywhere in the code page in HTML view and select Apply XML Formatting Rules on the pop-up menu. Any tags that are not closed or are incomplete will be changed to meet XML rules. FrontPage users can also reformat HTML code in HTML view to remove extra spacing in the page.

Reformatting HTML

Before you apply XML rules to the EMCPWebs pages, it is often a good idea to reformat the HTML code to remove any extra spacing between lines of code. To reformat HTML code, first access the HTML view. Right-click anywhere in the code and select the Reformat HTML command.

exercise 13 REFORMATTING HTML

1. Open the EMCPWebs index.htm Web page in HTML view.
2. Right-click anywhere inside the code window and select Reformat HTML.
3. Save the updated Web page.
4. Perform the same procedure for each of the other Web page files in the EMCPWebs FrontPage Web.

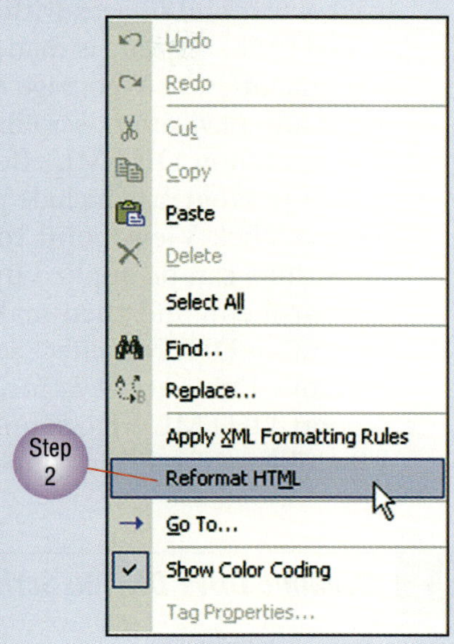

Applying XML Formatting Rules

XML is much more stringent than HTML in the matter of how tags are structured and entered. Tags that are missing or incomplete can cause the file not to function or to display improperly. When you apply the XML formatting rules, FrontPage searches the page for these missing or incomplete tags and automatically adds the tags for you.

exercise 14 APPLYING XML FORMATTING RULES

1. Open the EMCPWebs index.htm Web page in HTML view.
2. Right-click anywhere inside the code window and select Apply XML Formatting Rules.
3. Save the updated Web page.
4. Perform the same procedure for each of the other Web page files in the EMCPWebs FrontPage Web.

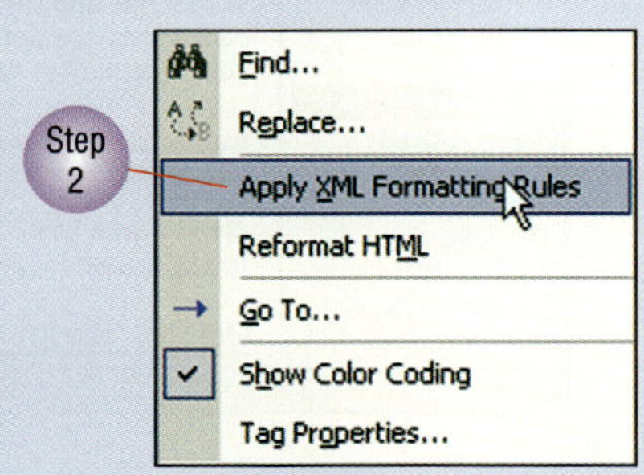

Applying DHTML Effects to a Web Page

Most pages on the World Wide Web are static, in that all users can do on the page is view text and images without much interaction or animation. Dynamic HTML, or DHTML, content is made up of interactive effects that allow Web designers to add animation to Web page elements. DHTML can include mouse over, Web page, menu and navigation, scrolling, browser, outlining, and other dynamic effects. The most common DHTML effects that can be performed on the DHTML Effects toolbar in FrontPage include page load and mouse over. To view the DHTML Effects toolbar, click View, point to Toolbars, and then click DHTML Effects. Page transitions can be applied by selecting the Page Transition command from the Format menu and then making selections in the Page Transitions dialog box. Interesting DHTML effect scripts can be found at many Web sites; one example is Dynamic Drive at www.emcp.net/dynamicdrive (see figure 9.5). Not all browsers support DHTML effects; only Internet Explorer and Netscape Navigator versions 4.0 and later currently support them.

FIGURE 9.5 **Dynamic Drive DHTML Script Web Site**

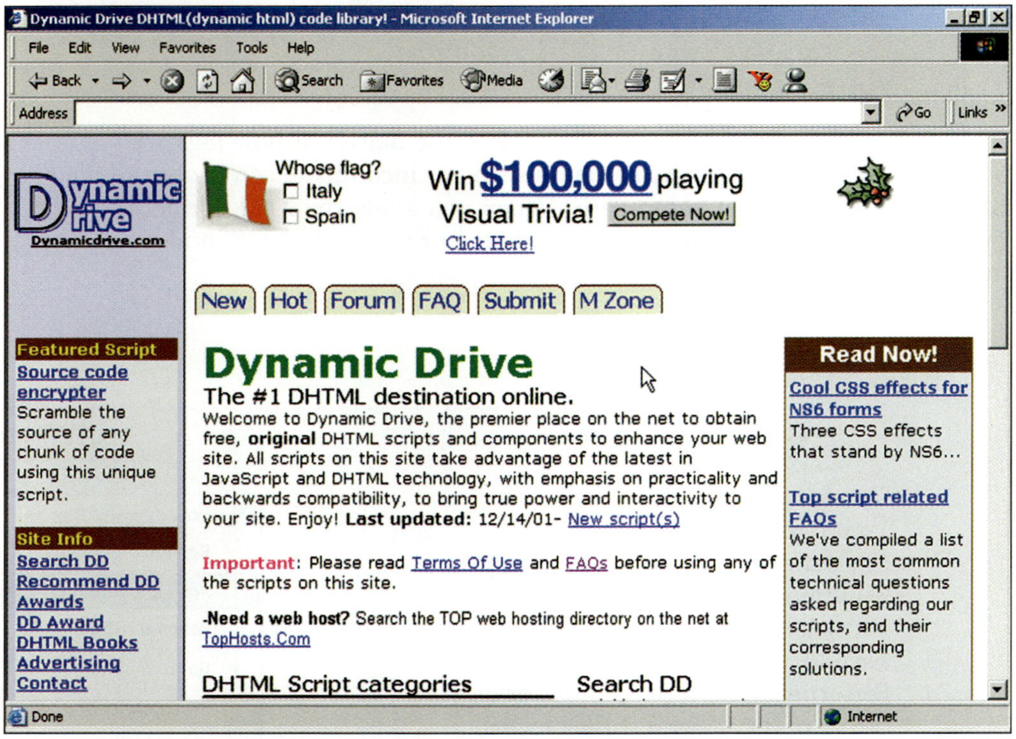

Applying DHTML Page Load and Transition Effects

Page load effects are similar in appearance to build effects in PowerPoint presentations. FrontPage 2002 offers seven different page load effects: Elastic, Fly in, Hop, Spiral, Wave, Wipe, and Zoom. Page transition effects are similar in appearance to slide transitions seen in PowerPoint presentations. FrontPage 2002 offers 25 different page transition options.

exercise 15

APPLYING DHTML PAGE LOAD EFFECTS

1. Open the EMCPWebs index.htm Web page in Page view.
2. Select the emcpwebs_collage.gif image in the upper left corner of the Web page.
3. Click View, point to Toolbars, and then click DHTML Effects.
4. On the DHTML Effects toolbar, click the down-pointing triangle next to <Choose an event> and select *Page load*.
5. Click the down-pointing triangle next to <Choose an effect> and select *Fly in*.
6. Click the down-pointing triangle next to <Choose Settings> and select *From right*.

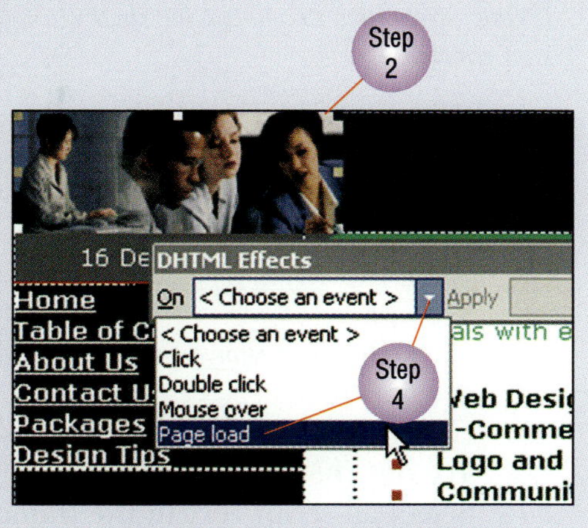

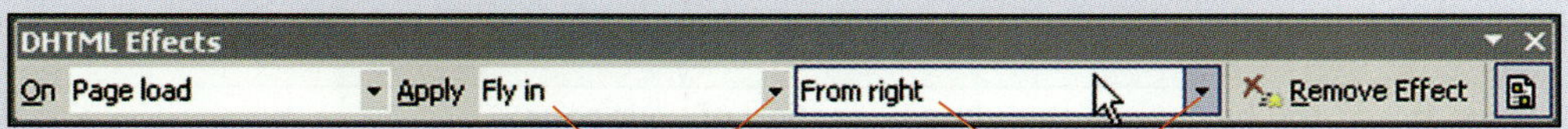

Step 5 Step 6

7. Save the updated home page.
8. Perform a Preview in Browser.

exercise 16

APPLYING DHTML PAGE TRANSITION EFFECTS

1. Open the EMCPWebs index.htm Web page in Page view.
2. Click Format and then click Page Transition.
3. At the Page Transitions dialog box, select the *Random dissolve* transition effect with a duration of 3 seconds.
4. Click the down-pointing triangle in the Event list box and select *Page Enter*.
5. Click the OK button.
6. Save the updated home page.
7. Perform a Preview in Browser.

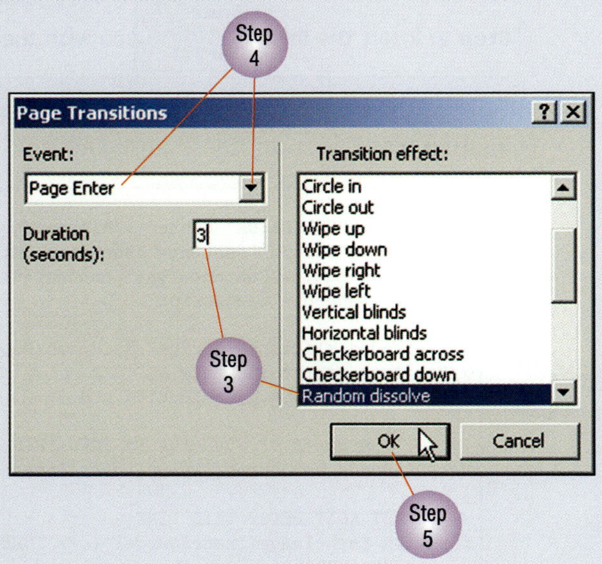

Creating a Web Page Slide Show Using DHTML

You have created slide shows incorporating a PowerPoint presentation, using the Photo Gallery Web component, and using the REFRESH meta tag. You will now create a slide show using DHTML script.

exercise 17

CREATING A WEB PAGE SLIDE SHOW USING DHTML (DYNAMIC DRIVE)

(Note: Web sites are noted for their changeability. The links cited were current at the time this text was written.)

1. With the EMCPWebs FrontPage Web open, click the Create a new normal page button on the Standard toolbar.
2. Access the Dynamic Drive Web site at www.dynamicdrive.com.

3. Click the *Terms Of Use* link and read through the Web page.
4. Click the *Slideshows* link in the DHTML Script categories area.
5. Click the *Preloaded slide show* link.
6. Try out the demo slide show on the Web page.
7. Select all script text in the frame at Step 1.
8. Right-click anywhere in the highlighted text and select Copy.

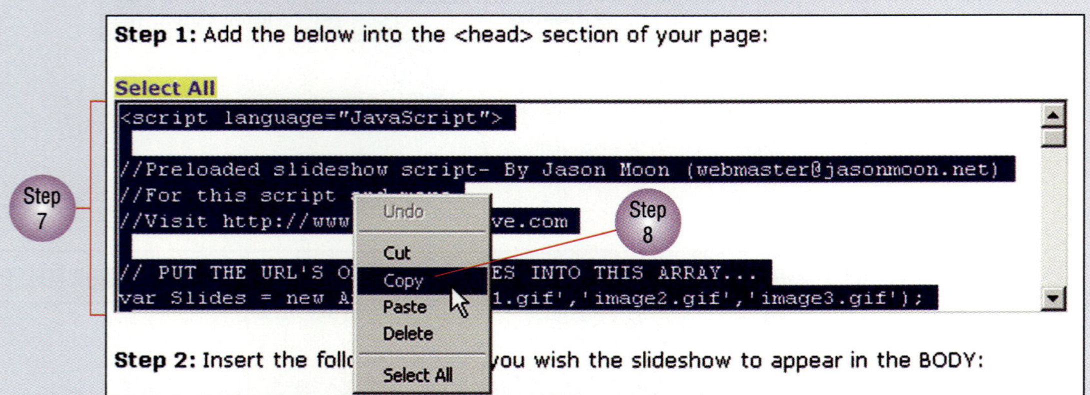

9. Return to the new Web page in FrontPage and click the HTML button.
10. Create a blank line on line 7 and click the Paste button on the Standard toolbar.

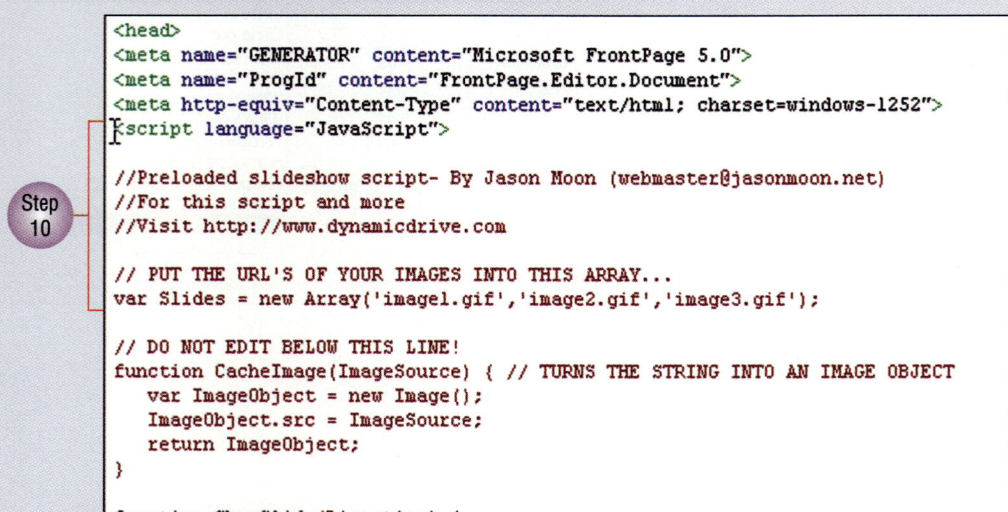

11. Return to the Dynamic Drive Web page and copy the script in the Step 2 frame.

12. Paste the script between the <BODY> tags in the HTML code.

Step 12

```
<title>New Page 1</title>
</head>

<body>

<form name="SlideShow">
<table>
<tr>
   <td colspan=2><img name="Screen" width=108 height=135></td>
</tr>
<tr>
   <td><input type="button" name="Previous"
value=" << "
onClick="ShowSlide(-1)"></td>
   <td align="right"><input type="button" name="Next"
value=" >> " onClick="ShowSlide(1)"></td>
</table>
</form>

</body>
```

13. Enter the script into the body as shown below. *(Note: You need to change the script to reference the images you want as well as to adjust the screen size of the images.*

Step 13

```
<body>

<body onLoad="StartSlideShow()">

<form name="SlideShow">
```

14. Replace the image file names in line 14 to match the illustration.

```
// PUT THE URL'S OF YOUR IMAGES INTO THIS ARRAY...
var Slides = new Array('design1.jpg','design2.jpg','design3.jpg', 'design4.jpg');
```

Step 14

15. Scroll down to the <BODY> section of the code and configure the "Screen" width to 320 and the height to 240.
16. Save the Web page as slideshow.htm with the page title *EMCPWebs DHTML Slideshow*.
17. Perform a Preview in Browser and test the slide show.

Applying Mouse Over Effects to Hyperlinks

Mouse over effects can alter font color, the font itself, and underline characteristics. Mouse over effects can be applied in the Background tab of the Page Properties dialog box as well as on the DHTML Effects toolbar. The DHTML Effects toolbar can be accessed by clicking View, pointing to Toolbars, and then selecting DHTML Effects. You will apply mouse over effects to hypertext links in the exercise.

1. Open the links.htm page in the EMCPWebs FrontPage Web.
2. Double-click the *Home* link.
3. Open the DHTML Effects toolbar from the View menu.
4. Click the down-pointing triangle next to <Choose an event> and select *Mouse over*.
5. Click the down-pointing triangle next to <Choose an effect> and select *Formatting*.
6. Click the down-pointing triangle next to <Choose Settings> and select *Choose font*.

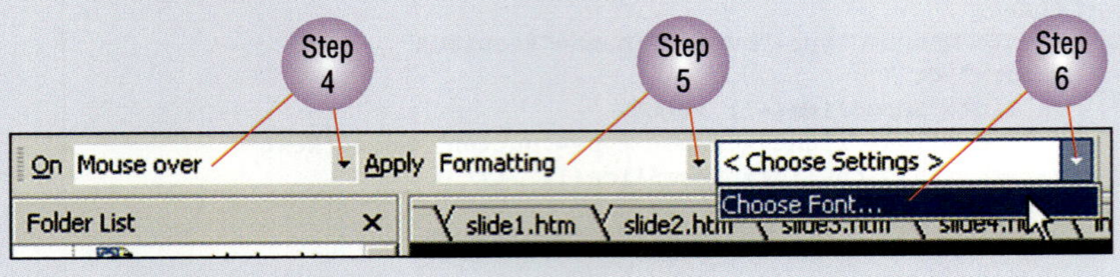

7. At the Font dialog box with the Font tab selected, in the Effects section, click in the No text decoration check box to insert a check mark and then click OK.

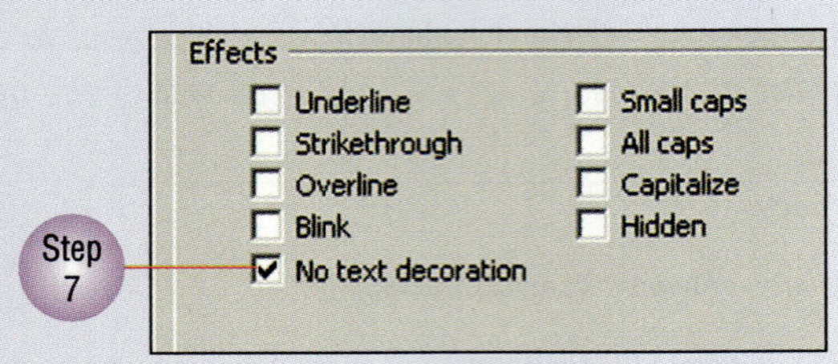

8. Repeat steps 2 through 7 to apply the No text decoration effect to the remaining hyperlinks.
9. Save the updated Web page.
10. Return to the index.htm page and perform a Preview in Browser and test the mouse over effects.

Applying JavaScripts to Web Pages

JavaScripts are very similar to DHTML effects; in fact, DHTML scripts are written in JavaScript. JavaScript was created by both Netscape Communications Corporation and Sun Microsystems. Before a script can be applied in a Web page, a <SCRIPT> tag is inserted in the <HEAD> of the HTML document. This basically tells the browser that JavaScript is being used and includes the functions that are to be used. The JavaScript tag shown in figure 9.6 would be located in the heading of an HTML document and informs the browser that mouse over effects are to be applied. Basic JavaScript fundamentals were applied when you performed exercise 17.

FIGURE 9.6 *Typical JavaScript Tag in the Heading of an HTML Document*

```
<script language="JavaScript" fptype="dynamicanimation">
<!—
function dynAnimation() {}
function clickSwapImg() {}
//—>
</script>
```

exercise 19 APPLYING JAVASCRIPTS TO WEB PAGES

(Note: These links were current at the time this text was written.)

1. With the EMCPWebs FrontPage Web open, click the Create a new normal page button on the Standard toolbar.
2. Access EarthWeb's JavaScript site at www.javascripts.com.
3. Click the *Games* link on the Web page.

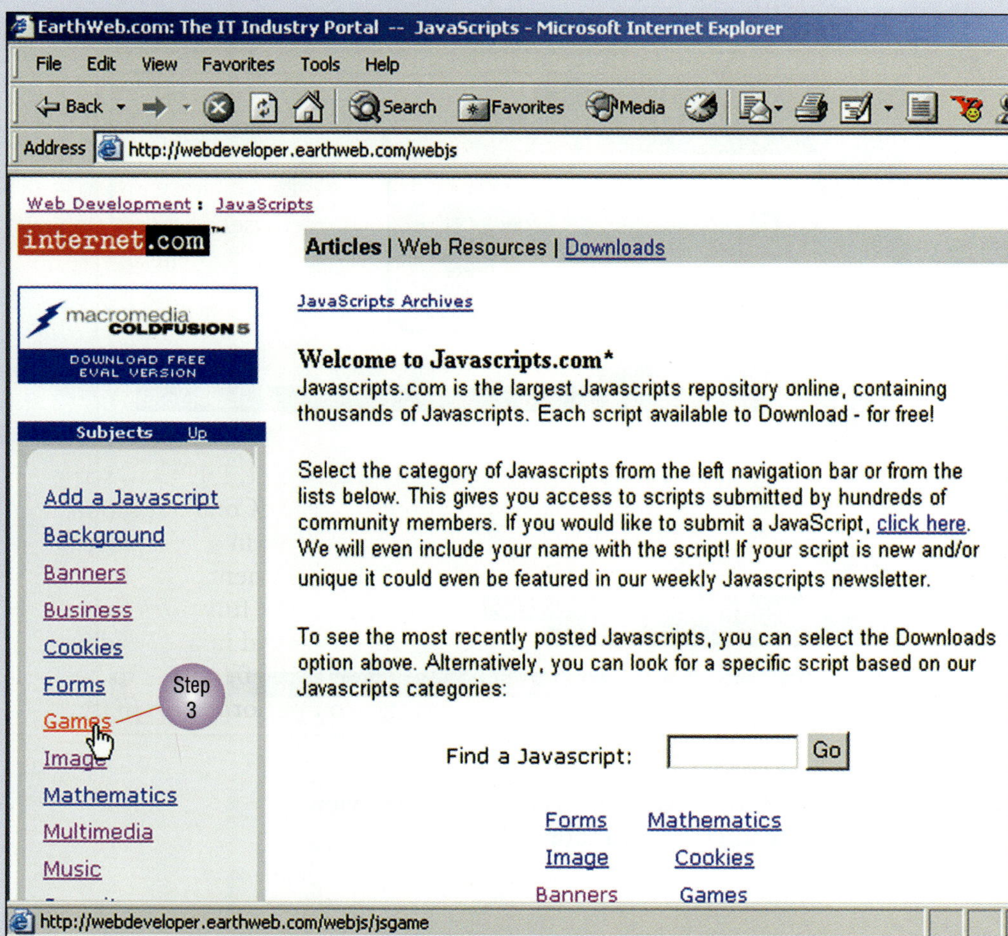

4. By scrolling and viewing subsequent pages, locate the *Irritating Button 2.0* hyperlink and then click the link.

5. Click the *Run the code* link and try out the JavaScript.
6. Click the Back button on the browser toolbar and then click the *See the code* link.

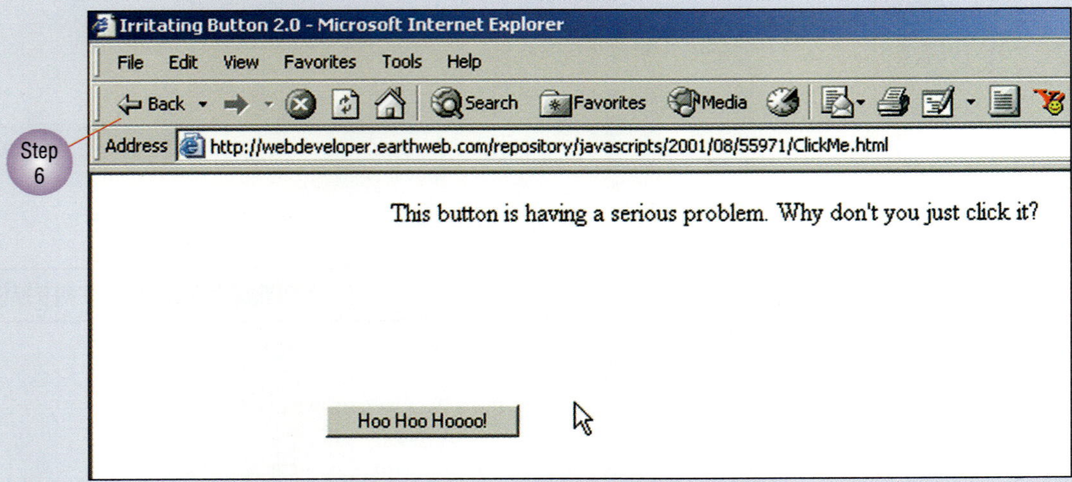

7. Copy all script text in the frame.

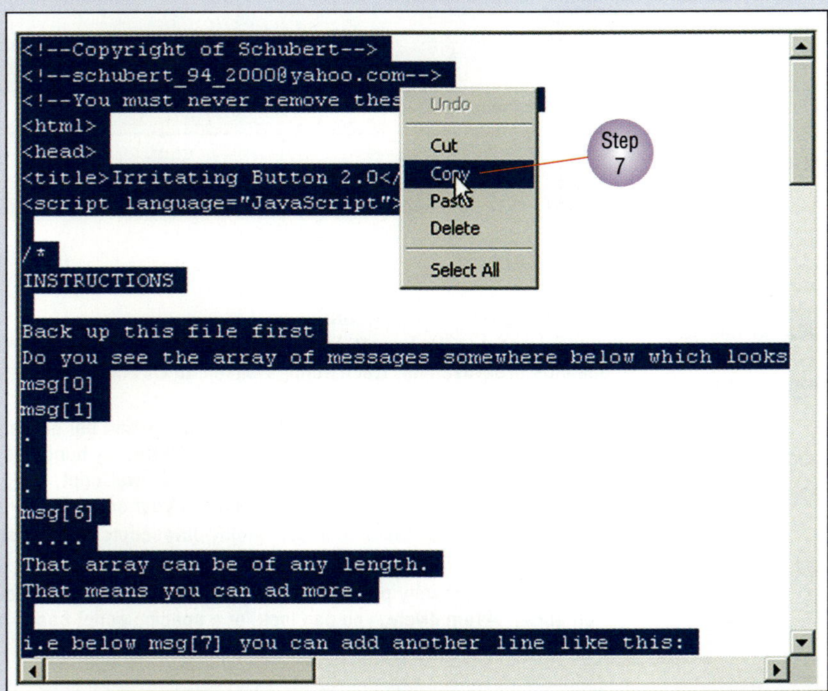

8. Return to the new EMCPWebs Web page in HTML view.
9. Delete all existing code in the window.

10. Paste the code and script into the HTML window.

Step 10

```
<!--Copyright of Schubert-->
<!--schubert_94_2000@yahoo.com-->
<!--You must never remove these lines-->
<html>
<head>
<title>Irritating Button 2.0</title>
<script language="JavaScript">

/*
INSTRUCTIONS

Back up this file first
Do you see the array of messages somewhere below which looks like...
msg[0]
msg[1]
.
.
.
msg[6]
.....
That array can be of any length.
That means you can add more.

i.e below msg[7] you can add another line like this:
```

11. Save the Web page as buttongame.htm with the page title *JavaScript Button Game*.
12. Perform a Preview in Browser and test the button game.

Working with Styles, Embedded Styles, and Cascading Style Sheets (CSS)

A style includes the formatting requirements for such page elements as text, headings, paragraphs, bullets, numbering, images, and tables. Once you have specified the formatting requirements for your Web page elements either in the Style dialog box in FrontPage or by entering the style rules and properties (inline styles) into the HTML code, your Web page elements will automatically adhere to those styles. The benefit to styles is that once they have been applied, the page elements are automatically updated. Web page styles are applied only to the current page. To apply styles to multiple pages, it might work best to insert embedded styles or reference an external cascading style sheet (CSS).

Creating and Using an External Style Sheet

With style sheets, Web designers can identify page element formats in a file that can be applied throughout the Web site. For example, a font family of Arial or Helvetica can be applied once in the style sheet and will be echoed throughout the site, whereas formatting text in HTML requires you to format each heading tag individually. Even using the Format Painter requires multiple applications to make an entire site consistent. To create a new style sheet, select the Page Templates link in the New Page or Web Task Pane, click the Style Sheets tab, and then select the Normal Style Sheet option.

exercise 20

CREATING AND USING AN EXTERNAL STYLE SHEET

1. With FrontPage open, click File, point to New, and then click Page or Web.
2. Select the *Empty Web* link in the New section of the New Page or Web Task Pane.
3. At the Web Site Templates dialog box, key **_:\styleweb** in the Specify the location of the new web text box and then click OK. (Substitute your preferred drive letter for the underscore.)
4. Click File and then click Import.
5. At the Import dialog box, click the Add File button.
6. From the *Style Web* folder in your *Chapter 9* folder, select the following Web page files using the Ctrl key: page2.htm, page3.htm, page4.htm, and default.htm.
7. Click the Open button.
8. Click the OK button.
9. Click File, point to New, and then click Page or Web.
10. Select the *Page Templates* link in the New from template section of the New Page or Web Task Pane.
11. Click the Style Sheets tab in the Page Templates dialog box.
12. Double-click the *Normal Style Sheet* icon.
13. Save the style sheet as stylesheet.css.
14. Key the hyperlink style rules and properties in the blank style sheet as shown.
15. Open the default.htm page in HTML view.
16. Key the link markup to the stylesheet.css style sheet as shown.
17. Save the updated Web page.
18. Perform a Preview in Browser and test the hyperlink style effects.

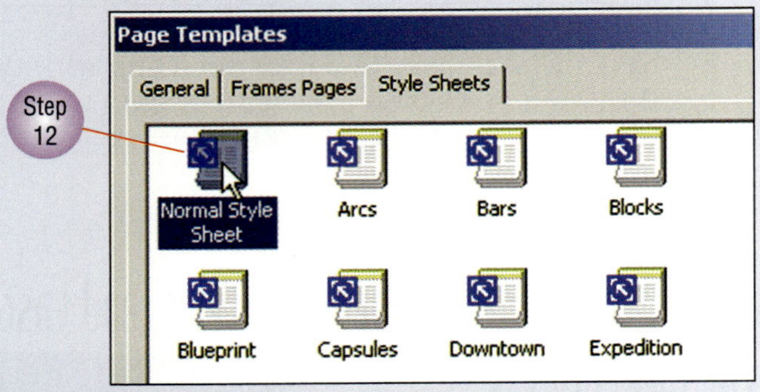

default.htm | stylesheet.css

Step 14

```
a:link {color:#FF0000}
a:hover {text-decoration: none; color:#000000}
a:visited {color:#FF9900}
a:active {color:#FFFF00}
```

```
<head>
<meta name="GENERATOR" content="Microsoft FrontPage 5.0">
<meta name="ProgId" content="FrontPage.Editor.Document">
<meta http-equiv="Content-Type" content="text/html; charset=windows-1252">
<link rel="stylesheet" href="stylesheet.css">
</head>
```

Step 16

Using the Style Toolbar to Add Style Sheet Styles

In addition to keying style rules in a style sheet, designers can click the Style button in the style sheet window to modify styles. There are 30 HTML tags to choose from, or users can create their own styles.

exercise 21

USING THE STYLE TOOLBAR TO ADD STYLE SHEET STYLES

1. Open the stylesheet.css page in Page view.
2. Click the Style button on the Formatting toolbar. If the Style button is not visible, click View, point to Toolbars, click Style, and then click Style.

3. At the Style dialog box, select *body* in the Styles list box and then click the Modify button.
4. At the Modify Style dialog box, click the Format button at the bottom of the dialog box and then click Font.

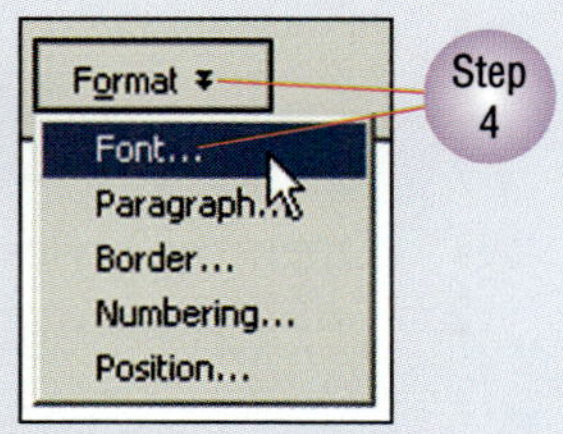

5. At the Font dialog box with the Font tab selected, change the font to Arial and Navy.
6. Click the OK button.
7. At the Modify Style dialog box, click the Format button and then click Border.
8. Click the Shading tab in the Borders and Shading dialog box.
9. Click the down-pointing triangle in the Background color list box and select More Colors.
10. Select the light green color.
11. Press the OK button in each dialog box to return to the style sheet.

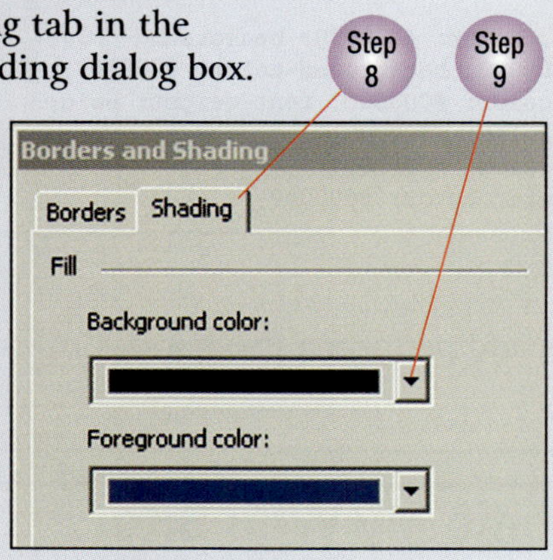

12. Remove the excess spacing in the style line to match the styles above.
13. Save the updated style sheet.
14. Return to the default.htm page and perform a Preview in Browser to test the styles.
15. Print the Web page.

Inserting an Embedded Style Sheet

Embedded styles are a quick way to format a Web page element throughout the page. For example, all Heading 3 fonts can be formatted to Arial, 14 points, bold, and Navy by entering an inline style into the heading section of the HTML code.

exercise 22 — INSERTING AN EMBEDDED STYLE SHEET

1. Open the stylesheet.css page in Page view.
2. Enter the remaining styles in the sheet as shown.

default.htm | stylesheet.css*

```
a:link {color:#FF0000}
a:hover {text-decoration: none; color:#000000}
a:visited {color:#FF9900}
a:active {color:#FFFF00}
body {font-family: Arial; color: #000080; background-color: #CCFFCC}
td {border: 4px solid #800000; background-color: #CCFFFF}
h1 {font-family: Arial; color: #008000; font-weight: bold}
h2 {font-family: Arial; color: #800000}
h3 {font-family: Arial; color: #008000}
ul {list-style-type: square; color: #008080}
```

Step 2

3. Save the updated style sheet.
4. Return to the default.htm page and perform a Preview in Browser.
5. Print the Web page.

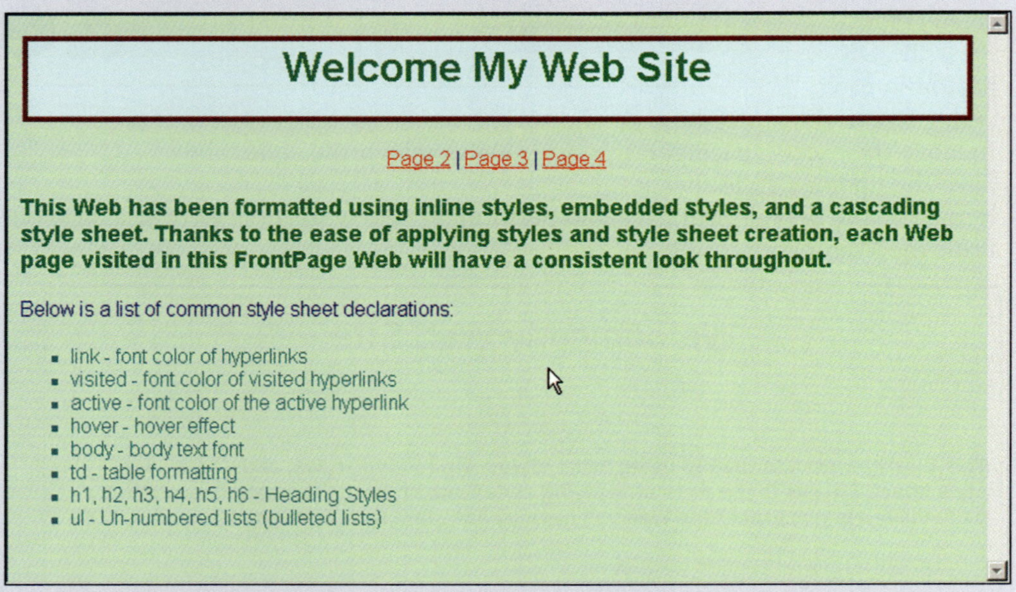

6. Return to the style sheet and copy lines 1 through 5.
7. Open the page2.htm page in HTML view.

8. Enter the embedded style tags and paste the copied styles into the HTML code as shown.

```
<html>

<head>
<meta name="GENERATOR" content="Microsoft FrontPage 5.0">
<meta name="ProgId" content="FrontPage.Editor.Document">
<title>Page 2</title>
<style type="text/css">
<!--
a:link {color:#FF0000}
a:hover {text-decoration: none; color:#000000}
a:visited {color:#FF9900}
a:active {color:#FFFF00}
body {font-family: Arial; color: #000080; background-color: #CCFFCC}
//-->
</style>
</head>

<body>

<div align="left">
  <table border="0" cellPadding="2" width="100%">
    <tbody>
      <tr>
        <td width="100%">
```

Step 8

9. Copy the entire embedded style and paste it into page3.htm and page4.htm.
10. Save all open Web page files and perform a Preview in Browser to test the page2.htm, page3.htm, and page4.htm pages.
11. Print page2.htm, page3.htm, and page4.htm.

Inserting an Inline Style

Inline styles are style formatting rules that are applied to elements within the body of the HTML code. To apply inline styles, simply enter the necessary style tags before and after the Web page element.

exercise 23

INSERTING AN INLINE STYLE

1. Open the default.htm page in HTML view.
2. Key the following underline <style> and numbered list <OL> into the HTML code.

```
  <li>h1, h2, h3, h4, h5, h6 - Heading Styles</li>
  <li>ul - Un-numbered lists (bulleted lists)</li>
</ul>

<div style="text-decoration:underline">
<ol>
  <li>Item 1</li>
  <li>Item 2</li>
  <li>Item 3</li>
</ol>
</style>

</body>
```

Step 2

3. Save the updated Web page and perform a Preview in Browser to view the underline style effect.
4. Print the Web page.

CHAPTER summary

- Hypertext Markup Language, or HTML, is an authoring language used to create Web pages for the World Wide Web.
- HTML is basically a text-based coding scheme that can be created using any text editing program.
- HTML tags instruct the encompassing text how to be displayed in the browser.
- HTML tags are surrounded by a less than (<) and a greater than (>) sign.
- The four basic HTML tags that make up a Web page document include <HTML>, <HEAD>, <TITLE>, and <BODY>.
- The <HTML> tag is read by the browser and indicates that the document is an HTML document.
- The <TITLE> tag is placed within the <HEAD> tag and tells the browser to place the title of the Web page on the browser Title bar.
- The <BODY> tag encompasses the actual content that appears on your Web page.
- The Reveal Tags feature, on the View menu, displays HTML tags in Page view.
- The HTML view is used to manually code HTML, styles, and scripts.
- The color coding of the elements in HTML view can be altered in the Page Options dialog box.
- The <FONT FACE="TIMES NEW ROMAN"> tag will format text to Times New Roman.
- The <FONT SIZE="5"> tag will format text to Heading 5 font size.
- The <FONT STYLE="font-size: 10 pt"> tag will format text to 10 points.
- The <BODY BGCOLOR="#FFFFCC"> tag will format the Web page background to a light yellow.
- The tag will format text to bold type.
- The <I> tag will format text to italic.
- The <U> tag will format text to underline.
- The <FONT COLOR="#008080"> tag will format text to Teal.
- Heading text can be applied using the <H1> through <H7> tags; <H1>=8 pt and <H7>=36 pt.
- The <BR> tag will insert a line break and force text to be placed directly under the line.
- The <CENTER> tag will format the paragraph to center alignment.
- The <RIGHT> tag will format the paragraph to right alignment.
- The <UL> tag initiates a bulleted list.
- The <LI> tag indicates the items in either a bulleted or numbered list.
- The <OL> tag initiates a numbered list.
- The <IMG SRC="image1.jpg"> tag inserts a JPEG image titled image.jpg into the Web page.
- The <A HREF="http://www.nytimes.com"> NY Times</a> tag creates a hyperlink on the text *NY Times* on the Web.
- The <TABLE> tag initiates a table.

- The <TR> tag is used to create rows in a table.
- The <TD> tag is used to create multiple columns in a table.
- The DESCRIPTION meta tag is used to provide search engines with a description of the Web site contents.
- The KEYWORDS meta tag is used to provide search engines with keywords that describe the contents of your Web site, enhancing search engine results.
- The REFRESH meta tag is used to automatically load another Web page after a specified amount of time.
- Meta tags can be added to an HTML document by accessing the Page Properties dialog box from the File menu.
- XML, or Extensible Markup Language, has the ability to define not only formatting of Web page content, but also the actual content of Web pages for use in other applications that require such data, object, or information.
- XML formatting rules can be applied to Web pages by right-clicking inside the code window in HTML view and selecting the Apply XML Formatting Rules command.
- HTML can be reformatted to remove unnecessary spaces and line spacing by right-clicking inside the code window and selecting the Reformat HTML command.
- Dynamic HTML, or DHTML, content is made up of interactive effects that allow Web designers to add animation to Web page elements such as mouse overs, page transitions, scrolling banners, and image effects.
- Page load effects can force Web page elements such as text and images to appear and exit from different locations on the screen.
- Page transition effects are similar to PowerPoint slide transitions and can be applied by selecting the Page Transition command on the Format menu.
- Page load and mouse over DHTML effects can applied by using the DHTML Effects toolbar accessed from the View menu.
- JavaScripts are similar to DHTML effects in that special effects and interactive components can be incorporated into a Web page.
- DHTML effects are written in JavaScript.
- Before a script can be applied in a Web page, a <SCRIPT> tag is inserted in the heading of the HTML document.
- A style includes the formatting requirements for such page elements as text, headings, paragraphs, bullets, numbering, images, and tables.
- An external Cascading Style Sheet (CSS) can be created that identifies the formatting requirements for various Web page elements and is referenced by a Web page at the code level.
- External style sheets can be created by selecting the Style Sheets tab in the Page Templates dialog box.
- Cascading style sheets must be saved with the .css extension.
- Embedded styles reference an external style sheet, but only for specific formatting elements.
- Inline styles are style rules that are applied directly to the Web page element in HTML without reference to an external style sheet file.

COMMANDS review

Command	Mouse/Keyboard
View HTML tags in Page view	Click View, Reveal Tags
View and edit HTML code in a Web page	Click HTML button at bottom of window
Alter HTML element color coding	Click Tools, Page Options
Insert meta data	Click File, Properties, Custom tab
Reformat HTML code	Right-click in HTML view, click Reformat HTML
Apply XML formatting rules	Right-click in HTML view, click Apply XML Formatting Rules.
Apply DHTML using DHTML Effects toolbar	Click View, point to Toolbars, click DHTML Effects
Apply page transition effects	Click Format, Page transition
Create an external Cascading Style Sheet (CSS)	Click File, point to New, click Page or Web, *Page Templates,* Style Sheets tab

CONCEPTS check

Completion: On a blank sheet of paper, indicate the correct term, command, or number for each item.

1. HTML is an authoring language used to create documents for this medium.
2. HTML documents must begin with this tag.
3. The Web page title should appear within this tag.
4. This FrontPage feature enables HTML tags to be displayed in Page view.
5. A font size of 18 points is the equivalent of this heading size.
6. Formatting text, table, and cell coloring in HTML is accomplished using this coding scheme.
7. Bulleted and numbered lists use this tag to separate the list items.
8. This tag is used to reference an image source to be displayed in a Web page.
9. A table must begin with this HTML tag.
10. This meta tag is used to provide search engines with a list of words and phrases to improve search engine rankings.
11. This coding markup language is used to define not only the content, but also the tags that identify how the content is displayed on the screen.
12. Use this FrontPage toolbar to apply page load and mouse over effects.

13. Page transition effects can be applied by clicking the Page Transition command on this menu.
14. Netscape Communications Corporation and Sun Microsystems developed this scripting language to create dynamic Web page content.
15. These are used to reference formatting requirements for such page elements as text, headings, paragraphs, bullets, numbering, images, and tables to create a consistent look throughout a Web site.

SKILLS check

Assessment 1

1. In a new blank Web page, key the following resume information. You may substitute your personal resume information if you already have a resume in electronic format.

JONATHAN B. DOE

9876 W. College Avenue - Anywhere, USA 77777 - 555.989.5150

CAREER OBJECTIVE

To obtain the position of Chief Web Designer at XYZ Corporation.

EDUCATION

Bachelor of Science: Business Information Technology, University of Denver, CO

Associate of Science, Nassau Community College, Garden City, NY

2. In HTML view, format the above text to the following specifications:

Line 13	Arial, 18 points, bold, and Blue (#003366)
Line 14	Arial, 12 points, italic
Line 15	Heading 3 Style, Arial, and Blue (#003366)
Line 16	Arial, 10 points
Line 17	Heading 3 Style, Arial, and Blue (#003366)
Line 18	Arial, 10 points
Line 19	Arial, 10 points

3. Key the title **HTML Assessment Activity** in line 8.
4. Save the Web page as htmlassessment.htm.
5. Preview the Web page in your browser, and then print.

Assessment 2

1. Open the htmlassessment.htm Web page file created in assessment 1.
2. In HTML view, format line 13 to center alignment and insert a line break between lines 13 and 14.
3. Key the text **Last Updated: November 12, 2003** in line 20.
4. Right align line 20 in HTML view.
5. Apply bullets to the two *EDUCATION* listings in HTML view.
6. Save the updated Web page.
7. Preview the Web page in your browser, and then print.

Assessment 3

1. In a new blank Web page, create the following table in HTML view:

Time	Saturday	Sunday
Morning (8-12)	College Orientation	Community Tours
Afternoon (1-5)	Campus Tours	Dormitory Assignments

2. Format the table background to Dark Purple (#330033).
3. Key the title **HTML Table Practice Document** in line 8.
4. Save the Web page document as tableassessment.htm.
5. Preview the Web page in your browser, and then print.

Assessment 4

1. Open the htmlassessment.htm Web page file created in assessment 1.
2. Insert a scanned or digital camera photograph of yourself at the top of the Web page in HTML view. *(Note: If your image file is located on a floppy, the HTML tag to reference the image would look something like <img border="0" src="file:///a:/jarrett_rebound.jpg" width="243" height="183">.)*
3. Add a space, dash (-), and another space after the phone number in line 14.
4. Enter your first and last names using an appropriate font color and create a hyperlink from your name to your e-mail in HTML view.
5. Create a blank line on line 21 and create a hyperlink to your personal or school Web page.
6. Save the updated Web page.
7. Preview the Web page in your browser, and then print.

Assessment 5

1. Open the htmlassessment.htm Web page file created in assessment 1.
2. Access HTML view and enter a DESCRIPTION meta tag that would best describe the resume Web page.
3. Enter a KEYWORDS meta tag that identifies a minimum of 10 and a maximum of 25 keywords that would best describe your personal objective, education, skills, qualifications, and so on.
4. Using the Page Properties dialog box, enter a COPYRIGHT meta tag that includes the current year and your name.
5. Save the updated Web page.
6. Preview the Web page in your browser, and then print.

Assessment 6

1. Open a new blank Web page in Page view.
2. Key the following text in the Web page: **The page you are looking for has been moved to www.emcp.com. You will be redirected to the appropriate Web page in five seconds. Please update your Favorites or Bookmarks.**
3. Enter a REFRESH meta tag that will automatically open the EMCParadigm home page after five seconds.
4. Save the Web page as refreshassessment.htm with the title *Refresh Meta Tag Assessment Activity.*
5. Preview the Web page in your browser to test the REFRESH meta tag.
6. Print the HTML code in HTML view.

Assessment 7

1. Open the transitionassessment FrontPage Web from your *Chapter 9* folder.
2. Open the index.htm Web page in Page view.
3. Format a page transition effect of Box in on Page Enter with a duration of three seconds.
4. Format a page transition effect of Box out on Page Exit with a duration of three seconds.
5. Save the updated Web page.
6. Preview the Web page in your browser and test the page transition effects.

Assessment 8

1. Open a new blank Web page in Page view.
2. Access the Dynamic Drive (www.dynamicdrive.com) Web site, read the terms of use, and then locate an interesting DHTML effect.
3. Incorporate a DHTML effect into the Web page.
4. Save the Web page as dhtmlassessment.htm with the title *DHTML Assessment Activity.*

Assessment 9

1. Create a new FrontPage Web titled resumeweb.
2. Key your resume information in the home page in Page view.
3. Ensure that you have the following page elements present. You may have to become inventive if you do not!
   - Bulleted list
   - Numbered list
   - Hypertext link
   - Table
4. Format the Web page text using the Heading (<H1><H7>) Style button.
5. Create an external style sheet titled stylesheet.css with your own formatting style rules for the following Web page elements:
   - Heading text
   - Hyperlink
   - Visited hyperlink
   - Active hyperlink
   - Body
   - Table

- Headings
- Bulleted lists
- Numbered lists

6. Reference the style sheet in the resumeweb home page HTML code.
7. Save the updated home page.
8. Perform a Preview in Browser and print the Web page.
9. Exit FrontPage.

CHAPTER 10

WORKING WITH FORMS AND DATABASES, AND MANAGING AND ANALYZING FRONTPAGE WEBS

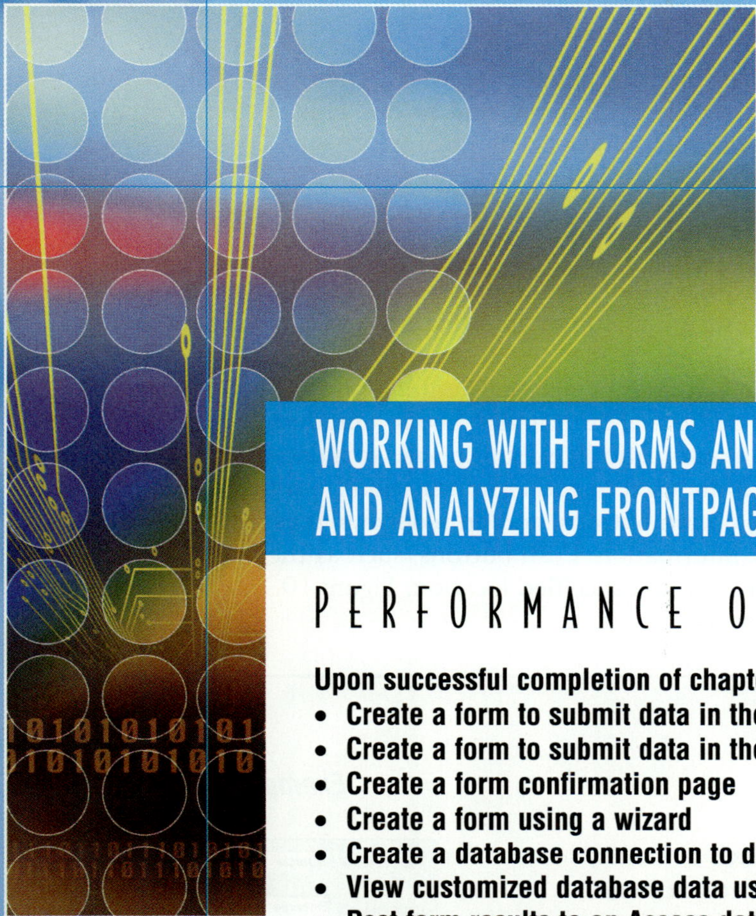

PERFORMANCE OBJECTIVES

Upon successful completion of chapter 10, you will be able to:

- **Create a form to submit data in the form of an e-mail**
- **Create a form to submit data in the form of a file**
- **Create a form confirmation page**
- **Create a form using a wizard**
- **Create a database connection to display database information in a Web page**
- **View customized database data using a Microsoft Access query**
- **Post form results to an Access database**
- **Analyze a Web using various FrontPage reports**
- **Set permissions for FrontPage Webs and subwebs**
- **Create a page template for site consistency**

Chapter 10 IRC

Interactive forms are an integral part of information gathering for individuals, organizations, and companies. Some of the methods used for information gathering include surveys, guest books, information requests, site searches, discussion groups, and purchases of goods and services through electronic commerce sites. FrontPage 2002 has a series of form templates that novice to advanced designers can use to compile information. The form-based template pages include Feedback Form, Guest Book, Search Page, User Registration, and a Confirmation Page. FrontPage 2002 even has a Form Page Wizard that allows you to customize your form inquiries based on your specifications.

Database-driven content is prevalent in many of today's Web sites. In this chapter you will connect to an Access database to view database information on a Web page. You will also use a form to post data to a Microsoft Access database.

There are many things to consider when designing, developing, and managing a Web site, especially if there are multiple persons working on the site. FrontPage 2002 has several site-management features aimed at assisting FrontPage Web developers in producing professional Webs. The Tasks view in FrontPage is basically an electronic notepad to document the aspects of your FrontPage Web that need to be created, updated, fixed, or deleted. Using the Reports view, pages, graphics, and files in your Web can be analyzed by running various reports. With the new usage analysis reports, FrontPage Web administrators can view monthly, weekly, and daily reports that monitor the number of hits, the number of users, operating systems and browsers used by visitors, referring domains, and so on. This chapter will also explore FrontPage Web permissions and page templates.

Using Forms to Collect and Disseminate Data

A Web page form is an excellent tool for obtaining information from a visitor. Personal information, requests for additional information, and comments are typical components of a Web page form. Simple form results are usually sent as an e-mail message. That information can then be manually entered into a database or used to contact the visitor with additional information about a product or service. More advanced uses of forms can automatically submit results to a database. Form fields are elements in a form that are used to gather information from the visitor. Form fields such as check boxes, option buttons, and drop-down menus allow visitors to make selections and enter information. Push buttons, such as the Submit button, will send selections and entries to a specified location. Figure 10.1 describes form fields used in Web page forms.

FIGURE 10.1 ***Form Fields***

Form Field	***Description***	***Example***
Textbox	Used to collect data such as names, addresses, or other short text items.	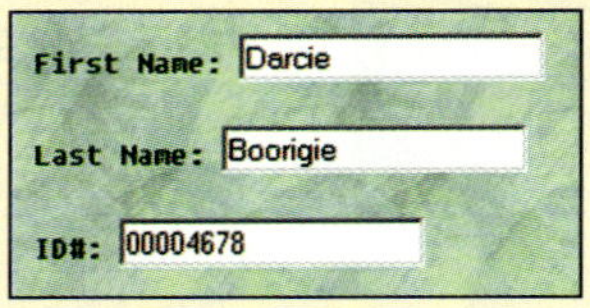
Text Area	Commonly used to collect multiple lines of text such as comments and questions from the visitor.	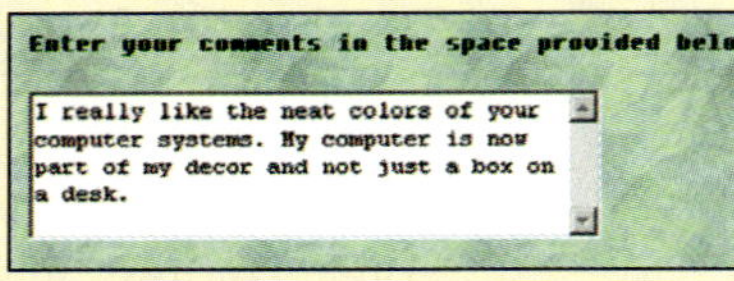
File Upload	A new form item that allows visitors to send files such as images and documents.	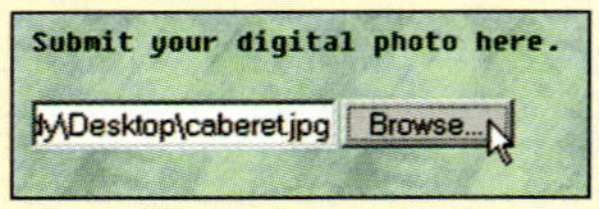
Checkbox	Gives the visitor a list of options from which multiple selections can be made.	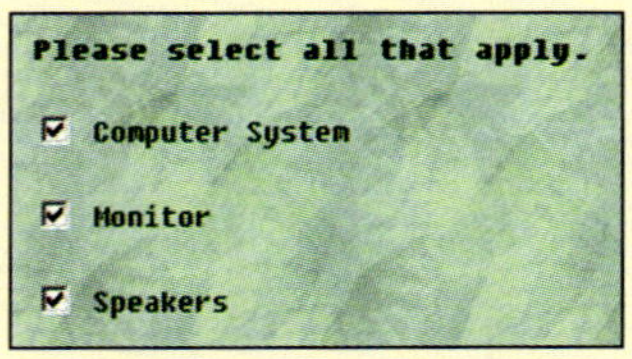
Option Button	Gives the visitor a list of options from which only one choice can be made.	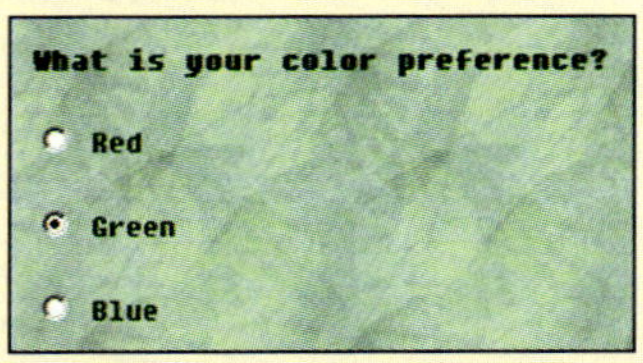

Group Box — Allows developers to separate a group of related controls or text from other information within the form or Web page.

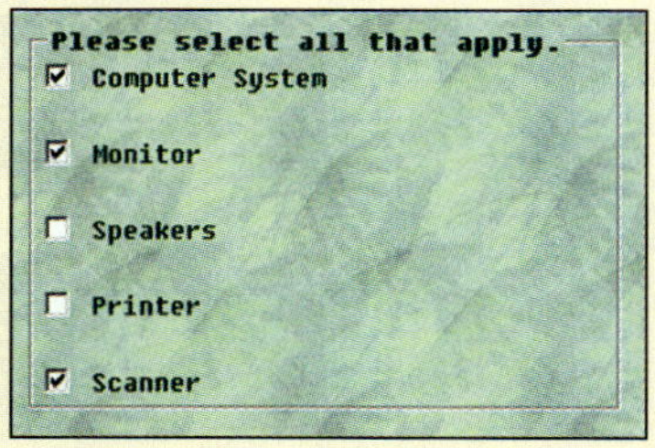

Drop-Down Box — Provides the visitor a list of options, similar to option buttons, from which to select; can be configured to allow single or multiple selections; takes up less space than group of option buttons or check boxes.

Push Button — Used to initiate an action; script must be written in HTML code or with the Script Wizard to execute the action.

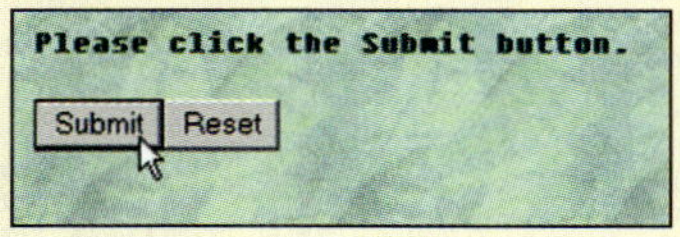

Advanced Button — Similar to a push button but can include content such as images, tables, and text inserted and formatted directly on the button.

Picture — Similar to the above buttons but uses an image to send or receive the form contents.

Label — Treats the text label next to a form field as a form field. The mouse pointer turns into a block arrow and the option button is selected even when the text *Blue* is clicked.

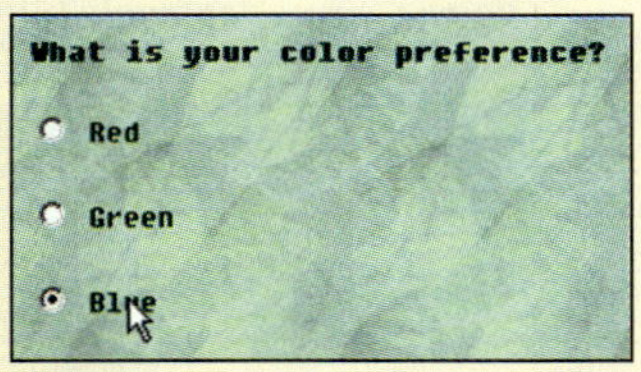

(Note: Before completing computer exercises, delete the Chapter 9 *folder on your disk. Next, download the Chapter 10 data files from the Internet Resource Center to the* Chapter 10 *folder you have created on your disk, and then make* Chapter 10 *the active folder.)*

exercise 1

CREATING A FRONTPAGE FORM

1. Open the EMCPWebs FrontPage Web.
2. Open the contactus.htm Web page in Page view.
3. Place the insertion point in the empty cell below the *Support Staff* drawing object.

4. Key the text **Request Information** and format it to Verdana, 18 points, bold, and dark gray.

5. With the insertion point one line below the text *Request Information,* click Insert, point to Form, and then click Form.
6. Press Enter and then press the up arrow key.
7. Change the font to Verdana, 10 points, and Black.
8. Key the text **Mr:** and then press the spacebar.
9. Click Insert, point to Form, and then click Option Button.
10. Double-click the inserted option button.

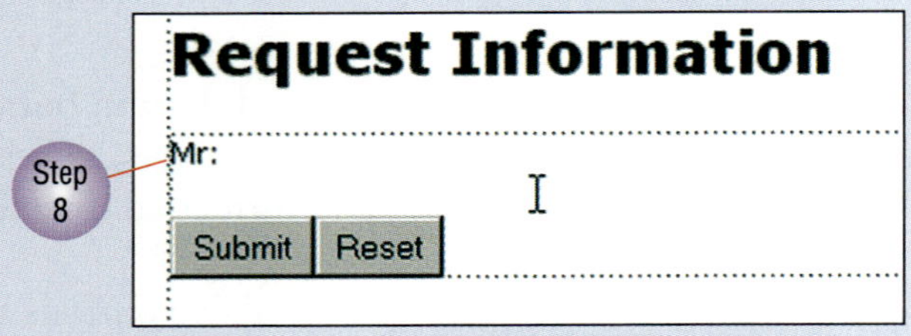

11. At the Option Button Properties dialog box, key **Title** in the Group name text box and **MR** in the Value text box. *(Note: For a group of option buttons, the Group name must be the same for each button property.)*

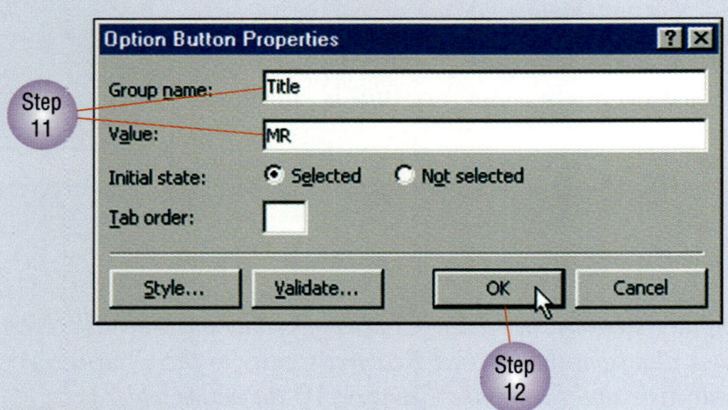

12. Click the OK button.
13. Press the spacebar twice after the option button.
14. Key the text **Ms:** and then press the spacebar once.
15. Using the table and illustration, enter the text labels and form objects and format the form object properties. Your finished form should look like the illustration.

Text Label	Form Object	Form Object Properties	
		Group Name	***Value***
Ms:	Option Button	Title	MS

		Name	***Width in Characters***
First Name:	Textbox	FIRSTNAME	15
Last Name:	Textbox	LASTNAME	15
Address:	Textbox	ADDRESS	20
City:	Textbox	CITY	20
State:	Textbox	STATE	2
ZIP:	Textbox	ZIP	10
Country:	Textbox	COUNTRY	20
E-mail Address:	Textbox	EMAIL	30
		Name	***Initial State***
TV	Checkbox	TV	Not checked
Radio	Checkbox	RADIO	Not checked
Web Search	Checkbox	SEARCH	Not checked
Banner Ad	Checkbox	BANNERAD	Not checked
		Name	***Choices***
Services	Drop-Down Box	SERVICES	Choose here... Selected: Yes
Services	Drop-Down Box	SERVICES	Web Design
Services	Drop-Down Box	SERVICES	Graphic Design
Services	Drop-Down Box	SERVICES	Logo Design
Services	Drop-Down Box	SERVICES	E-Commerce
Services	Drop-Down Box	SERVICES	Community Webs
Services	Drop-Down Box	SERVICES	Enterprise Solutions
		Name	***Width in Characters/ Number of Lines***
Comments/Questions	Text Area	COMMENTS	40/4

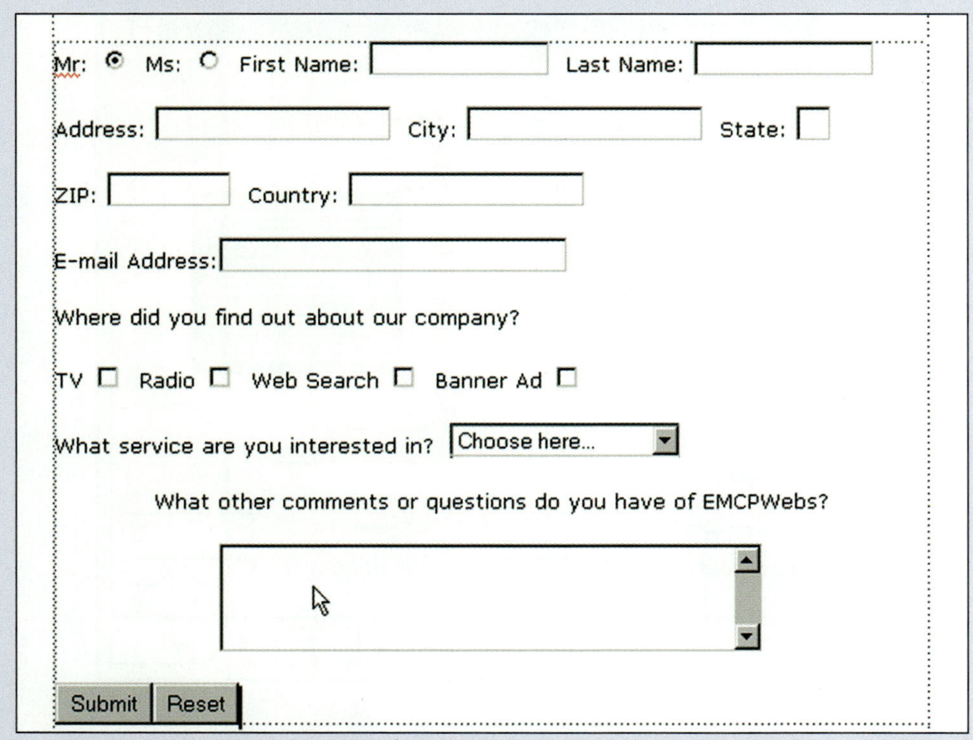

16. Save the updated Contact Us Web page.

exercise 2

VIEWING THE COLOR CODING IN HTML VIEW

1. With the contactus.htm Web page open in Page view, double-click the MR option button object.
2. At the Option Button Properties dialog box, click the Style button.
3. At the Modify Style dialog box, click the Format button and then click Border.

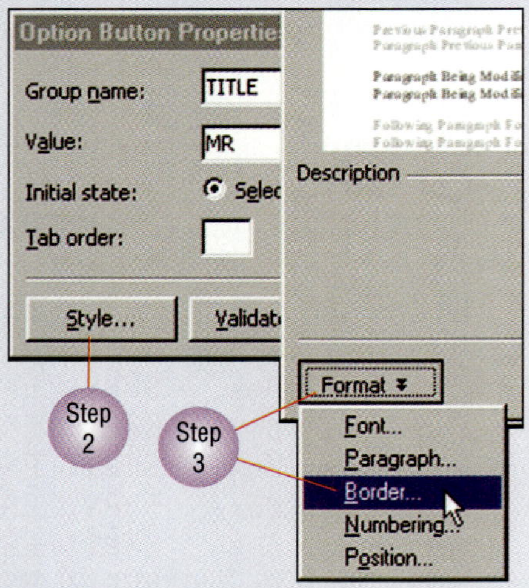

4. At theBorders and Shading dialog box with the Borders tab selected, format the border to 2 points width and dark gray.
5. Click the Shading tab and format the Background color to light green (33, 99, 66).

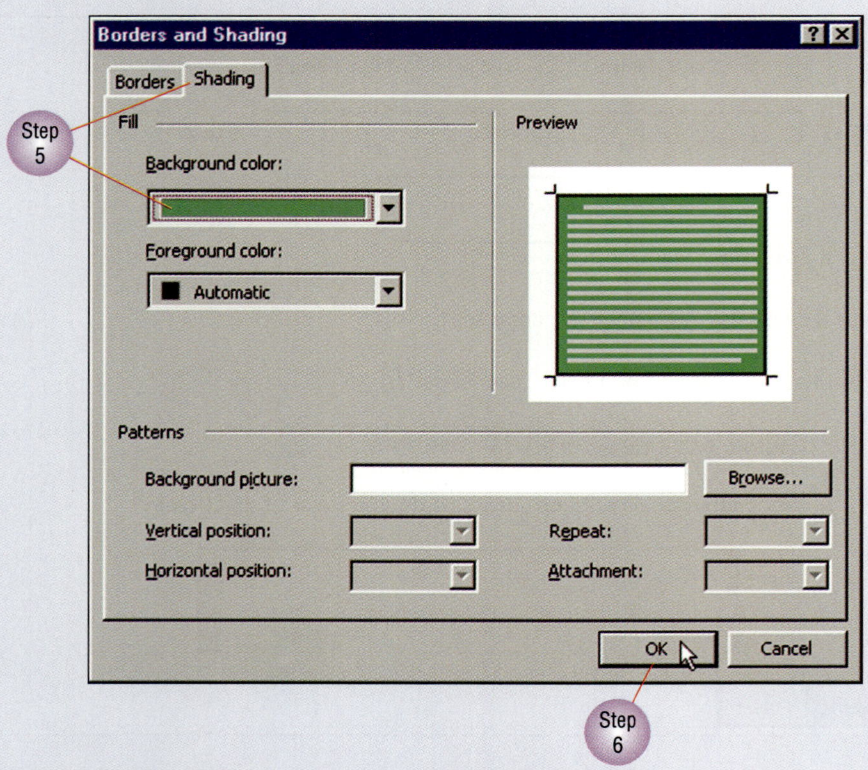

6. Click the OK button to return to the Modify Style dialog box.

7. Click the Format button and then click Font.
8. Format the font to Verdana, 10 points and black.
9. Click the OK button in each dialog box to return to Page view.
10. Repeat steps 1 through 9 to apply the dark gray border, light green shading, and Verdana, 10 points, White font to each of the remaining form field items.

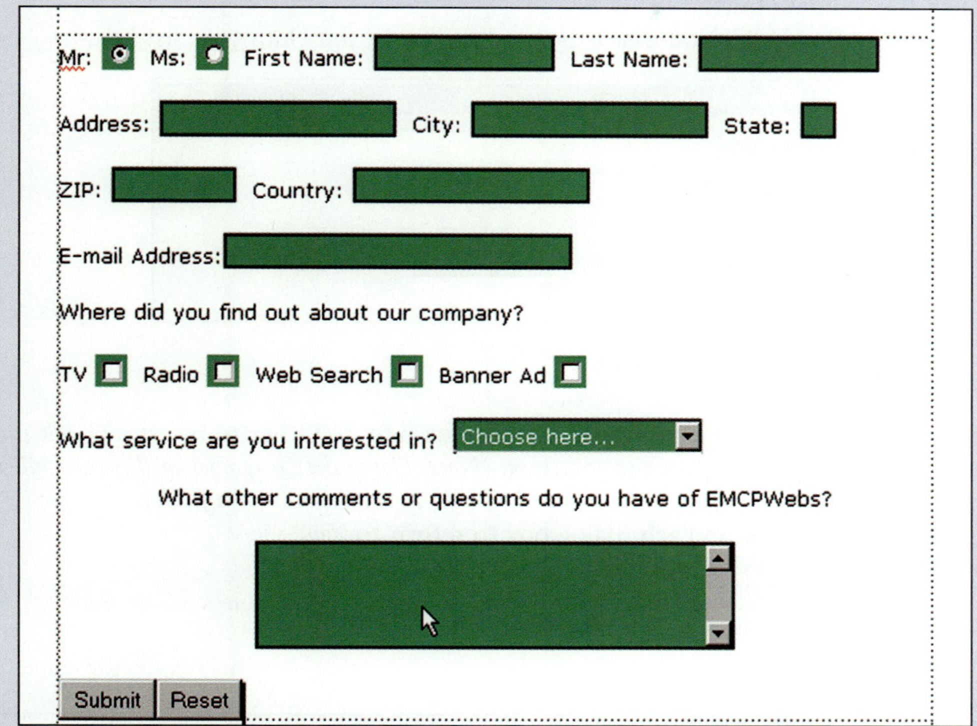

11. Select the text *TV* and the check box.

12. Click Insert, point to Form, and then click Label Button.
13. Repeat steps 11–13 to apply a label to the *Radio, Web Search,* and *Banner Ad* form fields.

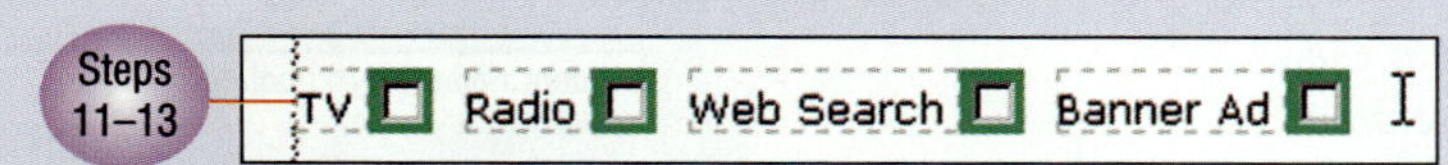

14. Save the updated Web page.
15. Perform a Preview in Browser and enter your personal and filler information.
16. Click the Submit button.
17. Read the component error page and then click the Back button on the browser toolbar.
18. Print the Web page.

exercise 3

VALIDATING FORM INPUT

1. With the contactus.htm Web page open in Page view, double-click the *E-mail* text box field object.
2. Click the Validate button.
3. At the Text Box Validation dialog box, select *Text* in the Data type list box.

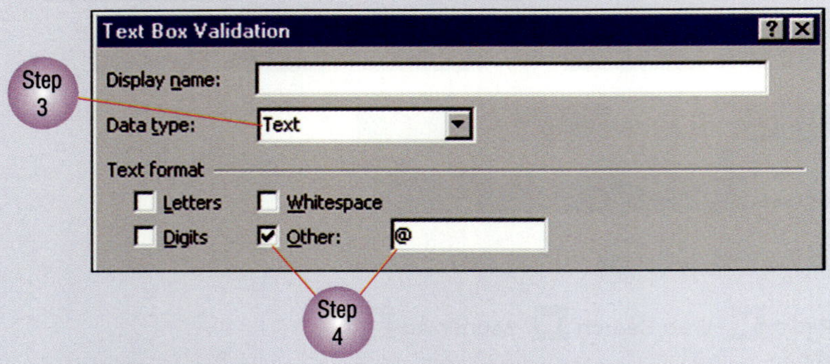

4. In the Text format section, click the check box next to Other to insert a check mark and enter the @ symbol in the text box. *(Note: Using the @ symbol in this case will not allow a form to be submitted without the @ symbol in the* E-mail *form field.)*
5. Click the OK button in each dialog box to return to Page view.
6. Save the updated Web page.

exercise 4

FORMATTING FORM RESULTS TO BE SENT TO AN E-MAIL ADDRESS

1. With the contactus.htm Web page open in Page view, right-click anywhere inside the form area.
2. Select the Form Properties command.
3. At the Form Properties dialog box, key your e-mail address in the E-mail address text box. *(Note: Using an e-mail address will send the form results from the visitor directly to someone's e-mail account. That information can then be used to add the data to a mailing list and/or identify requests for additional information or materials.)*

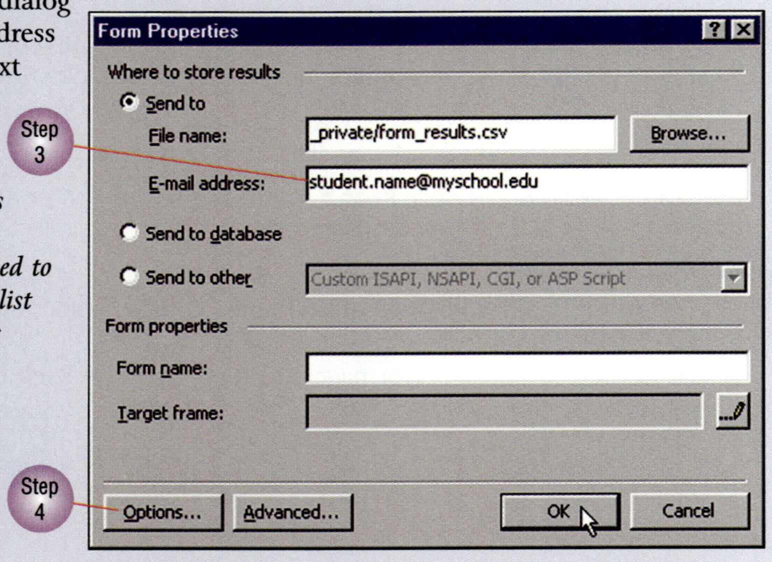

4. Click the Options button.
5. At the Saving Results dialog box, click the E-mail Results tab.

6. Key **Web Site Information Request** in the Subject line text box. *(Note: This will automatically enter* Web Site Information Request *in the subject line of the e-mail message as forms are completed and submitted.)*
7. Click the OK button in each dialog box.
8. Click the No button on the alert window, as you want to keep the e-mail recipient. *(Note: Since your Web is disk-based, you will not be able to test the form unless you are using the Microsoft Personal Web Server (PWS) or a Web server running the FrontPage server extensions.)*

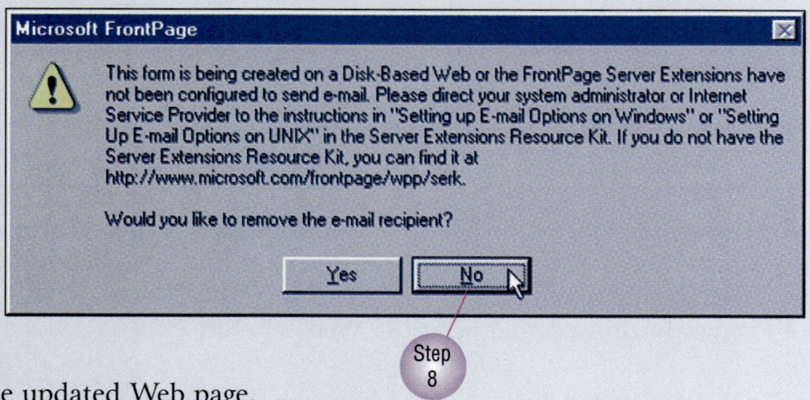

9. Save the updated Web page.

Creating a Form Confirmation Page

A confirmation page typically thanks the visitor for his or her interest in the product, service, or information, and allows the visitor to view form entries for accuracy. If an error was made, the visitor can then return to the form and resubmit the form as corrected. Confirmation fields must be identical to the form field on the bounding form. Just as with the regular form, a confirmation page will work only if your Web is running on a server with FrontPage server extensions.

exercise 5

CREATING A FORM CONFIRMATION PAGE

1. Open the bernard_brown.htm page in Page view.
2. Press Ctrl + A to select the entire page contents.
3. Press Ctrl + C to copy the contents.
4. Click the Create a new normal page button on the Standard toolbar.
5. Press Ctrl + V to paste the copied contents.
6. Format the background a dark gray to match the banner image, and format the margins to 0.
7. Change the font to Verdana and 10 points. Key the text **Dear** in the Web page and press the spacebar.

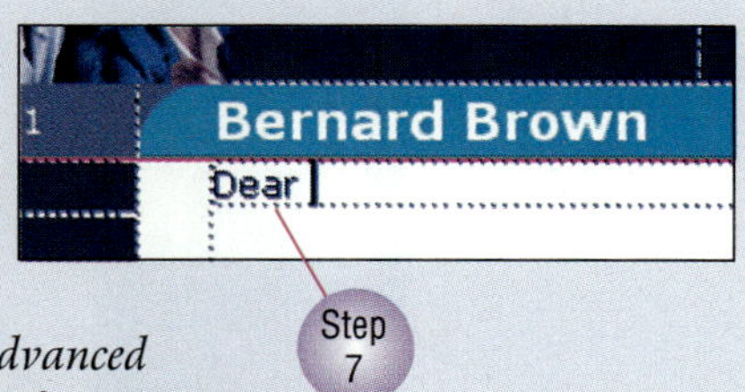

8. Click the Web Component button on the Standard toolbar.
9. At the Insert Web Component dialog box, select the *Advanced Controls* Component type and then double-click the *Confirmation Field* control option.
10. Key the field name **FIRSTNAME** in the Confirmation Field Properties dialog box.

11. Click the OK button.
12. Key the remaining text and confirmation fields as shown.

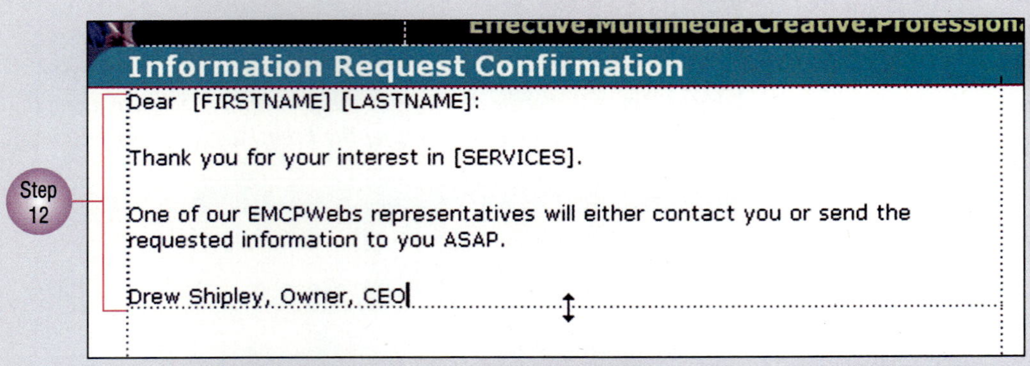

13. Replace the *Bernard Brown* text with **Information Request Confirmation**.
14. Save the Web page as confirmation.htm with the page title *EMCPWebs Request Information Form Confirmation.*
15. Perform a Preview in Browser and print the Web page.

Creating a Guest Book Form Using a Wizard

Guest books allow visitors to leave messages and comments on your Web site for other visitors to see. Guest book entries often serve as testimonials about the site or the company. Once the visitor enters his or her comments into the guest book form (see figure 10.2), that text is then saved in a Web page file called guestlog.htm in your FrontPage Web. You have ultimate control over the guestlog.htm file and can edit and/or delete unwanted comments. The guest book and guest log pages can also be formatted to match your Web design scheme. *(Note: Just as with a regular form, a FrontPage guest book will work only if your Web is running on a server with FrontPage server extensions.)*

FIGURE 10.2 ***Sample FrontPage Guest Book***

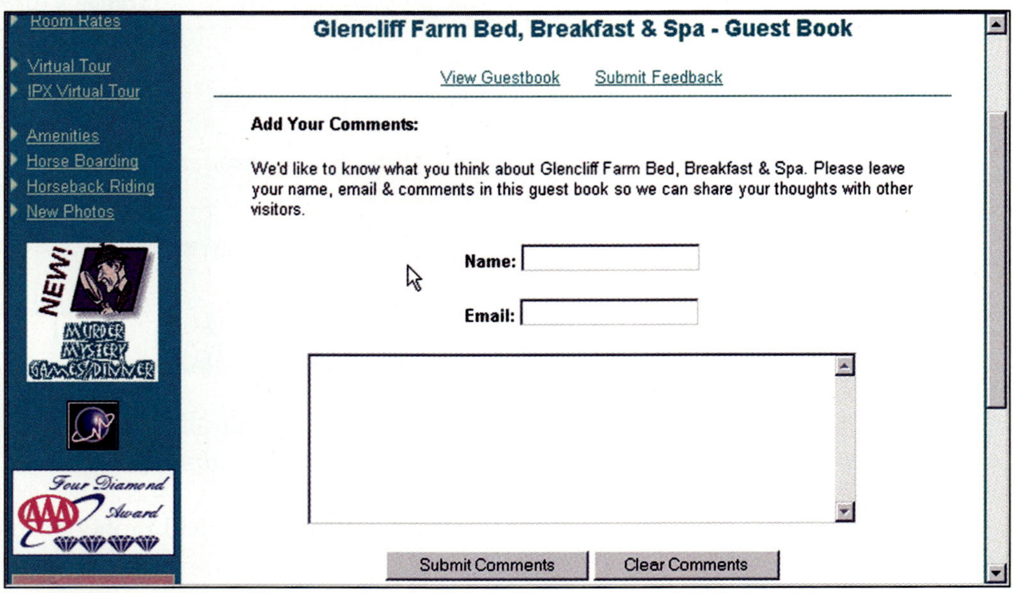

exercise 6

CREATING A GUEST BOOK FORM USING A WIZARD

1. Click File, point to New, and then click Page or Web.
2. At the New Page or Web Task Pane, click the *Page Templates* link.
3. At the Page Templates dialog box with the General tab selected, click the *Guest Book* icon and then click OK.
4. View the guest book page as created.

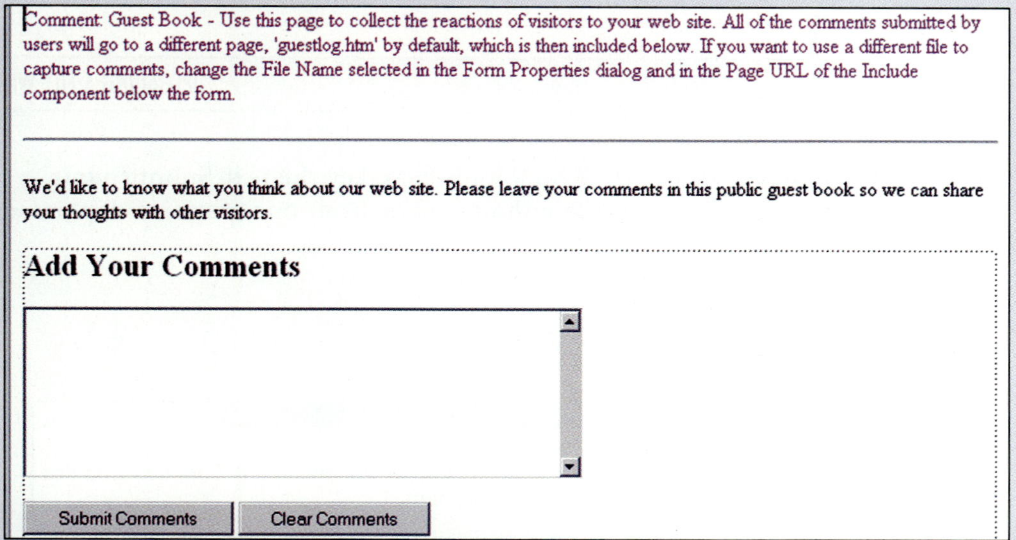

5. Copy and paste the bernard_brown.htm Web page contents into the guest book Web page.
6. Copy, paste, replace, format, and delete the guest book Web page contents to match the illustration.

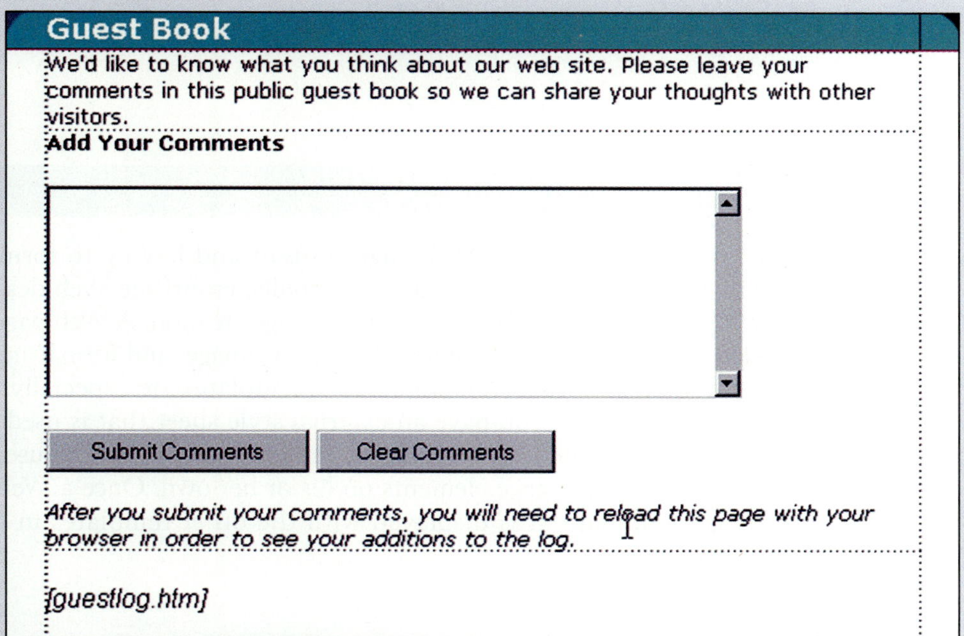

7. Save the Web page as guestbook.htm with the page title *Sign the EMCPWebs Guest Book.*
8. Perform a Preview in Browser and print the Web page.

Uploading a File with a Form

With the new file upload feature, visitors to a Web page can send files such as images, letters, spreadsheets, presentations, and other documents. One example would be a college athletic team using the file upload feature on a prospective student athlete form to submit photographs that showcase game action or physical attributes. *(Note: The file upload feature will work only if your Web is running on a server with FrontPage server extensions.)*

exercise 7 — UPLOADING A FILE WITH A FORM

1. Open the contactus.htm Web page in Page view.
2. On a blank line under the *COMMENTS* form field, key the text **Submit your company logo to receive a sample enhancement from our graphics department.** Press the Enter key.
3. Click Insert, point to Form, and then click File Upload.
4. Name the field FILEUPLOAD.
5. Format the box styles to match the other form field object properties.

Step 5

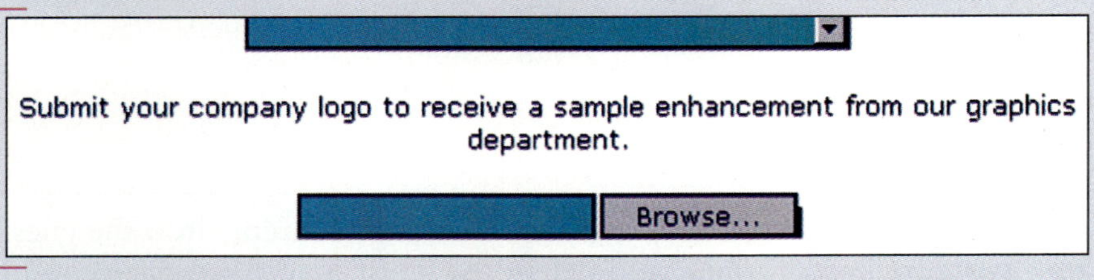

6. Save the updated Web page.
7. Perform a Preview in Browser and print the Web page.

Creating Page Templates

Instead of copying and pasting Web page content and having to format page properties (e.g., margins and background) manually, FrontPage Web designers can create a Web page template to be used in future page creation. A Web page template is a predesigned Web page that contains the layout, image, and formatting elements to create consistency among Web pages. Page templates are especially handy in multiuser environments. If you have an external style sheet that is used for your Web site, you can code the page template to reference the style. The user will thus not have to format certain page elements on his or her own. Once a Web page has been saved as a template, it is displayed with the other templates in the Page Template dialog box.

exercise 8

CREATING A PAGE TEMPLATE

1. Open the bernard_brown.htm Web page in Page view.
2. Select the entire page contents and copy it to the Clipboard.
3. Create a new Web page and paste the copied contents.
4. Change the margins to 0 and format the background to dark gray.
5. Change the page title to **Page Template** and key the text **Enter text here.** in the cell as shown.
6. Format **Enter text here.** to Verdana, 12 points, and Automatic Color.
7. Click File and then click Save As.
8. At the Save As dialog box, select *FrontPage Template* on the Save as type drop-down list.

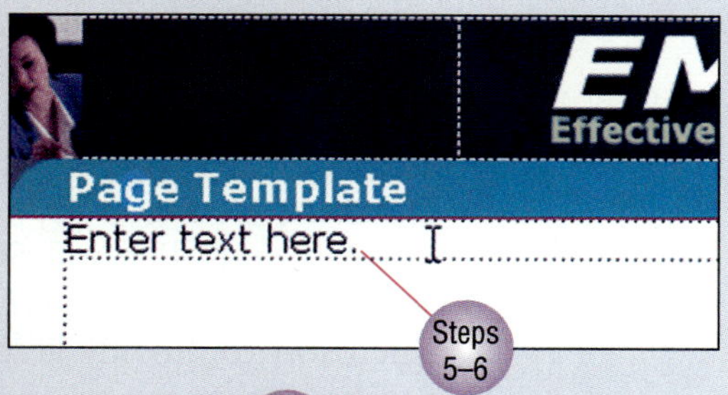

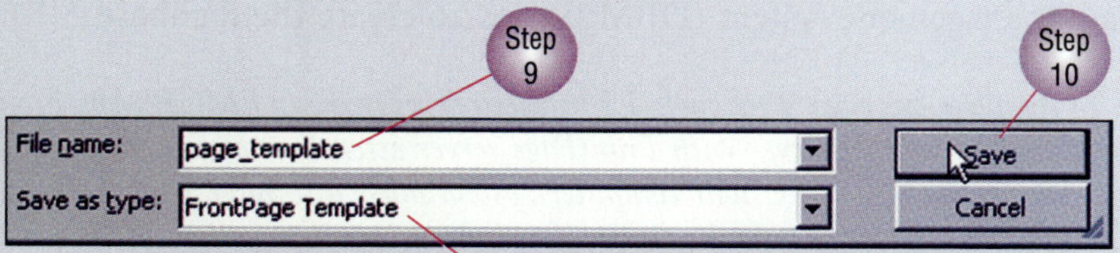

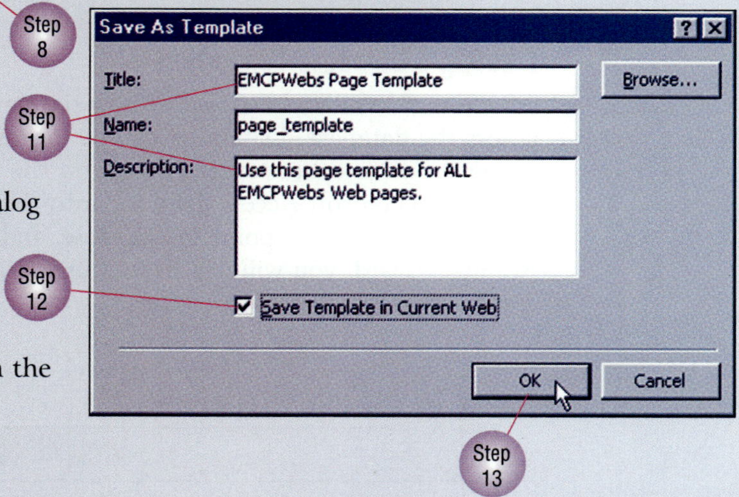

9. Key **page_template** in the File name text box.
10. Click the Save button.
11. At the Save As Template dialog box, key **EMCPWebs Page Template** in the Title text box, and key **Use this page template for ALL EMCPWebs Web pages.** in the Description text box.
12. Click the Save Template in Current Web check box to insert a check mark.
13. Click the OK button.
14. Click File, point to New, and then click Page or Web.
15. Click the *Page Templates* link in the New Page or Web Task Pane.
16. At the Page Templates dialog box with the General tab selected, select the *EMCPWebs Page Template* icon and then click OK.
17. Print the Web page template.
18. Do not save the Web page.

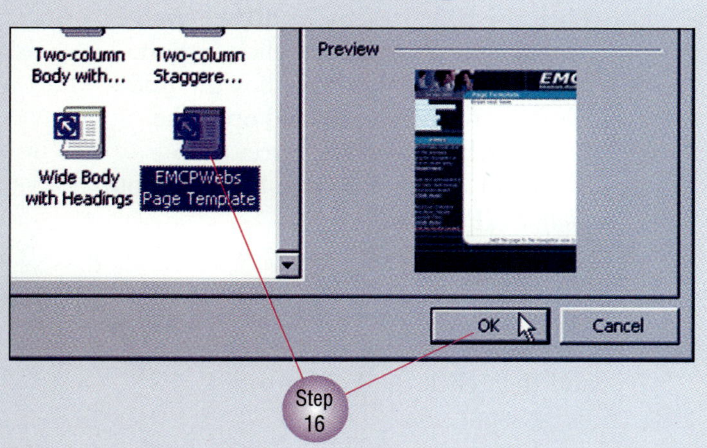

Working with Databases

Information management is the driving force of the computer and information technology industry. Database-driven Web sites are increasingly being utilized by all types of businesses for collecting and distributing information and selling goods and services. FrontPage 2002 offers several database management tools for sites that are data driven. Dynamic data-driven Web pages in FrontPage will automatically be saved as Active Server Pages (ASPs) with an *.asp* file extension. FrontPage 2002 will automatically create the files that reside in the FrontPage Web to enable visitors to access database content on the Web. You will be working with a Microsoft Access database to create Web pages that retrieve data from the database and post data to a database. While you will be using Microsoft Access as your database, any Open Database Connectivity (ODBC)-compliant database program such as FoxPro, Paradox, and Microsoft SQL Server could be used with FrontPage 2002 to retrieve and collect data. The ODBC standard is a database access method created by Microsoft to provide access to any data from any application, regardless of the database management system (DBMS) used to create the database.

(Note: To complete exercises 9 through 13 in their entirety, your EMCPWebs FrontPage Web must be stored on a Web server with FrontPage server extensions or one using the Microsoft Personal Web Server (PWS). Your computer system must also have Microsoft Access 2000 or 2002 installed. Refer to your instructor for appropriate instructions.)

Creating a Database Connection

To connect to a database and display data on a Web page, you must be able to access the database. Databases can be located within the root Web, on the Web server, or on another server located on the network. For this exercise, you will import a Microsoft Access database into the *emcpwebs* root Web. To connect to a database, click Insert, point to Database, and then click Results. From the Database Results Wizard, you will use an existing database connection to create a database results region on your Web page.

exercise 9

IMPORTING A DATABASE AND CREATING A DATABASE CONNECTION

1. With the EMCPWebs FrontPage Web open, click File and then click Import.
2. At the Import dialog box, click the Add File button, then locate and open the EMCPWebs Expert Resources.mdb Microsoft Access database file from your *Chapter 10* folder.
3. Click the OK button in the Import dialog box.
4. At the Add Database Connection dialog box, key **experts** in the Name text box and then click the Yes button.

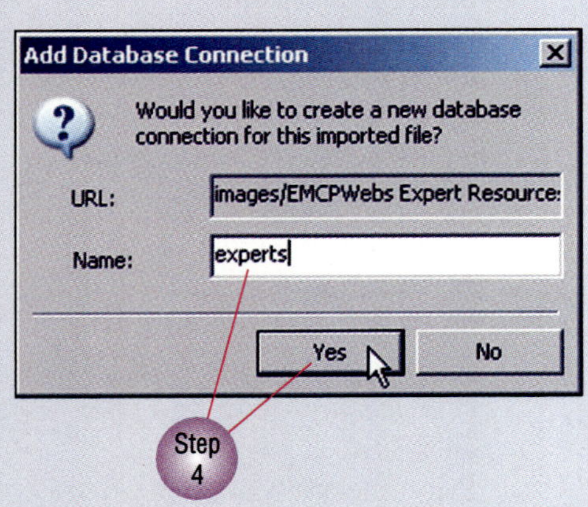

5. Click the Yes button on the alert dialog box to store the Access database file in the *fpdb* folder.
6. Access the Folders view and open the *fpdb* folder to view the database file.

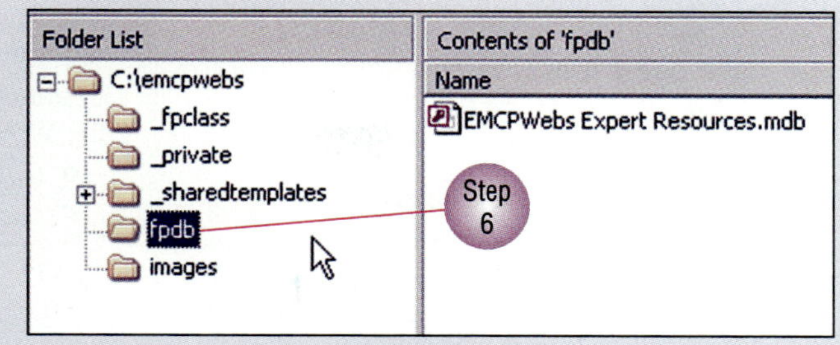

exercise 10

USING THE DATABASE RESULTS WIZARD TO DISPLAY DATABASE INFORMATION

1. Click File, point to New, and then click Page or Web.
2. Click the *Page Templates* link in the New Page or Web Task Pane.
3. At the Page Templates dialog box with the General tab selected, select the *EMCPWebs Page Template* icon and then click OK.
4. Change the page title to *EMCPWebs Expert Resources*.
5. Delete **Enter text here.**
6. Click Insert, point to Database, and then click Results.
7. At the Step 1 Database Results Wizard dialog box, click the Use an existing database connection option, ensure that *experts* appears in the text box, and then click Next.

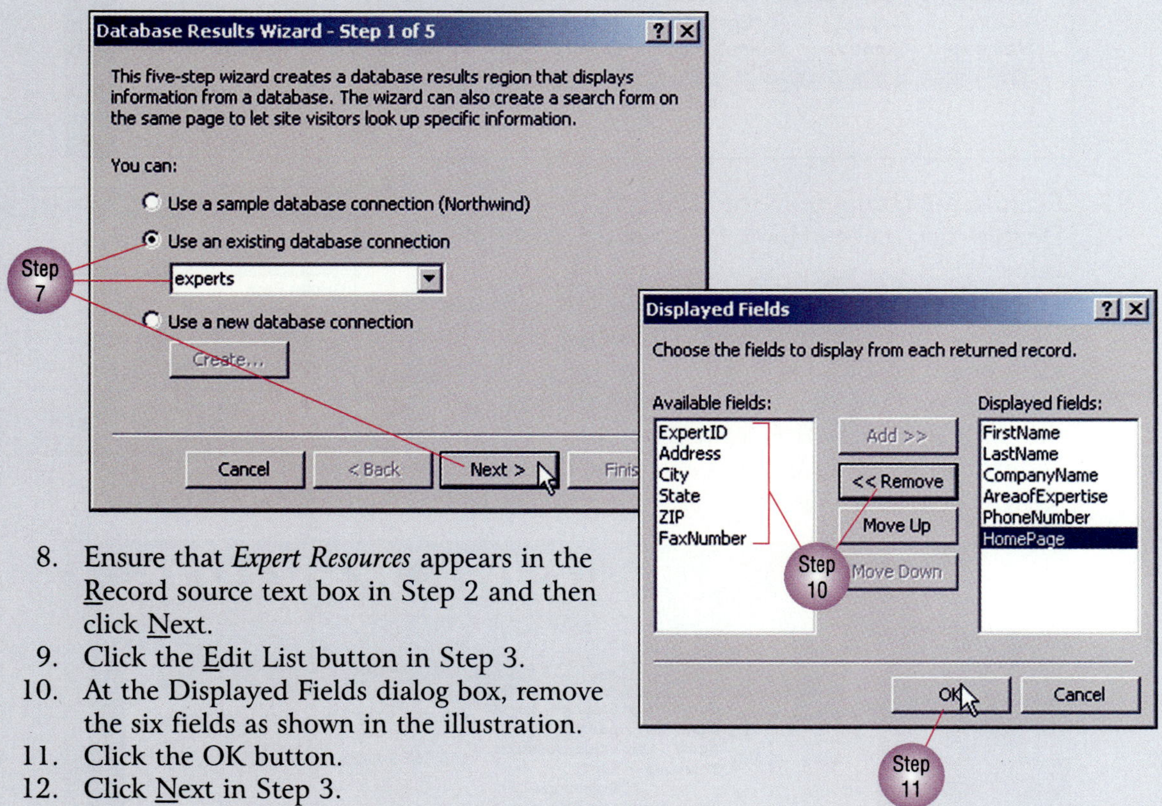

8. Ensure that *Expert Resources* appears in the Record source text box in Step 2 and then click Next.
9. Click the Edit List button in Step 3.
10. At the Displayed Fields dialog box, remove the six fields as shown in the illustration.
11. Click the OK button.
12. Click Next in Step 3.

13. Leave the default settings in Step 4 and then click Next.
14. Click the Display all records together option in Step 5 and then click Finish.
15. Select all cells in the database results table and change the font to Verdana and 10 points.
16. Format the top row cells of the table to mid gray (33, 33, 33), with a font color of White.

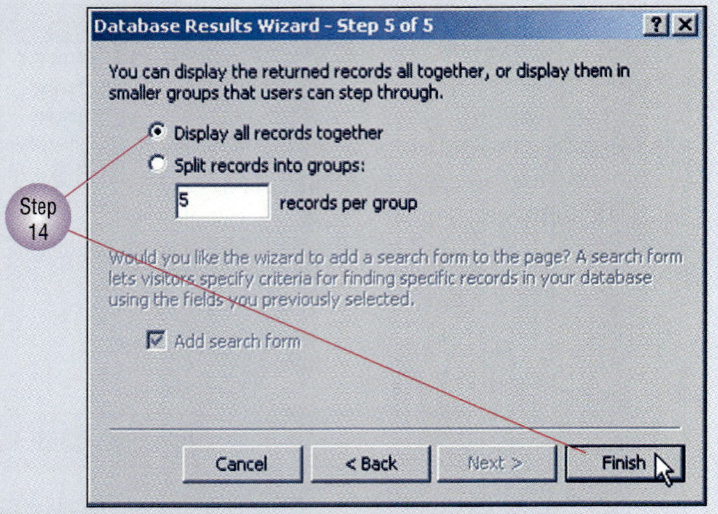

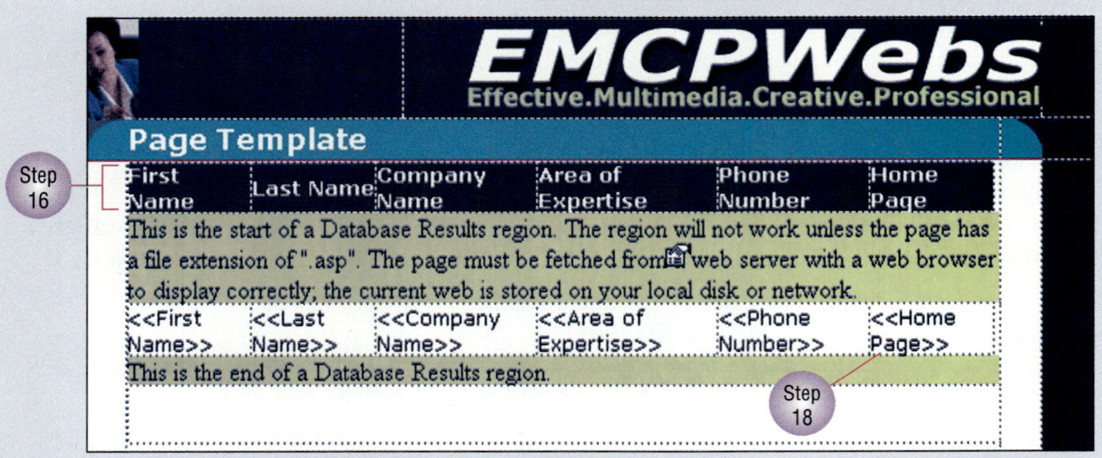

17. Remove the border from the table.
18. Double-click the <<Home Page >> database column value.
19. At the Database Column Value dialog box, click the Display as hyperlink check box to insert a check mark and then click OK.
20. Save the Web page as results.asp with the page title *EMCPWebs Expert Resources*.
21. Perform a Preview in Browser and print the Web page.

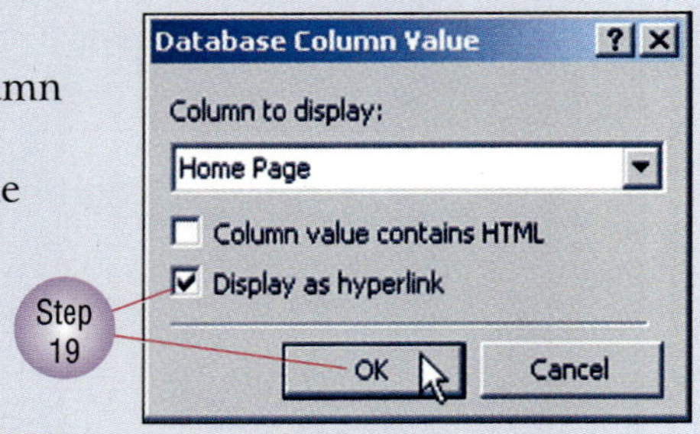

(Note: The following illustration shows the database results as published to a Web server.)

Using a Search Form to Query Database Results

With the Database Results Wizard, developers can set criteria to query database results. A query is defined as a request for information from a database. Comparison Criteria can be established in Step 3 of the Database Results Wizard by clicking the More Options button, the Criteria button, and then the Add button. In the Add Criteria dialog box, common comparison criteria include Equals, Greater Than, and Contains. With the Equals criterion, the search string must be identical to the field entry. The Contains criterion, on the other hand, requires only partial matches.

exercise 11

USING A SEARCH FORM TO QUERY DATABASE RESULTS

1. With the results.asp page open in Page view, double-click inside the yellow Database Results region.

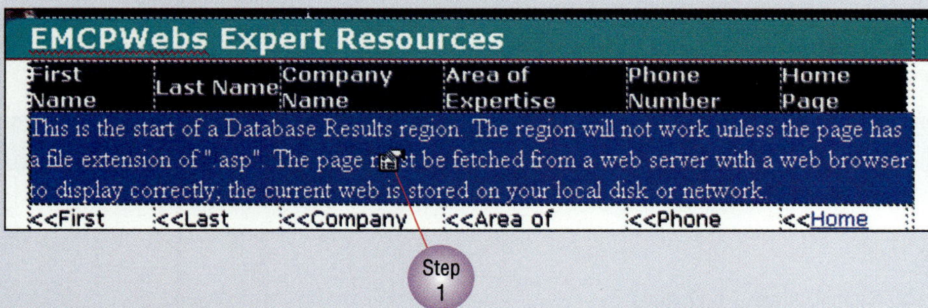

2. Click Next in the first two Database Results Wizard dialog boxes to access Step 3.
3. Click the More Options button.
4. Click the Criteria button in the More Options dialog box.
5. Click the Add button in the Criteria dialog box.
6. At the Add Criteria dialog box, select *Last Name* in the Field Name list box and *Equals* in the Comparison list box.
7. Click the OK button twice to return to the More Options dialog box.
8. Key the text **Search results found here** in the Message text box.
9. Click the OK button to return to the Database Results Wizard.
10. Click Next in each dialog box until you reach Step 5.

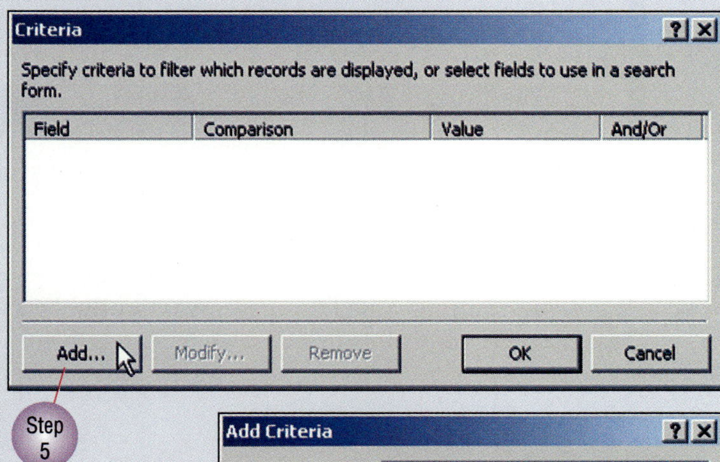

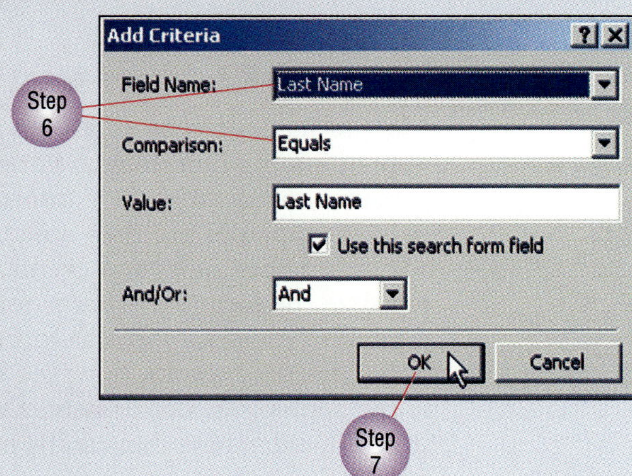

11. Select the Display all records together option and click the Add search form check box to insert a check mark.
12. Click Finish.
13. Select all cells in the database results table and change the font to Verdana and 10 points.
14. Format the top row cells of the table to mid gray (66, 66, 66), with a font color of White.
15. Remove the border from the table.
16. Save the updated Web page.
17. Perform a Preview in Browser and print the Web page. *(Note: The following illustration shows the database results as published to a Web server.)*

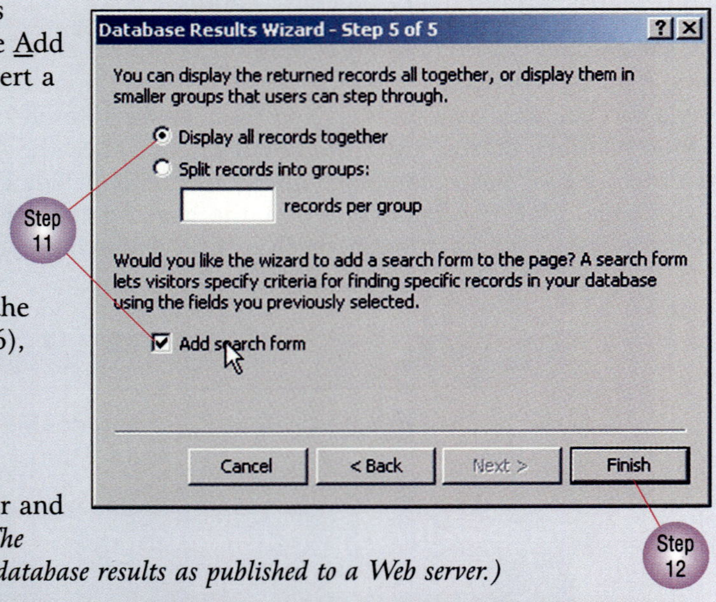

18. If you are running your FrontPage Web on the Personal Web Server or a server with FrontPage server extensions, test your search form.

Posting Form Results to an Access Database

Most of us have been to a Web site in which a company or organization has wanted information from and/or about us. The form requests on Web sites include personal and demographic information, product preferences, and even opinion polls. Companies are then able to use this data for such purposes as targeted advertisements, news and events distribution, and market research. How do you organize the form data that is returned? The information request form that you created in exercises 1–4 was formatted to send the results to an e-mail account. E-mail message results, however, must then be read, interpreted, and disseminated to the appropriate department. Data from form results, on the other hand, is often stored in a database that can be manipulated, queried, reported, and even exported to other sources such as mail merge documents, charts, and contact lists for e-mail purposes. You could use the existing experts database connection to add to the three records already in the database. For this exercise, however, you will create a new Microsoft Access database based on your form fields.

exercise 12

POSTING FORM RESULTS TO AN ACCESS DATABASE

1. Open the results.asp Web page in Page view.
2. Create the following form under the Database Results region:
   a. Format the text *Submit an Expert* to Verdana, Dark Gray, and 18 points.
   b. Format the text box fields as follows:

Field Name	***Width in Characters***
First Name	20
Last Name	20
Company Name	30
Areas of Expertise	50
Home Page	30

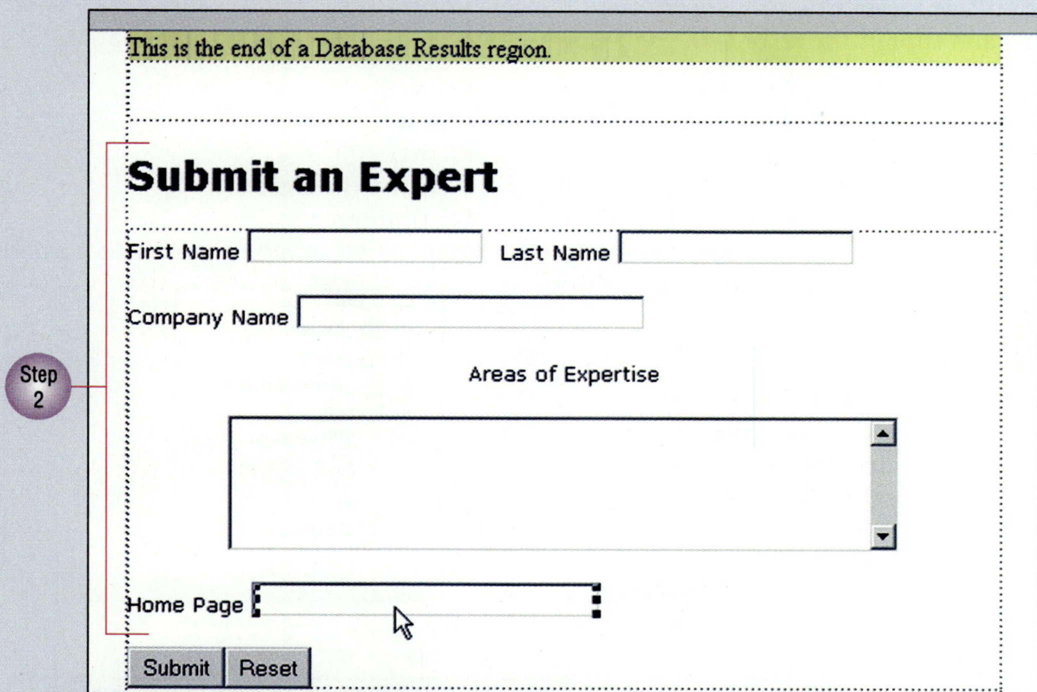

3. Right-click anywhere inside the form boundaries and click Form Properties on the pop-up menu.

4. At the Form Properties dialog box, click the Send to database option and then click the Options button.
5. At the Options for Saving Results to Database dialog box with the Database Results tab selected, click the Create Database button. *(Note: FrontPage will automatically create a database for you and place it in the* fpdb *folder.)*

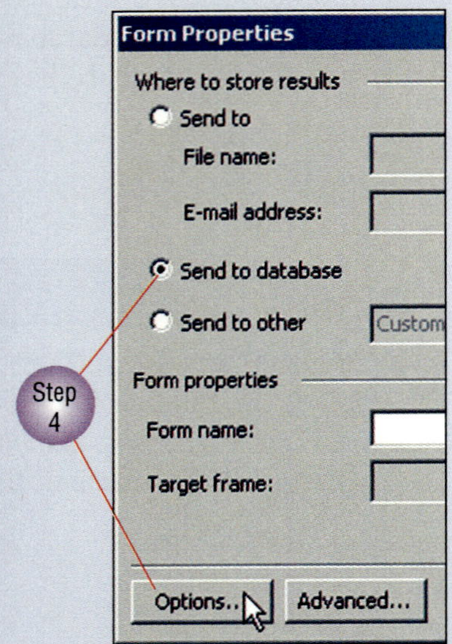

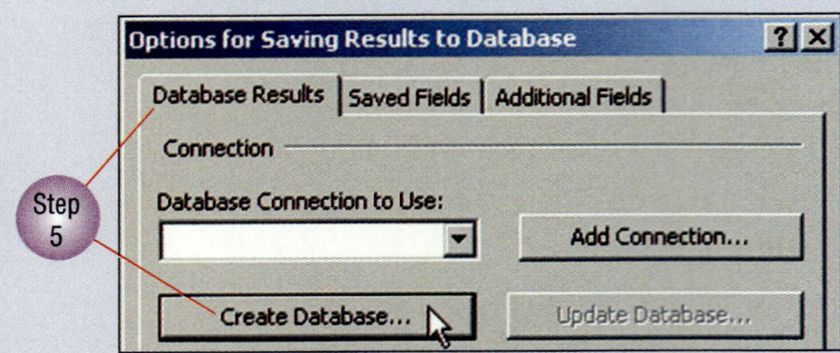

6. Read the Microsoft FrontPage alert window and then click OK.
7. Save the updated Web page.
8. If you are running your FrontPage Web on the Personal Web Server or a server with FrontPage server extensions, perform a Preview in Browser.
9. Key and submit the records in the following table:

Field	*Expert 1*	*Expert 2*
First Name	**Tim**	**Maria**
Last Name	**Davis**	**Picotti**
Company Name	**Tim Davis Consulting**	**Picotti-Commerce**
Areas of Expertise	**Enterprise Systems**	**E-Commerce**
Home Page	**http://www.emcp.net/ timdavisconsulting**	**http://www.emcp.net/picotticommerce**

10. Return to FrontPage and access the Folders view.
11. In the *fpdb* folder, double-click the results.mdb Access database file.
12. View the results table entries. Ask your instructor for further instructions.

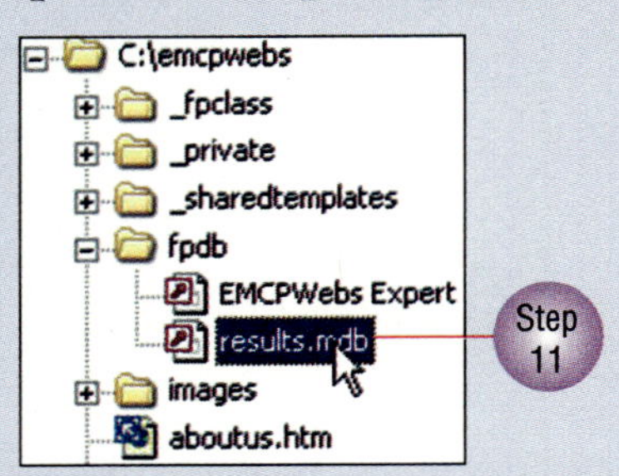

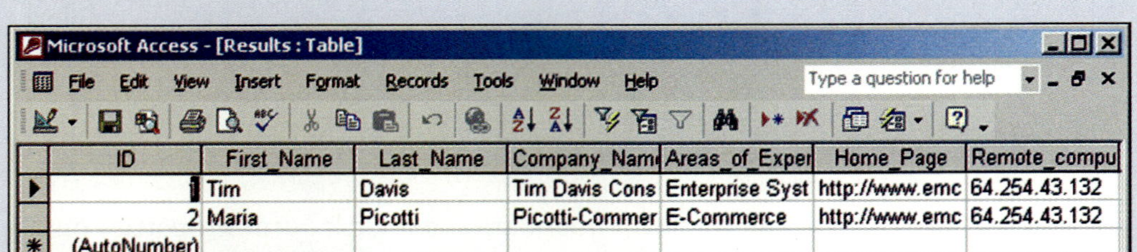

Using the Database Interface Wizard

The Database Interface Wizard, new to FrontPage 2002, creates an entire FrontPage Web or subweb based on a database. Within the wizard process, developers can select any combination of the following database interface options:

- The Results Page (results_page.asp) is similar to the Database Results region you created in exercise 10. This page displays the results of the database table or query.
- The Submission Form (submission_form.asp) Web page is similar to the form you created in exercise 12 to submit form data to the Microsoft Access database.
- The Database Editor (database_editor.asp) allows users to add, edit, and delete records within the database.

Users can opt to password protect the database editor interface. This will increase the security of the database and decrease the chance of its being unwittingly modified. The Database Editor Login page (login.asp) includes a comment that informs users how to change the user name and password if necessary. The home page (default.htm) is a simple Web page with descriptions of hyperlinks to the above database interface options.

exercise 13

CREATING A DATABASE INTERFACE USING A WIZARD

1. With FrontPage open, click File, point to New, and then click Page or Web.
2. Click the *Web Site Templates* link in the New Page or Web Task Pane.
3. Click the *Database Interface Wizard* icon in the Web Site Templates dialog box.
4. Key **__:\databaseweb** in the Specify the location of the new web text box. Replace the underscore (__) with your preferred drive location.
5. Click the OK button.

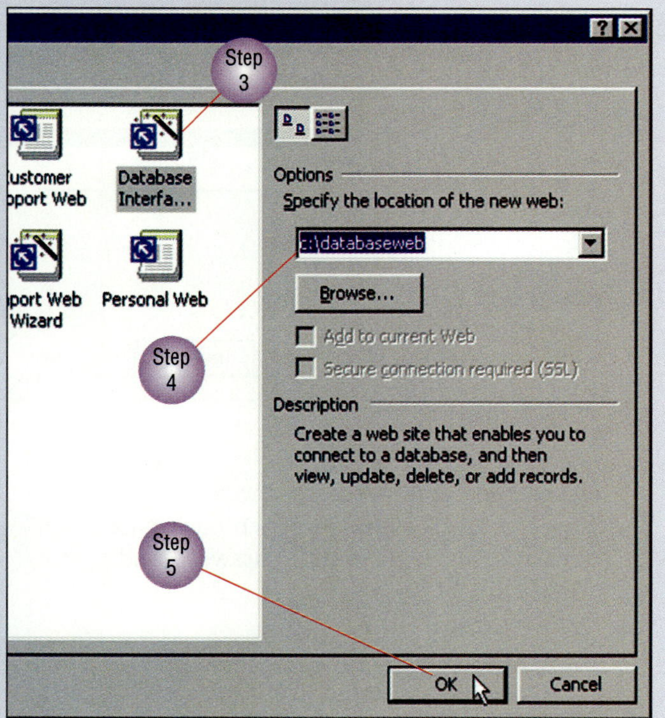

6. At the first Database Internet Wizard dialog box, click the Use a sample database connection (Northwind) option and then click Next.

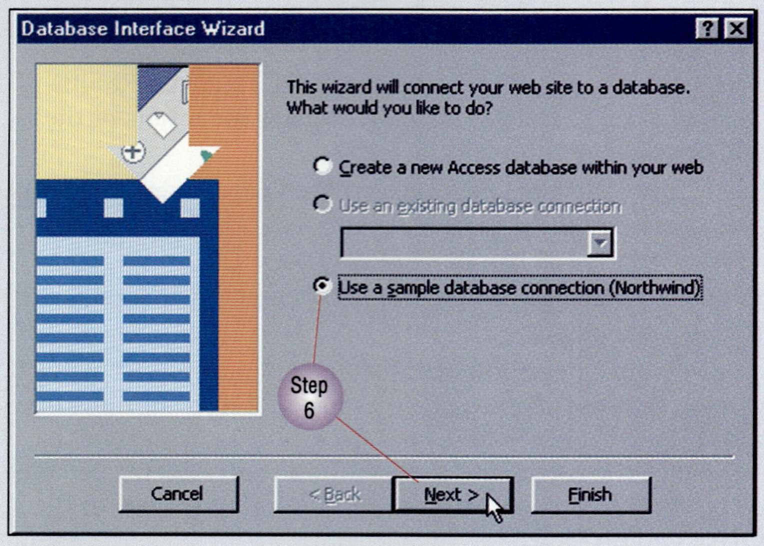

7. Once the database connection is established, click Next.
8. Select the *Products* table and then click Next.

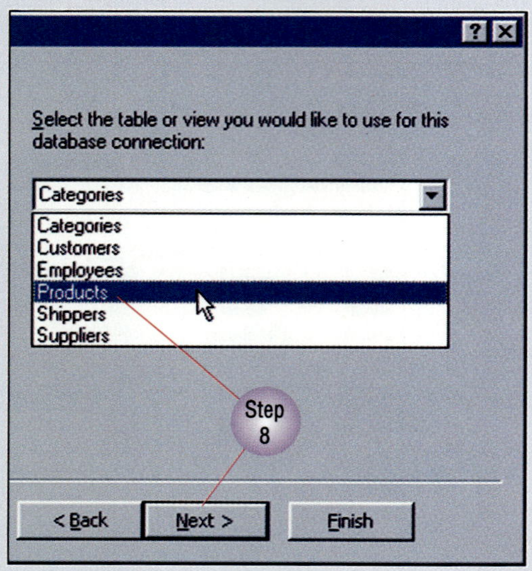

9. Click Next once again.
10. Click the *Database Editor* check box to insert a check mark and then click Next.
11. Enter a user name and a password and then click Next.
12. Click Finish.
13. Navigate through the page tabs to view the Database Interface Web pages.
14. Perform a Preview in Browser and test the Web pages.

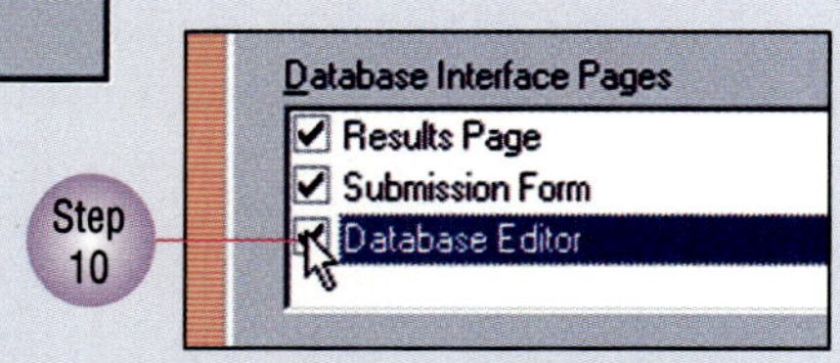

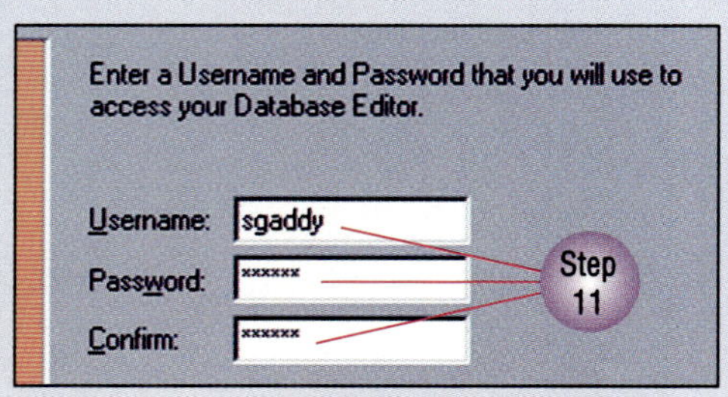

15. Print the first page of the Results Page.

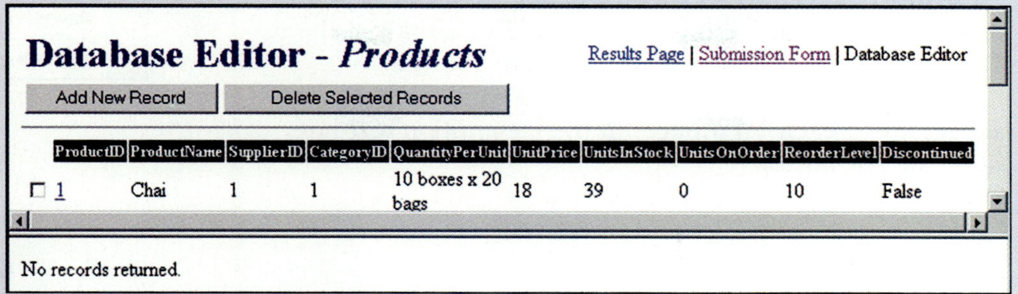

16. Close the browser and then close FrontPage.

Managing and Analyzing FrontPage Webs

Working with Tasks

Keeping track of tasks that need to be created, inserted, deleted, or fixed can be inefficient without a tasking system. The Tasks view allows users to determine tasks and assign them to specific designers. The Webmaster and other designers can assign tasks, establish priority levels, view and apply descriptions of the tasks, and view the date and time the tasks were established. Tasks can have a status of Not Started, In Progress, or Completed. Assignees can identify a task name and description as well as a priority level for their tasks.

exercise 14 — WORKING WITH TASKS

1. Open FrontPage and the EMCPWebs Web.
2. Click the Tasks button on the Views bar.
3. Click Edit, point to Tasks, and then click Add Task.
4. At the New Task dialog box, key **Staff Information** in the Task name text box.
5. Key your own name in the Assigned to text box.
6. Key **Obtain biographical information and photos for staff Web pages.** in the Description text box.
7. Click the OK button.

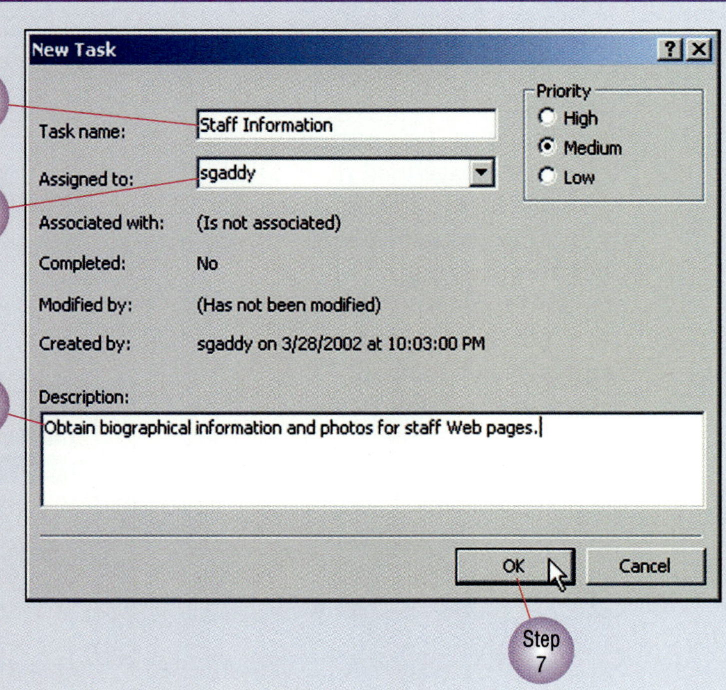

8. Right-click in an empty area of the task window and then click Add Task.
9. At the New Task dialog box, key **Phone/Fax/E-mail** in the Task name text box and assign the task to yourself.
10. Key **Add phone & fax number as well as e-mail addresses to each Web page.** in the Description text box.
11. Click the OK button.
12. Open the index.htm page in Page view.
13. Click Edit, point to Tasks, and then click Add Task.
14. At the New Task dialog box, key **Fly-in effect** in the Task name text box and assign the task to yourself.
15. Key **Remove the Fly-in effect on the top graphic.** in the Description text box.
16. Click the OK button.

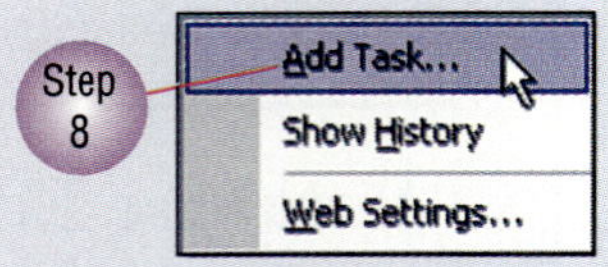

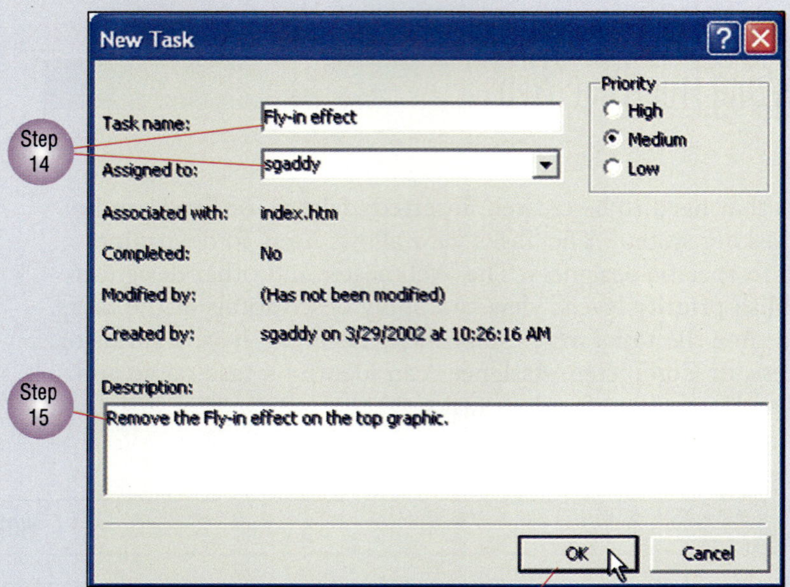

17. Return to the Tasks view.
18. Double-click the *Fly-in effect* task.
19. Click the Start Task button.
20. Remove the page load fly-in DHTML effect on the top image using the DHTML Effects toolbar.
21. Click the Save button on the Standard toolbar.
22. Click Yes in the Microsoft FrontPage alert box.
23. Return to the Tasks view.
24. Right-click the completed *Fly-in effect* task and then click Delete Task on the pop-up menu.
25. Click Yes in the alert box.

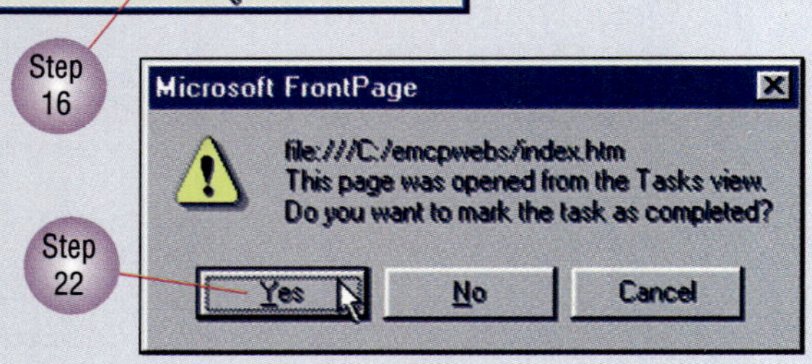

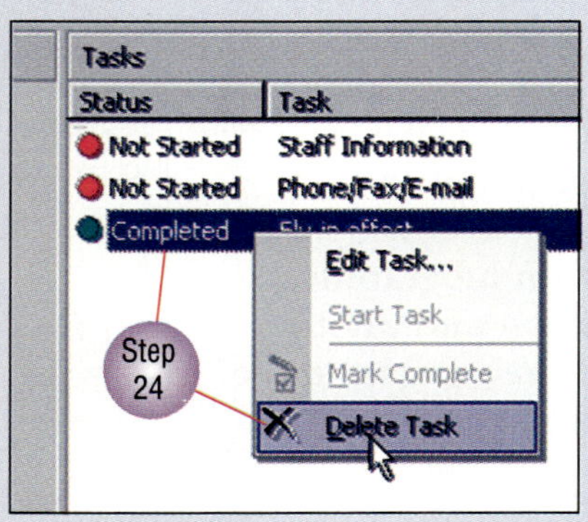

Analyzing a Web with Reports

Using the Reports view, pages, graphics, and files in your Web can be analyzed by running reports to list slow pages, unlinked pages, recently added or changed files, broken hyperlinks, component errors, uncompleted tasks, categories of files, and the published status of Web pages, graphics, and files. Reports can be copied and pasted to other documents by right-clicking inside a report and selecting the Copy Report command.

Exploring the Site Summary

The Site Summary is the command center for various reports such as slow pages, recently added files, unverified hyperlinks, broken hyperlinks, component errors, and uncompleted tasks. The Reporting toolbar (figure 10.3) appears each time you access the Reports view. The Reports drop-down list on the Reporting toolbar contains the Site Summary, Files, Problems, Workflow, and Usage categories of reports.

FIGURE 10.3 ***Reporting Toolbar in Reports View***

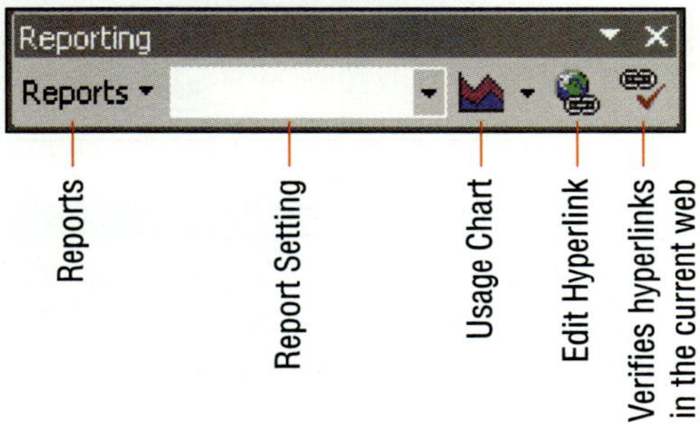

exercise 15 — VIEWING FILE REPORTS

(Note: Your report may vary from the illustrations, depending on the time frame during which you work on the chapter exercises.)

1. With the EMCPWebs FrontPage Web open, access the Reports view.
2. Click the Reports down-pointing triangle on the Reporting toolbar, point to Files, and then click Recently Added Files.

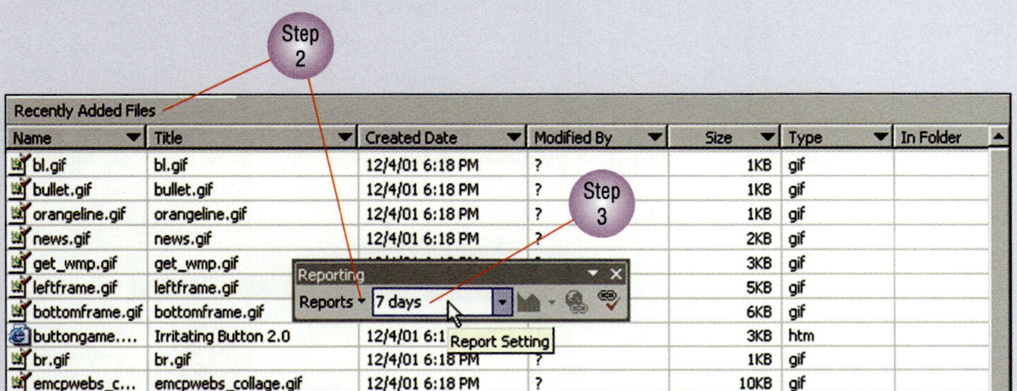

3. Change the Report Setting from 30 days to 7 days.

exercise 16

VIEWING PROBLEM REPORTS

1. Access the Reports view of the EMCPWebs FrontPage Web, if you are not there already.
2. Click the Reports down-pointing triangle on the Reporting toolbar, point to Problems, and then click Slow Pages.

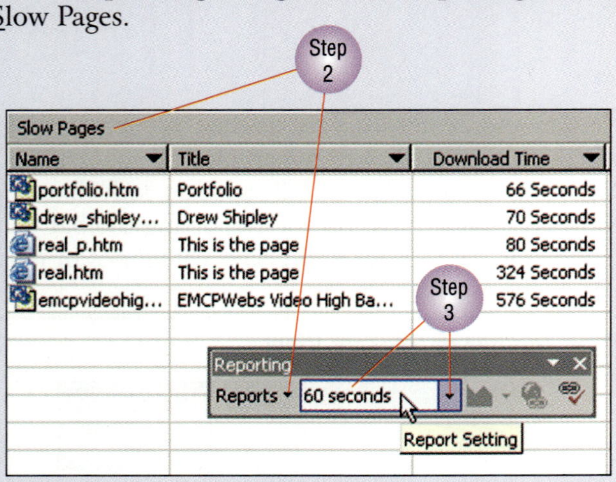

3. Change the Report Setting from 30 seconds to 60 seconds
4. Click the Reports down-pointing triangle on the Reporting toolbar, point to Problems, and then click Broken Hyperlinks.
5. Click Yes to verify the hyperlinks. *(Note: There should be no broken hyperlinks! If there is a broken hyperlink, double-click the broken hyperlink entry and replace it with the correct hyperlink.)*
6. Open the practicehtml.htm Web page and change the hyperlink to CNN.com to http://www.cnn.comm.
7. Save the Web page.
8. Return to the Reports view and click the Verifies hyperlinks in the current web button on the Reporting toolbar.
9. Double-click the broken hyperlink and enter the correct URL in the Edit Hyperlink dialog box.
10. Click the Replace button.

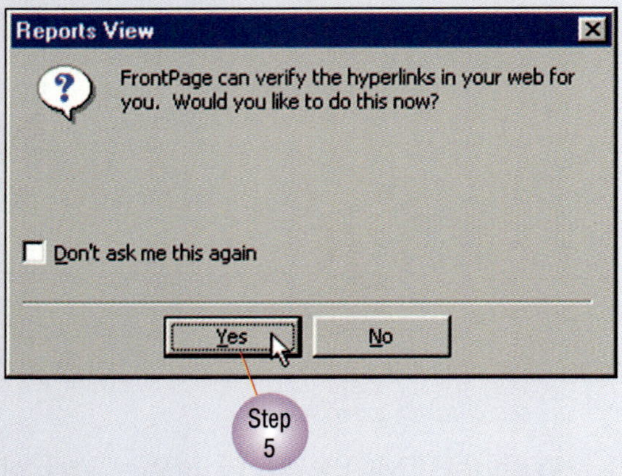

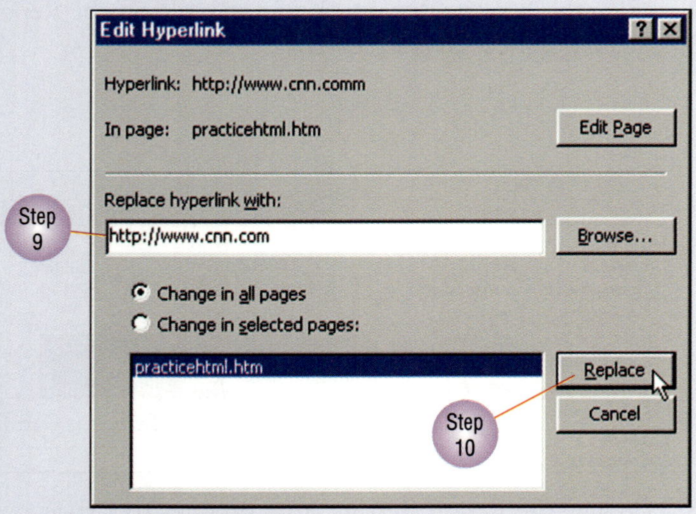

exercise 17 VIEWING WORKFLOW REPORTS

1. Access the Reports view of the EMCPWebs FrontPage Web, if you are not there already.
2. Click the Reports down-pointing triangle on the Reporting toolbar, point to Workflow, and then click Assigned To.

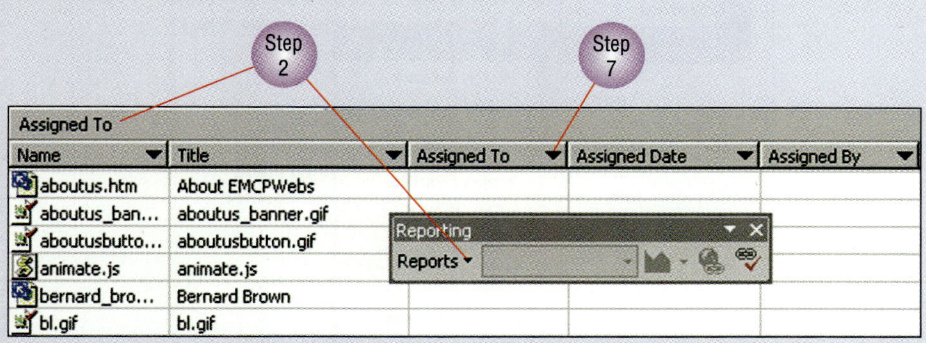

3. Right-click the index.htm entry and then click Properties.
4. Click the Workgroup tab in the index.htm Properties dialog box.
5. Key your name in the Assigned to text box.
6. Click the OK button.
7. Click the Assigned To drop-down filter button and select your name to list all files assigned to you.

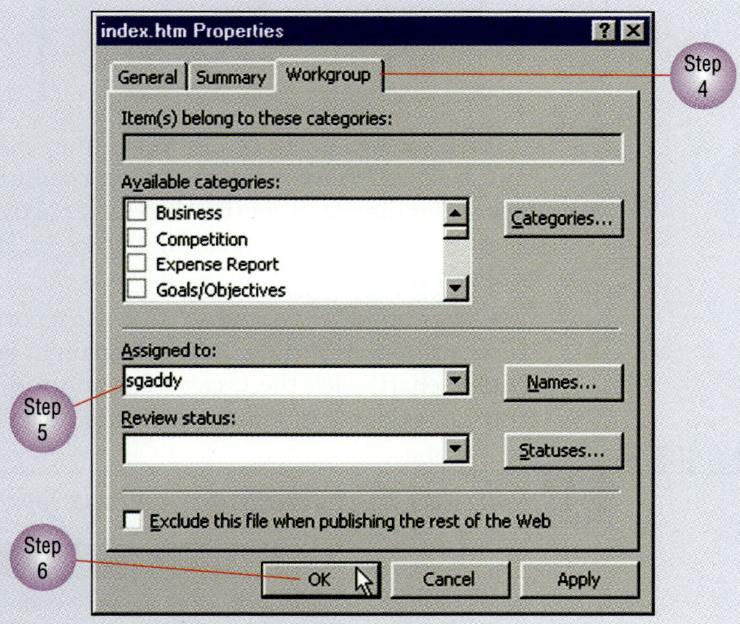

Exploring Usage Reports

Usage reports can give Web administrators valuable information about how many hits the site has received, the number of visiting users, types of operating systems and browsers used by visitors, referring domains, and other data. This data can be used to determine what browser(s) to develop the site toward and possibly how the navigation structure can be improved to increase lower tiered Web page hits.

The Usage Summary is similar to the Site Summary report in that it offers a broad overview of statistical values for the Web. To display the Usage Summary report, click the Reports down-pointing triangle on the Reporting toolbar, point to Usage, and then click Usage Summary (see figure 10.4).

FIGURE 10.4 *Usage Reports*

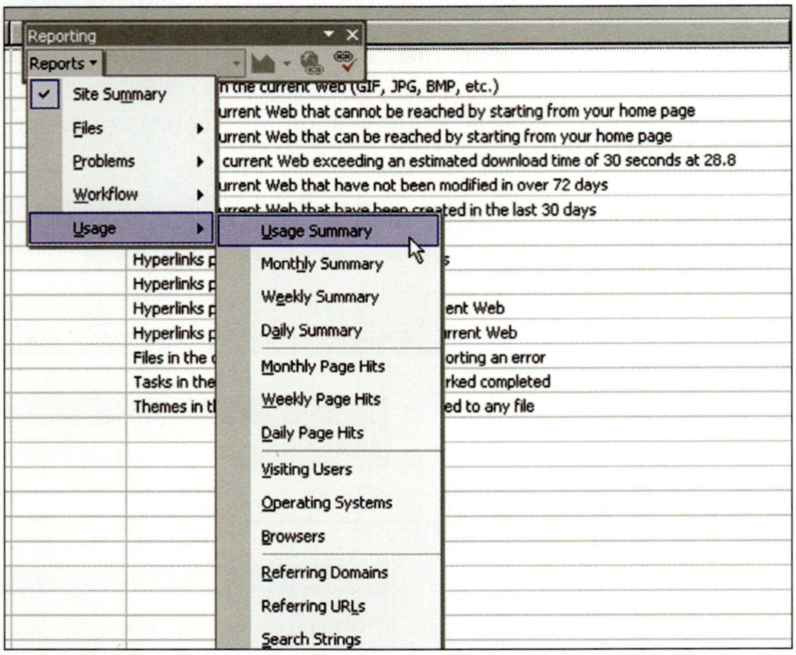

Web usage reports require that either the SharePoint Team Services or the FrontPage 2002 server extensions are running on the Web server. The usage report data comes directly from the Web server activity logs. Some of the usage data is not logged by the server automatically, however; these features will have to be activated on the Web server.

Once you have selected a particular report, the report data can then be charted. The chart options include area, bar, column, line, pie, and doughnut charts. To create a report chart, click the Usage Chart button on the Reporting toolbar. Figure 10.5 shows an example of a daily summary area chart.

FIGURE 10.5 *Daily Summary Area Chart (FrontPage Tour)*

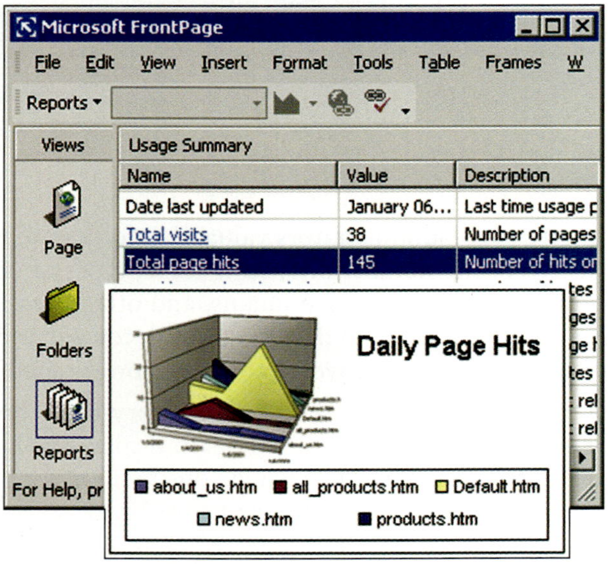

Exploring Permissions with FrontPage Webs

FrontPage 2002 FrontPage Web Server Permissions give Web administrators the ability to set group and user rights to (a) browse the particular Web, (b) author and browse, or (c) administer, author, and browse. To access FrontPage Web Server Permissions, click Tools, point to Server, and then click Permissions. The *Browse this web* permission allows visitors only to browse the Web (see figure 10.6, figure 10.7). In the Users tab of the Permissions dialog box, you can grant permission to specific users listed on the server. The *Author and browse* permission allows certain groups and/or users to author the FrontPage Web or subweb, but not to have total administrative authority over the Web. The *Administer, author, and browse* permission grants specified groups and/or users total control over the FrontPage Web, not only for creating, deleting, and modifying Webs, but also for creating and deleting subwebs and setting permissions for the Webs.

FIGURE 10.6 **Permissions Dialog Box**

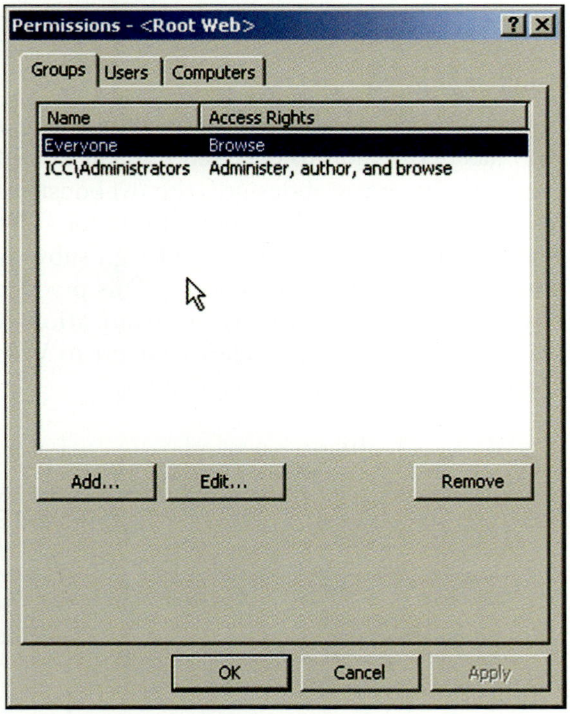

FIGURE 10.7 *Add Users Dialog Box*

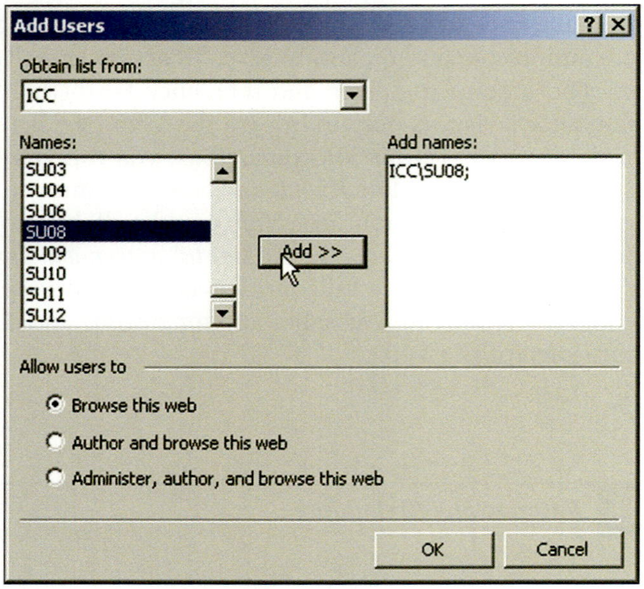

Converting a Folder into a Subweb

Having subwebs, or nested Webs, on your Web site will give you added control over content and over who has permission to edit and publish Web pages on your site. On the URL http://emcpwebs.com/webdesign/, the /webdesign path is a subweb within the EMCPWebs root web. What do subwebs mean for a Web site? Permissions can be granted to specific individuals for the /webdesign subweb without allowing access to EMCPWebs root web and other subwebs. This practice is common and can improve access security within a company or organization. To convert a folder to a subweb, right-click the folder and then click Convert to Web. Subwebs within the root web will open in a separate FrontPage window.

exercise 18 CONVERTING A FOLDER INTO A SUBWEB

1. Access the Folders view of the EMCPWebs FrontPage Web.
2. Right-click the *emcpwebs* root web folder on the Folder List, point to New, and then click Folder.
3. Name the folder *subweb*.

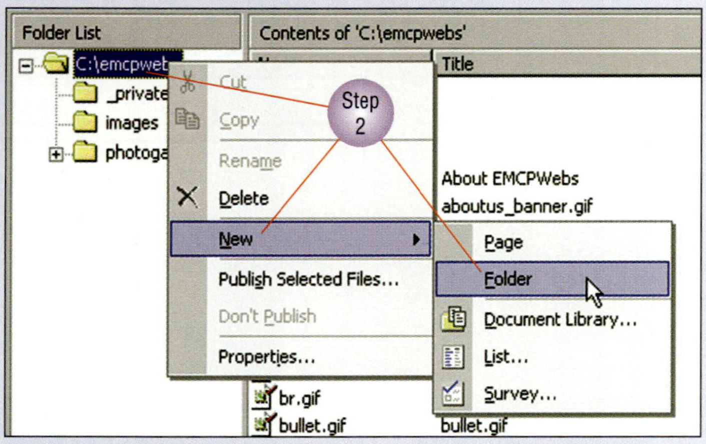

4. Right-click the *subweb* folder and then click Convert to Web.
5. Double-click the *subweb* folder icon to open it in a new window.
6. Close the subweb FrontPage window.

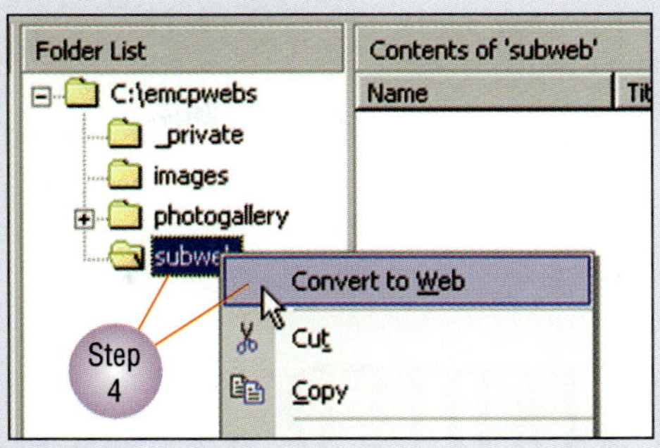

Tracking Web Size

Once you have registered your domain name, you need to find a site-hosting service to store your Web site contents. Web-hosting companies may have various packages from which to choose. These services may include traffic allowances, e-mail accounts, FrontPage server extensions, and Web size. Some hosting service companies charge more for larger Web sites or have a ceiling for Web site sizes. Therefore, it may be imperative to track your FrontPage Web size. The All Files summary in the Site Summary shows the overall size of the FrontPage Web, minus hidden files. To find the total file size of a FrontPage Web, click Tools and then click Web Settings. At the Web Settings dialog box, click the Advanced tab, and then click the Show hidden files and folders check box.

exercise 19 REPORTING TOTAL SIZE OF FRONTPAGE WEB (SHOW HIDDEN FILES)

1. With the EMCPWebs FrontPage Web open, access the Reports view.
2. Click the Reports down-pointing triangle on the Reporting toolbar and then click Site Summary to view the All files summary of the overall size of the EMCPWebs FrontPage Web.
3. Click Tools and then click Web Settings.
4. Click the Advanced tab in the Web Settings dialog box.
5. Click the Show hidden files and folders check box to insert a check mark.
6. Click the OK button.
7. Click the Yes button to refresh the Web.
8. View the updated All files size. It should have increased by approximately 35KB.
9. Exit FrontPage.

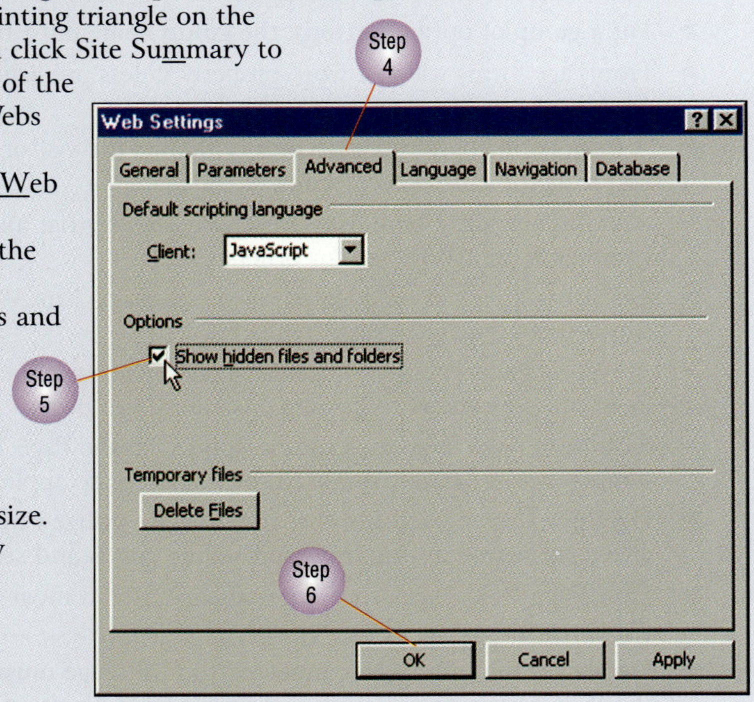

FrontPage also has a file check in and check out feature that prevents multiple users from editing the same file. To check out a file for editing, right-click the file icon in Folders view or on the Folder List and then click Check Out. To check a file back in for others to edit, right-click the file icon and select Check In. This feature must be enabled on the Web server.

CHAPTER summary

- A Web page form is used primarily to gather information from visitors.
- Simple form results are usually sent as e-mail messages once submitted.
- Forms can be used to submit data directly to a database.
- Form fields are the elements in a form that are used to gather information from the visitor.
- Text boxes are used to collect short amounts of textual data.
- Text area boxes are used to collect multiple lines of text.
- The file upload field item allows visitors to transmit files such as images and documents.
- Check boxes give the visitor a list of options from which multiple selections can be made.
- Option buttons give visitors a list of options from which only one choice can be made.
- Group boxes allow developers to separate a group of related controls or text from other information within the form or Web page.
- Drop-down boxes provide visitors a list of options similar to option buttons, but taking up a smaller amount of screen space.
- Push buttons are used to initiate an action such as with the Submit and Reset buttons.
- For a group of option buttons, the group name must be the same for each button property.
- FrontPage forms will not work properly unless published on a server running the Microsoft FrontPage server extensions.
- A form confirmation page typically thanks the visitor for his or her form submission and confirms the entries for accuracy.
- A FrontPage guest book is a Web page feature that allows visitors to post messages and comments on a Web site for others to see.
- Guest book entries are located on the guestlog.htm Web page created by the wizard and can be edited as necessary.
- A Web page template is a predesigned Web page that contains the layout, image, and formatting elements to create consistent Web pages.
- FrontPage page templates can be applied in the Page Templates dialog box just as other templates (e.g., Guest Book, Photo Gallery) are applied to new Web pages.
- Database-driven Web sites are increasingly utilized by all types of businesses for collecting and distributing information and selling goods and services.
- FrontPage Web pages that are database driven must be saved as Active Server Pages (ASPs), with an *.asp* file extension.
- Databases that are to be connected to FrontPage must be located within the root web, on the Web server, or on another server located on the network.

- A Database Results region displays database table and/or query data in a specified region of the Web page.
- Any Open Database Connectivity (ODBC)-compliant database program such as FoxPro, Paradox, and Microsoft SQL Server can be used with FrontPage 2002 to retrieve and collect data.
- Search forms can be added to Database Results regions to query database fields.
- FrontPage Database Results pages will not display properly unless published on a server running the Microsoft FrontPage server extensions.
- A query is defined as a request for information from a database.
- A Microsoft Access database can automatically be created by FrontPage based on the fields inserted in a Web page form.
- The Database Interface Wizard creates an entire FrontPage Web or subweb based on a database.
- The Results Page of a Database Interface Web displays the results of the database table or query.
- The Submission Form page of a Database Interface Web allows those with access to submit form data into the Microsoft Access database.
- The Database Editor page allows users to add, edit, and delete records within the database.
- The Database Interface home page (default.htm) contains descriptions of and hyperlinks to the Results Page, Submission Form, and Database Editor pages.
- The Tasks view is used by FrontPage Web designers to assign tasks to specific designers.
- Tasks can be added in the Tasks view as well as on the Edit menu of the Web page that needs a task assigned.
- The Reports view gives FrontPage Web developers the ability to view and analyze files, problems, workflow, and usage data.
- The Site Summary is the first report displayed in the Reports view and contains such data as slow pages, recently added files, unverified hyperlinks, broken hyperlinks, component errors, and uncompleted tasks.
- Usage reports can give Web administrators valuable information about how many hits the site has received, number of visiting users, operating systems and browsers used by visitors, referring domains, and other data.
- Web usage reports require that either the SharePoint Team Services or the FrontPage 2002 server extensions are running on the Web server.
- Even with FrontPage server extensions or SharePoint Team Services running on the Web server, some usage report data must be activated by the Web server administrator.
- Usage reports can be charted using the Usage Chart button on the Reporting toolbar.
- FrontPage Web Server Permissions give Web administrators the ability to set group and user rights to (a) Browse this web; (b) Author and browse; or (c) Administer, author, and browse.
- The Browse this web permission allows visitors only to browse the Web.
- The Author and browse permission allows certain groups and/or users to author the FrontPage Web or subweb, but not to have total administrative authority over the Web.
- The Administer, author, and browse this web permission grants specified groups and/or users total control over the FrontPage Web, including creating, deleting, and modifying Webs, and also creating and deleting subwebs and setting permissions for the Webs.

COMMANDS review

Command	Mouse/Keyboard
Insert a FrontPage form	Click Insert, point to Form, click Form
Insert a form field object	Click Insert, Form, then click desired form field object
Validate form input	Double-click form object, click Validate button
Send form data to an e-mail account	Right-click inside form area, click Form Properties, key e-mail address
Insert a confirmation field	Click Web Component button on Standard toolbar, select *Advanced Controls,* select *Confirmation Field*
Create a FrontPage guest book using a wizard	Click File, point to New, click Page or Web, *Page Templates*, *Guest Book* icon
Upload a file using a form	Click Insert, Form, File Upload
Save a Web page as a page template	Click File, Save As, select FrontPage template in Save as type drop-down list, key file name
Import a Microsoft Access database to create a database connection	Click File, Import, name the database connection, click Yes to store database in *fpdb* folder
Display database information using the Database Results Wizard	Click Insert, Database, Results, select database connection, continue wizard
Use a search form to query database results	Click More Options button in Step 3 of Database Results Wizard, click Criteria button, click Add button, add the criteria, check Add search form check box in Step 5
Post form results to a database	Right-click inside form area, click Send to database option button, make appropriate selections
Create a database interface using a wizard	Click File, point to New, click Page or Web, *Web Site Templates*, *Database Interface Wizard* icon
Create a task	Click Edit, point to Tasks, click Add Task
Mark a task as completed	Right-click completed task, click Mark Complete
Delete a task	Right-click completed task, click Delete Task
View the Site Summary report	Click Reports button on Views bar

View Files, Problems, Workflow, and Usage reports	Click Reports drop-down list on Reporting toolbar
View a usage report chart	Click Usage Chart drop-down list on Reporting toolbar
Set Browse, Author, and Administer permissions	Click Tools, point to Server, click Permissions
Convert a folder into a subweb	Right-click folder, click Convert to Web
Show hidden files for All files summary	Click Tools, Web Settings, Advanced tab, click Show hidden files and folders check box

CONCEPTS check

Completion: On a blank sheet of paper, indicate the correct term, command, or number for each item.

1. These are used on Web pages to obtain various types of information from visitors.
2. These objects are the elements in a form that are used to obtain information from visitors.
3. This type of form field is used to collect multiple lines of text from a visitor.
4. This type of form object uses an image file to submit form results rather than a typical push button.
5. Form results can be formatted to be sent to an e-mail account or database in this dialog box.
6. This type of Web page contains results of entered form data to verify that the data is correct and often thanks the visitor for completing the form.
7. This FrontPage feature allows visitors to post comments for other visitors to view on the guestlog.htm Web page.
8. A Web page can be saved as a page template by selecting this option in the Save as type drop-down list of the Save As dialog box.
9. A Database Results region can be inserted into a Web page by selecting this command on the Insert menu.
10. Database Results pages must be saved with this file extension.
11. Databases to be connected to FrontPage should be stored in this folder.
12. This view can be accessed to track duties that need to be created, inserted, deleted, or fixed in a FrontPage Web.
13. This is the initial report of the Reports view.
14. These types of reports give Web administrators valuable informaltion about how many hits the site has received, number of visiting users, types of operating systems and browsers used by visitors, referring domains, and other data.
15. Browse, author, and administer authorizations can be established in this dialog box.

SKILLS check

Assessment 1

1. Open Microsoft FrontPage.
2. Open the formweb10 FrontPage Web from your *Chapter 10* folder.
3. Create a form on the feedback.htm Web page using the following form requirements:

Text Label	Form Object	Form Object Properties	
		Name	***Width in Characters***
First Name:	Textbox	FIRSTNAME	15
Last Name:	Textbox	LASTNAME	20
Address:	Textbox	ADDRESS	20
City:	Textbox	CITY	20
State:	Textbox	STATE	2
ZIP:	Textbox	ZIP	10
Country:	Textbox	COUNTRY	20
E-mail Address:	Textbox	EMAIL	30
		Name	***Initial State***
Name on Shirt	Checkbox	NAME	Not checked
Logo on Shirt	Checkbox	LOGO	Not checked
Pinstripes	Checkbox	STRIPES	Not checked
		Name	***Choices***
Color	Drop-Down Box	COLOR	Choose here... Selected: Yes
Color	Drop-Down Box	COLOR	Red
Color	Drop-Down Box	COLOR	Orange
Color	Drop-Down Box	COLOR	Yellow
Color	Drop-Down Box	COLOR	Green
Color	Drop-Down Box	COLOR	Blue
Color	Drop-Down Box	COLOR	Purple
		Name	***Width in Characters/ Number of Lines***
	Text Area	SHIRTTEXT	40/4

4. Format the form field elements to Maroon with fonts of Times New Roman, 10 points, and White.
5. Validate each of the form fields by requiring data to be entered or selected.
6. Format the form data to be sent to your e-mail address.
7. Save the updated Web page.
8. Publish the formweb10 FrontPage Web to a Web server running the FrontPage server extensions, if possible.
9. Perform a Preview in Browser, test the form, and print the feedback.htm Web page.
10. Print the message sent to your e-mail account.

Assessment 2

(Note: This assessment requires FrontPage server extensions.)

1. Open the formweb10 FrontPage Web from your *Chapter 10* folder.
2. Insert the following text and confirmation fields into the confirmation.htm Web page:

    Thank you for your interest in our Personalized Shirts. Your [COLOR] shirt with the following features will be available for you in one week.

    [NAME]
    [LOGO]
    [STRIPES]

3. Format the feedback.htm Web page form to access the confirmation.htm confirmation page.
4. Save the updated Web pages.
5. Publish the formweb10 FrontPage Web to a Web server running the FrontPage server extensions, if possible.
6. Perform a Preview in Browser for the feedback.htm Web page and test the form to view the confirmation page.
7. Print the confirmation.htm Web page in your browser.

Assessment 3

1. Open the formweb10 FrontPage Web from your *Chapter 10* folder.
2. Open the template.htm Web page in Page view.
3. Reformat the following Web page elements: page background, table cell shading, fonts, font sizes, and font colors.
4. Save the Web page as a page template with the name *formweb10template*.
5. Create a new Web page based on the formweb10template page template.
6. Perform a Preview in Browser and print the Web page.

Assessment 4

(Note: This assessment requires FrontPage server extensions.)

1. Open the formweb10 FrontPage Web from your *Chapter 10* folder.
2. Open the database.htm Web page.
3. Complete the Database Results Wizard to display the following fields of the Products record source using the Northwind Sample data connection: *ProductID, ProductName, CategoryID, UnitPrice, and UnitsInStock.*
4. Save the updated database.asp Web page.
5. Publish the formweb10 FrontPage Web to a Web server running the FrontPage server extensions, if possible.
6. Test the database.asp Web page in a browser to view the chapter10 database table information.
7. Print the database.asp Web page in your browser.

Assessment 5

1. Open the formweb10 FrontPage Web from your *Chapter 10* folder.
2. Open the postdata.htm Web page.
3. Create a form to gather the following information from visitors:

Text Label	*Field Name*	*Form Object*	*Description*
Movie Name	moviename	Text box	30 characters
Genre	genre	Text box	30 characters
Main Actor	actor	Text box	30 characters
Description	description	Text area	40 char./5 lines

4. Format the form contents to be sent to a database.
5. Have FrontPage create the database to store the form results.
6. Save the updated Web page.
7. Publish the formweb10 FrontPage Web to a Web server running the FrontPage server extensions, if possible.
8. Test the form with a minimum of five movies.
9. Open the postdata.mdb database and view the Results table in Microsoft Access.
10. Print the table from within Microsoft Access.

Assessment 6

1. Open Microsoft FrontPage.
2. On your preferred storage device, create a database interface titled *webfavorites*.
3. Incorporate the following field requirements into your database: Web Site Title, URL, Color Scheme Description, Layout Design Description, Navigability Description, and Addition Site Comments.
4. Publish the formweb10 FrontPage Web to a Web server running the FrontPage server extensions, if possible.
5. Perform a Preview in Browser and enter a minimum of five critiques into the Database Interface Submission Form Web page.
6. Print the results_page.asp Web page.

Assessment 7

1. Open the formweb10 FrontPage Web from your *Chapter 10* folder.
2. Key the task name **Apply a Style Sheet to entire Web** and assign the task to yourself.
3. Key **Develop the style sheet and key in the code to reference the style sheet** in the Description text box.
4. Mark the task as complete.
5. Delete the task.
6. Open the index.htm Web page in Page view and key the task name **Change Telephone Numbers** with the description **Change all 316 area codes to 620**.
7. Complete the task by double-clicking the task in the Tasks view.

Assessment 8

1. With FrontPage open, create a new empty FrontPage Web titled *sitereport* on your preferred storage device.
2. Import a Web site from the World Wide Web.
3. Limit the total of the downloaded files to 750KB.
4. View the Site Summary and investigate the various reports.
5. Copy the Slow Pages report data and paste it into a new Web page in Page view.
6. Save the Web page as slowpages.htm with the title *Slow Pages Report*.
7. Perform a Preview in Browser and print the slowpages.htm Web page.
8. Exit FrontPage.

UNIT 2 PERFORMANCE ASSESSMENTS

Customizing FrontPage Webs and Pages and Working with Advanced Concepts

ASSESSING Proficiency

Unit 2 IRC

In this unit, you have explored many advanced concepts of FrontPage 2002, including creating and customizing tables; publishing FrontPage Webs and Web pages; working with FrontPage components; inserting plug-in media; creating and formatting frames; working with languages, scripts, and styles; working with forms and databases; and managing and analyzing FrontPage Webs.

(Note: Before completing unit assessments, delete the Chapter 10 *folder on your disk. Next, download the Unit 2 data files from the Internet Resource Center to the* Unit 2 *folder you have created on your disk, and then make* Unit 2 *the active folder.)*

Assessment 1

1. On your preferred storage device, create a One Page Web titled cityweb.
2. In Folders view, title the home page *Welcome to My City*.
3. Create the following Web page files in Folders view (replace blanks with your city's name):

File Name	***Title***
history.htm	*The History of* ______________
demographics.htm	______________ *Demographic Profile*
tourism.htm	______________ *Tourism and Recreation*
business.htm	______________ *Business and Industry*
lodging.htm	______________ *Hotels, Motels, and B&Bs*
econdevelop.htm	______________ *Economic Development*
travel.htm	______________ *Travel Agencies and Airport Information*
recreation.htm	______________ *Parks and Recreation*

4. Create the navigation structure for the Web in Navigation view.
5. Print the navigation structure.
6. Using your creativity and other sources of inspiration, sketch a layout for the Web pages on scratch paper based on the creation of a table for columnar layouts, using the following guidelines:
   - Web page must consist of at least three columns.
   - Table properties must conform to typical screen resolutions (by pixel or percent).

- Merge and split cells as needed.
- At least one cell must have a color background.
- At least one cell must have a border (top, bottom, left, or right).
- Web page must include a banner image.
- Web page must include a navigation bar (text or image; vertical or horizontal).
- Web page must include at least one photograph.
- Web page text must be easy to read and free of errors.
- Web page must include a copyright notice, time stamp, and author credits.

7. Using FrontPage, create the Web page table structure in the home page.
8. Key appropriate text for the home page.
9. Insert appropriate images.
10. Create the necessary hyperlinks to second-tier pages.
11. Save the updated home page.
12. Perform a Preview in Browser and print the home page.

Assessment 2

(Note: To complete this exercise you must have access to a Web server with FrontPage server extensions installed as well as authorized permission to publish. Ask your instructor for school-specific Web publishing instructions. If you are unable to complete this assessment, please read through the steps.)

1. On your preferred storage device, create a One Page Web titled familyweb.
2. Create the following Web page files in Folders view:

File Name	***Title***
history.htm	*The History of My Family*
photos.htm	*Family Photographs*
family.htm	*Living Family Members*

3. Create the navigation structure for the Web in Navigation view.
4. Print the navigation structure.
5. Using your creativity and other sources of inspiration, sketch a layout for the Web pages on scratch paper based on publishing a Web site to a server with FrontPage server extensions, using the following guidelines:
   - Web page must consist of at least three columns.
   - Table properties must conform to typical screen resolutions (by pixel or percent).
   - Merge and split cells as needed.
   - At least one cell must have a color background.
   - At least one cell must have a border (top, bottom, left, or right).
   - Web page must include a banner image.
   - Web page must include a navigation bar (text or image; vertical or horizontal).
   - Web page must include at least one photograph.
   - Web page text must be easy to read and free of errors.

- Web page must include a copyright notice, time stamp, and author credits.

6. Using FrontPage, create the Web page table structure in the home page.
7. Key appropriate text for the home page.
8. Insert appropriate images.
9. Insert a hit counter at the bottom of the home page.
10. Create the necessary hyperlinks to second-tier pages.
11. Create *The History of My Family* Web page.
12. Create *Family Photographs* Web page.
13. Create *Living Family Members* Web page using a table to organize individuals by First Name, Last Name, Age, Street Address, City, State, and ZIP.
14. Save the finished Web pages.
15. Publish the familyweb FrontPage Web onto a Web server running FrontPage server extensions.
16. Perform a Preview in Browser and print all Web pages.

Assessment 3

(Note: To complete this exercise you must have access to a Web server with FTP access and authorized permission to publish. Ask your instructor for school-specific Web publishing instructions. If you are unable to complete this assessment, please read through the steps.)

1. Open either the cityweb FrontPage Web from assessment 1 or the familyweb from assessment 2.
2. Click the Publish Web button on the Standard toolbar.
3. Key the appropriate FTP address in the Publish Destination dialog box and then click OK.
4. Follow the remaining steps as presented onscreen.
5. View the published Web site.

Assessment 4

1. On your preferred storage device, create an empty Web titled framesassessment.
2. Create a new Banner and Contents frames page.
3. Import the framesbanner.htm and bannerframe.gif files from your *Unit 2* folder into the framesassessment Web.
4. Set the banner page to framesbanner.htm.
5. Set a new page for the left side frame.
6. Set a new page for the main contents frame.
7. In the main contents frame, insert a digital image from file.
8. Create four new normal pages.
9. Insert one digital image from file into each new Web page.
10. Key a caption of the photograph above the image.
11. Save the Web pages with appropriate file names and page titles.
12. Create hypertext links on the left side frame to the five Web pages with images. Your home page might look something like the example on page 380.

FIGURE U2.1 • Assessment 4

Assessment 5

1. Using Notepad, re-create the Web page below:

Ristorante Italiano

Lunch Menu

Item	Price
Zuppa del Giorno	$6.99
Insalata di Pollo	$9.99
Linguine Pesto	$12.99

Dinner Menu

Item	Price
Zuppa del Giorno	$8.99
Linguine Venezia	$17.99
Paillard di Pollo	$21.99

Restaurants.com

FIGURE U2.2 • Assessment 5

2. Optimize the Web page by keying the following meta information:
   a. TITLE: **Welcome to Ristorante Italiano on the Web!**
   b. DESCRIPTION: **Ristorante Italiano is the best Italian restaurant in the country. Try our appetizers, pastas, meats, fish, and desserts. Lunch and dinner menus. Reservations, Groups, and Buses welcome.**
   c. KEYWORDS: **zuppe, soups, pasta, carni, meats, fish, desserts, wine, Italian, restaurant, ristorante, food, lunch, dinner**
3. Save the Web page as ristorante.htm.
4. Print the HTML code.
5. Open the Web page in your browser and print.

Assessment 6

1. Access the Dynamic Drive Web site at www.dynamicdrive.com.
2. Locate an interesting DHTML effect from one of the categories.
3. Copy the necessary code and paste it into FrontPage as directed.
4. Modify the code if necessary.
5. Save the Web page as unit2assess6.htm.
6. Perform a Preview in Browser and test the DHTML effect.

Assessment 7

1. Create a simple FrontPage form requesting information for a survey.
2. Use, at minimum, the following fields:
   - Text Box
   - Text Area
   - Check Box
   - Option Button
3. Format the field text labels to Times New Roman, 10 points.
4. Format the title text to Times New Roman, 12 points, and bold.
5. Format the form to be sent to your e-mail address.
6. Save the Web page as unit2assess7.htm.
7. Perform a Preview in Browser and print the Web page.

Assessment 8

(Note: This assessment activity requires Microsoft Access.)

1. On your preferred storage device, create a One Page Web titled databasesassessment.
2. Import the unit2assess7.htm file into the databasesassessment FrontPage Web.
3. Format your form to be sent to a database.
4. Create the database from within FrontPage.
5. Save the updated Web page.
6. Open the database file from the *fpdb* folder.
7. Print the Results table from within Microsoft Access.

WRITING Activities

Activity 1

There are many aspects to the development of Web sites, including: (1) design and layout; (2) content development; (3) photography and image development; (4) programming; and (5) site administration.

Prepare a research document of a minimum of five pages that identifies, explains, and draws conclusions about the types of duties and tasks that are involved in the development and management of a Web site.

Refer to your instructor for research document preparation and submission guidelines.

Activity 2

What certification opportunities are available for Web designers? In addition to a traditional education experience, there are industry standard certification course programs in Web design.

Prepare a research document of a minimum of five pages that identifies, explains, and draws conclusions about the types of certification opportunities that are available for current and aspiring Web designers.

Refer to your instructor for research document preparation and submission guidelines.

INTERNET Project

Access the CoolHomePages.com Web site at www.emcp.net/coolhomepages. Peruse the various categories of Web pages in the View Sites Grouped By section. Create a Web page with links to at least 15 Web sites that you find interesting.

Save the Web page as favoritepages.htm.

JOB Study

Creating a Knowledge Base FrontPage Web

In the Job Study assessment in unit 1, you created a Knowledge Base Web for various Web design techniques. For this project, you will create a Knowledge Base Web for a certification path of your choice.

You must research the Web for articles, test-taking tips, practice exams, and other matters relating to a certification path of your choice. The categorical Web pages will contain hyperlinks to the Web pages of the certification objectives. You must create a home page that introduces the Knowledge Base Web and includes appropriate textual formatting and images. Depending on your skill level, you may want to experiment with such image creation programs as Adobe PhotoShop or

Macromedia Fireworks for your page banners and navigation buttons. All Web pages must be consistent in layout design and formatting. Test your FrontPage Web for errors.

For those who have CD Rewritable (CD-RW) drives, you may want to move or copy your FrontPage Knowledge Base Web to a CD-RW disc. To make the home page open automatically when you insert the CD into the drive, you will need to create an autorun.inf file and place it on the CD-RW disc. To create the file, perform the following steps:

1. In Notepad, key the following text:

    [autorun]
    open=start index.htm

2. Save the document as autorun.inf on your CD-RW disc.

APPENDIX

This text is organized around the Microsoft Office User Specialist (MOUS) skills established by Microsoft Corporation. The pages on which these skills are covered are shown in the tables on page 385 (Core skills) and page 386 (Expert skills). To learn more about the Microsoft Office User Specialist program, visit www.mous.net.

MICROSOFT® FRONTPAGE 2002
CORE MOUS SKILLS

Reference No.	Skill	Pages
FP2002-1	**Creating and Modifying Web Sites**	
FP2002-1-1	Create and manage a FrontPage web	48-51, 140, 174-177, 178-179
FP2002-1-2	Create and Preview web pages	51-54, 79-80, 351
FP2002-1-3	Open, view, and rename web pages	15-16, 19-22, 53-54, 90, 153
FP2002-1-4	Rename a web page	53-54, 153
FP2002-1-5	Change the title for a web page on banners and buttons	226
FP2002-2	**Importing Web Content**	
FP2002-2-1	Insert text and images	66-70, 94-98, 151-152, 168-174, 189-190, 312
FP2002-2-2	Insert Office Drawings, AutoShapes, and WordArt	111-120
FP2002-3	**Formatting Web Pages**	
FP2002-3-1	Apply text and paragraph formats	72-74, 77-79, 180-81, 182, 184-188, 308-311, 328-331
FP2002-3-2	Insert hyperlinks	132-134, 136-138, 141-143, 146-150, 312
FP2002-3-3	Insert a date using shared borders	312
FP2002-3-4	Create and edit tables	208-218, 241-242, 252, 312-314
FP2002-3-5	Apply web themes	223-225
FP2002-4	**Formatting Web Pages**	
FP2002-4-1	Edit graphic elements	98-103, 105-111, 151-152
FP2002-4-2	Create image maps	146-147
FP2002-4-3	Add a FrontPage Web component to a web page	266-270, 272-276, 276-279, 281-287
FP2002-4-4	Add a Photo Gallery	121-125
FP2002-5	**Organizing and Viewing FrontPage Web Sites**	
FP2002-5-1	Use FrontPage views	12-22, 52-57, 125, 153-155, 156
FP2002-5-2	Manage web structures	54-57, 125
FP2002-5-3	Organize web files	14
FP2002-5-4	Manage tasks	361-362
FP2002-6	**Managing Web sites**	
FP2002-6-1	Publish a web page	231-233, 256
FP2002-6-2	Create Custom Reports	363, 365

MICROSOFT® FRONTPAGE 2002
EXPERT MOUS SKILLS

Reference No.	Skill	Pages
FP2002e-1	**Creating and Customizing Web Sites**	
FP2002e-1-1	Modify web page layout	245-246
FP2002e-1-2	Create Sub webs	368-369
FP2002e-1-3	Manage permissions for subwebs	367-368
FP2002e-1-4	Create and apply custom themes	227-229
FP2002e-1-5	Customize shared borders	230-231
FP2002e-1-6	Add and modify background images	57-58, 61-65
FP2002e-2	**Using Navigational Features**	
FP2002e-2-1	Manage the structure of a web	54-57, 125, 153-154
FP2002e-2-2	Add navigation bars to page banners	225-226
FP2002e-2-3	Add link bars	143-145, 226-227
FP2002e-3	**Customizing Tables**	
FP2002e-3-1	Format tables	215-218, 220-222, 242-245, 248-251, 253
FP2002e-3-2	Split tables	219-220
FP2002e-3-3	Apply table AutoFormats	247-248
FP2002e-3-4	Nest tables	246-247
FP2002e-4	**Inserting and Modifying FrontPage Components**	
FP2002e-4-1	Add FrontPage components to web pages	266-270, 272-276, 276-279, 281-287
FP2002e-4-2	Modify component properties	269
FP2002e-5	**Creating Customer and User Feedback Web pages**	
FP2002e-5-1	Create forms for user input	340-343, 346-350
FP2002e-5-2	Add search capabilities to web pages	272
FP2002e-6	**Integrating Databases**	
FP2002e-6-1	Connect a web site to a database	352-354, 359-361
FP2002e-6-2	Send form data to Access databases	357-358
FP2002e-6-3	Add query capabilities to web pages	355-356
FP2002e-7	**Using Collaboration Features**	
FP2002e-7-1	Check HTML files in and out	370
FP2002e-7-2	Manage web folders	368-369
FP2002e-8	**Inserting Frames**	
FP2002e-8-1	Create frames	287-295
FP2002e-8-2	Specify target content in frames	296
FP2002e-8-3	Create and customize banners	226, 229
FP2002e-9	**Generating Reports**	
FP2002e-9-1	Find broken hyperlinks	155
FP2002e-9-2	Locate most popular pages	270-271
FP2002e-9-3	Locate problems	364-365
FP2002e-10	**Publishing Web Sites**	
FP2002e-10-1	Publish web sites from one server to another	231-233, 253-254
FP2002e-10-2	Use Personal Web Servers	254
FP2002e-10-3	Publish a site from one location to another	253-254, 257, 259

INDEX

Q

R

S